The Handbook of
Adult Language
Disorders

The Handbook of

Adult Language

Disorders

Integrating Cognitive Neuropsychology,
Neurology, and Rehabilitation

Edited by

Argye E. Hillis

Psychology Press
New York   London   Hove

Published in 2002 by
Psychology Press
29 West 35th Street
New York, NY 10001

Published in Great Britain by
Psychology Press Ltd.
27 Church Road
Hove, East Sussex
BN3 2FA

Psychology Press is an imprint of the Taylor & Francis Group.

10 9 8 7 6 5 4 3 2 1

On the cover: *The Englishman (William Tom Warrener, 1861–1934) at the Moulin
Rouge* by Henri de Toulouse-Lautrec. The Metropolitan Museum of Art, bequest of
Miss Adelaide Milton de Groot (1876–1967), 1967. (67.187.108) Photography by
Malcolm Varon. Photograph © 1979 The Metropolitan Museum of Art.

Library of Congress Cataloging-in-Publication Data is available from the Library
of Congress.

ISBN 1-84169-003-1 (hbk)

This book is dedicated to HW, SJD, PM, HG, JJ, DW, and many others whose friendship and enthusiastic participation in my studies of language breakdown and recovery have brought joy and new ideas to my work, and to my daughter Lydia, whose boundless energy and passionate curiosity continuously inspire me.

Contents

About the Editor   xi
Contributors   xiii
Preface   xv

Part 1: Reading

1   MODELS OF THE READING PROCESS   3

Argye E. Hillis

2   NEUROANATOMICAL ASPECTS OF READING   15

Argye E. Hillis and Elizabeth Tuffiash

3   CLINICAL DIAGNOSIS AND TREATMENT
OF READING DISORDERS   27

Rhonda B. Friedman

Part 2: Spelling

4   UNCOVERING THE COGNITIVE ARCHITECTURE
OF SPELLING   47

Brenda Rapp

5   NEUROANATOMICAL CORRELATES OF SPELLING
AND WRITING   71

Steven Z. Rapcsak and Pelagie M. Beeson

6   CLINICAL DIAGNOSIS AND TREATMENT
OF SPELLING DISORDERS   101

Pelagie M. Beeson and Steven Z. Rapcsak

Part 3: Naming

7   MODELS OF NAMING   123

Doriana Chialant, Albert Costa, and Alfonso Caramazza

8   NEUROANATOMICAL ASPECTS OF NAMING   143

Christine Whatmough and Howard Chertkow

9   CLINICAL DIAGNOSIS AND TREATMENT
OF NAMING DISORDERS   163

Anastasia M. Raymer and Leslie J. Gonzalez Rothi

Part 4: Semantics

10   SEMANTIC MEMORY   185

Elaine Funnell

11   NEURAL SUBSTRATES OF SEMANTICS   207

John Hart, Jr., Lauren R. Moo, Jessica B. Segal,
Ellen Adkins, and Michael A. Kraut

12   "SEMANTIC THERAPY" IN DAY-TO-DAY CLINICAL
PRACTICE: PERSPECTIVES ON DIAGNOSIS AND
THERAPY RELATED TO SEMANTIC IMPAIRMENTS
IN APHASIA   229

Simon Horton and Sally Byng

Part 5: Auditory Discrimination and Recognition

13   MODELS OF SPEECH PROCESSING   253

Martha W. Burton and Steven L. Small

14   NEUROBIOLOGICAL BASES OF AUDITORY
SPEECH PROCESSING   269

Dana Boatman

15   DIAGNOSIS AND TREATMENT OF AUDITORY
DISORDERS   281

Dana Boatman

Part 6: Sentence Processing

16   SENTENCE COMPREHENSION DEFICITS:
INDEPENDENCE AND INTERACTION OF SYNTAX,
SEMANTICS, AND WORKING MEMORY   295

Randi C. Martin and Michelle Miller

17   MODELS OF SENTENCE PRODUCTION   311

Cynthia K. Thompson and Yasmeen Faroqi-Shah

18   THE NEURAL BASIS OF SYNTACTIC PROCESSING:
A CRITICAL LOOK   331

David Caplan

19   ASSESSMENT AND TREATMENT OF SENTENCE
PROCESSING DISORDERS: A REVIEW OF
THE LITERATURE   351

Jane Marshall

Part 7: Other Types of Models and Treatment Approaches

20   HOW CAN CONNECTIONIST COGNITIVE MODELS
OF LANGUAGE INFORM MODELS
OF LANGUAGE REHABILITATION?   375

Nadine Martin, Matti Laine, and Trevor A. Harley

21   BIOLOGICAL APPROACHES TO THE TREATMENT
OF APHASIA   397

Steven L. Small

22   ASSESSMENT AND TREATMENT OF PRAGMATIC
ASPECTS OF COMMUNICATION IN APHASIA   413

Audrey L. Holland and Jacqueline J. Hinckley

23   THE NATURE AND IMPLICATIONS OF RIGHT
HEMISPHERE LANGUAGE DISORDERS:
ISSUES IN SEARCH OF ANSWERS   429

*Connie A. Tompkins, Wiltrud Fassbinder,
Margaret T. Lehman-Blake, and Annette Baumgaertner*

Author Index   449
Subject Index   455

About the Editor

Argye E. Hillis is an Assistant Professor of Neurology and Cognitive Sciences at Johns Hopkins University. Prior to her medical training and neurology residency, she trained in the fields of speech-language pathology and cognitive neuropsychology and conducted research focusing on understanding and treating aphasia. Similarly, her current clinical research in neurology involves neuroimaging and cognitive studies of aphasia in patients with acute stroke, designed to learn how language functions are represented in the brain.

Contributors

Ellen Adkins
Department of Neurology
Johns Hopkins University, USA

Annette Baumgaertner
Communication Science and Disorders
University of Pittsburgh, USA

Pelagie M Beeson
National Center for Neurogenic Communication
  Disorders
University of Arizona, USA

Dana Boatman
Department of Neurology
Johns Hopkins University, USA

Martha Burton
Depatment of Neurology
University of Maryland, Baltimore, USA

Sally Byng
National Hospitals College of Speech Science
London, England

David Caplan
Neuropsychology Lab
Massachusetts General Hospital, USA

Alfonso Caramazza
Department of Psychology
Harvard University, USA

Howard Chertkow
Jewish General Hospital, Canada

Doriana Chialant
Department of Psychology
Harvard University, USA

Albert Costa
Department of Psychology
Harvard University, USA

Yasmeen Faroqi-Shah
Communication Sciences and Disorders
Northwestern University, USA

Wiltrud Fassbinder
Communication Science and Disorders
University of Pittsburgh, USA

Rhonda B. Friedman
Georgetown University Medical Center, USA

Elaine Funnell
Psychology Department
University of London, England

Leslie Gonzalez Rothi
VAMC, Gainesville, FL, USA

Trevor A. Harley
Department of Psychology
University of Dundee, Scotland

John Hart
Department of Neurology
Johns Hopkins Hospital, USA

Jacqueline J. Hinckley
Communication Sciences and Disorders
University of South Florida, USA

Audrey L. Holland
Department of Speech and Hearing Sciences
University of Arizona, USA

Simon Horton
Department of Language and Communication
  Science
City University, London, England

Michael A. Kraut
Department of Radiology
Johns Hopkins Hospital School of Medicine, USA

Matti Laine
University of Turku, Finland

Margaret T. Lehman-Blake
Department of Communication Sciences and
  Disorders
Syracuse University, USA

Jane Marshall
Department of Language and Communication
  Science
City University, London, England

Nadine Martin
Department of Neurology
Temple University School of Medicine, USA

Randi Martin
Psychology Department
Rice University, USA

Michelle Miller
Department of Psychology
Northern Arizona University, USA

Lauren R. Moo
Department of Neurology
Johns Hopkins University, USA

Steven Z. Rapcsak
VA Medical Center, Tucson, AZ, USA

Brenda Rapp
Cognitive Science Department
Johns Hopkins University, USA

Anastasia M. Raymer
Department of ESSE, Child Study Center
Old Dominion University, USA

Jessica B. Segal
Department of Neurology
Johns Hopkins Hospital, USA

Steven L. Small
Department of Neurology
University of Chicago, USA

Cynthia K. Thompson
Communication Sciences and Disorders
Northwestern University, USA

Connie A. Tompkins
Communication Science and Disorders
University of Pittsburgh, USA

Elizabeth Tuffiash
Department of Cognitive Science
Johns Hopkins University, USA

Christine Whatmough
McGill University, Canada

Preface

The breakdown of language after focal brain injury has captured the interest of investigators and clinicians for more than 150 years. This common interest has formed the basis for the emergence of aphasiology—a field of investigation devoted to characterizing language disorders that result from brain damage, and the implications of these disorders both for theories of the cognitive processes underlying language and for theories of how language is represented and processed in the brain. This handbook is meant to review the major areas of research undertaken by aphasiologists; that is, speech-language pathologists, clinical neuropsychologists, cognitive neuropsychologists, neurolinguists, computer scientists, and behavioral/cognitive neurologists who investigate acquired language impairments. Some have as their goal to characterize the types of cognitive representations and operations that underlie normal language, on the basis of how language breaks down after focal brain lesions. Others have as their goal to identify how or where these cognitive representations are carried out in the brain. Still others seek to develop and refine methods to improve language functions after they are disrupted by brain damage. But collaboration between investigators with these divergent goals has been crucial for all of them. For instance, the development of models of lexical processing that specified relatively independent functional components for representing information about spoken forms, written forms, and meanings of words laid the groundwork for identifying, through functional imaging and lesion studies, a variety of brain regions that are involved in a particular task such as naming. Without such models, investigators would likely have persisted in seeking a single "naming center" (versus a "reading center"), for example, or in seeking a simple dichotomy of language input versus output centers. The identification of focal brain regions responsible for specific cognitive functions, such as the phonological output lexicon versus the semantic lexicon, has guided diagnosis and even surgical intervention (for example, surgical treatment of intractable epilepsy). Cognitive models have also spurred the development of therapies that focus on restoring, or compensating for, the impaired components of a task such as naming, rather than applying the same therapy to patients whose naming (or reading, or sentence processing, say) is impaired at different levels of the process.

The organization of this handbook is unique in that it reflects a step toward integration of these various branches of aphasiology. There are several major sections, each devoted to a particular language task, such as naming, spelling, or sentence comprehension. Within each section, there is a chapter on models or theories of the cognitive processes involved in the task, a chapter on the neural structures underlying the task (as revealed by functional neuroimaging as well as lesion-behavior correlation studies), and a chapter on diagnosis and treatment of impairments of that task. For sentence comprehension and production, there are separate chapters on the models/theories of comprehension versus production, reflecting the vast quantity of research devoted to characterizing each. There are also chapters that do not fall into a single section, but apply to (or potentially apply to) a variety of language tasks. For instance, Nadine Martin and her colleagues discuss computational models of lexical processing, and touch on how such models might be useful in guiding therapy. Although it might be argued that there ought to be a chapter in each section on the computational models of the task, the field has not matured in every aspect of language. Instead, each chapter on theories/models of the language task at least briefly discusses computational models of that task, and the Martin, Laine, and Harley chapter addresses computational modeling in more detail. Steven L. Small discusses pharmacological interventions that might someday be applied to improving function in each of the tasks. Audrey L. Holland and Jacqueline J. Hinckley provide an important pragmatic perspective to the treatment of aphasia. Their chapter brings to light the fact that most patients with aphasia have impairment in more than one component, on more than one task, so that treatment cannot always address a single impaired component. Rather, treatment must serve to improve the aphasic patient's ability to communicate. This goal often transcends the details of the patient's particular deficit(s), although communication strategies might differ depending on the profile of the impairment(s). Finally, Connie A. Thompkins and her coauthors eloquently discuss the role of the right hemisphere in language and communication.

Even the main sections of this handbook are not fully integrated. For the most part, each chapter in a given section is written by a different author, often from a different background or backgrounds. The theoretical models discussed are not identical, even within a given section. As an editor, I encouraged this divergence, without apology. The variation in the models honestly reflects the state of the field, including the controversies and unknowns. It would be a disservice to the reader to present a completely "united front," as though any given language task were well understood. But there is a common thread, both within and across sections. That is, each chapter on neuroanatomy/neuroimaging and each chapter on therapy relies on a model of the language task that specifies functionally distinct components that have been postulated in order to account for impaired patterns of performance.

Consistent with the interdisciplinary approach to aphasia, several authors have training and expertise in more than one discipline, each contributing to that author's characterization of language and its disorders. For example, Dana Boatman is both an audiologist and a linguist; David Caplan is both a linguist and a cognitive neurologist; Steven L. Small is both a cognitive neurologist and a computer scientist. Nadine Martin is a speech-language pathologist with extensive experience in cognitive neuropsychology and computationalism. Other chapters are coauthored by investigators from different disciplines, such as the chapters by Pelagie M. Beeson (a speech-language pathologist) and Steven Z. Rapczak (a behavioral/cognitive neurologist). But irrespective of the discipline(s) in which each author received formal training, we all share a belief that interaction with the other disciplines is essential to making progress toward understanding aphasia. Interaction with yet other disciplines, such as basic neuroscience and molecular genetics, will be essential in future years, to specify the neurotransmitters, channels, hormones, and changes in gene expression that truly underlie impairment and recovery of language after brain injury.

Part 1

—

Reading

—

Models of
the Reading Process

Argye E. Hillis

The problem of how a printed word is understood and pronounced has been the focus of an explosion of research in cognitive neuropsychology, experimental psychology, and computational neuroscience since the 1970s. One attraction of this topic is that the task of reading a word can be disrupted by focal brain damage in a variety of recognizable ways that seem to transparently reflect damage to a discrete cognitive mechanism. And yet, many aspects of these impaired patterns of performance can be reproduced by computational models of reading without postulating the discrete cognitive mechanisms that have been proposed to account for impaired performance. Hence, the topic remains rich in controversy and unresolved questions. Nevertheless, there is widespread agreement on the basic computations that are essential to reading aloud and comprehending a printed word. Thus, a schemata of the mental representations and processes underlying reading can help us to understand disordered reading after brain lesions, and can provide a framework for focusing therapy. Furthermore, such a schemata is essential in determining the regions of the brain that are responsible for reading. That is, there is clearly not a single area of the brain that, when damaged, causes inability to read. Rather, a number of areas are likely to carry out separate components of the reading task, so that lesions in various brain regions disrupt the reading process in different ways. Therefore, an account of the components (representations and mechanisms) that underlie reading guides our investigation of the neural substrates that subserve these components.

To begin, let us consider the computational requirements of reading a familiar word. First, the lines and dots that comprise the letters must be resolved into letter shapes. Then, these letter shapes, which have a particular font and case, must access abstract letter identities (graphemes), so that strings of the same letters, such as TEAR and tear and *tear*, are recognized as strings of the same graphemes. Subsequently, this string of graphemes is recognized as a familiar word, when it accesses stored orthographic representation in the mental lexicon. Once recognized as familiar, the string of graphemes must access a the stored meaning, or semantic representation, appropriate to the context, so that the word *tear*, for instance, is understood differently in the context *a tear dropped* versus *tear the paper*. Whichever discrete semantic representation is activated (for example, <a droplet from the eye> versus <to rip>) must then be used to access a stored pronunciation, or phonological representation, corresponding to that meaning. Thus, the word *tear* in *tear the paper* will be pronounced in such a way that it rhymes with *bear* and not *fear*. (In some schema, words without homographs may access a phonological representation directly; this issue will be discussed in detail later in this chapter.) Lastly, this phonological representation must serve as the basis for activating particular motor programs for articulation. At some point in this process, either parallel to or prior to accessing a phonological representation, information about the syntactic role of the word is also activated, so that we know that the word *tear* is a noun in the context of the phrase *a tear dropped,* but is a verb in the context of the phrase *tear the paper.*

Now let us consider how we pronounce a word (or pseudoword or uncommon proper name) that we have never encountered. It is possible to assign a plausible pronunciation without accessing stored orthographic, semantic, or phonological representations, by using some sort of print-to-sound, or orthography-to-phonology, conversion mechanisms. For example, my first name, Argye, has elicited a variety of equally plausible pronunciations (/argi/, /argaI/, /arʤi/ /arʤai/) although just as often it is mispronounced as "Argyle" or "argue" (presumably because the written form activates an orthographically similar word in the lexicon).

These relatively independent components of the reading task are schematically represented in figure 1.1. It should be noted that this "model" of the reading process is not universally accepted. For example, alternative models assume that many of the proposed representations are activated in parallel (Plaut & Shallice, 1993) or in cascade (Humphreys, Riddoch, & Quinlan, 1988), or that there are not separate mechanisms for reading familiar and unfamiliar words (Seidenberg & McClelland, 1989). Others propose a "direct route" from orthographic o phonological lexicons, bypassing semantics (for example, Coslett, 1991). These controversies will be addressed below as each component of the model is discussed. Evidence that will be presented for each component of the reading process comes from neurologically impaired patients, whose pattern of performance in reading and other lexical tasks can be explained by proposing selective damage to that component. Most of the cited evidence will come from my own investigations, since these patients were tested on a relatively uniform battery of reading and other lexical tasks, and their divergent patterns of performance across stimuli and tasks can thus be directly compared and contrasted. However, it should be recognized that the same points could be made by citing data from patients who have been studied at least as thoroughly by other investigators.

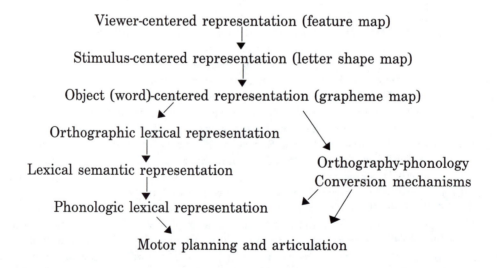

Figure 1.1. A schematic representation of the cognitive processes underlying reading.

LEVELS OF SPATIAL REPRESENTATION COMPUTED IN RECOGNIZING A PRINTED WORD

Viewer-Centered Representations

When a word on the upper left corner of a page is to be read, the first representation to be computed takes the form of lines and blobs and other variations in light intensities, represented in the upper left corner of a spatial map with viewer-centered coordinates (Monk, 1985; Marr & Nishihara, 1978). Computation of this level of representation can be disrupted by viewer-centered hemispatial neglect, in which stimuli or parts of stimuli on the side of the view contralateral to brain damage are not processed. This level of hemispatial neglect occurs most frequently (if not exclusively) after damage to the right hemisphere, affecting the left side of the view. To illustrate, patients CS, AS, and AWR failed to read words correctly if they were presented on the left side of their view, even if they were in the intact visual field (Hillis, Rapp, Benzing, & Caramazza, 1998). Moreover, the three patients each made more errors on letters that were further to the left of their view, whether the letters comprised the initial letters of the word (in standard print) or the final letters (in upside-down or mirror-reversed print). They each made similar visual errors on nonlexical stimuli presented in the left side of the view, and made no errors on words that were presented nonvisually (for example, spelled aloud to them), indicating that the deficit involved computation of a viewer-centered representation of visual stimuli.

Stimulus-Centered Representations

Other patients with left hemispatial neglect make errors on the left side of the word, irrespective of where the word is presented in their view. To illustrate, patients RW (Hillis & Caramazza, 1991a) and BPN (Hillis & Caramazza, 1995a) made errors on the initial letters of words in reading standard print, but not on the final letters of words (on the left side of the visual stimulus) in reading mirror-reversed print, and made no spatially specific errors in reading vertically printed words, whether the stimuli were presented on the left or right side of the body or visual field. For example, *bear* was read as "fear" in standard print and as "bead" in mirror-reversed print. Therefore, their errors seem to concern one side of visual/spatial representation defined by the coordinates of the stimulus, rather than by the location with respect to the viewer. We have called this level of representation the "stimulus-centered representation" because errors increase as a function of the distance (to the left) from the center of the visual stimulus (Caramazza & Hillis, 1990a; Hillis & Caramaza, 1991 & 1995b). To further illustrate, when a suffix was added to a word (for example, sad, sadness), the initial letter of the word was "pushed" further to the left of the center of the stimulus; and RW and BPN were more likely to make errors on the initial letter in this condition. That is, both were more likely to make errors on the *s* in *sadness* (for example, *sadness* → "badness") than on the *s* in *sad*. Furthermore, if a prefix was added to the word, pushing the initial letter of the root word closer to the center of the word, fewer errors were made on the initial letter of the root word. For instance, both RW and BPN were more likely to make an error on the *c* in *cook* (for example, *cook* → "look") than on the *c* in *precook*. There were similar findings with recognition of nonlexical stimuli: these patients made more errors in identifying/copying left sides of stimuli, irrespective of where the stimuli were presented with respect to the viewer. These results indicated that the deficit in RW and BPN concerned stimulus-centered representations of not only words, but also visual/spatial stimuli more generally (but see Patterson & Wilson, 1990, and Costello & Warrington, 1987, for possible cases of similar hemispatial errors in reading but not in nonlexical visuospatial tasks). Neither RW nor BPN made left-sided errors in recognizing words that were spelled aloud to them, indicating that their deficit concerned visuospatial representations rather than abstract grapheme or word-level representations. Other patients with patterns of performance indicating neglect at the level of stimulus-centered representations have been reported by Subbiah and Caramazza (2000), Haywood and Coltheart (2000); and Nichelli, Venneri, Pentore, and Cubelli (1993).

Word-Centered (Object-Centered) Representations

In contrast to all of the patients with hemispatial neglect described above, patient NG (who was left-handed, and nonaphasic after a left temporoparietal and thalamic stroke) made errors on the right side of words. More important, the frequency of her errors was a function of the letter position in the canonical representation of the word. That is, she made errors on the final letters of words, whether words were presented in standard print, mirror-reversed print, or vertical print (Hillis & Caramazza, 1990; Caramazza & Hillis, 1990b). She even made errors on the final letters of words when they were spelled aloud to her (or when she spelled aloud or wrote the word), as shown in table 1.1, indicating that her errors concerned the right side of an abstract representation of the word (the grapheme string) in its canonical orientation, independent of the orientation or modality of the stimulus. Her errors specific to the right side of a location-, orientation- and modality-independent representation were not specific to words—NG made comparable errors in recognizing or responding to nonlinguistic stimuli (Hillis & Caramazza, 1995a). As also described for RW and BPN, NG's error rate in reading words was a function of the distance from the center of the word; she made more errors on the final letter of a root word when a prefix was added (pushing the final letter further to the right from the center) and fewer errors when a suffix was added (pushing the final letters closer to the center of the word (Caramazza & Hillis, 1990a & 1990b). Similarly, she made fewer errors in copying the right side of an abstract figure when the abstract figure was expanded by adding a box around it, thereby "pushing" the right side of the original stimulus further toward the center of the modified stimulus (Hillis & Caramazza, 1995a). NG also made errors on the final letters of nonlexical letter and nonletter strings (Hillis & Caramazza, 1990). Additional patients have been reported whose patterns of performance on reading and/or spelling (Barbut & Gazzaniga, 1987; Baxter & Warrington, 1983; Hillis & Caramazza, 1995b) and nonlexical tasks (Bisiach & Luzzatti, 1978; Bisiach & Berti, 1987) indicated damage at the level of object-centered representations. These results provide evidence that a word/object-centered representation is computed from the visual stimulus and is used to access stored orthographic or canonical object representations.

Orthographic Representations (Units of the Orthographic Lexicon)

An overwhelming number of cases of impaired reading, in which patients do not recognize printed words and cannot distinguish real words from pronounceable pseudowords (for example, *samp*), have been reported. Most of the earliest cases (see Marshall & Newcombe, 1973; Patterson, Coltheart, & Marshall, 1985) were found to have spared reading (that is, plausible pronunciation) of pseudowords, and could "sound out" familiar words and unfamiliar words, according to common orthography-phonology correspondence (OPC) rules. Consequently, they read "regular" words better than "irregular" words, since regular words can be correctly pronounced just by applying the most frequent OPC rules. Such cases have been interpreted as manifesting impaired access to orthographic representations, but intact access to OPC procedures. Consider patient PS, who read pseudowords more accurately than words (since plausible pronunciations of pseudowords, based on OPC rules, are always accurate), and read regular words significantly better than irregular words (Hillis, 1993). He seemed to pronounce letter strings according to OPC mechanisms or "rules." For example, he read aloud *threat* as "threet"

Table 1.1
Example of NG's Errors in Various Lexical Tasks

Task	Stimulus	NG's response	
Oral reading: standard print	stripe	strip	
	study	stud	
	humid	human	
	chin	chew	
	sprinter	sprinkle	
Oral reading: vertical print (top-to-bottom)	rang	ran	
	forced	force	
	blending	blemish	
	risks	rich	
	common	comet	
Oral reading: vertical print (bottom-to-top)	friend	fright	
	candid	candle	
	agency	agenda	
	repeat	reply	
	barbeque	barbell	
Oral reading: mirror-reversed print	common	comet	
	greenish	greenery	
	joint	join	
	discovery	disco	
	dashes	dash	
Recognition of aurally spelled words	j-o-y-o-u-s	joy	
	f-i-x-e-d	fix	
	w-o-r-e	work	
	t-a-l-e-n-t	tall	
	e-a-r-n-s	earring	
Written spelling	pretty	pret	
	fact	fac	
	blame	bland	
	crow	croy	
	sneeze	sneed	
Oral spelling	spoke	s-p-o-k	(spok)
	priest	p-r-i-e-s	(pries)
	jury	j-u-r-i-o-n	(jurion)
	event	e-v-e-n-i-s	(evenis)
	soft	s-o-f-e	(sofe)
Backward oral spelling	absorb	n-w-o-s-b-a	(absown)
	sky	k-i-k-s	(skik)
	church	r-u-h-c	(chur)
	garbage	i-s-b-r-a-g	(garbsi)
	oyster	e-t-s-y-o	(oyste)

(rhyming with *beet*) and *stood* as "stewed." He also understood words as he pronounced them, indicating that he did not access semantics from the orthographic representation, but from the phonological representation activated by his application of OPC mechanisms. So, for example, he read the word *bear* as "beer" and understood it as something to drink at the bar. Therefore, he also had a great deal of trouble distinguishing the meaning of homophones, such as *beet* and *beat.* Therapy designed to reestablish orthographic representations of words, or access to them, in order to activate the corresponding semantic representations lead to improved reading of irregular words, homophones, and words with ambiguous pronunciations, such as *bear* (Hillis, 1993).[1] This pattern of performance (sometimes referred to as "input surface dyslexia"), along with the opposite pattern (better reading of familiar words than words, and phonologically dissimilar word substitutions in reading aloud words; sometimes referred to as "deep dyslexia"), can be interpreted as evidence for distinct cognitive mechanisms for reading familiar words versus unfamiliar words (or pseudowords). Familiar words are thought to be read via the orthographic lexicon, and pseudowords or unfamiliar words are read via OPC mechanisms (Coltheart, Patterson, & Marshall, 1980). However, this rather simple account has been challenged by authors who point to computer simulations of reading, in which both words and pseudowords can be correctly pronounced without postulating distinct word representations (Seidenberg & McClelland, 1989). Furthermore, some aspects of impaired performance, such as better reading of pseudowords than words or vice versa, can be simulated by creating damage to such a neural network (Plaut & Shallice, 1993). For example, plausible pronunciations of words (reported in cases of "surface dyslexia") and a pattern in which errors include visually similar words (for example, *ford* for *fork*), semantically similar words (for example, *spoon* for *fork*), as reported in cases of "deep dyslexia," have been simulated. However, the simulations fail to reproduce certain other reported patterns of performance, such as the production of only semantically related words (for example, by RGB in Caramazza & Hillis, 1990c) or the production of only phonologically or visually similar words (for example, Hillis, Boatman, Hart, & Gordon, 1999). Thus, only models that postulate separate cognitive mechanisms for lexical representations and OPC can account for the full spectrum of impaired reading patterns due to focal brain injury that have been reported. Nevertheless, certain features of these connectionist models or neural networks of the reading process, such as the interaction between separate levels of processing, are likely to capture important features of normal reading, as discussed in detail later in this chapter.

Lexical-Semantic Representations

Many patients have been described who make "regularization" errors similar to those of PS, but can nevertheless distinguish words from pseudowords, and can often extract some, although incomplete, meaning from familiar words. Moreover, their understanding of words is no better when the word is read aloud correctly. Consider, for example, JJ, who suffered a left posterior temporo-parietal infarct (Hillis & Caramazza, 1991b&c). He made "regularization errors," such as reading *pear* as "pier." Such regularization errors, along with his relatively accurate reading of pseudowords, indicate that JJ also read aloud via OPC mechanisms, at least when he failed to understand the words at all. But most printed words were partially understood. For example, he typically selected the correct printed word or a semantically related word to match a picture (for example, matched a pictured chair to the word *bed*). His rates and types of errors in word-picture matching were identical with spoken and written word stimuli, indicating that both forms accessed an incomplete semantic representation. JJ also made semantically related word errors in spoken and written naming (for example, JJ named a picture of a boat as "motor cycle"), with approximately the same frequency as his errors in comprehension tasks. JJ's pattern of performance across lexical tasks can be explained by proposing selective damage to the semantic component of the reading system. This semantic component is shared by reading, writing, naming, and comprehension tasks.

Although the semantic component is crucial in correctly reading homophones, such as

---

[1]Early after his brain damage, PS also had an impairment at the level of semantics, but this deficit only affected the semantic representations of animals and vegetables (Hillis & Caramazza, 1991b).

tear, in appropriate contexts, and in reading irregular words, the semantic component can be "bypassed" in oral reading of regular words by relying on OPC mechanisms. Reliance on OPC mechanisms alone results in correct oral reading of regular words. However, irregular words, such as *one,* are misread (as "own" in this example) when using OPC alone, as reported in JJ's case. Nevertheless, it was noted that JJ read aloud some irregular words correctly. Many of these words were probably read correctly via the semantic component, since he also understood these words. However, other irregular words were correctly read even though he failed to comprehend them completely. To illustrate, he read *one* correctly, although he defined it as "the number of ears I have." It was found that the only irregular words that JJ read aloud accurately were words that he understood at least partially. Irregular words that he failed to understand at all were misread as phonologically plausible errors. For instance, he read *quay* as /kweI/ or "kway" (rhyming with *kay*) and defined it as "I have no idea; it looks like a type of bird." It was therefore hypothesized that phonological representations for output can be accessed by a "summation" of partial information from the semantic component and partial information from OPC mechanisms (Hillis & Caramazza, 1991c & 1995e; see Patterson & Hodges, 1992, for a similar proposal about the interaction of semantics and OPC mechanisms). Additional evidence for this hypothesis is that the rare semantic errors JJ made in oral reading were all phonologically related, as well as semantically related, to the target. For example, JJ misread *skirt* as "shirt." However, other authors have proposed that correct oral reading of irregular words that are not understood provides evidence that phonological representations for output can be activated directly from orthographic representations; that is, that there is a "direct route" from the orthographic (input) lexicon to the phonological (output) lexicon (Schwartz, Marin, & Saffran, 1979; Coslett, 1991). Indeed, there have been cases reported in which irregular words are pronounced correctly without any apparent evidence of comprehension of the words (Greenwald & Berndt, 1998). Obviously, this "nonsemantic route" would not allow one to read homographs, such as *lead, read,* or *tear,* correctly in various contexts.

Other patients with impairment at the level of the semantic representation do not produce "regularization" errors. Rather, they make errors that are semantically related to the target. To illustrate, patient KE made semantically related errors in reading, oral naming, written naming, spoken word comprehension, and written word comprehension (for example, *onion* named as "carrot"; *jacket* read as "belt" [Hillis, Rapp, Romani, & Caramazza, 1990]). He showed no ability to use OPC mechanisms to read aloud familiar or unfamiliar words or pseudowords. If his OPC mechanisms had been spared at all, the phonological information yielded by OPC would likely have "blocked" the production of semantically related words in oral reading. The production of semantically related word errors in oral reading, along with the inability to read nonwords, is a pattern sometimes referred to as "deep dyslexia." However, it will be shown below that this pattern can be a consequence of damage to different components of the reading system, making it a heterogeneous class of disorders.

Phonological Representations

The semantic representation of a word (with or without input from OPC mechanisms) activates a phonological representation for spoken output. As noted above, it is also possible that OPC mechanisms and/or orthographic representations alone can activate a phonological representation for spoken output. Normally, only the target phonological representation is selected for output. But after focal brain damage the target phonological representation may be unavailable. There are at least two possible consequences of impaired access to the target phonological representations. First, if the patient has intact OPC mechanisms, he or she might rely on these mechanisms and will produce phonologically plausible errors. Consider, for example, patient HG. After severe left fronto-temporal-parietal damage, HG was unable to access correct phonological representations in any spoken task (spontaneous speech, oral naming, repetition, or oral reading). Her spontaneous speech consisted of fluent, low-volume jargon, with virtually no content. However, her OPC mechanisms were intact (at least after some brief training), and so she "sounded out" words slowly in oral reading tasks. For example, she read *feet* correctly and read *comb* as "sombe" (/soUmb/). In contrast, HG had relatively preserved access to orthographical representations for written output. Thus, in naming tasks she often wrote the correct word, but read aloud her own written word incorrectly (for example, *comb* as "sombe"). Furthermore, at times she would produce a phonologically plausible rendition of the orthographic stimulus, even though no written name was available. That is, she named *comb* as "sombe" in response to the object, even though she did not write or have available the written word. In conversation, her rare content words were often phonologically plausible renditions of the written form of the word. For example, she named *Broad St.* as "brode sssst" /brod st/. She apparently had no recollection that the abbreviation *St.* represented the word *street*. When *street* was written out, she pronounced it correctly, indicating that her mispronunciations were not due to motor programming or articulation problems. HG was able to learn the correct pronunciations of words (that is, to develop, or restore access to, phonological representations) only if they were spelled for her phonetically. Thus, learning to say *pizza* correctly was accomplished by spelling it as *peetsa* (Hillis, 1991). HG's case demonstrates that "regularization" errors can occur as a result of damage not only at the levels of the orthographic input lexicon or the semantic system, but also at the level of the phonological output lexicon; that is, damage anywhere along the "lexical route," sparing the OPC route.

A second reported pattern of errors that can result from impaired access to phonological representations for output is the production of semantically related words in oral reading and naming. In these cases, there has been severe impairment of OPC mechanisms, as well as impaired access to some phonological representations. One illustrative case is that of RGB (Caramazza & Hillis, 1990c; Hillis & Caramazza, 1995c). RGB had fluent, grammatical speech, with frequent circumlocutions and semantic paraphasias. But in contrast to patients JJ and KE, who made semantic errors in both oral naming and comprehension, RGB had perfectly intact comprehension of written and spoken words (as indicated by his 100 percent accurate word/picture verification, his accurate definitions of words, and so on). Nevertheless, he read aloud words as semantically related words. For instance, he read the word *red* as "yellow" but defined it as "the color of blood." RGB's oral reading and naming could not be improved by providing the phonetically spelled word, since he had no ability to use OPC mechanisms to read familiar or unfamiliar words. However, his oral reading and naming improved with a cuing hierarchy that increased production of the correct word (see chapter 9 in this book for discussion of cuing hierarchies). That is, it is thought that the availability of a phonological representation is dependent on its "threshold of activation," which is a function of the frequency of production of a word. Thus, cued production of the word likely increased its frequency of production and perhaps lowered its threshold of activation.

Why did RGB make semantic errors, rather than phonological errors, in reading and naming, since his semantic component was intact (as indicated by preserved comprehension)? One account for the production of semantic errors in the face of spared comprehension is the following: semantic representations are composed of all the semantic features that together define the meaning of the word, and each of these semantic features activates every phonological representation to which it corresponds. For example, the semantic representation of *mitten* might be composed of semantic features, such as <clothing>, <for hands>, <for cold weather>, <woolen or weather-resistant material>, <without separate parts for each digit>. These semantic features would each activate corresponding phonological representations. To illustrate, the feature <clothing> would activate phonological representations of *skirt, shirt, pants, sock, mitten,* and so on; while the feature <for hands> would activate phonological representations of words such as *mitten, glove, hand lotion,* and so on. Normally, only the target phonological representation would receive the most activation (from all of the semantic features) and would thus be selected for output. However, if that target phonological representation were to be unavailable (for example, in the case of RGB), one of the other phonological representations (for example, *glove*) activated by one or more of the semantic features, might be activated instead (see Hillis & Caramazza, 1995c & 1995d). In this way, the production of semantic errors in reading, along with impaired OPC mechanisms (the pattern known as "deep dyslexia"), can result from damage to either the phonological lexicon or the semantic component. In the latter case, semantic errors are likely to arise when one or more features of the semantic representations is damaged, such that the impoverished semantic representation is equally compatible with (and equally activates) several phonological representations. For instance, if the semantic representation of *mitten* were missing the feature <for hands>, the remaining features might equally activate *mitten* and *sock*. Whichever phonological representation had a lower threshold of activation (for example, higher frequency) would be selected for output. This account would explain the inconsistent production of semantic errors and correct names in oral reading and oral naming by patients with semantic impairments (for example, KE, described above).

Phonetic Selection

Many patients after brain damage fail to read aloud or name words correctly, even though they seem to "know" the correct pronunciation. That is, they appear to access the target phonologic representation, but then produce either a phonologically similar word (a "formal error"; for example, *mitten* → "kitten" [Martin, Saffran, & Schwartz, 1994]) or phonologically similar nonword (for example, *mitten* → "titten"). They may attempt to self-correct the phonological error. A case in point is that of JBN (Hillis et al., 1999). JBN had fluent, grammatical speech, with frequent phonological errors. Her comprehension of written words was intact, as indicated by printed word/picture verification tasks with both phonologically and semantically related foils, and by matching printed words to synonyms. She also seemed to access the correct phonological representation, as indicated by her ability to match rhyming words or pictures. Nevertheless, in oral reading (and oral naming), she made frequent phonological errors in producing the words. The problem was not in motor planning or articulation, since JBN correctly repeated nonsense syllables. Rather, her performance was explained by assuming impaired selection of the sequence of phonemes (or sublexical phonological units) to articulate.

Motor Programming and Articulation

Once the sequence of phonemes (or phonetic segments) is selected for output, it must be translated into the appropriate sequence of movements, through programming and coordination of the lips, tongue, jaw, soft palate, and vocal cords. Since this handbook concerns language (rather than speech production) disorders, a full discussion of the variety of motor deficits that can interfere with accurate oral reading is beyond the scope of this chapter. However, it is important to note that either dysarthria or apraxia can result in impaired, or difficult-to-understand, oral reading. Dysarthria is an impairment in the range, strength, rate, or coordination of movements of the articulators, due to upper and/or lower cranial nerve deficits or damage to the basal ganglia and/or cerebellum. Apraxia of speech is an impairment in programming or sequencing these complex movements, in the face of normal range, strength, and rate of movements.

SUMMARY

This review of the components of the reading process (schematically represented in figure 1.1) was meant to provide the reader with an overview of some of the major levels of representations and cognitive mechanisms underlying reading that have been identified through the study of neurologically impaired subjects. It is not comprehensive. For instance, some investigators would add a level of representation—the lemma—that mediates between semantics and phonological representations (Roelofs, 1992). This level of representation is further discussed in chapter 7 by Doriana Chialant, Albert Costa, and Alfonso Caramazza, who conclude that such a level of representation is not necessary to account for the spectrum of data presented in its favor, and in chapter 17 by Cynthia K. Thompson and Yasmeen Faroqi-Shah, who present a different view. Furthermore, a number of investigators would add more (or less) interaction between levels of representation. This topic, of the degree and type (feedforward, feedback, or both) of interaction, and between what levels of representation, is just beginning to receive attention (Rapp & Goldrick, 2000; Chialant et al., chapter 7 in this volume). Most computational models have assumed both feedforward and feedback interaction between all levels of representation; whereas most "serial" models have assumed virtually no interaction between components (but see Humphreys et al., 1988, and Hillis & Caramazza, 1991c & 1995e). Recent investigations indicate that the hypothesis of limited interaction between specific levels of representation may best account for the empirical evidence (Rapp & Goldrick, 2000).

Still other investigators would question the existence of one or more of the levels of representation or processing specified in figure 1. For example, many computational models have accounted for at least a subset of data from neurologically impaired subjects without proposing independent lexical and sublexical (OPC) mechanisms. It is not clear, however, how these models could be revised to account for patients like HG, who relied solely on OPC mechanisms, even to pronounce printed words that she understood. Nor could they account for the fact that HG could only learn correct pronunciations of printed irregular words when she was presented with the printed word misspelled phonetically. As mentioned, these computational models also fail to account for patients who make strictly one sort of error (either phonologically/visually similar errors or semantically related errors) in reading. Computational models that do specify lexical levels (or a lemma level) of representation separate from a semantic component can better account for the observed patterns of performance, but only if selective components of the system are "lesioned" (see chapter 7 in this volume). Other computational models would do away with an "object-centered" level of spatial representation (Mozer & Behrmann, 1990), but in so doing cannot account for patients, like NG, who make errors on one side of the "canonical" representation of a word, irrespective of its orientation or modality of presentation.

Although the components of the reading system are represented by discrete boxes in figure 1.1, it is highly likely that these functional entities consist of distributed representations in the brain. That is, a "semantic representation" almost certainly consists of coactivation of numerous regions of the brain (let alone thousands or millions of neurons) that represent separate features that jointly define the meaning of a given word. Similarly, an orthographic representation might be best thought of as coactivation of the component graphemes, together with ordering information, which may or may not be represented in a unified brain region. Nevertheless, there does seem to be a certain amount of localization of these separate cognitive components to specific brain regions, although there is assuredly not a single region of the brain that carries out the entire reading task. The localization of distinct operations in the reading process is discussed in chapter 2.

It was noted in this chapter that patients with selective damage to specific components of the reading system responded to different types of therapy to improve their reading. Specific remediation strategies for a number of the patients described in this chapter, along with other patients with damage to one or more levels of processing in reading, are described in more detail elsewhere (for example, in Beeson & Hillis, 2001; Hillis & Caramazza, 1994). More important, discussion of how a model of the reading task can focus therapy for patients with a variety of reading disorders is discussed in detail by Rhonda B. Friedman in chapter 3.

It is safe to conclude from the cases of impaired reading described in this chapter and elsewhere that reading is a complex process that entails activation of a number of different mental representations and operations that can be selectively impaired by focal brain damage. Many of these representations and operations are shared by other language tasks, such that damage—say, to the semantic component—is reflected not only in reading, but also in oral and written naming and in comprehension tasks. Thus, pinpointing and characterizing the level of impairment in reading often requires assessment of a variety of lexical tasks, with different input and output modalities. Reading sentences and narrative recruits additional processes, such as short-term memory and syntactic processes. Even so, evidence, of the type reported in this chapter, that single word reading consists of a number of functionally distinct components carried out by various regions of the brain, has played a crucial role in the development of cognitive neuroscience. Such evidence has been pivotal in further investigation of the neural substrates of reading and other lexical processes and investigation of the types of therapeutic interventions (see chapter 3) that might restore language function after brain damage.

REFERENCES

Barbut, D., & Gazzaniga, M. (1987). Disturbances in conceptual space involving language and speech. *Brain, 110*, 1487–1496.

Baxter, D. M., & Warrington, E. K. (1983). Neglect dysgraphia. *Journal of Neurology, Neurosurgery, and Psychiatry, 45*, 1073–1078.

Beeson, P., & Hillis, A. E. (2001). Comprehension and production of written words. In R. Chapey (Ed.), *Language intervention strategies in adult aphasia* (4th edition). Baltimore: Williams and Wilkin.

Bisiach, E., & Berti, A. (1987). Dyschiria: An attempt at its systemic explanation. In M. Jeannerod (Ed.), *Neuropsychological and physiological aspects of spatial neglect*. New York: Elsevier Science Publishers.

Bisiach, E., & Luzzatti, C. (1978). Unilateral neglect of representational space. *Cortex, 14*, 129–133.

Caramazza, A., & Hillis, A. E. (1990a). Levels of representation, coordinate frames, and unilateral neglect. In M. J. Riddoch (Ed.), *Neglect and the peripheral dyslexias, special issue of cognitive neuropsychology*, 391–445.

Caramazza, A., & Hillis, A.E. (1990b). Spatial representation of words in the brain implied by studies of a unilateral neglect patient. *Nature, 346*, 267–269.

Caramazza, A., & Hillis, A. E. (1990c). Where do semantic errors come from? *Cortex, 26*, 95–122.

Coltheart, M., Patterson, K., & Marshall, J. C. (Eds.). (1980). *Deep dyslexia*. London: Routledge and Kegan Paul.

Coslett, H. B. (1991). Read but not write "idea": Evidence for a third reading mechanism. *Brain and Language, 40*, 425–443.

Costello, A. de L., & Warrington, E. K. (1987). Dissociation of visuo-spatial neglect and neglect dyslexia. *Journal of Neurology, Neurosurgery, and Psychiatry, 50*, 1110–1116.

Greenwald, M., & Berndt, R. (1998). Letter-by-letter lexical access without semantics or specialized letter name phonology. *Brain and Language, 65*, 149–152.

Haywood, M., & Coltheart, M. (2000). Neglect dyslexia and the early stages of visual word recognition. *Neurocase, 6*, 33–44.

Hillis, A. E. (1991). Effects of separate treatments for distinct impairments within the naming process. In T. Prescott (Ed.), *Clinical Aphasiology* (Vol. 19). Austin, TX: Pro-Ed.

Hillis, A. E. (1993). The role of models of language processing in rehabilitation of language impairments. *Aphasiology, 7*, 5–26.

Hillis, A. E., Boatman, D., Hart, J., & Gordon, B. (1999). Making sense out of jargon: A neurolinguistic and computational account of jargon aphasia. *Neurology, 53*, 1813–1824.

Hillis, A. E., & Caramazza, A. (1990). The effects of attentional deficits on reading and spelling. In A. Caramazza (Ed.), *Cognitive neuropsychology and neurolinguistics: Advances in models of cognitive runction and impairment*. London: Lawruence Erlbaum Associates.

Hillis, A. E., & Caramazza, A. (1991a). Spatially-specific deficit to stimulus-centered letter shape representations in a case of "unilateral neglect." *Neuropsychologia, 29*, 1223–1240.

Hillis, A. E., & Caramazza, A. (1991b). Category-specific naming and comprehension impairment: A double dissociation. *Brain, 114*, 2081–2094.

Hillis, A. E., & Caramazza, A. (1991c). Mechanisms for accessing lexical representations for output: Evidence from a category-specific semantic deficit. *Brain and Language, 40*, 106–144.

Hillis, A. E., & Caramazza, A. (1994). Theories of lexical processing and theories of rehabilitation. In G. Humphreys & M. J. Riddoch (Eds.), *Cognitive neuropsychology and cognitive rehabilitation* (pp. 449–482). Hillsdale, NJ: Lawrence Erlbaum Associates.

Hillis, A. E., & Caramazza, A. (1995a). A framework for interpreting distinct patterns of hemispatial neglect. *Neurocase, 1*, 189–207.

Hillis, A. E., & Caramazza, A. (1995b). Spatially-specific deficits in processing graphemic representations in reading and writing. *Brain and Language, 48*, 263–308.

Hillis, A. E., & Caramazza, A. (1995c). The compositionality of lexical-semantic representations: Clues from semantic errors in object naming. *Memory, 3*, 333–358.

Hillis, A. E., & Caramazza, A. (1995d). Cognitive and neural mechanisms underlying visual and semantic processing. *Journal of Cognitive Neuroscience, 7*, 457–478.

Hillis, A. E., & Caramazza, A. (1995e). Converging evidence for the interaction of semantic and phonological information in accessing lexical information for spoken output. *Cognitive Neuropsychology, 12*, 187–227.

Hillis, A. E., Rapp, B., Benzing, L., & Caramazza, A. (1998). Dissociable coordinate frames of unilateral spatial neglect: Viewer-centered neglect. *Brain and Cognition, 37,* 491–526.

Hillis, A. E., Rapp, B. C., Romani, C., & Caramazza, A. (1990). Selective impairment of semantics in lexical processing. *Cognitive Neuropsychology, 7,* 191–244.

Humphreys, G. W., Riddoch, M. J., & Quinlan, P. T. (1988). Cascade processes in picture identification. *Cognitive Neuropsychology, 5,* 67–104.

Marr, D., & Nishihara, H. K. (1978). Representation and recognition of the spatial organization of three-dimensional shapes. *Proceedings of the Royal Society of London, 200,* 269–294.

Marshall, J. C., & Newcombe, F. (1973). Patterns of paralexia: A psycholinguistic approach. *Journal of Psycholinguistic Research, 2,* 175–199.

Martin, N., Dell, G. S., Saffran, E. M., & Schwartz, M. F. (1994). Origins of paraphasias in deep dysphasia: Testing the consequences of a decay impairment to an interactive spreading activation model of lexical retrieval. *Brain and Language, 47,* 609–660.

Monk, A. F. (1985). Co-ordinate systems in visual word recognition. *Quarterly Journal of Experimental Psychology, 37*(A), 613–625.

Mozer, M., & Behrmann, M. (1990). On the interaction of selective attention and lexical knowledge: A connectionist account of neglect dyslexia. *Journal of Cognitive Neuroscience,* 96–123.

Nichelli, P., Venneri, A., Pentore, R., & Cubelli, R. (1993). Horizontal and vertical neglect dyslexia. *Brain and Language, 44,* 264–283.

Patterson, K. E., Coltheart, M., & Marshall, J. C. (1985). *Surface dyslexia.* London: Lawrence Erlbaum Associates.

Patterson, K., & Hodges, J. (1992) Deterioration of word meaning: Implications for reading. *Neuropsychologia, 30,* 125–40.

Patterson, K., & Wilson, B. (1990). A ROSE is a ROSE or a NOSE: A deficit in initial letter identification. *Cognitive Neuropsychology, 7,* 447–477.

Plaut, D., & Shallice, T. (1993). Deep dyslexia: A case study of connectionist neuropsychology. *Cognitive Neuropsychology, 10,* 377–500.

Rapp, B. C., & Goldrick, M. (2000). Discreteness and interactivity in spoken word production. *Psychological Review, 107,* 460–499.

Roelofs, A. (1992). A spreading activation theory of lemma retrieval in speaking. *Cognition, 42,* 107–142.

Schwartz, M. F., Marin, O. S. M., & Saffran, E. M. (1979). Dissociations of language function in dementia: A case study. *Brain and Language, 7,* 277–306.

Seidenberg, M., & McClelland, J. L. (1989). A distributed, developmental model of visual word recognition and naming. *Psychological Review, 96*(4), 523–568.

Subbiah, I., & Caramazza, A. (2000). Stimulus-centered neglect in reading and object recognition. *Neurocase, 6,* 13–31.

2

Neuroanatomical Aspects
of Reading

Argye E. Hillis
Elizabeth Tuffiash

Despite the rich literature devoted to identifying the cognitive processes underlying reading (see chapter 1 for review), there is little agreement on the neural substrates underlying each of these component processes. Two major types of investigations have been devoted to the neuro-anatomical localization of the representations and mechanisms involved in reading: (1) lesion-deficit correlation studies, and (2) functional imaging studies. In both domains, studies have yielded conflicting results, as delineated below. However, there have been points of convergence as well. In this chapter, each method for identifying the neural bases of reading and the potential pitfalls of each method will be briefly reviewed. Then, candidate sites of each level of representation in the reading process will be discussed.

THE LESION-DEFICIT CORRELATION APPROACH

Since at least the mid-1800s, conclusions about where language is processed in the brain have been based largely on observations about deficits incurred by circumscribed brain lesions. The reasoning behind this approach is straightforward: if a lesion in a focal area of the brain causes impairment of a particular language process, that area of the brain must have been necessary for that language process. Early studies identified lesions (primarily strokes) at autopsy of patients with alexia—impairment of the reading task. Two areas of the brain were identified that resulted in alexia: left occipital and left temporo-parietal, including the angular gyrus (Dejerine, 1891 & 1892). It was noted that patients with temporo-parietal lesions had associated agraphia (writing impairment), but patients with occipital lesions did not. Although initially it was widely accepted that these two regions were the brain centers for reading, subsequent autopsy studies found frontal lesions in some alexic patients. Other individuals with frontal lesions, however, had intact reading. These observations led Freud (1891) to reject the leading theories of language localization.

One explanation for the conflicting results of lesion-deficit studies is that the characterization of reading impairment was too gross. As delineated in chapter 1, reading is a complex process requiring several relatively distinct mechanisms and levels of representation that might take place in different brain regions. Damage to any one of these components might disrupt the reading task (although in different ways). Hence, it is not surprising that a variety of sites of damage would result in alexia.

Another potential reason for contradictory findings in lesion-deficit correlation studies is that patients have generally been studied months or years after the initial brain injury. There is strong evidence that substantial reorganization of structure-function relationships occurs within weeks of onset of brain injury (Jenkins & Merzenich, 1987; Merzenich, Kaas, Wall, Nelson, Sur, & Felleman, 1983). Thus, even if a lesion (for example, in the frontal lobe) initially caused reading impairment, reading ability may have been recovered prior to studying the patient due to reorganization, with or without rehabilitation. Therefore, in studying patients with chronic lesions there may be little correlation between deficits at the time of investigation and the deficits initially caused by the lesion. Furthermore, studies of chronic stroke do not include patients whose deficits resolved quickly, or those who had no deficits after the brain injury. This selection bias precludes determination of the probability that a particular lesion will cause a specific deficit. That is, many patients who have the particular lesion but do not have the deficit are not included in the study.

To circumvent this problem, a number of investigators have attempted to identify the sites at which temporary lesions (caused by focal electrical stimulation) do or do not cause impaired reading. Such studies involve stimulation of electrodes placed directly on the cortex, used to guide surgery to remove a lesion or an area of the brain thought to be causing intractable epilepsy (Lesser, Luders, Dinner, Dinner, Klem, Hahn, & Harrison, 1986; Ojemann, 1994). Of course, these cortical stimulation studies can only be carried out in patients with lesions or chronic epilepsy, whose brains may have already undergone substantial reorganization due to the lesion or seizures. Ojemann (1994) reported that a variety of temporal and parietal sites resulted in impaired reading in these patients. Many sites affected both reading and naming, but a larger number of sites affected only one task or the other. Sites that interfered with both naming and reading generally caused slow, effortful reading, while sites that were specific to reading caused morpho-syntactic errors in reading. Of note, cortical stimulation studies investigate only areas of the brain being considered for resection (nearly always temporal and/or parietal regions, more than frontal or occipital), so sites outside of these areas that may be essential for reading cannot be investigated.

Another lesion-deficit approach that largely avoids the problems of reorganization and selection bias is the use of recent advanced imaging techniques to identify sites of lesion and poorly functioning brain regions, along with concurrent evaluation of reading, in patients with hyperacute stroke. Patients are studied within hours (less than twenty-four hours) of onset of stroke symptoms to identify which components of the reading process are impaired (as described in chapters 1 and 3). Within minutes or hours of this testing they undergo magnetic resonance diffusion-weighted imaging (DWI) and perfusion-weighted imaging (PWI) to identify the structural and functional brain lesions associated with the deficits. DWI is highly sensitive to infarct or densely ischemic tissue within minutes of onset, and PWI shows areas of poor blood flow, or hypoperfusion, that cause tissue dysfunction (Barber, Darby, Desmond, Yang, Gerraty, Jolley, Donnan, Tress, & Davis, 1998; Beaulieu, de Crespingy, Tong, Mosely, Albers, & Marks, 1999; Hillis, Barker, Beauchamp, Gordon, & Wityk, 2000). By studying all patients with symptoms of left hemisphere stroke prospectively, it is possible to determine the association between the presence or absence of a lesion and the presence or absence of a particular deficit at the time of onset. This has been the primary method we have used to identify sites of dysfunctional or damaged brain tissue associated with disruption of specific mechanisms underlying reading, as described in the following section. Results from a study of forty patients who had evaluation of reading, PWI, and DWI within twenty-four hours of onset of stroke are included in the following sections (see Hillis, Kane, Barker, Beauchamp, & Wityk, 2001, for details of the methodology).

FUNCTIONAL IMAGING

The two primary methods of evaluating regions of brain that are "activated" during specific components of the reading process in normal or brain-damaged subjects have been O^{15} PET and fMRI. Both types of studies have generally relied on the "subtraction method" to identify activated regions of cortex. In this method, subjects undergo imaging during a baseline task and during an experimental task. Then, areas that are activated during baseline are subtracted from areas that are activated during the experimental task. It is thus hoped that areas activated only during a particular component of the reading task can be isolated. For example, several studies have compared regional activation during viewing of real words versus viewing of unpronounceable letter strings. In this way, regions of activation associated with primary vision and spatial attention to letter strings are "subtracted out." The activation associated with the experimental task (viewing real words) minus baseline (viewing letter strings) thus corresponds to the activation associated with access to orthographic representations in the lexicon, and perhaps "automatic" access to the meaning of the words and/or the pronunciation of the words.

Results from functional imaging studies (like lesion studies) of reading have often been conflicting. There are many potential reasons for the discordant results. The most important is that many aspects of the particular experimental paradigm can substantially influence the results of functional imaging studies. For example, Peterson and colleagues reported results of a PET study indicating that passive viewing of real words or pronounceable pseudowords, compared to visual fixation of a crosshair, activated left extrastriate areas. In contrast, passive viewing of unpronounceable letter strings or strings of false fonts compared to visual fixation did not activate these regions (Peterson, Fox, Snyder, & Raichle, 1990; see also Peterson, Fox, Posner, Mintun, & Raichle, 1988). They concluded that access to orthographic representations of words in the lexicon occurs in the left extrastriate cortex. In contrast, Howard and coworkers (1992), using PET, found no activation of left extrastriate cortex in a task designed to isolate access to orthographic lexical representations. They compared an experimental task of reading real words aloud to a baseline task of saying the word *crime* when viewing false fonts. Again, this subtraction should isolate areas activated during access to the orthographic representations with or without "automatic" access to word meanings. Since the verbal response, early visual processing, and spatial attention were present in both the baseline and the experimental task, activation associated with these processes should have been subtracted out. In this study, access to orthographic lexical representations was associated with activation in the left posterior middle and inferior temporal area (Brodmann's area, or BA, 37), not the left extrastriate cortex.[1] Price and coworkers noted that the duration of exposure of stimuli was 150 msec in the Peterson et al. study and was 1000 msec in the Howard et al. study (Price, Wise, Watson, Patterson, Howard, & Frackowiak, 1994). They evaluated whether or not the conflicting results were due to different exposure durations by using similar tasks as in the previous studies, with exposure durations of both 150 msec and 1000 msec. The results of their PET study indicated that a verbal response to words minus a verbal response to pseudowords activated both left extrastriate and left temporal cortex with exposure duration of 150 msec, but activated neither region with exposure duration of 1000 msec. Furthermore, passive viewing of words compared to false fonts activated the left BA 37 with exposure duration of 150 msec or 1000 msec, but not did not activate left extrastriate cortex with either exposure duration. Additionally, other regions were activated at one exposure duration or the other. Thus, the results did not replicate either the Peterson et al. study or the Howard et al. study,

---

[1]Brodmann's areas are areas of the brain reported to have different cytoarchitetures. There are published templates that allow investigators to estimate areas of CT or MRI scans that correspond to each Brodmann's area.

but did show that exposure duration influenced results. Importantly, these results underscore the complication that functional imaging studies are very sensitive to both task selection and other variables of paradigm design (such as exposure duration) that are irrelevant to the question being studied. This complication is encountered at least equally in fMRI studies as in PET studies, and may account for many failures to replicate findings (see Grabowski & Damasio, 2000, and Chertkow and Bub, 1994, for further discussion).

Additionally, even the most robust results from functional imaging studies about the localization of cognitive mechanisms underlying reading often conflict with the most reliable results from lesion-deficit correlation studies. For example, a large number of PET studies and fMRI studies show activation of the right cerebellum during silent word reading tasks, although large lesions of the right cerebellum are not associated with deficits in silent word reading. One reason for such apparently contradictory results is that functional imaging studies show areas that are *active* during a particular task, whereas lesion-deficit studies reveal areas that are *essential* for the task. Some areas of "activation" may even be areas of active inhibition, since a large amount of neuronal firing in the brain (associated with changes in blood flow and oxygen consumption reflected in functional imaging studies) is inhibitory.

Despite the foregoing caveats about the methods used to localize specific cognitive functions, there is evidence for proposing that specific brain regions are essential for certain components of the reading process. The data and conclusions are reviewed for each of the cognitive processes and levels of representations underlying the complex task of word reading that are postulated in the model of reading outlined in chapter 1.

VIEWER-CENTERED, STIMULUS-CENTERED, AND OBJECT-CENTERED SPATIAL REPRESENTATIONS OF WORDS

Reading begins with construction of a sequence of spatial representations of the visual stimulus that are increasingly abstract, in order to match the computed representation of the stimulus with a stored, orthographic representation. Disruption of reading at these levels results in various forms of "neglect dyslexia"—impaired reading of words on the side of the *space* contralateral to brain damage, and/or errors on the side of the *word* contralateral to brain damage. Studies designed to specifically identify the neural basis of computing spatial representations of words with different coordinate frames have not been done. However, it is well known from lesion studies, functional imaging studies, and single cell recording studies in animals that one area of the brain with viewer-centered (for example, retinotopic) organization is the primary visual (striate) cortex. Unilateral lesions to the striate cortex cause homonymous hemianopia and can acutely cause errors in reading the sides of the words contralateral to the lesion, or "unilateral paralexias" (Benson, 1979). Nonetheless, most patients with isolated visual field cuts such as hemianopia quickly compensate for the deficit with eye movements, and eventually have normal reading except in experimental conditions (for example, tachistoscopic presentation of words to the affected hemifield or speeded reading). Furthermore, cortical ablations in monkeys (the most controlled type of lesion-deficit correlation study) and axonal transport of tracer substances have also identified intrahemispheric neuronal networks of spatial attention, with distinct spatial maps that are likely to account for various types of neglect and neglect dyslexia (Mesulam, 1981 & 1998; Vallar & Perani, 1985; von Giessen, Schlang, Steinmetz, Beneche, Freund, & Seitz, 1994; Rizzolatti, Gentilucci, & Matelli, 1985; Rizzolatti & Gallese, 1988). Likewise, single cell recording experiments reveal functionally discrete areas of frontal and parietal cortex of monkeys, where representations of space are encoded in different spatial coordinate frames: eye-centered, head-centered, reaching-related, grasp-related, and object-centered. For example, some neurons represent object-centered coordinates of space. These neurons respond to eye movements directed to the left end of a bar, and not to movements in the same trajectory but directed to the right end of a bar (Colby, 1998; Olson & Gettner, 1995). Other neurons have purely retinotopic or head-centered response fields (Andersen, Essick, & Siegel, 1985). These studies predict the occurrence of neglect and neglect dyslexia in distinct coordinate frames associated with parietal and/or frontal lesions (as reported by Chatterjee, 1994; Mennemeier, Chatterjee, & Heilman, 1994; and Hillis & Caramazza, 1995). Functional imaging studies have also indicated that extrastriate occipital cortex and regions in the "dorsal stream" (the "where pathway"; Mishkin, Ungerleider, & Macko, 1983) also have at least some viewer-centered organization (Haxby, Horowiz, Ungerleider, Maisong, Pietrini, & Grady, 1994). Consistent with the hypothesis that the occipital-parietal regions are crucial for computing viewer-centered spatial representations of words, reported patients with "viewer-centered" neglect dyslexia (reading errors contralesional[2] to the side of the viewer) have had right occipital and/or parietal lesions (Hillis, Rapp, Benzing, & Caramazza, 1998). Computation of stimulus-centered representations also likely occurs in these same regions. Consistent with this assumption, patients with "stimulus-centered" neglect dyslexia (errors on the contralesional side of the stimulus, irrespective of the location with respect to the viewer) have had occipital and/or parietal lesions (Hillis & Caramazza, 1991). Finally, there are parietal regions where neurons respond to stimuli particular regions of modality-independent object-centered spatial representations (Colby, 1998). Lesions in these regions have given rise to object-centered hemispatial neglect in patients (Hillis & Caramazza, 1990). Such patients make reading errors on the side of the abstract representation of the word that is contralateral to the parietal lesion, irrespective of the location, orientation, or the modality of the stimulus (Hillis & Caramazza, 1990 & 1995). In short, the computation of sequential spatial representations of written words, prior to accessing the corresponding stored lexical representations, likely occurs in the dorsal visual stream (occipital-parietal-frontal regions), with more abstract representations computed in modality-independent regions of the cortex (for example, parietal cortex).

ACCESS TO ORTHOGRAPHIC REPRESENTATIONS IN THE LEXICON

In order to recognize the printed word, a stored representation of the spelling of the word, or orthographic representation, must be accessed. Impairment at this level results in errors in written lexical decision (discriminating words from pseudowords), errors in comprehension of written words, and errors in oral reading of words, with production of visually and/or phonologically related errors and/or letter-by-letter reading. As noted above, results from functional imaging studies of the neural basis of the orthographic input lexicon have been controversial, but the majority of studies have revealed activation in the left middle temporal gyrus, angular gyrus, and temporo-occipital junction associated with access to orthographic representations during passive viewing of real words or oral reading of words. Chronic lesion studies have also demonstrated an association between lesions in left temporo-parietal regions, especially the angular gyrus, and impaired written word recognition (Benson, 1979; Black & Behrmann, 1994). Furthermore, we have found that in patients with hyperacute stroke, impairment at the level of the orthographic input lexicon was significantly associated with hypoperfusion of the angular gyrus (BA 39; χ^2 = 7.1; df1; p<.01) and the posterior middle and inferior temporal gyrus (BA 37; χ^2 = 5.7; df1; p<.02; Fisher=s exact: p<.03) (Hillis, Kane, Barker, Beauchamp, & Wityk, 2001). DWI and PWI scans of patients with hypoperfusion of these areas who have had concurrent impairment in accessing orthographic representations are shown in figure 2.1.

---

[2]The term *contralesional* refers to the side contralateral to the brain lesion.

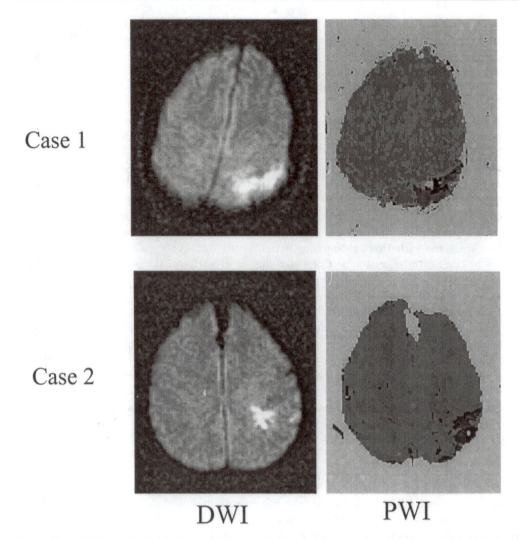

Figure 2.1. DWI and PWI scans of patients with hyperacute impairment at the level of the orthographic input lexicon (disturbances in lexical decision, reading comprehension, and oral reading), and concurrent hypoperfusion of the angular gyrus (BA 39). Dark areas correspond to hypoperfused regions in these figures.

Additionally, access to orthographic representations can be disrupted by a combination of lesions that prevents transmission of visual information to the left angular gyrus (BA 39) and BA 37. As first described by Dejerine in 1891, the co-occurrence of a lesion in the left occipital cortex (resulting in right homonymous hemianopia) and a lesion in the splenium of the corpus collosum, results in alexia without agraphia. In patients with this combination of lesions, all visual information is processed in the right occipital lobe (due to the lesion in the left occipital lobe), but cannot reach left hemisphere reading areas due to lesions of the splenium (which normally transfers visual information from one hemisphere to the other). Such patients may be able to read single letters (usually with some errors), and therefore attempt to read words in a letter-by-letter fashion. Sometimes, saying the letters aloud allows construction of an object-centered representation that can be used to access an orthographic representation in the lexicon (by hypothesis, represented and/or processed in BA 39 and 37).

LEXICAL-SEMANTIC REPRESENTATIONS

Following access to the orthographic representation of the word, access to the meaning—the lexical-semantic representation—is necessary to understand the written word. There is strong evidence from PET studies that access to lexical-semantic representations in response to either words or pictures activates Wernicke's area (BA 22; Vandenburghe, Price, Wise, Josephs, & Frackowiak, 1996; Demonet, Chollet, Ramsay, Cardebat, Nespoulous, Wise, Rascol, & Frackowiak, 1992). These studies also demonstrate activation in surrounding temporal and parietal regions as well (see chapter 11 for discussion of all of the various areas likely to be involved in semantic processing). It is likely that BA 22 is not the site at which lexical-semantic representations are *stored*, but a site that is crucial for linking widely distributed lexical-semantic representations to spoken and written words. Chronic lesion studies have also confirmed that lesions in BA 22 result in lexical-semantic impairments (Wernicke, 1874; Goodglass & Wingfield, 1997; Hart & Gordon, 1990). Convergent results have been obtained with cortical stimulation of BA 22, which causes impairment in word comprehension (Lesser et al., 1986). Finally, we found that in hyperacute stroke patients, lexical-semantic deficits were strongly associated with hypoperfusion of Wernicke's area (area 22; $\chi^2 = 26$; $df1$; $p << .00001$), and less strongly associated with surrounding areas, including the supramarginal gyrus (BA 40), the middle temporal lobe (BA 21 and 37), angular gyrus (BA 39), and visual association cortex (BA 19) (Hillis, Kane, Barker, et al., 2001). To illustrate, DWI and PWI scans of patients with severe impairment of lexical-semantics are shown in figure 2.2. In contrast, hypoperfusion of Wernicke's area was not at all associated with impairment to any other component of the reading process. Furthermore, reperfusion of BA 22 in acute stroke patients resulted in recovery of lexical-semantic deficits (Hillis, Kane, Tuffiash, Ulatowski, Barker, Beauchamp, & Wityk, 2002; Hillis, Barker, Beauchamp, Winters, Mirski, & Wityk, 2001). Also, the severity of hypoperfusion of BA 22 was strongly correlated with the severity of word comprehension deficit in eighty patients with acute stroke (Hillis, Wityk, Tuffiash, Barker, Beauchamp, Jacobs, & Selnes, 2001).

PHONOLOGICAL REPRESENTATIONS

To read a word aloud, it is necessary to access phonological representations in the output lexicon. Patients with damage at this level of processing will make errors not only in oral reading, but also in oral naming (but not in comprehension of spoken or written words). Errors may be phonologically or semantically related to the target. The neural substrates of accessing phonological representations of words for spoken output are discussed in chapter 8. I will add that in our study of reading in hyperacute stroke patients, impairment at the level of the phonological output lexicon was highly associated with hypoperfusion of the posterior middle and inferior temporal lobe (BA 37; $\chi^2 = 17.4$; $df1$; $p<.000001$; Hillis, Kane, Barker, et al., 2001). Furthermore, in some patients, impaired access to phonological representations for output was observed when BA 37 was hypoperfused, and recovered access to phonological representations was seen when blood flow was restored to BA 37 (Hillis, Kane, Tuffiash, et al., 2002; Hillis, Kane, Barker, et al., 2001). These results are consistent with chronic lesion studies indicating that damage to BA 37 results in anomic aphasia, which reflects impaired retrieval of phonological representations of words (Nielson, 1948; Alexander & Benson, 1991; Benson, 1994). However, these studies may be specific to accessing phonological representations of nouns, since only nouns were tested in our study and in many reports of anomic aphasia. Access to the phonological representation of verbs is likely to occur in the posterior frontal regions (Miceli, Silveri, Villa, & Caramazza, 1984; Berndt, Mitchum, Haendiges, & Sandson, 1997; Damasio & Tranel, 1993; Daniele, Giustolisi, Silveri, Colosimo, & Gainotti, 1994; Cappa, Binetti, Pezzini, Padovani, Rozzini, & Trabucchi, 1998; Shapiro, Pascual-Leone, Mottaghy, Gangitano, &

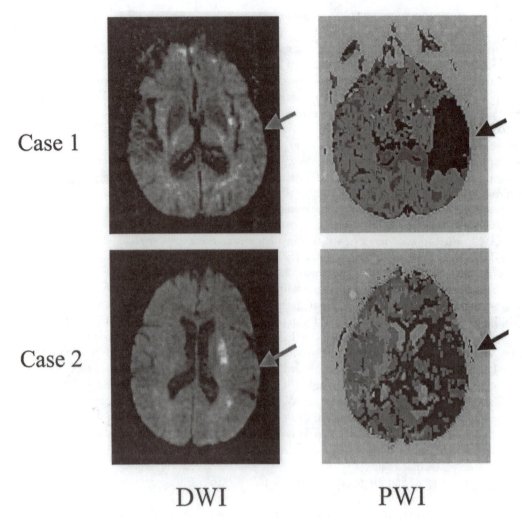

Figure 2.2. DWI and PWI scans of patients with hyperacute impairment at the level of the lexical-semantics and concurrent hypoperfusion of Wernicke's area (BA 22). The arrows point to BA 22.

Caramazza, in press; Tranel, Adolphs, Damasio, & Damasio, in press). This proposal may account for at least some of the cases of impaired oral reading due to frontal lesions.

ORTHOGRAPHY-TO-PHONOLOGY CONVERSION

Reading of unfamiliar words or pseudowords (for example, *glamp*) cannot be accomplished by accessing stored, orthographic representations alone, since there are no stored representations corresponding to stimuli that have not been previously encountered. Rather, the reader relies on orthography-to-phonology conversion (OPC) mechanisms. Damage at the level of OPC mechanisms results in inability to "sound out" pseudowords or unfamiliar words. Furthermore, patients who concurrently have impaired access to OPC mechanisms and to semantic or phonological representations are likely to make semantically related word errors in reading (for example, *stool* read as "chair"), because they cannot use OPC mechanisms to "block" semantic errors. There is a paucity of evidence for the neural basis of OPC mechanisms. However, one fMRI study of the effects of rehabilitation of alexia indicated that training to use OPC mechanisms was associated with increased activation of the left occipital and nearby temporal and parietal cortices, including BA 39 and 40 (Small, Flores, & Noll, 1997). Consistent with this proposed posterior temporo-parietal localization of OPC mechanisms, we found that hyperacute impairment of OPC mechanisms was associated with hypoperfusion of the angular gyrus (BA 39; χ^2 = 5.9; $df1$; $p<.02$) and the supramarginal gyrus (BA 40; χ^2 = 5.5; $df1$; $p<.02$) within hours of stroke onset (Hillis, Kane, Barker, et al., 2001).

SUMMARY

Data from functional imaging, chronic lesion-deficit correlation studies, acute lesion-deficit correlation studies (cortical stimulation studies and concurrent cognitive evaluation with DWI and PWI), and single cell recording studies have provided evidence for proposing the neural substrates of some of the cognitive processes underlying word reading. For many of the structure-function relationships, there has been convergent evidence from the various sources. The most reliable associations across modalities of investigation have been: (1) visual spatial representations of words and regions within the dorsal stream of visual processing (occipital-parietal-frontal regions); (2) the orthographic input lexicon and posterior temporal and parietal regions (including BA 37 and 39); (3) lexical-semantics and Wernicke's area (BA 22); (4) phonological output lexicon (at least for nouns) and posterior middle and inferior temporal gyri (BA 37); and (5) OPC mechanisms and the left angular gyrus (BA 39) and supramarginal gyrus (BA 40). Note that there is some overlap, in that some regions of the brain appear to be essential for more than one component of the reading process. For example, the left angular gyrus (BA 39) is crucial for both accessing orthographic representations in the lexicon and for OPC mechanisms. This finding is consistent with the observation that most patients with acquired alexia due to stroke have deficits in reading both irregular words (which depend on the orthographic input lexicon) and pseudowords (which depend on OPC mechanisms). In such cases of overlap, it is possible that there are specific cells, or specific regions within a given BA, that are specialized for a single one of these processes, but that large lesions involving the region will affect a number of separate processes. Furthermore, some processes, such as lexical-semantics, are likely to require a number of different regions, and damage to any one of the regions will cause partial impairment of the process. Such partial impairments may account for deficits at a given level of processing (for example, lexical-semantics) that are limited to a specific category of words. Finally, it should also be noted that the profile of performance (including production of semantic errors, functor substitutions, derivational errors, and better performance for nouns than verbs and for concrete words than abstract words, observed in patients with "deep alexia") has been hypothesized to reflect compensatory reading with the right hemisphere (Coltheart, 1980). Although there is little direct support for this hypothesis, functional imaging studies of alexic patients have often shown more activation of the right hemisphere than observed in normal subjects (for example, Small et al., 1997; but see also Price, 2000).

This chapter has focused on oral reading of single words, particularly nouns. Other cortical areas may be essential for fluent reading of word classes other than nouns and of sentences. Sentence reading requires not only reading of the individual words in all word classes, but also likely requires computation of a sentence planning frame, working memory, and other processes involved in sentence production (see chapter 17 for discussion).

ACKNOWLEDGMENTS

The research reported in this chapter was supported by an NIH grant, K23 DC00174-01, and the Charles A. Dana Foundation.

REFERENCES

Alexander, M. P., & Benson, D. F. (1991). The aphasia and related disturbances. In R. J. Yoynt (Ed.), *Clinical neurology* (Vol. 1). Philadelphia: Lippincott.

Andersen, R., Essick, G., & Siegel, R. (1985). Encoding spatial location by posterior parietal neurons. *Science, 230,* 456–458.

Barber, P. A., Darby, D. G., Desmond, P. M., Yang, Q., Gerraty, R. P., Jolley, D., Donnan, G., Tress, B. M., & Davis, S. M. (1998). Prediction of stroke outcome with echoplanar perfusion- and diffusion-weighted MRI. *Neurology, 51,* 418–426.

Beaulieu, C., de Crespingy, A., Tong, D. C., Mosely, M. E., Albers, G. W., & Marks, M. P. (1999). Longitudinal magnetic resonance imaging study of perfusion and diffusion in stroke: Evolution of volume and correlation with clinical outcome. *Annals of Neurology, 46,* 568–578.

Benson, D. F. (1979). *Aphasia, alexia, and agraphia.* New York: Churchill Livingsone, Inc.

Benson, D. F. (1994). Naming disorders. In S. Kennedy (Ed.), *Psychobiology of language.* Cambridge, MA: MIT Press.

Berndt, R. S., Mitchum, C. C., Haendiges, A. N., & Sandson, J. (1997). Verb retrieval in aphasia. *Brain and Language, 56,* 68–106.

Black, S., & Behrmann, M. (1994). Localization in alexia. In A. Kertesz (Ed.), *Localization and neuroimaging in neuropsychology.* San Diego: Academic Press.

Cappa, S. F., Binetti, G., Pezzini, A., Padovani, A., Rozzini, L., & Trabucchi, M. (1998). Object and action naming in Alzheimer's disease and frontotemporal dementia. *Neurology, 50,* 351–355.

Chatterjee, A. (1994). Picturing unilateral spatial neglect: Viewer versus object-centred reference frames. *Journal of Neurology, Neurosurgery, and Psychiatry, 57,* 1236–1240.

Chertkow, H., & Bub, D. (1994). Functional activation and cognition: The O¹⁵ PET subtraction method. In A. Kertesz (Ed.), *Localization and neuroimaging in neuropsychology.* New York: Academic Press.

Colby, C. (1998). Action-oriented spatial reference frames in cortex. *Neuron, 20,* 15–24

Coltheart, M. (1980) Deep dyslexia: A right hemisphere hypothesis. In M. Coltheart, K. E. Patterson, & J.C. Marshall (Eds.), *Deep dyslexia.* London: Routledge and Kegan Paul.

Damasio, A. R., & Tranel, D. (1993). Nouns and verbs are retrieved with differently distributed neural systems. *Proceedings of the National Academy of Sciences, 90,* 4957–4960.

Daniele, A., Giustolisi, L., Silver, M. C., Colosimo, C., & Gainotti, G. (1994). Evidence for a possible neuroanatomical basis for lexical processing of nouns and verbs. *Neuropsychologia, 32,* 1325–134

Dejerine, J. (1891). Sur un cas de cécité verbale avec agraphie, suivi d'autopsie. *Comptes Rendus Hebdomadaires des Séances et Mémoires de la Société de Biologie,* Ninth series, *3,* 197–201.

Dejerine, J. (1892). Contribution à l'étude anatomo-pathologique et clinique des différentes variétés de cécité verbale. *Mem. Soc. Biol., 4,* 61-90.

Demonet, J.-F., Chollet, F., Ramsay, S., Cardebat, D., Nespoulous, J.-L., Wise, R., Rascol, A., & Frackowiak, R. (1992). The anatomy of phonologic and semantic processing in normal subjects. *Brain, 115,* 1753–1768.

Freud, S. (1891, 1953). *On aphasia.* Trans. E. Stengl. New York: International University Press.

Goodglass, H., & Wingfield, A. (1997). Word-finding deficits in aphasia: Brain-behavior relations and symptomatology. In H. Goodglass (Ed.), *Anomia.* London: Academic Press.

Grabowski, T. J., & Damasio, A. R. (2000). Investigating language with functional imaging. In A. W. Toga & J. C. Mazziotta (Eds.), *Brain mapping: The systems.* San Diego: Academic Press.

Hart, J., & Gordon, B. (1990). Delineation of single-word semantic comprehension deficits in aphasia, with anatomical correlation. *Annals of Neurology, 27,* 226–231.

Haxby, J. V., Horowiz, B., Ungerleider, L. G., Maisong, J. M., Pietrini, P., & Grady, C. L. (1994). The functional organization of the human extrastriate cortex: A PET-rCBF study of selective attention to faces and locations. *Journal of Neuroscience, 14,* 6336–5633.

Hillis, A. E., Barker, P., Beauchamp, N., Gordon, B., & Wityk, R. (2000). MR perfusion imaging reveals regions of hypoperfusion associated with aphasia and neglect. *Neurology, 55,* 782–788.

Hillis, A. E., Barker, P., Beauchamp, N., Winters, B., Mirski, M., & Wityk, R. (2001). Restoring blood pressure reperfused Wernicke's area and improved language, *Neurology, 56,* 670–672.

Hillis, A. E., & Carmazza, A. (1990). The effects of attentional deficits on reading and spelling. In A. Caramazza (Ed.), *Cognitive neuropsychology and neurolinguistics: Advances in models of cognitive function and impairment.* London: Lawrence Erlbaum Associates.

Hillis, A. E., & Caramazza, A. (1991). Spatially-specific deficit to stimulus-centered letter shape representations in a case of "unilateral neglect." *Neuropsychologia, 29,* 1223-1240.

Hillis, A. E., & Caramazza, A. (1995). A framework for interpreting distinct patterns of hemispatial neglect. *Neurocase, 1,* 189–207.

Hillis, A. E., Kane, A., Barker, P., Beauchamp, N., & Wityk, R. (2001). Neural substrates of the cognitive processes underlying reading: evidence from magnetic resonance perfusion imaging in hyperacute stroke. *Aphasiology, 15,* 919–931.

Hillis, A. E., Kane, A., Tuffiash, E., Ulatowski, J. A., Barker, P., Beauchamp, N., & Wityk, R. (2002). Reperfusion of specific brain regions by raising blood pressure restores selective language functions in subacute stroke. *Brain and Language, 79,* 495–510.

Hillis, A. E., Rapp, B., Benzing, L., & Caramazza, A. (1998). Dissociable coordinate frames of unilateral spatial neglect: Viewer-centered neglect. *Brain and Cognition, 37,* 491–526.

Hillis, A. E., Wityk, R. J., Tuffiash, E., Barker, P. B., Beauchamp, N. J., Jacobs, M. A., & Selnes, O. A. (2001). Hypoperfusion of Wernicke's area predicts severity of semantic deficit in acute stroke. *Annals of Neurology, 50,* 561–566.

Howard, D., Patterson, K., Wise, R., Brown, W. D., Friston, K., Weiller, C., & Frackowiak, R. (1992). The cortical localization of the lexicons. *Brain, 115,* 1769–1782.

Jenkins, W. M., & Merzenich, M. M. (1987). Reorganization of neocortical representations after brain injury:

A neurophysiological model of the bases of recovery from stroke. *Progress in Brain Research, 71,* 249–266

Lesser, R., Luders, M., Dinner, N., Dinner, D.S., Klem, G., Hahn, J., & Harrison, M. (1986). Electrical stimulation of Wernicke's area interferes with comprehension. *Neurology, 36,* 658–663.

Mennemeier, M., Chatterjee, A., & Heilman, K. (1994). A comparison of the influences of body and environment centered reference frames on neglect. *Brain, 117,* 1013–1021.

Merzenich, M. M, Kaas, J. H., Wall, J. T., Nelson, R. J., Sur, M., & Felleman, D. (1983). Topographic reorganization of somatosensory cortical areas 3b and 1 in adult monkeys following restricted deafferentation. *Neuroscience, 8,* 33–55.

Mesulam, M.-M. (1981). A cortical network for directed attention and unilateral neglect. *Annals of Neurology, 10,* 309–325.

Mesulam, M.-M. (1998). From sensation to cognition. *Brain, 121,* 1013–1052.

Miceli, G., Silveri, M.C., Villa, G., & Caramazza, A. (1984). On the basis of agrammatic's difficulty in producing main verbs. *Cortex, 20,* 217–220.

Mishkin, M., Ungerleider, L. G., & Macko, K. A. (1983). Object vision and spatial vision: Two cortical pathways. *Trends in Neuroscience, 6,* 414–417.

Nielson, J. M. (1948) *Agnosia, apraxia, and aphasia.* New York: Hafner. (Original work published 1936).

Ojemann, G. A. (1994). *Cortical stimulation and recording in language.* London: Academic Press.

Olson, C. R., & Gettner, S. N. (1995). Object-centred direction selectivity in the macaque supplementary eye field. *Science, 269,* 985–988.

Peterson, S. E., Fox, P. T., Posner, M. I., Mintun, M., & Raichle, M. E. (1988). Positron emission tomography studies of the cortical anatomy of single word processing. *Nature, 331,* 585–589.

Peterson, S. E., Fox, P. T., Snyder, A. Z., & Raichle, M. E. (1990). Activation of extrastriate and frontal cortical areas by visual words and word-like stimuli. *Science, 249,* 1041–1044.

Price, C. (2000). Functional Imaging Studies of Aphasia.

In J. C. Massiotta, A. W. Toga, & R. S. J. Frackowiak (Eds.), *Brain mapping: The disorders.* San Diego: Academic Press.

Price, C. J., Wise, R. J. S., Watson, J. D. G., Patterson, K., Howard, D., & Frackowiak, R. S. J. (1994). Brain acitivity during reading: the effects of exposure duration and task. *Brain, 117,* 1255–1269.

Rizzolatti G., & Gallese, V. (1988) Mechanisms and theories of spatial neglect. In F. Boller & J. Grafman (Eds.), *Handbook of neurology* (Vol. 1). New York: Elsevier Science Publishers.

Rizzolatti, G., Gentilucci, M., & Matelli, M. (1985). Selective spatial attention: One center, one circuit, or many circuits? In M. I. Posner & O. S. M. Marin (Eds.), *Attention and performance XI.* Hillsdale, NJ: Lawrence Erlbaum Associates.

Shapiro, K. A., Pascual-Leone, A., Mottaghy, F. M., Gangitano, M., & Caramazza, A. (In press). Grammatical distinctions in the left frontal cortex. *Journal of Cognitive Neuroscience.*

Small, S. L., Flores, D., & Noll, D. C. (1997). Grapheme to phoneme conversion in acquired dyslexia: Neurobiological changes accompany therapy. *Brain and Language, 60,* 127–131.

Tranel, D., Adolphs, R., Damasio, H., & Damasio, A. R. (In press). A neural basis for the retrieval of words for actions. *Cognitive Neuropsychology.*

Vallar, G., & Perani, D. (1985). The anatomy of spatial neglect in humans. In M. Jeannerod (Ed.), *Neuropsychological and neuropsychological aspects of spatial neglect.* New York: Elsevier/North-Holland.

Vandenburghe, R., Price, C., Wise, R., Josephs, O., & Frackowiak, R. S. J. (1996). Functional anatomy of a common semantic system for both words and pictures. *Nature, 383,* 254–256.

Von Giesen, H. J., Schlaug, G., Steinmetz, H., Beneche, R., Freund, H. J., & Seitz, R. J. (1994). Cerebral network underlying unilateral motor neglect: evidence from positron emission tomography. *Journal of the Neurological Sciences, 125,* 29–38.

Wernicke, K. (1874). *Der aphasische symptomkomplex.* Breslau: Kohn and Neigat.

3

Clinical Diagnosis and Treatment
of Reading Disorders

Rhonda B. Friedman

ASSESSING THE UNDERLYING COGNITIVE DEFICIT

The activity of reading depends upon the integration of many component processes, both linguistic and visual. Thus there are many different ways for reading to break down following injury to the brain. A thorough assessment of reading begins with an examination of elementary visual processing, and proceeds through analyses of orthographic, phonologic, and semantic processing of single written words, to a final assessment of reading comprehension of text.

Visual Processing

Neglect

In searching for the cause of a patient's reading deficit, one must first ensure that the problem is not of a purely perceptual nature. That is, it is important to ascertain that the written letters are being perceived properly. One phenomenon that may interfere with the visual perception of the letters of a word is visual (hemispatial) neglect (Kinsbourne & Warrington, 1962). Since hemispatial neglect is usually associated with lesions of the right hemisphere, it most commonly has its effects on the left half of stimuli or stimuli that appear on the left side of the reader's body or field of vision (see chapter 1 of this book, for discussion of various types of hemispatial neglect, and how they affect reading). Left-handed (and occasionally right-handed) patients with left hemisphere lesions may show right neglect, affecting only the ends of words. If the patient shows a tendency to make errors at the beginnings (or ends) of words, and neglect is suspected, the patient should be asked to read words that are presented vertically; that is, top to bottom rather than left to right. If the problem is one of viewer-centered or stimulus-centered neglect, errors will not predominate at the beginnings (or ends) of vertically presented words. However, if the problem is object-centered neglect, the patient will continue to make errors on the neglected side of the "canonical" orientation of the word (for example, the initial letters in patients with left neglect dyslexia).

Selective Attention Deficit

Patients with impaired selective attention may have difficulty segregating words from other words in space. As a result, letters tend to "migrate" from adjacent words (Shallice & Warrington, 1977). There is no specific test for this deficit, other than being aware of the possibility that letter intrusion errors may have their source in neighboring words. Thus, when single word reading appears to be intact, yet text reading is impaired, it is worthwhile to carefully examine the patient's text reading for such intrusion errors from neighboring words.

Letter Knowledge

Naming and Pointing to Letters Named

As an initial test of letter knowledge, individual letters—both upper- and lowercase—should be presented to the patient for naming. The ability to attach a letter's name to its physical form is a good indication that knowledge of the letter's identity remains intact. However, failure to name letters may reflect a problem with word retrieval, not letter identification. Patients who fail to name letters accurately should be given a sheet of paper upon which all twenty-six letters are scattered. The patient is asked to point to each letter as the therapist names it. Success at this task demonstrates that a letter's form is still associated with its name, even if the patient cannot retrieve that name.

Identity

Even if a patient can no longer associate the names of letters with their shapes, it might still be possible to demonstrate intact knowledge of letters' abstract identities. This can be done with a cross-case matching task. Two letters, one uppercase and one lowercase, appear together, and the patient is asked to determine whether or not they represent the same letter. Patients who can perform this task, even for letters with different upper- and lowercase shapes (for example, Rr), retain information about the letters' identities. This is important, as it is letters' identities, and not necessarily their names, that are the foundation of successful reading in most situations.

Recognition

The simplest level of letter knowledge is recognition: that is, knowing that a particular written symbol is an actual letter of the alphabet. One easy way to test for this knowledge is with a forced choice task in which the patient must distinguish correct letters from mirror-reversed letters. This task does not require explicit identification of letters, only recognition of the correct shapes of real letters of the alphabet. Patients who cannot perform this task adequately are not likely to be good candidates for alexia treatment.

Integrity of Orthographic Representations

Lexical Decision

Difficulty accessing the correct internal orthographic representation of a written word may be revealed with a lexical decision task in which the word and nonword stimuli are carefully chosen. The real words should include words with regular spelling-to-sound correspondences—for example, *mint*—and words with irregular spelling-to-sound correspondences (orthography-to-phonology conversion)—for example, *pint*. The nonwords should include pseudowords that are homophonic with real words—for example, *sope*. Patients whose orthographic representations are not adequately activated tend to read all letter strings as they would be pronounced according to spelling-to-sound rules. Hence, they will have difficulty with such a lexical decision task. They will incorrectly accept the pseudohomophones (for example, *sope*) as being real words, because they sound like real words when pronounced; and they will incorrectly reject irregular words as being nonwords, because they do not sound like real words when pronounced according to spelling-to-sound rules ("/pInt/; that's not a word").

Homophones

A second means of assessing inadequate orthographic activation, related to the above lexical decision task, is a homophone definition task. The task is to present words that have homophones (for example, *oar, whole*) one at a time, and ask the patient to both read and define the words. Patients who are relying on the phonologic code derived from the orthography, rather than the orthographic representation itself, will have no way to distinguish *tacks* from *tax*, or *pray* from *prey*. This will be manifest in the patient's reading the word correctly, but defining it as its homophone (for example, defining *tacks* as money collected from people by the government).

The reliance on orthography-to-phonology conversion, resulting in better reading of regular words than irregular words and poor homophone comprehension, is commonly known as surface dyslexia. Surface dyslexia often results from impaired activation of orthographic representations (or impaired access to the orthographic lexicon), but may also result from damage at the level of the semantic system or at the level of accessing phonological representations for output. That is, any impairment in using the "lexical route" (orthographic representations → semantic system → phonological representations) to read can necessitate reliance on orthography-to-phonology correspondence to read aloud (see chapter 1 of this volume for illustrative cases).

Access to the Lexicon through the Visual Modality

Orthographic representations may remain intact, and other aspects of lexical knowledge may remain intact as well, in patients whose reading is impaired because they cannot access that knowledge through the visual modality. In these patients, whose reading disorder is known as pure alexia (or "alexia without agraphia," or "letter-by-letter reading"), the integrity of orthographic representations can be demonstrated through intact spelling or through intact recognition of orally spelled words. These patients often spontaneously compensate for their deficit by naming each letter of the word aloud or silently, which often allows them to recognize the word (hence "letter-by-letter reading").

Length Effect

Not all patients with pure alexia show outward signs of letter-by-letter reading. A second means of assessing difficulty with processing whole words as single units (or accessing the orthographic lexicon) is to examine for an effect of length on reading accuracy and/or reading speed. Patients should be asked to read a list of words that vary systematically in letter length. Words should be matched for frequency and part of speech across length, and should range from three letters to at least eleven letters. Substantial differences in accuracy as letter length increases is diagnostic of difficulty with accessing the orthographic representation. A more sensitive means of assessing length effects, for patients whose accuracy is high given unlimited time, is to look for increasing time required to read longer words. One way to do this is to create lists of words of different lengths, ten words to a list, and time the patient's reading of each list. While normal readers will show a slight increase in time to read longer words, simply because longer words take more time to articulate, patients with a whole word processing or lexical access deficit will require considerably more time to read the lists with the longer words.

Spelling

A patient's writing and spelling will likely be assessed as part of a comprehensive aphasia battery. For the purposes of demonstrating intact orthographic representations in the face of inability to access these representations visually, patients should be asked to write or orally spell words and pseudowords (PWs) that she or he has been asked to read (preferably in a separate testing session). Most patients with an alexic disturbance will perform more poorly on spelling than reading. Patients with pure alexia will show the opposite pattern: relatively better spelling than reading.

Recognition of Orally Spelled Words

Another means of ascertaining intact orthographic representations in a patient who cannot access these representations visually is to spell the words aloud to the patient, one letter at a time. Again, words and PWs that the patient has been asked to read should be used for this task. Words should not be so long as to exceed a normal verbal short-term memory span (approximately seven letters). Patients with pure alexia will perform normally on this task, recognizing words without regard to part of speech, and PWs as well. Importantly, performance on this task will exceed performance on reading these same words for pure alexic patients (or patients with damage to any component of visual processing of words, such as most forms of neglect dyslexia), but not for patients with damage to the reading process at a level beyond access to the orthographic lexicon.

Phonologic Processing

Reading Pseudowords

To evaluate the ability to access the phonology of written letter strings without regard to semantic processing, patients should be asked to read pseudowords; that is, orthographically legal, pronounceable nonwords. The key to identifying a phonological processing deficit is demonstrating that PW reading is not just impaired, but is actually worse than real word reading. It is recommended that a list of pseudowords be created from a list of real words, by changing a single letter from each of the real words. Difficulty reading the PWs in the list far exceeding any difficulty reading the real words in the matched list indicates a disturbance in orthography-to-phonology conversion or other phonological deficit (see below). This is never a modality-specific problem: a PW reading deficit seen for written words will also be apparent if PWs are spelled aloud to the patient.

Pseudoword Repetition

Impaired PW reading may reflect a deficit that is specific to reading, or it may be part of a more general phonological processing deficit. The most sensitive means of testing this is to ask the patient to repeat multisyllabic pseudowords. Impaired performance on this task suggests a general phonological processing deficit (for example, holding the sequence of phonemes in phonological short-term memory). Additionally, such a deficit may be picked up by asking patients to read and repeat real words of increasing syllable length and phonological complexity.

Digit Span

Patients with reduced short-term phonological memory may experience difficulty reading text, while showing little deficit in reading individual words. This disorder, termed phonological text alexia, is accompanied by difficulty reading PWs. To assess a patient's ability to hold multiple phonological codes in short-term memory, variations of a standard digit span test, such as that contained in the Wechsler Memory Scale, should be administered. This includes normal digits forward and backward, single noun span, single functor word span, and single PW span.

Semantic Representation

Word-picture Matching

The most direct method of testing access to semantics from the written word (that is, compre-hension of written words) is to use a word-picture matching task. A written word is presented, along with an array of pictures, one of which corresponds to the written word. The required response is to point to the picture corresponding to the word; no verbal output is required. Foils may be pictures that are unrelated to the target; this allows the patient to choose the correct picture even if she or he has access to incomplete semantic information about the word. To increase the difficulty of the task by requiring the patient to have more precise information about the word's meaning, picture foils should be chosen from the same superordinate cat-egory as the target.

Other Semantic Tasks

Milder impairments of semantic processing may affect only words of low imageability, or abstract words. Such semantic impairments may not be picked up with the word-picture match-ing task, which, by the nature of the task, uses only words that are high in imageability (that is, they are picturable). Other semantic decision tasks may be helpful in these instances. One such test is the odd-man-out test. Three words are presented (for example, *faith, belief, anger*), and the patient must point to the word that does not belong with the other two words. Alternatively, the patient may be asked whether the referent of a written word belongs to a particular category (for example, Is the word *sadness* an emotion?), or whether two written words are similar in meaning.

Concreteness Effects in Oral Reading

When semantic processing is impaired concurrently with phonological reading, the result may be an effect of concreteness in oral reading. Words with less stable or accessible semantic value—that is, words of lower concreteness—are read more poorly than words of high concrete-ness. To test for this effect, patients should be asked to read a list of words, half of which are high in concreteness and half of which are low in concreteness. High- and low-concreteness words should be matched for frequency and length. A significant advantage for reading highly concrete words is consistent with an impairment in semantic reading, although concreteness effects may also occur as a result of damage at different levels of processing, for different reasons, as discussed by Elaine Funnell in chapter 10 of this volume.

Semantic Paralexias

The production of a word that is related in meaning to the target word (for example, *dog* read as "cat") is known as semantic paralexias. Such errors sometimes reflect semantic processing that is close but not quite accurate. For instance, these errors may occur when the incorrect semantic representation is activated from the written word, or when an impoverished semantic representation is activated. However, they also sometimes occur as a result of difficulty accessing the correct phonologic representation of the word from the correct and intact semantic representation. One may attempt to tease apart these possibilities, using a two-step procedure (Friedman & Perlman, 1982). First, the patient is asked to read a written word aloud. Next, she or he is presented with an array of four pictures, and is asked to point to the referent of the word. The foils are all highly semantically related to the target. It is hoped that if the patient produces a semantic paralexia when reading the word, the referent of that paralexia will be among the picture foils. If it is, the patient's picture choice provides the clue needed to determine the source of the semantic paralexia. If the patient points to the correct picture, despite having read the word incorrectly, the conclusion is drawn that the paralexia was the result of an impairment in accessing the target phonologic representation from the correct semantic representation. If the patient points to the picture that corresponds to the paralexic error that she or he produced, it is concluded that the paralexia represents inaccurate activation of the semantic representation. Note that it is not always easy to choose the appropriate foils, as one has no way of knowing in advance what semantic paralexias are likely to be produced. Thus, the successful use of this two-step task is partly dependent upon wise prognostication and partly upon chance. Often, though, a patient who makes a semantic paralexia (for example, *dog* → "cat") will be willing to point to any semantically related picture (for example, cat, horse, fox). Such patients are likely to have accessed an impoverished semantic representation (see chapter 1 of this book for discussion). An alternative method for evaluating access to semantics in the presence of semantic paralexias, in patients with adequate speech production, is to ask the patient to define the word that he or she just read aloud. For example, patient RGB (see chapter 1) read aloud *red* as "yellow" but defined it as "the color of blood." He apparently accessed an intact semantic representation, but then activated the incorrect phonological representation for output.

Patients who make semantic paralexias in reading often are observed to also show several other features of reading: a concreteness effect, impaired orthography-to-phonology conversion (with difficulty reading PWs), grammatical word class effects (nouns read better than verbs or functors), and morphological errors (for example, *write* → "wrote"). This collection of characteristics has been labeled "deep dyslexia." However, the label does not pin down the level of disruption in the reading process, since (as just discussed) semantic paralexias may arise at the level of semantics or at the level of access to the phonological output lexicon. Furthermore, some of these features have been observed in patients who do not produce semantic paralexias. For example, selective impairment in orthography-to-phonology conversion, with predominantly impaired PW reading, occurs without the other features; this pattern of performance has been labeled "phonological dyslexia." Most patients with deep dyslexia, and some patients with phonological alexia, exhibit selective difficulty reading functors, and these patients may or may not show an advantage of nouns over verbs. Thus, understanding what component processes are impaired in an individual patient, based on convergence of evidence from error types, parameters that do and do not affect reading (for example, word class, concreteness, frequency, word length), and performance across various reading and semantic tasks, is more useful than applying a label.

Part of Speech Effects

Difficulty reading words of certain form class can be uncovered by asking the patient to read a list of words that have been created specifically for this purpose. The list should contain nouns, verbs, adjectives, and functors (prepositions, conjunctions, pronouns, auxiliary verbs). Words of the different form classes should be matched for letter length. It is difficult to match for frequency, as functors tend to be higher in frequency than other words. However, one should at least ensure that all nonfunctor words are as high frequency as possible. Results should be scored for accuracy of reading words of the different classes.

The finding of a part of speech effect has typically been interpreted in a manner similar to that of the concreteness effect, with which it is commonly associated. That is, functors are not as strongly represented within the semantic lexicon as nouns are, and hence are less likely to be accessed in reading by the "lexical-semantic route," particularly if there is an impairment within the semantic lexicon. However, selective impairment in accessing one grammatical class of words (for example, nouns or verbs) can also occur as a result of damage at the level of the phonological lexicon. In such cases, the patient reads aloud and orally names one class of words (say, verbs) poorly, but has no trouble comprehending written verbs or in written naming of verbs (see chapter 7, by Doriana Chialant, Albert Costas, and Alfonso Caramazza, in this volume, for illustrative cases and discussion). Furthermore, a part of speech effect may be the result of a syntactic processing deficit, particularly when the effect is seen solely within the context of text reading, a phenomenon that has been called phonological text alexia (Friedman, 1996). When a part of speech effect is seen in reading, one should always evaluate it within the context of the patient's speech: the deletion of functors (agrammatism) likely indicates a grammatical processing deficit.

Morphologic Paralexias

Closely tied to the part of speech effects seen in certain alexic patients is the phenomenon of the production of morphologic paralexias (also called derivational paralexias). These errors typically involve the substitution of one affix for another (for example, *lovely* for *loving*), or simply the deletion or addition of an affix (for example, *play* for *playing*). As with errors on functor words, morphologic paralexias are often attributed to a deficit in accessing phonology directly from orthography; the semantic pathway is simply unable to deal with these semantically weak morphemes. However, these errors may also be seen as orthographic errors; that is, errors in which the word produced is similar in spelling to the target word (and thus may occur as a result of hemispatial neglect or other visual processing deficit). Likewise, these errors may be seen as semantic paralexias; the meaning of *play* is certainly semantically similar to the meaning of *playing*. And, as with the part of speech effect, morphologic errors may be a reflection of a more pervasive grammatical problem.

As with all types of paralexias, it is difficult to devise a task specifically to elicit these errors. It is even more problematic to assess their prevalence, as it is difficult to know how many of such errors one should expect for a given set of words. One is best advised to include words with different affixes in a list of words presented to the patient, and to keep track of such errors (including additions of affixes to nonaffixed words) in all lists of words that the patient is asked to read. For details on how one might assess morphological errors in reading, see Badecker and Caramazza (1987).

Sentence and Text Reading

It is clearly the case that most patients who have difficulty reading single words will have difficulty reading text, although some patients may read text more accurately due to the contextual cues provided by the text. However, it is more common to encounter a patient who complains of difficulty reading text yet appears to have no difficulty reading single words. This dissociation may be a reflection of grammatical difficulties, and can be examined by presenting sentences of increasing grammatical complexity. Difficulty with text reading may also be caused by hemispatial neglect or other visual processing/eye tracking impairments, or phonologic processing deficits (which may result in increased difficulty with increasing sentence length). To determine the extent to which reading comprehension deficits truly reflect a problem specific to reading, it is important to compare reading comprehension of sentences and paragraphs with auditory comprehension of comparable sentences and paragraphs.

CLINICAL ASSESSMENT TOOLS

The previous section of this chapter suggested ways to assess those aspects of reading that are most likely to be disturbed in patients with acquired alexia. Here, we review some of the best known of the clinical assessment tools that may be useful in performing such an evaluation.

Psycholinguistic Assessment of Language Processing in Aphasia (PALPA), by Kay, Lesser, and Coltheart, 1992

This test of language function contains the most comprehensive assessment of reading function that we are aware of in a published test. The PALPA contains sixty subtests, many of which are devoted to written language processing. Each subtest has normative data, clear descriptions of the parameters being assessed, and well-organized answer sheets for efficient data analysis. A large number of the assessments discussed in the previous section are represented in the PALPA in some manner.

One disadvantage to using the PALPA is that it was normed only for British English; thus, some of the items are not appropriate for speakers of American English (for example, *pram*, *hosepipe*). Another potential disadvantage is the brevity of the word lists. This is desirable as a screening for potential deficits, but is somewhat inadequate for definitive affirmation of the presence of a particular deficit. Longer lists controlled for various parameters such as grammatical word class, word length, frequency, concreteness, and regularity are found in the Johns Hopkins University Dyslexia Battery (Goodman & Caramazza, 1986; published with permission in Beeson & Hillis, 2001).

New Adult Reading Test Revised (NART), by Blair and Spreen, 1989

This is the American version of the National Adult Reading Test (Nelson, 1982; Nelson & Willison, 1991). This test was designed as measure of premorbid IQ in patients with dementia. It consists of sixty-one words with irregular spelling-to-sound correspondences. The words in the test are arranged so as to decrease in word frequency, making the later words less likely to be read correctly than the earlier words. This test may be a useful source of irregular words, if surface alexia is suspected. However, the number of irregular words that a reader of normal IQ would be expected to read correctly is rather limited, which limits the usefulness of the test.

Gates-MacGinitie Reading Tests, by Gates and MacGinitie, 1965

This test was designed to assess single word comprehension, comprehension of short paragraphs of increasing difficulty, and speed and accuracy of reading one- to two-sentence paragraphs. The single words were not chosen on the basis of any psycholinguistic parameters, and so this part of the test is of little practical value. The speed and accuracy subtest evaluates accuracy by asking the subject to choose one of four written words that best completes a statement based on the short paragraph. It assesses speed by measuring how many such paragraphs can be completed in four minutes. This subtest, and the slightly longer paragraph subtest, can be useful in assessing oral reading and reading comprehension of text. As there are alternate forms of the test, it is also useful for comparing reading comprehension to auditory comprehension.

Reading Comprehension Battery for Aphasia, Second Edition (RCBA-2), by LaPointe and Horner, 1998

The original RCBA was designed to assess functional silent reading. Added to the second edition are tests of letter knowledge, lexical decision, and oral reading.

There are several letter knowledge tasks contained within the RCBA-2. At the simplest level, perceptual processing is assessed with a physical matching task; the subject decides whether two uppercase letters are identical or not. Tests for neglect are incorporated into a test of letter naming and a test of pointing to the letter named. There is no assessment of letter identity (cross-case matching), nor mirror-image recognition.

In the lexical decision task, the subject is asked to choose the real word from among a triad of one word and two pseudowords. The PWs are not created to be pseudohomophones of real words, and the real words are not chosen to assess regularity; thus this test will not be adequate to completely determine the integrity of orthographic representations.

Single word comprehension is assessed with a word-picture matching task, in which a single picture must be matched to one of three words, which are either orthographically similar, phonologically similar (and possibly orthographically similar as well), or semantically similar. A synonym matching task is included as well. There is also an assessment of "functional reading," which includes different formats such as labels, signs, and entries in phone books.

Oral reading of single words is assessed for nouns only. Oral reading of sentences is assessed for sentences of subject-verb-object structure only. The effect of context is incorporated into this task by including words from the single word oral reading task.

In a sentence comprehension task, the subject chooses one of three pictures that corresponds to a written sentence. In one subtest, the sentences are chosen to assess morphosyntactic reading. Another task tests short paragraph comprehension. Longer paragraphs are presented for comprehension in a test containing both factual and inferential questions.

Gray Oral Reading Test, Third Edition (GORT-3), by Wiederholt and Bryant, 1992

The GORT-3 was designed for use with school-age children. It assesses oral reading, identifies reading strengths and weaknesses, and is used to document reading progress and as a research tool for studying reading abilities in school-age children. The test consists of two alternate, equivalent versions, each consisting of thirteen increasingly difficult passages, which are each followed by five multiple choice questions. The test evaluates oral reading rate, accuracy, and comprehension, total oral reading ability, and oral reading miscues.

Rate is measured in terms of time to read each passage. Accuracy is measured in terms of number of oral reading errors. The two scores are then added to compute the passage score. Multiple choice questions are used to assess comprehension. The examiner reads aloud the question and response choices while the examinee reads along. The total number of correctly answered questions is the comprehension score. Total oral reading ability is computed by combining the passage score and the comprehension score into the oral reading quotient.

The passages were written to control for a variety of features of words and sentences.

Vocabulary was chosen from three published word lists that were based on school textbooks. Content is general, and not academic in nature. The authors did a good job of altering vocabulary in the comprehension questions so that the examinee cannot simply match words in order to choose the correct answer. Many of the questions require subjective interpretation of the passage and, therefore, do not strictly assess linguistic abilities.

Boston Diagnostic Aphasia Exam (BDAE), Revised, by Goodglass and Kaplan, 2000

The BDAE contains several subtests of reading that may be of some use in evaluating possible alexias. Reading test A1 requires the patient to match single letters and short words across case and font. This test of letter identity contains too few items to make any real determination about the patient's abilities in this area; poor performance would certainly suggest a problem, but success on these few items would not necessarily mean that competence has been demonstrated.

Also included in the BDAE are subtests dealing with morphology. One advantage of these subtests is that they do not require the patient to produce verbal output; a word is spoken by the examiner, and the patient points to the corresponding word, from a multiple choice list. Included are functors and words with bound grammatical and derivational morphemes. However, performance on these items is not compared with performance on nongrammatical words, making it difficult to identify a relative deficit for grammatical words. Further, as this is a screening test of reading embedded within a much larger language test, the number of items are insufficient to be sensitive to milder problems.

TREATMENT OF THE ALEXIAS

Controlled studies of treatments for the alexias have only recently begun appearing in the scientific journals. This appears to have followed directly from the development of cognitive neuropsychological models of reading and reading disorders. Prior to the 1970s, alexic disorders were not well differentiated (aside from pure alexia), and so clinical treatments did not take into account the nature of the specific deficit. The identification of various types of alexias, such as surface alexia and phonological alexia (Marshall & Newcombe, 1973), changed the way that many speech-language pathologists considered remediating reading. The current trend, then, is to identify the specific cognitive deficits that underlie the reading problem in an individual patient, and to devise a treatment program accordingly. A description of some of the treatment studies that have been published in the last two decades follows.

Treatment for Letter Recognition Deficit in Pure Alexia: Tactile-Kinesthetic Approach (Greenwald & Gonzalez Rothi, 1998; Kashiwagi & Kashiwagi, 1989; Lott, Friedman, & Lincbaugh, 1994; Lott & Friedman, 1999; Maher, Clayton, Barrett, Schober-Peterson, & Gonzalez-Rothi, 1998)

As mentioned above, patients with pure alexia may recover some reading function by learning to read in a serial letter-by-letter fashion. Use of letter-by-letter reading may be taught by the therapist (see, for example, Daniel, Bolter, & Longs, 1992), though it is often discovered by the patients themselves. However, some patients with pure alexia also have difficulty recognizing individual letters. If letters are misidentified, it follows that the word in which they are contained will be misread. A fairly successful remedy for this problem involves tactile-kinesthetic (T-K) letter identification.

The rationale for this technique is straightforward. Because the deficit in pure alexia is one of access to the orthographic lexicon when stimuli are presented in the visual modality, the

T-K technique is designed to provide a means for accessing orthographic lexical representations through other modalities—tactile and/or kinesthetic.

In a typical T-K treatment, the patient is first trained to recognize single letters in isolation. A letter is presented on a computer screen or an index card, and the patient is asked to trace or copy the letter, and then to name it. If the letter is copied onto the table or a piece of paper, as in the Maher et al. (1998) and Kashiwagi and Kashiwagi (1989) studies, only kinesthetic feedback is obtained. If the letter is copied onto the palm of the patient's other hand, as in the Lott et al. (1994) study, the patient receives both tactile and kinesthetic feedback. Once the patient has mastered single letter recognition, training proceeds to whole words, and eventually to sentences.

After the patient's accuracy of letter-by-letter reading has reached an acceptable level, training can next be geared toward improving speed of reading. Lott and Friedman (1999) employed a three-stage approach, which focused first on single letter naming. The patient was encouraged to use the T-K strategy to name letters aloud as rapidly as possible. Feedback regarding speed of letter naming was provided to the patient after every block of trials, and training continued until the patient's speed reached a plateau. The next phase involved the naming of letters in a letter string. This stage was inserted prior to the word reading stage, so the patient would develop the habit of naming every letter in a string prior to attempting to read a word. The final stage was single word reading. As before, the patient received feedback about his speed, and was encouraged to try to do better on successive blocks. The result of this treatment was substantial improvement in reading speed, with no sacrifice in accuracy.

Treatment for Impaired Whole Word Recognition in Pure Alexia: A Semantic Approach (Friedman & Lott, 2000; Gonzalez Rothi, & Moss, 1992; Maher et al., 1998)

It has been reported that some patients with pure alexia may be able to recognize words as wholes if the words are presented rapidly (Coslett & Saffran, 1989; Shallice & Saffran, 1986). The explanation for this finding is that a secondary reading system, based upon semantics, is available to the patients but only becomes available when the patient is prevented from employing a letter-by-letter reading strategy. It has been suggested (Coslett & Saffran, 1989) that patients can be trained to employ this alternate reading mechanism by presenting words tachistoscopically and focusing on tasks that emphasize semantic processing, such as category decision or other semantic judgments. This notion has been put into practice in several treatment studies.

Gonzalez Rothi and Moss (1992) used the semantic approach in treating the reading deficit of a patient with pure alexia using three separate tasks, all of which made use of tachistoscopically presented written words. The homophone task required the patient to determine whether a written homophonic word (for example, *reign*) matched the meaning of the word in an orally presented sentence (for example, "She will reign"). In the semantic decision task, the patient determined whether a written word was a member of an orally presented semantic category. The third task was a lexical decision task. Results revealed improved accuracy for the stimuli presented in all three tasks. Reading of untrained words showed some improvement in speed, but not accuracy. The authors report some success with this approach in one subsequent case, but failure in another case.

Further investigation of the training of whole word reading (Friedman & Lott, 2000) suggests that focusing on semantic processing may not be necessary for this strategy to be successful. Using 50 msec presentations of words, presented over many sessions with feedback, these investigators were able to train a patient, RS, to make accurate semantic judgments for trained but not untrained words. However, their patient also learned to recognize rapidly presented words when the task was simple oral reading, not categorization. Further, the patient learned words of lower semantic value (that is, functors) as rapidly as words high in semantic value (concrete nouns), again suggesting that the mechanism of learning may not be semantically based. This technique has since been used successfully with several other pure alexic patients; one patient failed to benefit from this therapy.

Given that it may be possible to train patients with pure alexia to recognize words rapidly, but that it is unrealistic to attempt to train all words of the language, a reasonable approach to treatment is to train the patient to recognize 125 to 150 of the most frequent words of the language, words that tend to appear repeatedly within typical sentences and paragraphs. Mastery of these words will take the patient a long way toward improved reading efficiency.

It is worth noting that this training paradigm has been implemented successfully on a computer (Friedman & Lott, 2000; Lott & Friedman, 1994), so that the patient can self-train at home between therapy sessions. The program is set up so that a word is flashed on the screen, and the patient reads the word. Following a key press, the computer presents the word auditorily, providing the necessary feedback.

Treatment for Inability to Access Orthographic Representation in Surface Alexia (Byng & Coltheart, 1986; Coltheart & Byng, 1989; Scott & Byng, 1989; Weekes and Coltheart, 1996)

A patient who consistently reads regular words (*home*) better than irregular words (*come*) and who defines words solely according to their derived pronunciation (*come* → "you use it to fix your hair") has difficulty accessing lexical orthographic representations of known words. In an attempt to ameliorate this problem in such a surface dyslexic patient, Byng and Coltheart (1986) developed a technique in which targeted irregular words were paired with semantic cues. For example, the word *through* was presented with an arrow drawn through it. The patient was given a set of cards with such pairings, and practiced reading the words at home. The patient's reading of words paired with semantic cues improved more than his reading of words that were not included in the treatment, but some generalization may have occurred as well. These results were replicated in a subsequent study by Weekes and Coltheart (1996).

A study focusing specifically on comprehension of homophones (Scott & Byng, 1989) employed context-rich whole sentences for training the meanings of homophonic words in a patient with surface alexia. On each training trial, a sentence appeared on the screen with the homophone deleted. Below the sentence were six choices, which included the correct word, its homophone, and a pseudohomophone of the correct word. The patient chose a response, and received feedback regarding accuracy. Following ten weeks of training, the patient showed improvement of the trained words. However, improvement of the untrained words on two of the three post-tests made interpretation of the results of this study problematic. In contrast, Hillis (1993) reported improved oral reading and comprehension (and spelling) of trained homophones (for example, *stake* and *steak*), without generalization to untrained homophones in a similar study. Hillis (1993) trained a patient with impaired access to the orthographic lexicon to read homophones, by having him read each trained word and its definition and then write it in a sentence.

Treating a Deficit in Accessing Phonology from Orthography by Training Grapheme-Phoneme Correspondence Rules (dePartz, 1986; Laine & Niemi, 1990; Mitchum & Berndt, 1991; Nickels, 1992)

Patients with "deep dyslexia" have difficulty reading many words that are low in concreteness, and are unable to use orthography-to-phonology correspondences to decode these words. One approach to reading remediation in these patients is to retrain the use of such correspondences. Therapy of this sort has been implemented by several investigators, with mixed results.

Several studies have focused on the retraining of grapheme-phoneme correspondence rules. In one such study, dePartz (1986) was successful in teaching her patient to use these rules. In the first stage of therapy, the patient was taught to associate one "relay" word with each letter of the alphabet (for example, "boy" for b). In the second stage, the patient was taught to elongate his pronunciation of the first phoneme in the relay word, and then to pronounce only the phoneme. After three months of practice, he was encouraged to produce only the initial phoneme, without first pronouncing the relay word. In the third stage, the patient produced short nonwords by first sounding each letter individually. This procedure was then employed for short real words.

At the end of this therapy program, which lasted a total of nine months, the patient's word reading accuracy had improved to 98 percent, compared with 28 percent prior to therapy. The success of this therapy program is impressive, yet three subsequent therapy programs for deep dyslexic patients (Laine & Niemi, 1990; Mitchum & Berndt, 1991; Nickels, 1992), modelled after this one, all met with considerably less success. The patient of Laine and Niemi and the patient of Mitchum and Berndt both learned to produce the appropriate phonemes for given graphemes with little difficulty. However, they were never able to successfully blend the phonemes into syllables, despite considerable attempts to teach them to do so. The authors of both studies consider the possibility that the problem with phoneme blending is attributable to a deficient phonological short-term memory. The interaction of short-term memory with success/failure of therapy of this type has yet to be systematically addressed. Another difference between these two patients and the patient of dePartz is that the former had nonfluent aphasia, while the latter had fluent aphasia. Thus, aphasia type (and lesion location) may also be relevant to success/failure of this therapy technique.

In noting that one result of the therapy was to reduce the number of semantic paralexias produced, Mitchum and Berndt (1991) suggested that a combination of lexical and nonlexical training may be beneficial to some patients. Such an approach was taken by Nickels (1992), who also used the relay word strategy to teach her patient to translate graphemes into phonemes. Like the others, Nickels's patient learned to assign the appropriate phonemes to graphemes, but could not learn to blend them into syllables. In the next phase of treatment, the patient was instructed to produce the initial phoneme of a word, then think about its meaning, then attempt to say the word. The patient learned this strategy promptly, and used it with success. Assessment two weeks after the end of therapy revealed a significant improvement in the reading of high imagebility words. This approach, then, may be of some value in training a patient to read high imageability words; however, patients who have trouble decoding phonology from orthography tend to have more trouble with low imageability words than high imageability words, a fact that renders this approach less useful.

Treating a Deficit in Accessing Phonology from Orthography by Training Bigraphs (Friedman & Lott, 1996, in press)

The failure of the grapheme-phoneme therapy discussed in the above section was the result of the patients' inability to blend individual phonemes into syllables. The therapy devised by Friedman and Lott (1996 & in press) was predicated on the premise that grapheme-phoneme conversion is not the most natural way to translate letters into sounds: in particular, many consonantal phonemes cannot actually be produced in isolation; a vowel (usually a schwa) must be produced as well. When blending these sounds, then, the schwa must first be inhibited, and this appears to be difficult for these patients (and for many young children as well; Rozin & Gleitman, 1977).

Friedman and Lott implemented a therapy that was based upon what they considered to be a more natural unit of pronunciation, the bigraph syllable. The patient was first trained to associate a set of bigraphs with their corresponding sounds. This was accomplished using the "relay" procedure, much like the one used by dePartz (1986): When presented with a two-letter bigraph (for example, *ma*), the patient was trained to produce a word that begins with those letters (for example, *match*), then cut it short so that only the appropriate bigraph syllable is produced (/mæʦ/ → /mæ/). After learning consonant-vowel (CV) bigraphs and vowel-consonant (VC) bigraphs, the patient learned to put CVs and VCs together into CVC words; for example, /mæ/ + /æt/ = mat. Two patients were able to learn the trained bigraphs. Further, both patients were able to combine those bigraphs in such a way as to read a large number of words on which they had not been specifically trained.

Bigraph therapy does appear to be a promising way to improve the phonological decoding skills of some alexic patients. However, it does have certain limitations. As with the use of any phonological decoding strategy with an irregular language such as English, there are many exceptions to contend with (producing /mæ/ at the beginning of the word *many* would lead to an incorrect reading). In addition, using such a strategy with multi-syllabic words may be problematic. Finally, the number of different bigraphs that must be trained is not insignificant. Despite these obstacles, providing patients with a means of decoding even short words or syllables may go a long way toward improving their overall reading, particularly if combined with other strategies, such as the semantic strategy employed by Nickels (1992).

Treatment for Impairment in Reading Certain Classes of Words Using Paired Associate Learning (Friedman, Sample, and Lott, 2000; Friedman, Lott, and Sample, 1998)

Patients with "phonological dyslexia" (predominant impairment in orthography-to-phonology conversion) often have difficulty reading functors and other words that are low in concreteness, while retaining fairly good reading of concrete words. Friedman et al. (2000) made use of two such patients' intact reading of content words to aid in their reading of functors and verbs. Words low in semantic value, and hence poorly read by these patients, are paired with words high in semantic value that are phonologically similar. The most perfect case of this type of pairing is the homophone: the word *be* is paired with the word *bee*. As most words do not have homophones, near-homophones were used as well (for example, *me*, *meat*).

In this treatment, the target word (*be*) was printed on the front of an index card; its homophone (*bee*), along with a picture of the homophone, appeared on the back of the card. During training, the patient was asked to read the target word. If the response was incorrect, the card was turned over, and the patient read/named the homophone (or near-homophone). In this way, the patients learned to pair the targets with their homophone or near-homophone, and eventually learned to read the target words before turning over the cards. No measurable improvement in overall text reading was seen following treatment. However, this study trained the patients on only sixty words, presented in isolation. Perhaps with a larger corpus of trained words, and possibly with the additional training of these words in sentences or text, a real improvement in functional reading might be achieved.

Treatment Focusing on Text Reading: The Multiple Oral Rereading Approach (Beeson, 1998; Beeson & Insalaco, 1998; Moody, 1988; Moyer, 1979; Tuomainen & Laine, 1991)

The multiple oral rereading (MOR) technique was developed by Moyer (1979) in an attempt to improve the reading speed of her pure alexic patient. The patient read aloud a simple (sixth grade level) six-hundred-word selection from a child's encyclopedia, then practiced reading it aloud for thirty minutes a day for one week. A new selection was introduced each week. Speed of reading the practiced selection and speed of reading an unpracticed selection were recorded each week. At the end of three months, the patient's speed of reading new selections had improved significantly.

Moody (1988) tested the efficacy of the MOR technique with three patients, one with pure alexia and two with phonologic alexia. The procedure was the same as that used by Moyer, but passages as well as daily practice time were shorter. Like Moyer, Moody found increased speed of reading novel text for her pure alexic patient. One of the phonologic alexic patients also showed improvement, although less than that of the pure alexic patient. The other phonologic alexic patient showed no improvement in reading unpracticed text.

Tuomainen and Laine (1991) found the MOR technique to be successful with two of their three pure alexic patients. They attributed their lack of success with the third patient to his additional visuospatial and memory deficits, and suggest that at least partial functioning of the visual word form system is necessary for the success of MOR therapy. Further, only one of the patients showed increased speed of reading single words, leading the authors to conclude that MOR does not affect the "underlying defect in pure alexia" but rather serves to improve top-down processing strategies in text reading.

Beeson (1998) replicated the findings of the previous study. Beeson's pure alexic patient showed improved speed of reading text following MOR therapy, but did not show improvement of single words. Beeson and Insalaco (1998) demonstrated successful use of the MOR technique with a patient whose alexia most resembled phonologic alexia, but with a significant word length effect. Following treatment, the patient's reading speed for text improved. A new treatment was then begun, in which the patient practiced reading text that was divided into phrases. After seven months of this treatment, the patient no longer showed a word length effect, and her reading speed for single words increased relative to her speed at the beginning of the MOR treatment; the increase was particularly salient for functors. The authors concluded that the patient showed "a generalized improvement in whole word recognition and a specific improvement in associating written functors to their corresponding phonological representations." Because the single word reading was retested only after both MOR and phrase-formatted treatment, it is impossible to know which of these treatments produced the increased reading speed for functors. A second patient also showed improved reading speed following MOR and phrase-formatted treatment, and particular improvement with functors. However, the patient continued to show improved reading speed when doing nothing more than spending thirty minutes per day reading new text, making it difficult to determine what the effect of the specific treatments had been. Improvement in overall language scores contributed to the difficulty in determining treatments' specific effects.

At present, then, the role of MOR therapy in the rehabilitation of pure alexia and phonologic alexia remains somewhat unclear. Its advantage over simply practice reading text has not yet been proven. In any case, therapy of this kind, whose beneficial effect is in speed but not accuracy of reading, is appropriate only for patients whose reading is already at a fairly high level of competence.

SUMMARY

Reading is a complex process that requires a number of relatively independent processing components. Individuals with focal brain damage often have impaired reading as a result of disruption of one or more of these processing components. A number of tests have been reviewed that allow the clinician to pinpoint which processing components are impaired in each case. Once the level of disruption has been identified, therapy can focus on specifically treating the impaired component, or can focus on using intact processing mechanisms to compensate for the impaired mechanism or level of representation. Such therapy is often, but not always, effective in improving reading, but the determinants of effectiveness have not yet been identified.

REFERENCES

Badecker, W., & Caramazza, A. (1987). The analysis of morphological errors in a case of acquired dyslexia. *Brain and Language, 32,* 278-305.

Beeson, P. M. (1998). Treatment for letter-by-letter reading: A case study. In N. H. Estabrooks & A. Holland (Eds.), *Approaches to the treatment of aphasia.* San Diego: Singular Publishing Group.

Beeson, P., & Hillis, A. E. (2001). Comprehension and production of written words. In R. Chapey (Ed.), *Language intervention strategies in adult aphasia* (4th ed.). Baltimore: Lippincott, Williams and Wilkens.

Beeson, P. M., & Insalaco, D. (1998). Acquired alexia: Lessons from successful treatment. *Journal of the International Neuropsychological Society, 4,* 621-635.

Blair, J. R., & Spreen, O. (1989). Predicting premorbid IQ: A revision of the National Adult Reading Test. *The Clinical Neuropsychologist, 3*(2), 129-136.

Byng, S., & Coltheart, M. (1986). Aphasia therapy research: methodological requirements and illustrative results. *Advances in Psychology, 34,* 191-213.

Coltheart, M., & Byng, S. (1989). A treatment for surface dyslexia. In X. Seron & G. Deloche (Eds.), *Cognitive approaches in neuropsychological rehabilitation.* Hillsdale, NJ: Lawrence Erlbaum Associates.

Coslett, H. B., & Saffran, E. M. (1989). Evidence for preserved reading in "pure alexia." *Brain, 112,* 327-359.

Daniel, M. S., Bolter, J. F., & Longs, C. J. (1992). Remediation of alexia without agraphia: A case study. *Brain Injury, 6*(6), 529-542.

dePartz, M.-P. (1986). Re-education of a deep dyslexic patient: Rationale of the method and results. *Cognitive Neuropsychology, 3*(2), 149-177.

Friedman, R. B. (1996). Phonological text alexia: Poor pseudoword reading plus difficulty reading functors and affixes in text. *Cognitive Neuropsychology, 13*(6), 869-885.

Friedman, R. B., & Lott, S. N. (1996). Phonologic treatment for deep dyslexia using bigraphs instead of graphemes. *Brain & Language, 55,* 116-118.

Friedman, R. B., & Lott, S. N. (2000). Rapid word identification in pure alexia is lexical but not semantic. *Brain and Language, 72*(3), 219-237.

Friedman, R. B., & Lott, S. N. (in press). Successful blending in a phonologic reading treatment for deep dyslexia. *Aphasiology.*

Friedman, R. B., Lott, S. N., & Sample, D. (1998). A reorganization approach to treating phonological alexia. *Brain and Language, 65,* 196-198.

Friedman, R. B., & Perlman, M. B. (1982). On the underlying causes of semantic paralexias in a patient with deep dyslexia. *Neuropsychologia, 20,* 559-568.

Friedman, R. B., Sample, D. M., & Lott, S. N. (2000). The role of level of representation in the use of paired associate learning for rehabilitation of alexia, *Neuropsychologia, 40,* 223-234.

Gates, A. I., & MacGinitie, W. H. (1965). *Gates-MacGinitie reading tests.* New York: Teachers College Press.

Gonzalez-Rothi, L. J., & Moss, S. (1992). Alexia without agraphia: Potential for model assisted therapy. *Clinics in Communication Disorders, 2,* 11-18.

Goodglass, H., & Kaplan, E. (2000). *The assessment of aphasia and related disorders* (3rd ed.). Philadelphia: Lea & Febiger.

Goodman, R. A., & Caramazza, A. (1986). *The Johns Hopkins dyslexia battery.* Baltimore: Johns Hopkins University Press.

Greenwald, M. L., & Gonzalez-Rothi, L. J. (1998). Lexical access via letter naming in a profoundly alexic and anomic patient: A treatment study. *Journal of the International Neuropsychological Society, 4,* 595-607.

Hillis, A. E. (1993). The role of models of language processing in rehabilitation of language impairments. *Aphasiology, 7,* 5-26.

Kashiwagi, T., & Kashiwagi, A. (1989). Recovery process of a Japanese alexic without agraphia. *Aphasiology, 3*(1), 75-91.

Kay, J., Lesser, R., & Coltheart, M. (1992). *PALPA: Psycholinguistic assessments of language processing in aphasia.* London: Lawrence Erlbaum Associates.

Kinsbourne, M., & Warrington, E. K. (1962). A variety of reading disability associated with right hemisphere lesions. *Journal of Neurology, Neurosurgery, and Psychiatry, 25,* 339-344.

Laine, M., & Niemi, J. (1990). Can the oral reading skills be rehabilitated in deep dyslexia? In M. Hietanen, J. Vilkki, M.-L. Niemi, & M. Korkman (Eds.), *Clinical neuropsychology: Excursions into the field in Finland.* Rauma, Finland: Suomen Psykologinen Seura.

LaPointe, L. L., & Horner, J. (1998). *Reading comprehension battery for sphasia, Second Edition (RCBA-2).* Austin, TX: PRO-ED, Inc.

Lott, S. N., & Friedman, R. B. (1994). Treatment for pure alexia via the information superhighway. *Brain and Language, 47,* 524-527.

Lott, S. N., & Friedman, R. B. (1999). Can treatment for pure alexia improve letter-by-letter reading speed without sacrificing accuracy? *Brain and Language, 67,* 188-201.

Lott, S. N., Friedman, R. B., & Linebaugh, C. W. (1994). Rationale and efficacy of a tactile-kinaesthetic treatment for alexia. *Aphasiology, 8*(2), 181-195.

Maher, L. M., Clayton, M. C., Barrett, A. M., Schober-Peterson, D., & Gonzalez-Rothi, L. J. (1998). Rehabilitation of a case of pure alexia: Exploiting residual abilities. *Journal of the International Neuropsychological Society, 4,* 636-647.

Marshall, J. C., & Newcombe, F. (1973). Patterns of paralexia: A psycholinguistic approach. *Journal of Psycholinguistic Research, 2,* 175-199.

Mitchum, C. C., & Berndt, R. S. (1991). Diagnosis and treatment of the non-lexical route in acquired dyslexia: an illustration of the cognitive neuropsychological approach. *Journal of Neurolinguistics, 6*(2), 103-137.

Moody, S. (1988). The Moyer Reading Technique re-evaluated. *Cortex, 24,* 473-476.

Moyer, S. B. (1979). Rehabilitation of alexia: A case study. *Cortex, 15,* 139-144.

Nelson, H. E. (1982). *The national adult reading test (NART): Test manual.* Windsor, UK: NFER-Nelson.

Nelson, H. E., & Willison, J. (1991). *National adult reading test (NART)* (2nd ed.). Windsor, UK: NFER-Nelson.

Nickels, L. (1992). The autocue? Self-generated phonemic cues in the treatment of a disorder of reading and naming. *Cognitive Neuropsychology, 9,* 155-182.

Rozin, P., & Gleitman, L. R. (1977). The structure and acquisition of reading II: The reading process and the acquisition of the alphabetic principle. In A. S. Reber & D. L. Scarborough (Eds.), *Toward a psychol-*

ogy of reading. Hillsdale, NJ: Lawrence Erlbaum Associates.

Scott, C., & Byng, S. (1989). Computer assisted remediation of a homophone comprehension disorder in surface dyslexia. *Aphasiology, 3*(3), 301–320.

Shallice, T., & Saffran, E. (1986). Lexical processing in the absence of explicit word identification: Evidence from a letter-by-letter reader. *Cognitive Neuropsychology, 3*, 429–458.

Shallice, T., & Warrington, E. K. (1977). The possible role of selective attention in acquired dyslexia. *Neuropsychologia, 15*, 31-41.

Tuomainen, J., & Laine, M. (1991). Multiple oral rereading technique in rehabilitation of pure alexia. *Aphasiology, 5*(4–5), 401–409.

Weekes, B., & Coltheart, M. (1996). Surface dyslexia and surface dysgraphia: Treatment studies and their theoretical implications. *Cognitive Neuropsychology, 13*(2), 277–315.

Part 2

—

Spelling

—

4

Uncovering the Cognitive Architecture of Spelling

Brenda Rapp

A variety of different patterns of spelling impairment may be observed subsequent to neurological damage. For example, *sauce* might be spelled as *soss* or as *soucf* or as *gravy*. Errors such as these, as well as other aspects of the spelling performance of dysgraphic individuals, have made fundamental contributions to our understanding of the nature and organization of the mental operations that are normally involved in spelling words. In this chapter I will first provide an overview of our current understanding of the normal spelling process. I will then illustrate, through a series of case studies, how the performance of dysgraphic individuals has been used in uncovering this cognitive architecture of spelling.

A COGNITIVE ARCHITECTURE OF THE SPELLING PROCESS

The term *cognitive architecture* is used to describe the organization of the various mental operations that are involved in a skill such as spelling. A cognitive architecture specifies not only the functions of the various cognitive processes but also the relationships among them. In this context it is important to distinguish between cognitive functions and behavioral tasks. A cognitive function is a mental operation or process that can be used in a number of tasks. For example, if cognitive function A involves searching memory for the spelling of a word, then we assume that cognitive function A is used in any task that requires that function. For example, searching memory for the spelling of a word is required for tasks such as spelling a word in response to a picture stimulus, spelling a word to dictation, or spelling a word in the course of writing a business letter. These tasks are similar in that they all make use of function A; however, they also differ in that each requires other cognitive processes that are not shared by all of the tasks. What is important to note is that there is not a one-to-one relationship between tasks and cognitive functions.

Figure 4.1 is a schematic depiction of the cognitive architecture of the spelling process that is assumed in most current work on spelling. In this section I will describe each of the cognitive components or functions that are assumed in this theory of spelling, grouping the functions into the categories of lexical, sublexical, and postlexical. The empirical bases for particular aspects of this architecture will be discussed in the following section.

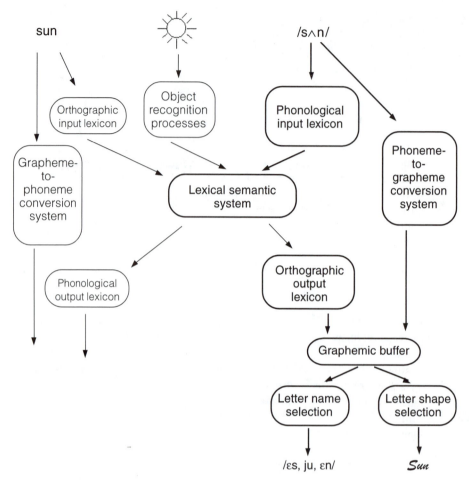

Figure 4.1. A schematic depiction of lexical, postlexical, and sublexical cognitive processes. Those processes specifically involved in spelling are bolded.

Lexical Processes

It is generally assumed that, as a result of experience in hearing a spoken word, a memory trace of the word's phonological form is laid down. The collection of all phonological word form memories is referred to as the phonological lexicon. A distinction is often drawn between an input and an output lexicon. The phonological input lexicon is involved in processing phonological input, in recognizing spoken words. By contrast, the phonological output lexicon is involved in producing spoken words.

The phonological input lexicon plays a role in the spelling process when the stimulus for spelling is a spoken word. When a person is asked to spell a word to dictation (or is taking notes in class or messages on the phone), the spoken stimulus is subjected to a series of prelexical auditory and phonological input processes that translate the acoustic stimulus to a phonological form. Subsequently, a process "searches" the phonological input lexicon for a memory trace that matches the phonological representation of the stimulus. If the search is successful it can be said that an entry in the phonological input lexicon has been "addressed" or "accessed." The phonological input lexicon is involved in a large number of tasks—in effect in any task that involves hearing a word and determining whether or not it is familiar. Examples of such tasks would include: spelling to dictation, spoken language comprehension, spoken word-picture matching, and so forth.

The lexical semantic system is the store of all the word meanings that an individual is familiar with. We assume that the same store of word meanings is involved regardless of the modality of presentation of a word (spoken, written, or pictorial) and regardless of the modality of production (spoken or spelled). After a word is accessed in the phonological input lexicon, and in order for the word to be understood, the memory of its meaning must be contacted in the lexical semantic system. This will be true of tasks that involve simply understanding a spoken word as well as tasks such as spelling to dictation where the word must first be understood and then spelled. The lexical semantic system is, therefore, required for virtually all word comprehension and production tasks.

The orthographic output lexicon is the repository of all familiar word spellings. It is assumed to be specifically involved in the production of word spellings. By contrast, the recognition of word spellings in tasks such as reading is often assumed to make use of the orthographic input lexicon.[1] As Figure 4.1 indicates, once a word's meaning has been accessed or activated, its semantic representation can serve as the basis for searching the orthographic output lexicon for the corresponding spelling. According to this architecture, it is not necessary to go from a word's meaning to its phonology in order to retrieve its spelling; instead, orthography can be retrieved independently of phonology. In other words, phonological mediation between word meaning and orthographic form is not required. The evidence supporting this claim will be discussed in detail below.

Thus, the orthographic output lexicon is required for any task that involves going from word meaning to word spelling, regardless of the form of the input. This includes the task of spelling to dictation, but is not limited to it since accessing the orthographic output lexicon will also be necessary if one simply writes down a word whose meaning one has in mind while writing a letter, a poem, or a grocery list. In addition, addressing the orthographic output lexicon from the lexical semantic system will be necessary if the stimulus for spelling is a picture or an object. For spelling the name of a picture or a visually presented object (the task of written naming), additional cognitive components are required for processing the visual stimulus and then accessing the lexical semantic system (see figure 4.1).

Some theorists posit a direct connection between the phonological input lexicon and the orthographic output lexicon (Patterson, 1986; Roeltgen, Rothi, & Heilman, 1986). This is sometimes referred to as the "direct route" or the "nonsemantic route." There is some evidence that subjects who apparently do not understand the meanings of words with highly irregular spellings (for example, *yacht* or /jat/) may nonetheless spell them. This evidence is still somewhat controversial, and alternative accounts of the data that do not require positing a direct route have been proposed (Hillis & Caramazza, 1991). For these reasons we will not discuss the proposal further.

Postlexical Processes

A number of processes are required for going from the point at which a word's spelling is contacted in the orthographic output lexicon to actually producing a spelling. Spelling knowledge can be expressed in a variety of ways: written spelling, oral spelling, typing, arranging toothpicks in the shapes of letters and words, and so on. Here we will be concerned with the two most common means of spelling: oral and written. In oral spelling a word's orthography is

---

[1]Figure 4.1 depicts the fairly standard theory in which there are two orthographic lexicons—one for input and one for output. There is considerable controversy regarding whether reading and spelling actually depend on different lexical stores, and some researchers have proposed a single-lexicon model (for example, Allport & Funnel, 1981; Behrmann & Bub, 1992; Coltheart & Funnel, 1987). The single-lexicon model predicts that lexical orthographic damage should necessarily result in an association of impairments in reading and spelling, while the two-lexicon model predicts that there need not be such an association. This debate is ongoing and unresolved, so I have chosen here to adopt the two-lexicon model, which is somewhat easier to depict and discuss.

expressed by saying the names of letters (for example, *cat* (picture) → /si, ei, ti/), whereas in written spelling it is expressed by producing letter shapes (for example, *cat* (picture) → CAT). In written spelling there are a number of letter shape types that may be used: CAT, cat, *cat*.

Given that spelling knowledge can be expressed in such a wide range of formats the following question arises: In what format are word spellings represented in the orthographic output lexicon? For a number of reasons it is assumed that information about word spellings is stored in the orthographic output lexicon in an abstract format-independent manner. That is, our memories of the letter combinations that make up word spellings do not consist of letter shapes or letter names; rather, they consist of abstract letter representations, or graphemes.

The abstract graphemic representations retrieved from the orthographic output lexicon are given form by postlexical processes that are dedicated to translating graphemes into specific letter shapes (in written spelling) or letter names (in oral spelling). Postlexically, therefore, there is a bifurcation of processes into those that are specific to written spelling and those that are specific to oral spelling.

For written spelling, the letter shape selection process (sometimes referred to as the allographic conversion process) translates each grapheme of a word's spelling into a letter shape representation. These letter shape representations specify the case (upper/lower) and font (print/cursive) corresponding to each grapheme. The letter shape representations serve as the "blueprint" for complex motor processes that send commands to specific muscles that generate the movements required to produce the target shapes.

For oral spelling, the letter name selection process translates abstract, graphemic representations into their corresponding letter names. The phonological representations that are the output of the letter name selection process serve as the basis for the motor, articulatory plans that produce the movements of the oral articulators necessary for pronouncing the target letter names. (Note that the letter name selection process yields phonological representations corresponding to letter names and not the names of the words themselves.)

Producing a word's spelling (either orally or in writing) is a time-consuming, serially executed process. When a word's spelling is activated in the orthographic output lexicon it must remain active and available throughout the relatively slow process of converting the abstract, graphemic code to letter shapes or letter names and then executing the appropriate motor actions. The graphemic buffer, is the mechanism or process dedicated to maintaining abstract graphemic codes active throughout the spelling process. Graphemic buffering is required for both written and oral spelling and, as a result, is located after the orthographic output lexicon and prior to the letter name and letter shape selection processes.

Sublexical Processes

In addition to being able to spell familiar words, we are also able to produce reasonable spellings for words that we have never heard before (for example, proper names). Thus, if you take a phone message from a Mrs. /f l i p/, you will note that a Mrs. Flepe, Fleep, Fleap, or Phlepe called. The cognitive system containing the knowledge required to derive a plausible spelling for an unfamiliar phonological form is referred to as the phoneme-grapheme conversion system (or PG system).

It is typically assumed that the PG system consists of at least two processes: phonological parsing and phoneme-grapheme assignment. The phonological parsing process takes the output of prelexical auditory and phonological processes and parses (or organizes) the phonological representation into smaller phonological units (perhaps individual phonemes or syllabically defined units). The phoneme-grapheme assignment process then selects a plausible spelling for each phoneme. For example,

/f l i p/:
    /f/ → F or PH
    /l/ → L
    /i/ → E_E, EE, or EA
    /p/ → P

Thus the PG system contains the knowledge of the regularities in the relationship between sounds and letters in English. It is referred to as a sublexical system because the units that are represented and manipulated are smaller than the whole-word or morpheme-sized units that are manipulated by the lexical system. Presumably, PG conversion knowledge is laid down as a result of accumulated experience in spelling the words of the language.

Interestingly, evidence from cognitively intact subjects as well as from dysgraphic individuals indicates that the PG system contains knowledge of the multiple ways in which the sounds of English may be spelled; that is, not simply that /f/ may be spelled with F but that it may be spelled with F or PH. Furthermore, the evidence indicates that these multiple PG mappings (for example, /f/ → F) are weighted in the PG system according to their frequency in the language. For example, 85 percent of all the words of English with syllable-initial /f/ are spelled with an initial F, while only 11 percent of such words are spelled with PH. There is some evidence that PG mappings are selected according to their frequency or mapping probability. Given this, the PG system is far more likely to generate a spelling for Mrs. /f l i p/ that begins with F than with PH.

As can be seen in figure 4.1, the PG system shares with the lexical system not only the early prelexical components involved in processing an auditory stimulus, but also the postlexical processes involved in buffering the graphemes generated by the PG system and the conversion processes required to translate these into letter names or letter shapes for the written or oral spelling of unfamiliar words (sometimes also referred to as nonwords or pseudowords).

HOW PATTERNS OF DYSGRAPHIC PERFORMANCE REVEAL THE ARCHITECTURE OF THE SPELLING PROCESS

In the case of the spelling system, patterns of performance of dysgraphic individuals have formed the primary source of evidence regarding the organization of the system. In the next sections, I review a number of case studies[2] that specifically illustrate how dysgraphic performance has contributed to the development of the cognitive architecture just described.

The Question of Orthographic Autonomy: RGB (Caramazza and Hillis, 1990)

A long-standing issue in written language research has been the relationship among orthography, phonology, and semantics. In the context of spelling, the question has been: If we have the meaning of a word in mind, do we need to access the word's spoken form in order to retrieve its spelling? According to the hypothesis of obligatory phonological mediation, the retrieval of a word's spelling requires the prior retrieval of its phonological form (see figure 4.2[a]). According to this hypothesis, activation of a word's meaning is followed by activation of its phonology and only then can access to its orthography take place. This hypothesis is based on the traditional assumption that written language knowledge is entirely dependent on spoken language knowledge (Brown, 1972; Geschwind, 1969; Grashey, 1885; Head, 1926; Hecaen & Angelergues, 1965; Lichtheim, 1885; Luria, 1966; Wernicke, 1886; Frith, 1979; Hotopf, 1980;

---

[2]For a discussion of the role of case studies in addressing questions of cognitive processing and representation see Caramazza & McCloskey, 1988.

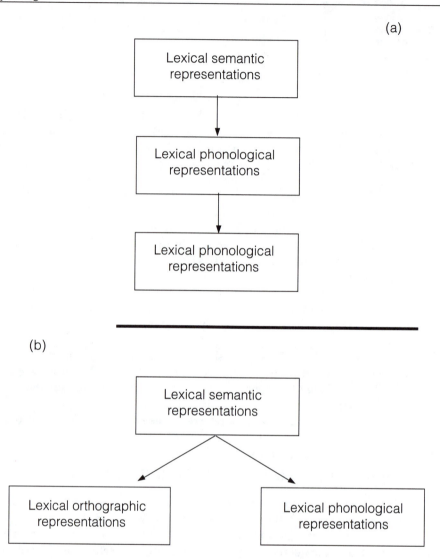

Figure 4.2. A schematic depiction of the hypotheses of obligatory phonological mediation and orthographic autonomy.

Van Orden, Johnston, & Hale, 1988). An alternative hypothesis, that of orthographic autonomy, proposes that, although orthography builds on phonology in the course of written language acquisition, in the fully developed system, orthography can be retrieved directly from meaning, without phonological mediation (see figure 4.2[b]). This direct relationship between orthography and semantics is assumed in the spelling architecture depicted in figure 4.1.

Dysgraphic performance has been especially useful in adjudicating between these two hypotheses, because the two make clearly different predictions regarding the performance patterns that should be possible subsequent to damage. According to the hypothesis of obligatory phonological mediation, a deficit that affects the ability to access the phonological output lexicon should necessarily have consequences for spelling. In contrast, according to the hypothesis of orthographic independence, a deficit that affects phonological retrieval need not have any consequences for orthographic retrieval. In order to evaluate these hypotheses, it will be necessary to consider cases of individuals with damage affecting the phonological output lexicon or access to it. According to the obligatory phonological mediation hypothesis, in such cases spelling should also be affected; according to orthographic autonomy hypothesis, it need not be.

The case of RGB (Caramazza & Hillis, 1990) provides a strong test of these predictions. RGB was a sixty-two-year-old, right-handed retired personnel manager with a high school education. He suffered a left middle cerebral artery occlusion four years prior to the investigation, with CT scans revealing a large, left fronto-parietal infarct. He had dense hemiplegia but no cranial nerve deficits.

RGB showed intact access to semantic knowledge from both spoken and written word stimuli as well as from pictures. This was demonstrated by flawless performance on comprehension tasks requiring him to provide definitions for printed words or verifying whether written or spoken words match pictures (table 4.1). This performance indicates that RGB's lexical semantic system was intact.

Interestingly, however, RGB made frequent semantic errors in spoken production tasks, such as oral naming of pictures and oral reading (table 4.1). For example, a picture of a kangaroo was named as "raccoon," mittens as "socks," clam as "octopus"; *kangaroo* was read as "giraffe," *mittens* as "gloves," and *banana* as "pineapple." The fact that the lexical semantic system was intact rules it out as the source of the errors; the fact that semantic errors (rather than phonological errors) were produced makes a postlexical phonological deficit unlikely. This indicates that the semantic errors in spoken naming arose from difficulties in activating the correct phonological representation in the phonological output lexicon. To account for the occurrence of semantic errors at this level of the system, Caramazza and Hillis (1990) proposed that a semantic representation (for example, pronged, eating utensil, for spearing) serves as the basis for the activation of a set of representations in the phonological output lexicon to varying degrees depending upon the extent to which they match the semantic features of the target (for example, "fork," "spoon," "knife," "pitchfork"). The most active representation, normally the correct word, is selected for output. If for some reason (for example, neurological damage) the target word is not available, the most highly activated member of the set will be produced, and a semantic error will be observed (for example, *fork* → "spoon").

A postsemantic deficit locus is consistent with the fact that in oral reading, on the same

Table 4.1
RGB's Performance on Comprehension, Spoken Production,
and Written Production Tasks

Task	Correct* (%)	Semantic (%)	Definitions (%)	Morph (%)	Other (%)
Defining printed words (n = 200)	100				
Auditory word/picture matching (n = 144)	100				
Printed word/picture matching (n = 144)	100				
Oral reading (n = 144)	69	12	14	5	
Spoken picture naming (n = 144)	68	15	16	1	
Writing to dictation (n = 144)	94				6
Written picture naming (n = 144)	94				6

*For written responses this includes clearly recognizable responses such as SQUAH for "squash."

trials that RGB produced semantic errors he was able to correctly define the target word. For example, *records* was read as "radio" but defined as "you play 'em on a phonograph . . . can also mean notes you take and keep"; *volcano* was read as "lava" and defined as "fire comes of it . . . a big thing . . . a mountain." Thus, RGB constitutes a case where neurological damage has interrupted access to correct lexical phonological forms—a case with just the characteristics for testing the orthographic autonomy and phonological mediation hypotheses.

RGB's spelling accuracy is critical for adjudicating between these two hypotheses. As table 1 indicates, contrary to the prediction of the obligatory phonological mediation hypothesis, RGB's accuracy was excellent on written production tasks. RGB never produced semantic errors in either writing to dictation or written picture naming tasks. In these tasks, he sometimes produced recognizable misspellings (for example, "donkey" spelled as DOKNY or a picture of celery spelled as CELEY). His only errors, however, occurred on 6 percent of items where he was able to provide only the initial letter.

In order to account for the pattern of intact spelling in the face of semantic errors in spoken production, it is necessary to assume a cognitive architecture in which lexical orthographic forms can be retrieved directly from semantic representations without a mediating role for phonology. Thus, the hypothesis of orthographic autonomy can account for the data, while the hypothesis of obligatory phonological mediation cannot. In this way, RGB's performance serves to uncover a very basic aspect of the organization of the cognitive processes within the architecture of the spelling system (for other relevant cases, see Rapp, Benzing, & Caramazza, 1997; Nickels, 1992; Basso, Taborelli, & Vignolo, 1978; Hillis & Caramazza, 1995b; Miceli, Benvegnu, Capasso, & Caramazza, 1997; Hanley & McDonnell, 1997; Bub & Kertesz, 1982; Hier & Mohr, 1977; Levine, Calvanio, & Popovics, 1982).

The Distinction between Lexical and Sublexical Processing: RG (Beauvois & Derouesne, 1981) and PR (Shallice, 1981)

The architecture depicted in figure 4.1 assumes that different processes are involved in the spelling of familiar and unfamiliar words (or pseudowords). An alternative hypothesis is that words and pseudowords are spelled in the same way, making use of the same cognitive functions. Although the hypothesis of a single route or common procedures for the processing of familiar words and pseudowords has not been extensively discussed in the context of spelling, it has played an important role in debates and research on reading (Seidenberg & McClelland, 1989; Glushko, 1979; Marcel, 1980). Evidence for the independence of processes involved in spelling familiar words and pseudowords comes from observations indicating that neurological damage may affect one of these skills and not the other.

Beauvois and Derouesne (1981) described the case of RG, a French-speaking, right-handed man who had been an agricultural machinery sales manager until undergoing surgery for a left parieto-occipital angioma. RG's IQ remained in the average range and, except for reading and spelling deficits and difficulties in naming tactile stimuli, his language comprehension and production were normal.

With regard to spelling, RG's ability to spell pseudowords was unaffected: he was accurate with both short two-phoneme pseudowords (for example, *ka*) and longer six-phoneme ones. In contrast, he had considerable difficulty correctly spelling words (table 4.2). This pattern (often referred to as surface dysgraphia) is difficult to understand without assuming that processes for spelling words are sufficiently distinct from those for spelling nonwords that they can be selectively affected by neurological damage. In this way, these findings support a distinction between lexical and nonlexical spelling processes (for other similar cases see also Baxter & Warrington, 1987; Behrmann & Bub, 1992; De Partz, Seron, & Van der Linden, 1992; Goodman

Table 4.2
Contrasting Patterns of Word and Nonword Spelling Accuracy for RG
(Beauvois & Derouesne, 1981) and PR (Shallice, 1981)

	Words (%)	Nonwords (%)
RG	61	99
PR	94	18

& Caramazza, 1986; Goodman-Shulman & Caramazza, 1987; Hatfield & Patterson, 1983; Parkin, 1993; Sanders & Caramazza, 1990; Weekes & Coltheart, 1996).

Within the lexical route, RG's difficulties in word spelling could not be attributed to a deficit in processing the phonological input in writing to dictation, as both word repetition and spoken word comprehension were intact. Furthermore, the same spelling difficulties he experienced in writing to dictation were observed in spontaneous writing where there is no phonological input. Peripheral difficulties with letter shape selection were ruled out as he exhibited the same difficulties in written and oral spelling. The absence of an effect of word length also rules out a deficit at the level of graphemic buffering. On this basis, RG's deficit is best described as affecting his ability to retrieve word spellings from the orthographic output lexicon. Damage of this sort is almost invariably sensitive to the frequency of the stored information, with higher frequency words (more common words) being less susceptible to disruption than lower frequency words. Consistent with this, RG's spelling exhibits a significant effect of lexical frequency: high-frequency words were 70 percent correct; low-frequency were 53 percent correct.

There are a number of other very specific characteristics of the spelling errors that RG produced that provide further support for the spelling architecture depicted in figure 4.1. RG's errors in word spelling consisted entirely of nonwords that had the same pronunciation as the target word (for example, "rameau" spelled as RAMO; an English-language example would be spelling *sauce* as SOSS). Such errors are generally referred to as phonologically plausible errors or PPEs. These kinds of errors can be understood if we assume that they are generated by the sublexical system subsequent to a failure in accessing the word's spelling from the orthographic output lexicon. The sublexical system should generate a plausible spelling for phonological stimuli, treating words and pseudowords in the same manner. In addition, if we are correct in assuming that the sublexical system is sensitive to the frequency with which a phoneme-grapheme relationship occurs in the language, the sublexical system should actually produce correct spellings for words with very common (high-frequency) phoneme-grapheme mappings (also referred to as high-probability PG mappings). This should manifest itself in greater accuracy with words containing only high-probability mappings (for example, in English, words such as *cat, fender, town*) than words containing low-probability PG mappings (for example, *once, yacht, aisle*). Indeed, as indicated in table 4.3, RG's accuracy in spelling words containing only high-probability PG mappings was very high (91 percent), while his accuracy with low-probability PG words was only 30 percent.

Table 4.3
RG's Spelling Accuracy, Revealing a Probability-by-Frequency Interaction

	Low frequency (%)	High frequency (%)	Total (%)
Low probability	19	44	30
High probability	90	92	91
Total	53	70	

It is important to note that while the lexical frequency effect mentioned above reflects the fact that high-frequency words are, at the level of the orthographic output lexicon, less suscep- tible to damage, the PG probability effect is not a reflection of the robustness of the lexical representations. Instead, this effect is based simply on the likelihood that the sublexical pro- cess will generate a spelling that happens to correspond to the lexical spelling. As a result of these properties of the lexical and sublexical systems, we should expect to see an accuracy interaction between word frequency and PG probability. Specifically, although low-frequency words should be comparably affected in the orthographic output lexicon regardless of their PG mapping probabilities, they will surface as errors depending on their PG mapping probabilities. Thus, frequency effects should be masked for words with only high PG mappings, but clearly visible for words containing low PG mappings. This interaction is clearly depicted in table 4.3. The fact that as many 44 percent of high-frequency, low-probability words resulted in errors suggests that there was considerable damage to the orthographic lexicon. The fact that 92 percent of high-frequency, high-probability words were correctly written indicates that the sublexical system is intact and able to produce appropriate spellings. The most vulnerable category of words is the set of low-frequency, low-probability words. Because of their lexical frequency, these words have a higher likelihood of suffering damage at the level of the ortho- graphic output lexicon; because of their low PG mapping status, they have very little chance of being correctly spelled via the sublexical system.

The proposed distinction between lexical and sublexical processes predicts that it should be possible to observe the dissociation complementary to that exhibited by RG: impaired pseudoword spelling in the face of preserved word spelling. Just such a pattern was reported by Shallice (1981). PR's spelling of words was excellent, with 94 percent accuracy (table 4.2). His word spelling was not affected by word frequency or PG probability. In contrast, his spelling of pseudowords was severely impaired (18 percent correct). The pattern of essentially intact word spelling in the face of severely affected pseudoword spelling is sometimes referred to as phonological dysgraphia. PR's difficulties in nonword spelling were not readily attributable to difficulties in processing or remembering the pseudoword stimulus: although he was able to correctly spell only 27 percent of the nonwords, he was able to correctly repeat 77 percent of them after misspelling them. He experienced important difficulties (30 percent correct) in writing even short (vowel-consonant) nonwords, and his performance was comparable in oral and written spelling. On this basis his deficit was localized to the sublexical spelling system (for other similar cases see Bub & Kertesz, 1982; Goodman-Shulman & Caramazza, 1987; Roeltgen, 1985; Roelgen, Sevush, & Heilman, 1983).

PR's ability to spell both high- and low-PG probability words (also referred to as regular and irregular words, respectively) also has implications for debates concerning the contents of the orthographic output lexicon. One possibility is that only those words that cannot be correctly derived by the sublexical system are stored in the sublexical system. Under that scenario, low-PG-probability words would be spelled through the lexical system and spelling of high-PG-probability words would rely on the sublexical system. This leads to the prediction that an individual with a deficit to the sublexical system should have difficulty spelling both pseudowords and highly regular words. The fact that this was not observed with PR provides support for the hypothesis that the orthographic output lexicon stores the spellings of all familiar words, regardless of their regularity.

In summary, the complementary patterns of spelling accuracy (double dissociation) exhib- ited by RG and PR constitute strong evidence that words and pseudowords are spelled by cognitive processes whose neural substrates are sufficiently different that they can be selec- tively affected by neural damage. In addition to the accuracy differences in spelling words and pseudowords, various specific attributes of the errors of these individuals provide further support for this distinction.

The Relationship between Oral and Written Spelling: JGE (Rapp & Caramazza, 1997) and JP (Kinsbourne & Warington, 1965)

In the theory being reviewed, a distinction is drawn between the abstract, format-independent graphemic representations manipulated by lexical and sublexical systems through the level of the graphemic buffer and the modality-specific representations of letter shape and letter name that are involved in written and oral spelling respectively. An alternative possibility might be that spellings are stored in the orthographic lexicon in one modality-specific format (letter shapes or letter names) and then translated to the other. However, the organization depicted in figure 4.1 is motivated by the observation of selective deficits to either modality of spelling output.

JGE (Rapp & Caramazza, 1997) was a right-handed man with a master's degree who worked as a high school business teacher until his retirement. At age seventy-three he suffered a large left occipital and posterior temporal lobe infarct (confirmed by MRI). There was also evidence of prior (undetected) infarcts affecting the right occipital lobe extending to the calcarine fissure as well as the supra and peri-ventricular white matter and left thalamus. JGE's spoken language comprehension and production were excellent, and he showed no signs of visual neglect. However, he had a right visual field cut, right hemiparesis, and significant difficulties in object recognition and reading as well as in written spelling.

Although JGE used his nondominant left hand in writing, his writing was easily legible, and his ability to copy figures with his left hand appeared to be intact (figure 4.3). Nonetheless, he

JGE left hand "eye," "arrow"

JGE copy (left hand)

JGE drawing (left hand) "airplane"

Figure 4.3. Examples of JGE's drawing and writing with his nondominant left hand.

made numerous errors in written spelling, errors that were largely absent from his oral spelling. JGE was administered the same set of 356 words for written and oral spelling. In terms of word-level errors (semantic errors, orthographically similar word errors, or phonologically plausible errors), JGE produced few errors in both written and oral spelling—three phonologically plausible errors in written spelling and four in oral spelling. This rate of PPEs was within the range of normal controls and allows us to rule out any significant deficit affecting lexical processes.

In contrast, written and oral spelling were markedly different with regard to letter-level errors (letter substitutions, additions, deletions, and transpositions). In oral spelling he produced only 17 letter errors, while in written spelling he produced 123 of these errors (table 4.4). The highly significant difference between the two modalities reflects an impairment that arose primarily (or entirely) from a process specific to the written modality. The fact that written production was legible and that well-formed letters were always produced rules out a very peripheral locus involving motor execution. Instead, the results indicate a deficit affecting the translation of abstract graphemes to specific letter shapes at the level of the letter shape selection process. This conclusion is consistent with the observation that in performing written spelling, JGE would often produce an erroneous written response while simultaneously producing a correct oral spelling. For example, he would correctly say "t-a-b-l-e" (/ti, ei bi, ɛl, i/) while writing "F-A-P-L-E" (for other relevant cases see Anderson, Damasio, & Damasio, 1990; Baxter & Warrington, 1986; De Bastiani & Barry, 1989; Black, Behrmann, Bass, & Hacker, 1989; Freidman & Alexander, 1989; Goodman & Caramazza, 1986; Kinsbourne & Rosenfield, 1974; Patterson & Wing, 1989; Rapp & Caramazza, 1989; Rothi & Heilman, 1981; Zangwill, 1954).

Rapp and Caramazza (1997) examined JGE's written letter substitution errors to determine the nature of letter shape representations at the level of the letter shape selection process. Specifically they examined whether substituted letters were similar to target letters in terms of visuo-spatial features or stroke features. For example, uppercase F and P were considered to be visually similar as they have been found to be visually confusable (see Gilmore, Hersh, Caramazza, & Griffin, 1979, and van der Heijden, Malhas, and van den Roovaart, 1984), but they share only one stroke (a downward vertical). In contrast, T and L are not visually confusable, but their component strokes are highly similar (a downward vertical and a left-right horizontal). The analyses revealed that while 30 percent of JGE's written target/error pairs could be classified as being similar in terms of stroke features, only 10 percent could be classified as visually similar. Furthermore, the observed rate of visual similarity was well within the range generated by a random pairing of 1000 target letters and errors, whereas the observed stroke similarity rate was never generated by this random process. The authors concluded that JGE's deficit originated primarily in the misselection of similar letter shapes within a system that represented letter shape in a stroke-based format.

A contrasting pattern of accuracy in oral and written spelling to that displayed by JGE was

Table 4.4
Frequency of JGE's Letter Errors in Written and Oral Spelling

	Written spelling	Oral spelling
Substitution	66	3
Transposition	5	3
Addition	7	3
Deletion	36	8
Other	9	0
Total	123/1899	17/1899

exhibited by JP (Kinsbourne & Warrington, 1965). JP was a car maintenance worker who suffered an infarct in the territory of the left middle cerebral artery. He exhibited no sensory loss or field defect. His spoken language comprehension was unimpaired, as was his single word reading, although he had moderate difficulties in spoken language production and very specific difficulties in spelling. With regard to spelling, JP was 93 percent correct in the written spelling of three-, four-, and five-letter words that were dictated to him. However, he was only 7 percent correct in orally spelling the same set of words (also see Bub & Kertesz, 1982). Thus, JP exhibited a striking dissociaiton between impaired oral and intact written spelling.

The combined patterns exhibited by JGE and JP create difficulties for hypotheses that propose that our knowledge of the spellings of words is represented in either a letter name or letter shape format. If in a letter-name format, then JP's ability to write down spellings he cannot orally produce cannot be readily explained; if in a letter-shape format, then JGE's ability to orally spell using letter names whose shapes have been incorrectly selected is left unaccounted for. However, both patterns are easily interpretable within the architecture depicted in figure 4.1 that assumes that word spellings are stored in an abstract graphemic code and then given specific form by distinct and independently lesionable letter shape and letter name selection processes.

Graphemic Buffering and Insights into the Nature of Orthographic Representation: LB (Caramazza, Miceli, Villa, & Romani, 1987)

The graphemic buffering component or process is assumed to be shared by lexical and sublexical processes, regardless of modality or format of output. The buffering process is assumed to be responsible for maintaining activation levels of the abstract graphemic representations that have been addressed in the orthographic output lexicon or assembled by the sublexical phonology-to-orthography conversion system, while the slower, serial processes involved in letter shape or letter name production are executed. Given its position within the spelling architecture, damage to the graphemic buffer should result in highly similar deficits in oral and written spelling of both words and pseudowords. Furthermore, given that the graphemic buffer is a short-term memory process, it is expected that longer words will stress the capacity of the buffer more than shorter words. Given this, a disruption to the graphemic buffer should manifest itself in a higher error rate for longer versus shorter words. These predictions were borne out in the case of LB (Caramazza et al., 1987). LB was a sixty-five-year-old, Italian-speaking, right-handed man who had university degrees in engineering and mathematics. He suffered a stroke that, according to CT scans, affected pre- and postrolandic areas in the left hemisphere. LB's language abilities were essentially normal except for reading and spelling.

Caramazza and colleagues (1987) reported LB's spelling abilities across a range of tasks with words and nonwords four to twelve letters in length (table 4.5). First, a clear effect of length was observed for both word and nonword stimuli in both written and oral spelling. The length effect suggests a deficit at the level of a component (such as the graphemic buffer) that is sensitive to word length. A length effect is not ubiquitous in dysgraphia; for example, it was not observed either in the case of RG (Beauvois & Derouesne, 1981), who had an orthographic output lexicon deficit, or in the case of JGE (Rapp & Caramazza, 1997), who suffered from damage at the level of letter shape selection. Second, the fact that both the spelling of words and the spelling of nonwords were affected in both written and spoken output modalities suggests damage to a mechanism shared across these processes. Error rates, although similar, were not identical across word and nonword spelling and oral and written spelling. Nonetheless, as indicated in table 4.6, the distribution of error types for words and nonwords was virtually identical.

Table 4.5

LB's Error Rate in Spelling Words and Nonwords

Length	Writing-to-dictation (%)	Oral spelling (%)	Written naming (%)
		Words	
4–5	15	25	25
6–7	34	69	42
8–9	67	100	91
10/12	41	69	52
Mean	52	69	57
		Nonwords	
4–5	27	31	–
6–7	51	88	–
8–9	75	88	–
10/12	100	100	–
Mean	63	77	–

In order to account for the similarities in performance across these tasks and modalities Caramazza and colleagues (1987) proposed damage to the graphemic buffer. An alternative hypothesis would require assuming fairly comparable levels of damage to both the lexical and sublexical systems. This hypothesis not only would be less parsimonious in terms of number of damaged loci, it would not readily account for the length effect for words observed in LB's case but not in the case of individuals who otherwise exhibit the characteristics of a lexical deficit. Furthermore, a lexical deficit would predict that PPEs should at least occasionally be observed (unless the sublexical system is largely eliminated); however, PPEs were not observed in LB's case nor in many of the other graphemic buffer cases that have been reported (Miceli, Silveri, & Caramazza, 1985; Caramazza & Miceli, 1990; Jonsdottir, Shallice, & Wise, 1996; Katz, 1991; Kay & Harley, 1994; McCloskey, Badecker, Goodman-Shulman, & Aliminosa, 1994; Posteraro, Zinelli, & Mazzucchi, 1988). It is in this manner that LB's performance provides support for the hypothesis of a component dedicated to graphemic buffering that is shared across lexical and sublexical systems and across modalities.

Caramazza and Miceli (1990), in a further study of LB's spelling performance, carried out further analysis of LB's spelling errors in order to gain some understanding of the nature and internal organization of the graphemic representations themselves that are being buffered. The default assumption had been that orthographic representations contain letter identity and position represented as a linear string (the spelling of *table* is represented as T+A+B+L+E). On the basis of observations of LB's spelling errors, Caramazza and Miceli (1990) proposed that orthographic representations are internally more complex and nonlinear (see also McCloskey et al., 1994; Badecker, 1996). Here I will highlight two aspects of their findings.

Table 4.6

LB's Distribution of Errors in Writing Words
and Nonwords to Dictation

	Words (%)	Nonwords (%)
Substitutions	37	36
Insertions	8	9
Deletions	34	37
Transpositions	21	18

LB's most frequent type of error was letter substitutions: on the list of 5,089 words administered to him, LB made 741 letter substitutions, with about half of the errors on consonants and half on vowels. What was striking was the fact that in 99.3 percent of the substitutions, vowels were substituted for vowels and consonants for consonants. Apparently, although on many occasions LB did not know the identity of a letter, he did know whether or not it was a consonant or a vowel. This observation (see also McCloskey et al., 1994) led Caramazza and Miceli (1990) to propose that orthographic representations contain information not only about letter identity and order but also about consonant/vowel status (figure 4.4). When the graphemic buffer is stressed, information may be lost; the fact that C/V status and letter identity information are independent of one another allows one type of information to be lost and not the other.

A second set of observations concerns LB's performance with double letters (or geminates). Caramazza and Miceli (1990) noted that LB would sometimes incorrectly produce double letters that did not belong in a word. This could happen as a geminate shift ("sorella" [sister] → SORRELA) a geminate duplication ("abisso" [abyss] → abbisso) or a geminate substitution ("marrone" [brown] → MAZZONE). These errors occured almost exclusively in words containing a double letter. That is, it was not the case that LB would introduce double letters at random in his error responses, producing doubling errors on words without geminates. Responses such as "verita" (truth) → VETTIVA occurred on only 0.2 percent of LB's errors. It was this observation that led Caramazza and Miceli to propose that information regarding doubling is also independent from letter identity information (figure 4.4). The double "feature" may be dissociated from its proper position and reassigned to another, leading to a geminate shift or even a duplication. Furthermore, geminate substitutions can be accounted for by assuming that they occur on those occasions where information regarding identity is lost while doubling information is retained. The independent representation of doubling and identity information would also account for observations indicating that double letters behave as a unit. These occurred in movement errors involving geminates, such as exchange errors ("cellula" [cell] → LECCULA) or shifts ("palazzao" [palace] → PALLAZO). In these errors both elements of the geminates always "traveled" together (never LECULULA or PALALZO). The fact that both elements of a geminate move together is hard to account for if double letters are assumed to be represented simply as a linear sequence of two consonants, comparable to the consonants within a consonant cluster (see also Tainturier & Caramazza, 1996).

Thus, a detailed examination of LB's errors provides insights not only into questions concerning the extent to which graphemic buffering is shared across components, but also into fundamental questions concerning the representation and organization of the graphemic mate-

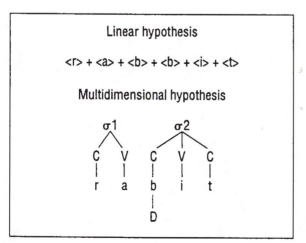

Figure 4.4. A schematic depiction of orthographic representations, including the representation of consonant/vowel status and letter doubling.

rial that is being buffered. This serves as an example of the more general point that the performance of dysgraphic subjects can provide information not only regarding the basic organization of a cognitive system but also regarding extremely detailed aspects of its functioning.

Feedback from Graphemes to Lexical Representations: CM (McCloskey, Macaruso, & Rapp, 1999)

The spelling process has been described thus far as a series of independent processing steps such that processing in one component drives processing in the next component and so on—a strictly forward flow of processing. Another possibility is that processing does not occur only in a forward direction; instead, some components of the system may be interactive, in the sense that processing in a later component may begin before processing is finished in an earlier one. Furthermore, processing in the later component may exert an influence on the earlier one—feedback interactivity. Evidence of feedback interactivity was reported by McCloskey and colleagues (1999). Specifically, McCloskey and colleagues argued for a feedforward-feedback (bidirectional) flow of information between the grapheme and lexeme levels of the graphemic buffer and the orthographic output lexicon (figure 4.1).

McCloskey and colleagues (1999) reported on CM, a sixty-three-year-old man with a Ph.D. in electrical engineering who suffered a left middle cerebral artery stroke. This left him with severely impaired spoken and written language production; both written and spoken language comprehension were intact.

Although CM correctly understood the words dictated to him, his error rate in spelling was 45 percent, and performance was comparable whether he wrote or typed his responses. There were two noteworthy aspects of his errors. First, they were characterized by numerous intrusions of letters that were not in the target word (for example, "skirt" → SKINT, "from" → FROBEN). Second, about a third of CM's errors were lexical substitutions (for example, "tool" → TOOK; "dignify" → DEFINE). I will briefly discuss each of these observations in turn.

McCloskey and colleagues determined that for any given error the intruded letters tended to be letters that appeared in CM's preceding spelling responses. Specifically, they established that intruded letters occurred in the five preceding responses at rates far greater than would be expected by chance. For example, for the error "fit" → FILTER, the L, E, and R are intruded letters. These letters occurred seven times in the five responses that CM produced immediate preceding *filter*: WEPT, TOPLES, WILTEN, BOLT, CASKET. Table 4.7 reports the overall likelihood that an intruded letter appeared in the five preceding responses. In contrast to the observed rates ranging from .36 to .48, the chance probability of such occurrences ranges between .28 and .29. Thus, it is clear that the observed occurrence of intruded letters in preceding responses is far greater than would be expected by chance. McCloskey and colleagues found that this pattern of intrusions was not specific to format of output, as it occurred with both writing and typing. Furthermore, it was not dependent on visual input from his responses, as the same pattern occurred whether CM's eyes were open or closed while spelling. On this basis, McCloskey and colleagues argued that CM's deficit was one where the abstract

Table 4.7
The Probability with Which an Intruded Letter That Occurred
in CM's Response to a Target Word Occurred in the Five
Preceding Responses

Target	−1	−2	−3	−4	−5
	.48	.41	.38	.38	.36

letter representations involved in spelling persisted in their activation beyond the point in time at which a response was executed. As a result, when attempting to spell a word there would often be interference from "persisting" graphemes.

If letter activation at the level of the graphemic buffer was persisting such that earlier letters sometimes intruded into later responses, one might expect that nonwords would be the most likely response. This was indeed CM's most common type of error. In addition, of course, an intruding letter should occasionally happen to make a word and, therefore, word responses should also have been observed at rates expected by the *chance* intrusion of letters. Interestingly, however, CM's rate of lexical substitutions was quite high, making up one-third of his errors. Such a high rate of word errors would seem unlikely according to the hypothesis that word errors arise only when intruding letters just happen to form a word. In order to quantitatively evaluate whether or not CM's errors really occurred at above chance rates, McCloskey and colleagues carried out an analysis based on all of the word errors that CM produced that involved letter substitutions (for example, "chain" → CHAIR). For each error, they listed the set of possible substitution errors that could have occurred based on the random intrusion of the letters that were available from the five preceding responses. They looked at each possible error that was generated in this way and categorized it as a word or nonword. This provided an estimate of the number of word and nonword responses that would be expected if preceding letters were randomly intruding into a response. When this rate was compared to CM's actual rate of word errors, it was shown that chance intrusion errors could, at most, account for half of the observed word errors.

If not by the chance intrusion of persisting letters, how might such large numbers of lexical errors have come about? Lexical substitutions suggest that a target word (for example, FIT from the example above) is in competition with other words that share letters from previous responses (for example, FILTER). The question is, how do competitors such as FILTER enter into the game? Recall that earlier it was noted that a set of candidate lexical entries in the orthographic output lexicon is activated according to semantic similarity with the target. This assumption was necessary to account for, among other things, those individuals who produce semantic errors in the absence of a semantic deficit. Given this, we would expect semantically related words to be in competition with one another; this assumption does not provide a mechanism by which formally related words would be activated.

McCloskey and colleagues suggest that by assuming feedback connections from graphemes to lexical entries we can understand how lexical errors that include letters from preceding responses would occur at above chance rates. The argument goes as follows: if CM is asked to spell the word *bench,* the graphemes B, E, N, C, H might be activated; if a subsequent stimulus is *arm,* then the letters A, R, M will be activated and some of the letters from B, E, N, C, H may still remain active. All of these active letters would feed activation back to all lexical representations that include some of these letters, including words such as *beach, amber, barn,* and so on. These lexical representations would, in turn, feedforward activation to their constituent letters. It is in this way that lexical entries such as *amber* enter into the competition. Eventually, as the system settles into a stable state of activation, some sets of letters will be maximally active and will drive letter name or letter shape selection processes. The set of maximally active letters may correspond to the letters of the correct response (ARM), a nonsense-word mix of letters from the target and previous responses (AMBECH), or the letters of one of the words activated as a result of feedback activity from the letter level back to lexical representations (AMBER).

In the area of spoken language production, the occurrence of formally related lexical substitutions at rates higher than would be expected by the random substitution of individual phonemes has received a similar explanation in terms of feedback connectivity from the level of phonological segments back to lexical representations (Dell, 1986).

Integration of Lexical and Sublexical Processes:
LAT (Rapp, Epstein, & Tainturier, 2002), JJ (Hillis & Caramazza, 1991), and RCM (Hillis, Rapp, & Caramazza, 1999)

In an earlier section the empirical motivation for positing independently lesionable lexical and sublexical processes was discussed. However, the fact that the two processes are independent (in the sense that neither requires or subsumes the other), doesn't mean that they do not interact in any way. A number of patterns of dysgraphic performance indicate that lexical and sublexical systems integrate their outputs at the level of the graphemic buffer (see figure 4.1).

LAT (Rapp, Epstein, & Tainturier, 2002) was a seventy-eight-year-old, right-handed man who was diagnosed with probable Alzheimer's disease. LAT was a college graduate and retired engineer. MRI scans at the time of diagnosis showed diffuse cortical atrophy and prominent ventricles as well as increased signal intensity in the periventricular white matter. SPECT scans showed generalized cortical hypo-perfusion, especially affecting both temporo-parietal regions.

LAT had no difficulty in repeating each dictated stimulus before and after spelling it, and he produced written responses easily without struggling or hesitation. His ability to spell nonwords was excellent, with accuracy ranging from 90 to 98 percent correct. In contrast, he had greater difficulties in spelling words. Although he was able to provide excellent definitions for dictated words ("Martyr—a martyr is someone who will sacrifice himself for a particular concept"), his word spelling exhibited effects of word frequency and PG probability. As discussed earlier, these are characteristics of a deficit within the lexical system. Further confirmation of this was the fact that LAT's errors in word spelling were almost entirely phonologically plausible errors ("persuit" → PERSUTE; "pretty" → PRITY). Thus, LAT would correctly define a stimulus word and then produce a PPE in spelling it (for example, "Knowledge—knowledge is the accumulation of important information K-N-O-L-E-G-E").

LAT's good nonword spelling ruled out a postlexical deficit locus and his good word comprehension and definitions indicated intact processing through the lexical semantic system. On this basis, Rapp and colleagues concluded that LAT's deficit lay in accessing the correct spellings of words in the orthographic output lexicon.

If LAT's PPEs arose when he was unable to access the correct spelling in the orthographic output lexicon, his PPE's should reflect the functioning of the PG system. However, one thing that was striking about LAT's PPEs was that they sometimes included extremely unusual, low-probability PG mappings. For example, *bouquet* was spelled as BOUKET; *autumn* was spelled as AUTOMN. It is not surprising that the PG system would produce K for /k/ (in BOUKET) since this is the most common spelling for the phoneme /k/; however, it is somewhat surprising that the PG conversion system would yield ET as a spelling for /ei/ and MN for /m/. Although low-probability spellings such as /ei/ → ET should occur very occasionally under the assumption that the frequency with which the PG system produces spellings corresponds to their occurrence in the English language, such low-probability spellings should not be produced often. Also relevant is the fact that the low-frequency mappings in LAT's PPEs were often "lexically correct." That is, it is not just that ET is a low-probability spelling for /k/, it is the spelling that is correct for the lexical target *bouquet*. Thus, Rapp and colleagues were interested in accounting for the observation that LAT's PPEs often included both highly frequent PG mappings such as /k/ → K as well as relatively unusual—yet lexically correct—spellings such as /ei/ → ET.

One hypothesis was that the PPEs were generated entirely by the PG system but that LAT's PG system was unusual in that low-probability mappings were represented more strongly than would be expected on the basis of their distribution in the language; this can be referred to as the idiosyncratic PG system hypothesis. Another hypothesis was that LAT's PPEs reflected a combination of information from both lexical and sublexical systems—the lexical/sublexical integration hypothesis. According to this hypothesis, word stimuli might activate lexical spellings sufficiently to contribute activation to their respective letters, although not sufficiently to yield a correct response. Under this hypothesis, in the spelling BOUKET, the PG system generated activation supporting K, the lexical system supported ET, and either or both systems might have contributed to the remaining letters.

The idiosyncratic PG system hypothesis predicts that low-probability spellings should appear at comparable rates in LAT's phonologically plausible errors to word stimuli as well as in his spelling of comparable nonwords. That is, according to this hypothesis a PPE in response to /bukei/ and a plausible spelling of the nonword /lukei/ (rhyming with *bouquet*) should be equally likely to include ET. In contrast, according to the lexical/sublexical integration hypothesis one might expect to find higher rates of low-probability, lexically correct spellings in the PPEs than in the spellings of matched pseudowords. Rapp and colleagues tested these hypotheses by administering a list of ninety-seven word stimuli that each contained at least one low-probability PG mapping (for example, /n/ → KN in *knowledge*) and a matched set of pseudowords that differed from each word by only one phoneme (for example, /pɔlədʒ/, rhyming with knowledge, as a control for "knowledge").

The results clearly supported the integration hypothesis: low-probability, lexically correct PG mappings were used in 52 percent of cases in LAT's phonologically plausible errors, but in only 36 percent of cases in his responses to matched pseudowords. Thus, the evidence is clearly consistent with the integration hypothesis and difficult to account for under alternative accounts.[3]

Other patterns of dysgraphia also find explanation if lexical/sublexical integration is assumed. Hillis and Caramazza (1991) described the case of JJ, who made 30 to 40 percent errors in written and spoken naming to picture stimuli and comprehension of items from all semantic categories (except animals). His naming and comprehension errors were semantic errors. This pattern indicates a deficit at the level of the lexical semantic system. Interestingly, however, he produced no semantic errors in spelling to dictation.

Why should written picture naming and spelling to dictation yield such different results? If JJ relied only on the lexical system for spelling, given his semantic-level deficit, he should have produced semantic errors in both written naming and writing to dictation. Hillis and Caramazza accounted for the absence of semantic errors in JJ's spelling to dictation by assuming that JJ was able to combine the outputs of lexical and sublexical processes to eliminate semantic errors. For example, as a result of lexical semantic damage, the picture of a pear might generate an impoverished semantic representation (for example, yellow, fruit) that would be consistent with, and thus lead to the activation of, multiple lexical candidates in the orthographic output lexicon (for example, *apple, pear, banana*). In written picture naming one of these candidates would be selected for output, sometimes resulting in a semantic error—*apple* or *banana*. In writing to dictation, however, the phonological input from the stimulus (/pɛr/) would be processed by the sublexical system that would generate a plausible spelling such as P-A-I-R. Hillis and Caramazza argued that the sublexically generated output, although incorrect, would be sufficient to select among the multiple lexically generated candidates (*apple, banana, pear*) and yield the correct response (see also Hillis & Caramazza, 1995a).

Hillis and Caramazza did not describe a specific mechanism for the combination of lexical and sublexical information that would lead to such a result. However, the features of lexical/sublexical integration at the level of the graphemic buffer in combination with feedback from

---

[3]Rapp and colleagues (2002) reanalyzed the errors produced by RG (Beauvois & Derouesne, 1981) in order to determine if there was evidence in those errors of lexical/sublexical integration. Consistent with the lexical/sublexical integration hypothesis, Rapp and colleagues found that RG indeed produced lexically correct mappings more often than would be expected according to the PG mapping probabilities in French. However, because matched nonwords were not administered, it is not possible to rule out the idiosyncratic PG system hypothesis. No other published cases include data in the appropriate form to permit a reanalysis.

letters to lexical representations provide an independently motivated account of JJ's pattern of performance. First, sublexical/lexical integration provides a means by which information from the sublexical system can make contact with letter-level information generated by the lexical system. Second, in the earlier discussion of feedback connectivity we have seen how the selection of lexical representations in the orthographic output lexicon is influenced not only by semantically driven activation but also by activation provided via the feedback connections from graphemes to lexical representations. In JJ's case we must assume that in spelling to dictation the auditory stimulus /pɛr/ ("pear") results in the activation of the lexical candidates *pear, banana,* and *apple,* and also that the sublexical system generates activation of candidate letters such as P-A-I-R. Feedback from these letters to the lexical level will increase the activation of *pear* relative to *banana* or *apple,* tipping the balance in favor of the correct response rather than a semantic error. This critical input to the orthographic output lexicon via the feedback connections is unavailable in written picture naming where there is no auditory stimulus to drive the sublexical system.[4]

According to this account the sublexical system plays a crucial role in eliminating semantic errors in writing to dictation. This makes very specific predictions regarding what would be expected if the sublexical system were unavailable or if it were unavailable and then were recovered. These predictions were tested in Hillis et al. (1999).

Hillis and colleagues described the case of RCM, an eighty-two-year-old, right-handed woman who suffered a subacute infarct in the left frontal cortex. Spoken and written word comprehension were normal, and she exhibited only mild word-finding difficulties and somewhat reduced word fluency. Performance on oral picture naming and oral reading was excellent, with accuracy levels of 100 percent and 95 percent, respectively. Her spelling, in contrast, was considerably impaired and characterized by numerous semantic errors. On this basis her spelling deficit was localized to the orthographic output lexicon

RCM was evaluated during two time periods. Study 1 took place in the first week after her stroke, study 2 took place two weeks later. At the time of study 1, 56 percent of RCM's errors in spelling were semantic errors (table 4.8). Importantly, for the hypothesis under examination, her sublexical system was severely compromised: no pseudowords were spelled correctly. Many of her errors in response to pseudowords bore no resemblance to the target ("besk" → TO) and others were phonologically or orthographically related words ("pon" → POWDER, "teef" → BEEF). Scoring of pseudoword spelling according to individual phonological segments (rather than the whole stimulus string) yielded 58 percent errors. Further evidence of a severely impaired sublexical system is the fact that no phonologically plausible errors were observed.

In contrast, at the time of study 2, RCM's rate of semantic errors had dropped sharply to only 10 percent of her spelling errors. There were various indications that this drop was related to increased sublexical input. First, spelling of nonwords improved somewhat such that 3 percent of pseudowords were now correctly spelled and the error rate on segments dropped from 58 percent in study 1 to 33 percent in study 2. Furthermore, RCM occasionally produced phonologically plausible responses to word stimuli. Finally, although the rate of semantic errors dropped, the rate of orthographically and phonologically similar errors (for example, "myth" → METHOD) increased. This latter effect would be expected under an integration hypothesis. By way of the letter-lexeme feedback connections the sublexically generated input contributes to the activation of not only the target, but also of words that share the letters generated by the sublexical system. For example, the stimulus "myth" might yield sublexically generated activation of the letters M-I-T-H. Through letter-lexeme feedback, words such as *method, myth, math* should receive activation. In a situation where there continues to be

---

[4]That is, unless the individual him or herself can generate a phonological representation of the picture stimulus that may serve as input to the sublexical process. In JJ's case this was not possible since spoken naming was equally affected by the deficit at the level of the lexical semantic system.

Table 4.8

RCM's Error Rates and Distribution of Errors for Words and Nonwords
and Two Different Time Points for Spelling

	Study 1 (%)	Study 2 (%)
Error rate: words	49	37
Semantic	56	10
Ortho/phon similar	21	49
PPE	0	4
Other nonword	21	36
Other	3	1
Error rate (by segments): nonwords	58	33

disruption at the level of the orthographic output lexicon, the correct response may still not be the most highly activated one, and orthographically similar words might be produced instead.

In sum, RCM's performance is consistent with very specific predictions of the hypothesis of lexical/sublexical integration and, in this way, provides further support for this aspect of the architecture depicted in figure 4.1 (for other relevant papers see Beeson, 1998; Hillis and Caramazza, 1995b; Miceli, Capasso, & Caramazza, 1994).

CONCLUSIONS

As indicated earlier, spelling is perhaps the cognitive domain where the study of deficits has most prominently contributed to an understanding of the organization and functioning of the component mental processes. In this chapter I hope to have shown how case study research with dysgraphic individuals has been used to test specific hypotheses regarding both the organization of the system and the content of the representations that are manipulated and generated in the course of spelling. This work has revealed a highly structured cognitive system that manipulates representations with a rich internal structure.

The following chapters in this volume, by Rapcseck and Beeson and Beeson and Rapcseck, make use of this theory of the spelling process as a framework within which to discuss the neural bases of the various cognitive functions that have been posited and the manner in which deficits of spelling can be diagnosed and remediated.

ACKNOWLEDGMENTS

Writing of this chapter was made possible by the support of NIMH grant R29MH55758.

REFERENCES

Allport, D. A., & Funnel, E. (1981). Components of the mental lexicon. *Philosophical Transactions of the Royal Society of London, B 295*, 397–410.

Anderson, S. W., Damasio, A. R., & Damasio, H. (1990). Troubled letters but not numbers: Domain specific cognitive impairments following focal damage in frontal cortex. *Brain, 113*, 749–766.

Badecker, W. (1996). Representational properties common to phonological and orthographic output systems. *Lingua, 99*, 55–83.

Basso, A., Taborelli, A., & Vignolo, L. A. (1978). Dissociated disorders of speaking and writing in aphasia.

Journal of Neurology, Neurosurgery, and Psychiatry, 41, 556–563.

Baxter, D. M., & Warrington, E. K. (1986). Ideational agraphia: A single case study. *Journal of Neurology, Neurosurgery, and Psychiatry, 49*, 369–374.

Baxter D. M., & Warrington, E. K. (1987). Transcoding sound to spelling: Single or multiple sound unit correspondences? *Cortex, 23*, 11–28.

Beauvois, M. F., & Derouesne, J. (1981). Lexical or orthographic agraphia. *Brain, 104*, 21–49.

Beeson, P. M. (1998). Problem-solving in acquired agraphia: How do you spell relief? Paper presented at the Meeting of the Academy of Aphasia. Santa Fe, NM.

Behrmann, M., & Bub, D. (1992). Surface dyslexia and dysgraphia: Dual routes, single lexicon. *Cognitive Neuropsychology, 9*, 209-251.

Black, S. E., Behrmann, M., Bass, K., & Hacker, P. (1989). Selective writing impairment: Beyond the allographic code. *Aphasiology, 3*(3), 265-277.

Brown, J. W. (1972). *Aphasia, apraxia, and agnosia.* Springfield, IL: Charles C Thomas.

Bub, D., & Kertesz, A. (1982). Evidence for lexicographic processing in a patient with preserved written over oral single word naming. *Brain, 105*, 697-717.

Caramazza, A., & Hillis, A. (1990). Where do semantic errors come from? *Cortex, 26*, 95-122.

Caramazza, A., & McCloskey, M. (1988). The case for single-patient studies. *Cognitive Neuropsychology, 5*(5), 517-528.

Caramazza, A., & Miceli, G. (1990). The structure of graphemic representations. *Cognition, 37*, 243-297.

Caramazza, A., Miceli, G., Villa, G., & Romani, C. (1987). The role of the graphemic buffer in spelling: Evidence from a case of acquired dysgraphia. *Cognition, 26*, 59-85.

Coltheart, M., & Funnel, E. (1987). Reading and writing: One lexicon or two? In D. A. Allport, D. McKay, W. Prinz, & E. Scheerer (Eds.), *Language perception and production: Common processes in listening, speaking, reading, and writing.* London: Academic Press.

De Bastiani, P., & Barry, C. (1989). A cognitive analysis of an acquired dysgraphic patient with an "allographic" writing disorder. *Cognitive Neuropsychology, 6*(1), 25-41.

Dell, G. (1986). A spreading activation theory of retrieval in sentence production. *Psychological Review, 93*, 283-321.

De Partz, M. P., Seron, X., & Van der Linden, M. (1992). Re-education of a surface dysgraphic with a visual imagery strategy. *Cognitive Neuropsychology, 9*, 369-401.

Friedman, R. B. & Alexander, M. (1989). Written spelling agraphia. *Brain and Language, 36*, 503-517.

Frith, U. (1979). Reading by eye and writing by ear. In P. A. Kolers, M. Wrolstad, & H. Bouma (Eds.), *Processing of visible language, I.* New York: Plenum Press.

Geschwind, N. (1969). Problems in the anatomical understanding of aphasia. In A. L. Benton (Ed.), *Contributions of clinical neuropsychology.* Chicago: University of Chicago Press.

Gilmore, G. C., Hersh, H., Caramazza, A., & Griffin, J. (1979). Multidimensional letter similarity derived from recognition errors. *Perception & Psychophysics, 25*(5), 425-431

Glushko, R. J. (1979). The organization and activation of orthographic knowledge in reading aloud. *Journal of Experimental Psychology: Human Perception and Performance, 5*, 674-691.

Goodman, R. A., & Caramazza, A. (1986). Aspects of the spelling process: Evidence from a case of acquired dysgraphia. *Language and Cognitive Processes, 1*, 263-296.

Goodman-Shulman, R. A., & Caramazza, A. (1987). Patterns of dysgraphia and the nonlexical spelling process. *Cortex, 23*, 143-148.

Grashey, H. (1885). On aphasia and its relations to perception (Über Aphasie und ihre Beziehungen zur Wahrnehmung). *Archiv für Psychiatire und Nervenkrankheiten, 16*, 654-688. (English version: *Cognitive Neuropsychology, 6*(1989), 515-546.

Hanley, J. R., & McDonnell, V. (1997). Are reading and spelling phonologically mediated? Evidence from a patient with a speech production impairment. *Cognitive Neuropsychology, 14*(1), 3-33.

Hatfield, F. M., & Patterson, K. E. (1983). Phonological spelling. *Quarterly Journal of Experimental Psychology, 35A*, 451-458.

Head, H. (1926). *Aphasia and kindred disorders of speech.* London: Cambridge University Press.

Hecaen, H., & Angelergues, R. (1965). *Pathologie du language, vol. 1.* Paris: Larousse.

Hier, D. B., & Mohr, J. P. (1977). Incongruous oral and written naming. *Brain and Language, 4*, 115-126.

Hillis, A., & Caramazza, A. (1991). Mechanisms for accessing lexical representations for output: Evidence from a category-specific semantic deficit. *Brain and Language, 40*, 106-144.

Hillis, A., & Caramazza, A. (1995a). Converging evidence for the interaction of semantic and sublexical phonological information in accessing lexical representations for spoken output. *Cognitive Neuropsychology, 12*(2), 187-227.

Hillis, A., & Caramazza, A. (1995b). "I know it but I can't write it": Selective deficits in long- and short-term memory. In R. Campbell (Ed.), *Broken memories: Neuropsychological case studies.* London: Blackwell.

Hillis, A.., Rapp, B., & Caramazza, A. (1999). When a rose is a rose in speech but a tulip in writing. *Cortex, 35*, 337-356.

Hotopf, N. (1980). Slips of the pen. In U. Frith (Ed.), *Cognitive processes in spelling.* London: Academic Press.

Jonsdottir, M. K., Shallice, T., & Wise, R. (1996). Phonological mediation and the graphemic buffer disorder in spelling: Cross language differences? *Cognition, 59*, 169-197.

Katz, R. B. (1991). Limited retention of information in the graphemic buffer. *Cortex, 27*, 111-119.

Kay, J., & Harley, R. (1994). Peripheral spelling disorders: The role of the graphemic buffer. In G. D. A. Brown & N. C. Ellis (Eds.), *Handbook of spelling: Theory, process, and intervention.* New York: Wiley.

Kinsbourne, M., & Rosenfield, D. B. (1974). Agraphia selective for written spelling. *Brain and Language, 1*, 215-225.

Kinsbourne, M., & Warrington, E. K. (1965). A case showing selectively impaired oral spelling. *Journal of Neurology, Neurosurgery, and Psychiatry, 28*, 563-567.

Levine, D. N., Calvanio, R., & Popovics, A. (1982). Language in the absence of inner speech. *Neuropsychologia, 4*, 391-409.

Lichtheim, L. (1885). On aphasia (Über Aphasie). *Deutsches Archiv für klinische Medizin, 36*, 204-268. (English version: *Brain, 7*, 433-485.)

Luria, A. R. (1966). *Higher cortical functions in man.* New York: Basic Books.

Marcel, A. J. (1980). Surface dyslexia and beginning reading: A revised hypothesis of the pronunciation of print and its impairments. In M. Coltheart, K. E. Patterson, & J. C. Marshall (Eds.), *Deep dyslexia.* London: Routledge and Kegan Paul.

McCloskey, M., Badecker, W., Goodman-Shulman, R. A., & Aliminosa, D. (1994). The structure of graphemic representations in spelling: Evidence from a case of acquired dysgraphia. *Cognitive Neuropsychology, 2*, 341-392.

McCloskey, M., Macaruso, P., & Rapp, B. (1999). Grapheme-to-lexeme feedback in the spelling system: Evidence from dysgraphia. Paper presented at the Academy of Aphasia. Venice, Italy.

Miceli, G., Benvegnù, B., Capasso, R., & Caramazza, A. (1997). The independence of phonological and orthographic lexical forms: Evidence from aphasia. *Cognitive Neuropsychology, 14,* 35–69.

Miceli, G., Capasso, R., & Caramazza, A. (1994). The interaction of lexical and sublexical processes in reading, writing, and repetition. *Neuropsychologia, 32,* 317–333

Miceli, G., Silveri, C., & Caramazza, A. (1985). Cognitive analysis of a case of pure dysgraphia. *Brain and Language, 25,* 187–221.

Nickels, L. (1992). The autocue? Self-generated phonemic cues in the treatment of a disorder of reading and naming. *Cognitive Neuropsychology, 9,* 155–182.

Parkin, A. J. (1993). Progressive aphasia without dementia: A clinical and cognitive neuropsychological analysis. *Brain and Language, 44,* 201–220.

Patterson, K. (1986). Lexical but nonsemantic spelling? *Cognitive Neuropsychology, 3,* 341–367.

Patterson, K., & Wing, A. M. (1989). Processes in handwriting: A case for case. *Cognitive Neuropsychology, 6*(1), 1–23.

Posteraro, L., Zinelli, P., & Mazzucchi, A. (1988). Selective impairment of the graphemic buffer in acquired dysgraphia: A case study. *Brain and Language, 35,* 274–286.

Rapp, B., Benzing, L., & Caramazza, A. (1997). The autonomy of lexical orthography. *Cognitive Neuropsychology, 14,* 71–104

Rapp, B., & Caramazza, A. (1989). Letter processing in reading and spelling: Some dissociations. *Reading and Writing, 1,* 3–23.

Rapp, B., & Caramazza, A. (1997). From graphemes to abstract letter shapes: Levels of representation in written spelling. *Journal of Experimental Psychology: Human Perception and Performance, 23,* 1130–1152.

Rapp, B., Epstein, C., & Tainturier, M. J. (2002). The integration of information across lexical and sublexical processes in spelling. *Cognitive Neuropsychology, 19,* 1–29.

Roeltgen, D. P., (1985). Agraphia. In K. M. Heilman & E. Valenstein (Eds.), *Clinical neuropsychology* (2nd ed.). New York: Oxford University Press.

Roeltgen, D. P., Rothi, L. G., & Heilman, K. M. (1986). Linguistic semantic agraphia: A dissociation of the lexical spelling system from semantics. *Brain and Language, 27,* 257–280.

Roeltgen, D. P., Sevush, S., & Heilman, K. M. (1983). Phonological agraphia: Writing by the lexical-semantic route. *Neurology, 33,* 755–765.

Rothi, L. J., & Heilman, K. M. (1981). Alexia and agraphia with spared spelling and letter recognition abilities. *Brain and Language, 12,* 1–13.

Sanders, R. J., & Caramazza, A. (1990). Operation of the phoneme-to-grapheme conversion mechanism in a brain injured patient. *Reading and Writing, 2,* 61–82.

Seidenberg, M., & McClelland, J. L. (1989). A distributed developmental model of word recognition and naming. *Psychological Review, 96,* 523–568.

Shallice, T. (1981). Phonological agraphia and the lexical route in writing. *Brain, 104,* 413–429.

Tainturier, M. J., & Caramazza, A. (1996). The status of double letters in graphemic representations. *Journal of Memory and Language, 35,* 53–73.

Van der Heijden, A. H. C., Malhas, M. S. S., & van den Roovaart, B. P. (1984). An empirical interletter confusion matrix for continuous-line capitals. *Perception and Psychophysics, 35,* 85–88.

Van Orden, G. C., Johnston, J. C., & Hale, B. L. (1988). Word identification in reading proceeds from spelling to sound to meaning. *Journal of Experimental Psychology: Learning, Memory, and Cognition, 14,* 371–386.

Weekes, B., & Coltheart, M. (1996). Surface dyslexia and surface dysgraphia: Treatment studies and their theoretical implications. *Cognitive Neuropsychology, 13,* 277–315

Wernicke, C. (1886). Neurology: Recent contributions on aphasia (Nervenheilkunde: Die neueren Arbeiten über Aphasie). *Fortschritte der Medizin, 4,* 463–482. (English version: *Cognitive Neuropsychology, 6*(6 [1989]), 547–569.)

Zangwill, O. L. (1954). Agraphia due to a left parietal glioma in a left-handed man. *Brain, 77,* 510–520.

5

Neuroanatomical Correlates of Spelling and Writing

Steven Z. Rapcsak
Pelagie M. Beeson

> It is evident that writing can be disordered by circumscribed lesions of widely differ-
> ent areas of the cerebral cortex, but in every case the disorder in writing will show
> qualitative peculiarities depending on which link is destroyed and which primary
> defects are responsible for the disorder of the whole functional system.
>
> —A. R. Luria

INTRODUCTION

The first descriptions of writing impairment following focal brain damage appeared during the second half of the nineteenth century. A particularly important early contribution was the report of Ogle (1867), which explicitly argued for the anatomical independence of writing from speech based on clinical observations of a double dissociation between agraphia and aphasia. This paper also introduced the first classification system of agraphia by drawing a critical distinction between linguistic impairments of spelling and motor disorders of writing. The publication of Ogle's seminal work was soon followed by attempts to localize the brain regions involved in various aspects of the writing process. These efforts culminated in the development of neuroanatomical models that postulated two distinct cortical writing centers. Following Dejerine's suggestion (1891), it was generally assumed that orthographic information relevant to the correct spelling of familiar words was stored in the dominant angular gyrus. In addition, Exner (1881) postulated the existence of a cortical center responsible for controlling the skilled movements of handwriting located at the foot of the second frontal convolution. Although the putative writing centers were conceptualized as being physically separate from the cortical speech areas identified by Broca and Wernicke, this neuroanatomical arrangement did not always imply complete functional independence. In fact, many theorists considered written expression to be parasitic upon speech and maintained that it necessarily required phonological mediation. In particular, some investigators proposed that writing involved subword-level phonological-to-orthographic transcoding (that is, phoneme-grapheme conversion) (Grashey, 1885; Wernicke, 1886), whereas others believed that orthographic representations for familiar words could be activated only indirectly via the spoken form of the word (Wernicke, 1874; Dejerine, 1914). However, there were also those who considered writing an autonomous language skill that depended on the coordinated activity of the parietal and frontal writing centers without the obligatory participation of the cortical speech areas (Charcot, 1883; Pitres, 1894; Bastian, 1897).

The modern era in the neuropsychological study of writing was ushered in by two major developments. The first of these was the introduction of new structural (that is, CT, MRI) and functional (that is, PET, fMRI) neuroimaging techniques during the last three decades of the twentieth century. The widespread availability of structural brain imaging has made it possible to obtain precise in vivo lesion localization information in a large number of neurological patients with focal brain damage. As a valuable complement to the neuropsychological lesion data, functional neuroimaging has permitted the study of regional brain activation in normal individuals engaged in various cognitive tasks.

The second important development had to do with the systematic application of a cognitive information processing approach to the study of agraphia. The cognitive method of analysis seeks an explanation of complex language skills such as writing by postulating a set of potentially independent processing components that are assigned distinct computational roles. A typical example of a cognitive model of spelling and writing is presented in figure 5.1. Due to the essentially modular architecture of the model, damage to individual components is expected to result in characteristic and predictable combinations of impaired and preserved cognitive abilities, making it possible to interpret the abnormal writing performance of agraphic patients within this type of theoretical framework. Furthermore, the fact that focal brain damage can produce highly selective functional deficits suggests that the proposed processing modules may be localizable to specific anatomical regions. Since writing involves several linguistic, motor, perceptual, and spatial operations, it can be disrupted by damage to a variety of cortical areas, the integrated activity of which is essential for normal performance (Luria, 1980).

In this chapter we review what is currently known about the neuroanatomical substrates of spelling and writing. In doing so, we will draw primarily on CT and MRI lesion data obtained in patients with various forms of agraphia and, when appropriate, seek additional confirmation from functional neuroimaging studies in normal subjects.

CEREBRAL LOCALIZATION OF THE COGNITIVE SYSTEMS INVOLVED IN SPELLING AND WRITING

From a neuropsychological perspective, the writing process can be subdivided into central and peripheral components (Ellis, 1988). Central processing components are responsible for selecting the appropriate words for written output and for providing information about their correct spelling. Central components can also be used to generate plausible spellings for unfamiliar words or pronounceable nonwords (for example, *doke*). According to the model depicted in figure 5.1, there are two major sources of input to orthography: semantic and phonological. Functionally linked central processing components involved in activating or computing orthographic representations in response to these two types of codes are referred to as the lexical-semantic and the phonological spelling routes. The lexical-semantic route is the dominant pathway used for spelling familiar words, whereas the phonological route can be used for spelling both familiar words and unfamiliar words or nonwords. The orthographic representations generated by central spelling routes are temporarily stored in the graphemic buffer—a working memory system that occupies a strategic position between the central and peripheral components of the model. Peripheral processing components located downstream from the graphemic buffer in figure 5.1 are responsible for converting abstract orthographic information into concrete neuromuscular commands for handwriting movements. The neuroanatomical substrates of the various central and peripheral cognitive systems are discussed below.

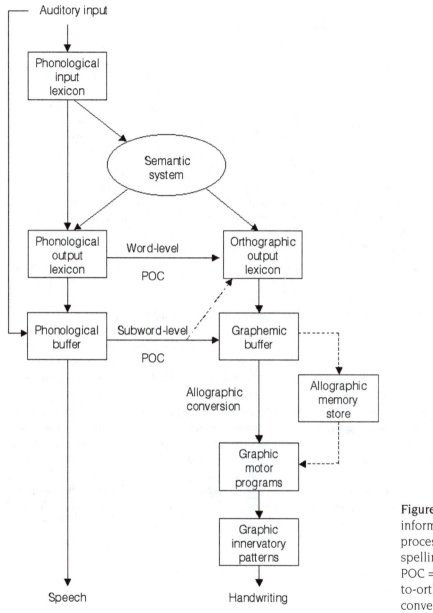

Figure 5.1. Cognitive information processing model of spelling and writing. POC = phonological-to-orthographic conversion.

Central Components

Lexical-Semantic Spelling Route

Generating written output via the lexical-semantic spelling route is based on an interaction between the semantic system and the orthographic output lexicon (figure 5.1). The semantic system is a component of long-term memory that contains knowledge of objects, facts, concepts, and word meanings. The orthographic output lexicon provides information about the graphemic structure of familiar words and thus functions as the memory store of learned spellings.

We will only comment here briefly on the possible cortical localization of the semantic system, since this functional component is not specific to writing and the neuroanatomical aspects of semantic processing are covered elsewhere in this volume. However, observations in patients with semantic agraphia (Roeltgen, Rothi, & Heilman, 1986; Rapcsak & Rubens, 1990) are directly relevant to our understanding of the neural substrates of lexical-semantic spelling. In semantic agraphia, the lexical-semantic spelling route is dysfunctional, either because of damage to the semantic system or because of impaired transmission of information between the semantic system and the orthographic output lexicon. Since the lexical-semantic route provides the only mechanism for incorporating meaning into writing, conceptually driven writing tasks such as spontaneous writing and written naming may be significantly compromised. By contrast, writing to dictation can be relatively spared. The preservation of writing to dictation is probably attributable to the fact that this task can also be accomplished by direct phonological-to-orthographic transcoding, which need not involve obligatory semantic mediation (figure 5.1). The disruption of semantic influence on spelling, however, produces significant difficulties in writing homophones to dictation. Homophones have identical sound pattern, but they are spelled differently and have different meanings (for example, *seen* → *scene*). The correct spelling of homophonic words depends critically on semantic context (for example, "he has *seen* the movie" versus "he made a terrible *scene*"). Patients with semantic agraphia cannot use contextual information to disambiguate dictated homophones reliably and, therefore, frequently produce the semantically inappropriate orthographic word form.

Semantic agraphia and homophone confusions have been described in association with both frontal and temporo-parietal left-hemisphere lesion sites that typically spare the perisylvian language zone (that is, Wernicke's area, the supramarginal gyrus, and Broca's area) (Roeltgen & Heilman, 1984; Roeltgen et al., 1986; Rapcsak & Rubens, 1990). Similar writing impairment has been documented in patients with neurodegenerative disorders characterized by prominent semantic memory dysfunction, including Alzheimer's disease (AD) (Glosser & Kaplan, 1989; Neils, Roeltgen, & Constantinidou, 1995) and semantic dementia (Schwartz, Marin, & Saffran, 1979; Naida Graham, personal communication). In AD, the neocortical pathology primarily involves extrasylvian temporo-parietal association cortex (Braak & Braak, 1991). In semantic dementia, the most striking structural changes are seen in anterior and inferolateral temporal cortex (Hodges, Patterson, Oxbury, & Funnell, 1992; Breedin, Saffran, & Coslett, 1994; Patterson & Hodges, 1995), although pathological involvement of posterior temporo-parietal cortex has also been documented in some cases (Harasty, Halliday, Code, & Brooks, 1996). In both AD and semantic dementia, the perisylvian language areas remain relatively preserved until the later stages of the illness. In both disorders, the semantic memory impairment has been linked to left temporal lobe dysfunction (Martin, 1987; Patterson & Hodges, 1995).

The neuroanatomical observations in semantic agraphia are consistent with recent functional imaging studies in normal subjects that demonstrated activation of specific left-hemisphere extrasylvian cortical areas during language tasks requiring semantic processing (for example, Demonet, Chollet, Ramsey, et al., 1992; Vandenberghe, Price, Wise, Josephs, & Frackowiak, 1996; Binder, Frost, Hammeke, Cox, Rao, & Prieto, 1997; Price, Wise, Watson, Patterson, Howard, & Frackowiak, 1997). The main sites of semantic activation included inferolateral temporal and posterior parietal cortex, as well as inferior prefrontal cortex. With respect to the writing process, these findings suggest that the generation of a semantic code that can subsequently be used to activate the appropriate representation in the orthographic output lexicon is mediated by a distributed neural system that includes both extrasylvian temporo-parietal cortex and frontal lobe association areas. Within this network, the temporo-parietal cortical areas may act primarily as storage sites of semantic knowledge, whereas the prefrontal regions may be involved in implementing strategic search and selection procedures and may also be responsible for monitoring the product of semantically guided lexical retrieval to ensure that it is consistent with the message the writer wishes to communicate. Thus, although left temporo-parietal and frontal cortical lesions may both interfere with semantically based activation of representations in the orthographic output lexicon, the neuropsychological mechanism of the ensuing writing disorder may vary as a function of lesion location. One important difference may be that semantic knowledge per se is preserved following frontal lobe lesions (Rapcsak & Rubens, 1990), whereas temporo-parietal lesions may produce a genuine loss or degradation of semantic memory representations (Alexander, Hiltbrunner, & Fischer, 1989; Hart & Gordon, 1990; Patterson & Hodges, 1995).

Information about the possible cortical localization of the orthographic output lexicon comes primarily from neuroanatomical observations in patients with lexical or surface agraphia (Beauvois & Dérouesné, 1981). In lexical agraphia, the spelling of ambiguous or irregular words (for example, *choir*) is significantly impaired, whereas regular word and nonword spelling is characteristically preserved. Spelling errors are usually phonologically plausible (for example, *circuit–serkit*). In addition to the strong effect of orthographic regularity, spelling accuracy is typically influenced by word frequency, with an advantage of high-frequency words over low-frequency ones. Within the framework of the model presented in figure 5.1, lexical agraphia is best accounted for by postulating an impairment at the level of the orthographic output lexicon. Due to the loss or unavailability of word-specific orthographic information, patients are forced to rely on spelling by a nonlexical phonological strategy (that is, phoneme-grapheme conversion), which can be successful when dealing with regular words and nonwords but which leads to regularization errors in spelling ambiguous or irregular words.

In most reported cases of lexical agraphia, the responsible lesion involved the left temporo-parieto-occipital junction (Beauvois & Dérouesné, 1981; Hatfield & Patterson, 1983; Roeltgen & Heilman, 1984; Vanier & Caplan, 1985; Goodman & Caramazza, 1986a; Behrmann, 1987; Croisile, Trillet, Laurent, Latombe, & Schott, 1989; Rapp & Caramazza, 1997, Case 2). In particular, damage to the angular gyrus (Brodmann area 39) and posterior middle and inferior temporal gyrus (Brodmann area 37) is a common finding. In some patients, lexical agraphia was observed following left ventral temporo-occipital lesions (Patterson & Kay, 1982; Rapcsak, Rubens, & Laguna, 1990) (figure 5.2). The writing disorder in these cases was probably related to damage to the posterior fusiform gyrus (ventral component of Brodmann area 37). The proposed role of the left fusiform gyrus in orthographic processing is also supported by the finding that cortical electrical stimulation of this basal temporal lobe region can produce transient impairments of spelling (Lüders et al., 1991).

The degradation of word-specific orthographic knowledge and the relative preservation of phonological spelling has also been documented in AD (Rapcsak, Arthur, Bliklen, & Rubens, 1989; Platel et al., 1993; Croisile, Carnoi, Adeleine, & Trillet, 1995; Croisile et al., 1996; Hughes, Graham, Paterson, & Hodges, 1997) and in patients with semantic dementia or possible Pick's disease (Hodges et al., 1992; Snowden, Neary, Mann, Goulding, & Testa, 1992; Parkin, 1993; Kertesz, Davidson, & McCabe, 1998; Graham, Patterson, & Hodges, 1997, 2000). The difficulty in spelling irregular words in AD has been shown to correlate with reduced metabolic activity in the left angular gyrus (Brodmann area 39) (Peniello et al., 1995). The lexical spelling deficit in semantic dementia may also be attributable to direct pathological involvement of the left posterior temporo-parietal region (Brodmann areas 37 and 39) (Harasty et al., 1996). Alternatively, it has been proposed that the prominent anterior temporal lobe structural changes in semantic dementia may produce functional disconnection of anatomically preserved posterior inferior temporal cortex (Brodmann area 37) (Mummery et al., 1999). Regardless of the exact pathophysiological mechanisms involved, it would appear that lexical agraphia in the setting of neurodegenerative disorders reflects dysfunction of the same left-hemisphere temporo-parietal cortical areas that are implicated in patients with focal brain lesions.

To summarize, lexical agraphia is typically associated with extrasylvian left hemisphere pathology involving the angular gyrus and/or posterior lateral and ventral temporal cortex.

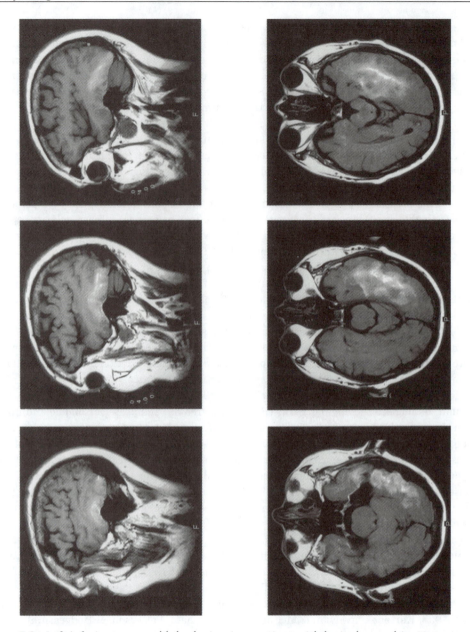

Figure 5.2. Left inferior temporal lobe lesion in a patient with lexical agraphia. Note sparing of the perisylvian language zone.

These observations suggest that information relevant to the graphemic structure of familiar words is stored in a posterior cortical region extending from the angular to the fusiform gyrus, making this area a possible neural substrate of the orthographic output lexicon. The relative preservation of phonological spelling following damage to this cortical zone is most likely attributable to the fact that the responsible lesions generally spare the perisylvian language areas important for phonological processing (see below). In addition to the lesion data obtained from patients with lexical agraphia, the critical role of posterior temporal cortex in orthographic processing is supported by the results of a PET study in which writing to dictation in normal subjects was associated with activation of left Brodmann area 37 (Petrides, Alivisatos,

& Evans, 1995). Activation of the left posterior inferior temporal region was also documented in a recent fMRI study during written production and mental recall of Kanji orthography in Japanese subjects (Nakamura et al., 2000). Damage to left Brodmann area 37 is associated with selective agraphia for Kanji—a writing disorder that is considered to be the Japanese equivalent of lexical agraphia in European languages (Soma, Sugishita, Kitamura, Maruyama, & Imanaga, 1989).

The close anatomical/functional relationship between semantic and orthographic processing is illustrated by the fact that features of semantic and lexical agraphia are sometimes observed in combination. For instance, patients with lexical agraphia may produce homophone errors in writing to dictation (Hatfield & Patterson, 1983; Roeltgen & Heilman, 1984; Goodman & Caramazza, 1986a; Behrmann, 1987) consistent with reduced semantic influence on spelling. Similarly, some patients diagnosed with semantic agraphia have demonstrated regularity effects in homophone spelling tasks (Roeltgen et al., 1986), indicating a possible impairment of word-specific orthographic knowledge. Concurrent semantic and lexical spelling impairments are also observed in AD and in semantic dementia. The cooccurrence of semantic and lexical spelling deficits in neurological patients could of course simply reflect the anatomical proximity of semantic and orthographic processing regions within left extrasylvian temporo-parietal cortex. According to this view, any association observed between semantic impairment and lexical agraphia is merely coincidental and is the result of simultaneous damage to adjacent or partially overlapping semantic and orthographic cortical processing modules. However, the results of a recent study documenting a strong correlation between measures of semantic ability and spelling performance in patients with semantic dementia suggest that the orthographic regularity and word frequency effects that characterize lexical agraphia may be directly attributable to the loss of semantic memory representations (Graham et al., 2000). Based on these observations, Graham and colleagues (2000) proposed that accurate and complete activation of orthographic representations for low-frequency irregular words normally depends on input from the semantic system, because lexical items containing unpredictable phoneme-grapheme correspondences cannot be spelled correctly by relying exclusively on the phonological spelling route (that is, direct phonological-to-orthographic transcoding). According to these authors, the degradation of semantic memory representations alone is sufficient to produce all the main features of lexical agraphia, without the need for postulating additional damage to the orthographic output lexicon.

The findings of the Graham et al. (2000) study have important theoretical implications because they indicate a potential causal relationship between semantic memory deficits and orthographic regularity/frequency effects, thus raising the possibility that lexical agraphia may arise as a result of damage to a component of the cognitive architecture that is not specific to spelling (that is, the semantic system). There are some caveats, however. First, reports of patients who can spell irregular words correctly without adequate comprehension of their meaning (for example, Patterson, 1986; Roeltgen et al., 1986; Hall & Riddoch, 1997; Cipolotti & Warrington, 1995) suggest that there may be individual differences in the degree of reliance on semantic support during writing to dictation. Apparently, in some persons the capacity of the phonological spelling route operating in isolation from the semantic system is sufficient to guarantee accurate spelling of irregular words. Second, most cases of lexical agraphia following focal brain damage do not display evidence of the pervasive central semantic impairment typically seen in patients with semantic dementia. Although patients with lexical agraphia are usually anomic, indicating an additional impairment in gaining access to representations in the phonological output lexicon, auditory comprehension is generally well preserved, and some patients could provide accurate definitions for the words they were subsequently unable to spell (for example, Goodman & Caramazza, 1986a, 1986b).

Taken together, these observations suggest that lexical agraphia is probably not a single entity, and that variations in clinical presentation may reflect differences in the level of breakdown within the lexical-semantic spelling route. It may be the case that, as suggested by Graham and colleagues (2000), the difficulty in spelling irregular words in some patients is directly attributable to the loss of semantic memory representations. These patients should also show evidence of semantic agraphia (that is, significant impairment of spontaneous writing and written naming, homophone confusions in writing to dictation) and should perform poorly on all input and output language tasks requiring semantic processing. In other patients, lexical agraphia may result from a disconnection between the semantic system and the orthographic output lexicon. Although these patients may demonstrate features of semantic agraphia, they should not show evidence of a central semantic impairment. In particular, they should be able to comprehend and provide accurate definitions for the words they cannot spell correctly. Finally, in some patients lexical agraphia may result from selective damage to the orthographic output lexicon. These patients should show a strong effect of orthographic regularity and frequency in spelling, but they should not exhibit signs of semantic agraphia and should perform normally on all tasks of semantic processing. The validity of this classification system and the exact nature of the functional interaction between semantic and orthographic representations in spelling require additional study.

The precise neuroanatomical localization of the cortical systems involved in semantic versus orthographic processing must also await further investigation. Although semantic and orthographic cortical modules may partially overlap, the lesion data in patients with different forms of lexical agraphia seem to indicate some degree of anatomical segregation between the two processing domains. Specifically, lexical agraphia without significant semantic memory impairment is usually associated with damage to the left posterior temporo-parietal region (Brodmann areas 37 and 39) (for example, Beauvois & Dérouesné, 1981; for anatomical details of this case see Beauvois, Saillant, Meininger, & Lhermitte,1978; Croisile et al., 1989; Rapp & Caramazza, 1997, Case 2). The spelling deficit in these patients may be primarily attributable to damage to the orthographic output lexicon. By contrast, lexical agraphia in the setting of profound semantic memory dysfunction is typically observed following structural damage to anterior temporal cortex (Brodmann areas 20, 21, and 38) (for example, Behrmann & Bub, 1992; for anatomical details of this case see Vanier & Caplan, 1985; Hodges et al., 1992; Graham et al., 2000). An intriguing possibility is that anterior temporal lobe lesions produce lexical agraphia indirectly by depriving the orthographic processing regions located within posterior temporal cortex from semantic input (see Mummery et al., 1999; Graham et al., 2000).

Additional evidence for the proposed anatomical segregation of semantic versus orthographic processing along the anterior-posterior axis of the left temporal lobe comes from intracranial evoked potential studies of visual word recognition (Nobre, Allison, & McCarthy, 1994; Nobre & McCarthy, 1995; McCarthy, Nobre, Bentin, & Spencer, 1995). These studies have identified a region within posterior fusiform gyrus that responded equally to words and nonwords, and was unaffected by the semantic properties of the word stimuli. By contrast, responses recorded from anterior fusiform gyrus were sensitive to semantic content and the sentence context in which words were presented. These findings suggest that posterior temporal cortex plays an essential role in the perceptual identification of visually presented letter strings and thus may mediate the functions ascribed to the orthographic input lexicon in cognitive models of reading. On the other hand, the anterior temporal lobe regions seem to be more involved in gaining access to conceptual knowledge relevant to the word's meaning and therefore may represent one of the neural substrates of semantic processing.

Another aspect of the neuroanatomical data on lexical agraphia that deserves commentary is the relationship between the orthographic representations used in spelling versus reading. Dejerine (1891) originally proposed that the same lexical representations supported both functions, and this position has also been embraced by a number of current investigators (Allport & Funnell, 1981; Coltheart & Funnell, 1987; Behrmann & Bub, 1992). Others, however, have argued for the existence of independent orthographic input and output lexicons subserving reading and spelling (Morton & Patterson, 1980; Campbell, 1987; Patterson & Shewell, 1987). Although not conclusive, certain neuroanatomical observations seem to favor the single ortho-graphic lexicon view. Specifically, functional imaging studies in normal subjects have docu-mented activation of left fusiform gyrus, posterior middle and inferior temporal gyrus, and angular gyrus (Brodmann areas 37 and 39) during various reading tasks, suggesting that these functionally linked extrasylvian cortical regions may be the neural substrate of the ortho-graphic input lexicon (for example, Howard et al., 1992; Price et al., 1994; Bookheimer, Zeffiro, Blaxton, Gailland, & Theodore, 1995; Menard, Kosslyn, Thompson, Alpert, & Rauch, 1997; Beauregard et al., 1996; Horwitz, Rumsey, & Donohue, 1998; Cohen et al., 2000). The anatomi-cal areas activated by visually presented words are very close to and perhaps identical with the putative cortical location of the orthographic output lexicon, as inferred from lesion studies of patients with lexical agraphia. Furthermore, as noted earlier, PET and fMRI studies have reported activation of left Brodmann area 37 during the performance of writing tasks that presumably required the retrieval of representations from the orthographic output lexicon (Petrides et al., 1995; Nakamura et al., 2000). Also consistent with the single orthographic lexicon hypothesis is the finding that patients with lexical agraphia frequently exhibit the complementary reading disorder known as surface dyslexia (that is, difficulty in reading ir-regular words with relative preservation of regular word and nonword reading, phonologically plausible errors) (Patterson, Marshall, & Coltheart, 1985; Hodges et al., 1992; Patterson & Hodges, 1992; Behrmann & Bub, 1992; Graham et al., 2000). Taken together, these observa-tions are compatible with the view that a common lexicon subserves reading and spelling and provide further support for the critical role of left posterior temporo-parietal cortex in ortho-graphic processing.

Phonological Spelling Route(s)

In addition to the lexical-semantic route, dual-route models of spelling also postulate the existence of a nonlexical or phonological route that is used primarily to generate plausible spellings for unfamiliar words and pronounceable nonwords. Unlike the lexical-semantic route that relies on a whole-word retrieval process from the orthographic output lexicon, phonologi-cal spelling presumably utilizes a subword-level algorithmic procedure based on phoneme-grapheme conversion rules. Specifically, in spelling by the phonological route the novel audi-tory stimulus is first broken down into its component sounds, following which each phoneme is converted into the corresponding grapheme. It has been proposed, however, that subword-level phonological-to-orthographic translations can also be based on units larger than individual phonemes and graphemes (Baxter & Warrington, 1987). Furthermore, some investigators have suggested that a variety of sizes may be involved in phonological spelling, ranging from pho-nemes to whole words (Shallice, 1988). In contrast to the multilevel phonological spelling route hypothesis, "three-route" models of spelling distinguish separate linguistic routines for subword- and word-level phonological-to-orthographic transcoding, with the latter procedure being imple-mented by direct word-specific connections between the phonological and the orthographic output lexicons (Margolin, 1984; Patterson & Shewell, 1987) (figure 5.1). Fortunately, the resolution of this theoretical debate is not critical to our discussion. What is important for our purposes, however, is the notion that there are spelling routines that rely on phonological codes in generating orthographic output and that these linguistic procedures may be function-ally and anatomically independent from the lexical-semantic spelling system. Consequently, we will use the terms *subword-level* and *word-level phonological spelling* without addressing further the controversial issue of whether different levels of phonological-to-orthographic conversion are mediated by distinct systems.

Dysfunction of the subword-level phonological spelling procedure is considered to be the hallmark of the writing disorder known as phonological agraphia (Shallice, 1981). Patients with phonological agraphia are unable to spell unfamiliar words or nonwords, but real word spelling, including words containing irregular sound-to-spelling correspondences, is relatively preserved. Several observations suggest that real word spelling in phonological agraphia is mediated primarily by a lexical-semantic strategy. For instance, patients may be unable to spell words to dictation unless they have access to their meaning (Shallice, 1981; Bub & Kertesz, 1982a). Furthermore, spelling performance may be influenced by lexical-semantic variables, such as word frequency (high frequency > low frequency), concreteness (concrete > abstract), and grammatical word class (content words > functors). By contrast, orthographic regularity has no appreciable effect on spelling accuracy. Spelling errors on real words are usually phonologically implausible, but they often retain visual/orthographic similarity to the target (for example, *secret* → *securt*) consistent with partial lexical knowledge (Ellis, 1982). Morphological errors (for example, *works* → *worked*) and functor substitutions (for example, *where* → *what*) are also frequently observed.

Phonological agraphia is associated with damage to the perisylvian language zone (Shallice, 1981; Bub & Kertesz, 1982a; Langmore & Canter, 1983; Roeltgen, Sevush, & Heilman, 1983a; Roeltgen & Heilman, 1984; Baxter & Warrington, 1985; Bolla-Wilson, Speedie, & Robinson, 1985; Goodman-Schulman & Caramazza, 1987; Alexander, Loverso, & Fischer, 1992). The responsible lesions typically involve Wernicke's area (Brodmann area 22), the supramarginal gyrus (Brodmann area 40), and Broca's area (Brodmann area 44) in various combinations (figure 5.3). Roeltgen and colleagues (Roeltgen et al., 1983a; Roeltgen & Heilman, 1984, 1985; Roeltgen, 1993) have proposed that the critical neuroanatomical substrate of phonological agraphia is damage to the anterior supramarginal gyrus or the insula underlying this cortical region. An alternative interpretation is that phonological agraphia may be produced by damage to a variety of perisylvian cortical areas that are components of a distributed neural network dedicated to phonological processing. This hypothesis takes into account the fact that subword-level phonological-to-orthographic conversion requires several mental computations that are unlikely to be mediated by a single cortical region. These closely related functions include not only the phonological segmentation and phoneme-grapheme conversion components alluded to earlier, but also phoneme discrimination, phonological short-term memory, and subvocal rehearsal. It is possible that these cognitive operations are subserved by distinct perisylvian cortical areas and that selective damage to these regions results in different clinical forms of phonological agraphia. In any event, the neuroanatomical findings in phonological agraphia are consistent with functional imaging studies in normal subjects that demonstrated activation of Wernicke's area, the supramarginal gyrus, and Broca's area in a variety of experimental tasks requiring phonological processing (for example, Demonet et al., 1992; Zattore, Evans, Meyer, & Gjedde, 1992; Paulesu, Frith, & Frackowiak, 1993; Paulesu et al., 1996; Price, Moore, Humphreys, & Wise, 1997).

From a neuroanatomical perspective, the relative preservation of real word spelling in phonological agraphia is most likely attributable to the fact that the responsible lesions generally spare the extrasylvian cortical areas implicated in lexical-semantic spelling. It should be noted, however, that real word spelling ability shows considerable variation across different patients, ranging from near normal (Shallice, 1981; Bub & Kertesz, 1982a; Bolla-Wilson et al., 1985) to moderately impaired (Roeltgen et al., 1983a; Alexander, Friedman, Loverso, & Fischer, 1992). One possibility is that this variability reflects differences in lesion configuration. Specifically, real word spelling may be significantly compromised in those patients whose lesions extend outside the narrow confines of the perisylvian region and encroach upon the neuroanatomical areas important for lexical-semantic spelling. The presence of additional damage to the lexical-semantic spelling route may explain the frequency, concreteness, and grammatical word class effects observed in many patients with phonological agraphia. Furthermore, damage to or insufficient activation of representations in the orthographic output lexicon may account for the high incidence of visually similar misspellings characterized by letter omissions, substitu-

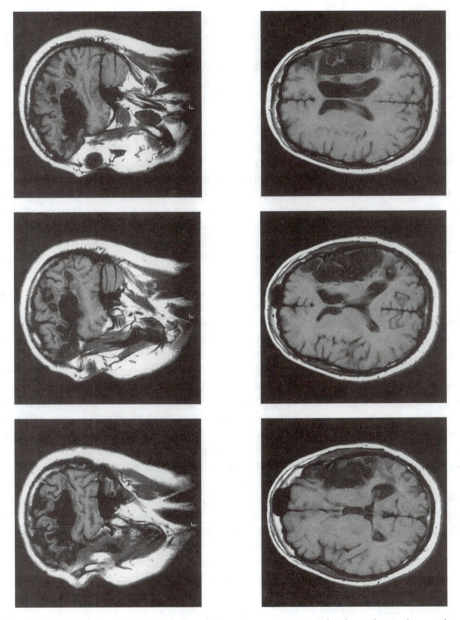

Figure 5.3. Extensive left perisylvian lesion in a patient with phonological agraphia.

tions, additions, and transpositions (that is, errors of partial lexical knowledge). Alternatively, such spelling errors may reflect dysfunction of the graphemic buffer (see below). The latter hypothesis is supported by the word length and letter position effects documented in some patients with phonological agraphia (Langmore & Canter, 1983; Roeltgen et al., 1983a; Baxter & Warrington, 1985; Alexander, Friedman, Loverso, & Fischer, 1992).

We must also consider the possibility that the pattern of real word spelling impairment seen in phonological agraphia is related to the loss of phonological influence on orthographic selection. It has been proposed that representations in the orthographic output lexicon are activated not only by the semantic system but also by input from subword-level (Hillis & Caramazza, 1991) or word-level (Margolin, 1984; Patterson & Shewell, 1987) procedures for phonological-to-

orthographic conversion (figure 5.1). We have already noted that perisylvian lesions can interfere with subword-level phonological spelling. However, such lesions also have the potential for
compromising lexical phonological representations, as demonstrated by the prominent speech
production deficits of aphasic patients with damage to Wernicke's area, the surpramarginal
gyrus, and Broca's area (Albert, Goodglass, Helm, Rubens, & Alexander, 1981; Cappa, Cavallotti,
& Vignolo, 1981). Therefore, perisylvian damage may disrupt not only subword-level phonological input to orthography but also the ability to spell by using representations in the phonological output lexicon to activate the corresponding entries in the orthographic output lexicon
(figure 5.1). The word-level phonological spelling procedure could also be rendered inoperative
by lesions that disrupt word-specific connections between the phonological and orthographic
output lexicons, and in these cases speech production may be relatively preserved.

The loss of phonological influence on orthographic selection may create difficulties in spelling linguistic items that have impoverished semantic representation, including abstract words,
functors, and bound morphemes. For these items, the semantic code alone may be insufficient
to uniquely specify the correct representation in the orthographic output lexicon. In this
hypothesis, the concreteness and grammatical word class effects, functor substitutions, and
morphological errors in phonological agraphia need not imply the presence of additional damage to the lexical-semantic system. Instead, these linguistic features may reflect the functional
limitation of the lexical-semantic spelling route when this system must operate in isolation
without support from subword- or word-level phonological input to orthography. From a neuroanatomical point of view, this interpretation does not require that the lesions in phonological
agraphia extend outside the perisylvian language zone in order to produce the lexical-semantic
effects on spelling performance. Instead, the presence or absence of such effects would be
determined by the extent to which the perisylvian lesions compromised subword- and word-
level phonological-to-orthographic conversion, and perhaps also by individual differences in the
degree to which this type of phonological mediation contributed to spelling performance
premorbidly. Additional studies are needed to distinguish between the different neuropsychological accounts of the real word spelling deficit in phonological agraphia.

Phonological agraphia is closely related to deep agraphia (Bub & Kertesz, 1982b). The two
writing disorders have several features in common, including the severe difficulty in spelling
unfamiliar words and nonwords, the strong effect of lexical-semantic variables on real word
spelling (that is, frequency, concreteness, grammatical word class), and the presence of functor
substitutions, morphological errors, and visually similar misspellings. However, deep agraphia
is empirically distinguishable from phonological agraphia by the frequent occurrence of semantic errors in writing (for example, *sister* → *daughter*).

Semantic errors in written production are indicative of dysfunction within the lexical-semantic spelling route and they may have several different underlying mechanisms. For instance,
semantic errors may be caused by damage to the semantic system, reflecting impaired transmission of information between the semantic system and the orthographic output lexicon, or
they may arise as a consequence of damage to the orthographic output lexicon itself (Hillis,
Rapp, & Caramazza, 1999). Dysfunction of the lexical-semantic spelling route alone, however, is
not sufficient to produce semantic errors in writing to dictation, because the correct spelling of
the target word could potentially be generated by direct phonological routes to orthography
that are capable of functioning independently of the semantic system (figure 5.1). In particular,
subword- or word-level phonological-to-orthographic conversion could block the production of
overt semantic errors by imposing constraints on the selection of representations from the
orthographic output lexicon. Therefore, the necessary conditions for semantic spelling errors
arise when the faulty output of the lexical-semantic spelling route remains completely unconstrained by phonological input to orthography. As a result, an adequate linguistic explanation
of deep agraphia requires that we postulate independent functional deficits affecting both the
lexical-semantic spelling route and the various phonologically mediated routes to orthography.

An alternative hypothesis is that semantic errors reflect the normal instability of the lexical-semantic spelling route operating without any support from phonology (see Coltheart, Patterson, & Marshall, 1980). According to this view, the loss of the phonological spelling route alone may be sufficient to produce most of the characteristic features of deep agraphia.

Not surprisingly, the close linguistic relationship between phonological and deep agraphia is accompanied by a similar overlap with respect to neuroanatomical substrates. In all reported cases of deep agraphia, there has been evidence of damage to the perisylvian language areas (Marin, 1980; Assal, Buttet, & Jolivet, 1981; Bub & Kertesz, 1982b; Nolan & Caramazza, 1983; Hatfield, 1985; Rapcsak, Beeson, & Rubens, 1991; Beaton, Guest, & Ved, 1997; Miceli, Benvegnu, Capasso, & Caramazza, 1997; Shelton & Weinrich, 1997; Rapp, Benzing, & Caramazza, 1997). In most patients the perisylvian cortical involvement was quite extensive, although cases with more circumscribed lesions have also been described (Hillis, Rapp, & Caramazza, 1999). As noted earlier, damage to the perisylvian language areas can account for the pervasive impairment of subword- and word-level phonological spelling. The presence of semantic errors may reflect extension of the lesion into the extrasylvian temporo-parietal or frontal cortical association areas important for spelling by a lexical-semantic strategy. Alternatively, semantic errors may be attributable to the inherent instability of the lexical-semantic route operating without the constraints normally imposed on orthographic selection by the phonological spelling route. In this account, semantic errors in deep agraphia reflect the complete loss of phonological influence on spelling caused by damage to the perisylvian language areas.

The substantial overlap between phonological and deep agraphia suggests that it may not be justifiable to consider these writing disorders as taxonomically distinct entities (see Glosser & Friedman, 1990, for similar views on the relationship between phonological and deep dyslexia). Instead, it may be more appropriate to conceptualize phonological and deep agraphia as representing endpoints along a clinical continuum of increasingly severe phonological and lexical-semantic spelling deficits. The continuum model receives further support from the observation that deep agraphia may evolve into a profile more consistent with phonological agraphia during the recovery process (Kremin, 1987; Hillis et al., 1999).

So far, we have interpreted the phonological/deep agraphia continuum as writing disorders that reflect the output of the damaged left-hemisphere spelling system. However, the extensive destruction of left-hemisphere language areas documented in some patients (figure 5.4) raises the possibility that in these individuals writing may have been mediated by the intact right hemisphere. According to this hypothesis, phonological/deep agraphia reflects the intrinsic functional limitations of the normal right-hemisphere language system. Neuropsychological studies of right-hemisphere language ability in split-brain and dominant hemispherectomy patients are generally consistent with this view (for reviews see Zaidel, 1990; Rapcsak et al., 1991; Weekes, 1995; Ogden, 1996). For instance, investigations of auditory and written word comprehension in this patient population have provided evidence that the semantic system of the right hemisphere lacks the precise functional organization of the left-hemisphere semantic network, making it susceptible to semantic errors. These studies have also revealed that the right-hemisphere lexicon is biased toward high-frequency, concrete words, and may have limited representation of low-frequency, abstract words, functors, and bound morphemes. In addition, the right hemisphere seems to have limited phonological competence and may completely lack the ability to perform subword-level phonological operations. Perhaps most important, it has been demonstrated that the isolated right hemisphere is capable of generating elementary written expression, with a linguistic profile that is consistent with phonological/deep agraphia. Taken together, these observations suggest that right-hemisphere writing is a viable explanation of phonological/deep agraphia in patients with extensive left-hemisphere damage. However, the fact that many patients with large left-hemisphere lesions and global aphasia cannot produce meaningful writing at all suggests that right-hemisphere writing capacity may be subject to considerable individual variation. The respective contribution of left- versus right-

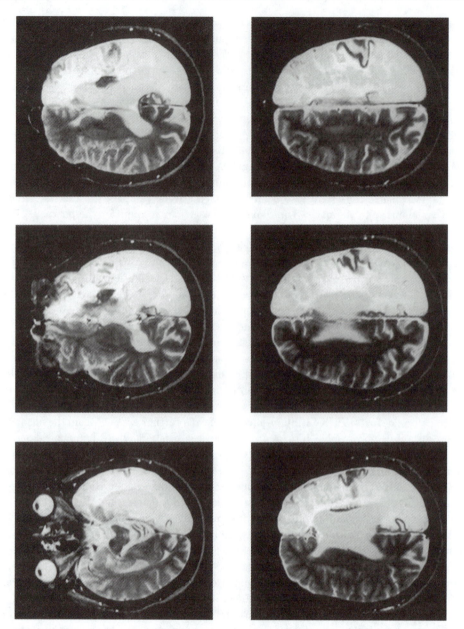

Figure 5.4. Massive destruction of left-hemisphere language areas in a patient with deep agraphia.

hemisphere cortical structures to spelling performance in patients with agraphia can now be studied directly by using functional neuroimaging techniques (Beeson, Rapscak, Hirsch, Plante, & Trouard, 1999).

Graphemic Buffer

The graphemic buffer is a working memory system that temporarily stores the abstract ortho-graphic representations generated by central spelling routes while they are being converted into motor output by the peripheral components of the writing process. Damage to the buffer interferes with the processing of all stored graphemic representations, irrespective of lexical status (that is, words versus nonwords), lexical-semantic features (that is, frequency, concreteness, grammatical word class), or orthographic regularity. Stimulus length, however, has a strong effect on performance because each additional grapheme imposes further demands on limited storage capacity. Dysfunction of the buffer results in the loss of information relevant to the serial order and identity of stored graphemes, leading to letter substitutions, omissions, additions, and transpositions (Caramazza, Miceli, Villa, & Romani, 1987). These grapheme-level errors give rise to phonologically inaccurate misspellings that frequently retain visual similarity to the target. The distribution of errors may be influenced by letter position. Specifically, some patients produce errors primarily on letters located at the end of the word, consistent with a serial left-to-right read-out process operating over a rapidly decaying orthographic memory trace (Chédru & Geschwind, 1972; Katz, 1991). In other cases, errors mostly involved letters in the middle of the word (Caramazza et al., 1987; Posteraro, Zinelli, & Mazzucchi, 1988; Trojano & Chiacchio, 1994), presumably because letters in internal positions are more susceptible to interference from neighboring items than letters located at either end (Wing & Baddeley, 1980). In addition to memory storage capacity, the retrieval of information from the graphemic buffer may also be influenced by attentional factors. For instance, it has been demonstrated that some patients with unilateral neglect produce more errors on the side of the word opposite their lesion, regardless of stimulus length and modality of output, and independent of whether they spell in conventional left-to-right order or in reverse (Baxter & Warrington, 1983; Caramazza & Hillis, 1990; Hillis & Caramazza, 1989, 1995). These observations are consistent with a unilateral disruption of attention over an internal graphemic representation in which the order of graphemes is spatially coded within a word-centered coordinate frame (Caramazza & Hillis, 1990).

Lesion sites in patients with agraphia due to dysfunction of the graphemic buffer have been somewhat variable, and most case reports unfortunately do not provide detailed anatomical information. Nonetheless, it appears that damage to left posterior parietal cortex in or near the angular gyrus is a fairly common finding (figure 5.5). As noted earlier, the left posterior temporo-parietal region plays an important role in orthographic processing, and damage to this cortical area would be expected to reduce the ability to maintain activated or computed graphemic representations in a high state of accessibility. According to this view, temporary storage capacity for graphemic information is intrinsic to the operations of the cortical module specialized for orthographic processing (compare Monsell, 1984), rather than being mediated by a separate functional subcomponent of the writing process as implied by the model presented in figure 5.1. Consistent with the hypothesis that the same cortical areas are involved in processing orthographic information in reading and spelling, it has been suggested recently that a common graphemic buffer may subserve both functions (Hillis & Caramazza, 1995; Caramazza, Capasso, & Miceli, 1996). Interestingly, the behavioral evidence used to support the common graphemic buffer proposal came primarily from observations in patients with parietal lobe damage. We do not wish to imply, however, that posterior parietal cortex is the only brain region involved in orthographic working memory. In fact, recent neuroimaging studies have shown that working memory operations are implemented by distributed neural systems that include functionally linked domain-specific regions within posterior temporo-parieto-occipital cortex and lateral prefrontal cortex (Salmon et al., 1996; Smith & Jonides, 1998; Ungerleider, Courtney, & Haxby, 1998; Crosson, Rao, Woodley, et al., 1999). Therefore, we expect that relatively isolated frontal lobe lesions could also result in graphemic buffer dysfunction—a hypothesis that receives some support from the literature (Posteraro et al., 1988; Cubelli, 1991; Roeltgen, 1994; Margolin & Goodman-Schulman, 1992).

Word length effects and spelling errors suggestive of graphemic buffer dysfunction have also been documented in patients with phonological/deep agraphia (for example, Nolan & Caramazza, 1983; Langmore & Canter, 1983; Roeltgen et al., 1983a; Baxter & Warrington, 1985; Alexander,

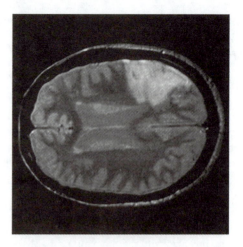

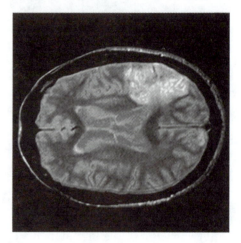

Figure 5.5. Left temporo-parietal lesion in a patient with evidence of graphemic buffer dysfunction.

Friedman, Loverso, & Fischer, 1992; Rapp et al., 1997). To account for this finding, we suggest that the perisylvian lesions in these patients may have interfered with the generation or maintenance of phonological codes that can normally be used to prevent the rapid decay of orthographic information from the graphemic buffer. Specifically, it has been proposed that the contents of the graphemic buffer need to be "refreshed" by input from the phonological buffer, either through subword- or word-level phonological-to-orthographic transcoding (Nolan & Caramazza, 1983; Miceli, Silveri, & Caramazza, 1987). Functional imaging studies in normal subjects have provided evidence that the left supramarginal gyrus plays a critical role in the short-term storage of phonological information (for example, Paulesu et al., 1993; Smith & Jonides, 1998). The maintenance of information in the parietal phonological store requires subvocal rehearsal—a function that is probably mediated by Broca's area. Damage to these cortical regions can lead to a reduction of phonological short-term memory capacity and it can also disrupt phonological-to-orthographic transcoding. As a result, perisylvian lesions may prevent phonological working memory systems from "refreshing" the orthographic short-term memory store by interactions mediated via the phonological spelling route.

So far, we have considered two potential sources of graphemic buffer dysfunction: direct damage to orthographic processing regions and the loss of phonological support necessary for preventing the rapid decay of orthographic information. However, neither of these mechanisms offers a principled explanation of the finding that spelling errors in some patients show evidence of a unilateral spatial bias (Caramazza & Hillis, 1990; Hillis & Caramazza, 1989, 1995). As noted earlier, spatially selective spelling deficits suggest a unilateral breakdown in the allocation of attention during the read-out process from the graphemic buffer, or they may result from an inability to activate or compute the contralesional side of orthographic representations. Posterior parietal cortex plays a critical role in spatial attention, and damage to this area is associated with contralateral neglect that may affect the processing of internal representations as well as the ability to report, respond, or orient to external environmental stimuli (Heilman, Watson, & Valenstein, 1993). The anatomical proximity of spatial attention and orthographic working memory systems within posterior parietal cortex, therefore, may explain the presence of spatially selective spelling deficits in some patients with graphemic buffer impairment. Specifically, parietal damage may reduce the capacity of the buffer to maintain orthographic information in a high state of accessibility, and it may also interfere with processing the contralesional side of stored graphemic representations. However, because orthographic working memory and spatial attention systems are anatomically distinct, graphemic buffer agraphia and neglect-induced errors in spelling are potentially dissociable (Hillis & Caramazza, 1989, 1995). Finally, although we have focused here on posterior parietal cortex, it is conceivable that contralateral attentional gradients in spelling can also be produced by frontal lobe lesions, consistent with the notion that spatial attention functions are mediated by distributed fronto-parietal cortical networks (Heilman et al., 1993).

Peripheral Components

Allographic Conversion

The first peripheral stage in producing writing is known as the allographic conversion process, during which the abstract orthographic representations held in the graphemic buffer are assigned specific letter shapes (Goodman & Caramazza, 1986b). In handwriting, letters can be realized in different case (that is, upper versus lower) or style (that is, print versus script). The various physical shapes each letter of the alphabet can take are referred to as allographs (Ellis, 1982).

The precise nature of the representations involved in allographic conversion has not been determined conclusively. Some investigators have suggested that allographs are stored in long-term memory as abstract visuospatial representations of letter shape (Ellis, 1982; Margolin, 1984), whereas others have proposed that allographs correspond to letter-specific graphic motor programs (Shallice, 1988; Van Galen, 1991; Rapp & Caramazza, 1997). According to the latter hypothesis, shape information is specified not in terms of visuospatial features but with reference to the sequence of strokes necessary to produce a given letter.

In general, allographic disorders are characterized by an inability to activate or select the appropriate letter shapes for written production. The breakdown of the allographic conversion process can take different clinical forms, and individual patients may show more than one type of impairment. For instance, in some patients the difficulty primarily involved the production of lowercase letters (Patterson & Wing, 1989; Kartsounis, 1992; Weekes, 1994; Shuren, Maher & Heilman, 1996; Hughes et al., 1997; Graham et al., 1997), whereas others were mostly impaired when attempting to write in uppercase (De Bastiani & Barry, 1986; Trojano & Chiacchio, 1994; Destreri et al., 2000). Various lowercase writing styles may also be differentially affected (Hanley & Peters, 1996). Although these dissociations are consistent with independent neural representation of letter case and style information, it should be pointed out that problems involving the production of lowercase letters are far more common in neurological patients than impairments affecting writing in uppercase (for a review, see Graham et al., 1997). Therefore, the possibility exists that other factors, such as graphomotor complexity, may also play a role in determining the pattern of the letter production deficit.

Allograph-level impairments can also lead to difficulties in restricting letter production to the intended allographic repertoire, resulting in an uncontrollable mixing of upper- and lower-case letters in handwriting (De Bastiani & Barry, 1989). Finally, in some patients with allographic disorders letter case and style specification procedures are relatively preserved, but written spelling is nonetheless characterized by numerous well-formed letter substitution errors (Kinsbourne & Rosenfield, 1974; Rothi & Heilman, 1981; Kapur & Lawton, 1983; Friedman & Alexander, 1989; Goodman & Caramazza, 1986b; Black, Behrmann, Bass, & Hacker, 1989; Lambert, Viader, Eustache, & Morin, 1994; Rapp & Caramazza, 1997; Destreri et al., 2000). It has been demonstrated that substitution errors generally involve the production of letter shapes physically similar to the target. Although similarity effects in letter substitution errors may be based on shared visual features (Zesiger, Pegna, & Rilliet, 1994; Weekes, 1994), in some patients they are more likely to represent confusions between letter-specific graphic motor programs containing similar stroke sequences (Lambert et al., 1994; Rapp & Caramazza, 1997; Destreri et al., 2000).

Disruption of the allographic conversion process is typically observed following damage to the left posterior temporo-parieto-occipital region (figure 5.6). The lesion sites partially overlap with the extrasylvian cortical areas implicated in lexical agraphia, and this anatomical proximity may explain the frequent cooccurrence of lexical and allographic spelling deficits in neurological patients (Goodman & Caramazza, 1986b; Friedman & Alexander, 1989; Weekes, 1994;

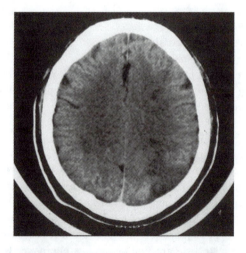

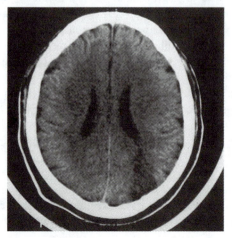

Figure 5.6. Left dorsal parieto-occipital lesion in a patient with allograph-level writing impairment and preserved oral spelling.

Hughes et al., 1997; Rapp & Caramazza, 1997; Graham et al., 1997). As a possible alternative to this neuroanatomical hypothesis, Graham and colleagues (1997) suggested that connectionist models incorporating bidirectional interactions between word- and letter-level processes in spelling could also account for this association. Within the framework of such models, the degradation of word-specific orthographic representations would be expected to disrupt letter selection and production because of a reduction in top-down activation. Although reciprocal interactions between word- and letter-level procedures may certainly occur in spelling, it is not clear whether damage to lexical orthographic representations inevitably leads to difficulties in letter production. Furthermore, in patients with selective damage to the allographic conversion process oral spelling is characteristically spared, indicating preserved word-specific orthographic knowledge and thus confirming the postlexical locus of the written spelling deficit.

In principle, allographic writing disorders could result from impaired access or damage to abstract letter shape representations within the putative allographic long-term memory store (Ellis, 1982; Margolin, 1984), or they may be caused by lesions that disrupt functional connections between orthographic representations and letter-specific graphic motor programs (figure 5.1). In our view, the latter hypothesis is more convincing for a number of reasons. First, it is not entirely clear why one would need the additional step of retrieving abstract visuospatial information about letter shape once the characteristic stroke patterns of different letters are firmly established in procedural memory and writing becomes an automatic motor task. Second, it has been demonstrated that letter production can be relatively preserved even when letter recognition and letter shape imagery are severely compromised (Shuren et al., 1996; Destreri et al., 2000). These observations suggest that access to stored knowledge about the visuospatial features of letters may not be critical for writing. Third, as discussed earlier, letter substitution errors in some patients with allographic disorders seem to be based on motor rather than visual similarity to the target (Lambert et al., 1994; Rapp & Caramazza, 1997; Destreri et al., 2000). Finally, the dorsal parieto-occipital lesions documented in a number of patients with allograph-level writing impairment (figure 5.6) are well situated for disrupting the flow of information between the inferior temporo-parietal cortical regions involved in orthographic processing and the posterior-superior parietal areas implicated in the motor programming of handwriting movements (see below). The close relationship between letter shape selection and motor programming is also indicated by the finding that letter substitution errors and errors of letter morphology often coexist in the written productions of patients with dorsal parietal damage (for example, Baxter & Warrington, 1986; Crary & Heilman, 1988; Levine, Mani, & Calvanio, 1988).

In conclusion, it seems to us that there are no compelling theoretical or empirical reasons for postulating that an independent level of visual letter shape representations is mediating between the orthographic and motor components of writing. Allographic writing disorders are more parsimoniously explained by assuming that the lesions in these patients interfere with the procedures by which graphemic representations are directly mapped onto the appropriate letter-specific graphic motor programs.

Motor Programming and Neuromuscular Execution

Similar to other complex motor skills, the neural control of handwriting movements is hierarchically organized, with the general plan of the movement represented at the highest level and lower levels regulating increasingly specific details of neuromuscular execution. As shown in figure 5.1, the highest level of control is implemented by graphic motor programs. Graphic motor programs contain information about abstract spatio-temporal movement attributes, including the sequence, position, direction, and relative size of the strokes necessary for producing specific letters (Ellis, 1982, 1988). However, graphic motor programs do not specify concrete movement parameters such as absolute stroke size or duration. Graphic motor programs are also effector-independent in the sense that they do not determine which muscle groups are to be recruited for movement execution. Writing can be performed by using different limbs (for example, left versus right hand or foot), or by using different muscle combinations of the same limb (for example, distal muscles in writing with a pen versus proximal muscles when writing on the blackboard). The fact that writing produced by different effector systems displays striking similarities with respect to overall letter shape is consistent with the notion of effector-independent graphic motor programs (Merton, 1972; Wright, 1990).

Defective motor control of handwriting movements is the central abnormality in the writing disorder known as apraxic agraphia. Clinically, apraxic agraphia is characterized by poor letter formation that cannot be accounted for by elementary sensorimotor (that is, weakness, deafferentation), basal ganglia (that is, tremor, rigidity), or cerebellar (that is, dysmetria, ataxia) dysfunction affecting the writing limb. Typical errors of letter morphology include spatial distortions, stroke omissions, and the insertion of anomalous strokes resulting in nonletters. In severe cases, all writing attempts may result in the production of illegible scrawl.

From a neuropsychological perspective, the writing impairment in apraxic agraphia is attributable to damage to graphic motor programs, or it may reflect an inability to translate the information contained in these programs into motor commands to specific muscle effector systems (Rapcsak, 1997). Apraxic agraphia is dissociable from limb apraxia, suggesting that motor programs for writing movements are distinct from programs for other types of skilled limb movements (Roeltgen & Heilman, 1983; Margolin & Binder, 1984; Coslett, Rothi, Valenstein, & Heilman, 1986; Baxter & Warrington, 1986; Anderson, Damasio, & Damasio, 1990; Papagno, 1992).

In right-handers, apraxic agraphia is associated with specific left-hemisphere lesion sites. The most common neuroanatomical correlate is damage to cortical areas surrounding the intraparietal sulcus, including the superior parietal lobule and the superior portions of the supramarginal and angular gyri (for example, Roeltgen, Sevush, & Heilman, 1983b; Coslett et al., 1986; Alexander, Fischer, & Friedman, 1992; Papagno, 1992; Otsuki, Soma, Arai, Otsuki, & Tsuji, 1999). Similar writing impairment has been documented in patients with neurodegenerative disorders characterized by focal atrophy of the superior parietal region (Ross et al., 1996). Apraxic agraphia has also been reported following lesions that involved the dorsolateral premotor area located at the foot of the second frontal convolution known as Exner's writing center (for example, Anderson et al., 1990; Hodges, 1991). Finally, apraxic agraphia has been described in association with damage to the supplementary motor area (SMA) (Rubens, 1975; Watson, Fleet, Rothi, & Heilman, 1986). Taken together, the lesion data suggest that the motor programming of writing is mediated by a distributed neural network that includes posterior-superior parietal cortex and dorsolateral and medial frontal premotor cortex. Within this network, the posterior-superior parietal regions may contain abstract spatio-temporal codes for writing movements (that is, graphic motor programs), whereas the frontal cortical areas may be responsible for generating the appropriate motor commands for neuromuscular execution.

The existence of a distributed fronto-parietal cortical system involved in the motor programming of handwriting is also supported by functional imaging studies in normal subjects (figure 5.7). These studies have consistently demonstrated activation of posterior-superior parietal cortex (that is, the region of the intraparietal sulcus), dorsolateral premotor cortex, and the SMA across a variety of writing tasks (Petrides et al., 1995; Sugishita, Takayama, Shiona, Yoshikawa, & Takahashi, 1996; Seitz et al., 1997; Kato et al., 1999). Interestingly, similar anatomical areas are activated during imagined writing movements (Decety, Philippon, & Ingvar, 1988; Sugishita et al., 1996), suggesting that mentally executed and real graphomotor gestures are controlled by partially overlapping neural networks.

In most right-handers the left hemisphere is dominant for writing. Left-hemisphere damage in these individuals typically produces agraphia affecting both hands, although the right hand may not be testable due to paralysis. By contrast, damage to the corpus callosum may result in

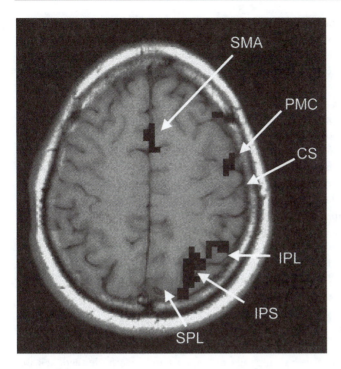

Figure 5.7. fMRI scan of a normal right-handed individual demonstrating the cortical network involved in the motor production of handwriting. Regions of activation reflect a writing fluency task (generating written words from different semantic categories) minus a control task of drawing circles. SMA = supplementary motor area; PMC = premotor cortex (Exner's area); CS = central suclus; IPL = inferior parietal lobule (angular and supramarginal gyri); IPS = intraparietal sulcus; SPL = superior parietal lobule.

unilateral agraphia of the left hand, indicating that writing with the nondominant hand normally requires interhemispheric transfer of information (for example, Liepmann & Maas, 1907; Geschwind & Kaplan, 1962; Watson & Heilman, 1983). Neuroanatomical observations in patients with callosal agraphia suggest that information critical to the motor programming of handwriting movements is transferred through the body of the corpus callosum (Liepmann, 1920; Geschwind, 1975; Watson & Heilman, 1983), whereas linguistic information relevant to spelling is transferred more posteriorly through the fibers of the splenium (Yamadori, Osumi, Ikeda, & Kanazawa, 1980; Sugishita, Toyokura, Yoshioka, & Yamada, 1980; Gersh & Damasio, 1981; Yamadori, Nagashima, & Tamaki, 1983; Kawamura, Hirayama, & Yamamoto, 1989).

The final stage in the motor control of handwriting involves the translation of the information encoded in graphic motor programs into graphic innervatory patterns containing sequences of motor commands to specific muscle effector systems (figure 5.1). It is at this stage that the proper combination of agonist and antagonist muscle groups are selected and concrete kinematic parameters specifying absolute stroke size, duration, and force are inserted into the program. Damage to motor systems involved in generating graphic innervatory patterns results in defective control of writing force, speed, and amplitude. A typical example of this kind of motor production deficit is the micrographia of patients with Parkinson's disease, characterized by a striking reduction in handwriting size (McLennan, Nakano, Tyler, & Schwab, 1972; Margolin & Wing, 1983; Oliveira, Gund, Nixon, Marshall, & Passingham, 1997).

Micrographia in Parkinson's disease reflects basal ganglia dysfunction attributable to the loss of striatal dopamine. Dopaminergic projections to the striatum originate in the substantia nigra of the midbrain. It has been demonstrated that focal lesions of the substantia nigra can produce micrographia of the contralateral hand (Kim, Im, Kwon, Kang, & Lee, 1998). Basal ganglia structures exert their influence on motor behavior through connections to frontal premotor areas via a major reentrant basal ganglia-thalamocortical motor loop (Alexander, DeLong, & Strick, 1986). Operating as a functional unit, the cortical and subcortical components of this neural network play a critical role in controlling movement force, speed, and amplitude. Consistent with this hypothesis, micrographia has been observed following focal damage to various components of this motor loop, including the striatum, thalamus, and the SMA (Lewitt, 1983; Martinez-Vila, Artedia & Obeso, 1988; Klatka, Depper, & Marini, 1998; Murray, Llinas, Caplan, Scammell, & Pascual-Leone, 2000).

Defective motor execution is also characteristic of the writing produced by patients with cerebellar lesions (Haggard, Jenner, & Wing, 1994). Similar to the basal ganglia, the cerebellum is functionally linked to frontal premotor areas through reentrant neural circuitry (Brooks, 1986). The striking disruption of motor behavior following cerebellar lesions (Holmes, 1939) suggests that cortico-cerebellar systems are critically involved in selecting and implementing the appropriate kinematic parameters for skilled limb movements, including the graphic innervatory patterns required for the smooth and automatic production of handwriting movements.

To summarize, basal ganglia-thalamocortical and cerebello-cortical networks are possible neural substrates of the system responsible for generating specific motor commands for handwriting movements. This hypothesis receives support from functional imaging studies in normal subjects that demonstrated activation of premotor cortex, basal ganglia, and cerebellum during the performance of various writing tasks (Lauritzen, Henriksen, & Lassen, 1981; Mazziotta, Phelps, & Wapenski, 1985; Decety, Philippon, & Ingvar, 1988; Petrides et al., 1995; Seitz et al., 1997).

Afferent Control Systems

Handwriting is a complex motor activity that depends on visual and kinesthetic feedback for maximum speed and accuracy. When normal subjects are deprived of appropriate visual feedback, they produce characteristic writing errors that include the duplication or omission of letters or strokes (Smith, McCrary, & Smith, 1960; Lebrun, 1976; Smyth & Silvers, 1987). These errors are especially common when writing sequences of similar items (for example, words with double letters, such as *rubber* may be written as "rubbber" or "ruber," strokes may be added or deleted when writing single letters containing repeated stroke cycles, such as *w* or *m*). Based on these findings, it has been proposed that monitoring afferent sensory information plays an important role in updating graphic motor programs as to which letters or strokes have already been executed (Margolin, 1984). In addition to this "place-keeping" function, afferent feedback is also required to maintain the correct spacing between letters and words and for keeping the line of writing properly oriented on the page (Lebrun, 1976, 1985; Smyth & Silvers, 1987).

Damage to neural systems involved in monitoring sensory feedback during handwriting results in a disorder known as afferent or spatial dysgraphia (Lebrun, 1976, 1985; Marcie & Hécaen, 1979; Ellis, Young, & Flude, 1987; Ardila & Rosselli, 1993; Silveri, 1996; Croisile & Hibert, 1998; Seki et al., 1998; Cubelli & Lupi, 1999). The written productions of patients with afferent dysgraphia contain numerous letter/stroke duplications and omissions, similar to those observed in normal subjects under experimental conditions that interfere with the efficient use of sensory feedback. Patients also frequently have difficulty keeping the correct spacing between letters or words and may not be able to write in a straight horizontal line.

Afferent dysgraphia is typically seen following right parietal lobe damage, suggesting that this cortical area plays an essential role in monitoring visual and kinesthetic information relevant to the motor production of handwriting movements (Marcie & Hécaen, 1979; Lebrun, 1985; Ardila & Rosselli, 1993; Silveri, 1996; Croisile & Hibert, 1998). Right parietal lesions also frequently produce contralateral neglect (Heilman et al., 1993). However, errors attributable to general left-sided visual neglect, such as the tendency to write on the right side of the page and the failure to cross t's and dot i's at the beginning of the word, are dissociable from feedback-related errors that are specific to handwriting and include letter/stroke duplications and omissions (Ellis et al., 1987; Silveri, 1996; Croisile & Hibert, 1998; Seki et al., 1998; Cubelli & Lupi, 1999). Afferent control of stroke and letter production may also be separate from control over other nonlateralized visuospatial aspects of writing, such as maintaining the correct spacing between letters and words and keeping the line of writing properly oriented on the page. Therefore, the core deficit in afferent dysgraphia may be the inability to use sensory feedback to keep track of the number of letters or strokes produced in handwriting (see Cubelli & Lupi, 1999), whereas the associated clinical findings may reflect simultaneous damage to functionally independent visuoperceptual and spatial attention modules located in close anatomical proximity within parietal cortex. Finally, we note that features of afferent dysgraphia have also been documented in patients with right frontal (Ardila & Rosselli, 1993; Seki et al., 1998) or cerebellar lesions (Silveri, Misciagna, Leggio, & Molinari, 1997), suggesting that the afferent control of handwriting movements requires the coordinated activity of several distinct brain regions. The specific contribution of these different anatomical areas requires further study.

CONCLUSIONS

A comprehensive theory of writing must make an effort to identify possible neural substrates for the various central and peripheral processing components postulated by cognitive models. In fact, we believe that lesion data obtained from patients with agraphia combined with imaging studies in normal subjects can impose important neurobiological constraints on cognitive theories about the functional architecture of the writing process. In our view, the neural systems involved in writing are best described in terms of four broad processing domains that include orthography, semantics, phonology, and motor execution. As we have seen, left extrasylvian temporo-parietal cortex plays a critical role in orthographic processing. Orthographic representations are activated, computed, and temporarily maintained in a high state of accessibility within this cortical region in response to input from semantics and/or phonology. Semantic processing is mediated by a distributed neural system that includes specialized regions within left extrasylvian frontal and temporo-parietal cortex. Functional interactions between cortical areas dedicated to semantic and orthographic processing constitute the neural substrate of the lexical-semantic spelling route. Extrasylvian left-hemisphere lesions may disrupt spelling by a lexical-semantic strategy and result in various combinations of semantic and lexical agraphia. By contrast, the subword- and word-level phonological codes used in spelling are generated by perisylvian cortical areas. Perisylvian lesions may interfere with the operations of the phonological spelling route (that is, phonological-to-orthographic transcoding) and produce phonological/deep agraphia. It should be emphasized that although they are conceptualized here as being anatomically distinct and therefore functionally independent, the lexical-semantic and phonological spelling routes operate in a highly interactive fashion under normal circumstances. Functional interactions can also occur between partially damaged central spelling routes and may play an important role in shaping the performance of neurological patients with agraphia (Hillis & Caramazza, 1991).

As far as the different peripheral processing components are concerned, the evidence suggests that the motor programming of writing is controlled by a distributed neural network that includes posterior-superior parietal cortex, dorsolateral premotor cortex, and the SMA, whereas specific kinematic parameters for writing movements are generated by basal ganglia-thalamo-cortical and cerebello-cortical motor loops. The monitoring of afferent feedback relevant to the execution of handwriting movements is mediated primarily by right-hemisphere neural systems.

In closing, we wish to emphasize that the neuroanatomical model of spelling and writing presented here is preliminary and will require further empirical validation. It is our hope that future studies will provide the appropriate combination of behavioral and anatomical data needed to accomplish this goal.

ACKNOWLEDGMENTS

This work was supported by the Cummings Endowment Fund to the Department of Neurology at the University of Arizona and the National Multipurpose Research and Training Center Grant DC-01409 from the National Institutes on Deafness and Other Communication Disorders. The functional neuroimaging was supported by the Small Grants Program from the Vice President for Research at the University of Arizona. The authors also express their appreciation to Cynthia Ochipa, Ph.D., for sharing the brain scan from one of her agraphic patients with us.

REFERENCES

Albert, M. L., Goodglass, H., Helm, N. A., Rubens, A. B., & Alexander, M. P. (1981). *Clinical aspects of dysphasia*. Wien: Springer-Verlag.

Alexander, G. E., DeLong, M. R., & Strick, P. L. (1986). Parallel organization of functionally segregated circuits linking basal ganglia and cortex. *Annual Review of Neuroscience, 9*, 357-381.

Alexander, M. P., Fischer, R. S., & Friedman, R. (1992). Lesion localization in apractic agraphia. *Archives of Neurology, 49*, 246-251.

Alexander, M. P., Friedman, R. B., Loverso, F., & Fischer, R. S. (1992). Lesion localization in phonological agraphia. *Brain and Language, 43*, 83-95.

Alexander, M. P., Hiltbrunner, B., & Fischer, R. S. (1989). Distributed anatomy of transcortical sensory aphasia. *Archives of Neurology, 46*, 885-892.

Allport, A., & Funnell, E. (1981). Components of the mental lexicon. *Philosophical Transactions of the Royal Society of London, B295*, 397-410.

Anderson, S. W., Damasio, A. R., & Damasio, H. (1990). Troubled letters but not numbers: Domain specific cognitive impairments following focal damage in frontal cortex. *Brain, 113*, 749-766.

Ardila, A., & Rosselli, M. (1993). Spatial agraphia. *Brain and Language, 22*, 137-147.

Assal, G., Buttet, J., & Jolivet, R. (1981). Dissociations in aphasia: A case report. *Brain and Language, 13*, 223-240.

Bastian, C. H. (1897). Some problems in connexion with aphasia and other speech defects. *Lancet, 1*, 1005-1017.

Baxter, D. M., & Warrington, E. K. (1983). Neglect dysgraphia. *Journal of Neurology, Neurosurgery, and Psychiatry, 46*, 1073-1078.

Baxter, D. M., & Warrington, E. K. (1985). Category specific phonological dysgraphia. *Neuropsychologia, 23*, 653-666.

Baxter, D. M., & Warrington, E. K. (1986). Ideational agraphia: A single case study. *Journal of Neurology, Neurosurgery, and Psychiatry, 49*, 369 374.

Baxter, D. M., & Warrington, E. K. (1987). Transcoding sound to spelling: Single or multiple sound unit correspondence? *Cortex, 23*, 11-28.

Beauregard, M., Chertkow, H., Bub, D., Murtha, S., Dixon, R., & Evans, A. (1997). The neural substrate for concrete, abstract, and emotional word lexica: A positron emisson tomography study. *Journal of Cognitive Neuroscience, 9*, 441-461.

Beauvois, M.-F., & Dérouesné, J. (1981). Lexical or orthographic agraphia. *Brain, 104*, 21-49.

Beauvois, M.-F., Saillant, B., Meininger, V., & Lhermitte, F. (1978). Bilateral tactile aphasia: A tacto-verbal disconnection. *Brain, 101*, 381-401.

Beaton, A., Guest, J., & Ved, R. (1997). Semantic errors in naming, reading, writing, and drawing following left-hemisphere infarction. *Cognitive Neuropsychology, 14*, 459-478.

Beeson, P. M., Rapcsak, S. Z., Hirsch, F. M., Plante, E., & Trouard, T. P. (1999). Broca's aphasia from the right hemisphere: A functional neuroimaging study. Paper presented at the American Speech-Language-Hearing Association Annual Convention, San Francisco, CA.

Behrmann, M. (1987). The rites of righting writing: Homophone mediation in acquired dysgraphia. *Cognitive Neuropsychology, 4*, 365-384.

Behrmann, M., & Bub, D. (1992). Surface dyslexia and dysgraphia: Dual routes, single lexicon. *Cognitive Neuropsychology, 9*, 209-251.

Binder, J. R., Frost, J. A., Hammeke, T. A., Cox, R. W., Rao, S. M., & Prieto, T. (1997). Human brain language areas identified by functional magnetic resonance imaging. *Journal of Neuroscience, 17*, 353-362.

Black, S. E., Behrmann, M., Bass, K., & Hacker, P. (1989). Selective writing impairment: Beyond the allographic code. *Aphasiology, 3*, 265-277.

Bolla-Wilson, K., Speedie, L. J., & Robinson, R. G. (1985). Phonologic agraphia in a left-handed patient after a right-hemisphere lesion. *Neurology, 35*, 1778-1781.

Bookheimer, S. Y., Zeffiro, T. A., Blaxton, T., Gaillard, W., & Theodore, W. (1995). Regional cerebral blood flow during object naming and reading. *Human Brain Mapping, 3*, 93-106.

Braak H., & Braak, E. (1991). Neuropathological staging of Alzheimer-related changes. *Acta Neuropathology., 82*, 239-259.

Breedin, S. D., Saffran, E. M., & Coslett, H. B. (1994). Reversal of the concreteness effect in a patient with semantic dementia. *Cognitive Neuropsychology, 11*, 617-660.

Brooks, V. B. (1986). *The neural basis of motor control*. New York: Oxford University Press.

Bub, D., & Kertesz, A. (1982a). Evidence for lexicographic processing in a patient with preserved written over oral single word naming. *Brain, 105*, 697-717.

Bub, D., & Kertesz, A. (1982b). Deep agraphia. *Brain and Language, 17*, 146-165.

Campbell, R. (1987). One or two lexicons for reading and writing words: Can misspellings shed any light? *Cognitive Neuropsychology, 4*, 487-499.

Cappa, S., Cavallotti, G., & Vignolo, L. A. (1981). Phonemic and lexical errors in fluent aphasia: Correlation with lesion site. *Neuropsychologia, 19*, 171-177.

Caramazza, A., & Hillis, A.E. (1990). Spatial representation of words in the brain implied by studies of a unilateral neglect patient. *Nature, 346,* 267–269.

Caramazza, A., Capasso, R., & Miceli, G. (1996). The role of the graphemic buffer in reading. *Cognitive Neuropsychology, 13,* 673–698.

Caramazza, A., Miceli, G., Villa, G., & Romani, C. (1987). The role of the graphemic buffer in spelling: Evidence from a case of acquired dysgraphia. *Cognition, 26,* 59–85.

Charcot, J. M. (1883). Des différentes formes de l'aphasie: De la cécité verbale. *Progrés Médicale, 11,* 441–469.

Chédru, F., & Geschwind, N. (1972). Writing disturbances in acute confusional states. *Neuropsychologia, 10,* 343–353.

Cipolotti, L., & Warrington, E. K. (1995). Semantic memory and reading abilities: A case report. *Journal of the International Neuropsychological Society, 1,* 104–110.

Cohen, L., Dehaene, S., Naccache, L., Lehéricy, S., Dehaene-Lambertz, G., Hénaff, M. A., & Michel, F. (2000). The visual word form area: Spatial and temporal characterization of an initial stage of reading in normal subjects and posterior split-brain patients. *Brain, 123,* 291–307.

Coltheart, M., & Funnell, E. (1987). Reading and writing: One lexicon or two? In D. A. Allport, D. G. MacKay, W. Prinz, & E. Scheerer (Eds.), *Language perception and production: Shared mechanisms in listening, speaking, reading and writing.* London: Academic Press.

Coltheart, M., Patterson, K., & Marshall, J. C. (1980). *Deep dyslexia.* London: Routledge & Kegan Paul.

Coslett, H. B., Rothi, L. J. G., Valenstein, E., & Heilman, K. M. (1986). Dissociations of writing and praxis: two cases in point. *Brain and Language, 28,* 357–369.

Crary, M. A., & Heilman, K. M. (1988). Letter imagery deficits in a case of pure apraxic agraphia. *Brain and Language, 34,* 147–156.

Croisile, B., Brabant, M.-J., Carmoi, T., Lepage, Y., Aimard, G., & Trillet, M. (1996). Comparison between oral and written spelling in Alzheimer's disease. *Brain and Language, 54,* 361–387.

Croisile, B., Carmoi, T., Adeleine, P., & Trillet, M. (1995). Spelling in Alzheimer's disease. *Behavioral Neurology, 8,* 135–143.

Croisile, B., & Hibert, O. (1998). Spatial or afferent agraphia without left-sided neglect. *Aphasiology, 12,* 147–159.

Croisile, B., Trillet, M., Laurent, B., Latombe, B., & Schott, B. (1989). Agraphie lexicale par hematome temporoparietal gauche. *Revue Neurologique, 145,* 287–292.

Crosson, B., Rao, S. M, Woodley, S. J., et al. (1999). Mapping of semantic, phonological, and orthographic working memory in normal adults with functional magnetic resonance imaging. *Neuropsychology, 13,* 171–187.

Cubelli, R. (1991). A selective deficit for writing vowels in acquired dysgraphia. *Nature, 353,* 258–260.

Cubelli, R., & Lupi, G. (1999). Afferent dysgraphia and the role of vision in handwriting. *Visual Cognition, 6,* 113–128.

De Bastiani, P., & Barry, C. (1986). After the graphemic buffer: Disorders of peripheral aspects of writing in Italian patients. Cited in Patterson, K., & Wing, A. M. (1989). Processes in handwriting: A case for case. *Cognitive Neuropsychology, 6,* 1–23.

De Bastiani, P., & Barry, C. (1989). A cognitive analysis of an acquired dysgraphic patient with an allographic writing disorder. *Cognitive Neuropsychology, 6,* 25–41.

Decety, J., Philippon, B., & Ingvar, D. H. (1988). rCBF landscapes during motor performance and motor ideation of a graphic gesture. *European Archives of Psychiatry and Neurological Sciences, 238,* 33–38.

Dejerine, J. (1891). Sur un cas de cécité verbale avec agraphie, suivi d'autopsie. *Mém. Soc. Biol. 3,* 197–201.

Dejerine, J. (1914). *Sémiologie des affections du systéme Nerveux.* Paris: Masson et Cie.

Demonet, J.-F., Chollet, F., Ramsay, S., et al. (1992). The anatomy of phonological and semantic processing in normal subjects. *Brain, 115,* 1753–1768.

Destreri, N. D. G., Farina, E., Alberoni, M., Pomati, S., Nichelli, P., & Mariani, C. (2000). Selective uppercase dysgraphia with loss of visual imagery of letter forms: A window on the organization of graphomotor patterns. *Brain and Language, 71,* 353–372.

Ellis, A. W. (1982). Spelling and writing (and reading and speaking). In A.W. Ellis (Ed.), *Normality and pathology in cognitive functions.* London: Academic Press.

Ellis, A. W. (1988). Normal writing processes and peripheral acquired dysgraphias. *Language and Cognitive Processes, 3,* 99–127.

Ellis, A. W., Young, A. W., & Flude, B. M. (1987). "Afferent dysgraphia" in a patient and in normal subjects. *Cognitive Neuropsychology, 4,* 465–486.

Exner, S. (1881). *Untersuchungen über die Localisation der Functionen in der Grosshirnrinde des Menschen.* Wien: W. Braunmüller.

Friedman, R. B., & Alexander, M. P. (1989). Written spelling agraphia. *Brain and Language, 36,* 503–517.

Gersh, F., & Damasio, A. R. (1981). Praxis and writing of the left hand may be served by different callosal pathways. *Archives of Neurology, 38,* 634–636.

Geschwind, N., & Kaplan, E. (1962). A human cerebral deconnection syndrome: A preliminary report. *Neurology, 12,* 675–685.

Glosser, G., & Friedman, R. B. (1990). The continuum of deep/phonological alexia. *Cortex, 26,* 343–359.

Glosser, G., & Kaplan, E. (1989). Linguistic and nonlinguistic impairments in writing: A comparison of patients with focal and multifocal CNS disorders. *Brain and Language, 37,* 357–380.

Goodman, R. A., & Caramazza, A. (1986a). Aspects of the spelling process: evidence from a case of acquired dysgraphia. *Language and Cognitive Processes, 1,* 263–296.

Goodman, R. A., & Caramazza, A. (1986b). Dissociation of spelling errors in written and oral spelling: The role of allographic conversion in writing. *Cognitive Neuropsychology, 3,* 179–206.

Goodman-Schulman, R., & Caramazza, A. (1987). Patterns of dysgraphia and the nonlexical spelling process. *Cortex, 23,* 143–148.

Graham, N. L., Patterson, K., & Hodges, J. R. (1997). Progressive dysgraphia: Co-occurrence of central and peripheral impairments. *Cognitive Neuropsychology, 14,* 975–1005.

Graham, N. L., Patterson, K., & Hodges, J. R. (2000). The impact of semantic memory impairment on spelling: Evidence from semantic dementia. *Neuropsychologia, 38,* 143–163.

Grashey, H. (1885). Über Aphasie und ihre Beziehungen zur Wahrnehmung. *Archiv für Psychiatrie und Nervenkrankheiten, 16,* 654–688.

Haggard, P., Jenner, J., & Wing, A. (1994). Coordination of aimed movements in a case of unilateral cerebellar damage. *Neuropsychologia, 32,* 827–846.

Hall, D. A., & Riddoch, J. M. (1997). Word meaning deafness: Spelling words that are not understood. *Cognitive Neuropsychology, 14,* 1131–1164.

Hanley, J. R., & Peters, S. (1996). A dissociation between the ability to print and write cursively in lower-case letters. *Cortex, 32,* 737–745.

Harasty, J. A., Halliday, G. M., Code, C., & Brooks, W. S. (1996). Quantification of cortical atrophy in a case of progressive fluent aphasia. *Brain, 119,* 181–190.

Hart, J., & Gordon, B. (1990). Delineation of single-word semantic comprehension deficits in aphasia, with anatomical correlation. *Annals of Neurology, 27,* 226–231.

Hatfield, F. M. (1985). Visual and phonological factors in acquired dysgraphia. *Neuropsychologia, 23,* 13–29.

Hatfield, F. M., & Patterson, K. (1983). Phonological spelling. *Quarterly Journal of Experimental Psychology, 35A,* 451–468.

Heilman, K. M., Watson, R. T., & Valenstein, E. (1993). Neglect and related disorders. In K. M. Heilman & E. Valenstein (Eds.), *Clinical neuropsychology.* New York: Oxford University Press.

Hillis, A. E., & Caramazza, A. (1989). The graphemic buffer and attentional mechanisms. *Brain and Language, 36,* 208–235.

Hillis, A. E., & Caramazza, A. (1990). Where do semantic errors come from? *Cortex, 26,* 95–122.

Hillis, A. E., & Caramazza, A. (1991). Mechanisms for accessing lexical representations for output: Evidence from a category-specific semantic deficit. *Brain and Language, 40,* 106–144.

Hillis, A. E., & Caramazza, A. (1995). Spatially specific deficits in processing graphemic representations in reading and writing. *Brain and Language, 48,* 263–308.

Hillis, A. E., Rapp, B. C., & Caramazza, A. (1999). When a rose is a rose in speech but a tulip in writing. *Cortex, 35,* 337–356.

Hodges, J. R. (1991). Pure apraxic agraphia with recovery after drainage of a left frontal cyst. *Cortex, 27,* 469–473.

Hodges, J. R., Patterson, K. Oxbury, S., & Funnell, E. (1992). Semantic dementia: Progressive fluent aphasia with temporal lobe atrophy. *Brain, 115,* 1783–1806.

Holmes, G. (1939). The cerebellum of man. *Brain, 62,* 1–30.

Horwitz, B., Rumsey, J. M., & Donohue, B. C. (1998). Functional connectivity of the angular gyrus in normal reading and dyslexia. *Proceedings of the National Academy of Sciences, 95,* 8939–8944.

Howard, D. Patterson, K., Wise, R., Brown, W. D., Friston, K., Weiller, C., & Frackowiak, R. (1992). The cortical localization of the lexicons. *Brain, 115,* 1769–1782.

Hughes, J. C., Graham, N., Patterson, K., & Hodges, J. R. (1997). Dysgraphia in mild dementia of Alzheimer's type. *Neuropsychologia, 35,* 533–545.

Kapur, N., & Lawton, N. F. (1983). Dysgraphia for letters: a form of motor memory deficit. *Journal of Neurology, Neurosurgery, and Psychiatry, 46,* 573–575.

Kartsounis, L. D. (1992). Selective lower-case letter ideational dygraphia. *Cortex, 28,* 145–150.

Kato, C., Isoda, H., Takehara, Y., Matsuo, K., Moriya, T., & Nakai, T. (1999). Involvement of motor cortices in retrieval of kanji studied by functional MRI. *NeuroReport, 10,* 1335–1339.

Katz, R.B. (1991). Limited retention of information in the graphemic buffer. Cortex, 27, 111-119.

Kawamura, M., Hirayama, K., & Yamamoto, H. (1989). Different interhemispheric transfer of Kanji and Kana writing evidenced by a case with left unilateral agraphia without apraxia. *Brain, 112,* 1011–1018.

Kertesz, A., Davidson, W., & McCabe, P. (1998). Primary progressive semantic aphasia: A case study. *Journal of the International Neuropsychological Society, 4,* 388–398.

Kim, J. S., Im, J. H., Kwon, S. U., Kang, J. H., & Lee, M. C. (1998). Micrographia after thalamo-mesencephalic infarction: Evidence for striatal dopaminergic dysfunction. *Neurology, 51,* 625–627.

Kinsbourne, M., & Rosenfield, D. B. (1974). Agraphia selective for written spelling: An experimental case study. *Brain and Language, 1,* 215–225.

Klatka, L. A., Depper, M. H., & Marini, A. M. (1998). Infarction in the territory of the anterior cerebral artery. *Neurology, 51,* 620–622.

Kremin, H. (1987). Is there more than ah-oh-oh? Alternative strategies for writing and repeating lexically. In M. Coltheart, G. Sartori, & R. Job (Eds.), *The cognitive neuropsychology of language.* London: Lawrence Erlbaum.

Lambert, J., Viader, F., Eustache, F., & Morin, P. (1994). Contribution to peripheral agraphia: A case of post-allographic impairment? *Cognitive Neuropsychology, 11,* 35–55.

Langmore, S. E., & Canter, G. J. (1983). Written spelling deficit of Broca's aphasics. *Brain and Language, 18,* 293–314.

Lauritzen, M., Henriksen, L., & Lassen, N. A. (1981). Regional cerebral blood flow during rest and skilled hand movements by Xenon-133 inhalation and emission computerized tomography. *Journal of Cerebral Blood Flow and Metabolism, 1,* 385–389.

Lebrun, Y. (1976). Neurolinguistic models of language and speech. In H. Whitaker & H. A. Whitaker (Eds.), *Studies in neurolinguistics, Vol. 1.* New York: Academic Press.

Lebrun, Y. (1985). Disturbances of written language and associated abilities following damage to the right hemisphere. *Applied Psycholinguistics, 6,* 231–260.

Levine, D. N., Mani, R. B., & Calvanio, R. (1988). Pure agraphia and Gerstmann's syndrome as a visuospatial-language dissociation: An experimental case study. *Brain and Language, 35,* 172–196.

Lewitt, P. A. (1983). Micrographia as a focal sign of neurological disease. *Journal of Neurology, Neurosurgery, and Psychiatry, 46,* 1152–1157.

Liepmann, H., & Maas, O. (1907). Fall von Linksseitiger Agraphie und Apraxie bei Rechsseitiger Lähmung. *Journal für Psychologie und Neurologie, 10,* 214–227.

Lüders, H., Lesser, R. P., Hahn, J., Dinner, D. S., Morris, H. H., Wyllie, E., & Godoy, J. (1991). Basal temporal language area. *Brain, 114,* 743–754.

Luria, A. R. (1980). *Higher cortical function in man* (2nd ed.). New York: Basic Books.

Marcie, P., & Hécaen, H. (1979). Agraphia: writing disorders associated with unilateral cortical lesions. In K. M. Heilman & E. Valenstein (Eds.), *Clinical neuropsychology.* New York: Oxford University Press.

Margolin, D. I. (1984). The neuropsychology of writing and spelling: Semantic, phonological, motor and perceptual processes. *Quarterly Journal of Experimental Psychology, 36A,* 459–489.

Margolin, D. I., & Binder, L. (1984). Multiple component agraphia in a patient with atypical cerebral dominance: An error analysis. *Brain and Language, 22,* 26–40.

Margolin, D. I., & Wing, A. M. (1983). Agraphia and

micrographia: Clinical manifestations of motor programming and performance disorders. *Acta Psychologica, 54*, 263-283.

Margolin, D. I., & Goodman-Schulman, R. (1992). Oral and written spelling impairments. In D. I. Margolin (Ed.), *Cognitive neuropsychology in clinical practice*. New York: Oxford University Press.

Marin, O. S. M. (1980). CAT scans of five deep dyslexic patients. In M. Coltheart, K. Patterson, & J. C. Marshall (Eds.), *Deep dyslexia*. London: Routledge and Kegan Paul.

Martin, A. (1987). Representation of semantic and spatial knowledge in Alzheimer's patients: Implications for models of preserved learning in amnesia. *Journal of Clinical and Experimental Neuropsychology, 9*, 191-224.

Martinez-Vila, E., Artieda, J., & Obeso, J. A. (1988). Micrographia secondary to lenticular h e m a t o m a. *Journal of Neurology, Neurosurgery, and Psychiatry, 51*, 1353-1356.

Mazziotta, J. C., Phelps, M. E., & Wapenski, J. A. (1985). Human cerebral motor system metabolic responses in health and disease. *Journal of Cerebral Blood Flow and Metabolism, Supplement 1*, S213-S214.

McCarthy, G., Nobre, A. C., Bentin, S., & Spencer, D. D. (1995). Language related field potentials in the anterior-medial temporal lobe: I. Intracranial distribution and neural generators. *Journal of Neuroscience, 15*, 1080-1089.

McLennan, J. E., Nakano, K., Tyler, H. R., & Schwab, R. S. (1977). Micrographia in Parkinson's disease. *Journal of the Neurological Sciences, 15*, 141-152.

Menard, M. T., Kosslyn, S. M., Thompson, W. L., Alpert, N. M., & Rauch, S. L. (1996). Encoding words and pictures: A positron emission tomography study. *Neuropsychologia, 34*, 185-194.

Merton, P. A. (1972). How we control the contraction of our muscles. *Scientific American, 226*, 30-37.

Miceli, G., Benvegnu, B., Capasso, R., & Caramazza, A. (1997). The independence of phonological and orthographic lexical forms: Evidence from aphasia. *Cognitive Neuropsychology, 14*, 35-69.

Miceli, G., Silveri, M. C., & Caramazza, A. (1987). The role of the phoneme-to-grapheme conversion system and of the graphemic buffer in writing. In M. Coltheart, G. Sartori, & R. Job (Eds.), *The cognitive neuropsychology of language*. London: Lawrence Erlbaum.

Monsell, S. (1984). Components of working memory underlying verbal skills: a "distributed capacities" view. A tutorial review. In H. Bouma & D. G. Bouwhuis (Eds.), *Attention and performance X: Control of language processes*. Hillsdale, NJ: Lawrence Erlbaum.

Morton, J., & Patterson, K. (1980). A new attempt at an interpretation, or, an attempt at a new interpretation. In M. Coltheart, K. Patterson, & J. C. Marshall (Eds.), *Deep dyslexia*. London: Routledge & Kegan Paul.

Mummery, C. J., Patterson, K., Wise, J. S. R., Vandenbergh, R., Price, C. J., & Hodges, J. R. (1999). Disrupted temporal lobe connections in semantic dementia. *Brain, 122*, 61-73.

Murray, B. J., Llinas, R., Caplan, L. R., Scammell, T., & Pascual-Leone, A. (2000). Cerebral deep venous thrombosis presenting as acute micrographia and hypophonia. *Neurology, 54*, 751-753.

Nakamura, K., Honda, M., Okada, T., Hanakawa, T., Toma, K., Fukuyama, H., Konishi, J., & Shibasaki, H. (2000). Participation of the left posterior inferior temporal cortex in writing and mental recall of kanji orthography: A functional MRI study. *Brain, 123*, 954-967.

Neils, J., Roeltgen, D. P., & Constantinidou, F. (1995). Decline in homophone spelling associated with loss of semantic influence on spelling in Alzheimer's disease. *Brain and Language, 49*, 27-49.

Nobre, A. C., Allison, T., & McCarthy, G. (1994). Word recognition in the human inferior temporal lobe. *Nature, 372*, 260-263.

Nobre, A. C., & McCarthy, G. (1995). Language related field potentials in the anterior-medial temporal lobe: II. Effects of word type and semantic priming. *Journal of Neuroscience, 15*, 1090-1098.

Nolan, K. N., & Caramazza, A. (1983). An analysis of writing in a case of deep dyslexia. *Brain and Language, 20*, 305-328.

Ogden, J. A. (1996). Phonological dyslexia and phonological dysgraphia following left and right hemispherectomy. *Neuropsychologia, 34*, 905-918.

Ogle, J. W. (1867). Aphasia and agraphia. *Report of the Medical Research Counsel of St. George's Hospital (London), 2*, 83-122.

Oliveira, R. M., Gurd, J. M., Nixon, P., Marshall, J. C., & Passingham, R. E. (1997). Micrographia in Parkinson's disease: The effect of providing external cues. *Journal of Neurology, Neurosurgery, and Psychiatry, 63*, 429-433.

Otsuki, M., Soma, Y., Arai, T., Otsuka, A., & Tsuji, S. (1999). Pure apraxic agraphia with abnormal writing stroke sequences: Report of a Japanese patient with a left superior parietal hemorrhage. *Journal of Neurology, Neurosurgery, and Psychiatry, 66*, 233-237.

Papagno, C. (1992). A case of peripheral dysgraphia. *Cognitive Neuropsychology, 9*, 259-270.

Parkin, A. J. (1993). Progressive aphasia without dementia: A clinical and cognitive neuropsychological analysis. *Brain and Language, 44*, 201-220.

Patterson, K. (1986). Lexical but nonsemantic spelling? *Cognitive Neuropsychology, 3*, 341-367.

Patterson, K., & Hodges, J. R. (1992). Deterioration of word meaning: implications for reading. *Neuropsychologia, 30*, 1025-1040.

Patterson, K., & Hodges, J. R. (1995). Disorders of semantic memory. In A. D. Baddeley, B. A. Wilson, & F. N. Watts (Eds.), *Handbook of memory disorders*. Chichester: John Wiley and Sons.

Patterson, K. E., & Kay, J. (1982). Letter-by-letter reading: Psychological descriptions of a neurological syndrome. *Quarterly Journal of Experimental Psychology, 34A*, 411-441.

Patterson, K. E., Marshall, J. C, & Coltheart, M. (1985). *Surface dyslexia: Neuropsychological and cognitive studies of phonological reading*. London: Lawrence Erlbaum.

Patterson, K., & Shewell, C. (1987). Speak and spell: Disssociations and word-class effects. In M. Coltheart, G. Sartori, & R. Job (Eds.), *The cognitive neuropsychology of language*. London: Lawrence Erlbaum.

Patterson, K., & Wing, A. M. (1989). Processes in handwriting: a case for case. *Cognitive Neuropsychology, 6*, 1-23.

Paulesu, E., Frith, C. D., & Frackowiak, R. S. J. (1993). The neural correlates of the verbal component of working memory. *Nature, 362*, 342-345.

Paulesu, E., Frith, U., Snowling, M., Gallagher, A., Morton, J., Frackowiak, R. S. J., & Frith, C. D. (1996). Is developmental dyslexia a disconnection syndrome? Evidence from PET scanning. *Brain, 119*, 143-157.

Peniello, M.-J., Lambert, J., Eustache, F., Petit-Taboué,

M. C., Barré, L., Viader, F., Morin, P., Lechevalier, B., & Baron, J.-C. (1995). A PET study of the functional neuroanatomy of writing impairment in Alzheimer's disease: the role of the left supramarginal and angular gyri. *Brain, 118,* 697–707.

Petrides, M., Alivisatos, B., & Evans, A. C. (1995). Functional activation of the human ventrolateral frontal cortex during mnemonic retrieval of verbal information. *Proceedings of the National Academy of Sciences, 92,* 5803–5807.

Pitres, A. (1894). Rapport sur la question des agraphies. Bordeaux: Congres Francais de Médecine Interne.

Platel, H., Lambert, J., Eustache, F., Cadet, B., Dary, M., Viader, F., & Lechevalier, B. (1993). Characteristic evolution of writing impairment in Alzheimer's disease. *Neuropsychologia, 31,* 1147–1158.

Posteraro, L., Zinelli, P., & Mazzucchi, A. (1988). Selective impairment of the graphemic buffer in acquired dysgraphia: a case study. *Brain and Language, 35,* 274–286.

Price, C. J., Moore, C. J., Humphreys, G. W., & Wise, R. J. S. (1997). Segregating semantic from phonological processes during reading. *Journal of Cognitive Neuroscience, 9,* 727–733.

Price, C. J., Wise, J. S. R., Watson, J. D. G., Patterson, K., Howard, D., & Frackowiak, R. S. J. (1994). Brain activity during reading: The effect of exposure duration and task. *Brain, 117,* 1255–1269.

Rapcsak, S. Z. (1997). Disorders of writing. In L. J. G. Rothi & K. M. Heilman (Eds.), *Apraxia: The neuropsychology of action.* Hove, England: Psychology Press.

Rapcsak, S. Z., Arthur, S. A., Bliklen, D. A., & Rubens, A. B. (1989). Lexical agraphia in Alzheimer's disease. *Archives of Neurology, 46,* 66–68.

Rapcsak, S. Z., Beeson, P. M., & Rubens, A. B. (1991). Writing with the right hemisphere. *Brain and Language, 41,* 510–530.

Rapcsak, S. Z., & Rubens, A. B. (1990). Disruption of semantic influence on writing following a left prefrontal lesion. *Brain and Language, 38,* 334–344.

Rapcsak, S. Z., Rubens, A. B., & Laguna, J. F. (1990). From letters to words: Procedures for word recognition in letter-by-letter reading. *Brain and Language, 38,* 504–514.

Rapp, B., Benzing, L., & Caramazza, A. (1997). The autonomy of lexical orthography. *Cognitive Neuropsychology, 14,* 71–104.

Rapp, B., & Caramazza, A. (1997). From graphemes to abstract letter shapes: Levels of representation in written spelling. *Journal of Experimental Psychology: Human Perception and Performance, 23,* 1130–1152.

Roeltgen, D. P. (1993). Agraphia. In K. M. Heilman & E. Valenstein (Eds.), *Clinical neuropsychology.* New York: Oxford University Press.

Roeltgen, D. P. (1994). Localization of lesions in agraphia. In A. Kertesz (Ed.), *Localization and neuroimaging in neuropsychology.* San Diego: Academic Press.

Roeltgen, D. P., & Heilman, K. M. (1983). Apractic agraphia in a patient with normal praxis. *Brain and Language, 18,* 35–46.

Roeltgen, D. P., & Heilman, K. M. (1984). Lexical agraphia: Further support for the two-system hypothesis of linguistic agraphia. *Brain, 107,* 811–827.

Roeltgen, D. P., & Heilman, K. M. (1985). Review of agraphia and a proposal for an anatomically-based neuropsychological model of writing. *Applied Psycholinguistics, 6,* 205–230.

Roeltgen, D. P., Rothi, L. G., & Heilman, K. M. (1986).

Linguistic semantic agraphia: A dissociation of the lexical spelling system from semantics. *Brain and Language, 27,* 257–280.

Roeltgen, D. P., Sevush, S., & Heilman, K. M. (1983a). Phonological agraphia: Writing by the lexical-semantic route. *Neurology, 33,* 755–765.

Roeltgen, D. P., Sevush, S., & Heilman, K. M. (1983b). Pure Gerstmann's syndrome from a focal lesion. *Archives of Neurology, 40,* 46–47.

Ross, S. J. M., Graham, N., Stuart-Green, L., Prins, M., Xuereb, J., Patterson, K., & Hodges, J. R. (1996). Progressive biparietal atrophy: An atypical presentation of Alzheimer's disease. *Journal of Neurology, Neurosurgery, and Psychiatry, 61,* 388–395.

Rothi, L. J., & Heilman, K. M. (1981). Alexia and agraphia with spared spelling and letter recognition abilities. *Brain and Language, 12,* 1–13.

Rubens, A. B. (1975). Aphasia with infarction in the territory of the anterior cerebral artery. *Cortex, 11,* 239–250.

Salmon, E., Van der Linden, M., Collette, F., Delfiore, G., Maquet, P., Degueldre, C., Luxen, A., & Franck, G. (1996). Regional brain activity during working memory tasks. *Brain, 119,* 1617–1625.

Schwartz, M. F., Marin, O. S. M., & Saffran, E. M. (1979). Dissociations of language function in dementia: A case study. *Brain and Language, 7,* 277–306.

Seitz, R. J., Canavan, A. G. M., Yaguez, L., Herzog, H., Tellmann, L., Knorr, U., Huang, Y., & Homberg, V. (1997). Representations of graphomotor trajectories in the human parietal cortex: Evidence from controlled processing and automatic performance. *European Journal of Neuroscience, 9,* 378–389.

Seki, K., Ishiai, S., Koyama, Y., Sato, S., Hirabayashi, H., & Inaki, K. (1998). Effects of unilateral spatial neglect on spatial agraphia for kana and kanji letters. *Brain and Language, 63,* 256–275.

Shallice, T. (1981). Phonological agraphia and the lexical route in writing. *Brain, 104,* 413–429.

Shallice, T. (1988). *From neuropsychology to mental structure.* Cambridge: Cambridge University Press.

Shelton, J. R., & Weinrich, M. (1997). Further evidence of a dissociation between output phonological and orthographic lexicons: A case study. *Cognitive Neuropsychology, 14,* 105–129.

Shuren, J. E., Maher, L. M., & Heilman, K. M. (1996). The role of visual imagery in spelling. *Brain and Language, 52,* 365–372.

Silveri, M. C. (1996). Peripheral aspects of writing can be differentially affected by sensorial and attentional defect: Evidence from a patient with afferent dysgraphia and case dissociation. *Cortex, 32,* 155–172.

Silveri, M. C., Misciagna, S., Leggio, M. G., & Molinari, M. (1997). Spatial dysgraphia and cerebellar lesion: A case report. *Neurology, 48,* 1529–1532.

Smith, E. E., & Jonides, J. (1998). Neuroimaging analyses of human working memory. *Proceedings of the National Academy of Sciences, 95,* 12061–12068.

Smith, W. M., McCrary, J. W., & Smith, K. U. (1960). Delayed visual feedback and behavior. *Science, 132,* 1013–1014.

Smyth, M. M., & Silvers, G. (1987). Functions of vision in the control of handwriting. *Acta Psychologica, 65,* 47–64.

Snowden, J. S., Neary, D., Mann, D. M. A., Goulding, P. J., & Testa, H. J. (1992). Progressive language disorder due to lobar atrophy. *Annals of Neurology, 31,* 174–183.

Soma, Y., Sugishita, M., Kitamura, K., Maruyama, S., & Imanaga, H. (1989). Lexical agraphia in the Japanese language: Pure agraphia for Kanji due to left posteroinferior temporal lesions. *Brain, 112,* 1549–1561.

Sugishita, M., Takayama, Y., Shiono, T., Yoshikawa, K., & Takahashi, Y. (1996). Functional magnetic resonance imaging (fMRI) during mental writing with phonograms. *NeuroReport, 7,* 1917–1921.

Sugishita, M., Toyokura, Y., Yoshioka, M., & Yamada, R. (1980). Unilateral agraphia after section of the posterior half of the truncus of the corpus callosum. *Brain and Language, 9,* 215–225.

Trojano, L., & Chiacchio, L. (1994). Pure dysgraphia with relative sparing of lower-case writing. *Cortex, 30,* 499–507.

Ungerleider, L. G., Courtney, S. M., & Haxby, J. V. (1998). A neural system for human working memory. *Proceedings of the National Academy of Sciences, 95,* 883–890.

Vandenberghe, R., Price, C., Wise, R., Josephs, O., & Frackowiak, R. S. J. (1996). Functional anatomy of a common semantic system for words and pictures. *Nature, 383,* 254–256.

Van Galen, G. P. (1991). Handwriting: issues for a psychomotor theory. *Human Movement Science, 10,* 165–192.

Vanier, M., & Caplan, D. (1985). CT correlates of surface dyslexia. In K. E. Patterson, J. C. Marshall & M. Coltheart (Eds.), *Surface dyslexia: Neuropsychological and cognitive studies of phonological reading.* London: Lawrence Erlbaum.

Watson, R. T., Fleet, W. S., Rothi, L. J. G., & Heilman, K. M. (1986). Apraxia and the supplementary motor area. *Archives of Neurology, 43,* 787–792.

Watson, R. T., & Heilman, K. M. (1983). Callosal apraxia. *Brain, 106,* 391–403.

Weekes, B. S. (1994). A cognitive-neuropsychological analysis of allograph errors from a patient with acquired dysgraphia. *Aphasiology, 8,* 409–425.

Weekes, B. (1995). Right hemisphere writing and spelling. *Aphasiology, 9,* 305–319.

Wernicke, C. (1874). *Der Aphasische Symptomenkomplex.* Breslau: Cohn & Weigert.

Wernicke, C. (1886). Nervenheilkunde: Die neueren Arbeiten über Aphasie. *Fortschritte der Medizin, 4,* 463–482.

Wing, A. M., & Baddeley, A. D. (1980). Spelling errors in handwriting: A corpus and a distributional analysis. In U. Frith (Ed.), *Cognitive processes in spelling.* London: Academic Press.

Wright, C. E. (1990). Generalized motor programs: re-evaluating claims of effector independence in writing. In M. Jeannerod (Ed.), *Attention and performance,* Vol. XXIII. Hillsdale, NJ: Lawrence Erlbaum.

Yamadori, A., Nagashima, T., & Tamaki, N. (1983). Ideogram writing in a disconnection syndrome. *Brain and Language, 19,* 346–356.

Yamadori, A., Osumi, Y., Ikeda, H., & Kanazawa, Y. (1980). Left unilateral agraphia and tactile anomia: Disturbances seen after occlusion of the anterior cerebral artery. *Archives of Neurology, 37,* 88–91.

Zaidel, E. (1990). Language functions in the two hemispheres following complete cerebral commissurotomy and hemispherectomy. In F. Boller & J. Grafman (Eds.), *Handbook of neuropsychology: Vol. 4.* Amsterdam: Elsevier Science Publishers.

Zattore, R. J., Evans, A. C., Meyer, E., & Gjedde, A. (1992). Lateralization of phonetic and pitch discrimination is speech processing. *Nature, 256,* 846–849.

Zesiger, P., Pegna, A., & Rilliet, B. (1994). Unilateral dysgraphia of the dominant hand in a left-hander: A disruption of graphic motor selection. *Cortex, 30,* 673–683.

6

Clinical Diagnosis and Treatment of Spelling Disorders

Pelagie M. Beeson
Steven Z. Rapcsak

INTRODUCTION

Daily needs for spelling range from jotting down lists of items to buy at the store or "things to do," to composition of electronic mail messages, to carefully crafted literary prose or scholarly papers. While these activities require varying degrees of linguistic competence, they all depend on the ability to spell single words. Clearly some individuals are more dependent on the written word than others, so that an acquired impairment of spelling will have varied impact in accordance with one's lifestyle. Isolated impairments of spelling or writing can result in significant reduction in one's ability to exchange information, leading to marked changes in vocational and personal activities. More often, acquired agraphia is part of a central language impairment, as is common in aphasia. In that context, the loss or impairment of written communication compounds the difficulties posed by disturbances of spoken communication.

Given that spoken language is the primary means of daily commerce for most people, it is not surprising that aphasia treatment typically is focused on spoken rather than written communication. That fact does not diminish the importance of clinical assessment and treatment of writing at the appropriate time in the rehabilitation process. In fact, in some cases of aphasia, writing may be better preserved than spoken language so that it becomes the dominant means of communication (Ellis, Miller, & Sin, 1983; Levine, Calvanio, & Popovics, 1982). Similarly, writing may prove to be more amenable to remediation than speech in some patients (Beeson, 1999; Hillis Trupe, 1986). Writing also may serve to facilitate spoken productions, so that it may be an important aspect of strategic compensation for impaired communication abilities (De Partz, 1986; Holland, 1998; Nickels, 1992). Thus, the clinical assessment and treatment of writing may be motivated by varied goals: to provide a substitute for spoken communication, to serve as an adjunct or stimulant for spoken language, or to reestablish premorbid writing skills.

In this chapter, we will describe clinical tasks that allow the examination of the cognitive processes necessary for writing that were detailed in chapters 4 and 5, followed by a review of evidence-based approaches to agraphia treatment. It is our premise that careful determination of the status of the component processes for writing should lead to the formulation of hypotheses regarding the locus (or loci) of impairment and an understanding of preserved processes. In turn, this information provides the rationale for the selection or development of particular agraphia treatment approaches. An individual's response to treatment may further clarify the nature of the impairment, and thus offer additional insight to direct the rehabilitation efforts.

CLINICAL EVALUATION OF SPELLING

A comprehensive evaluation of spelling should include a variety of tasks and stimulus materials designed to examine the status of central and peripheral spelling processes. As indicated in table 6.1, different spelling tasks rely on certain processes and representations but not others, so that comparative performance across several tasks helps to isolate the locus of impairment. The relationships among the processes that support spelling and writing are depicted in figure 6.1, which is an elaborated version of the model presented in chapter 5 of this volume, including the various input and output modalities that may be examined during clinical evaluation. As discussed in chapter 5, the central components include the lexical-semantic and phonological spelling routes and the graphemic buffer. The lexical-semantic route supports conceptually mediated spelling that is critical for spontaneous written communication and is based on the association between word meanings and orthographic word forms (indicated in figure 6.1 by the arrow from the semantic system to the orthographic output lexicon). The phonological route can be used for spelling both familiar words and unfamiliar words or nonwords, and depends on direct transcoding between phonological and orthographic representations. Although a word-level phonological spelling route has been postulated (Margolin, 1984; Patterson, 1986; Patterson & Shewell, 1987; indicated as word-level POC in figure 6.1), there are no clinical tasks that allow for direct examination of this route, nor is an impairment of this route specifically targeted in rehabilitation efforts. Therefore, in this chapter we will use the term *phonological spelling* to refer only to procedures that are operating at the subword level (that is, phoneme-grapheme conversion). Orthographic information derived from subword-level phonological procedures is held in the graphemic buffer as graphic motor programs are activated; however, it is also likely that such information interacts with the orthographic output lexicon (as indicated in figure 6.1 by the dashed arrow from subword-level phonological-to-orthographic conversion [POC]).

A detailed analysis of impaired and preserved spelling processes and an examination of spelling errors should provide a clear picture of the agraphia profile. It also should be possible to determine whether the patient fits the diagnostic criteria of the various agraphia syndromes reviewed in chapter 5 and summarized in table 6.2. We acknowledge that the use of syndrome labels can be justifiably criticized for the potential oversimplification of the nature of the impairment and for the fact that a given syndrome may reflect damage to different components of the spelling process (as will be discussed below). Despite these limitations, however, syndrome classifications provide the benefit of a shorthand to communicate the presence of a symptom cluster and are useful in a clinical context. For that reason, we refer to the syndrome labels, but note their limitations and emphasize that many individual patterns of acquired agraphia fail to conform to a recognized syndrome and are best characterized by the description of the impaired and preserved processes.

Assessing the Lexical-Semantic Route

The lexical-semantic spelling route supports all conceptually driven writing tasks, so it is critical for most everyday writing activities. To determine the functional status of this spelling route, it is useful to obtain a sample of self-generated written communication before proceeding with a structured assessment of single-word writing. Spontaneous writing can be elicited as a descriptive narrative or as a picture description task, such as written description of standard stimuli like the "cookie theft" picture from the *Boston Diagnostic Aphasia Examination* (Goodglass

Table 6.1

Tasks Used for the Assessment of Spelling. Check Marks Indicate Those Processes or Representations that are Necessary to Accomplish the Various Tasks.

| | Central spelling processes | | | | Peripheral spelling processes | | |
| | Lexical-semantic processes | | Phonological processes | Central-peripheral interface | | | |
Tasks	Semantic representation	Orthographic output lexicon	Phoneme-grapheme conversion	Graphemic buffer	Allographic conversion	Graphic motor programs	Letter name selection
Written Naming	√	√		√	√	√	
Dictation							
Writing to dictation	√[a]	√		√	√	√	
Writing homophones	√	√		√	√	√	
Typing or anagram spelling	√[a]	√		√	√[b]		
Oral spelling	√[a]	√		√			√
Writing nonwords			√	√	√	√	
Copy							
Delayed copy		√		√	√	√	
Direct copy		√[c]			√[c]	√	
Case conversion					√		

[a] These tasks typically activate the semantic representation, but may be accomplished via word- or subword-level phonological spelling procedures, therefore bypassing semantics.

[b] Typing and anagram spelling could be accomplished with reliance on recognition (rather than selection) of letter shape.

[c] Direct copy may be accomplished without activation of orthographic output lexicon, letter shape selection, or graphic motor programs if performed in a pictorial (nonlinguistic) fashion.

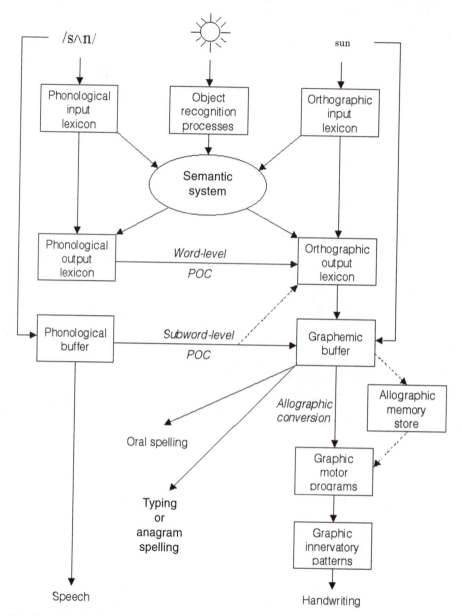

Figure 6.1. Cognitive information processing model of spelling that depicts several output modalites (oral spelling, handwriting, and typing or anagram spelling). POC = phonological-to-orthographic conversion.

& Kaplan, 1976/1983) or the "picnic scene" from the *Western Aphasia Battery* (Kertesz, 1982). Written narratives may provide a sample of spelling errors and reveal the types of words that are spelled in error or omitted. This information provides clues regarding the nature of the spelling impairment that may be further investigated using carefully constructed word lists. Written narratives also allow for examination of lexical retrieval, syntactic structure, and other linguistic and cognitive abilities that are not the focus of this chapter but clearly are of interest as well. Writing should be compared to spoken language to determine if the observed agraphia reflects impairments to lexical-semantic processes that are common to writing and speaking, or whether the impairment is specific to writing.

Table 6.2

Observed Effects on Spelling Accuracy Typically Associated with Impairment to Certain Spelling Processes, and the Syndrome Labels Associated with the Spelling Profile.

HF = high frequency; LF = low frequency; HI = high imagery; LI = low imagery; N = nouns; F = functors; reg = regularly spelled; irregular = irregularly spelled.

Locus of Damage	Syndrome label	Effect								
		Dictation> spont. writing	Word freq. HF>LF	Image HI>LI	Gram. class N>F	Semantic errors	Homo-phone errors	Unable to spell nonwords	Regularity reg> irregular	Length short> long
Semantic system	*Semantic agraphia*	√	√				√			
Orthographic output lexicon	*Lexical agraphia*		√						√	
Phonological spelling route	*Phonological agraphia*		√	√	√			√		
Phonological and lexical-semantic spelling routes	*Deep agraphia*		√	√	√	√		√		
Graphemic buffer	*Buffer impairment*									√

Written Naming

Just as written narratives and picture descriptions allow for the assessment of conceptually motivated spellings, written naming of pictured stimuli allows for examination of spellings derived from semantic representations. Relatively common, concrete nouns are typically used as picture stimuli for a written naming task. Adequate visual perception and object recognition must occur in order to activate the appropriate semantic representation for the pictured item, which should in turn activate the appropriate entry in the orthographic output lexicon. It is likely that presentation of pictured items evokes overt or subvocal spoken naming, but the written naming task can be accomplished without activation of the phonological representation (Ellis et al., 1983; Levine et al., 1982). Failure to correctly write the name of a visually perceived item may reflect impairment to any of the necessary central or peripheral spelling processes indicated in table 6.1. Clues regarding the locus of impairment may be derived from a comparison of written naming to writing to dictation. For example, if written naming is impaired relative to writing to dictation, it may reflect damage to the semantic system or a failure of the semantic system to activate the appropriate representation in the orthographic output lexicon, a profile that is characteristic of semantic agraphia (Roeltgen, Rothi, & Heilman, 1986; Rapcsak & Rubens, 1990).

Writing to Dictation

Writing familiar words to dictation is typically accomplished via the lexical-semantic route in which the phonological input lexicon activates the appropriate semantic representation that in turn addresses the corresponding entry in the orthographic output lexicon (see figure 6.1). If the phonological input lexicon is selectively damaged or fails to appropriately address the semantic system, then writing to dictation will be impaired relative to tasks that do not depend on auditory input, such as spontaneous writing, written picture description, and written naming. Adequate processing of auditory input can be confirmed by means of spoken word-to-picture matching tasks. Written spelling to dictation should be contrasted with other output modalities, such as oral spelling, typing, or spelling with anagram letters. A central spelling impairment will result in similar spelling errors for a given patient across modalities because they all depend upon information from the lexical-semantic system. In contrast, a peripheral agraphia may result in modality-specific errors such as the case in which poor written spelling is accompanied by preserved oral spelling.

Writing single words to dictation allows for control over a number of lexical-semantic features that may influence spelling accuracy, such as word frequency, imageability (or concreteness), grammatical class, and morphological complexity. A number of research laboratories have created controlled word lists to be used for testing spelling, and several are available in published form, including the *Psycholinguistic Assessments of Language Processing in Aphasia* (PALPA; Kay, Lesser, & Coltheart, 1992) and *The Johns Hopkins University Dysgraphia Battery* (Goodman & Caramazza, 1986a, published in Beeson & Hillis, 2001). It is assumed that most literate adults are familiar with the words included in such lists and can spell them with relatively high accuracy so that spelling is not significantly affected by linguistic variables. This assumption is supported by normative data in the PALPA (Kay et al., 1992); however, it is important to take into consideration premorbid spelling abilities and to tailor the selection of stimuli accordingly. For instance, it is not uncommon for neurologically normal individuals to occasionally produce phonologically plausible errors in spelling irregular words (for example, *February* → *Febuary*), so that these types of errors may be more common in patients who were poor spellers premorbidly.

In competent spellers, spelling accuracy is not significantly affected by orthographic regularity; that is, the extent to which sounds map onto orthography in a predictable manner.[1] Therefore, a comparison of spelling accuracy for orthographically regularly versus irregular words provides clues as to whether spelling is accomplished via lexical-semantic or the phonological spelling route. When spelling accuracy is significantly better for regularly versus irregularly spelled words, it is suggestive of dependence on the phonological spelling route due to damage to the lexical-semantic route. Spellings that are assembled using knowledge of sound-to-letter correspondences (that is, the phoneme-grapheme conversion mechanism) often reflect phonologically plausible renditions of the target word (for example, *circuit → serkit*). Such errors are characteristic of lexical (or surface) agraphia (Beauvois & Dérouesné, 1981; Behrmann, 1987; Goodman-Schulman & Caramazza, 1987; Roeltgen & Heilman, 1984). When there is reliance on phonological spelling and a lack of semantic mediation, homophone errors may occur (*suite → sweet*) as observed in semantic agraphia (Roeltgen et al., 1986; Rapcsak & Rubens, 1990).

When spelling is accomplished by exclusive reliance on the lexical-semantic route, performance may be influenced by lexical-semantic variables such as word frequency[2] (better spelling of high-frequency words like *dollar* or *sister* compared to low-frequency words like *fabric* or *bugle*; Ellis & Young, 1996; Morton, 1969), grammatical word class (better spelling of nouns than of function words; Badecker, Hillis, & Caramazza, 1990; Baxter & Warrington, 1985; Hillis & Caramazza, 1994) and concreteness (better spelling of concrete words such as *table* than of abstract words such as *wish*). These effects are typically observed in agraphia syndromes characterized by damage to the phonological spelling route, including phonological and deep agraphia (Shallice, 1981; Bub & Kertesz, 1982a; Roeltgen, Sevush, & Heilman, 1983; Roeltgen & Heilman, 1984; Baxter & Warrington, 1985; Goodman-Schulman & Caramazza, 1987). Semantic errors (for example, *sister → daughter*), which are the hallmark of deep agraphia, are thought to reflect impairment of the lexical-semantic spelling route that is concomitant with an impaired phonological route (Bub & Kertesz, 1982b; Marshall & Newcombe, 1966; Newcombe & Marshall, 1984; Nolan & Caramazza, 1983; Hatfield, 1985). In addition to the error types described above, damage to the lexical-semantic route may result in substitution of orthographically similar words (for example, *grass → grade*), and phonologically implausible spellings that may or may not reflect partial lexical knowledge (for example, *brother → bothr; brother → sivnre*).

Assessing the Phonological Spelling Route

The integrity of the phonological spelling route can be examined in a relatively direct manner with the spelling of pronounceable nonwords (that is, pseudowords like *flig*). If nonword spelling is good, it can be assumed that the ability to convert sounds to corresponding graphemes is intact, and thus the phonological spelling route is available. If nonword spelling is notably impaired relative to real word spelling, it suggests a deficit at some level of the phoneme-grapheme conversion process. Nonword spelling will be poor for both written and oral spelling because they depend on the same phonological processes. Attempts at spelling nonwords may be phonologically implausible (*flig → poame*) or may reflect the substitution of phonologically or orthographically similar real words (*merber → member*). Such lexicalization errors suggest

---

[1]Researchers have calculated phoneme-grapheme probabilities based on norms such as those provided by Hanna, Hanna, Hodges, and Rudorf (1966). For example, Goodman and Caramazza (1986a) defined high-probability words as those with greater than 50 percent probability of being accurately spelled by use of phoneme-grapheme correspondence mappings and low-probability words as those with less than 10 percent probability of being accurately spelled by use of phoneme-grapheme correspondence.

[2]High- versus low-frequency distinctions have been set, for example, as greater than fifty occurences per million and fewer than twenty-five occurences per million, respectively (Goodman & Caramazza, 1986a).

persistent attempts to spell nonwords via a lexical-semantic strategy. To further assess pho-neme-grapheme conversion abilities, characteristic sounds for single letters may be presented orally for translation to the appropriate grapheme. Preserved phoneme-grapheme conversion for single sounds but not for words or pseudowords suggests impairment in the ability to segment words into their constituent sounds (Roeltgen et al., 1983; Bolla-Wilson, Speedie, & Robinson, 1985).

When real word and nonword spelling are both impaired, it may reflect concomitant impair-ment to lexical-semantic and phonological spelling routes, or damage to any of the more peripheral spelling processes that are common to both real word and nonword spelling, includ-ing the graphemic buffer, letter selection processes, or graphomotor control. Assessment of the graphemic buffer and the peripheral spelling processes should add the necessary information to further isolate the impairment.

Assessing the Graphemic Buffer

Graphemic representations derived from either the lexical-semantic or phonological spelling routes must be held in a short-term storage mechanism, referred to as the graphemic buffer, while peripheral writing processes are planned and implemented (Miceli, Silveri, & Caramazza, 1985; Caramazza, Miceli, Villa, & Romani, 1987). The graphemic buffer serves as an interface between central and peripheral spelling processes, so impairment at this level will affect the spelling of words and nonwords in all output modalities (for example, writing, typing, oral spelling). Given that word length is an important determinant of the amount of time an item needs to be held in the buffer, errors are expected to be more frequent with longer words when the buffer is impaired. Additionally, letters at the beginning of words tend to be better pre-served, with errors occurring most often toward the end or in the middle of words (Katz, 1991; Caramazza et al., 1987). Word lists that are controlled for word length (and balanced for other lexical-semantic features such as frequency, imagery, and grammatical class) can be used to test the integrity of the graphemic buffer.

When the graphemic buffer is impaired, spelling errors typically take the form of letter substitutions (*water* → *waten*), additions (*apple* → *appler*), deletions (*airplane* → *airplne*), and transpositions (*chapter* → *chatper*). If the impairment is specific to the graphemic buffer, then no lexical-semantic effects (that is, frequency, imagery, or grammatical class) should be ob-served. Similarly, if the peripheral writing processes are spared, performance on the direct copy and the transcoding of letter case should be intact, but performance for delayed copy is likely to be impaired relative to direct copy because of the demand for temporary storage of graphemic information.

Assessing Peripheral Writing Processes

In order for abstract graphemic information to be realized as a written word, the appropriate letter shapes must be selected and the motor programs implemented to achieve the necessary movements of the pen (Ellis, 1982; Goodman & Caramazza, 1986b). Figure 6.1 depicts the peripheral processes for handwriting as they follow the central spelling processes. The allographic conversion process involves not only the determination the appropriate letter identity but the specification of the particular physical characteristics including case (upper versus lower) and style (print versus cursive). To assess the ability to select correct letter shapes, a transcoding task can be administered that requires conversion of words (or individual letters) from upper-to lowercase letters, and vice versa. Impaired access or damage to information about letter shapes (that is, allographs) can result in errors in letter selection and disorders of letter production that will be evident on all tasks requiring written spelling (for example, writing words and nonwords to dictation, written naming, spontaneous written narrative, and transcoding tasks). In marked contrast, oral spelling of dictated words and nonwords will be preserved.

Direct copying tasks provide an examination of writing without demands on central spelling processes, and provide a means to examine the motor aspects of writing. Attention should be paid to overall legibility, letter size, and morphology. Observation of direct copying attempts should provide evidence of impaired afferent control and defective spatial organization, as well as poor control of force, speed, and amplitude of pen movements. It should also be evident whether copying is accomplished in a lexical, graphemic (that is, nonlexical), or pictorial fashion (Ellis, 1982). Whereas lexical copying reflects activation of the orthographic input lexicon via the reading system and subsequent writing of the word by access to the orthographic output lexicon, graphemic copying is mediated by recognition of single letters and activation of the corresponding allographic representation. Both lexical and graphemic copying are implemented using the stored graphic motor programs for individual letters. In contrast, pictorial copying of letters may be accomplished in the same way that one would copy nonlinguistic visual patterns and does not benefit from stored graphic motor programs. Pictorial copying is slow and fragmented and is accomplished in a stroke-by-stroke fashion with heavy reliance on visual feedback.

As noted earlier, peripheral agraphia may be confirmed if spelling is significantly better using another output modality, such as oral spelling or anagram arrangement, that does not require written production of letters. Anagram spelling may be a particularly useful task with patients who also have letter-naming difficulty, as is common in aphasia.

TREATMENT APPROACHES TO SPELLING IMPAIRMENTS

The clinical assessment of writing should provide information regarding impaired and preserved processes and representations that will be considered as treatment plans are devised. Writing treatment may be directed toward strengthening weakened processes (and representations) in an attempt to restore premorbid spelling procedures, and may serve to establish alternative spelling procedures or strategies. Within this framework, treatment may target the lexical-semantic spelling route, the phonological spelling route, and/or peripheral spelling processes, as indicated. Writing treatment may strengthen orthographic representations so that spelling may be improved in an item-specific manner (that is, word by word), or the intervention may address spelling rules or compensatory strategies that influence spelling for a variety of words. Whereas the latter approach is clearly more efficient, it is not always possible, as will become evident in the discussion below.

We focus here on a number of rationally devised treatment approaches for acquired agraphia that are directed toward various component processes necessary for spelling. The review is intended to be representative rather than exhaustive. It is clear that no one treatment approach will work for all individuals with acquired agraphia even when the impairment appears to be the same (Hillis, 1992). Individual variability in response to treatment conceivably reflects the unique pattern of damaged and preserved cognitive processes following brain damage, as well as differences in premorbid language abilities and the supporting neural architecture. For those reasons, individual responses to treatment should be monitored closely to determine if treatment is effective and in what ways treatment should be adjusted to better suit the needs of the patient. Clinical management and decision-making are also influenced by intrinsic and extrinsic factors that are unique to each patient, including medical, psychosocial, cultural, and contextual factors. As we proceed to discuss various treatment approaches, it is with the understanding that cognitive approaches to spelling treatment should be applied in a manner that enhances the functional communication skills of the individual patient (see Holland & Hinckley, this volume).

Strengthening the Lexical-Semantic Route

When it is evident that lexical-semantic processes are impaired, writing treatment may be directed toward strengthening semantic and/or orthographic representations, or improving access to those representations. Given that the semantic system is central to all modalities of language processing, treatment to improve semantics is likely to be given high priority when clinical assessment implicates damage to that component.

Treatment to Improve Semantics

Working from the assumption that semantic representations for specific items consist of a unique cluster of features that "define" the concept, it follows that treatment that clarifies those features may serve to strengthen semantics (Caramazza & Hillis, 1990). For example, if *apple* were written as *orange*, it would appear that the overlapping features of <fruit> and <round> were activated, but a distinguishing feature, such as <red>, was not. In that case, the clarification that *apple* represents <fruit>, <round>, <red>, in contrast to *orange* as <fruit>, <round>, <orange>, should improve the semantic distinction between the two items. Treatment employing this sort of semantic feature specification to clarify the distinctions among semantically related items was described by Hillis (1991, 1992) with patient HG, who exhibited impairment to the semantic system. A written naming task was used to elicit single word spellings, and when semantic errors were made, a semantic specification procedure was used. For example, if the word *pants* was written in response to a picture of a shirt, corrective feedback was given using gestures, pointing, and simple verbal explanations to highlight the semantic differences between *pants* and *shirt*. Using a single-subject multiple baseline design, Hillis (1991) documented improved written naming of targeted word sets in response to this semantic treatment. Improved performance was noted for trained items on other tasks, including oral naming and comprehension, providing evidence that improvement occurred at the level of semantics rather than specific orthographic representations. In addition, HG showed improved written naming of untrained items from the treated semantic categories, suggesting that treatment served to enhance representations within a given semantic category, thus allowing for more accurate distinctions among category members. As expected, there was no improvement for words from untreated, semantically unrelated categories.

Treatments that include less explicit clarification of semantic concepts also can serve to strengthen semantic representations for some patients. For example, Hillis and Caramazza (1994) reported that a task that involved matching printed words to pictures (with corrective feedback) served to reduce semantic errors in oral naming for patient JJ, who had a well-documented semantic impairment (Hillis & Caramazza, 1991). As JJ mastered the word-picture matching task for targeted items, his oral naming performance improved for untrained, semantically related items without the need for explicit semantic feature elaboration. In addition, his written naming improved simultaneously with his improved performance on the word-picture matching task. Therefore, it appeared that the task served to strengthen semantic representations even though treatment did not involve specific attention to semantic distinctions between items.

Another treatment approach that proved successful for addressing semantic impairment was reported for patient KE, who, like HG and JJ, showed semantic errors in all modalities (Hillis, 1989; Hillis & Caramazza, 1994). Implementation of a cueing hierarchy designed to elicit correct written naming of targeted items resulted in a reduction of written semantic errors. The cueing procedure included increasing support for correct spelling in the following sequence: scrambled anagram letters (with distractor letters) → scrambled anagram letters (without distractor letters) → initial letter cue → spoken word → delayed copy. A multiple baseline design showed that KE's written *and* oral naming improved with treatment. Generalization was observed to a set of untreated nouns in the same semantic category, with no generalization to a set of untreated verbs. Therefore, it appeared that cueing and reinforcement of the correct written responses (to the exclusion of other responses) served to strengthen semantic representations. This finding was somewhat surprising given that the treatment appeared to focus more on the orthographic representations than on the underlying semantic concepts; however, the repeated exposure to targeted pictures and their associated name apparently served to resolve semantic underspecification initially exhibited by KE.

The treatment outcomes for HG, JJ, and KE demonstrate that it is possible to strengthen semantics and thus improve single word writing. The semantic specification approach used with HG appeared to most directly address the semantic system; however, treatment that simply facilitated repeated linking of semantic and orthographic representations also served to reduce semantic errors.

Strengthening Orthographic Representations

When brain damage degrades or prevents access to the store of learned spellings in the orthographic output lexicon, semantic representations may not successfully activate spelling knowledge. In such cases, treatment may be directed toward relearning spellings in an item-specific manner. Several case reports support the potential value of treatments designed to strengthen specific orthographic representations for writing (Aliminosa, McCloskey, Goodman-Schulman, & Sokol, 1993; Beeson, 1999; Behrmann, 1987; Hillis & Caramazza, 1987; Carlomagno, Iavarone, & Colombo, 1994; Seron, Deloche, Moulard, & Rousselle, 1980). These treatments vary with regard to the precise nature of the cues used to elicit correct responses, but they share the common feature of repeated, corrected practice for spelling targeted words.

One of the earlier treatment studies by Seron and colleagues (1980) employed a computer-based treatment to improve single word spelling through reinforcement of correct choice and ordering of letters. The treatment resulted in a significant reduction of spelling errors in the five aphasic subjects, although follow-up testing showed some lack of stability after the treatment ended. More recent treatment studies, by Beeson (1999) and Hillis (1989), demonstrated lasting treatment effects using cueing hierarchies for spelling that included letter ordering tasks. Hillis (1989) described the arrangement of component letters in an anagram task as part of a cueing hierarchy that served to improve spelling in two aphasic patients. Beeson (1999) also employed a cueing hierarchy for spelling that included an anagram task. The manipulation of component letters and repeated opportunity to examine and judge the resultant spellings provided a problem-solving task that appeared to strengthen specific orthographic representations. Using a multiple baseline design, Beeson (1999) documented the effectiveness of the anagram and copy treatment (ACT) with patient ST, who had severe, chronic Wernicke's aphasia and was able to write only his name and numbers prior to treatment. The anagram treatment procedure included letter arrangement as well as repeated copy of the word, followed by delayed recall of spelling. The treatment was supplemented by daily homework that required repeated copy of target words followed by self-directed attempts to recall the spelling without the model present (referred to as copy and recall treatment: CART). Using ACT and CART, ST was able to master the spelling of over one hundred targeted words. Subsequent work with other agraphic patients demonstrated that a homework-based program using CART alone can also be effective for strengthening orthographic representations for targeted written words (Beeson & Hirsch, 1998) suggesting the value of repeated exposure and copy of orthographic representations. These findings were consistent with the case reported by Aliminosa and colleagues (1993) showing the effectiveness of a treatment that included study of the written target followed by delayed copy of each word. Their patient, JES, with nonfluent aphasia of moderate severity, showed word-specific improvement of spelling for trained words and no improvement for untrained words.

Carlomagno and colleagues (1994) described a treatment that similarly provided visual cues (along with semantic cues) to evoke correct spelling of targeted words. Their cueing hierarchy moved from greatest support to least support as follows: direct copy of target words → delayed copy of target words → serial ordering of letters with various visual cues provided (for example, number of letters, word contour, prepositioning of some letters) → semantic cues (for example, describing the object's function). They found that three of six aphasic patients with acquired agraphia responded to this visual-semantic cueing approach. The three patients who did not benefit from the visual-semantic treatment were responsive to an alternative treatment paradigm that focused on strengthening the phonological spelling route (described below). This differential response to treatment served to clarify the availability of preserved processes for specific individuals that was not apparent prior to treatment.

Behrmann (1987) reported another item-specific treatment designed to improve spelling of homophonic word pairs (for example, *main* versus *mane*) in patient CCM, who showed an impairment in the lexical-semantic spelling route with reliance on phoneme-grapheme conversion rules for spelling. Following stable baseline performance by CCM, Behrmann (1987) employed a picture-to-written-word matching task followed by written naming of each picture to reestablish the link between semantic meaning and orthography for targeted homophones. Homework was included that required the correct selection of written words to appropriately complete printed sentences—for example, "After Christmas the shops have a big (sail/sale)." Following treatment, CCM showed improved, stable performance in the ability to correctly spell the targeted homophones. Untrained homophone pairs did not improve; however, CCM showed surprising improvement on untrained irregularly spelled words following treatment. Behrmann offered the plausible explanation that CCM improved use of a lexical checking strategy employed during treatment so that she improved her ability to evaluate the correctness of irregularly spelled words relative to her orthographic input lexicon. This lexical check did not benefit homophone spellings, which must rely on semantics for disambiguation. Behrmann and Byng (1992) reported on a subsequent treatment to improve spelling of irregular words that similarly stressed lexical-semantic processing rather than phonological spelling. The procedures proved successful for the reestablishment of item-specific links from semantics to orthography for irregularly spelled words.

De Partz, Seron, and Van der Linden (1992) used a somewhat different approach to assist their patient, LP, to relearn the spelling of irregular words. LP's spelling showed reliance on the phonological route, with resultant spelling errors for ambiguous and irregularly spelled words. A visual imagery treatment was designed that took advantage of LP's relative strength for visual memory. For this treatment, each target word was written in the context of a drawing that was semantically related to the word. The drawing served to cue LP to the correct spelling because the shape of error letters was integrated into the drawing. For example, LP spelled *pathologie* (pathology) as *patologie* (lacking the *h*), so the word was written with the letter *h* integrated into the drawing of a bed (as a hospital bed, denoting illness). This creative approach proved adequate to cue LP to the correct spelling of targeted words, and the word-specific improvement was maintained over a long period of time.

Taken together, these case reports suggest that orthographic representations can be strengthened in some patients with acquired agraphia. The treatment procedures shared the common feature of repeated exposure to targeted orthographic representations (that is, reading the word) as well as practice writing (or copying) the words. It is assumed that repeated reading and writing of target words serve to lower the activation threshold for specific orthographic representations, and thus result in improved spelling for targeted words (Hillis, 1992; Morton, 1969). Of course, every time a word is read or spelled, its semantic representation should be activated as well, so it is likely that orthographic treatments stimulate both lexical and semantic representations. It is not clear whether repeated reading *and* writing of target words are necessary components of treatment, or whether repeated exposure to the written word alone would be adequate to improve spelling. This question relates the controversial issue of whether there are separate orthographic input and output lexicons (see discussion in Rapcsak & Beeson, this volume; Weekes & Coltheart, 1996). If, in fact, there is one orthographic lexicon, repeated exposure to written word targets (without repeated copy) may be adequate to improve spelling. A recent experiment with normal adults literate in Italian who were taught to spell French words with irregular orthography showed that repeated exposure to written words supported rapid acquisition of written spelling (Basso, Burgio, & Prandoni, 1999); however, this effect awaits empirical support in agraphic individuals. From a clinical perspective, we advocate combined stimulation of repeated reading and writing of target words in order to maximize activation of orthographic representations.

Lexical Relay Strategy

Hatfield (1983) contributed some of the earliest writing treatment studies that were based on the premise that writing procedures could be reorganized to take advantage of spared processes. She reported on three deep dysgraphic patients who could write some content words, but had limited ability to write functors. A lexical relay strategy was employed whereby specific content words were used as links to relearn the spelling of functors in individuals with deep agraphia. For example, retrieval of the word *inn* was used to establish the relearning of the homophone *in*, and *Ron* was used to retrieve the spelling for *on*. This strategic approach was necessarily item-specific, but was successfully used to circumvent retrieval failure for specific functors. The concept of using preserved words as "relay" or "code" words to cue the spelling of other words, or to derive graphemes from phonology, has been subsequently used by other researchers, as discussed below (Carlomagno & Parlato, 1989).

Strengthening the Phonological Spelling Route

The phonological spelling route that depends upon phoneme-grapheme conversion processes provides an alternative (or supplement) to lexical-semantic spelling processes. Spelling treatment may be designed to strengthen and facilitate the use of these processes, particularly in cases where lexical-semantic spelling is impaired. Numerous case reports have documented success in retraining sound-to-letter correspondences to facilitate spelling via the phonological route in individuals with acquired agraphia (Cardell & Cheney, 1999; Hillis & Caramazza, 1994; Carlomagno & Parlato, 1989; Carlomagno et al., 1994). The task of translating phonemes to graphemes requires several steps, including segmenting the word into sounds or syllables, categorizing each sound into its phoneme category, and mapping the phoneme to the corresponding grapheme.

Hillis and Caramazza (1994) described the spelling treatment to strengthen the phonological route with patient SJD, who had an impairment of lexical-semantic spelling with preserved oral naming ability. Although SJD could say the words that she wanted to write, her ability to make sound-to-letter conversions was limited, so that she could not derive information from phonology to guide her spelling. In order to increase her use of the phonological spelling route, SJD was trained in thirty sound-to-letter correspondences. The treatment procedure employed a "key word" approach, whereby SJD associated a word that she was able to spell for each sound-letter correspondence. So, for example, she was able to recall that the sound /b/ is the first sound of the key word *baby* and that *baby* starts with the letter *b*. After treatment to establish key words and consistent association of sound-to-letter correspondences, SJD was able to use those skills to derive the first letter or two of words she could not spell using the lexical-semantic route. The initial letter(s) then served to cue her retrieval of spellings and to block semantic errors in writing.

A similar procedure was shown to be successful with patient JS, who was not able to say the target words due to severe oral-verbal apraxia (Hillis Trupe, 1986). JS mastered three sets of ten phoneme-grapheme correspondences, which allowed her to formulate plausible spellings of words. Although the phoneme-grapheme conversion approach did not yield correct spelling for irregularly spelled words, JS was able to type the plausible spellings into a portable computer with text-to-speech capability, which resulted in synthesized spoken utterances.

Carlomagno and Parlato (1989) reported on the training of a lexical relay strategy, whereby a patient was trained to make use of a corpus of preserved proper nouns that served as "code words" to derive spellings of syllables. For example, to retrieve the spelling for the syllable /ro/, the patient recalled and wrote the word *Roma*, and then segmented the syllables in order to retrieve *ro*. Using this procedure, the patient mastered thirty consonant-vowel syllables. Following treatment, the patient showed generalization of the lexical relay strategy to spontaneous writing using self-dictation of each syllable followed by retrieval of the proper code word, segmentation, and writing of the syllable. Subsequent work by Carlomagno and colleagues (1994) with six agraphic individuals further supported the lexical relay treatment. Five of their six subjects significantly improved their spelling of real words and nonwords in response to the phonological treatment strategy. Two of those subjects also benefited from a visual-semantic strategy to strengthen lexical orthography (described above), but three subjects were responsive only to the phonological treatment.

It is apparent that spelling can be enhanced by increased reliance on and improved function of the phonological spelling route. In reality, however, many dysgraphic patients derive only partial orthography from phonology, or they make regularization errors as they rely too heavily on sound-to-letter correspondences. In such cases, treatment may be implemented that strives to maximize the use of partial lexical and phonological spelling information, as described below.

Interactive Use of Lexical and Phonological Spelling Routes

It makes sense that agraphic patients should bring all available information to bear as they attempt to resolve spelling difficulties. Partial information derived from the lexical-semantic route may be supplemented by orthographic information derived from the phonological route (Hillis & Caramazza, 1991); conversely, spellings that are assembled via phoneme-grapheme conversion may be self-corrected as they are compared to entries in the orthographic lexicon (as indicated by the dashed arrow from subword-level POC to orthographic output lexicon in figure 6.1). Beeson and colleagues (Beeson, Rewega, Vail, & Rapcsak, 2000) reported a treatment approach designed to maximize interactive use of lexical and phonological spelling routes in two patients (SV and SW) with mild anomic aphasia and persistent spelling problems. Both SV and SW were often capable of generating partial spellings or phonologically plausible spellings. The focus of treatment was to develop problem-solving strategies to maximize the use of partial orthographic information combined with sound-letter correspondences to generate and self-correct spellings. Both patients also made use of an electronic speller that was accepting of plausible misspellings to resolve spelling difficulties when their own self-correction efforts failed. The treatment outcome was of interest not only because the problem-solving strategies were useful for self-correction of spelling errors, but also because both patients showed generalized improvement in spelling abilities following treatment. Thus, treatment appeared to strengthen orthographic representations as well as improve self-correction strategies.

Treatment for Impairment of the Graphemic Buffer

When orthographic representations are activated but they are not adequately retained in the graphemic buffer, spelling accuracy notably declines as word length increases due to the increased time demands to write longer compared to shorter words (Caramazza et al., 1987;

Katz, 1991; Miceli et al., 1985). Under normal circumstances representations held in ortho-graphic short-term memory should be refreshed as needed by the available orthographic or phonological information (Nolan & Caramazza, 1983; Rapcsak & Beeson, this volume). There-fore, treatment for impairment to the graphemic buffer might be expected to strengthen the buffer directly or to improve the ability to refresh orthographic information as it decays. The few reports of treatment for individuals with apparent impairments to the graphemic buffer do not appear to reflect improved function of orthographic short-term memory per se. Rather, improved spelling appears to result from strengthening orthographic representations so that they are more resistant to degradation, or from the use of strategies to circumvent the short-term memory deficit (Hillis, 1989; Hillis & Caramazza, 1987).

Hillis (1989) reported a patient with an apparent impairment of the graphemic buffer who benefited from treatment using a cueing hierarchy for written naming that was also effective to improve spelling in a patient with a well-documented semantic impairment. The cueing hierar-chy (as described above in the context of lexical-semantic treatments) included anagram letter arrangement, provision of initial letter, writing to dictation, and delayed copy—all tasks that should serve to strengthen orthographic representations. A multiple baseline design showed improvement in written naming for targeted words, so that the word length effect was elimi-nated for trained words, but remained for untrained words. Had the treatment served to improve the overall function of the graphemic buffer, generalized improvement in spelling should have been observed for untrained items. The item-specific response to treatment sug-gested that strengthening orthographic representations may have provided input that was less subject to decay, and thus yielded correct spelling for trained items. Hillis (personal communi-cation) also suggested that the patient learned to compensate for the impaired buffer by parsing words into shorter components that did not exceed the demands of the buffer, such as *carrot = car + rot.*

Another treatment approach to compensate for apparent decay of orthographic representa-tions employed the training of self-directed strategies to detect and correct spelling errors. Such an approach was shown to be effective for patient DH, who had a mild anomic aphasia with persistent spelling impairment affecting about half of all written words (Hillis & Caramazza, 1987). DH made predominantly single letter spelling errors on the ends of words on all spelling tasks (written naming, writing to dictation, and oral spelling). Treatment was devised to take advantage of DH's preserved ability to use phonological spelling procedures and relatively intact orthographic output lexicon. DH was trained to use a search strategy to detect errors (that is, to compare his spellings to representations in his orthographic lexicon). He also was guided to focus on the ends of words (where most of his errors occurred), and to sound out each word as it was written to call attention to phonologically implausible misspellings. DH was responsive to this treatment; he ultimately improved his self-correction of spelling in written narratives. Although DH still made many spelling errors, his ability to self-correct his errors allowed him to return to previous employment.

Other reports of reduced word length effects have been noted when treatment was directed toward central spelling processes. For example, a single case treatment study reported by Aliminosa and colleagues (1993) showed that successful treatment to strengthen orthographic representations served to eliminate word length effects for trained items. Similarly, a patient with multiple levels of impairment reported by Cardell and Cheney (1999) responded to seman-tic and phonological treatments so that targeted real word and nonword spellings were mas-tered, but word length effects persisted for untrained items. Therefore it appeared that as orthographic representations were strengthened, they persisted long enough for peripheral writing processes to be accomplished. The finding that treatments directed toward improving orthographic representations may eliminate length effects in spelling is consistent with the proposal that temporary storage of graphemic information is intrinsic to the orthographic processing module, as discussed in chapter 15.

Treatment for Impairments to Peripheral Spelling Processes

Relatively little attention has been given to treatment that is specific to peripheral agraphias. This is not surprising given that the incidence of acquired writing impairments without significant language impairment is relatively rare. A review of five hundred left-hemisphere-damaged individuals yielded only two who were considered to have pure agraphia (Basso, Taborelli, & Vignolo, 1978). In contrast, the cooccurrence of central and peripheral writing impairments is a far more common finding, owing to lesions that damage neuroanatomical regions critical to lexical-semantic, phonological, and peripheral spelling processes. In cases of concomitant impairment to central and peripheral writing processes, the peripheral impairments must be overcome in order to realize the effects of treatment for central spelling processes. Although empirical evidence is lacking, it is likely that peripheral processes are strengthened in the context of treatments for central spelling processes such as those reviewed above. In particular, repeated copy and delayed copy of target words are likely to facilitate retraining of allographic conversion processes and the execution of the appropriate motor programs for handwriting.

Taking Advantage of Output Modalities Other than Handwriting

Cases in which oral spelling is preserved relative to written spelling provide a useful context in which to examine treatment for impairments of allographic conversion processes. Several case reports address attempts to remediate written spelling in cases with relatively preserved oral spelling (Lesser, 1990; Pound, 1996; Ramage, Beeson, & Rapcsak, 1998). Lesser's patient failed to respond to a treatment that employed self-dictation of oral spelling as a means to guide written spelling, despite the patient's preserved ability to write single letters to dictation and to orally spell words with fair accuracy. In contrast, patient JA, reported by Pound (1996) and patient LL, reported by Ramage and colleagues (1998) responded positively to self-dictation treatments. JA was trained to orally spell each target word before attempting to write it, then self-dictated each letter to write, and finally examined the written words one letter at a time as she orally spelled the word again. JA also was prompted to self-correct detected errors and to use an alphabet card if a model was needed for letter shapes. This procedure proved effective in improving JA's written spelling, and although her spelling was not flawless, it more closely approximated her oral spelling, which tended to show regularity effects.

The self-dictation procedure reported by Ramage and colleagues (1998) similarly resulted in improved written spelling in an individual with preserved oral spelling. The patient (LL) also had a marked word length effect in written spelling, but as the self-dictation treatment ensued and written spelling improved, LL's word length effect dissipated. These results were best explained by assuming that LL's allographic impairment placed excessive demands on the graphemic buffer so that information failed to persist long enough for letter shape assignment to be implemented fully. As LL's allographic conversion processes improved, demands on the graphemic buffer decreased, thus resolving what might be considered a pseudo-impairment of the graphemic buffer.

Individuals with intact central spelling processes who experience selective impairment of peripheral spelling processes may be able circumvent their handwriting difficulty by using a typewriter or word processor. For example, a patient reported by Black and colleagues (Black, Behrmann, Bass, & Hacker, 1989) with a selective impairment to allographic conversion processes showed nearly normal ability to type. Similarly, individuals with damage to graphic motor programs (that is, apraxic agraphia) or damage to neural systems involved in monitoring sensory feedback during handwriting (that is, afferent agraphia) may retain the ability to use a keyboard for written communication because such movements do not require the same level of skilled motor control as that needed for handwriting. In such cases, where an effective alternative to written spelling is available, rehabilitation of the peripheral writing impairment may be unwarranted.

Treatment for Impaired Graphomotor Control

Treatments for apraxic agraphia and afferent agraphia have not been documented in the literature. Given that copying skills may be relatively preserved in apraxic agraphia, we suggest that treatment should include repeated direct and delayed copying tasks to reestablish the ability to write letters and words. A task hierarchy should initially include slow, deliberate, and feedback-dependent writing to regain graphomotor control, followed by repeated tasks to improve the automaticity of motor programs for writing. Reliance on visual checking and self-correction should be emphasized in cases of afferent dysgraphia.

There has been some work reported relative to treatment for the excessively small handwriting size that often accompanies Parkinson's disease (that is, micrographia; Oliveira, Gurd, Nixon, Marshall, & Passingham, 1997). Treatment includes the provision of parallel lines or a template to facilitate the recalibration of the range and force of movement necessary to achieve increased letter size. With the eventual fading of external cues, maintenance of normal letter size requires continuous monitoring of writing movements. Oliveira and colleagues (1997) also demonstrated that a constant verbal reminder to "write big" was as effective as the provision of parallel lines to reduce micrographia; however, there was no documentation that the beneficial effects of this strategy were maintained.

Many individuals with acquired writing impairments also have hemiparesis affecting their ability to write with the dominant hand, so that they must shift to writing with the nondominant hand. Several investigators have reported on the use of various writing prostheses for the paralyzed right hand, with the intriguing finding that written composition produced with the aided hemiparetic right hand was linguistically superior to that written with the nondominant left hand (Leischner, 1983, 1996; Brown, Leader, & Blum, 1983; Lorch, 1995a, 1995b). Leischner (1983) used a special pen grip and assisted the patient with movement of the hand after each stroke. Brown and colleagues (1983) used a pen holder in combination with a skateboard device supporting the forearm, which allowed independent movement of the arm by proximal shoulder muscles. Whurr and Lorch (1991) advocated the use of a device that reduced the spasticity of the right hand and wrist, enabling use of the right hand for writing. In all cases, there was evidence of improved written spelling and more elaborate and accurate linguistic production when using the supported right hand. The precise mechanisms underlying this phenomenon are a matter of discussion and debate (Brown, 1995; Goldberg & Porcelli, 1995; Rothi, 1995; Lorch, 1995a, 1995b; Sasanuma, 1995; Leischner, 1996), but it appears that aided right-handed writing is worthy of further investigation and clinical consideration because of the potential support for central as well as peripheral writing impairments.

CONCLUSIONS

Clinical assessment of individuals with acquired agraphia should provide insight into the status of orthographic, semantic, phonological, and sensorimotor processes necessary for spelling and writing. The observed performance profile across a range of spelling tasks allows the formulation of hypotheses regarding the locus of the spelling impairment and the contribution from spared processes. As we have reviewed in this chapter, information derived from the assessment can subsequently guide the selection and planning of agraphia treatment directed toward specific components of central or peripheral spelling processes. This includes strengthening semantic and orthographic representations (and their links), improving the use of the phonological spelling route, and reestablishing peripheral spelling processes.

Although the literature regarding agraphia treatment is not extensive, there is strong evidence in the form of well-controlled, single-subject experiments to show that spelling and writing may be improved even at times long after the onset of agraphia. Our approach was to examine treatments directed toward specific processes and representations; however, it is apparent that the treatment tasks typically engage numerous cognitive processes, so that the stimulation provided by the treatment was rarely limited to isolated processes. For that reason, it is not surprising that a given treatment approach may serve to strengthen several cognitive processes. For example, the arrangement of anagram letters and repeated copy of target words (in the presence of pictured stimuli) may serve to strengthen the orthographic representation, but may also strengthen the link between semantics and orthography, or improve allographic conversion processes. We acknowledge that this lack of treatment specificity undermines the precise application of a cognitive neuropsychological approach to rehabilitation. This is a drawback from a theoretical perspective, but not from a clinical point of view. In other words, it may be difficult to determine with certainty that treatment influenced a particular spelling process to the exclusion of others; however, the fact that treatment improves the function of several components of the spelling process makes for an efficacious clinical approach.

In closing, we return to the issue of the functional value of spelling and writing treatment. We recognize that it is not enough to simply improve cognitive processes if such treatment has no significant impact on the functional outcome or quality of life for a given patient. Clearly the clinical treatment of writing should be influenced by patient needs and should include the necessary bridge between clinical activities and real life. Although our review of treatment approaches focused on the procedures for strengthening spelling and writing abilities, many of the case reports also include evidence of the functional impact of treatment. For example, patient DH, reported by Hillis and Caramazza (1987), was able to return to work following writing treatment. Patient ST, reported by Beeson (1999), developed a repertoire of single words that allowed on-line written communication that was not possible prior to treatment. The improved spelling skills achieved by patient SV (Beeson et al., 2000) allowed her to return to her lifelong hobby of writing fiction. Cases such as these exemplify how the application of rational treatment approaches serve to improve the cognitive processes to support written communication with consequent positive functional outcomes.

ACKNOWLEDGMENTS

This work was supported in part by National Multipurpose Research and Training Center Grant DC-01409 from the National Institute on Deafness and Other Communication Disorders to the University of Arizona, and by the Cummings Foundation Endowment to the Department of Neurology at the University of Arizona. The authors appreciate the assistance of Jullyn Chargualaf and Anne Chung in the preparation of this manuscript.

REFERENCES

Aliminosa, D., McCloskey, M., Goodman-Schulman, R., & Sokol, S. (1993). Remediation of acquired dysgraphia as a technique for testing interpretations of deficits. *Aphasiology, 7*, 55–69.

Badecker, W., Hillis, A., & Caramazza, A. (1990). Lexical morphology and its role in the writing process: Evidence from a case of acquired dysgraphia. *Cognition, 35*, 205–243.

Basso, A., Burgio, F., & Prandoni, P. (1999). Acquisition of output irregular orthographic representations in normal adults: An experimental study. *Journal of the International Neuropsychological Society, 5*, 405–412.

Basso, A., Taborelli, A., & Vignolo, L. A.(1978). Dissociated disorders of speaking and writing in aphasia.

Journal of Neurology, Neurosurgery, & Psychiatry, 41, 556–563.

Baxter, D. M., & Warrington, E. K. (1985). Category specific phonological dysgraphia. *Neuropsychologia, 23*, 653–666.

Baxter, D. M., & Warrington, E. K. (1987). Transcoding sound to spelling: Single or multiple sound unit correspondence? *Cortex, 23*, 11–28.

Beauvois, M.-F., & Dérousné, J. (1981). Lexical or orthographic agraphia. *Brain, 104*, 21–49.

Beeson, P. M. (1999). Treating acquired writing impairment. *Aphasiology, 13*, 367–386.

Beeson, P. M., & Hillis, A. E. (2001). Comprehension and production of written words. In. R. Chapey (Ed.).

Language intervention strategies in adult aphasia (4th ed.). Baltimore: Lippencott, Williams, & Wilkins.

Beeson, P. M., & Hirsch, F. M. (1998). Writing treatment for severe aphasia. Presentation at the Annual Convention of the American Speech-Language-Hearing Association. San Antonio, TX: November.

Beeson, P. M., Rewega, M., Vail, S., & Rapcsak, S. Z. (2000). Problem-solving approach to agraphia treatment: interactive use of lexical and sublexical spelling routes. *Aphasiology, 14,* 551–565.

Behrmann, M. (1987). The rites of righting writing: Homophone mediation in acquired dysgraphia. *Cognitive Neuropsychology, 4,* 365–384.

Behrmann, M., & Byng, S. (1992). A cognitive approach to the neurorehabilitation of acquired language disorders. In D. I. Margolin (Ed.), *Cognitive neuropsychology in clinical practice.* New York: Oxford University Press.

Black, S. E., Behrmann, M., Bass, K., & Hacker, P. (1989). Selective writing impairment: beyond the allographic code. *Aphasiology, 3,* 265–277.

Bolla-Wilson, K., Speedie, L. J., & Robinson, R. G. (1985). Phonologic agraphia in a left-handed patient after a right-hemisphere lesion. *Neurology, 35,* 1778–1781.

Brown, J. (1995). What dissociation should be studied? *Aphasiology, 9,* 277–279.

Brown, J. W., Leader, B. J., & Blum, C. S. (1983). Hemiplegic writing in severe aphasia. *Brain and Language, 19,* 204–215.

Bub, D., & Kertesz, A. (1982a). Evidence for lexicographic processing in a patient with preserved written over oral single word naming. *Brain, 105,* 697–717.

Bub, D., & Kertesz, A. (1982b). Deep agraphia. *Brain and Language, 17,* 146–165.

Caramazza, A., & Hillis, A. E. (1990). Where do semantic errors come from? *Cortex, 26,* 95–122.

Caramazza, A., Miceli, G., Villa, G., & Romani, C. (1987). The role of the graphemic buffer in spelling: Evidence from a case of acquired dysgraphia. *Cognition, 26,* 59–85.

Cardell, E. A., & Cheney, H. J. (1999). A cognitve neuropsychological approach to the assessment and remediation of acquired dysgraphia. *Language Testing, 16,* 353–388.

Carlomagno, S., Iavarone, A., & Colombo, A. (1994). Cognitive approaches to writing rehabilitation: From single case to group studies. In M. J. Riddoch & G. W. Humphreys (Eds.), *Cognitive neuropsychology and cognitive rehabilitation.* Hillsdale, NJ: Lawrence Erlbaum.

Carlomagno, S., & Parlato, V. (1989). Writing rehabilitation in brain damaged adult patients: A cognitive approach. In G. Deloche (Ed.), *Cognitive approaches in neuropsychological rehabilitation.* Hillsdale, NJ: Lawrence Erlbaum.

De Partz, M.-P. (1986). Re-education of a deep dyslexic patient: Rationale of the method and results. *Cognitive Neuropsychology, 3,* 147–177.

De Partz, M.-P., Seron, X., & Van der Linden, M. V. (1992). Re-education of surface dysgraphia with a visual imagery strategy. *Cognitive Neuropsychology, 9,* 369–401.

Ellis, A. W. (1982). Spelling and writing (and reading and speaking). In A. W. Ellis (Ed.), *Normality and pathology in cognitive runctions.* London: Academic Press.

Ellis, A. W., Miller, D., & Sin, G. (1983). Wernicke's aphasia and normal language processing: A case study in cognitive neuropsychology. *Cognition, 15,* 111–144.

Ellis, A. W., & Young, A. W. (1996). *Human cognitive neuropsychology: A textbook with readings.* London: Lawrence Erlbaum.

Goldberg, G., & Porcelli, J. (1995). The functional benefits: How much and for whom? *Aphasiology, 9,* 274–277.

Goodglass, H., & Kaplan, E. (1976). *The assessment of aphasia and other disorders.* Philadelphia: Lea & Feabiger.

Goodman, R. A., & Caramazza, A. (1986a). *The Johns Hopkins University dyslexia and dysgraphia batteries.* Unpublished.

Goodman, R. A., & Caramazza, A. (1986b). Aspects of the spelling process: Evidence from a case of acquired dysgraphia. *Language and Cognitive Processes, 1,* 263–296.

Goodman-Schulman, R., & Caramazza, A. (1987). Patterns of dysgraphia and the nonlexical spelling process. *Cortex, 23,* 143–148.

Hanna, P. R., Hanna, J. S., Hodges, R. E., & Rudorf, E. H. (1966). *Phoneme-grapheme correspondences as cues to spelling improvement.* Washington, D.C., U.S. Department of Health, Education, and Welfare.

Hatfield, F. M. (1983). Aspects of acquired dysgraphia and implication for re-education. In C. Code & D. J. Muller (Eds), *Aphasia therapy.* London: Edward Arnold Publisher.

Hatfield, F. M. (1985). Visual and phonological factors in acquired dysgraphia. *Neuropsychologia, 23,* 13–29.

Hillis Trupe, A. E. (1986). Effectiveness of retraining phoneme to grapheme conversion. In R. H. Brookshire (Ed.), *Clinical aphasiology.* Minneapolis, MN: BRK Publishers.

Hillis, A. E. (1989). Efficacy and generalization of treatment for aphasic naming errors. *Archives of Physical Medicine and Rehabilitation, 70,* 632–636.

Hillis, A. E. (1991). Effects of separate treatments for distinct impairments within the naming process. *Clinical Aphasiology, 19,* 255–265.

Hillis, A. E. (1992). Facilitating written production. *Clinics in Communication Disorders, 2,* 19–33.

Hillis, A. E., & Caramazza, A. (1987). Model-driven treatment of dysgraphia. In R. H. Brookshire (Ed.), *Clinical aphasiology.* Minneapolis, MN: BRK Publishers.

Hillis, A. E., & Caramazza, A. (1991). Mechanisms for accessing lexical representations for output: Evidence from a category-specific semantic deficit. *Brain and Language, 40,* 106–144.

Hillis, A. E., & Caramazza, A. (1994). Theories of lexical processing and rehabilitation of lexical deficits. In M. J. Riddoch & G. W. Humphreys (Eds.), *Cognitive neuropsychology and cognitive rehabilitation.* Hillsdale, NJ: Lawrence Erlbaum.

Holland, A. (1998). A strategy for improving oral naming in an individual with a phonological access impairment. In N. Helm-Estabrooks & A. L. Holland (Eds.), *Approaches to the treatment of aphasia.* San Diego: Singular Press.

Katz, R. B. (1991). Limited retention of information in the graphemic buffer. *Cortex, 27,* 111–119.

Kay, J., Lesser, R., & Coltheart, M. (1992). *Psycholinguistic assessments of language processing in aphasia* (PALPA). East Sussex, England: Lawrence Erlbaum.

Kertesz, A. (1982). *Western aphasia battery.* New York: Grune and Stratton.

Leischner, A. (1983). Side differences in writing to dictation of aphasics with agraphia: A graphic disconnection syndrome. *Brain and Language, 18,* 1–19.

Leischner, A. (1996). Word class effects upon the

intrahemispheric graphic disconnection syndrome. *Aphasiology, 10,* 443–451.

Lesser, R. (1990). Superior oral to written spelling: Evidence for separate buffers? *Cognitive Neuropsychology, 7,* 347–366.

Levine, D. N., Calvanio, R., & Popovics, A. (1982). Language in the absence of inner speech. *Neuropsychologia, 20,* 391–409.

Lorch, M. P. (1995a). Laterality and rehabilitation: Differences in left and right hand productions in aphasic agraphic hemiplegics. *Aphasiology, 9,* 257–271.

Lorch, M. P. (1995b). Language and praxis in written production: A rehabilitation paradigm. *Aphasiology, 9,* 280–282.

Margolin, D. I. (1984). The neuropsychology of writing and spelling: Semantic, phonological, motor and perceptual processes. *Quarterly Journal of Experimental Psychology, 36A,* 459–489.

Marshall, J. C. & Newcombe, F. (1966). Syntactic and semantic errors in paralexia. *Neuropsychologia, 4,* 169–176.

Miceli, G., Silveri, M. C., & Caramazza, A. (1985). Cognitive analysis of a case of pure dysgraphia. *Brain and Language, 25,* 187–212.

Morton, J. (1969). Interaction of information in word recognition. *Psychological Review, 76,* 165–178.

Newcombe, F., & Marshall, J. C. (1984). Task and modality-specific aphasias. In F. C. Rose (Ed.), *Advances in neurology: Vol. 42. Progress in aphasiology.* New York: Raven Press.

Nickels, L. (1992). The autocue? Self-generated phonemic cues in the treatment of a disorder of reading and naming. *Cognitive Neuropsychology, 9,* 155–182.

Nolan, K. N., & Caramazza, A. (1983). An analysis of writing in a case of deep dyslexia. *Brain and Language, 20,* 305–328.

Oliveira, R. M., Gurd, J. M., Nixon, P., Marshall, J. C., & Passingham, R. E. (1997). Micrographia in Parkinson's disease: The effect of providing external cues. *Journal of Neurology, Neurosurgery, and Psychiatry, 63,* 429–433.

Patterson, K. (1986). Lexical but nonsemantic spelling? *Cognitive Neuropsychology, 3,* 341–367.

Patterson, K., & Shewell, C. (1987). Speak and spell: Dissociations and word-class effects. In M. Coltheart., G. Sartori, & R. Job (Eds.), *The cognitive neuropsychology of language.* London: Lawrence Erlbaum.

Pound, C. (1996). Writing remediation using preserved oral spelling: A case for separate output buffers. *Aphasiology, 10,* 283–296.

Ramage, A., Beeson, P. M., & Rapcsak, S. Z. (1998). Dissociation between oral and written spelling: clinical characteristics and possible mechanisms. Presentation at the Clinical Aphasiology Conference, June.

Rapcsak, S. Z., & Beeson, P. M. (2000). Agraphia. In L. J. G. Rothi, B. Crosson, & S. Nadeau (Eds.), *Aphasia and language: Theory and practice.* New York: Guilford.

Rapcsak, S. Z., & Rubens, A. B. (1990). Disruption of semantic influence on writing following a left prefrontal lesion. *Brain and Language, 38,* 334–344.

Rapp, B., & Caramazza, A. (1997). From graphemes to abstract letter shapes: levels of representation in written spelling. *Journal of Experimental Psychology: Human Perception and Performance, 23,* 1130–1152.

Roeltgen, D. P. (1993). Agraphia. In K. M. Heilman & E. Valenstein (Eds.), *Clinical neuropsychology.* New York: Oxford University Press.

Roeltgen, D. P., & Heilman, K. M. (1984). Lexical agraphia: Further support for the two-system hypothesis of linguistic agraphia. *Brain, 107,* 811–827.

Roeltgen, D. P., Rothi, L. G., & Heilman, K. M. (1986). Linguistic semantic agraphia: A dissociation of the lexical spelling system from semantics. *Brain and Language, 27,* 257–280.

Roeltgen, D. P., Sevush, S., & Heilman, K. M. (1983). Phonological agraphia: Writing by the lexical-semantic route. *Neurology, 33,* 755–765.

Rothi, L. J. (1995). Are we clarifying or contributing to the confusion? *Aphasiology, 9,* 271–273.

Sasanuma, S. (1995). The missing data. *Aphasiology, 9,* 273–274.

Seron, X., Deloche, G., Moulard, G., & Rousselle, M. (1980). A computer-based therapy for the treatment of aphasic subjects with writing disorders. *Journal of Speech and Hearing Disorders, 45*(1), 45–58.

Shallice, T. (1981). Phonological agraphia and the lexical route in writing. *Brain, 104,* 413-429.

Weekes, B., & Coltheart, M. (1996). Surface dyslexia and surface dysgraphia: Treatment studies and their theoretical implications. *Cognitive Neuropsychology, 13,* 277–315.

Whurr, M., & Lorch, M. (1991). The use of a prosthesis to facilitate writing in aphasia and right hemiplegia. *Aphasiology, 5,* 411–418.

Part 3

—

Naming

—

7

Models of Naming

Doriana Chialant
Albert Costa
Alfonso Caramazza

INTRODUCTION

The study of the performance of individuals with brain damage represents a rich source of information for the understanding of the organization and functioning of the human cognitive system. The detailed analysis of patients' performance may help us to constrain hypotheses about the nature of both the representations and the mechanisms involved in various cognitive functions. In this chapter we focus on the analysis of the performance of patients with naming deficits.

Naming of a visual stimulus, such as a picture, begins with early visual processing and recognition (accessing a stored structural description), and procedures for accessing a semantic representation from vision, as discussed in chapter 8 and in chapter 10 of this volume. Here, we focus on those mechanisms required for spontaneously producing a name of a concept (specifically, an object or action). The main components involved in the production of a *written* name are: the semantic system, the lexical level of representation (the orthographic output lexicon), and more peripheral spelling processes (see chapter 4 of this volume, for discussion). The production of a *spoken* name from a concept involves the semantic system, the phonological output lexicon, the phonological level (phonological subunits that constitute the phonological lexical representation), and motor speech processes. The first step in this process is the selection of the semantic representation that comprises the message that the speaker wants to convey. In the second stage this preverbal message must be translated into the appropriate lexical representations or nodes (words) that correspond to the conceptual information. Once this selection has been achieved, the speaker has to retrieve the phonological subunits that correspond to the selected lexical items, and articulate these sounds. As discussed below, another level of representation, the lemma level, has been postulated to mediate between the semantic and the lexical levels. However, we argue that the data garnered to support this proposal can be accounted for without assuming this additional level of representation.

In this chapter we first discuss how many levels of representation are computed in producing a name from a concept. Then we focus on two main issues regarding the functional architecture of naming that are currently under debate: (1) the nature and organization of the representations involved in the semantic and lexical system; and (2) the temporal dynamics in accessing those representations. The following chapters in this section describe the neural substrates of the levels of representation involved in naming and rehabilitation of impairments at each level.

LEVELS OF PROCESSING

How many levels of representation are there in lexical access? And how are representations activated and selected? In the last few years there has been an intense debate about how lexical representations are accessed when speaking or writing. In this section we will discuss theories of lexical access and issues related to the number of independent levels of representation. We will return later to the issue of the time course and mechanisms of lexical activation and selection.

There is little debate that naming requires at least two relatively independent levels of representation, a semantic representation (meaning) and a lexical representation. Evidence for this proposal comes from neurologically impaired patients whose performance across tasks can be explained by assuming damage to one level of representation or the other. For example, the production of semantic errors (for example, dog → cat) of the same type and frequency across tasks of oral naming, written naming, and word comprehension, resulting from brain damage, can be understood by assuming selective damage to the one component process shared by all of these tasks—the lexical-semantic system (Hillis, Rapp, Romani, & Caramazza, 1990). In contrast, modality-specific naming deficits—that is, disproportionate naming errors in one modality of output—can be understood by assuming selective damage at the level of the phonologic or orthographic output lexicon. For example, there have been reports of patients who produce semantic errors in only one modality of output, the oral modality (RGB; Caramazza & Hillis, 1990) or the written modality (RCM; Hillis, Rapp, & Caramazza, 1999), while being relatively spared in the other modality. Their errors cannot be due to impaired motor speech or more "peripheral" spelling processes, because their errors were well-produced, semantically related words. Thus, there is strong evidence that the semantic and lexical levels can be independently disrupted by brain damage. The debate arises on the issue of whether lexical representations are accessed directly from the semantic system, or whether there is a modality-independent representation, or lemma, that mediates lexical access. The existence of modality-specific semantic errors may shed light on this debate, and thereby constrain hypotheses about functional architecture of the naming system.

The Debate on the Modality-Neutral-Level Hypothesis

Two of the most influential theories of lexical access in speech production (Levelt, Roelofs, & Meyer, 1999; Dell, 1986) assume that lexical access entails the successful retrieval of two different lexical representations: lemma nodes and lexeme nodes. A modality-neutral lexical representation (lemma), which is activated by the semantic system, is linked to the word's grammatical properties. Access to the modality-specific lexical nodes (orthographic or phonological lexemes) is always mediated by prior access to a modality-neutral lexical node (lemma) (see figure 7.1[a]). To illustrate the role of lemma representations, consider the simple case of picture naming (for ease of exposition we will focus on the variant proposed by Levelt et al., 1999). According to the proponents of this type of lexical system architecture, after having accessed the semantic representation of a picture (for example, of a dog), the lemma corresponding to that semantic representation is retrieved (for example, *dog*). Access to the lemma node allows the selection of the grammatical properties of the word (for example, noun, count). Only after the selection of that lemma and the retrieval of its grammatical features does activation spread to the corresponding modality-specific lexeme (this is the so-called syntactic mediation hypotheses; see more on this below). When naming orally, the phonological lexeme is retrieved (for example, "dog") and when naming in writing the orthographic lexeme is

a.   b.

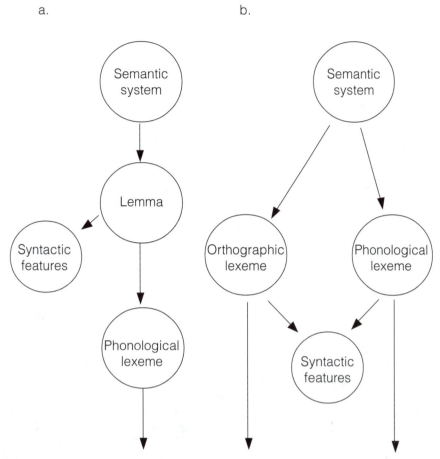

Figure 7.1. Schematic representation of modality-neutral lemma models (a) and of modality-specific lexeme models (b).

retrieved (for example, <DOG>). There are two important features in this model. First, when producing a word, the semantic system activates several semantically related lemma nodes (multiple activation principle). The lemma node with the highest level of activation is eventually selected. Second, activation of modality-specific representations (lexemes) only occurs after the selection of the lemma node and its grammatical properties have been achieved. Furthermore, only the lexeme corresponding to the selected lemma is activated at the modality-specific level of representation. According to these assumptions, a semantic error can arise either at the level of semantic representation or as the result of misselection of a modality-neutral lexical node or lemma. In this model, semantic errors cannot arise at the level of modality-specific lexical nodes (lexemes), because at that level only one lexical node is activated—the one that has been selected at the lemma level.

In contrast to this model, there are types of models in which semantic representations are linked directly to modality-specific lexical nodes (Caramazza, 1997; Starreveld & La Heij, 1996), without the intervention of any modality-neutral level of representation or lemma level (see figure 7.1[b]). In these models, the modality-specific lexical nodes (which correspond to a conflation of the lemma and lexeme levels in the preceding models) are connected to the semantic system, to either phonological or orthographic sublexical information, and to their grammatical properties. As in the previous theory, in this framework it is assumed that the semantic system activates multiple lexical representations (modality-specific representations in this case), and that the selection of the lexical node would then be followed by the selection of its grammatical and phonological features. According to the latter models, a semantic error is explained in terms of either a problem at the semantic level or misselection of modality-specific lexical nodes corresponding to the target semantic representation.

In summary, the major difference between the two architectures of the lexical system shown in figure 7.1 is the existence or not of an intermediate modality-neutral level of representation (lemma level) between the semantic level and the modality-specific level (lexeme level). In the following section we will address this issue by considering the performance of patients with modality-specific lexical deficits.

Constraints Imposed by Modality-Specific Deficits on the Number of Processing Layers

As we have seen, the existence of a lemma level has consequences in terms of the existence or not of activation of multiple lexical nodes at the modality-specific level of representation. The performance of patients with modality-specific naming deficits help us adjudicate between these two possibilities.

Consider, for example, the naming performance of patient RGB (Caramazza & Hillis, 1990). RGB was quite impaired in naming pictures orally (68 percent correct). His erroneous responses were basically semantically related words or descriptions of the target object. For example, RGB named *lemon* as "sour," *clam* as "octopus," and *banana* as "pineapple." Furthermore, RGB also produced semantic errors when the objects to be named were presented in different modalities (98 percent semantic errors in visual presentation; 100 percent of semantic errors in tactile presentation). One possible interpretation of RGB's impairment is that he sustained damage at the semantic level. However, that interpretation can be dismissed, since RGB performed flawlessly in other comprehension tasks that required semantic processing. Furthermore, when he produced a semantic error, he was asked to define the meaning of his response. On these occasions he defined the meaning of the target stimulus rather than that of his response (for example, he read *anchor* as "boat" and defined it as "what you would have on a boat that holds it down"), which indicates that he had accessed the target word's semantic representation.

Another feature of RGB's performance is relevant here: his written naming. Although he produced semantic errors in oral naming, he did not produce any such errors in written naming. When asked to write down the name of a picture, RGB only made orthographic errors but he never produced a semantic error. Therefore, RGB's semantic errors were restricted to one modality of output—oral production.

Interestingly, these modality-specific deficits have been observed in several patients for whom the modality at which the semantic errors arose was not always the same (Caramazza & Hillis, 1991; Hillis, Rapp, & Caramazza, 1999). For example, RCM produced a large number of semantic errors when asked to write down the names of pictures (42 percent of the responses were semantic errors), while she was able to name orally all the pictures flawlessly. How can the models presented above account for these modality-specific dissociations?

A major assumption of the models that postulate a modality-neutral lemma level is that semantic activation does not directly activate modality-specific lexical nodes (phonological and orthographic lexical nodes). Instead, it activates an amodal lemma node, which in turn connects to the corresponding lexical nodes (lexemes) in the two different output modalities. Therefore, in this model a semantic error can only arise at the level at which lemmas are selected. Accordingly, a semantic error produced as a consequence of damage at the lemma level (or at the connections that link the semantic system and the lemma level), would necessarily be translated into semantic errors in both oral and written naming. This is because the same lemma node mediates access of the modality-specific lexical nodes of a word. Therefore, the naming performance of patients like RGB and RCM, who produced semantic errors in only one modality of output, poses serious problems for theories that postulate that oral and written naming are mediated by access to a modality-neutral lexical representation.

Modality-specific naming deficits find a more natural explanation in the models that postulate that the semantic system directly activates phonological and orthographic lexical nodes. Recall that those models assume that in the course of naming (or writing) a picture's name, several semantically related modality-specific lexical nodes are activated from the semantic system. Therefore, if the phonological (or orthographic) lexical nodes, or the links between the semantic system and one of the two modality-specific lexicons, were to be damaged, semantic substitutions would be observed only in the damaged modality of output.

In summary, the striking performance of patients with naming impairments specific to a single output modality argues against the existence of a modality-neutral lemma level that mediates between the semantic system and modality-specific lexical nodes. Other arguments favoring the lemma level of representation (in the context of sentence production) are discussed by Cynthia K. Thompson and Yasmeen Faroqi-Shah in chapter 17 of this volume.

THE ORGANIZATION OF CONCEPTUAL KNOWLEDGE: SEMANTIC CATEGORY-SPECIFIC DEFICITS

One approach that has proven useful in characterizing the organization of the semantic system in the brain is the analysis of patients' patterns of spared and impaired performance in naming and in other tasks that implicate access to meaning. An important source of information comes from the investigation of patients with so-called category-specific deficits. These patients are severely impaired in naming and in processing the semantic information of items within restricted semantic categories, while their knowledge of other semantic categories may be virtually intact.

Some of the first well-studied cases of category-specific deficits were reported by Warrington and colleagues (Warrington & Shallice, 1984; Warrington & McCarthy, 1983). Warrington and Shallice (1984) reported four patients recovering from herpes simplex encephalitis who were disproportionately impaired in producing and understanding the names of living things (see Elaine Funnell, chapter 10 of this volume, for details, and see John Hart and colleagues, chapter 11, for a review of studies reporting category-specific semantic deficits and their neuroanatomical substrates).

Other studies have shown more discrete dissociations, such as the selective impairment (Hart & Gordon, 1992; Caramazza & Shelton, 1998) or sparing (Hillis & Caramazza, 1991) of animals relative to all other categories, including fruits and vegetables. For example, patient KR (Hart & Gordon, 1992) was disproportionately worse at naming animals (30 to 60 percent correct) regardless of the type of presentation (auditory or visual) or response route (verbal or written), but had no difficulty with other living things or objects (86 to 99 percent correct). Although these striking dissociations invite the conclusion that semantic information is stored in a category-like fashion in the brain, other possibilities have been entertained.

Are Category-Specific Deficits Artifacts of Poor Experimental Control?

Some researchers have claimed that the specific difficulties in processing the names of living things may simply reflect the lower frequency, lower familiarity, and higher complexity of this semantic category in comparison to others (Funnell & Sheridan, 1992; Stewart, Parkin, & Hunkin, 1992; Gaffan & Heywood, 1993). In other words, seemingly categorical deficits may be due to other uncontrolled variables that happen to correlate with specific semantic categories.

For example, if the members of the category *animals* are used less frequently than the members in the category *artifacts*, then a patient who has special problems with low-frequency items would show a disproportionate impairment in processing animals versus artifacts—a pattern of performance that would look like a category-specific effect. Although these confounding variables could be the basis of the category-specific deficits observed in some patients (see Funnell, chapter 10, this volume), they cannot account for the category-specific dissociations observed in studies that controlled for these variables (Laiacona, Barbarotto, & Capitani, 1993; Caramazza & Shelton, 1998; Lambon-Ralph, Howard, Nightingale, & Ellis, 1998; Moss, Tyler, Durrant-Peatfield, & Bunn, 1998; Samson, Pillon, & De Wilde, 1998). For example, Laiacona and colleagues (1993) carried out a systematic investigation of the oral naming and verbal comprehension of a patient with disproportionate difficulty in naming living things. They found that variables such as word frequency (a measure of written word occurrence in the language), familiarity (a measure of conceptual frequency), prototypicality (measured in terms of frequency of occurrence of each item in a category fluency task by 442 normal subjects), question difficulty (rated by 60 normal elderly and 10 young subjects), image agreement (a measure of correspondence between the picture and a subject's mental image of the target item), and visual complexity (a measure of the amount of detail or intricacy of lines in the picture) affected to different extents naming and comprehension *overall*, but not selectively or predominantly for any of the categories tested. In fact, FM showed a category effect with a predominant impairment for living things on all tasks even when the effects of all of the above variables had been partialled out.

Furthermore, the fact that the direction of the dissociation is not always the same (for example, some patients have special problems with the category *animals* while others have more problems with the category *artifacts*), excludes an interpretation of these deficits in terms of the overall difficulty in processing the elements of a given category. Therefore, regardless of the ultimate explanation for the category-specific deficits, it seems that the reported phenomenon is in itself reliable and not a by-product of poorly controlled experiments (at least for some patients).

Reducing Categorical Distinctions to Effects of Semantic Features

Given the existence of reliable category-specific semantic deficits, the question then becomes what these deficits can tell us about the organization of semantic information in the brain. The interpretations that have been put forward for these deficits can be broadly divided in two types: categorical versus noncategorical explanations.

Noncategorical explanations of category-specific deficits assume that they result from damage to types of object properties, such as visual properties like being "furry." Properties of this sort tend to distinguish among elements of different semantic categories. For example, "furry" things tend to be animals. Thus categorical distinctions are reduced to emergent properties of the distribution of semantic features that define the members of a category. These accounts appeal to the notion that semantic space is not uniform. Because similar kinds of things tend to share similar properties, certain features tend to cooccur more often within a category than across categories. Therefore, it is because properties of similar kinds of things cluster together in semantic space that damage to one area of this space may produce disproportionate impairments for items within rather than across categories (Caramazza, Hillis, Rapp, & Romani, 1990). Here we consider two types of feature theories of category-specific semantic deficits.

The Sensory Functional Hypothesis

The sensory functional hypothesis (SFH) was first proposed by Warrington and Shallice (1984; see also Silveri & Gainotti, 1988; Farah & McClelland, 1991; Hart & Gordon, 1992; De Renzi & Lucchelli, 1994; Gainotti & Silveri, 1996). The SFH is based on two basic assumptions. The first is that semantic knowledge is organized into modality-specific subsystems: the visual and the functional/associative. The visual subsystem stores information about the visual-semantic properties of objects (for example, chairs have four legs), whereas the functional/associative subsystem stores information about an object's function and other nonsensory properties (for example, chairs are for sitting). The second assumption is that visual and functional/associative properties are not equally important for the meaning of living and nonliving things. Living things are mostly defined in terms of visual features, and nonliving things in terms of functional/associative features. Under these assumptions, damage to the visual semantic subsystem may result in a category-like deficit for living things and damage to the functional/associative subsystem in a category-like deficit for nonliving things.

Explanations of this type make two interesting sets of predictions about how different semantic categories are affected by selective damage to either the visual or the functional/associative semantic subsystems. One set of predictions concerns the categories that are expected to be affected following selective damage to a specific semantic subsystem. For example, since the assumption is that "visual semantics" plays a crucial role in determining the meaning of living things as well as that of certain other categories (for example, musical instruments), the expectation is that damage to this subsystem will result in damage to all these semantic categories. In this view, if the category of animals is impaired, the categories of fruits, vegetables, and musical instruments must be as well. Another set of predictions also stems from the hypothesized modality-specific nature of the underlying deficit. These predictions concern the type of knowledge that should be affected in patients with category-specific deficits. For example, if a patient has a deficit for living things, which presumably is a consequence of damage to the visual semantic subsystem, we would expect the patient to have greater difficulties with the visual rather than the functional properties of living items (see Caramazza & Shelton, 1998, for detailed discussion). Along the same lines, this patient should also have more difficulties with visual rather than functional properties for elements belonging to the category of nonliving things. In addition, the reverse pattern of relation between type of damage and affected semantic categories should also hold. That is, patients with measurable deficits affecting visual knowledge of objects should manifest a category-like impairment to living versus nonliving things.

All three sets of predictions are at odds with empirical observations. There are several reports showing that the category of living things fractionates; animals can be damaged independently of fruit and vegetables, and vice versa (see Caramazza, 1998, for review). Also, there is recent evidence that the category of musical instruments groups with artifacts and not living things (Barbarotto, Capitani, Spinnler, & Trivelli, 1995) and that the category of body parts can be damaged or spared selectively (see Shelton & Caramazza, 1999, for review). Thus, the categorical distinctions revealed by category-specific deficits are not those predicted by the SFH.

There are reports of patients who have selective deficits for living things who nonetheless show equal deficits for visual *and* functional attributes of these items. In addition, these patients are equally unimpaired for both types of attributes for nonliving items (for example, Laiacona et al., 1993; Caramazza & Shelton, 1998; Lambon-Ralph et al., 1998; Moss et al., 1998). Furthermore, patients with disproportionate difficulties in processing the visual attributes of objects do not show a correspondingly disproportionate impairment in processing living things (Lambon-Ralph et al., 1998). For example, Lambon-Ralph and colleagues (1998) report the performance of two patients affected by dementia. One patient presented with relatively poor performance on living things. Her performance on a word-picture matching task administered in both the written and the auditory modality was 79 percent correct (76/96) for living things, and 99 percent correct (103/104) for nonliving things. Her naming performance (collapsing across tests) was 57 percent correct (35/62) for living things, and 90 percent correct (56/62) for nonliving things. However, on a definition task where she was required to match a perceptual definition (for example, cow: "a four-legged animal that has udders and moos") or an associative definition (for example, cow: "a farm animal that supplies us with milk and meat") to one item out of a set of five she failed to show a difference between knowledge of visual-perceptual and associative-functional information. She performed at 100 percent correct on each type of feature (perceptual and associative) for artifacts, but only 69 percent correct for each type of feature for animals. The other patient had poor knowledge of visual attributes but failed to exhibit a category-specific deficit for animate items. In fact, her comprehension and naming of living things were significantly better for animate than for inanimate items.

Two conclusions can be drawn from these cases. First, categorical effects are not the by-product of damage to either the visual or the functional properties of subsets of semantic features. Second, the evidence speaks against a modality-specific organization of the semantic system. Therefore, theories that try to reduce the seemingly categorical semantic deficits in some patients to differential damage to the object's visual and functional properties do not capture the wide variety of results reported in the literature.

The Organized Unitary Content Hypothesis

Another type of noncategorical theory explains the existence of category-specific deficits by appealing to the fact that members of a semantic category have many more properties in common than do objects from different semantic categories. The main assumptions of these theories are that semantic properties are not distributed uniformly across categories but tend to cluster together, independently of their modality, and that objects within a category share many more properties than do objects across categories (Keil, 1989; Keil, Smith, Simons, & Levine, 1998; Rosh, Mervis, Gray, Johnson, & Royes-Braem, 1976). For example, animals are generally capable of particular types of motion, have particular types of shapes and odors, are found in particular types of environments, and so on. Damage to a part of the brain that represents a crowded region of semantic space will result in a category-like semantic deficit. One such theory is the organized unitary content hypothesis (OUCH) (Caramazza et al., 1990; for similar accounts see Devlin, Gonnerman, Andersen, & Seidenberg, 1998; Moss et al., 1998; Riddoch, Humphreys, Coltheart, & Fannell, 1998).

OUCH-like theories account for two major datasets from category-specific deficits. They can account for the existence of more fine-grained category distinctions than between living and nonliving things, and for evidence that these deficits are not necessarily associated with selective impairment to a modality-defined type of knowledge. Thus, for example, the prediction of fine-grained dissociations of semantic categories might follow from the possibility that the categories of animals and of fruit and vegetables are distinguished by sets of highly intercorrelated features. As already noted, animate objects are capable of self-initiated motion, tend to be made of certain types of substances, are sentient, engage in certain types of behaviors with their young, and so on, properties that clearly distinguish them from other living things such as fruits and vegetables. OUCH-like theories provide a rich source of hypotheses about the organization of conceptual knowledge and therefore remain the dominant type of theory in accounting for the existence of category-specific deficits.

Domain-Specific Theories of Category-Specific Deficits

Category-specific effects could of course reflect the categorical organization of conceptual knowledge in the brain. Caramazza and Shelton (1998) recently entertained just this possibility. This proposal, which is based largely on earlier suggestions by Gelman (1990) and Premack (1990), argues that conceptual knowledge is organized in broad domains that reflect evolutionarily salient distinctions. Their claim is based on the assumption that evolutionary pressures may have resulted in the development of neural mechanisms dedicated to processing of specific kinds of objects. This would have led to the categorical organization of knowledge about those objects. The most likely domains for such organization are animate objects, plants, and artifacts. It is important to note that this proposal predicts the occurrence of category-specific deficits for each of the specified domains, but also does *not* exclude the existence of other levels of organization of conceptual knowledge within these domains. The available data on category-specific deficits are consistent with the domain-specific hypothesis. The hypothesis predicts the major dissociations that have been reported—the selective impairments of animals, fruits and vegetables, and artifacts (and possibly also body parts). It also is consistent with the fact that damage to a given semantic category results in damage to all types of attributes of objects, including both visual and functional/associative attributes.

The analysis of category-specific impairments has been instrumental in determining the structure and organization of conceptual knowledge in the brain. It is clear from this brief review of the cases reported in the literature that at least one explanation of the existence of category-specific semantic deficits—the SFH—cannot be right. A corollary of this conclusion is that the reported results also undermine multiple semantics theories of the organization of conceptual knowledge in the brain (Shallice, 1988). However, the available data do not allow a choice between domain-specific accounts and OUCH-like theories of the organization of conceptual knowledge in the brain. From a methodological point of view, this discussion illustrates how the observation of dissociations may be open to several explanations, and only detailed investigations can allow more precise conclusions about the functional and neural organization of cognitive systems.

In the following section we extend this argument by looking at the information that one can gather from the study of other seemingly categorical deficits in naming, namely the grammatical category deficits.

THE ORGANIZATION OF THE LEXICON: GRAMMATICAL CATEGORY-SPECIFIC DEFICITS

All languages are characterized by the presence of different types of words that carry different grammatical functions. Although grammatical categories correlate with semantic domains (for example, nouns tend to refer to objects and verbs to actions), grammatical information cannot be reduced to semantic representations. Furthermore, words in different categories follow, to some extent, different processing principles. For example, while the lexical node corresponding to a noun (for example, *pear*) can be retrieved directly from the semantic system, the retrieval of the lexical node corresponding to an article (for example, *the*), at least in some languages, depends on both semantic properties *and* grammatical properties of the noun (for example, its gender). Therefore, the mechanisms involved in the selection of these two types of words, or at least the information required for that mechanism to function, need to be somewhat different. In fact, data from aphasia support this hypothesis.

The dissociation between open-class words (nouns and verbs) and closed-class words (function words) is well known (Andreewsky & Seron, 1975; Caramazza, Berndt, & Hart, 1981; Gardner & Zurif, 1975; Rapp & Caramazza, 1997). There are also numerous reports of patients who can produce nouns much better than verbs and/or function words (Berndt, Mitchum, Haendiges, & Sandson, 1997; Caramazza & Hillis, 1991; Damasio & Tranel, 1993; Kohn, Lorch, & Pearson, 1989; McCarthy & Warrington, 1985; Miceli, Silveri, Villa, & Caramazza, 1984; Myerson & Goodglass, 1972). Similarly, there are many reports of patients who can name verbs significantly better than nouns (Baxter & Warrington, 1985; Berndt et al., 1997; Breedin & Martin, 1996; Hillis & Caramazza, 1995; Damasio & Tranel, 1993; De Renzi & Di Pellegrino,

1995; Miceli, Silveri, Nocentini, & Caramazza, 1988; Zingeser & Berndt, 1988). For example, Berndt and colleagues (1997) report several patients with noun/verb naming dissociations. Of the eleven aphasic patients included in their study, five presented significantly more impaired performance in naming pictures and videotapes of actions than of objects (for example, patient LR was 45 percent correct on action naming and 88 percent on object naming, and patient EA was 28 percent correct on actions and 47 percent correct on objects). Conversely, two of their patients were significantly more impaired in naming pictures and videotapes of objects than of actions (patient HF was 82 percent correct on action naming and 46 percent on object naming, and patient HY was 67 percent correct on actions and 44 percent correct on objects).

What can we learn about the representation of grammatical information from these dissociations? What is the origin of these grammatical-class effects? Here we consider the case of the noun/verb dissociations.

Following the same argument as in the case of the semantic category-specific deficits, an interpretation of the grammatical class deficits in terms of different levels of difficulty (let us say that verbs are more difficult to process than nouns) can be dismissed right away. This is because the words that are most impaired in these patients do not always correspond to the same grammatical category. In some patients the disproportionately impaired category corresponds to verbs while in others it corresponds to nouns.

Despite this first approximation there is no consensus about the real cause of noun/verb deficits. Although these striking dissociations seem to invite an explanation in terms of categorical grammatical representations, this is not the only tenable explanation. Indeed, there is not even agreement among researchers about the level of representation at which these deficits are occurring. For some authors these deficits reflect damage at the lexical level at which grammatical information is computed/represented, while for others they are the result of damage to semantic characteristics that are correlated with the different grammatical categories. We examine these alternative explanations below.

Grammatical Class Deficits: A By-Product of a Selective Semantic Deficit?

Verbs and nouns vary, among other things, in their semantic representations. One straightforward theory of noun and verb dissociations is therefore one that views these deficits as occurring at the semantic level, and assumes that semantic representations for these two classes of items are categorically distinguished. One such interpretation is that of McCarthy and Warrington (1985), who have explained these deficits in terms of differential damage to the semantic representations corresponding to actions and objects. However, nouns and verbs vary also in terms of their level of abstraction. If one were to place them along a continuum of abstraction, verbs would tend to take more abstract values than nouns. Therefore, damage to the more abstract concepts could result in greater difficulties in processing verbs than nouns. Alternatively, damage to the more concrete concepts would result in greater difficulties in the processing of nouns in comparison to verbs. Some authors (Breedin, Saffran, & Schwartz, 1998; Marshall, Pring, Chiat, & Robson, 1996a; Marshall, Chiat, Robson, & Pring, 1996b) have argued that the grammatical-category deficits could be the result of differential damage to more or less abstract concepts.

These proposals share the idea that the grammatical-category deficits have their origins in a semantic impairment rather than in a lexical-grammatical impairment. Furthermore, according to the second explanation, the categorical deficits are accounted for by appealing to damage to certain values of a continuous variable (the concrete-abstract continuum). Therefore, these authors argue that the grammatical-category deficits do not require an explanation in terms of categorical representations.

Although these explanations could account for the deficits of some patients, especially those who present the same dissociation in comprehension and production tasks (Berndt et al., 1997;

McCarthy & Warrington, 1985; Miceli et al., 1988), they fail to account for the performance of other patients with grammatical-category deficits.

The performance of some patients who show a grammatical-category effect in only one modality of output (or input) poses a special problem for this interpretation. It is reasonable to assume that if the locus of the grammatical-category deficits is the semantic system, a patient would show the same dissociation in all tasks that require semantic processing. However, there have been reports of patients with a modality-specific grammatical class effect (Caramazza & Hillis, 1991; Hillis & Caramazza, 1995; Rapp & Caramazza, 1997, 1998). Consider, for example, the performance of patients HW and SJD, reported by Caramazza and Hillis (1991). These patients had difficulties with verbs in only one modality of output, oral and written production, respectively. HW's difficulties in orally producing words were much more severe for verbs than for nouns (22 percent versus 56 percent correct), and SJD's difficulties in writing words were more severe for verbs than for nouns (70 percent versus 99 percent correct). These effects persisted even when the stimuli were homonyms (for example, *crack*, as in "there is a *crack* in the mirror" and "don't *crack* nuts in here"), thus ruling out the possibility that the effects depended on item-specific differences. Moreover, the patients' greater difficulty for verbs was not the result of a frequency effect because the same pattern was obtained even when the verb form of a homonym pair was more frequent than the noun form.

The performance of these patients is difficult to explain in terms of damage to the semantic system, since their performance in other tasks that required semantic processing (written naming in the case of HW and oral naming in the case of SJD) and comprehension tasks (entirely normal in both patients) did not show any grammatical class effect. Therefore, their grammatical class impairments must be related to the grammatical information linked to the modality-specific lexical representations (the orthographic and phonological representations).

What plausible explanations can be given for these modality-specific grammatical class effects? One possibility is to assume that grammatical class information is represented independently in the phonological and orthographic output lexicons (more on this issue is discussed above). In this scenario, the grammatical features of different grammatical classes could be differentially damaged in only one of the output lexicons (let's say the phonological output lexicon in the case of HW). However, it is still possible to account for these deficits without appealing to grammatical categories. It may be argued that the links between some semantic representations and their respective modality-specific lexical items are damaged. For example, damage to the connections between abstract semantic representations and their corresponding orthographic lexical nodes could result in a grammatical class effect (for example, verb production worse than noun production) in only one modality of output (for example, written naming).

Another way to address whether the grammatical class effects have a lexical-grammatical basis rather than a semantic basis is to explore whether these deficits correspond to other lexical-grammatical impairments that cannot be interpreted in terms of damage to the semantic level. In the following section we will present some data showing that grammatical class effects may correlate with impairments in morphological processing, and we will argue that these observations suggest that grammatical class effects may have their origin in damage to the grammatical information represented at the lexical level.

Grammatical Class Effects:
A Product of Grammatical Organization in the Lexicon

A word's grammatical properties determine the type of morphological transformation the word can undergo. If the grammatical information of one type of lexical item were damaged (for example, nouns) it is possible that the morphological processing of that type of words would also be affected. For example, it is reasonable to assume that if a patient has relatively more problems in processing nouns than verbs, he or she will also have relatively more difficulties in the morphological processing of nouns than of verbs. This pattern of results would reveal that a deficit in the production of words of one grammatical category cooccurs with a more general lexical-grammatical deficit that cannot be attributed to semantic variables. And, therefore, this would suggest that the grammatical class effects have a grammatical basis rather than a semantic basis.

In a recent study, Shapiro, Shelton, and Caramazza (2000) reported the performance of an aphasic patient with problems in processing nouns in comparison to verbs, in many different production tasks, such as repetition, picture naming, and sentence production. An explanation of JR's performance in terms of damage at the semantic system is unlikely for two reasons. First, in some comprehension tasks JR showed the opposite effects to those he showed in production: in comprehension he was better in processing nouns compared to verbs, while the opposite pattern was observed in production. Second, JR made more errors with abstract than concrete nouns. These data show that JR is not especially worse with concrete nouns, as it would be predicted if the noun/verb dissociation were actually an abstract/concrete dissociation.

Furthermore, these authors analyzed the performance of JR in tasks that require the morphological processing of verbs and nouns. They asked JR to produce the plural form of singular nouns and the singular form of plural nouns, and the third person of the singular of verbs presented in the third person plural and the third person plural form of third person singular verbs. For example, JR had to produce the plural word (two) *judges* when presented with the singular noun (one) *judge* and he had to produce the third person of the singular (he) *judges* when presented with the third person plural (they) *judge*. Notice that the use of verb/noun homonyms allowed the authors to keep the response word the same for verbs and nouns (*judges*), and even to maintain the phonological transformation the same across the two grammatical classes (for example, add an *s* to the root). The morphological production of JR was much better with verbs (93 percent) than with nouns (65 percent). The same pattern was also observed when JR was asked to make the morphological transformations on nonwords that function as nouns (55 percent; (one) *wug*, (two) *wugs*) or verbs (83 percent; (they) *wug*, (he) *wugs*). This pattern of results replicates the grammatical class effects observed in JR in the production of verbs and nouns, and therefore confirms the idea that a grammatical class deficit may cooccur with more general problems in lexical processing of certain types of words. Taken together, these results indicate that JR's difficulties in the processing of noun morphology cannot be due to a general morphological deficit (his verbal morphology is much better preserved), a general phonological deficit (he is able to produce the words when they correspond to verbs), or a semantic deficit (he does not show the same dissociation in comprehension tasks). Therefore the authors concluded that the cause of JR's problems in the production of nouns has a grammatical basis, and that grammatical knowledge seems to be represented categorically in the brain.

In summary, the results reviewed in this section indicate that grammatical effects cannot be reduced to a semantic deficit. Rather, these effects may arise at some level of lexical processing, and suggest that grammatical knowledge is categorically represented.

MECHANISMS OF LEXICAL ACTIVATION AND SELECTION

Thus far we have focused on the overall architecture of the lexical system involved in spoken naming, and we have seen how theories differ significantly in the assumptions they make concerning the number of processing layers between the semantic level and the phonological level. We will now discuss the major assumptions about the processing dynamics in models of lexical access; that is, the temporal properties of the spreading of activation between the different levels of representation. There are two main proposals about the time course of lexical access in speech production: the discrete serial activation assumption and the cascaded activation assumption.

Discrete versus Cascade Processing

Discrete serial models of lexical access (for example, Levelt, 1989; Levelt, Roelofs, & Meyer, 1999; Roelofs, 1992; Schriefers, Meyer, & Levelt, 1990) propose that activation flows from layer to layer in a strictly serial way. Accordingly, while multiple lexical nodes are activated from the semantic system, only one of them (the selected lexical node) will send activation to the phonological layer of representation. Furthermore, the phonological properties of the selected lexical node would only receive activation *after* the lexical selection process is fully completed. In short, phonological activation is restricted to the selected lexical node. In contrast, there are other models that assume that activation flows continuously from the lexical layer to the phonological layer in a cascaded fashion (for example, Caramazza, 1997; Dell, 1986; Dell & O'Seaghdha, 1991; Harley, 1993; Humphreys, Riddoch, & Quinlan, 1988; Peterson & Savoy, 1998). According to these models, all the lexical nodes activated through the semantic system spread some proportional activation to their corresponding phonological segments, regardless of which node will eventually be selected. Therefore, phonological activation is *not* restricted to the selected lexical node.

Most of the evidence in favor of either discrete serial or cascaded models comes from analyses of unimpaired subjects' performance in different experimental tasks. Although earlier studies (Levelt et al., 1991; Schriefers et al., 1990) suggested that the time course of lexical access follows a discrete serial processing, more recent evidence seems to support the cascaded activation models of lexical access (Costa, Caramazza, & Sebastian-Galles, in press; Peterson & Savoy, 1998).

There is an important difference between two types of cascaded activation models: feed-forward and interactive models. Feed-forward models (Humphreys et al., 1988) assume that activation spreads unidirectionally from the semantic system to the phonological system. That is, the activation of phonological representations does not send back activation to higher representations (for example, lexical nodes, or semantic representations). In contrast, interactive models assume not only feed-forward activation but also backward activation from the phonological to the semantic level. According to this view, when a speaker intends to name the picture of a dog, for example, the semantic system activates the target lexical node *dog* along with other semantically related lexical nodes (for example, *cat, horse*, and so on). Because of the assumption of cascaded processing, all activated lexical nodes send some proportional activation to their phonological properties (/d/, /o/, /g/; /k/, /a/, /t/; and so on). The activated phonological segments send back activation to all lexical nodes with which they are connected. Thus, the segment /k/ reactivates the lexical node *cat*, as well as other phonologically related nodes such as *car, cap*, or *carpet*. In the same way, a phoneme that belongs to the target word (for example, /d/) would reactivate the target word (*dog*) but also other phonologically related words (for example, *doll*). Note that all this processing takes place before the target lexical node (*dog*) is selected, and therefore when lexical selection takes place not only semantically related competitors are activated (*cat, horse*) but also phonologically related ones (*doll, cap*, and so on).

Interactive processing was originally proposed to account for two basic findings from spontaneous and experimentally elicited speech errors: the mixed error effect and the lexical bias effect. The lexical bias effect stands for the observation that speech errors that arise as a consequence of misselection of phonological segments of a target word (for example, substituting /p/ or /t/ for /g/) lead to the production of a word (for example, *dot*) more often than what we would expect by chance. That is, errors like *dot* for *dog* (as opposed to *dop* for *dog*) occur more frequently than would be expected if these errors arose by randomly substituting one phoneme for another. This observation may be summarized as indicating that the lexical system is biased toward the production of words over nonwords. The mixed error effect refers to the observation that a lexical/semantic error results in a word that is similar *in both meaning and form* to the target more often than would be expected by chance. That is, the probability that a speaker produces *hog* instead of *dog* is greater than what we should expect if lexical selection errors were completely independent from a word's phonological properties.

An explanation of these two effects emerges naturally from the assumptions of interactive models. For example, as in the case of the production of the lexical node *dog*, the phonological segments of this word send back activation to all the words with which they are connected (for example, *dot* and *doll*), which in turn send activation to their phonological segments (/d/, /o/, /l/, /t/). In this scenario, the segments /t/ and /l/ that are not associated with the target word *dog* would nonetheless be activated to some extent. Under the assumption that the probability of misselecting a given segment that is not part of the target word depends on its level of activation, the segments /t/ and /l/ from *dot* and *doll* are more likely to be selected than other segments such as /k/ or /f/. And, as a consequence, the probability of producing *doll* is greater than that of producing *dof*.

Along the same lines, the over-representation of mixed errors in speech production corpora can naturally be explained by interactive models. Consider the above example in which the speaker intends to produce *dog* and finally produces a mixed error such as *hog*. If selection of a lexical node depends on its activation level, in case of failure to retrieve the target lexical node the probability of retrieving a semantically and phonologically related word would be higher than expected by chance. This is because the semantically and phonologically related word (for example, *hog*) receives activation from two sources: the semantic system (by virtue of its semantic relationship with the target word) and the phonological layer system (by virtue of its phonological relationship with the target word). In contrast, a semantically related word (for example, *cat*) only receives activation from the semantic system. Therefore, other things being equal, the probability of producing a mixed error (*hog*) is greater than expected by chance.

Mixed and lexical bias effects and their implications for processing dynamics have been challenged on both empirical and theoretical grounds. From an empirical point of view, the existence of these effects remains the target of much debate, as measurements rest crucially on the definition of clear classification criteria for errors and the definition of agreed-upon measurements of chance levels in producing words and nonwords by randomly substituting phonemes for one another (Stemberger, 1985; Rapp & Goldrich, 2000). Thus, despite several studies dedicated to assessing the reliability of such effects by looking at the performance of both unimpaired (Baars, Motley, & McKay, 1975; Baars, 1980; Berg, 1986; Dell, 1988; Dell & Reich, 1981; Fromkin, 1980; Stemberger, 1985) and aphasic speakers (Best, 1996; Blanken, 1998; Buckingham, 1980; Gagnon, Schwartz, Martin, Dell, & Saffran, 1997; Garrett, 1992; Soderpalm, 1979, 1980), the existence of these effects remains the target of much debate. From a theoretical point of view, proponents of noninteractive views have implemented alternative mechanisms to account for these effects.

Regardless of the final outcome of this debate, the exploration of these potential properties of lexical access mechanisms has led both to the development of more fine-grained theories of processing dynamics and therefore of new sources of data that could help characterize contending proposals of lexical access dynamics. In particular, one recent proposal by Dell, Schwartz, Martin, Saffran, and Gagnon (1997) attempted to expand the range of data accounted for by their model of lexical access by looking at error distributions in the oral naming of aphasic patients. In the following we will discuss the claims and evidence presented by these researchers in favor of the interactivity assumption and its implications for theories of aphasia.

Testing the Interactivity Assumption

Dell and colleagues (1997) proposed a computational model of word retrieval that aims at explaining the processes involved in both impaired and normal word production. These researchers tried to validate their model's assumptions by simulating the distributional properties of the naming errors produced by twenty-one fluent aphasics on a single picture-naming task.

The model is a variant of a more general theory of lexical processing proposed by Dell (1986) and it postulates three layers of nodes—semantic, lexical, and phonological. Accordingly, word retrieval entails the following main steps: (1) the retrieval of the semantic representation that a speaker wants to convey; (2) the selection of the appropriate lexical node; and (3) the retrieval of a target's phonological segments. Dell and colleagues (1997) assume that the dynamics of these processes follow a cascaded activation principle and that the different representational levels interact with each other; that is, their model is interactive. The selection of a node in this system is obtained through a mechanism that picks out the node with the highest level of activation at a given moment in time.

The computational implementation of this model in the context of aphasic language is based on two main parameters that govern the flow of activation between different levels of representation, and the activation levels of the representations themselves. The first parameter, termed the *connectivity strength*, is the strength of the connections between any interconnected representations. In a normal situation the strength of the connections is enough to guarantee that, for example, a selected semantic representation sends enough activation to the proper lexical node to cause its selection. The second parameter, called *decay rate*, is the speed with which the activation of a given representation (represented by nodes in the model) decays over time. Under normal circumstances, the decay rate is sufficiently high to allow speakers to select the appropriate lexical nodes and the appropriate phonological segments.

Dell and colleagues (1997) have claimed that the pattern of errors produced by fluent aphasics may be explained by altering the optimal values that the two parameters take under normal circumstances. If the connectivity strength between the representations is weaker than normal, the selection of a lexical node would not necessarily lead to the selection of the phonological nodes with which it is linked. In the same way, if the decay rate of a representation is too fast, when selection takes place nodes other than the target ones may be the most active, and an error is produced.

The authors further argue that whenever the values of any of these parameters is altered, all processing levels of the system are altered accordingly. If, for example, the connectivity strength is altered, it will affect both the connections between the semantic representations and the lexical nodes and those between the lexical nodes and the phonological segments. This assumption is what Dell and collaborators call the *globality assumption*, which states that different patterns of naming errors in fluent aphasics can be explained by assuming that brain damage affects all levels of lexical processing equally.

In order to test these assumptions Dell and collaborators analyzed the picture-naming performance of twenty-one fluent aphasics and classified the errors according to five types: semantic, formal (that is, phonologically similar lexical), mixed, unrelated word substitutions, and neologisms. For each patient they then attempted to determine whether there were values of the connection and decay parameters that allowed the model to reproduce the patient's distribution of errors. The authors interpreted the fit of their simulations to the patient data to be quite good and concluded that the results provided support for the two main assumptions in their model, the interactivity and the globality assumptions. However, these findings and conclusions have been criticized on several grounds.

Does the Model Really Fit the Data from Fluent Aphasics?

How can we assess whether the computational model proposed by Dell and colleagues (1997) provides a good account of the naming performance of fluent aphasics? Two approaches to this question are detailed below.

First, one could compare the model's fit of the data of the different patients' profiles with the model's fit of sets of random numbers. Dell and collaborators took this approach and showed that their model fits the patients' performance better than the sets of random numbers. However, this is an indirect and weak measure of how well the model performed in fitting the patient data, because the fact that the model fits the patients' data better than the random numbers does not necessarily mean that the fit is good in either case. Indeed, both fits can be quite poor. Therefore the weight of evidence generated by their approach is not high.

The second approach is to carry out an extensive investigation of the different patterns of errors that the model can account for. That is, by manipulating all the possible values that the decay and the connection strength parameters can take, one could derive the space of the possible patterns of errors that the model can account for. One could then assess whether the patients' error profiles fall inside or outside the model's space of possible outcomes. If the model does indeed reflect the distribution of errors produced by fluent aphasics, one should expect that the patients' error profiles would fall inside the space of the model's predicted profiles. The observation of patients' error profiles falling outside the boundaries of the model's prediction would indicate that at least one of the assumptions adopted in the model is incorrect. This approach has recently been taken by Ruml and Caramazza (2000) in assessing whether Dell and collaborators' model does indeed account for the performance of fluent aphasics. Interestingly, the results of these analyses have shown that a large number of the patients tested by Dell and collaborators produced error profiles that fall outside the range predicted by the model, and even that certain types of error profiles seem "impossible" to account for within this model. This is especially evident when one considers the performance of patients who make only one type of errors (for example, only semantic, or only phonological errors). For instance, consider the performance of DM, a fluent aphasic whose oral production was characterized by many phonological errors and essentially no semantic errors. When DM's error profile is plotted against the range of possible error distributions that Dell and collaborators' model can account for, it becomes apparent that the patient's performance falls well outside the predicted range. Note that the reverse pattern of errors (for example, many semantic errors without phonological errors) is also incompatible with Dell and collaborators' model (Cuetos, Aguado, & Caramazza, 2000).

What are the implications of these observations for the assumptions adopted by the model of lexical access in fluent aphasia proposed by Dell and collaborators? Which of the two core assumptions (or both) of this model is incorrect? The fitting approach used by the model does not allow in the case of poor fit to determine which assumption is incorrect. A more informative approach is to try to find independent evidence separately for the plausibility of the interactivity and globality assumptions.

There is already independent evidence in the literature that the globality assumption cannot be correct. The starkest evidence is provided by the existence of patients with modality-specific naming deficits who make semantic errors either only in oral naming (for example, RGB) or only in written naming (for example, RCM). These patients' profiles of naming performance clearly indicate that their naming failures cannot be due to a deficit at the semantic level, for otherwise they would have produced errors in both oral and written naming. Furthermore, as already noted, these patients show normal comprehension performance. We are led to conclude that their deficit must be restricted to difficulties in accessing modality-specific lexical forms. An implication of this conclusion is that these patients' damage to the lexical system cannot be global but must be restricted to a postsemantic level of processing. In other words, these patients' performance is at odds with the globality assumption.

Can we then retain the interactivity assumption? There is nothing in Dell and colleagues' (1997) results that compels us to do so, since the model does not account for many of the patients' error profiles. However, as already noted, we have independent reasons for rejecting the globality rather than the interactivity assumption. One way to test whether interactivity can be a valid assumption is to implement it in a model in which globality is not assumed. Foygel and Dell (2000) have developed a new model in which the globality assumption is not implemented but interactive processing is still assumed, thereby allowing for the system to be damaged selectively at only one level of representation. This new model has been found to account for a larger number of patients' errors profiles than the previous model. However, as demonstrated by Ruml and collegues (2000), this model, too, fails to account for many patients' error profiles. Furthermore, the new model still has major difficulties in accounting for the error profiles of patients with highly selective deficits, such those of DM (Caramazza, Papagno, & Ruml, 2001), or DP (Cuetos, Aguado, & Caramazza, 2000). This failure is not surprising, since a natural result of an interactive model is that a lesion to one layer of the system, let's say the lexical layer, would affect other layers as well. This is because activation reverberates in the system, and alterations to one level of representation have carryover effects to other layers. Thus, damage to a highly interactive system would lead to a certain degree of "global damage," leading to the production of different types of naming errors.

One possible solution is to assume that the reverberating activation is not very strong. That is, it could be assumed that the activation of lower layers of processing (phonological layers) only weakly affects upper layers of processing. In such models, damage to one layer of representation would not have a large impact on other layers. If one took such a step (that is, very limited interactive processing), it would be unclear how the model may account for the mixed error and the lexical bias effects. This outcome would possibly undermine one of the most interesting properties of interactive models, namely their elegant account of the lexical bias and mixed error effects.

In sum, neither the original model proposed by Dell and colleagues (1997) nor the variant proposed by Foygel and Dell (2000) successfully simulates the error performance of a wide range of fluent aphasics. Therefore, these simulations cannot be taken as evidence supporting the notions of globality and interactivity.

In this section we have addressed the question of whether the dynamics of the lexical access system are based on discrete or cascaded activation. There is growing evidence in support of the view that lexical access involves cascaded instead of discrete processing. However, at present the extent to which cascaded processing is only feed-forward is unclear.

CONCLUSIONS

This chapter has presented a highly selective review of current findings on the performance of individuals affected by semantic and lexical language deficits in spoken naming. The detailed analyses of brain-damaged individuals in language tasks has revealed categorical effects in both semantic and grammatical processing and the presence of modality-specific deficits.

The existence of deficits restricted to one modality of output sets precise constraints on the possible forms of organization of the lexical system. The presence of patients who produce semantic errors in only one modality of output is inconsistent with models that interpose a modality-neutral lexical node between the semantic component and modality-specific lexical nodes (for example, the model proposed by Levelt et al., 1999). Furthermore, since modality-specific naming deficits allow the conclusion that the semantic system is intact in at least some fluent aphasics, we can conclude that the pattern of performance of such patients does not result from global lesions that equally affect all levels of the lexical system (as suggested by Dell et al., 1997).

ACKNOWLEDGMENT

We would like to thank Xavier Alario for his helpful comments on earlier versions of this chapter.

REFERENCES

Andreewsky, E., & Seron, X. (1975). Implicit processing of grammatical roles in a classical case of agrammatism. *Cortex, 11*, 379–390.

Baars, B. J. (1980). On eliciting predictable speech errors in the laboratory. In V. A. Fromkin (Ed.), *Errors in linguistic performance: Slips of the tongue, ear, pen, and hand*. New York: Academic Press.

Baars, B. J., Motley, J. T., & McKay, D. (1975). Output editing for lexical status from artificially elicited slips of the tongue. *Journal of Verbal Learning and Verbal Behavior, 14*, 382–391.

Barbarotto, R., Capitani, E., Spinnler, H., & Trivelli, C. (1995). Slowly progressive semantic impairment with category specificity. *Neurocase, 1*, 107–119.

Baxter, D. M., & Warrington, E. K. (1985). Category-specific phonological dysgraphia. *Neuropsychologia, 23*, 653–666.

Berg, T. (1986). The problems of language control: Editing, monitoring, and feedback. *Psychological Research, 48*, 133–144.

Berndt, R. S., Mitchum, C. S., Haendiges, A. N., & Sandson, J. (1997). Verb retrieval in aphasia 1: Characterizing single word impairments. *Brain and Language, 56*, 68–106.

Best, W. (1996). When racquets are baskets but baskets are biscuits, where do words come from? A single case study of formal paraphasic errors in aphasia. *Cognitive Neuropsychology, 13*, 443–480.

Blanken, G. (1998). Lexicalisation in speech production: Evidence from form-related word substitutions in aphasia. *Cognitive Neuropsychology, 15*, 321–360.

Breedin, S. D., & Martin, R. C. (1996). Patterns of verb impairment in aphasia: an analysis of four cases. *Cognitive Neuropsychology, 13*, 51–91.

Breedin, S. D., Saffran, E. M., & Schwartz, M. F. (1998). Semantic factors in verb retrieval: An effect of complexity. *Brain and Language 63*(1), 1–31.

Buckingham, H. (1980). On correlating aphasic errors with slips-of-the-tongue. *Applied Psycholinguistics, 1*, 199–220.

Caramazza, A. (1997). How many levels of processing are there in the lexical access? *Cognitive Neuropsychology, 14*, 177–208.

Caramazza, A. (1998). The interpretation of semantic category-specific deficits: What do they reveal about the organization of conceptual knowledge in the brain? *Neurocase, 4*, 265–272.

Caramazza, A., Berndt, R. S., & Hart, J. (1981). "Agrammatic" reading. In F. J. Pirozzolo & M. C. Wittrock (Eds.), *Neuropsychological and cognitive processing in reading*. New York: Academic Press.

Caramazza, A., & Hillis, A. E. (1990). Where do semantic errors come from? *Cortex, 26*, 95–122.

Caramazza, A., & Hillis, A. (1991). Lexical organization of nouns and verbs in the brain. *Nature, 349*, 788–790.

Caramazza, A., Hillis, A., Rapp, B., & Romani, C. (1990). The multiple semantics hypothesis: multiple confusions? *Cognitive Neuropsychology, 7*(3), 161–189.

Caramazza, A., Papagno, C., & Ruml, W. (2001). The selective impairment of phonological processing in speech production. *Brain and Language, 75*, 428–450.

Caramazza, A., & Shelton, J. R. (1998). Domain-specific knowledge systems in the brain: The animate-inanimate distinction. *Journal of Cognitive Neuroscience, 10*, 1–34.

Costa, A., Caramazza, A., & Sebastian-Galles, N. (2000). The cognate facilitation effect: Implications for models of lexical access. *Journal of Experimental Psychology: Learning, Memory, and Cognition, 26*, 1283–1296.

Cuetos, F., Aguado, G., & Caramazza, A. (2000). Dissociation of semantic and phonological errors in naming. *Brain and Language, 75*, 451–460.

Damasio, A. R., & Tranel, D. (1993). Nouns and verbs are retrieved with differentially distributed neural systems. *Proceedings of the National Academy of Sciences, 90*, 4957–4960.

De Renzi, E., & Di Pellegrino, G. (1995). Sparing of verb and preserved but ineffectual reading in a patient with impaired word production. *Cortex, 31*(4), 619–636.

De Renzi, E., & Lucchelli, F. (1994). Are semantic systems separately represented in the brain? The case of living category impairment. *Cortex, 30*, 3–25.

Dell, G. S. (1986). A spreading-activation theory of retrieval in sentence production. *Psychological Review, 93*, 283–321.

Dell, G. S. (1988). The retrieval of phonological form in production. Test of prediction from a connectionist model. *Journal of Memory and Language, 27*, 124–142.

Dell, G. S., & O'Seaghdha, P. G. (1991). Mediated and convergent lexical priming in language production: A comment on Levelt et al. (1991). *Psychological Review, 98*, 604–614.

Dell, G. S., & Reich, P. A. (1981). Toward a unified model of slips of the tongue. In V. A. Fromkin (Eds.), *Errors in linguistic performance: Slips of the tongue, ear, pen, and hand*. New York: Academic Press.

Dell, G. S., Schwartz, M. F., Martin, N. M., Saffran, E. M., & Gagnon, D. A. (1997). Lexical access in apahsic and nonaphasic speakers. *Psychological Review, 104*, 801–838.

Devlin, J. T., Gonnerman, L. M., Andersen, E. S., & Seidenberg, M. S. (1998). Category-specific semantic deficits in focal and widespread brain damage: A computational account. *Journal of Cognitive Neuroscience, 10*, 77–94.

Farah, M. J., & McClelland, J. L. (1991). A computational model of semantic memory impairment: Modality specificity and emergent category specificity. *Journal of Experimental Psychology: General, 120*, 339–

357.

Foygel, D., & Dell, G. (2000). Models of impaired lexical access in speech production. *Journal of Memory and Language, 43,* 182–216.

Fromkin, V. A. (1980). *Errors in linguistic performance: Slips of the tongue, ear, pen, and hand.* New York: Academic Press.

Funnell, E., & Sheridan, J.S. (1992). Categories of knowledge? Unfamiliar aspects of living and non-living things. *Cognitive Neuropsychology, 9,* 135–153.

Gaffan, D., & Heywood, C.A. (1993). A spurious category-specific visual agnosia for living things in normal humans and non-human primates. *Journal of Cognitive Neurosciences, 5,* 118–128.

Gainotti, G., & Silveri, M. C. (1996). Cognitive and anatomical locus of lesion in a patient with a category-specific semantic disorders: A critical survey. In R. A. McCarthy (Ed.), *Semantic knowledge and semantic representations. Memory,* vol. 3, issues 3 and 4, 247–264. Hove, England: Erlbaum and Taylor and Francis.

Gagnon, D. A., Schwartz, M. F., Martin, N., Dell, G. S., & Saffran, E. M. (1997). The origins of form-related paraphasias in aphasic naming. *Brain and Language, 59,* 450–472.

Gardner, H., & Zurif, E. (1975). Bee, but not be: Oral reading of single words in aphasia and alexia. *Neuropsychologia, 27,* 193–200.

Garrett, M. (1992). Disorders of lexical selection. *Cognition, 42,* 143–180.

Gelman, R. (1990). First principles organize attention to and learning about relevant data: Number and the animate-inanimate distinction as examples. *Cognitive Science, 14,* 79–106.

Harley, T. A. (1993). Phonological activation of semantic competitors during lexical access in speech production. *Language and Cognitive Processes, 8,* 291–309.

Hart, J., & Gordon, B. (1992). Neural subsystems for object knowledge. *Nature, 359,* 60–64.

Hillis, A. E., & Caramazza, A. (1991). Category specific naming and comprehension impairment: A double dissociation. *Brain, 114,* 2081–2094.

Hillis, A. E., & Caramazza, A. (1995). The representation of grammatical categories of words in the brain. *Journal of Cognitive Neuroscience, 7,* 396–407.

Hillis, A. E., Rapp, B. C., Romani, C. & Caramazza, A. (1990). Selective impairment of semantics in lexical processing. *Cognitive Neuropsychology, 7,* 191–244.

Hillis, A. E., Rapp, B. C., & Caramazza, A. (1999). When a rose is a rose in speech but a tulip in writing. *Cortex, 35,* 337–356.

Humphreys, G., Riddoch, M. J., & Quinlan, P. T. (1988). Cascade processes in picture identification. *Cognitive Neuropsychology, 5,* 67–104.

Keil, F. C. (1989). *Concepts, kinds, and cognitive development.* Cambridge, MA: MIT Press.

Keil, F. C., Smith, W. C., Simons, D. J., & Levin, D. T. (1998). Two dogmas of conceptual empiricism: Implications for hybrid models of the structure of knowledge. *Cognition, 60,* 143–171.

Kohn, S. E., Lorch, M. P., & Pearson, D. M. (1989). Verb finding in aphasia. *Cortex, 25,* 57–69.

Laiacona, M., Barbarotto, R., & Capitani, E. (1993). Perceptual and associative knowledge in category specific impairment of semantic memory: A study of two cases. *Cortex, 29,* 727–740.

Lambon-Ralph, M. A., Howard, D., Nightingale, G., & Ellis, A. (1998). Are living and non-living category-specific deficits causally linked to impaired percep-tual or associative knowledge? Evidence from a category-specific double dissociation. *Neurocase, 4,* 311–338.

Levelt, W. J. M. (1989). *Speaking: From intention to articulation.* Cambridge, MA: MIT Press.

Levelt, W. J. M., Roelofs, A., & Meyer, A. S. (1999). A theory of lexical access in speech production. *Brain and Behavioral Sciences , 22,* 1–75.

Levelt, W. J., Schriefers, H., Vorberg, D., Meyer, A. S., Pechmann, T., & Havinga, J. (1991). Normal and deviant lexical processing: Reply to Dell and O'Seaghdha (1991). *Psychological Review, 98,* 615–618.

Marshall, J., Pring, T., Chiat, S., & Robson, J. (1996a). Calling a salad a federation: An investigation of semantic jargon. Part 1: Nouns. *Journal of Neurolinguistics, 9,* 237–250.

Marshall, J., Chiat, S., Robson, J., & Pring, T. (1996b). Calling a salad a federation: An investigation of semantic jargon. Part 2: Verbs. *Journal of Neurolinguistics, 9,* 251–260.

McCarthy, R., & Warrington, E. K. (1985). Category specificity in an agrammatic patient: The relative impairment of verb retrieval and comprehension. *Neuropsychologia, 23*(6), 709–727.

Miceli, G., Silveri, M. C., Nocentini, U., & Caramazza, A. (1988). Patterns of dissociation in comprehension and production of nouns and verbs. *Aphasiology, 2,* 351–358.

Miceli, G., Silveri, M. C., Villa, G., & Caramazza, A. (1984). On the basis for the agrammatic's difficulty in producing main verbs. *Cortex, 20*(2), 207–220.

Moss, H. E., Tyler, L. K., Durrant-Peatfield, M., & Bunn, E. M. (1998). Two eyes of a see-through: Impaired and intact semantic knowledge in a case of selective deficit for living things. *Neurocase, 4,* 291–310.

Myerson, R., & Goodglass, H. (1972). Transformational grammars of three agrammatic patients. *Language and Speech, 15,* 305–328.

Peterson, R. R., & Savoy, P. (1998). Lexical selection and phonological encoding during language production: Evidence for cascaded processing. *Journal of Experimental Psychology: Learning, Memory, and Cognition, 24,* 539–557.

Premack, D. (1990). The infant's theory of self-propelled motion. *Cognition, 36,* 1–16.

Rapp, B., & Caramazza, A. (1997). The modality-specific organization of grammatical categories: evidence from impaired spoken and written sentence production. *Brain and Language, 56*(2), 248–286.

Rapp, B., & Caramazza, A. (1998). A case of selective difficulty in writing verbs. *Neurocase, 4,* 127–140.

Rapp, B., & Goldrich, M. (2000). Discreteness and interactivity in spoken word production. *Psychological Review, 107,* 460–499.

Riddoch, M. J., Humphreys, G. W., Coltheart, M., & Funnell, E. (1998). Semantic systems or system? Neuropsychological evidence re-examined. *Cognitive Neuropsychology, 5,* 3–25.

Roelofs, A. (1992). A spreading-activation theory of lemma retrieval in speaking. *Cognition, 42,* 107–142.

Rosh, E., Mervis C. B., Gray, W. D., Johnson, D. M., & Boyes-Braem, P. (1976). Basic objects in natural categories. *Cognitive Psychology, 8,* 382–439.

Ruml, W., & Caramazza, A. (2000). An evaluation of a computational model of lexical access: Comments on Dell et al. (1997). *Psychological Review, 197,* 609–634.

Samson, D., Pillon, A., & De Wilde, V. (1998). Impaired knowledge of visual and non-visual attributes in a

patient with a semantic impairment for living entities: A case of a true-category specific deficit.
Neurocase, 4, 273-306.

Schriefers, H., Meyer, A. S., & Levelt, W. J. M. (1990).
Exploring the time-course of lexical access in produc-
tion: Picture-word interference studies. *Journal of
Memory and Language, 29,* 86-102.

Shallice, T. (1988). *From neuropsychology to mental structure.* Cambridge: Cambridge University Press.

Shapiro, K., Shelton, J., & Caramazza, A. (2000). Grammatical class in lexical production and morphological
processing: Evidence from a case of fluent aphasia.
Cognitive Neuropsychology, 17, 665-682.

Shelton, J., & Caramazza, A. (1999). Deficits in lexical
and semantic processing: Implications for models of
normal language. *Psychonomic Bulletin and Review,
6*(1), 5-27.

Silveri, M. C., & Gainotti, G. (1988). Interaction between
vision and language in category-specific impairment.
Cognitive Neuropsychology, 5, 677-709.

Soderpalm, E. (1979). *Speech errors in normal and pathological speech.* (Travaux de l'Institut de Linguistique
de Lund–XIV). Lund: Gleerup.

Soderpalm, E. (1980). Slips of the tongue in normal and
pathological speech. In V. A. Fromkin (Ed.), *Errors in
linguistic performance: Slips of the tongue, ear, pen,
and hand.* New York: Academic Press.

Starreveld, P. A., & La Heij, W. (1996). Time-course analysis of semantic and orthographic context effects in
picture naming. *Journal of Experimental Psychology:
Learning, Memory, and Cognition, 22,* 896-918.

Stemberger, J. P. (1985). Bound morpheme loss errors in
normal and agrammatic speech: One mechanism or
two? *Brain and Language, 25,* 246-256.

Stewart, F., Parkin, A. J., & Hunkin, N. M. (1992). Naming impairments following recovery from herpes simplex encephalitis: Category-specific? *Quarterly Journal of Experimental Psychology, 44A,* 261-284.

Warrington, E. K., & McCarthy, R. (1983). Category specific access dysphasia. *Brain, 106,* 859-878.

Warrington, E. K., & Shallice, T. (1984). Category specific semantic impairments. *Brain, 107,* 829-854.

Zingeser, L. B., & Berndt, R. S. (1988). Grammatical
class and context effects in a case of pure anomia:
Implications for models of language production. *Cognitive Neuropsychology, 5,* 473-516.

8

Neuroanatomical Aspects of Naming

Christine Whatmough
Howard Chertkow

INTRODUCTION

Object naming is systematically used in the neuropsychological examination of patients. As with most neuropsychological tools, it calls into play multiple levels of processing. When used in conjunction with other basic tasks, it is usually possible to determine whether the principal cause of naming deficits are perceptual, semantic, or language output impairments. Thus, although classical neurology viewed naming deficits to be nonlocalizing in the aphasic patient (Benson, 1979), its regular use on a wide range of patient types has provided the basic functional-anatomical correlates of this cognitive task. Picture naming is a task that has also been frequently examined in brain imaging studies as well, and there is considerable agreement across studies as to which areas are preferentially activated. This chapter reviews the evidence from both lesion studies and imaging studies concerning the neural correlates of the major functional stages of object naming.

Lesion-based and functional imaging research each furnish different types of information concerning cognitive processes and each has its own particular limitations. While lesion studies have the potential to indicate areas that are essential to a task, they are subject to the imprecisions of the lesioning process itself. This is a particular difficulty with regards to research into the frontal lobes, where focal lesions are rare. Further limiting factors of lesion studies are the vagaries of vascular anatomy, individual variability, and the fact that lesions affect not only cortical structures under scrutiny but underlying fiber tracts that may be connected to cortical regions other than the cortical area of interest. Imaging studies, for their part, can provide rather precise localizing information concerning the relative involvement of one area with respect to another, under one set of task conditions more than another. They do not, however, indicate if an area is essential to the task. Furthermore, the nature of the processing taking place in the areas of relatively increased activation can only be understood in the most general terms, and this by taking into account the results of a large number of other studies using a variety of experimental paradigms.

The foregoing listing of the limitations with regards to lesion and imaging studies are not given to discourage the reader as to the value of either type of research but rather to emphasize that no one study can in and of itself answer a particular question. Each study must be looked at in the context of other studies that approached the question from different angles.

With the increased precision of imaging techniques and the ever greater capacities to store and rapidly access vast amounts of information, lesion studies of both single cases and groups have become more informative. Imaging studies, for their part, have benefited from techniques that produce temporary lesions and can be carried out under certain circumstances on normal individuals. In particular, the use of preoperative electrical stimulation on epileptic patients and transmagnetic stimulation on normal subjects are of growing interest (Stewart, Meyer, Frith, & Rothwell, 2001).

The principal components of the object naming process that are covered in this chapter follow the model of lexical processing provided by Doriana Chialant, Albert Costa, and Alfonso Caramazza in chapter 7 and by Anastasia M. Raymer and Leslie Gonzalez Rothi in chapter 9 (see also Elaine Funnell, chapter 10). They denoted stages of visual perceptual processing, visual object recognition, semantic analysis, retrieval of the associated verbal label from the phonological output lexicon, and finally speech initiation and articulation. In this chapter, we examine areas of the brain associated with each of these tasks. In addition, we will consider the functions associated with "atypical" language areas in the basal and polar areas of the temporal lobes. In all cases we will separate out lesion and imaging results for clarity.

The process of visual object naming appears to proceed in the brain in a posterior-anterior direction. Benson (1979) described the neuroanatomical pathway of naming as proceeding from primary visual cortex to visual association cortex (Brodmann's areas, or BA, 18 and 19). From here proceeded three pathways: callosal, frontal (less necessary for naming), and inferotemporal for object recognition, and a direct link to angular gyrus. Benson (1979) suggested that, because of its location, the angular gyrus was ideal for the crossmodal associations that were essential to naming. The time course of picture naming appears to have been fairly well defined. Levelt, Praamstra, Meyer, Helenius, and Salmelin (1998), relying on experimental data from a variety of sources including behavioral and event-related potential (ERP) experiments, determined that the time course for confrontation naming was as follows: 0 to 150 msec for the visual processing and accessing of the lexical concept (that is, semantics), the 150- to 275-msec interval for lemma selection (the syntactic information of the word), the 275- to 400-msec interval for phonological encoding, and finally the 400- to 600-msec interval for phonetic and articulatory processing. Their analyses of magnetic response patterns (MEG) during a picture naming task showed a progression through these time intervals from early occipital activation, via parietal and temporal, to frontal activation.

PERCEPTUAL PROCESSES

Lesion Studies

The first stage in the process of object naming requires the formation of a perceptual representation of the object. Several studies of patients with naming deficits due to perceptual impairments have been published over the last century. Such individuals fall within the clinical spectrum of apperceptive agnosia. These individuals have preserved elementary visual function, inasmuch as their visual acuity and visual fields are not worse than those of other patients who are not agnosic. Furthermore, they can detect changes in luminance and movement and perceive depth and color. However, on tasks of copying or matching simple drawings they are grossly deficient and, in some cases, are unable to identify basic geometric forms (Kertesz, 1987). They can identify objects by other senses such as touch or audition. Other than that there is a range of varied deficits across patients.

Campion (1987) reviewed the deficits of three cases of apperceptive agnosia, all of whom had suffered from an episode of carbon monoxide poisoning. In one case a computerized axial tomography (CAT) scan was carried out and revealed a diffuse lesion more prominent in the left hemisphere above the calcarine sulcus, extending into striate and prestriate cortex. There was also some involvement of the prestriate cortex in the right cortex. Bilateral occipital lobe lesions have been shown to produce impaired form discrimination and apperceptive visual agnosia in the majority of cases (Kertesz, 1987; Warrington & James, 1988). From a processing point of view, apperceptive visual agnosia is a condition wherein specific visual feature maps for color, shape, and motion remain intact, but cannot be synthesized into a meaningful percept (Coslett & Saffran, 1992). Farah (1990) carried out an exhaustive review of all lesion cases reported, to which we direct the interested reader.

Imaging Studies

The contribution of functional imaging to our understanding of neuroanatomy is complex, and relies heavily on the robustness of theoretical processing models. Imaging studies support the proposal of a visual object processing stream that proceeds in a posterior-anterior direction along the ventral surface of the occipito-temporal, reaching up into the lateral surface of the posterior temporal cortex lobes (Haxby et al., 1991; Ungerleider & Mishkin, 1982). Areas involved in basic visual perceptual processing ought to be activated by just about any visual stimulus. Indeed, compared to a rest condition, most visual stimuli produce activation of basic occipital visual cortex bilaterally (Kertesz, 1994; Frackowiak, Friston, Frith, Dolan, & Mazziotta, 1997).

VISUAL OBJECT RECOGNITION

Lesion Studies

In classical behavior neurology since the time of Lissauer, the ability to copy an object demonstrated attainment of a "percept," which then had to be associated with an object's meaning for object recognition to occur. Thus, two stages of agnosia were described: an apperceptive agnosia (no percept attained, therefore unable to copy drawings) and an associative agnosia (an intact percept is unable to contact the stored meaning). An individual with a naming impairments who was good at copying and visually discriminating between objects and yet could not recognize objects was referred to as having associative agnosia (Geschwind, 1967). Such recognition impairments are specific to one input modality, usually vision (visual agnosia). Rarely, patients with tactile agnosia have been described also.

A more modern taxonomy of object processing has arisen over the past twenty years, largely motivated by attempts to develop computer vision systems (Biederman, 1987; Marr, 1980). These models focus on the multiplicity of processing stages that are needed to go from simple visual feature maps that encode for lines, angles, and edges to a stored description of each seen object's structure (Coslett & Saffran, 1992). Such a processing system must contain "grouping procedures" for developing a coherent representation of the seen object from the multiple feature maps. Once grouped together, an ever-changing "viewer-based" representation captures the visual features of the whole object on a moment-by-moment basis. A visual buffer is necessary to maintain such a representation over time and perform computations on objects seen from unusual views and in unusual lighting. This level of processing is then used to activate a more permanent "object-based" representation, which is abstract and independent of the momentary flux of light and angle. This final "presemantic" representation would be a fully described stored structural description of an object, analogous to the lexicon of stored word identities (Humphreys, Riddoch, & Price, 1997; Humphreys, Riddoch, & Quinlan, 1988). Current debate surrounds the degree to which such stored structural identities are independent of meaning, and how they interact with our semantic system.

Unfortunately, the lesion data rarely have involved sufficiently detailed cognitive assessments to delineate the level of visual processing actually impaired in any individual's case.

What we do have are classical studies of patients with associative visual agnosia, which is a rather overinclusive category. Such individuals generally have bilateral inferior occipitotemporal lesions (Kertesz, 1987). Striatal lesions (BA 17) alone generally produce hemianopsia but not visual agnosia. Rarely, unilateral lesions accompanied by significant compromise of the callosal fibers can produce associative agnosia. Several agnosic patients with lesions to the right inferior parietal and adjacent right occipital cortex have been described by De Renzi (De Renzi, Scotti, & Spinnler, 1969; De Renzi & Spinnler, 1966; Warrington & James, 1988). These patients demonstrated very good visual processing in tasks that required discriminating forms and detecting shapes. They also could answer questions that probed their visual semantic knowledge, indicating that it is sometimes possible to access a semantic representation from an incomplete 3D description. The patients failed, however, on tasks that required access to the three-dimensional structural description of an object, tasks such as recognizing objects or silhouettes from unconventional views.

Imaging Studies

In figure 8.1, the type of visual stimuli that produce increased activity in this posterior ventral area of the brain are noted along with the areas activated. As can be seen, patterns of disjointed line segments (that is, abstract patterns, or scrambled features) cause increased activity in the ventral occipital lobe. In addition, line drawings of structured objects, whether real or novel, activate areas further anterior to the occipital lobes in the fusiform gyri and inferior temporal gyri (Murtha, Chertkow, Beauregard, & Evans, 1999). Activation in these areas is not contingent on naming or verbally responding to the stimuli, as demonstrated by the research of Kanwisher and colleagues (Kanwisher, Woods, Iacoboni, & Mazziotta, 1997), in which the rate of stimulus presentation was quite rapid (two pictures per second) to discourage verbalization.

Together these studies indicate that the fusiform responds better to structured objects, real or not, than to discontinuous fragments of objects. The fusiform also responds better to pictures of known (real) objects than unknown (Martin, Wiggs, Ungerleider, & Haxby, 1996; Moore & Price, 1999a). Moore and Price (1999a) found that a posterior region of the ventral occipito-temporal cortex was activated by meaningful objects and not by printed words for objects, whereas both objects and printed words activated a common area in the left anterior (Tailarach coordinate, y = −40; see Tailarach & Tournoux, 1988) medial fusiform region. A simple interpretation of such results would be that the processes involved in higher visual processing, up to the level of structural descriptions of objects, are instantiated in overlapping regions of the fusiform gyri and inferior occipito-temporal cortices. Certainly there would be convergence in this conclusion between the imaging and lesion results. Recent imaging studies, however, have demonstrated that the role of these brain regions is far more subtle and complex than this.

In recent studies, a large range of stimuli have been found to specifically activate fusiform and and inferior occipito-temporal cortices. Activation within the fusiform and occipito-temporal gyrus has been shown to vary topographically according to certain broad semantic categories, such as faces, animals, and artifacts (Chao, Haxby, & Martin, 1999; Kanwisher, McDermott, & Chun, 1997; McCarthy, Puce, Gore, & Allison, 1997; Whatmough et al., 1999). Functional MRI studies have found that the fusiform face area is activated by thresholded black-and-white photos (Kanwisher et al., 1997), gray-tone photos, and sketches of faces (Halgren et al., 1999) more than to gray-tone photos of cars or line drawings of inanimate objects.

The fact that the ventral occipito-temporal area displays sensitivity to semantic categories and responds to printed words has encouraged some to conclude that it is an area for the semantic knowledge of objects rather than simply visual object processing. There are, however, other explanations that could limit the activity in this area to processing or storage of the

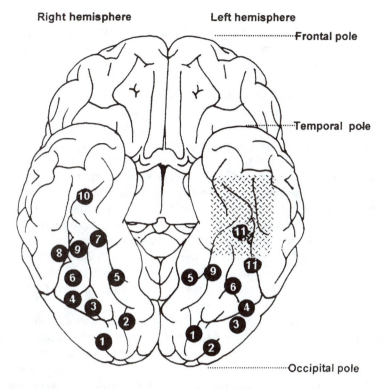

Figure 8.1. The ventral surface of the cerebral hemispheres depicting the approximate loci of peak activity during naming and naming-related tasks. Cross-hatched area indicates basal temporal language area as determined by Luders et al. (1991). See text for further details.

Key	Comparison	Study
1	**Abstract patterns**[a] (collages of patterns) minus **plus signs**[b]	Murtha et al. (1999)
2	**Abstract patterns**[a] (scrambled and disjointed picture elements) minus **plus sign**[a]	Whatmough et al. (1999) 4530
3	**Nonsense objects**[b] minus **visual noise**[b]	Martin et al. (1996) 495
4	**Animal**[c] minus **abstract patterns**[a]	Murtha et al. (1999)
5	**Tools**[c] minus **animals**[c]	Whatmough et al. (1999)
6&7*	**Novel** and/or **familiar objects**[d] more than scrambled features[d]	Kanwisher, Wood, et al. (1997)
8	**Animals**[c] minus **tools**[c]	Whatmough et al. (1999)
9	**Real object**[e] minus **nonsense objects**[d]	Martin et al. (1996)
10	**Multicomponent real objects**[e,f] (i.e., animals) > **simple objects**[e,f]	Moore & Price (1999a)
11	**Objects**[e] minus **nonobjects**[a]	Moore & Price (1999b)

Task: [a]responding "yes or okay" to each stimulus; [b]passive viewing; [c] picture naming; [d]passive viewing with rapid stimulus presentation; [e]silent naming; [f]word-to-picture matching. *The homologous left area was not a region of interest in this study.

structural description of objects. Category differences could be due to inherent differences in the visual analysis required to recognize objects from different categories. For example, faces are distinguished by fine details such as the relative proportions of facial features, whereas tools are recognized by the configuration of parts. Activation in the area induced by probe questioning could be due to some type of imagining strategy used by the subjects during probe questioning.

One way to understand the level of processing that is taking place in the fusiform is to determine the factors that affect the strength of its activation. Moore and Price (1999a) found that the right temporo-occipital and fusiform cortices were affected by the number of components that composed the object or nonobject. Maximal activity was demonstrated for multicomponent nonobjects and animals and the least activity for simple man-made objects. They also found that naming black-and-white line drawings brought out category differences in activity bilaterally in the anterior temporal cortex (ventral surface) that did not appear when the pictures were appropriately colored, indicating that activation increases when visual recognition is more difficult. Gerlach, Law, Gade, and Paulson (1999) found that rCBF increased significantly in the posterior part of the right inferior temporal (and anterior fusiform) gyrus in an object decision task that varied the class of real objects (natural versus artifacts) and the degree of nonobject discriminability (novel versus chimerical). The behavioral results indicated that subjects were slower to recognize real natural objects than artifacts and slower when the nonobjects were chimerical (that is, nonobjects composed of real object parts) than when they were an entirely novel composition. Regional CBF increased for chimerical versus novel objects in the extreme posterior part of right inferior temporal gyrus (Tailarach coordinates 54, -62, -12). They attributed this area to presemantic visual processing (structural processing) that involves either matching visual forms to memory or accessing the structural description of objects.

In an attempt to tease apart the contributions of presemantic and semantic visual processing to the fusiform activity during picture naming, Whatmough and colleagues (1999) carried out a picture naming task using PET techniques and focusing on the fact that picture familiarity reflects the strength of an item's semantic representation. They found that although the ventral and posterior inferior lateral temporal cortices were sensitive to variations in semantic category (animals versus tools), these regions were not sensitive to variations in object familiarity or success at naming. They suggested that the lack of familiarity effects in the fusiform indicated that the category effects seen on the ventral surface were probaby related more to the structural differences between object categories than to higher order semantic differences between categories.

Together, these results suggest that, indeed, the processes involved in higher visual processing, up to the level of structural descriptions of objects, are instantiated in overlapping regions of the fusiform gyri and inferior occipito-temporal cortices. In addition, we now have a more sophisticated recognition of subtle anatomic variations of such processing related to the different structural features of different categories of stimuli.

SEMANTIC PROCESSING IN NAMING

Lesion Studies

It is generally held that naming an object requires access to some sort of semantic representation to specify the concept that will then be tagged with the correct verbal label. Our knowledge of how concepts are actually stored in semantic memory remains rudimentary, and models of semantic memory are conflicting and imprecise (Caramazza, Hillis, Rapp, & Romani, 1990; Caramazza & Shelton, 1998). For instance, is the semantic knowledge needed to identify a picture of a lion for naming the same as that needed to answer the question "Which animal is the king of beasts?" Is the semantic knowledge needed to identify a picture of a lion for naming the same as the semantic knowledge activated when one merely reads the word *lion*? Such important distinctions have been variously characterized in terms of visual versus verbal semantics (McCarthy & Warrington, 1988), in terms of "identification procedures" for picture naming versus associative semantics (Chertkow, Bub, & Caplan, 1992), or in terms of preferential treatment of biological concepts (Caramazza & Shelton, 1998).

There have been a number of attempts to localize the lesions responsible for semantic deficits leading to naming problems, and an interesting set of studies applying brain imaging approaches to elucidate such localization. These approaches, we believe, have been broadly converging in their demonstration of the posterior left temporal lobe region as a critical focus for the semantic knowledge that is accessed during object naming.

Three forms of brain lesions have been investigated in terms of semantic deficits and naming difficulties: focal brain lesions producing aphasia (usually from cerebral infarction), herpes encephalitis (with lesions generally being localized but often being bilateral or less circumscribed), and degenerative dementias such as Alzheimer's disease or semantic dementia. In the case of the latter two forms of pathology, loss of semantic knowledge is probably the principal cause of the word finding difficulties encountered (Chertkow & Bub, 1990a, 1990b; Warrington & McCarthy, 1987; Warrington & Shallice, 1984). In the anomia of the aphasic patient, an "output-level" anomic impairment may be seen in conjunction with poor semantic information concerning the object (Butterworth, Howard, & McLoughlin, 1984).

Aphasic individuals had been long known to perform poorly on tests of association knowledge, although the processing level involved remained indeterminate (Goodglass & Baker, 1976; Goodglass, Wingfield, & Ward, 1997). In an influential study, Caramazza and colleagues demonstrated that a subgroup of aphasic individuals were impaired in their nonverbal semantic classification of simple objects (Caramazza, Berndt, & Brownell, 1982). Chertkow, Bub, Deaudon, and Whitehead (1997) examined eight aphasic patients with anomia who had verbal comprehension deficits on word-to-picture matching tasks. Five of these individuals also had nonverbal comprehension deficits despite demonstrating no general intellectual impairment. This pointed to a disruption in an amodal semantic system. The region of common lesion overlap in these five patients was on the lateral surface of the posterior temporal lobe, including the superior, middle, and inferior temporal lobes (BA 21, 22, and 37) and extending more anteriorly along the middle temporal gyrus. In the case of the three aphasic patients whose deficits were restricted to verbal comprehension, their brain lesions were posterior and dorsal to this posterior temporal region. This suggests that BA 37 and 22 in the left lateral temporal region are part of a neural network for an amodal semantic memory, which comes into play during picture naming. Hart and Gordon (1990) tested twelve aphasics—three with pervasive semantic deficits and one who was impaired on some semantic tests. They found that all had lesions in the posterior left temporal lobe, extending into the left inferior parietal lobule. None of the eight aphasics in the study who performed normally on the semantic tests had lesions in this area. All of the aphasics made more than 25 percent errors on the Boston Naming Test.

Another set of studies have induced artificial, temporary disruption of brain function as a means of elucidating the neural substrate of language mechanisms. While intriguing, such studies presuppose particular models of naming and semantic processing to guide interpretation, usually models that are underdeveloped. Certainly Ojemann and Whitaker (1978) have succeeded in producing speech arrest and interference with picture naming during electrical brain stimulation. They suggest that the middle temporal gyrus may be more important for naming than Wernicke's area in eliciting anomia. Schwartz, Devinsky, Doyle, and Perrine (1999) used subdural grid stimulation on the lateral surface of the left temporal lobe and found that speech-arrest sites were in the posterior third of the superior temporal gyrus, roughly in the area of the classical Wernicke's area. Regions that elicited naming errors and not simple speech arrest or reading errors were found in the posterior aspects of the superior, middle, and inferior temporal gyri, extending into the middle region of the middle temporal gyrus. There was a fairly consistent organization of language functions among subjects tested in this manner, although there was some variability as to the location of the posterior language area. This variability, and the conflicting results among studies, may reflect "normal" individual variability in structure function relationships or variability in structure-function relationships induced by lesions or seizure foci, since all patients in these studies have abnormal brains due to tumors or intractable seizures. Sites eliciting errors in both naming and reading were even more variable and widely distributed, extending more anteriorly into the temporal cortex. Again, the interpretation of these results depends on the model of semantics utilized. The authors chose to interpret regions affecting both naming and reading as corresponding to a "semantic lexicon," whereas areas affecting naming only were taken as indicative of a "visual-representation lexicon." Recently, Stewart et al. (2001) found that naming responses could be slowed 200 msec after transcranial magnetic stimulation of the posterior temporal zone (BA 37, similar to the "common semantic" region of Chertkow and colleagues [1997]). Since reading of the words was not similarly affected, the authors concluded that the region must be involved in visual object recognition processing rather than at the level of semantics. Again, we would argue that semantic activation is complex, and is not simply an "all-or-none" affair across all language tasks. The component of semantic memory activated during picture naming need not be identical with the semantics activated by reading the same word. Or, even if the semantic information is identical in the two tasks, the subject with a posterior temporal "lesion" that disrupts semantics may be able to read the word correctly on the basis of orthography-to-phonology (OPC) mechanisms or on the basis of partially disrupted semantics in conjunction with OPC mechanisms (see chapter 1 of this volume for discussion). In either case, we need not abandon the notion that the left posterior temporal region is critical for semantic identification of the seen item during picture naming, based on the claims of electrical stimulation or TMS studies to date.

A separate but important issue is that of category effects in picture naming. Goodglass originally brought attention to the presence of category-specificity in the anomia of many aphasics (Goodglass & Baker, 1976; Goodglass, Klein, & Jones, 1966). The level of representation responsible as well as the neural substrate of category specificity has remained controversial (Gainotti, Miceli, & Masullo, 1981). The theoretical interpretation of category specificity remains an active area of research (Caramazza & Shelton, 1998; Hodges & Patterson, 1997). Much of the literature concerning semantic-level impairments has focused on the category specificity issue, which is addressed in other chapters of this volume. Since a large proportion of the responsible lesions have been herpes encephalitis or degenerative dementia, little is known from lesion studies about the neural substrate underpinning such category effects. Some authors have focused on concrete objects versus action naming as categories of knowledge differentially affected by brain damage. Perani and colleagues report studies (1999) that suggest that patients with object naming deficits have left temporal lobe lesions, whereas patients with action naming deficits have large lesions extending into the frontal lobes as well.

Tranel, Damasio, and Damasio (1997) proposed that in object recognition visual input activates intermediary areas that in turn activate early sensory and motor representations associated with an object. For example, tool recognition would involve activation of representations of the tool in space, of its relationship to the hand, of its characteristic sounds, and of the typical motor patterns associated with its use. They propose that the intermediary areas that activate the ensemble of physical attributes associated with the objects varies categorically because the members of a semantic category will tend to activate similar areas of sensorimotor cortex or require similar contextual links. They support their proposal with patient lesion data that show that poor recognition of animals, tools, and faces are each associated with lesions to different brain areas. They found poor animal recognition to be associated with lesions to the mesial occipital cortex (bilaterally) and the left ventral temporal cortex, poor tool recognition with damage to the left occipital-temporal-parietal junction, and poor face recognition with right temporal pole lesions (including in several cases the hippocampus). It should be noted, however, that the patients with category deficits could in most cases recognize the majority of the objects presented from their defective category. For this reason, these intermediary areas are thought not to be essential but rather to optimize retrieval of conceptual knowledge.

Imaging Studies

The contribution of brain imaging studies in elucidating the neural basis of semantic memory involved in picture naming has been complex to date. A host of semantic tasks have been used during PET experimentation, dating back to the original studies of Posner, Petersen, and Raichle, who utilized a verb generation task (Posner, Petersen, & Raichle, 1988; Posner, Sandson, & Shulman, 1989). The most common resulting activation has been in the left inferior frontal lobe (for reviews see Cabeza & Nyberg, 1997, 2000). On the surface, such imaging studies diverge radically from the lesion evidence, which points robustly to involvement of the temporal lobes during semantic memory tasks as well as during picture naming. The emerging notion is that the frontal lobe activation represents processes of semantic search, or semantic "working memory," rather than storage of semantic representations themselves (Demb et al., 1995; Gabrieli et al., 1996).

Imaging the neural basis of semantic representations active in picture naming may be difficult because such representations are activated during many (if not all) baseline conditions as well. More subtle approaches to functional neuroimaging are probably necessary. The previously mentioned naming study by Whatmough and colleagues (1999) focused on the notion that more difficult processing at a particular level of representation is accompanied by greater activation of its associated neural tissue. Processing of more difficult or less familiar stimuli has been shown to result in much greater focal changes in cerebral blood flow, reflecting the necessity of recruiting larger regions of relevant cortex for the task (Jernigan et al., 1998; Raichle et al., 1994; Woodard et al., 1998). Whatmough and colleagues studied picture naming with PET imaging while presenting blocks of pictures at two levels of familiarity, in order to delineate through regression analysis brain regions specifically activated by decreasing picture familiarity (and increasing naming difficulty). When subjects found picture naming more difficult a corresponding increase in rCBF was found in the left posterior middle temporal gyrus (Tailarach coordinates x, y, z: -50, -47, -2, roughly corresponding to BA 37). This semantic difficulty effect was also reflected in CBF changes in the prefrontal cortex, left medial superior gyrus (BA 6), left middle frontal gyrus (BA 10), and right inferior frontal gyrus (BA 45/47), as well as in the thalamus. Whatmough and colleagues attributed the left posterior middle temporal gyrus activation to semantic processing of the picture stimuli, and the prefrontal activation to more general semantic search mechanisms. Figure 8.2 maps the areas of activation found across several studies on the lateral surface of the left hemisphere during picture naming.

A corollary to this result emerges from a PET activation study involving Alzheimer's disease patients carrying out the same task. There is now substantial evidence that the picture naming deficit of such individuals reflects the deterioration of their object representations in semantic memory (Chertkow & Bub, 1990a; Hodges & Patterson, 1995; Hodges, Salmon, & Butters, 1991). Chertkow and colleagues (2000) found that when Alzheimer's patients performed a picture naming task, they activated many of the same areas as normal elderly subjects (visual cortex, left lateral inferior frontal cortex, anterior cingulate). However, the Alzheimer's patients did not show the left posterior middle temporal gyrus activity that was associated with increasing difficulty in naming in the normal subjects. Thus, impairment at the level of semantic memory was accompanied by a specific failure to activate posterior middle temporal gyrus— the presumed substrate for semantic memory representations necessary for accurate picture naming.

A number of functional activation studies have addressed the question of category specificity, searching for differences between activations associated with naming animals and tools. We have earlier noted category effects in activation studies that localized to the fusiform and inferior occipital regions, presumably reflecting differences in the visual processing of different classes of stimuli. A series of studies by Martin, Chao, and colleagues have delineated category effects in wide ranging areas (Chao et al., 1999; Chao & Martin, 1999; Martin, Haxby,

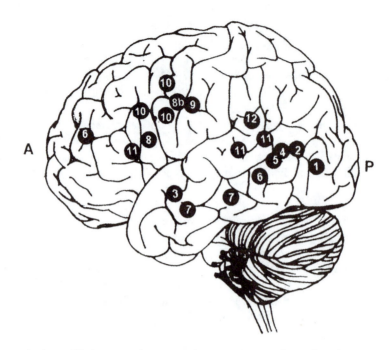

Figure 8.2. The lateral left cortex depicting the approximate loci of peak activity during naming and naming-related tasks. A = anterior, P = posterior.

Key	Comparison	Study
1	**Animal naming** minus **tool naming**	Whatmough et al. (1999)
2	**Animal naming** minus **tool naming**	Chao et al. (1999)
3	**Natural objects** minus **man-made objects** (naming and word-to-picture matching)	Moore & Price (1996a)
4	**Tool naming** minus **animal naming**	Chao et al. (1999)
5	**Tool naming** minus **animal naming**	Martin et al. (1996)
6	**Hard naming** (i.e., naming less familiar objects) minus **easy naming**	Whatmough et al. (1999)
7	**Category fluency** minus **letter fluency**	Mummery et al. (1996)
8 & 8b	**Naming objects** minus **saying "okay" to nonobjects**	Moore & Price (1999b)
8b &9	**Letter fluency** minus **category fluency**	Mummery et al. (1996)
10	**View objects** minus **view nonobjects** (i.e., covert naming, phonological code)	Zelkowicz et al. (1998)
8 & 11	**Objects naming** > **word discrimination**	Cannestra et al. (2000)
12	**Word discrimination** > **object naming**	Cannestra et al. (2000)
13	**View object** minus **view nonobject** (i.e., covert naming,	Zelkowicz et al. (1998);
(insula, not shown)	phonological code)	Martin et al. (1996)

*More common on the right homologous area.

Lalonde, Wiggs, & Ungerleider, 1995; Martin, Ungerleider, & Haxby, 1999; Martin et al., 1996). Besides activation in the ventral occipito-temporal region, pictures of real objects (as opposed to novel stimuli) activated the medial occipital lobes, particularly for animals. Tools and tool knowledge activated left posterior temporal regions as well as frontal motor strip. Martin, Wiggs, Ungerleider, and Haxby (1996) found greater activation in the calcarine sulcus (primary visual areas) for animal naming than for tool naming. Moore and Price (1999a) found that medial extrastriate cortex responded in the right hemisphere more to multicomponent objects (real or unreal) than to simple objects, and in the left hemisphere there was greater response to man-made than natural objects. These studies have led to controversial conclusions. Category differences may reflect differential storage of semantic features, differences in their presemantic visual processing, differences in the neural localization of storage for semantic categories, as well as task differences. Further data in this exciting area are emerging on a monthly basis.

To summarize: there is a coherent body of research pointing to the importance of the left posterior temporal lobe region in supporting the aspect or component of semantic memory necessary for picture naming. In addition, there are left inferior frontal regions involved in semantic access and search, as well as a host of regions associated with various aspects of category specificity (see chapter 11 of this book, for further discussion). The status of these latter regions and their involvement in picture naming remain to be clarified.

ACTIVATION OF PHONOLOGY AND WORD RETRIEVAL

Lesion Studies

Naming deficits are a feature of nearly all aphasic syndromes. Benson (1979, 1988) maintained that there were particular error patterns associated with word-finding difficulties encountered in the different classical aphasia syndromes such as Broca's and Wernicke's aphasias (but see Kremin, 1988). One difficulty in analyzing these older classifications is their emphasis on utilizing classical aphasia syndromes as the critical correlation with clinical symptomatology. Nevertheless, one can make an effort to distinguish among the naming disorders encountered in the various classical syndromes associated with damage to particular vascular territories.

Confrontation naming is poor in Wernicke's aphasia, and prompting is of little help. Verbal output in patients with Wernicke's aphasia is characterized by word-finding pauses, semantic paraphasias (for example, dog → "cat") and neologisms, and there are prominent word comprehension deficits. Thus, their naming deficits are likely to arise at the level of the semantic representation rather than at the level of the phonological representation. The pathology associated with Wernicke's aphasia involves the posterior third of the superior temporal gyrus, which we have already argued is crucial for the semantic level of naming. Unlike individuals with Wernicke's aphasia, those with anomic aphasia (also known as pure anomia, or amnesic aphasia) recognize words but cannot name. They make circumlocutions or self-corrected semantic paraphasias in naming attempts (for example, dog → "not a cat, but the one that barks"). In most cases, anomic aphasia emerges at the level of activation of the phonological representation for words or pictures, or even later stages in speech output. In Benson's scheme, pure anomia resulted from damage to BA 37, or the middle gyrus of the left temporal lobe, the inferior parietal lobe, and the lower angular gyrus. In contrast to both Wernicke's and anomic aphasias, in conduction aphasia, phonemic substitutions (literal paraphasias; for example, dog → "bog") are the most common type of naming error. Naming is abnormal because of substitution of phonemes or syllables. Conduction aphasia is attributed by Benson to damage in the anterior inferior parietal area between Broca's and Wernicke's areas. This area may be important for maintaining the phonological representation of the word while it is being articulated. Finally, in Broca's aphasia, naming is poor but can be aided by phonological cueing or by contextual priming. The problem appears to be one of access to output phonology or difficulty mapping phonology onto motor speech. The pathology associated with Broca's aphasia involves large areas of left posterior inferior frontal lobe (Benson, 1988). Interestingly, Broca's area has also been demonstrated to be involved in language production independent of motor speech output in a deaf signer. Cortical stimulation of Broca's area just anterior to the mouth and face area of the motor cortex and the supramarginal gyrus (BA 40) elicited signing errors in naming and repetition (Corina et al., 1999). Errors involved laxed hand articulations with repeated nonspecific movements with no effort to self-correct. Thus, Broca's area may be crucial for mapping from a lexical phonological representation to motor output (whether spoken or signed). Unfortunately, the neurolinguistic analysis of subjects with lesions in Broca's area in these studies has generally been insufficient to comment on the status of other processes, such as lexical-semantic representations.

Imaging Studies

A multiplicity of imaging techniques have been used to study speech output, but we will focus on those relevant to picture naming. With the use of MEG, Levelt and colleagues (1998) found that a region in the left posterior temporal lobe, roughly the location of Wernicke's area, showed prominent activation attributable to the stage of phonological encoding starting about 200 msec after picture onset and peaking at about 350 msec. A series of studies have examined activation of phonology using different tasks. Importantly, Zatorre and colleagues (Zatorre, Evans, Meyer, & Gjedde, 1992; Zatorre, Meyer, Gjedde, & Evans, 1996) produced activation in Broca's area during tasks such as judging whether two syllables had or did not have the same sound, or whether they rhymed. Since rhyme judgments activate the phonological representation of a word without activating a motor speech response, these data provide strong evidence that a word's sound form itself is instantiated in Broca's area. Mummery, Patterson, Hodges, and Wise (1996) contrasted verbal fluency for initial letters with verbal fluency for semantic categories. Initial letter fluency activated the left precentral sulcus (BA 44/6) and the primary sensorimotor cortex, similar to Zatorre and colleagues, which (Zatorre et al., 1996) they attribute to prearticulatory phonological processing.

Other studies have examined brain regions utilizing exquisitely sensitive techniques, but the very richness leads to results daunting in their complexity, as described below.

Naming to Verbal Description

Bookheimer and colleagues (1998) carried out a PET experiment that included tasks of naming to description, listening to nonsense phrases, hearing short word descriptions of objects (for example, tall pink bird), and hearing and naming the objects described by short phrases. They found that hearing the short descriptions without the requirement to name activated the medial visual cortex bilaterally (BA 17), lateral BA 18 on the right and the left fusiform gyrus. It also activated, when compared with hearing nonsense words, the language areas (left posterior superior temporal gyrus [BA 42], extending into the temporal-parietal junction [BA 39/40], and the superior temporal sulcus [BA 21/22], which includes Wernicke's area). Besides activating Broca's area (BA 44), hearing descriptions activated two other specific areas in the left prefrontal cortex (BA 46 and 6). When the naming scans were compared with the hearing-only scans, bilateral activation was found in the motor cortex, premotor cortex, insula, cerebellum, and thalamus and right activation of the putamen. The requirement to overtly name the defined object produced activation of motor-related areas and perhaps additional auditory input areas, but did not activate language areas above and beyond the hearing-only condition. This study indicates that auditory descriptions of objects produce activation in visual areas and object recognition areas.

Naming to description was also investigated by Cannestra and colleagues (2000). They explored optical imaging of intrinsic signals (OIS) while subjects performed tasks of visual and auditory confrontation naming and word discrimination (auditory lexical decision). Cannestra and colleagues focused specifically on Broca's and Wernicke's areas. They found increased activation in the pars operculis and the anterior portion of the pars triangularis of Broca's region during object naming, irrespective of input modality. Certainly this is compatable with the view that phonological access involves this region. It proves difficult, however, to distinguish phonological access from activation of the motor phoneme pattern itself. The word discrimination task, on the other hand, engaged the posterior part of pars triangularis of Broca's area, suggesting that the more posterior areas are engaged in articulation and phonological processes whereas the more anterior areas may have a lexical role. For instance, it is possible that the posterior region is more engaged in segmented phonemics, whereas the more anterior areas are involved in the retrieval of whole word phonology (a lexical representation).

The same study found increased activation for visual naming in the inferior margin of the left superior temporal gyrus and the left middle temporal gyrus. Naming to auditory description produced additional increased blood flow in the superior and middle temporal gyri with the center of activity .6 +/-0.2 cm posterior to the center for visual object naming, indicating differences related to modality of input. Auditory word discrimination produced activation that had a center superior to both object naming tasks, in the superior temporal gyrus and the supramarginal gyrus. Cannestra additionally found that the temporal profile over the 20s blocks of testing was different in each speech area. In Broca's area all activation had a "boxcar profile" (that is, a sustained plateau of activation) similar to orofacial activation in motor cortex. The posterior language area (Wernicke's area) responded more dynamically to stimulus input. There was an initial rapid rise in activation, which then declined to a plateau phase, a profile that is similar to that reported for the sensory and visual cortices. They suggest that around Wernicke's area, regions involved with phonemic word processing and semantic word processing can be found. Clearly, once one is able to reliably compare effects of input modality and variations in activation over blocks of stimuli, and utilize multiple tasks, the complexities of untangling the contributions of different levels of representation to the regional brain activation becomes a major challenge.

SPEECH INITIATION AND ARTICULATION

Lesion Studies

Speech initiation is linked to the medial supplementary motor area (Kertesz, 1994). In a minority of left-handers and a few right-handers these areas are in the right hemisphere. The classical syndrome of transcortical motor aphasia is seen in patients who can name but often need articulatory prompts to initiate speech, and for whom both phonemic and contextual cues are helpful. The syndrome results from infarction of the left anterior cerebral artery territory and is believed to result from disconnection of the supplementary motor area from the motor speech area (Freedman, Alexander, & Naeser, 1984). Lesion studies indicate that the executive functions of initiation, selection, and activation of speech arise from the supplementary motor area on the medial surface of the frontal lobe (superior to the anterior cingulate, BA 8) (Kertesz, 1994). The subcortical components of this initiation network are the ventral lateral nucleus of the thalamus and the periaqueductal gray matter of the mesencephalon. Johnson and Ojemann (2000) propose that the dominant ventrolateral thalamus generates a specific alerting response. In language tasks, this alerting response acts as a gating mechanism that controls input and the retrieval of specific items from memory. Notably, electrical stimulation of this area results in naming errors, omissions, and first syllable repetition, with a retained capacity to talk.

There is widely converging evidence from lesion studies (Kertesz, 1999) that the left inferior posterior frontal lobe (including Broca's area, or BA 44) is involved in articulation. Mohr and colleagues (1978) also reviewed a large number of cases that involved infarction of Broca's area or its surrounding area. They found that the prominent deficit of these lesions was not the agrammatism of "Broca's aphasia" but a motor speech impairment, affecting the programming or mechanics of speech (generally termed aphemia or apraxia of speech). These findings indicate that high-level articulatory programming or coding occurs in Broca's area (Kertesz, 1994). A persistent apraxia for facial, oropharyngeal, and lingual functions often accompanies such lesions.

Imaging Studies

Imaging studies have demonstrated that both verbalization and subvocalization activate motor processes, including those involved in articulation. Moore and Price (1999b) found that mouthing the names of printed words and pictures, as opposed to silently viewing the same, activated left frontal operculum, the left precentral cortex, and the right midline cerebellum and attribute this to phonological processing. Zelkowicz, Herbster, Nebes, Mintun, and Becker (1998) came to rather different conclusions. In their study, when naming of pictures was compared with producing the nonsense verbal response "hiya" in response to the nonsense figures, there was activation bilaterally in the ventral occipital procession stream but no activation in frontal or other language areas other than the right insula. Instead, the left inferior frontal regions were activated when viewing real objects compared to nonsense figures, without a verbal response. These results are rather perplexing. Presumably, in the naming task, both meaningful and meaningless verbal responses had generated similar activations in the left inferior frontal lobe. When no verbal response was called for, viewing of real but not nonsense objects resulted in unintentional subvocalization of the name in the left inferior frontal lobe, hence its activation, even during silent picture viewing.

These results suggest that there is perhaps a spectrum in the strength of activation (that is, CBF change) seen in the inferior frontal lobule (including Broca's area), ranging from mild activation during subvocalization to more robust activation during overt picture naming or phonological activity. This was in fact the finding of Rosen, Ojemann, Ollinger, and Petersen (2000), who compared silent (that is, covert naming) and spoken (that is, overt) word retrieval in a task of stem completion under fMRI. They found that both conditions activated the motor strip, although percent change was greater in the spoken condition. Both conditions activated the frontal operculum bilaterally and both conditions activated the dorsal lateral frontal area bilaterally, significantly more on the left. Interesting differences were also found at the subcortical level. The thalamus was more active on the left in both conditions. The putamen was active bilaterally for the overt condition, but activity was greatly reduced on the right during the silent word retrieval condition. This suggests that the participation of the left putamen in the word retrieval task is not strictly motor related but of a higher order.

NAMING DEFICITS ASSOCIATED WITH THE BASAL TEMPORAL LANGUAGE AREA AND TEMPORAL POLE LESIONS

Lesion Studies

There are a number of other regions, outside the standard language areas, that have been suggested to have a role in picture naming as well as other language functions. The evidence for involvement of these areas, as well as the level of processing implicated, remain controversial; and therefore we will explore evidence for involvement of these regions in a separate section. Anterior temporal lobe resections for control of refractory epilepsy typically include the temporal pole and mesially the parahippocampal gyrus and hippocampus. Bell, Davies, Hermann, and Walters (2000) found that a subgroup of epileptic patients (seventeen of forty-three subjects) who underwent left anterior temporal lobe resection experienced a significant decline in picture naming and verbal episodic memory in the presence of a preservation of other language functions and of general intellect. The remaining patients, who demonstrated no decline in naming after surgery, had an earlier age of seizure onset (mean of 8.8 years) than those who demonstrated some decline in language function (mean age of seizure onset of 17.0 years), and most (94 percent) had moderate to severe hippocampal sclerosis. Thus, the normal involvement of this area in picture naming might have been altered in the presence of early-onset temporal lobe damage; in early cases the language functions might have been transferred to alternate brain regions while brain plasticity was still maximal. These data argue for a role of the temporal pole in normal picture naming.

The basal temporal language zone is a region along the inferior ventral aspect of the temporal lobe. Luders and colleagues (1991) determined by electrial stimulation that, in those epileptic patients where such a language area could be demonstrated, it was located from 3 to 3.5 cm posterior (to the temporal pole) to 4 and 7 cm posterior (to the temporal pole). This area is represented in figure 8.1. Resection of the basal temporal language area as determined by cortical stimulation can result in anomia but frequently does not. Some, therefore, have classified this area along with the temporal pole as "atypical language areas" (Bell et al., 2000; Burnstine et al., 1990; Malow et al., 1996). The critical lesion is a little uncertain; in cases where it does cause anomia, the resection has often included lateral temporal areas as well.

Damasio, Grabowski, Tranel, Hichwa, and Damasio (1996) have documented brain lesions in a similar inferior temporal region that result in mild naming output problems. The three categories they tested in brain-lesioned subjects were unique person identities, animals, and tools. They found impaired word retrieval for the names of persons to be maximally impaired in patients with left temporal pole lesions including mesial temporal lobe. They found impaired word retrieval for animal stimuli to correlate with lesions in the left anterior and middle inferior temporal region (posterior to the persons area), and for naming tools they found a correlation with lesion location in the posterior inferior temporal and anterior lateral occipital area, extending up into the temporo-occipito-parietal junction. Based on their analyses, the authors concluded that these areas were not involved in semantic memory or phonological representations per se, but mediated between the two during the process of picture naming. All of these lesion locations are inferior to what is generally considered to be the "language zone" of the left hemisphere (Caplan, 1988). In light of these and other findings Damasio and colleagues (1996) postulate that lexical retrieval for picture naming involves higher order association cortex that mediates between concept knowledge and phonemic production. These areas of lexical retrieval would not hold the explicit form of names of persons or objects but rather, upon activation by concept knowledge, would instruct sensorimotor structures how to reconstruct the correct phonological pattern. These intermediary zones, which lie outside the classical language areas (that is, Broca's and Wernicke's area), exist in different areas for different categories of concepts. It should be noted that in their study, a variety of different lesion types were assessed, with few details as to the underlying pathology. It should also be noted that a word retrieval deficit was defined as performance that was more than 2 sd below normal performance (which was very high) and as such could include patients who could name as many as 88 percent of the objects in the affected category. These intermediary areas are therefore required for completely effective and efficient naming. Many individuals with lesions in these zones nevertheless seem capable of quite good naming and recognition of objects (Biederman, Gerhardstein, Cooper, & Nelson, 1997).

Temporal lobe epilepsy patients have experienced "word selection" deficits in visual and auditory confrontation naming tasks during electrical stimulation of the inferior temporal cortex (Malow et al., 1996). They experienced a "tip-of-the-tongue" state and could gesture or describe the target items. However, they also were poorer in picture selection tasks, which suggests a problem in precise object recognition. Lateral temporal stimulation also produced poorer naming and picture selection. The superior temporal gyrus was the only area that produced deficits in auditory confrontation naming alone.

Devinsky and colleagues (2000) examined the correlation between language sites as determined by cortical stimulation, and the cognitive function of epilepsy patients. They found that patients with language sites in the anterior or inferior temporal cortex had fewer years of education and had poorer verbal learning and fluency than those with language sites in the posterior superior temporal-inferior parietal area. In general the number of language sites was negatively correlated with full-scale IQ and measures of naming, verbal fluency, and immediate verbal memory. This study is important, inasmuch as the bulk of literature concerning the inferior temporal lobe and basal temporal language zone has concerned seizure subjects, whose neural localization may be atypical and related to disease factors that have influenced general brain organization.

Imaging Studies

There have been a number of imaging studies relevant to the question of involvement of the basal temporal lobe and temporal pole in picture naming. Moore and Price (1999b) found that the lateral and posterior (y = −62) inferior temporal region (the left basal language zone) was activated during both naming pictures of objects, as well as reading printed words.

Damasio and colleagues (1996) found that name retrieval of unique persons, animals, and tools each had a unique locus of increased activity on PET, which corresponded with their conclusions about language localization from lesion studies. PET picture naming was compared with responding "up" or "down" when presented with pictures of unfamiliar faces. These were presented randomly either correctly positioned or upside-down. This is an unusual subtraction baseline, which arguably complicates interpretation of any findings considerably. They limited their statistical search area to the temporal pole and the inferior temporal lobe. Naming unique persons activated the left ventrolateral TP, tool naming activated the posterior middle and inferior temporal cortex, and animal naming activated the inferior temporal gyri. Damasio and colleagues (1996) maintain that this converges with their lesion studies and indicate that the area plays a mediatory role between concept knowledge and the explicit representation of word phonology.

In summary, there is considerable evidence now for some role of this inferior temporal region in naming, but the exact level of processing involved remains controversial.

CONCLUSION

In this chapter we have reviewed a large number of investigations into picture naming, based on brain lesions (transient as well as permanent) as well as multiple brain imaging modalities. Each level of processing postulated to occur based on work in cognitive neuropsychology has been found to be accompanied by a core set of converging studies pointing with reasonable robustness to a small set of implicated neural regions. At the same time, this general convergence of results has been accompanied by multiple confusions. There has been confusion in the literature because most lesion studies preceded the era of processing diagrams and relied instead on correlations with classical aphasic syndromes. There has been confusion in the imaging literature because of technical problems that accompany novel brain imaging methods, and the poverty of our understanding of the underlying cognitive processes we are depicting. In some of the above sections, specifically that regarding semantic processing, we have tried to demonstrate the degree to which misinterpretation of imaging data flows from errors in the theoretical underpinning of a particular experiment.

At the same time, we hope to have presented, albeit briefly, the essential manner in which lesion data and imaging data will increasingly come to reinforce each other and generate ever more accurate models of complex linguistic processes such as picture naming.

REFERENCES

Bell, B. D., Davies, K. G., Hermann, B. P., & Walters, G. (2000). Confrontation naming after anterior temporal lobectomy is related to age of acquisition of the object names. *Neuropsychologia, 38*(1), 83-92.

Benson, D. F. (1979). Neurologic correlates of anomia. In H. Whitaker (Ed.), *Studies in Neurolinguistics* (Vol. 4). New York: Academic Press.

Benson, D. F. (1988). Classical syndromes of aphasia. In F. E. Boller, J. Grafman, J., et al. (Eds.), *Handbook of neuropsychology* (Vol. 1). Amsterdam: Elsevier Science Publishing Co.

Biederman, I. (1987). Recognition-by-components: A theory of human image understanding. *Psychological Review, 94*(2), 115-147.

Biederman, I., Gerhardstein, P. C., Cooper, E. E., & Nelson, C. A. (1997). High level object recognition without an anterior inferior temporal lobe. *Neuropsychologia, 35*(3), 271-287.

Bookheimer, S. Y., Zeffiro, T. A., Blaxton, T. A., Gaillard, W. D., Malow, B., & Theodore, W. H. (1998). Regional cerebral blood flow during auditory responsive naming: Evidence for cross-modality neural activation. *Neuroreport, 9*(10), 2409-2413.

Burnstine, T., Lesser, R., Hart, J., Jr, Uematsu, S., Zinreich, S., Krauss, G., Fisher, R., Vining, E., & Gordon, B. (1990). Characterization of the basal temporal language area in patients with left temporal lobe epilepsy. *Neurology, 40*(6), 966-970.

Butterworth, B., Howard, D., & McLoughlin, P. (1984). The semantic deficit in aphasia: The relationship between semantic errors in auditory comprehension and picture naming. *Neuropsychologia, 22*, 409-426.

Cabeza, R., & Nyberg, L. (1997). Imaging cognition: An empirical review of PET studies with normal subjects. *Journal of Cognitive Neuroscience, 9*(1), 1-26.

Cabeza, R., & Nyberg, L. (2000). Imaging cognition II: An empirical review of 275 PET and fMRI studies. *Journal of Cognitive Neuroscience, 12*(1), 1-47.

Campion, J. (1987). Apperceptive agnosia: The specification and description of constructs. In G. W. Humphreys & M. J. Riddoch (Eds.), *Visual object processing: A cognitive neuropsychological approach*. Hove, England: Lawrence Erlbaum Associates.

Cannestra, A. F., Bookheimer, S. Y., Pouratian, N., O'Farrell, A., Sicotte, N., Martin, N. A., Becker, D., Rubino, G., & Toga, A. W. (2000). Temporal and topographical characterization of language cortices using intraoperative optical intrinsic signals. *Neuroimage, 12*(1), 41-54.

Caplan, D. (1988). The language zone. In E. Newmeyer (Ed.), *Linguistics: The Cambridge survey* (Vol. 4). Cambridge: Cambridge University Press.

Caramazza, A., Berndt, R. S., & Brownell, H. H. (1982). The semantic deficit hypothesis: perceptual parsing and object classification by aphasic patients. *Brain and Language, 15*, 161-189.

Caramazza, A., Hillis, A., Rapp, B., & Romani, C. (1990). The multiple semantic hypothesis: Multiple confusions? *Cognitive Neuropsychology, 7*, 161-189.

Caramazza, A., & Shelton, J. (1998). Domain-specific knowledge systems in the brain: The animate-inanimate distinction. *Journal of Cognitive Neuroscience, 10*(1), 1-34.

Chao, L. L., Haxby, J. V., & Martin, A. (1999). Attribute-based neural substrates in temporal cortex for perceiving and knowing about objects. *Nature Neuroscience, 2*(10), 913-919.

Chao, L. L., & Martin, A. (1999). Cortical regions associated with perceiving, naming, and knowing about colors. *Journal of Cognitive Neuroscience, 11*(1), 25-35.

Chertkow, H., & Bub, D. (1990a). Semantic memory loss in Alzheimer-type dementia. In M. F. Schwartz (Ed.), *Modular deficits in Alzheimer-type dementia: Issues in the biology of language and cognition*. Cambridge, MA: MIT Press.

Chertkow, H., & Bub, D. (1990b). Semantic memory loss in dementia of Alzheimer's type: What do various measures measure? *Brain, 113*(2), 397-417.

Chertkow, H., Bub, D., & Caplan, D. (1992). Constraining theories of semantic memory processing: Evidence from dementia. *Cognitive Neuropsychology, 9*(4), 327-365.

Chertkow, H., Bub, D., Deaudon, C., & Whitehead, V. (1997). On the status of object concepts in aphasia. *Brain & Language, 58*(2), 203-232.

Chertkow, H., Murtha, S., Whatmough, C., McKelvey, R., et al. (2000). *Altered activation of cerebral cortex in Alzheimer's disease during picture naming: A positron emission tomographic study*. Paper presented at the Cognitive Neuroscience Society, San Francisco.

Corina, D. P., McBurney, S. L., Dodrill, C., Hinshaw, K., Brinkley, J., & Ojemann, G. (1999). Functional roles of Broca's area and SMG: Evidence from cortical stimulation mapping in a deaf signer. *Neuroimage, 10*(5), 570-581.

Coslett, H. B., & Saffran, E. M. (1992). Disorders of higher visual processing: Theoretical and clinical perspectives. In D. I. Margolin (Ed.), *Cognitive neuropsychology in clinical practice*. New York: Oxford University Press.

Damasio, H., Grabowski, T. J., Tranel, D., Hichwa, R. D., & Damasio, A. R. (1996). A neural basis for lexical retrieval [published erratum appears in *Nature* 1996 Jun 27; 381(6595): 810]. *Nature, 380* (6574), 499-505.

De Renzi, E., Scotti, G., & Spinnler, H. (1969). Perceptual and associative disorders of visual recognition: Relationship to the side of the cerebral lesion. *Neurology, 19*(7), 634-642.

De Renzi, E., & Spinnler, H. (1966). Visual recognition in patients with unilateral cerebral disease. *Journal of Nervous and Mental Disorders, 142*(6), 515-525.

Demb, J. B., Desmond, J. E., Wagner, A. D., Vaidya, C. J., Glover, G. H., & Gabrieli, J. D. (1995). Semantic encoding and retrieval in the left inferior prefrontal cortex: A functional MRI study of task difficulty and process specificity. *Journal of Neuroscience, 15*(9), 5870-5878.

Devinsky, O., Perrine, K., Hirsch, J., McMullen, W., Pacia, S., & Doyle, W. (2000). Relation of cortical language distribution and cognitive function in surgical epilepsy patients. *Epilepsia, 41*(4), 400-404.

Farah, M. J. (1990). *Visual agnosia: Disorders of object recognition and what they tell us about normal vision*. Cambridge, MA: MIT Press.

Frackowiak, R. S. J., Friston, K. J., Frith, C. D., Dolan, R. J., & Mazziotta, J. C. (1997). *Human brain function*. San Diego: Academic Press.

Freedman, M., Alexander, M. P., & Naeser, M. A. (1984). Anatomic basis of transcortical motor aphasia. *Neurology, 34*(4), 409-417.

Gabrieli, J. D. E., Desmond, J. E., Demb, J. B., Wagner, A. D., et al. (1996). Functional magnetic resonance imaging of semantic memory processes in the frontal lobes. *Psychological Science, 7*(5), 278–283.

Gainotti, G., Miceli, G., & Masullo, C. (1981). The relationship between type of naming error and semantic-lexical discrimination in aphasic patients. *Cortex, 17,* 401–410.

Gerlach, C., Law, I., Gade, A., & Paulson, O. B. (1999). Perceptual differentiation and category effects in normal object recognition: A PET study. *Brain, 122*(11), 2159–2170.

Geschwind, N. (1967). The varieties of naming errors. *Cortex, 3,* 97–112 .

Goodglass, H., & Baker, E. (1976). Semantic field, naming, and auditory comprehension in aphasia. *Brain and Language, 3,* 359–374.

Goodglass, H., Klein, B. C. P., & Jones, K. J. (1966). Specific semantic word categories in aphasia. *Cortex, 2,* 74–89.

Goodglass, H., Wingfield, A., & Ward, S. E. (1997). Judgments of concept similarity by normal and aphasic subjects: Relation to naming and comprehension. *Brain & Language, 56*(1), 138–158.

Halgren, E., Dale, A. M., Sereno, M. I., Tootell, R. B. H., Marinkovic, K., & Rosen, B. R. (1999). Location of human face-selective cortex with respect to retinotopic areas. *Human Brain Mapping, 7*(1), 29–37.

Hart, J., Jr., & Gordon, B. (1990). Delineation of single-word semantic comprehension deficits in aphasia, with anatomical correlation. *Annals of Neurology, 27*(3), 226–231.

Haxby, J. V., Grady, C. L., Horwitz, B., Ungerleider, L. G., Mishkin, M., Carson, R. E., Herscovitch, P., Schapiro, M. B., & Rapoport, S. I. (1991). Dissociation of object and spatial visual processing pathways in human extrastriate cortex. *Proceedings of the National Academy of Sciences of the United States of America, 88*(5), 1621–1625.

Hodges, J. R., & Patterson, K. (1995). Is semantic memory consistently impaired early in the course of Alzheimer's disease? Neuroanatomical and diagnostic implications. *Neuropsychologia, 33*(4), 441–459.

Hodges, J. R., & Patterson, K. (1997). Semantic memory disorders. *Trends in Cognitive Sciences, 1,* 17.

Hodges, J. R., Salmon, D. P., & Butters, N. (1991). The nature of the naming deficit in Alzheimer's disease. *Brain, 114*(4), 1547–1558.

Humphreys, G. W., Riddoch, M. J., & Price, C. J. (1997). Top-down processes in object identification: evidence from experimental psychology, neuropsychology, and functional anatomy. *Philosophical Transactions of the Royal Society of London, Series B: Biological Sciences, 352*(1358), 1275–1282.

Humphreys, G. W., Riddoch, M. J., & Quinlan, P. T. (1988). Cascade processes in picture identification. *Cognitive neuropsychology, 5,* 67–103.

Jernigan, T. L., Ostergaard, A. L., Law, I., Svarer, C., Gerlach, C., & Paulson, O. B. (1998). Brain activation during word identification and word recognition. *Neuroimage, 8*(1), 93–105.

Johnson, M. D., & Ojemann, G. A. (2000). The role of the human thalamus in language and memory: Evidence from electrophysiological studies. *Brain and Cognition, 42*(2), 218–230.

Kanwisher, N., McDermott, J., & Chun, M. M. (1997). The fusiform face area: A module in human extrastriate cortex specialized for face perception. *Journal of Neuroscience, 17*(11), 4302–4311.

Kanwisher, N., Woods, R. P., Iacoboni, M., & Mazziotta, J. C. (1997). A locus in human extrastriate cortex for visual shape analysis. *Journal of Cognitive Neuroscience, 9*(1), 133–142.

Kertesz, A. (1987). The clinical spectrum and localisation of visual agnosia. In G. W. Humphreys & M. J. Riddoch (Eds.), *Visual object processing: A cognitive neuropsychological approach.* Hove, England: Lawrence Erlbaum.

Kertesz, A. (1994). *Localization and neuroimaging in neuropsychology.* San Diego: Academic Press.

Kertesz, A. (1999). Language and the frontal lobes. In B. L. Miller (Ed.), *The human frontal lobes: Functions and disorders: The science and practice of neuropsychology series.* New York: Guilford.

Kremin, H. (1988). Naming and its disorders. In F. E. Boller, J. Grafman, J., et al. (Eds.), *Handbook of neuropsychology* (Vol. 1). Amsterdam: Elsevier Science Publishing Co.

Levelt, W. J., Praamstra, P., Meyer, A. S., Helenius, P., & Salmelin, R. (1998). An MEG study of picture naming. *Journal of Cognitive Neuroscience, 10*(5), 553–567.

Luders, H., Lesser, R. P., Hahn, J., Dinner, D. S., Morris, H. H., Wyllie, E., & Godoy, J. (1991). Basal temporal language Area. *Brain, 114*(2), 743–754.

Malow, B. A., Blaxton, T. A., Sato, S., Bookheimer, S. Y., Kufta, C. V., Figlozzi, C. M., & Theodore, W. H. (1996). Cortical stimulation elicits regional distinctions in auditory and visual naming. *Epilepsia, 37*(3), 245–252.

Marr, D. (1980). Visual information processing: The structure and creation of visual representations. *Phil. Trans. R. Soc. Lond., B290,* 199–218.

Martin, A., Haxby, J. V., Lalonde, F. M., Wiggs, C. L., & Ungerleider, L. G. (1995). Discrete cortical regions associated with knowledge of color and knowledge of action. *Science, 270*(5233), 102–105.

Martin, A., Ungerleider, L. G., & Haxby, J. V. (1999). Category-specificity and the brain: The sensory-motor model of semantic representations of objects. In M. S. Gazzaniga (Ed.), *The cognitive neurosciences, 2nd ed.* Cambridge, MA: MIT Press.

Martin, A., Wiggs, C. L., Ungerleider, L. G., & Haxby, J. V. (1996). Neural correlates of category-specific knowledge. *Nature, 379*(6566), 649–652.

McCarthy, G., Puce, A., Gore, J. C., & Allison, T. (1997). Face-specific processing in the human fusiform gyrus. *Journal of Cognitive Neuroscience, 9*(5), 605–610.

Mohr, J. P., Pessin, M. F. S., et al. (1978). Broca aphasia: Pathologic and clinical. *Neurology, 28,* 311–324.

Moore, C. J., & Price, C. J. (1999a). A functional neuroimaging study of the variables that generate category-specific object processing differences. *Brain, 122*(5), 943–962.

Moore, C. J., & Price, C. J. (1999b). Three distinct ventral occipitotemporal regions for reading and object naming. *NeuroImage, 10,* 181–192.

Mummery, C. J., Patterson, K., Hodges, J. R., & Wise, R. J. (1996). Generating "tiger" as an animal name or a word beginning with T: Differences in brain activation [published erratum appears in Proc R Soc Lond B Biol Sci 1996 Dec 22; 263 (1377): 1755-6]. *Proceedings of the Royal Society of London, Series B: Biological Sciences, 263*(1373), 989–995.

Murtha, S., Chertkow, H., Beauregard, M., & Evans, A. (1999). The neural substrate of picture naming. *Journal of Cognitive Neuroscience, 11*(4), 399–423.

Ojemann, G. A., & Whitaker, H. A. (1978). Language localization and variability. *Brain and Language, 6*(2), 239–260.

Perani, D., Cappa, S. F., Schnur, T., Tettamanti, M., Collina, S., Rosa, M. M., & Fazio, F. (1999). The neural correlates of verb and noun processing: A PET study. *Brain, 122*(12), 2337–2344.

Posner, M. I., Petersen, S., & Raichle, M. E. (1988). Localization of cognitive operations in the human brain. *Science, 240*, 1627–1631.

Posner, M. I., Sandson, J. D. M., & Shulman, G. L. (1989). Is word recognition automatic? A cognitive-anatomical approach. *Journal of Cognitive Neuroscience, 1*, 50–60.

Raichle, M. E., Fiez, J. A., Videen, T. O., MacLeod, A. M., Pardo, J. V., Fox, P. T., & Petersen, S. E. (1994). Practice-related changes in human brain functional anatomy during nonmotor learning. *Cerebral Cortex, 4*(1), 8–26.

Rosen, H. J., Ojemann, J. G., Ollinger, J. M., & Petersen, S. E. (2000). Comparison of brain activation during word retrieval done silently and aloud using fMRI. *Brain and Cognition, 42*(2), 201–217.

Schwartz, T. H., Devinsky, O., Doyle, W., & Perrine, K. (1999). Function-specific high-probability "nodes" identified in posterior language cortex. *Epilepsia, 40*(5), 575–583.

Stewart, L., Meyer, B., Frith, U., & Rothwell, J. (2001). Left posterior BA 37 is involved in object recognition: A TMS study. *Neuropsychologia, 39*(1), 1–6.

Tailarach, J., & Tournoux, P. (1988). *Co-planar stereotaxic atlas of the human brain: 3-Dimensional proportional system: An approach to cerebral imaging.* Stuttgart: George Thieme Verlag.

Tranel, D., Damasio, H., & Damasio, A. R. (1997). A neural basis for the retrieval of conceptual knowledge. *Neuropsychologia, 35*(10), 1319–1327.

Ungerleider, L. G., & Mishkin, M. (1982). Two cortical visual systems. In D. J. Ingle, M. A. Goodale, & R. J. V. Mansfield (Eds.), *Analysis of visual behaviour.* Cambridge, MA: MIT Press.

Warrington, E. K., & James, M. (1988). Visual apperceptive agnosia: A clinico-anatomical study of three cases. *Cortex, 24*(1), 13–32.

Warrington, E. K., & McCarthy, R. A. (1987). Categories of knowledge: Further fractionations and an attempted integration. *Brain, 110*, 1273–1296.

Warrington, E. K., & Shallice, T. (1984). Category specific semantic impairments. *Brain, 107*, 829–854 .

Whatmough, C., Chertkow, H., Murtha, S., Whitehead, V., Fung, D., & Templeman, D. (1999). *Separable effects of familiarity and semantic category on picture naming: An oxygen-15 PET study.* Paper presented at the Society for Neuroscience, Miami.

Woodard, J. L., Grafton, S. T., Votaw, J. R., Green, R. C., Dobraski, M. E., & Hoffman, J. M. (1998). Compensatory recruitment of neural resources during overt rehearsal of word lists in Alzheimer's disease. *Neuropsychology, 12*(4), 491–504.

Zatorre, R. J., Evans, A. C., Meyer, E., & Gjedde, A. (1992). Lateralization of phonetic and pitch discrimination in speech processing. *Science, 256*(5058), 846–849.

Zatorre, R. J., Meyer, E., Gjedde, A., & Evans, A. C. (1996). PET studies of phonetic processing of speech: Review, replication, and reanalysis. *Cerebral Cortex, 6*(1), 21–30.

Zelkowicz, B. J., Herbster, A. N., Nebes, R. D., Mintun, M. A., & Becker, J. T. (1998). An examination of regional cerebral blood flow during object naming tasks. *Journal of the International Neuropsychological Society, 4*(2), 160–166.

9

Clinical Diagnosis and Treatment of Naming Disorders

Anastasia M. Raymer
Leslie J. Gonzalez Rothi

INTRODUCTION

Impairments of word retrieval (anomia) are common among individuals with aphasia. The functional impact is devastating in that word-finding failures disrupt the ability to carry on a meaningful, effective, efficient conversation. While the impact of anomia is difficulty in maintaining verbal interactions, the clinical assessment and treatment of word retrieval impairments are most typically accomplished through the use of picture confrontation naming tasks. As reviewed by Doriana Chialant, Albert Costa, and Alfonso Caramazza (see chapter 7), the process of picture naming requires not only the retrieval of the lexical phonological forms for words, but also mechanisms for visual object and semantic processing (figure 9.1). Presumably, it is the semantic and phonological stages that are critical for the process of word retrieval in conversation, and impairments of these processes are associated with aphasia. Deficits affecting the mechanisms for visual object processing (the agnosias) may cooccur with aphasia, further complicating the picture in naming assessment and treatment.

Christine Whatmough and Howard Chertkow (see chapter 8) have explored the neural correlates of the complex process of picture naming distributed throughout the neural cortex. Disparate cortical regions may contribute different processes or types of information to a composite functional outcome of picture naming. They note that impairments in picture naming may result from dysfunction of a number of cortical regions.

Thus, the distributed architecture of word retrieval processing is compatible with a multicomponential, functional model. Many clinical researchers have advocated the use of multicomponent cognitive models, such as the model of naming described in figure 9.1, to provide a strategic theoretical rationale for clinical decision-making in the management of patients with acquired language disorders (Byng, Kay, Edmundson, & Scott, 1990; Coltheart, 1984; Hillis, 1993; Howard & Patterson, 1989; Raymer, Rothi, & Greenwald, 1995). In turn, information garnered from treatment studies may lead to modifications in cognitive models (Berndt, 1992).

In this chapter we focus specifically on the model of naming described in figure 9.1 and its implications for assessment and management of impairments of word retrieval. Although disruption of mechanisms of visual object processing may impair picture naming performance,

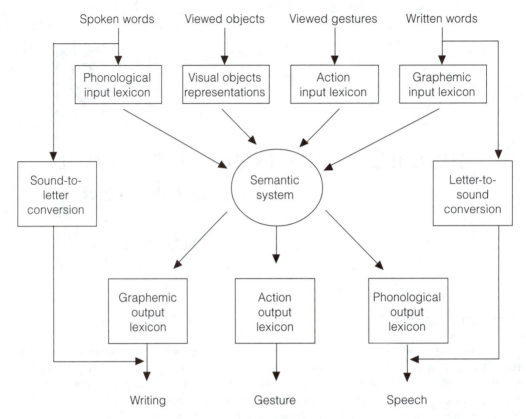

Figure 9.1. Model of lexical processing.

these impairments fall into the category of sensory-specific, prelinguistic processing, which is beyond the scope of this chapter. We concentrate primarily on dysfunction of semantic and phonological stages of lexical processing as they undermine word retrieval functions in conversational and picture naming tasks in individuals with aphasia. For each stage in the process of naming, we describe assessment procedures to characterize word retrieval impairments with respect to the model of naming. We also review studies in which researchers use this framework to develop rational treatments that either target impaired naming mechanisms or take advantage of spared mechanisms to circumvent naming impairments (Rothi, 1998). To exemplify this process in practice, we will describe the assessment and treatment of one patient, AW, who had significant word-finding difficulties.

CONSIDERATIONS IN ASSESSMENT

The goal of the assessment process we describe is to characterize a patient's word retrieval impairment with respect to dysfunction at some stage in the naming model in figure 9.1. Raymer, Rothi, and Greenwald (1995) illustrated how this approach may provide a more focused assessment of naming abilities in contrast to the standard methods used at that time. Two patients, both demonstrating anomia in standardized assessment, had distinct differences in the mechanisms for their word retrieval impairments. One patient, HH, had an impairment affecting semantic activation of the output lexicons characterized by intact performance in auditory comprehension tasks and severe cross-modality anomia in all verbal and written naming tasks (Raymer, Foundas, et al., 1997). The other, SS, had impairments affecting at least two stages of lexical processing: visual object activation of the semantic system, and semantic activation of the output lexicons (Raymer, Greenwald, Richardson, Rothi, & Heilman, 1997). Thus, in addition to cross-modality anomia, SS had inordinate naming difficulty for picture stimuli. Assessment results using this model-driven strategy led to a targeted word retrieval treatment in the second patient, SS, as we trained word retrieval using the auditory-verbal input modality rather than the impaired visual input system (Greenwald, Raymer, Richardson, & Rothi, 1995). Below, we describe the type of assessment procedures that help to identify the underlying cognitive impairment(s) in individual patients.

Cross-Modality Comparisons

A key notion incorporated in the assessment geared to identify impairments in the naming system is cross-modality comparison. The naming assessment should include a variety of single word processing tasks in which the clinician systematically varies input (written words, spoken words, viewed objects, viewed gestures) and output modalities (speech, written spelling, gesture), and then analyzes patterns of performance for tasks sharing modalities of processing. As shown in table 9.1, the assessment typically will include a set of key tasks that assess comprehension and production of single words in phonological and graphemic forms. Published psycholinguistic tests are available that allow systematic assessment of lexical processing (for example, Psycholinguistic Assessment of Language Processing Abilities; Kay, Lesser, & Coltheart, 1992). In addition, researchers have developed experimental batteries of lexical tasks for use in their studies of naming impairments as well (for example, Florida Semantics Battery; Raymer & Rothi, 2000).

If the functioning of a lexical mechanism is disturbed by neurologic disease, modality comparisons should demonstrate that performance is impaired in all tasks dependent upon that mechanism. For example, to the extent that the processing of meaning is required to comprehend and produce words, a deficit of semantic processing will affect performance in all comprehension and naming tasks (modality consistency) (for example, Hillis, Rapp, Romani, & Caramazza, 1990). In comparison, to the extent that the phonological output lexicon supports spoken word production, a dysfunction of that mechanism will result in impairment in all verbal production tasks (for example, oral naming of pictures and oral reading of single words if sublexical processes also are impaired) (Caramazza & Hillis, 1990). In the case of phonological output dysfunction, it is not necessary for comprehension or the written modality of output to be deficient (modality inconsistency).

Lexical Stimuli

A second consideration in naming assessment is the selection of appropriate stimuli to use across lexical tasks. For example, we use the same set of 120 nouns across all tasks in our Florida Semantics Battery (Raymer & Rothi, 2000). In this way, differences observed across

Table 9.1
Battery of Key Tasks to Include in Lexical Assessment

Oral picture naming
Written picture naming
Oral naming to spoken definitions
Oral word reading
Writing to dictation
Auditory word-to-picture matching or verification
Written word-to-picture matching or verification

tasks can be attributed to the modality of processing rather than differences inherent to the stimulus items. There will be times when the clinician wants to evaluate performance for contrasting sets of words from different semantic (for example, animals versus tools) or grammatical categories (for example, nouns versus verbs). However, additional factors such as word frequency, imageability, length, familiarity, and age of acquisition (Feyereisen, Van Der Borght, & Seron, 1988; Hirsh & Ellis, 1994; Lambon Ralph, Graham, Ellis, & Hodges, 1998; Nickels & Howard, 1994, 1995) may influence naming abilities across sets. Thus, clinicians should select an array of stimuli to represent these lexical variables and evaluate their influence on naming abilities.

Error Patterns

The assessment of naming abilities also includes a consideration of the errors produced across lexical tasks, as patterns of errors may provide clues to the mechanism of naming failure. The same qualitative pattern of errors should be observed in all tasks that require processing by the suspected impaired mechanism. For example, a deficit of semantic processing may lead to semantic errors (for example, *orange* for *apple*) in comprehension as well as naming tasks (for example, Hillis et al., 1990). A phonological output lexicon dysfunction may result in parallel patterns of phonological errors (/apsIl/ for "apple") that span verbal production tasks (for example, oral naming of pictures and oral reading of single words if sublexical processes also are impaired).

Examination of error type is not sufficient to distinguish the level of lexical impairment responsible for the naming error, however. Semantic errors in picture naming are a case in point (Hillis & Caramazza, 1995b). For example, for the target picture of a carrot, semantic naming errors may include responses such as "vegetable" (superordinate), "celery" (coordinate), or "rabbit" (associated). Whereas in some patients semantic errors represent semantic system impairment (Hillis et al., 1990; Raymer, Foundas, et al., 1997; Howard & Orchard-Lisle, 1984), semantic errors also can occur from impairment at the phonological retrieval stage (Caramazza & Hillis, 1990), or during visual-to-semantic activation (Hillis & Caramazza, 1995a; Raymer, Greenwald, et al., 1997). These observations suggest the need to analyze error patterns across lexical tasks to develop a more accurate hypothesis regarding the source of the lexical error as, for example, semantic errors do not necessarily imply semantic dysfunction (Raymer & Rothi, 2000).

Final Comments on Assessment

In addition to specifying the basis for dysfunction in lexical processing leading to naming failure, the approach we describe has other advantages (Raymer, Rothi, & Greenwald, 1995). Many patients with extensive neurological lesions have dysfunction affecting multiple levels in the naming process. An in-depth assessment will frequently suggest not only what mechanisms are impaired, but also what mechanisms are spared in lexical processing, information that may be beneficial as the clinician turns toward devising treatments for each patient. Retained lexical processing in alternative mechanisms not typically part of the naming process—for example, reading and gesture mechanisms—may be implemented in compensatory or vicariative methods (Rothi, 1995) to improve word retrieval and, thereby, communication abilities.

A clear disadvantage of this approach is the increased length of assessment that we have advocated. Although some clinicians may find lengthy assessments unrealistic in clinical practice, it is possible for clinicians to adapt these methods using a more circumscribed set of available materials. For example, clinicians may select a small set of stimuli representing a variety of semantic or grammatical categories and vary modality for key lexical processing tasks. For example, one might use this set of stimuli for oral and written naming, oral reading, writing to dictation, repetition, and word-picture matching. The systematic assessment may indeed be more cost-effective than the standard of care as clinicians characterize both their patients' impairments and retained abilities, and hence direct treatments in the most targeted manner.

PRINCIPLES OF TREATMENT

As is found with aphasia assessment, a number of clinical researchers have expressed enthusiasm for applying this model-guided approach to aphasia treatment (Coltheart, 1984; Mitchum, 1992; Raymer et al., 1995; Riddoch & Humphreys, 1994; Seron & Deloche, 1989), although others have voiced some caution (Caramazza & Hillis, 1993). Naming models provide a sound basis for leading some, though by no means all, treatment decisions. In particular, naming models are well suited to the view that the type of intervention strategy to apply should relate to the chronicity of the naming impairment. Rothi (1995) proposed that restitutive strategies, which encourage restoration of functioning in a manner compatible with normal language processing, are appropriate in early stages when neurophysiologic processes of recovery are maximal. Substitutive strategies that attempt to circumvent naming dysfunction using intact cognitive mechanisms may be beneficial during acute and chronic stages of recovery. Following the systematic lexical assessment, clinicians may choose to direct restitutive treatments at impaired semantic or phonological stages in the naming process. Alternatively, clinicians may train substitutive strategies that take advantage of intact output modes to circumvent or to vicariatively mediate word retrieval processes through gesture or reading.

SEMANTIC IMPAIRMENTS

Assessment

Word retrieval difficulties in some individuals may arise due to dysfunction of the semantic stage of naming. A patient with a semantic impairment will have difficulty performing any tasks that require semantic mediation (that is, modality consistency). Therefore, of the tasks listed in table 9.1, patients should have difficulty in comprehension of spoken words and spoken naming, not just for seen objects, but for all modalities of input (objects, spoken definitions, and so on) (Ellis, Kay, & Franklin, 1992). All modes of output will be affected as well (gesture, writing, and so on). Because sublexical letter-sound conversion mechanisms may be available for decoding or encoding written words, performance in oral word reading and writing to dictation may be less affected than naming or comprehension.

Assuming that the semantic system is structured in a similar fashion for all modalities of processing, individuals with brain damage that yields semantic system impairment should demonstrate quantitatively and qualitatively similar impairments across lexical tasks requiring semantic mediation. Researchers have described this association of impairments in some patients with vascular lesions (Hillis et al., 1990; Howard & Orchard-Lisle, 1984) and progressive neurological impairments (Chertkow, Bub, & Seidenberg, 1989; Hodges & Patterson, 1996; Lambon Ralph, Ellis, & Franklin, 1995; Raymer & Berndt, 1996).

Semantic Tasks

In practice, it may be possible for a neurological lesion to cause extensive damage to lexical input and output stages simultaneously, leading to modality consistency of impairments that mimic semantic dysfunction. Therefore, it can be beneficial to administer additional semantic tasks that require more specific processing of semantic attributes of stimuli or that avoid the use of lexical stimuli. Patients with semantic dysfunction should have difficulty in these types of tasks as well, whereas individuals with cooccurring input modality/output modality impairments may perform somewhat better in some of these semantic tasks that circumvent verbal disturbances. In this regard, semantic picture category sorting tasks can be useful. However, it is critical that patients sort pictures from closely related semantic categories that require patients to accomplish more specific semantic processing for successful performance (for example, fruits versus vegetables, winter clothing versus summer clothing). When required to sort distant semantic categories, patients may be able to accomplish the task by recognizing only visual characteristics or more superficial semantic information, and thereby may be able to complete the task in spite of semantic impairment.

Another useful task to assess semantic processing requires patients to match semantically associated pictures. *Pyramids and Palm Trees* (Howard & Patterson, 1992) is a useful published test of this sort. We have included a semantic associate subtest in the *Florida Semantics Battery* (Raymer & Rothi, 2000). This task requires subjects to match a target item (for example, carrot) to a semantically related item from three choices (for example, associate—rabbit; distractors—squirrel, duck). This type of associate task may be sensitive to more subtle impairments in semantic activation (for example, Raymer, Greenwald, et al., 1997). It is also useful to contrast performance in the associate task for matching spoken words and matching viewed pictures to delineate impairments related to phonological input or semantic stages of lexical processing. Semantic impairments are associated with difficulty whether stimuli are presented as words or pictures.

Researchers have also described individuals with aphasia whose naming and comprehension impairments fractionate, demonstrating selective preservation or selective impairment, for specific semantic categories. Patients have demonstrated impairments for categories such as living and nonliving things (Bunn, Tyler, & Moss, 1998; Montanes, Goldblum, & Boller, 1995; Silveri et al., 1997; Warrington & McCarthy, 1983), fruits and vegetables (Hart, Berndt, & Caramazza, 1985; Farah & Wallace, 1992), tools (Ochipa, Rothi, & Heilman, 1989), animals (Caramazza & Shelton, 1998; Ferreira, Giusiano, & Poncet, 1997; Hart & Gordon, 1992; Hillis & Caramazza, 1991), and medical terminology (Crosson, Moberg, Boone, Rothi, & Raymer, 1997). Because we know that semantic impairments can be category-specific, it is useful to include assessment tasks that are structured according to this dimension. We have incorporated semantic category distinctions into the *Florida Semantics Battery*, as we test items from twelve different semantic categories. Within standard aphasia tests currently available, an astute examiner may notice either impaired or spared performance related to selective semantic categories by noting errors and exploring the possibility of a category-specific dysfunction with additional testing materials representing that semantic category. Results of testing that identifies selective categories of difficulty for a patient may allow the clinician to streamline efforts in rehabilitation, focusing on impaired categories and taking advantage of retained processing for other categories.

Semantic Treatments for Naming Impairments

Because semantic dysfunction may lead to naming impairments, researchers have investigated a number of treatment approaches that exploit semantic functioning in an attempt to improve naming abilities (table 9.2). Some of the techniques tend to activate semantic processing, whereas others encourage the reconstitution of semantic representations. Although we cannot definitively state that the techniques are restitutive in nature, the methods seem to encourage semantic processing according to principles that parallel what is known of normal semantic processing and thus appear to be primarily restitutive.

Table 9.2
Types of Naming Treatments That Have Been Tested

	Restitutive
Semantic treatments	Phonological treatments
Semantic comprehension tasks	Phonological judgment tasks
Semantic distinctions	Phonological cueing hierarchy
Semantic matrix training	Oral word reading
	Word repetition
	Rhyme treatment

Substitutive
Letter-sound conversion self-cues
Verbal-gestural

Semantic Comprehension Treatments

Because the semantic system plays a role in both word comprehension and word selection, a number of researchers have investigated the utility of comprehension treatments to facilitate naming abilities. Byng and colleagues (1990) described a treatment for a patient with severe aphasia that implicated a semantic impairment. The patient participated in semantic processing tasks requiring picture categorization with increasingly related categories, and word-picture matching with increasingly difficult semantic distractors (closer semantic relationship to the target). Following this semantic treatment, the patient demonstrated improvement in naming for trained words.

A number of investigations subsequently have evaluated the effects that practice with semantic comprehension tasks (auditory word-picture matching, written word-picture matching, or answering yes/no questions about semantic details of a picture) have on naming abilities (Davis & Pring, 1991; Marshall, Pound, White-Thomson, & Pring, 1990; Nickels & Best, 1996; Pring, White-Thomson, Pound, Marshall, & Davis, 1990). However, in these studies the patients also said the words during the performance of the comprehension tasks, adding a phonological component to the treatment. Following semantic comprehension practice, subjects with impairments related to either semantic or phonologic dysfunction demonstrated significant improvement in naming abilities.

Two subsequent studies have contrasted treatments in which semantic comprehension tasks were performed with and without phonologic production of target words to determine the role that the phonologic component plays in treatment outcome (Drew & Thompson, 1999; Le Dorze, Boulay, Gaudreau, & Brassard, 1994). In both studies, subjects benefited maximally during training in which comprehension tasks were paired with phonologic output during training (oral reading, repetition), in keeping with the normal process of semantic-phonological activation in lexical output.

Semantic Distinctions Treatment

Some patients may produce semantic errors in naming because of dysfunction wherein semantic representations become underspecified (Hillis, 1991, 1998). To target such a problem, Hillis used a training protocol in which she provided her patient, HG, with semantic information about target pictures the patient was unable to name, and contrasted those features with the semantic features of a closely related object. Ochipa, Maher, and Raymer (1998) used a similar semantic distinctions treatment with their patient with naming impairment stemming from dysfunction at a somewhat later stage in naming, in the course of semantic representations activating subsequent lexical mechanisms. In both studies, the patients demonstrated significant improvements in naming trained pictures as well as generalization to untrained pictures and untrained lexical tasks requiring semantic processing (written word production).

Semantic Feature Matrix Training

Another type of naming treatment, developed on the basis of cognitive theories of how semantic representations are structured, incorporates a semantic feature matrix (Haarbauer-Krupa, Moser, Smith, Sullivan, & Szekeres, 1985). Clinicians teach subjects to use a viewed matrix of printed cue words (for example, function, properties, category, and so on) surrounding a target picture to assist in retrieving semantic information about the picture along with its name (Boyle, 1997; Boyle & Coelho, 1995; Lowell, Beeson, & Holland, 1995; McHugh, Coelho, & Boyle, 1997). Following semantic feature matrix training, subjects have demonstrated improved naming of trained pictures as well as generalization of the strategy to naming of some untrained pictures. For example, Boyle and Coelho (1995) noted that semantic matrix training improved the naming abilities of their patient with Broca's aphasia (the cognitive basis for naming failures was not specified). Lowell and colleagues (1995) reported that semantic matrix training was effective in two of three individuals with word retrieval deficit stemming from phonological stages of naming.

Summary

Overall, a number of investigators have evaluated treatment schemes that appear to target semantic processing, recognizing aspects of the normal process of semantic activation and representation of semantic knowledge. These treatments have been effective for improving naming for patients whose impairments arise at a semantic stage of processing. The semantic treatments have sometimes been effective for remediating some impairments arising at postsemantic stages in the naming process as well. Because the semantic training protocols often included a phonologic component to the training, however, this finding is perhaps not unexpected. In studies examining the importance of the phonological step in semantic training, findings indicated that the phonologic component was particularly critical for treatment effectiveness (Drew & Thompson, 1999; Le Dorze et al., 1994). Hence, training that encompasses semantic and phonologic information, as in the normal process of word retrieval, appears to be the most effective in the remediation of naming impairments.

Another observation among semantic training studies for naming is that, to some extent, generalization of training to untrained words may be possible. The semantic matrix training protocol, which seems to encourage a process of semantic activation of pieces of semantic information, was somewhat promising in this respect. However, with only guarded optimism, we would recommend that clinicians plan for little generalization to untrained words and should accordingly select training stimuli that are functional and relevant to the individual patient.

PHONOLOGIC IMPAIRMENTS

Assessment

Word retrieval difficulties in other patients stem from dysfunction at the level of the phonological output lexicon. In the case of phonological dysfunction, the patient will be impaired in all verbal tasks dependent upon the integrity of stored phonological representations. In the initial assessment battery (table 9.1), patients will have difficulty in oral naming to pictures and definitions. They may have difficulty in oral reading, particularly for exception words (for example, *colonel, bread*), as sublexical processes are often insufficient to derive accurate pronunciations for those words. Production errors may take a variety of forms, including semantic errors (Caramazza & Hillis, 1991), phonemic paraphasias (Kay & Ellis, 1987), neologisms (Kohn, Smith, & Alexander, 1996), and no response (Miceli, Giustollisi, & Caramazza, 1991). This variation in the form that verbal errors may take represents the spectrum of impairments that may occur in the phonological output lexicon. Some individuals may produce semantic errors or no response because of difficulty accessing the phonological output lexicon (Caramazza & Hillis, 1991; Le Dorze & Nespoulous, 1989; Miceli et al., 1991). Others may produce neologistic responses or phonemic paraphasias related to disturbance of the internal structure of representations (Kohn et al., 1996) or postlexical phonemic processes (Ellis et al., 1992).

A key distinction that presumably is represented at the level of the phonological output lexicon is grammatical category (Caramazza & Hillis, 1991). Dissociations in naming performance may be evident, as some patients with fluent aphasia and more posteriorly placed lesions may be more impaired for noun naming. Others with nonfluent aphasia and more anterior lesions may be more impaired for verb naming (Damasio & Tranel, 1993; Ellsworth & Raymer, 1998; Miceli, Silveri, Villa, & Caramazza, 1984; Zingeser & Berndt, 1990). Naming assessment then should incorporate tasks to explore grammatical category differences in naming. An initial step in assessing grammatical class in naming can be accomplished with the Boston Naming Test (Kaplan, Goodglass, & Weintraub, 1983) and the Action Naming Test (Nicholas, Obler, Albert, & Goodglass, 1985). However, those two published measures are not equated on variables such as word frequency that may influence word retrieval (Williamson, Adair, Raymer, & Heilman, 1998). An alternative useful resource to evaluate naming nouns and verbs can be found in Zingeser and Berndt (1990). They provided an appendix of their noun and verb word lists equated for factors that may affect word retrieval. Clinicians may wish to develop lexical tasks incorporating these carefully selected sets of nouns and verbs. Using these noun and verb naming stimuli, we developed corollary comprehension tasks (Williamson, Raymer, Adair, Schwartz, & Heilman, 1995). This noun-verb battery allows us to explore semantic versus phonological influences on word retrieval for nouns and verbs.

Phonological Tasks

In the initial lexical assessment, tasks requiring spoken word production will require activation of the phonological output lexicon. Impairment in oral naming, oral word reading, or repetition tasks in the context of good performance in auditory and reading comprehension, written naming, and writing to dictation leads one to suspect impairment of the phonological output lexicon (Caramazza & Hillis, 1990). However, this dissociation between spoken and written output may arise with subsequent phonological planning impairments (for example, apraxia of speech).

Although comparable impairments for spoken and written naming often represent semantic dysfunction, it is possible to develop cooccurring naming impairments from dysfunction of both the phonological and graphemic output lexicons (Miceli et al., 1991). On the basis of the lexical assessment, clinicians should be able to distinguish these two distinct deficits, however. With semantic dysfunction, naming impairments should be accompanied by difficulties in lexical comprehension tasks as well. In contrast, patients with naming impairment due to parallel dysfunctions of the phonological and graphemic output lexicons should demonstrate relatively preserved performance in comprehension tasks.

To distinguish among oral naming impairments related to phonologic lexical versus subsequent phonologic planning deficits, it may be necessary to administer tasks that specifically tax phonologic lexical processing without motor speech. One such task is a homophone task in which subjects must decide whether two pictures have the same name (for example, bow: violin bow and ribbon tied as a bow) (Caplan, 1993). A somewhat more difficult task is rhyme verification for picture pairs. In this task, the patient views two pictures and must determine whether their names rhyme (for example, *whale, nail*). Alternatively, a written homophone task in which subjects must decide whether two written words are pronounced the same (for example, *pear, pair*) may be useful. These three tasks will prove difficult for individuals who fail to activate a full lexical representation for the pictures. Comparison in the repetition of words versus nonwords may also help distinguish whether an impairment stems from the phonological output lexicon or beyond. Patients with postlexical impairments may have greater difficulty repeating nonword stimuli (Kahn, Stannard, & Skinner, 1998), whereas patients with lexical deficits alone may have less difficulty with nonword stimuli.

Phonologic Treatments

Recognizing that word retrieval abilities depend upon the integrity of the phonological stage of naming, a number of studies have used treatment protocols incorporating phonologic information in an attempt to restore naming abilities in patients with word retrieval impairments (table 9.2).

Reading and Repetition

In the naming model, the same phonologic output representation may be activated in oral reading, word repetition, and oral picture naming. Realizing this relationship, Miceli, Amitrano, Capasso, and Caramazza (1996) had their patient repeatedly practice reading aloud or repeating sets of words. Both types of practice resulted in improved picture naming for the corresponding words in their subject with phonologically based word retrieval failure. Mitchum and Berndt (1994) also used repetition practice in their patient with selective verb retrieval impairment. Following repetition training, their patient demonstrated improvements in naming trained verbs, but little progress in sentence formulation for the trained verbs.

Phonologic Cueing Hierarchy

Other treatment studies have incorporated phonologic cueing hierarchies in training to improve word retrieval impairments. In this type of protocol, patients systematically practice naming as they are given different types of phonologic information as they attempt to retrieve a target word. An example of a cueing hierarchy adapted from an earlier study is shown in table 9.3 (Raymer, Thompson, Jacobs, & leGrand, 1993). A number of patients who received training with cueing hierarchies have demonstrated improvements in word retrieval for trained words, with little generalization to untrained words (Greenwald et al., 1995; Hillis, 1993, 1998).

Table 9.3
Example of a Phonological Cueing Hierarchy (after Raymer et al., 1993)

At each step, patient attempts to retrieve the target word. If correct, the patient moves to the next picture after rehearsing the correct word multiple times. If incorrect, the patient is given the next cue.

1. Patient attempts to name target picture (for example, table).
2. Initial phoneme cue: "It starts with /t/."
3. Rhyme cue: "It sounds like *fable*."
4. Oral reading cue: Present word for oral reading.
5. Repetition cue: "Say table."

Among these studies, treatment was effective for subjects with either semantic or phonologic word retrieval dysfunction, although in one study improvements were more limited in patients with cooccurring semantic impairment (Raymer et al., 1993). Hillis (1998) noted, however, that treatment with a phonologic cueing hierarchy was not as effective as semantic distinctions treatment in her patient with a semantically based naming impairment.

Because of concerns that the phonologic hierarchy was effective simply because of a final repetition phase in their treatment, Greenwald and colleagues (1995) also administered a simple rehearsal (repetition) phase of treatment for a different set of stimuli. Only minimal naming improvement was evident following simple rehearsal, compared to the more noticeable effects of the phonemic cueing hierarchy treatment in both of their patients with naming impairments related to disturbance in semantic activation of the output lexicons.

Phonological Judgment Treatment

Robson, Marshall, Pring, and Chiat (1998) used a different type of phonologic training scheme that paralleled the procedures described earlier for semantic comprehension treatment. Their patient practiced a number of tasks requiring judgments about phonologic information for words, such as the number of syllables and the initial phoneme of words, to encourage activation of phonologic output representations. Their subject, with a naming impairment arising at a phonological stage of lexical processing, demonstrated improvement in naming pictures trained with this strategy and showed some generalization of the process in naming untrained pictures as well.

In a paradigm using the elements of semantic and phonological training, Marshall, Pring, and Chiat (1998) used a combination of semantic comprehension tasks and phonological judgment tasks to train verb retrieval for their subject with selective verb naming impairment. Following treatment, their subject not only improved naming for trained verbs, but also increased the use of grammatical sentences incorporating those verbs.

Semantic Category Rhyme Therapy

Recognizing the interactive nature of semantic and phonological information in the process of word retrieval, Spencer and colleagues (2000) devised a treatment for their patient, NR, whose naming impairment stemmed from failure at the phonological output lexicon. In their treatment, the clinician gave NR the semantic category and a rhyming word, aspects of semantic and phonologic information, for practice retrieving the labels corresponding to target pictures. NR demonstrated improvement in naming both trained and untrained pictures.

Summary

Overall, a number of researchers have investigated treatment protocols encompassing phonologic aspects of words to improve naming abilities. These phonologic treatments appear to be effective in patients with impairments related to either phonological or semantic stages of naming; however, effects may be reduced in individuals with semantic impairment (Raymer et al., 1993). Preliminary data suggest that the use of a phonologic cueing hierarchy is more effective than simple repetition practice in remediating word retrieval impairments (Greenwald et al., 1995). However, a cueing hierarchy may not be as effective as an alternative semantic treatment in individuals with semantically based naming impairments (Hillis, 1998). Finally, generalization of treatment effects to untrained stimuli were much more limited in the phonologic training investigations than in semantic training protocols, again suggesting the need to select stimuli carefully for functional relevance to the individual patients.

NAMING TREATMENTS: REMAINING ISSUES

Substitutive Naming Treatments

An alternative approach to rehabilitation of naming impairments to which lexical models may contribute is the development of substitutive treatments that either circumvent an impaired lexical mechanism or vicariatively mediate word retrieval using other cognitive mechanisms. For example, the use of semantic circumlocution to describe a concept when a naming failure occurs is a substitutive semantic strategy to circumvent failure at the subsequent stage of phonologic lexical retrieval. Some treatment studies have evaluated the effects of methods to vicariatively activate word retrieval using alternative cognitive mechanisms.

Graphemic Mechanisms

Some patients with naming impairments arising at the level of the phonological output lexicon nevertheless may be able to access the word's spelling. In turn, the patient may use print-to-sound conversion processes to generate the appropriate spoken word. Bruce and Howard (1987) used this strategy with their patient who had some retained spelling knowledge for words he was unable to say. The patient typed the letters into a computer, which then generated the initial phoneme of the word to cue naming. Over time the patient improved in naming practiced words even without computer-generated cues.

A number of studies have described similar procedures in which the patient self-generates the written letter to self-cue spoken naming. Nickels (1992) reported that her patient improved word retrieval skills using a graphemic training technique, in spite of impaired print-to-sound conversion abilities. Translation of the initial letter to phoneme was sufficient to self-cue the correct spoken form of the word. Bastiaanse, Bosje, and Franssen (1996) also described a patient who was trained to use the compensatory method of writing the first letter of the word and then generating a phonemic cue to retrieve the spoken word. Over time, the patient was able to generate the phonemic cue without writing.

Holland (1998) described the process of training her patient, RR, to use graphemic information to generate the spoken form of words during conversation. RR was adept at writing the words he was unable to retrieve and learned to generate spoken names of words during picture naming tasks. However, he did not use this strategy during conversational word retrieval failures. It was not until the strategy was practiced in a generative semantic category naming task (for example, writing words in a particular category such as animals) that RR made gains in using the strategy in functional communication.

Hillis (1998) described an extraordinary patient, HG, who spontaneously used retained print-to-sound conversion abilities and access to graphemic representations to support her attempts at oral naming. HG often mispronounced words using regularized pronunciations (for example, "breed" for bread). Familiar listeners could often perform a reverse translation for her technique and determine the word HG was saying. To circumvent this maladaptive strategy, Hillis taught HG to pronounce words by memorizing regularized spellings of common words with exceptional spellings (for example, *kwire* for *choir*), which she in turn used in oral naming of the same words.

Gesture

An alternative method that researchers have applied to mediate word retrieval is the use of the action output lexicon through pantomime. Luria (1970) originally referred to such a process as "intersystemic gestural reorganization," using intact gesture abilities to activate the impaired language system. Cognitive models that recognize the interactive nature of verbal and gestural output processing (Rothi, Ochipa, & Heilman, 1991, 1997) suggest a means for gesture to mediate activation of lexical retrieval. A desirable outgrowth of gestural training is that the patient has learned an alternative functional communication mode should verbal improvements not develop. A number of studies using traditional therapy procedures have demonstrated positive effects of verbal-gestural training in individuals with aphasia (for example, Hoodin & Thompson, 1983; Kearns, Simmons, & Sisterhen, 1982; Pashek, 1997; Raymer & Thompson, 1991). Recent studies have examined factors that may optimize gestural training effects. Pashek (1998), recognizing the differences in neural-cognitive representation for different classes of words, compared the effectiveness of verbal-gestural training for nouns versus verbs. Her findings in one subject with mild limb apraxia indicated that, whereas gestural training led to improvements in both word classes, naming performance was greater for verbs than for nouns.

Summary

Intact graphemic and gestural mechanisms of the lexical system may be used to support communication attempts in individuals with naming impairments. Some substitutive treatments may over time act vicariatively to improve spoken naming. At other times, the substitutive strategy remains the primary means of communication, as naming improvement is not forthcoming. It is crucial that clinicians evaluate the potential for alternative communication modes as a means to circumvent lexical impairments, particularly in individuals in more chronic stages of recovery from neurological injury (Rothi, 1995).

Contrasting Naming Treatments

A fairly broad literature has now demonstrated the effectiveness of a variety of treatments for naming impairments. And in these studies there has been no clear one-to-one relationship between type of impairment and type of treatment that is effective (Hillis, 1993). However, to evaluate this consideration more carefully, it is helpful to compare the effects of different treatments within the same patients to determine the most effective strategy. Howard and colleagues (1985) sequentially evaluated separate naming treatments requiring subjects to answer questions about either semantic or phonologic information for target pictures. Their group results indicated that both treatments led to improved naming for trained words, with an advantage of semantic over phonologic treatment. However, the mechanism of the naming impairments in their subjects was not well described, so it is not possible to evaluate the relationship between impairment and treatment on the basis of their results.

Ellsworth and Raymer (1998) used a training paradigm in which they contrasted phonologic and semantic question training for one subject, WR, who had a selective verb naming impairment. Intact performance in comprehension tasks and significant impairment across oral naming tasks indicated that the impairment arose at a phonologic retrieval stage in naming. In the semantic question hierarchy, WR answered yes/no questions about a coordinate action and an associated object for each trained verb. To illustrate, in training the verb *to paddle*, she was asked questions such as: Is it similar to rowing? Does it have to do with paddles? In the phonologic question hierarchy, WR answered yes/no questions about the initial phoneme and a rhyming word for each training word. So when training the verb *to cook*, she was asked questions such as: Does it start with /k/? Does it sound like *book*? A final repetition practice phase followed both treatments. Both semantic and phonologic treatments led to improvements in verb retrieval for trained verb naming and production of accurate sentences using those trained verbs. Maintenance of improvement was greatest for the phonologic treatment of verbs, in keeping with the phonologic basis to her verb retrieval impairment.

Ennis and colleagues (2000) completed a study contrasting the effects of a similar semantic question hierarchy versus a phonologic question hierarchy in their patient AS, with a noun retrieval impairment related to phonological dysfunction. In this case, the semantic question hierarchy included yes/no questions regarding coordinate, associate, and semantic category, whereas the phonologic question hierarchy queried as to initial phoneme, rhyming word, and number of syllables. Both treatments ended with a common rehearsal phase. Although both treatments were effective in improving noun retrieval, semantic treatment had an advantage over phonologic, in spite of the fact that AS had a naming impairment that arose at a phonologic stage of processing.

In contrast to patients with primarily phonologic impairment in word retrieval (Ellsworth & Raymer, 1998; Ennis et al., 2000), Wambaugh, Doyle, Linebaugh, Spencer, and Kalinyak-Fliszar (1999) contrasted phonologic and semantic cueing treatments in a patient, FS, with a semantic-phonologic basis for her naming impairment. And as in the other two studies, FS responded positively to both phonologic and semantic treatments. To some extent, however, generalization to untrained naming was more evident following semantic treatment.

On the basis of these preliminary findings, restitutive semantic and phonological treatments appear to be effective in improving word retrieval for trained words. However, there seems to be little direct relationship between type of naming impairment (semantic or phonologic) and most effective treatment (Hillis, 1993). Either semantic or phonologic treatment seems to improve naming in individuals with either semantic or phonologic impairment, although the treatment may be effective for different reasons in the two cases. For example, providing a phonological cue to a patient with a semantic deficit may help to activate the target phonological representation among many competing phonological representations activated by the damaged semantic representation. In contrast, providing a phonological cue to a patient with a deficit at the level of the phonological lexicon may provide the additional activation needed to the target lexical representation (which would have received full activation from the semantic system, but still did not quite reach threshold for selection due to damage at this level), such that the target is activated just above its threshold. This proposal is compatible with the interactive nature of semantic and phonologic processing in the course of lexical activation (Humphreys, Riddoch, & Quinlan, 1988). In fact, the best restitutive treatments appear to be those that combine semantic and phonologic components during training to encourage the process of word retrieval.

Case Example

We exemplify this approach to assessment and treatment with a description of a study we completed with our patient AW. He was a fifty-nine-year-old gentleman who was six months post onset of a left fronto-parietal stroke. AW was a retired railroad engineer with reported developmental reading and spelling difficulties that complicated his clinical presentation. On standardized aphasia testing with the Western Aphasia Battery (Kertesz, 1982), AW presented with a mild Broca's aphasia that was evolving toward conduction aphasia as he experienced more difficulty with repetition tasks and produced semantic and phonemic paraphasias in naming tasks. On the Boston Naming Test (Kaplan, Goodglass, & Weintraub, 1983) he had correct responses in only eight of sixty items, indicating a significant naming impairment.

We examined AW's naming impairment further using the Florida Semantics Battery (Raymer & Rothi, 2000), a set of lexical tasks assessing performance for 120 nouns. AW was unable to respond in the oral reading and written picture naming subtests, presumably due to his developmental problems. Results displayed in table 9.4 indicated that in the two oral naming subtests, significant difficulties were evident, as AW provided correct names for only 43.3 percent of pictures and 35.8 percent of definitions. In both oral naming tasks, AW made a significant portion of "no response" errors and a smaller portion of semantic errors (superordinate

Table 9.4

AW's Responses on the Florida Semantics Battery

Task	N	Correct (%)	Semantic related (%)	No resp. (%)	Other (%)
Oral picture naming	120	43.3	16.7	26.7	9.2
Oral naming to spoken definition	120	35.8	10.8	51.7	1.7
Semantic picture associate matching	90	56.7	36.7	1.1	—
Auditory word-picture natching	120	90.0	10.0	—	—
Written word-picture matching	120	20.0	78.3	1.7	—
Written picture naming		could not attempt			
Oral reading		could not attempt			

words and descriptions). His other responses in oral naming were unrelated words or complex phonemic paraphasias (differed from target words by more than one phoneme). His pattern of errors in oral naming implicate an impairment at either semantic or phonologic stages in lexical retrieval. To contrast these levels of processing, we considered his performance in comprehension tasks. His performance in auditory word-picture matching (90 percent correct) and semantic picture associate tasks (56.7 percent correct) is below cutoff levels observed in control subjects, suggesting that a mild semantic impairment contributed to his naming problem. This proposal is further supported by the observation that AW was somewhat worse in the name to definition subtest that places substantial demands on semantic processing. However, the significant difficulty in both oral naming tasks along with many "no response" errors and some complex phonemic errors suggest an additional measure of impairment related to the phonological retrieval stage in lexical processing. Thus, both semantic and phonologic stages of lexical retrieval appeared to be affected as a result of his stroke, and a significant naming impairment resulted.

AW then participated in an experimental treatment study in which we contrasted the effects of semantic and phonologic treatments for his naming impairment. Table 9.5 highlights the steps incorporated in the two treatment protocols, in which we asked a series of questions designed to help AW search for pieces of information that would help him to retrieve words when a naming failure occurred. Each question sequence was followed by a common rehearsal phase for consolidation of target word production. We examined AW's performance in naming three sets of pictures and a control word repetition task over the two treatment phases. Table 9.6 displays the mean accuracy level across three final sessions in each treatment phase. After low levels of baseline performance across probe measures, we initiated the phonologic questions treatment with one set of pictures. After ten treatment sessions, the accuracy of naming increased by 65 percent for trained items. Improvement for the two untrained picture naming

Table 9.5

Question Hierarchy Used in Phonologic and Semantic Training for Patient AW

Semantic questions (for example, apple)
1. Coordinate question: Is it similar to an orange?
2. Superordinate question: Is it in the category of fruits?
3. Associate question: Does it have to do with juice?

Phonologic questions (or example, stool)
1. Initial phoneme question: Is the first sound /s/?
2. Syllable question: Does it have one syllable?
3. Rhyme question: Does it sound like school?

Table 9.6
Average Correct Performance for AW in Final Three Sessions of Each Treatment
Phase for Experimental Probe Tasks

Task	Baseline (%)	Phonologic (%)	Semantic (%)	Maintenance (%)
Oral naming				
Phonologic set	13.3	78.3	56.7	50.0
Semantic set	13.3	41.7	55.0	55.0
Control set	13.3	40.0	28.3	10.0
Control word repetition	10.0	35.0	41.7	35.0

sets and the word repetition tasks was less than 30 percent, suggesting a noticeable effect of the phonologic training beyond either spontaneous recovery or repeated exposure to probe stimuli. When the semantic question protocol was instituted with a second set of pictures, naming improved an additional 15 percent for those items after ten training sessions, and AW never reached ceiling levels. In a final maintenance probe two months after the completion of treatment, AW had maintained some improvement for the two trained sets, whereas performance for untrained pictures had returned to baseline levels.

Therefore, AW, who presumably had both semantic and phonologic dysfunction underlying his significant naming impairment, had somewhat different responses to the two naming treatments. His immediate improvement in the phonologic treatment phase noticeably surpassed his progress following semantic treatment. However, the longer-term effects of the two treatments, as indicated in the follow-up observation, were similar. These results were not simply effects of spontaneous recovery or generalization of the first phonologic treatment to the second semantic training set, as AW showed no improvement for untrained pictures. Apparently, both phonologic and semantic question treatment had a modest influence on AW's naming abilities.

CLOSING COMMENTS

A substantial body of literature now exists to support the clinical utility of a model-guided approach to assessment and treatment of naming impairments. Clinicians have demonstrated that a number of different treatment methods may induce naming improvements in individuals with either semantic or phonological stages of dysfunction. However, a general conclusion that perhaps is contrary to early expectations for the use of this type of approach in treatment is that there is no direct relationship between type of impairment and type of treatment that will be most effective for those stage-specific impairments (Hillis, 1993). Some patients with semantic impairments benefit from phonological treatment and vice versa. Overall, the most effective naming treatments appear to be those that encourage semantic plus phonological processing within one treatment protocol, in keeping with the normal process of lexical activation.

One critical area for which further investigation is warranted in studies of naming treatments is the functional outcomes for patients in daily communication activities. The primary dependent variable in treatment studies for lexical impairments in aphasia has been percent improvement in the trained lexical task or in other lexical tasks sharing the same lexical mechanism. Fewer studies have investigated the generalization of lexical improvements to functional communication settings beyond anecdotal reports of the helpfulness of clinical training (Hillis, 1998). Boyle and Coelho (1995) reported no changes in conversational speech measures of words per minute and information units conveyed per minute following successful semantic matrix training for noun retrieval. However, a family member judged that the patient improved on a rating scale of communicative effectiveness (Lomas et al., 1989), which may indicate the functional gains of lexical treatment. Ellsworth and Raymer (1998) examined conversational output following verb naming treatment in their patient with aphasia. Using quantitative production analysis of lexical and grammatical use (Saffran, Berndt, & Schwartz, 1989), they noted changes toward more normal proportions of lexical categories within sentences following treatment. Overall, however, the functional consequences of treatments using a model-guided approach have not been well studied.

Knowledge gained from studies of the cognitive neuropsychological bases for word retrieval impairments certainly have influenced clinical practice in positive ways. A number of innovative treatment strategies have been developed on the basis of normal models of lexical and semantic processing. And it appears that treatments that respect the normal process of lexical retrieval are most beneficial in treatment effects. Although the model-guided approach to assessment and treatment requires a substantial investment of time and energy in the clinical process, patients may anticipate maximum benefits as a result. Certainly cognitive models do not provide a sufficient basis upon which to base our clinical practice, as a number of medical and social factors must be considered in the clinical decision-making process (Hillis, 1993). However, this approach has the potential to guide and influence clinical practice in practical ways as we continue to study methods and determine who, what, and how to assess and treat naming impairments in aphasia.

ACKNOWLEDGMENTS

We thank Lee Ennis for her assistance in preparation of materials for AW's treatment study. Preparation of this chapter was supported in part by NIH grant P50 DC03888-01A1.

REFERENCES

Bastiaanse, R., Bosje, M., & Franssen, M. (1996). Deficit-oriented treatment of word-finding problems: Another replication. *Aphasiology, 10,* 363–383.

Berndt, R. S. (1992). Using data from treatment studies to elaborate cognitive models: Non-lexical reading, an example. In NIH Publication no. 93-3424: *Aphasia treatment: Current approaches and research opportunities.*

Boyle, M. (1997). Semantic feature analysis treatment for dysnomia in two aphasia syndromes. Poster presented at the annual meeting of the American Speech-Language-Hearing Association, Boston, MA, November.

Boyle, M., & Coelho, C.A. (1995). Application of semantic feature analysis as a treatment for aphasic dysnomia. *American Journal of Speech-Language Pathology, 4,* 94–98.

Bruce, C., & Howard, D. (1987). Computer-generated phonemic cues: An effective aid for naming in aphasia. *British Journal of Disorders of Communication, 22,* 191–201.

Bunn, E. M., Tyler, L. K., & Moss, H .E. (1998). Category-specific semantic deficits: The role of familiarity and property type reexamined. *Neuropsychology, 12,* 367–379.

Byng, S., Kay, J., Edmundson, A., & Scott, C. (1990). Aphasia tests reconsidered. *Aphasiology, 4,* 67–91.

Caplan, D. (1993). *Language: Structure, processing, and disorders.* Cambridge, MA: MIT Press.

Caramazza, A., & Hillis, A. E. (1990). Where do semantic errors come from? *Cortex, 26,* 95–122.

Caramazza, A., & Hillis, A. E. (1991). Lexical organization of nouns and verbs in the brain. *Nature, 349,* 788–790.

Caramazza, A., & Hillis, A. (1993). For a theory of remediation of cognitive deficits. *Neuropsychological Rehabilitation, 3,* 217–234.

Caramazza, A., & Shelton, J. R. (1998). Domain-specific knowledge systems in the brain: The animate-inanimate distinction. *Journal of Cognitive Neuroscience, 10,* 1–34.

Coltheart, M. (1984). Editorial. *Cognitive Neuropsychology, 1,* 1-8.

Crosson, B., Moberg, P. J., Boone, J. R., Rothi, L. J. G., & Raymer, A. M. (1997). Category-specific naming deficit for medical terms after dominant thalamic/capsular hemorrhage. *Brain and Language, 60,* 407–440.

Damasio, A. R., & Tranel, D. (1993). Nouns and verbs are retrieved with differently distributed neural systems. *Proceedings of the National Academy of Sciences, USA, 90,* 4957–4960.

Davis, A., & Pring, T. (1991). Therapy for word-finding deficits: More on the effects of semantic and phonological approaches to treatment with dysphasic patients. *Neuropsychological Rehabilitation, 1,* 135–145.

Drew, R. L., & Thompson, C. K. (1999). Model-based semantic treatment for naming deficits in aphasia. *Journal of Speech, Language, and Hearing Research, 42,* 972–989.

Ellis, A. W., Kay, J., & Franklin, S. (1992). Anomia: Differentiating between semantic and phonological deficits. In D. I. Margolin (Ed.), *Cognitive neuropsychology in clinical practice.* New York: Oxford University Press.

Ellsworth, T. A., & Raymer, A. M. (1998). Contrasting treatments for verb retrieval impairment in aphasia: A case study. *ASHA Leader, 3*(16), 84 (abstract).

Ennis, M. R., Raymer, A.M., Burks, D.W., Heilman, K.M., Nadeau, S.E., & Rothi, L.J.G. (2000). Contrasting treatments for phonological anomia: Unexpected findings. *Journal of the International Neuropsychological Society, 6,* 240–241 (abstract).

Farah, M. J., & Wallace, M. A. (1992). Semantically-bounded anomia: Implications for the neural implementation of naming. *Neuropsychologia, 30,* 609–621.

Ferreira, C. T., Giusiano, B., & Poncet, M. (1997). Category-specific anomia: Implication of different neural networks in naming. *Neuroreport, 6,* 1595–1602.

Feyereisen, P., Van Der Borght, F., & Seron, X. (1988). The operativity effect in naming: A re-analysis. *Neuropsychologia, 26,* 401–415.

Greenwald, M. L., Raymer, A. M., Richardson, M. E., & Rothi, L. J. G. (1995). Contrasting treatments for severe impairments of picture naming. *Neuropsychological Rehabilitation, 5,* 17–49.

Haarbauer-Krupa, J., Moser, L., Smith, G., Sullivan, D. M., & Szekeres, S. F. (1985). Cognitive rehabilitation therapy: Middle stages of recovery. In M. Ylvisaker (Ed.), *Head injury rehabilitation: Children and adolescents.* San Diego: College Hill Press.

Hart, J., Berndt, R. S., & Caramazza, A. (1985). Category specific naming deficit following cerebral infarction. *Nature, 316,* 439–440.

Hart, J., & Gordon, B. (1992). Neural subsystems for object knowledge. *Nature, 359,* 60–64.

Hillis, A. E. (1991). Effects of separate treatments for distinct impairments within the naming process. In T. Prescott (Ed.), *Clinical aphasiology, Vol. 19.* San Diego: College Hill Press.

Hillis, A. E. (1993). The role of models of language processing in rehabilitation of language impairments. *Aphasiology, 7,* 5–26.

Hillis, A. E. (1998). Treatment of naming disorders: New issues regarding old therapies. *Journal of the International Neuropsychological Society, 4,* 648–660.

Hillis, A. E., & Caramazza, A. (1991). Category-specific naming and comprehension impairment: A double dissociation. *Brain, 114,* 2081–2094.

Hillis, A. E., & Caramazza, A. (1995a). Cognitive and neural mechanisms underlying visual and semantic processing: Implications from "optic aphasia." *Journal of Cognitive Neuroscience, 7,* 457–478.

Hillis, A. E., & Caramazza, A. (1995b). The compositionality of lexical semantic representations: Clues from semantic errors in object naming. *Memory, 3,* 333–358.

Hillis, A. E., Rapp, B., Romani, C., & Caramazza, A. (1990). Selective impairment of semantics in lexical processing. *Cognitive Neuropsychology, 7,* 191–243.

Hirsh, K. W., & Ellis, A. W. (1994). Age of acquisition and lexical processing in aphasia: A case study. *Cognitive Neuropsychology, 11,* 435–458.

Hodges, J. R., & Patterson, K. (1996). Nonfluent progressive aphasia and semantic dementia: A comparative neuropsychological study. *Journal of the International Neuropsychological Society, 2,* 511–524.

Holland, A. L. (1998). A strategy for improving oral naming in an individual with a phonological access impairment. In N. Helm-Estabrooks & A. L. Holland (Eds.), *Approaches to the treatment of aphasia.* San Diego: Singular Publishing.

Hoodin, R. B., & Thompson, C. K. (1983). Facilitation of verbal labeling in adult aphasia by gestural, verbal, or verbal plus gestural training. In R. H. Brookshire (Ed.), *Clinical aphasiology conference proceedings.* Minneapolis, MN: BRK Publishers.

Howard, D., & Orchard-Lisle, V. (1984). On the origin of semantic errors in naming: Evidence from the case of a global aphasic. *Cognitive Neuropsychology, 1,* 163–190.

Howard, D., & Patterson, K. (1992). *Pyramids and palm trees.* Bury St. Edmunds: Thames Valley Publishing.

Howard, D., Patterson, K., Franklin, S., Orchard-Lisle, V., & Morton, J. (1985). Treatment of word retrieval deficits in aphasia. *Brain, 108,* 817–829.

Humphreys, G. W., Riddoch, M. J., & Quinlan, P. T. (1988). Cascade processes in picture identification. *Cognitive Neuropsychology, 5,* 67–103.

Kahn, H. J., Stannard, T., & Skinner, J. (1998). The use of words versus nonwords in the treatment of apraxia of speech: A case study. *ASHA Special Interest Division 2: Neurophysiology and Neurogenic Speech and Language Disorders, 8*(3), 5–10.

Kaplan, E., Goodglass, H., & Weintraub, S. (1983). *The Boston naming test.* Philadelphia: Lea & Febiger.

Kay, J., & Ellis, A. (1987). A cognitive neuropsychological case study of anomia: Implications for psychological models of word retrieval. *Brain, 110,* 613–629.

Kay, J., Lesser, R., & Coltheart, M. (1992). *PALPA: Psycholinguistic assessments of language processing in aphasia.* East Sussex, England: Lawrence Erlbaum.

Kearns, K. P., Simmons, N. N., & Sisterhen, C. (1982). Gestural sign (Amer-Ind) as a facilitator of verbalization in patients with aphasia. In R. Brookshire (Ed.), *Clinical aphasiology conference proceedings.* Minneapolis, MN: BRK Publishers.

Kertesz, A. (1982). *Western sphasia battery.* Orlando, FL: Grune & Stratton.

Kohn, S. E., Smith, K. L., & Alexander, M. P. (1996). Differential recovery from impairment to the phonological lexicon. *Brain and Language, 52,* 129–149.

Lambon Ralph, M. A., Graham, K. S., Ellis, A. W., & Hodges, J. R. (1998). Naming in semantic dementia: What matters? *Neuropsychologia, 36,* 775–784.

Le Dorze, G., Boulay, N., Gaudreau, J., & Brassard, C. (1994). The contrasting effects of a semantic versus a formal-semantic technique for the facilitation of naming in a case of anomia. *Aphasiology, 8,* 127–141.

Le Dorze, G., & Nespoulous, J.-L. (1989). Anomia in moderate aphasia: Problems in accessing the lexical representation. *Brain and Language, 37,* 381–400.

Lomas, J., Pickard, L., Bester, S., Elbard, H., Finlayson, A., & Zoghaib, C. (1989). The communicative effectiveness index: Development and psychometric evaluation of a functional communication measure for adult aphasia. *Journal of Speech and Hearing Disorders, 54,* 113–124.

Lowell, S., Beeson, P. M., & Holland, A. L. (1995). The efficacy of a semantic cueing procedure on naming performance of adults with aphasia. *American Journal of Speech-Language Pathology, 4,* 109–114.

Luria, A. R. (1970). *Traumatic aphasia.* The Hague: Mouton.

Marshall, J., Pound, C., White-Thomson, M., & Pring, T. (1990). The use of picture/word matching tasks to assist word retrieval in aphasic patients. *Aphasiology, 4,* 167–184.

Marshall, J., Pring, T., & Chiat, S. (1998). Verb retrieval and sentence production in aphasia. *Brain and Language, 63,* 159–183.

McHugh, R. E., Coelho, C. A., & Boyle, M. (1997). Semantic feature analysis as a treatment for dysnomia: A replication. Poster presented at the annual convention of the American Speech-Language-Hearing Association, Boston, MA, November.

Miceli, G., Amitrano, A., Capasso, R., & Caramazza, A. (1996). The treatment of anomia resulting from output lexical damage: Analysis of two cases. *Brain and Language, 52,* 150–174.

Miceli, G., Giustollisi, L., & Caramazza, A. (1991). The interaction of lexical and non-lexical processing mechanisms: Evidence from anomia. *Cortex, 27,* 57–80.

Miceli, G., Silveri, M. C., Villa, G., & Caramazza, A. (1984). On the basis for the agrammatic's difficulty in producing main verbs. *Cortex, 20,* 207–220.

Mitchum, C. C. (1992). Treatment generalization and the application of cognitive neuropsychological models in aphasia therapy. In NIH Publication no. 93-3424: *Aphasia treatment: Current approaches and research opportunities.*

Mitchum, C., & Berndt, R. S. (1994). Verb retrieval and sentence construction: Effects of targeted intervention. In M. J. Riddoch & G. Humphreys (Eds.), *Cognitive neuropsychology and cognitive rehabilitation.* Hove: Erlbaum.

Montanes, P., Goldblum, M. C., & Boller, F. (1995). The naming impairment of living and nonliving items in Alzheimer's disease. *Journal of the International Neuropsychological Society, 1,* 39–48.

Nicholas, M., Obler, L., Albert, M., & Goodglass, H. (1985). Lexical retrieval in healthy aging. *Cortex, 21,* 595–606.

Nickels, L. (1992). The autocue? Self-generated phonemic cues in the treatment of a disorder of reading and naming. *Cognitive Neuropsychology, 9,* 155–182.

Nickels, L., & Best, W. (1996). Therapy for naming disorders (part II): Specifics, surprises, and suggestions. *Aphasiology, 10,* 109–136.

Nickels, L., & Howard, D. (1994). A frequent occurrence: Factors affecting the production of semantic errors in aphasic naming. *Cognitive Neuropsychology, 11,* 289–320.

Nickels, L., & Howard, D. (1995). Aphasic naming: What matters? *Neuropsychologia, 33,* 1281–1303.

Ochipa, C., Maher, L. M., & Raymer, A. M. (1998). One approach to the treatment of anomia. *ASHA Special Interest Division 2: Neurophysiology and Neurogenic Speech and Language Disorders, 15*(3), 18–23.

Ochipa, C., Rothi, L. J. G., & Heilman, K. M. (1989). Ideational apraxia: A deficit in tool selection and use. *Annals of Neurology, 25,* 190–193.

Pashek, G. V. (1997). A case study of gesturally cued naming in aphasia: Fominant versus nondominant hand training. *Journal of Communication Disorders, 30,* 349–366.

Pashek, G. V. (1998). Gestural facilitation of noun and verb retrieval in aphasia: A case study. *Brain and Language, 65,* 177–180.

Pring, T., White-Thomson, M., Pound, C., Marshall, J., & Davis, A. (1990). Picture/word matching tasks and word retrieval: Some follow-up data and second thoughts. *Aphasiology, 4,* 479–483.

Raymer, A. M., Foundas, A. L., Maher, L. M., Greenwald, M. L., Morris, M., Rothi, L. J. G., & Heilman, K. M. (1997) Cognitive neuropsychological analysis and neuroanatomic correlates in a case of acute anomia. *Brain and Language, 58,* 137–156.

Raymer, A. M., Greenwald, M. L., Richardson, M. E.,

Rothi, L. J. G., & Heilman, K. M. (1997). Optic aphasia and optic apraxia: Case analysis and theoretical implications. *Neurocase, 3,* 173–183.

Raymer, A. M., & Rothi, L. J. G. (2000). Semantic system. In S. Nadeau, B. Crosson, & L. J. G. Rothi (Eds.), *Aphasia and language: Theory to practice.* New York: Guilford Press.

Raymer, A. M., Rothi, L. J. G., & Greenwald, M. L. (1995). The role of cognitive models in language rehabilitation. *NeuroRehabilitation, 5,* 183–193.

Raymer, A. M., & Thompson, C. K. (1991). Effects of verbal plus gestural treatment in a patient with aphasia and severe apraxia of speech. In T. E. Prescott (Ed.), *Clinical aphasiology, Vol. 12.* Austin, TX: Pro-Ed.

Raymer, A. M., Thompson, C. K., Jacobs, B., & leGrand, H. R. (1993). Phonologic treatment of naming deficits in aphasia: Model-based generalization analysis. *Aphasiology, 7,* 27–53.

Riddoch, M. J., & Humphreys, G. W. (1994). Cognitive neuropsychology and cognitive rehabilitation: A marriage of equal partners? In M. J. Riddoch & G. W. Humphreys (Eds.), *Cognitive neuropsychology and cognitive rehabilitation.* London: Lawrence Erlbaum.

Robson, J., Marshall, J., Pring, T., & Chiat, S. (1998). Phonologic naming therapy in jargon aphasia: Positive but paradoxical effects. *Journal of the International Neuropsychological Society, 4,* 675–686.

Rothi, L. J. G. (1995). Behavioral compensation in the case of treatment of acquired language disorders resulting from brain damage. In R. A. Dixon & L. Mackman (Eds.), *Compensating for psychological deficits and declines: Managing losses and promoting gains.* Mahwah, NJ: Lawrence Erlbaum.

Rothi, L. J. G. (1998). Cognitive disorders: Searching for the circumstances of effective treatment: Introduction by the symposium organizer. *Journal of the International Neuropsychological Society, 4,* 593–594.

Rothi, L. J. G., Ochipa, C., & Heilman, K. M. (1991). A cognitive neuropsychological model of limb praxis. *Cognitive Neuropsychology, 8,* 443–458.

Rothi, L. J. G., Ochipa, C., & Heilman, K. M. (1997a). A cognitive neuropsychological model of limb praxis and apraxia. In L. J. G. Rothi & K. M. Heilman (Eds.), *Apraxia: The neuropsychology of action.* East Sussex, England: Psychology Press.

Saffran, E. M., Berndt, R. S., & Schwartz, M. F. (1989). The quantitative analysis of agrammatic production: Procedure and data. *Brain and Language, 37,* 440–479.

Seron, X., & Deloche, G. (Eds.) (1989). *Cognitive approaches in neuropsychological rehabilitation.* Hillsdale, NJ: Lawrence Erlbaum.

Silveri, M. C., Gainotti, G., Perani, D., Cappelletti, J. Y., Carbone, G., & Faxio, F. (1997). Naming deficits for non-living items: Neuropsychological and PET study. *Neuropsychologia, 35,* 359–367.

Spencer, K. A., Doyle, P. J., McNeil, M. R., Wambaugh, J. L., Park, G., & Carroll, B. (2000). Examining the facilitative effects of rhyme in a patient with output lexicon damage. *Aphasiology, 14,* 567–584.

Wambaugh, J. L., Doyle, P. J., Linebaugh, C. W., Spencer, K. A., & Kalinyak-Fliszar, M. (1999). Effects of deficit-oriented treatments on lexical retrieval in a patient with semantic and phonological deficits. *Brain and Language, 69,* 446–450.

Warrington, E. K., & McCarthy, R. A. (1983). Category-specific access dysphasia. *Brain, 100,* 1273–1296.

Williamson, D. J. G., Adair, J. C., Raymer, A. M., & Heilman, K. M. (1998). Object and action naming in Alzheimer's disease. *Cortex, 34,* 601–610.

Williamson, D. J. G., Raymer, A. M., Adair, J. C.,

Schwartz, R. L., & Heilman, K. M. (1995). Florida Noun-Verb Battery (unpublished test).

Zingeser, L. B., & Berndt, R. S. (1990). Retrieval of nouns and verbs in agrammatism and anomia. *Brain and Language, 39,* 14–32.

Part 4

—

Semantics

—

10

Semantic Memory

Elaine Funnell

INTRODUCTION

Standard definitions of semantic memory refer to factual knowledge shared by members of a community: the sort of information that would be found in an encyclopedia or dictionary. Encylopedias do not include personal experience and, in this respect, they observe the distinction, first drawn by Tulving (1972), between semantic knowledge for facts and episodic knowledge of personal events. As Tulving makes clear, this distinction is intended to be a useful guideline, and not necessarily to reflect differences in memory storage for the two types of knowledge. Nevertheless, the study of semantic memory has concentrated on encyclopedic knowledge, most commonly of single entities, such as objects. On the whole, theories of semantic memory and episodic memory have evolved separately.

Squeezed between episodic memory and semantic memory, and almost forgotten, is a memory for factual knowledge concerning common events—such as going to a restaurant, visiting the dentist (Schank & Abelson, 1977; Schank, 1982). This knowledge is also generally not considered to be part of semantic memory, despite the fact that it is shared by those who belong to the same culture and, in this respect, fits the standard definition of semantic memory. Kintsch (1980) has argued forcibly that knowledge of entities and events is not distinct, but forms the end points on a continuum of meaning from the least to the most context-bound. The separation of semantic memory from context will be one aspect that will be discussed in this chapter.

The scientific investigation of the organization of semantic memory has been driven in recent years by the study of semantic disorders following brain damage. Double dissociations have been reported between the processing of different types of material (pictures and words); different input modalities (visual, auditory, tactile); different types of words (concrete and abstract; nouns and verbs); different categories of objects; and different types of semantic features (visual and functional). Such findings have raised a series of questions about the organization of semantic memory that mainly revolve around one issue: is there one semantic system or many? Separable semantic systems have been proposed for processing different types of material, different input modalities, and different types of content. The main goal of this chapter will be to review the evidence that has given rise to these claims. The chapter will close with a model of semantic memory that attempts to integrate the representation of isolated entities with that of context into a continuum of levels of meaning.

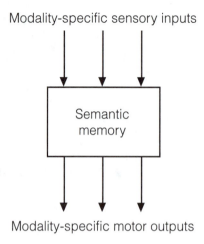

Figure 10.1. Basic unimodal model of semantic memory.

SEPARABLE SEMANTIC SYSTEMS?

Let us start with the simplest theory possible about semantic memory, illustrated in figure 10.1. It is a parsimonious model consisting of a single semantic system that can be accessed by all types of incoming information; for example, by words, pictures, and environmental sounds. It can activate responses in the form of linguistic output, drawing, and physical actions relating to object use. The model predicts that a disorder that affects semantic memory should disrupt the ability to comprehend all types of input and to express understanding in all types of output.

The case for a single semantic system has had serious challenges. In a seminal paper, Warrington (1975) investigated the residual semantic knowledge of two patients (AB and EM) who had a specific loss of semantic memory. Both patients defined spoken words to a similar level, but when the same items were presented visually as pictures for naming, AB was relatively impaired while EM achieved significantly superior scores.[1] To account for these differences in performance given either visual or verbal materials, Warrington argued that semantic knowledge must be represented in partially separable semantic systems: a visual system specialized for pictorial material and a verbal system for written and spoken words.

Methods Used for Identifying Semantic Memory Deficits

Warrington and Shallice (1984) argued that if the semantic representation for a particular object is damaged, then there should be errors each time the defective information is accessed. Likewise, if the semantic representation for a particular object is intact, a correct response should be expected each time that representation is accessed. Using this logic, they examined the consistency of responses across repeated tests using either pictorial or verbal material in two patients (JBR and SBY) who had semantic knowledge deficits. JBR and SBY showed consistent, item-specific effects across tests using visually presented objects, and SBY also showed consistent effects across tests using spoken object names. But neither patient showed a consistent relationship when responses made to visual and verbal material were compared. Instead, different items were affected in the two tests. From this, Warrington and Shallice

---

[1]AB and EM both obtained higher scores on the pictorial version of the test when the total sum of scores across all the test questions is compared. As Riddoch, Humphreys, Coltheart, and Funnell (1988) point out, this result is hard to reconcile with the claim that AB has a specific loss of visually accessed semantic information.

argued that the semantic information accessed from pictorial material and spoken words must be distinct.

Some methodological aspects of Warrington and Shallice's study undermine the conclusions (see Riddoch, Humphreys, Coltheart, & Funnell, 1988; and Rapp & Caramazza, 1993). First, JBR was not given repeated tests using spoken words. Thus, his consistency within the auditory domain was assumed rather than demonstrated.[2] Second, in one of four comparisons, SBY produced a consistent performance across tests. Furthermore, Rapp and Caramazza (1993) questioned the assumption that damage to conceptual representations must necessarily produce consistent responses to the same items across tests. They argue that if damage affects a subset of semantic features, the remaining features might activate a set of related responses that include the correct response. In this case the correct response might be produced on some occasions and a related error response on others, and so produce inconsistent responses across tests (see also Chertkow & Bub, 1990).

Response consistency is just one of a set of five characteristics that have been argued to signify damage to stored representations (Shallice, 1988a). The remaining characteristics are a strong effect of word frequency, a lack of response to priming, better access to shared properties than to specific properties of objects, and no effect of presentation rate on performance. However, as Rapp and Caramazza (1993) point out, few patients have been fully examined on all the characteristics and, even when fully tested, do not always show patterns of performance that support clear distinctions between deficits of access and storage. For each characteristic proposed to reflect semantic damage, Rapp and Caramazza propose plausible alternative frameworks in which the assumption that performance patterns reflect damage to stored representations do not hold.

Theoretical Accounts of Separable Material-Specific Semantic Systems

The distinction between visual and verbal systems has been defended by Shallice (1988a, 1988b) on the basis that the systems process different types of information. Visual semantic representations process visual scenes and scenarios, while verbal semantic representations are involved in interpreting sentences by identifying propositions and determining the sense of the words. At the level of object recognition and single object names, Shallice argues that some semantic properties of objects, such as their function, might be accessed frequently from both verbal and visual input, and for these properties the distinction between visual and verbal semantic systems is more difficult to sustain. He suggests, instead, that semantic knowledge of these properties might be represented in a network in which specific regions form subsystems specialized for different types of processing. Such subsystems may be determined by the connections that each region has to process concerned with intention and action (see Allport, 1985).

Caramazza, Hillis, Rapp, and Romani (1990, p. 162) organize previous arguments and claims into a set of four hypotheses concerning the organization of separable semantic systems for visual pictorial material and verbal material. These are as follows:

The modality-specific format hypothesis is concerned with the form in which the semantic information is stored in the separable semantic systems. Visual information is stored in a "visual/imagistic code," while verbal information is stored in symbolic or propositional form (see also Paivio, 1978). This theory, however, lacks theoretical motivation and empirical evidence.

---

[2]JBR has subsequently demonstrated consistent responses across tests of visual object naming and spoken name definitions (Funnell & de Mornay Davies, 1996).

The modality-specific input hypothesis proposes that the visual and verbal semantic systems contain the same material. According to this hypothesis, "visual" and "verbal" capture differences in the nature of the input material rather than semantic distinctions (see also Riddoch et al., 1988). Caramazza and colleagues argued that this hypothesis could not account for data from neurologically impaired subjects who made identical types and rates of semantic errors across all input modalities. For example, their patient KE made errors of the type, dog → cat, in oral reading, oral naming, writing to dictation, written naming, spoken word comprehension, and written word comprehension. These comprised 25 to 30 percent of his responses, and virtually all of his errors, in all of these tasks. The only way to account for this pattern of errors within a model that proposes separate semantic systems for each input modality is to assume that KE had identical damage to each of these semantic systems (Hillis, Rapp, Romani, & Caramazza, 1990).

The modality-specific content hypothesis distinguishes between different types of content for the visual and verbal systems. The visual system contains the visually specified attributes (for example, object shape) and associations between objects seen together. The verbal system contains information about abstract relations (for example, class membership) expressed through language. Both systems also include information derived in the context of the object. Caramazza and colleagues conclude that the modality-specific content hypothesis might account for data that "suggest that it is possible to access part of a semantic representation (e.g., 'visual' semantics) without necessarily having access to other parts of the semantic representation of a term (e.g., 'verbal' semantics)" (p. 174). But they also propose that the same data might be explained within an organized unitary content hypothesis (OUCH), in which a single semantic memory system has privileged access from particular inputs to particular types of semantic information.

The hypothesis of content organization within a single semantic system, such as OUCH, represents meaning as a set of semantic predicates in amodal form (see figure 10.2). In OUCH, semantic predicates are linked together, and those that are more highly associated have stronger links than others. The full set of semantic information associated with an object can be accessed as a complete unit from both words and pictures. However, pictures also have "privileged" access to the semantic predicates that represent the perceptual attributes of an object. For example, the tines of a visually presented fork will access the semantic feature "tines" or "for spearing" directly, whereas the word *fork* will access the feature "tines" or "for spearing" only indirectly as a component of the complete semantic representation of fork. The authors argue that if semantic damage affects a random set of semantic predicates, access to the complete semantic description will be compromised given either pictorial or verbal input. But, since pictures also have privileged access to semantic perceptual predicates, an advantage for visual pictorial input might be expected when the task requires access to only partial semantic information (such as gesture, which might be formed on the basis of the feature "for spearing" alone). This hypothesis is further discussed in chapter 7 of this volume.

OUCH, as Shallice (1993) points out, shares many characteristics with the account of visual and verbal semantic subsystems put forward earlier (Shallice, 1988a), in which the semantic system can be viewed as an interconnected system in which subregions are more specialized for particular types of input procedure. Theoretical differences may depend upon the nature of the connections between different types of input and different "regions" within an integrated semantic memory system, rather than separations between connections linking different sorts of semantic content.

In conclusion, the strong form of the visual-verbal semantic distinction has not stood up well. First, the evidence for a distinction between semantic knowledge systems for pictorial and

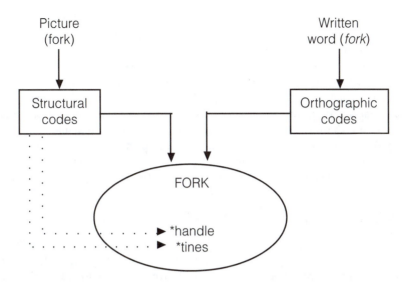

Figure 10.2. The OUCH model of semantic memory (redrawn from Caramazza et al., 1990).

verbal material is weak. Second, the theory of partial separation between visual and verbal semantics is not sufficiently well defined to be testable. As Caramazza and colleagues have shown, an account based on a single semantic system with additional privileged links to perceptual units from pictured inputs could provide a viable alternative. Nevertheless, the proposal of separable semantic systems is not settled. Each of the last three hypotheses regarding this issue, with evidence from more recent studies, are further discussed in the following sections.

Modality-Specific Input Hypothesis

The main source of evidence for proposing separate semantic systems distinguished by modality of input comes from optic aphasia, a rare disorder that particularly affects the naming of objects presented in the visual modality. Objects are named significantly more successfully when presented in other modalities, such as by a spoken description of the object, or by holding and manipulating the object with eyes closed. Surprisingly, patients can usually demonstrate some knowledge of the visually presented object that they are unable to name. For example, they may be able to gesture the object's use, or show knowledge of the category to which the object belongs, or its function. The fact that objects that can be identified but not named from vision can, in other modalities, be both identified *and* named provides a challenge to current unitary models of semantic memory. Three different theories of optic aphasia have been put forward. These are discussed in turn.

Disconnection between Verbal Semantics and Visual Semantics

Beauvois (1982) and Beauvois and Saillant (1985) suggested that optic aphasia occurs when the links between visual and verbal semantics are impaired. This theory was based initially on findings from a patient, MP, who had an optic aphasia for color resulting from a stroke affecting the posterior cerebral artery resulting in damage to the left occipital pole and medial area of the left temporal lobe. The patient, a well-educated woman, had good color discrimination, but her ability to name colors and point to colors named for her was very poor.

A series of tests showed that MP's difficulty with colors emerged when the tasks involved *both* visual and verbal processing. She could provide associated names in verbal tasks (for example, she was able to give the alternative name *jambon blanc* for *jambon de Paris*), and in purely visual tests she could point to the correctly colored version of visually presented objects. However, in visual-verbal tasks, she made errors when asked to point to a picture colored according to the color name associated with the object (for example, a "very orange" orange, rather than a more appropriate shade). She also made errors when naming the color of objects, such as a gherkin, that are not automatically associated with a color name and are argued to require visual imagery for the color to be identified. The authors argued that MP had suffered a disconnection between visual semantics, which contained information about the color of objects, and verbal semantics, which contained conceptual and linguistic attributes.

Optic Aphasia and Right Hemisphere Semantics

A second patient with an optic aphasia for colors, reported by Coslett and Saffran (1989), did not fit Beauvois's theory. Like MP, this patient was unable to name colors or point to the correct color given the spoken name, but he was able to name to a high level the color of named objects argued by Beauvois (1982) to require visualization (for example, "What color is a lime?"). Thus, he could carry out tasks that involved both verbal and visual domains. Investigations suggested that his disorder could not be put down to impairments to early visual processes or semantic access. For example, he was able to distinguish between correctly drawn objects (for example, a turtle) and incorrectly drawn objects composed of parts taken from two objects belonging to the same semantic category (for example, a turtle with a chicken's head). He could sort pictures perfectly into categories of animals and objects, and pair together pictures of different objects sharing either the same function (for example, a zipper and a button) or an associated function (for example, pen and paper). To account for these findings, Coslett and Saffran (1989) proposed that optic aphasia arises from a disconnection between a visual semantic system located in the right cerebral hemisphere and the speech processing system located in the left hemisphere.[3]

Optic Aphasia and a Unitary Semantic System

The remaining theoretical account explains optic aphasia within a single semantic memory system. There are a variety of forms of this theory: the dual route theory (Ratcliff & Newcombe, 1982); the semantic access theory (Riddoch & Humphreys, 1987); and the superadditive deficit theory (Farah, 1990; Campbell & Manning, 1996). All theories have in common a specialized set of structural descriptions for object recognition that enables an object to be identified as a familiar sensory form but does not provide associated information such as knowledge of object function. These structural systems have the same function as the visual knowledge attribute systems (Coltheart et al., 1998), referred to earlier. Thus, there are sets of structural descriptions for visually processed components of objects, tactile components, and auditory components of environmental sounds associated with objects. Each set of structural descriptions has access to the central, unimodal semantic system, from whence the spoken name of the object can be retrieved (see figure 10.3).

---

[3]Although naming via a right hemisphere semantic system appears to solve the problem of optic aphasia in Coslett and Saffran's patient (and also the reading pattern found in deep dyslexia; Coltheart, Patterson, & Marshall, 1980), the possibility of separable right and left hemisphere semantic systems complicates the study of semantic memory. At present, knowledge of the properties of each semantic system is rudimentary. Any complete semantic model will require a better understanding of the nature and function of each system and their interrelationship.

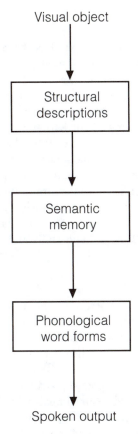

Figure 10.3. A standard model of visual object naming.

The Dual Route Theory

This theory (Ratcliffe & Newcombe, 1982) proposes that each sensory input has access to a further, nonsemantic pathway from structural descriptions to naming that provides a more precise access to the name than the semantic pathway, which is prone to error. However, Coslett and Saffran (1989) argued that their patient's performance could not be accounted for by the dual coding theory because he could name the same objects correctly from verbal descriptions, indicating that intact semantic processing can alone support accurate naming.

The Semantic Access Theory

This theory (Riddoch & Humphreys, 1987) proposes that optic aphasia arises from a deficit to a single pathway that accesses the semantic system from the visual structural descriptions. This theory was based upon a patient, JB, who suffered damage to the left parietal/occipital region as a result of a road traffic accident. He had marked difficulties when naming common objects by vision alone although he was able to gesture the use of many of them. He was considerably more successful at naming the same items from touch and from auditory definition.

Tests indicated that the visual processes leading up to and including the visual structural descriptions were intact: for example, he copied objects well, and matched objects successfully across different views. He also demonstrated well-preserved semantic knowledge when accessed through the auditory modality. His problems arose when he was required to access the semantic system from vision, particularly when objects from semantic categories containing many structurally similar neighbors were presented. Riddoch and Humphreys (1987) argued that JB's naming problem for objects belonging to categories containing many structurally similar objects indicated an impairment to the access mechanisms to semantic information from vision. They suggested that the effects of this impairment could be explained within an interactive system in which processing at an earlier stage affects later processing stages. Supporting this view, Arguin, Bub, and Dudek (1996) have shown that, in visual agnosia, structural similarity is a problem only if the structurally similar items belong to the same semantic category. A simulation of optic aphasia, in which the connections linking visual with semantic information were damaged, produced errors to items that were visually, and visually and semantically similar to the targets (Plaut & Shallice, 1993a). These authors proposed that a visual-semantic access account could explain optic aphasia. For additional evidence favoring this account, see DeRenzi and Saetti (1997) and Hillis and Caramazza (1995).

The Superadditive Theory

Farah (1990) doubted that a disorder affecting visual access only could explain optic aphasia and suggested instead that "superadditivity" between two mild disorders, one affecting visual input, the other affecting spoken output, was necessary. Neither disorder would be great enough to cause problems on its own, but when combined would disrupt processing in tasks involving both sets of processes.

An optic aphasic patient, AG, provides some support for the superadditivity theory (Campbell & Manning, 1996). AG showed a mild visual impairment in tasks that required access to information about the visual characteristics of objects when these were obscured in a picture. In addition, a naming impairment was revealed in verbal fluency tests, in which object names belonging to a category must be recalled, although his naming of objects presented in domains other than vision was good. From these results, Campbell and Manning argued that superadditive effects of mild disorders to visual access and naming output could account for AG's optic aphasia. They pointed out, however, that the data would also fit the single visual access theory of Riddoch and Humphreys. Other patients, such as DHY, reported by Hillis and Caramazza (1995), have had normal verbal naming and fluency.

Perhaps the most important conclusion to be drawn from the studies by Riddoch and Humphreys and Campbell and Manning is that deficits of visual access to semantics have been demonstrated when, hitherto, it has been argued that visual to semantic processing in optic aphasia is unimpaired. In the case of AG, the visual-to-semantic deficit was mild, revealing itself only in visual tasks in which the information was degraded. In JB, the deficits appeared when specific information was sought, or when decisions concerning the functional relationships between objects were made difficult by the addition of a semantically (but not functionally related) distractor. Previous studies have not used such demanding tasks. It is possible, therefore, that all cases of optic aphasia might reveal deficits in visual-semantic processing if the tests given are sufficiently stringent.

Modality-Specific Content Hypothesis

Saffran and Schwartz (1994) argue forcefully that the data from neuropsychology require distinctions between sensory information and conceptual representations, and suggest that the neural substrates of object concepts differ according to the modality in which the information was acquired. As Saffran and Schwartz observe, there is plenty of evidence in the neuropsychological literature to indicate that different perceptual systems, such as those used for color and movement, can break down independently, indicating functionally separable systems.

Allport (1985) and Coltheart, Inglis, Cupples, et al. (1998) suggest that each perceptual domain—visual, auditory, olfactory, tactile—has a dedicated knowledge base containing the perceptual properties of objects. Each knowledge base functions both as a recognition device and as a store of perceptual information. For example, a visual attribute domain is used for recognizing visually presented objects and for retrieving visual attribute knowledge.[4] Damage to any sensory attribute domain gives rise to attribute-specific semantic impairments. For example, damage to the visual knowledge base will give rise to failure to recognize visually presented objects and to loss of knowledge pertaining to specific visual attributes. Allport argues that perceptual domains link together to form a distributed parallel processing system that links perceptual information with knowledge of action and lexical knowledge. Coltheart suggests that perceptual attribute domains are not linked directly. Instead, each perceptual domain accesses an additional store of nonperceptual knowledge organized according to functional properties, such as "dangerous." The visual domain also accesses a system dedicated to knowledge about actions (see figure 10.4).

Coltheart et al. (1998) provided evidence for a specific visual semantic attribute system from a patient, AC, who had a left hemisphere stroke affecting the area of the left middle cerebral artery. CT scans also revealed small lesions in the white matter throughout the cerebral hemispheres. Assessments indicated that AC's early visual processes were intact. Nevertheless, he had difficulty accessing structural descriptions of animals from vision. Given pictures of real animals and nonsense animals, created by recombining heads and bodies of real animals, his performance in distinguishing real and nonsense animals was close to chance, while performance on the same test using objects was within the normal range.

AC was profoundly anomic and unable to read or write. Testing of his semantic memory for

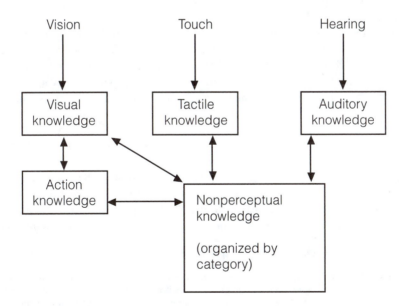

Figure 10.4. The representation of object knowledge (adapted from Coltheart et al., 1998).

---

[4]Coltheart, Inglis, Cupples, and colleagues (1998) refer to the sensory attribute domains as semantic, rather than perceptual.

animals and objects therefore used spoken questions that probed specific semantic attributes. He was unable to respond above chance level to questions such as "Does a worm have legs?" "Does a bicycle have wheels?" "Is a bubble round?" "Is a crow colored or not?" In contrast, he answered, above chance, olfactory and auditory questions, such as "Does coffee have a characteristic smell?" "Does a star make a noise?" He was also able to answer nonperceptual questions to a high level, such as "Is a snake dangerous or not?" "Is an elephant Australian?" "Does an oyster live in water?" "Do people usually eat eagles?" On the basis of these results, Coltheart and colleagues argued that AC had an attribute-specific semantic deficit in the visual domain.[5]

In one important aspect, AC's performance does not fit the theory. The theory states that the same set of information is responsible for visual object recognition *and* visual-conceptual knowledge. Thus, AC's spared visual recognition for object classes other than animals predicts that he should be able to answer visual attribute questions for these spared object classes. The fact that he was unable to do so indicates that his difficulty with answering visual attribute questions arises not in the visual recognition system, but elsewhere. Within Coltheart and colleagues' model, this could arise from a problem with accessing the visual structural descriptions from the nonperceptual knowledge system. In this case, it would not be surprising if only visual attribute knowledge was affected.

Content Organization within a Single Semantic System

We now turn to a set of theories that propose that the semantic system is organized according to the content of the information. The first of these theories separates information associated with different categories of objects; the second separates object knowledge from action knowledge; and the third separates concrete from abstract word meanings. These theories will be examined in turn.

Category-Specific Disorders for Objects

Disorders affecting particular categories of objects have been widely reported. Two contrasting cases, JBR and VER, reported by Warrington (1981), began the flowering of interest in the theoretical bases of these disorders. One of these patients, JBR (referred to earlier), appeared to have a particularly marked problem with objects in the realm of living things (see also Warrington & Shallice 1984). He named one of a set of pictures of animals and plants, but named over half of a set of man-made objects. His definitions of living things were generally empty of detailed information (for example, daffodil → "plant"; ostrich → "unusual"), while definitions of man-made objects were well informed (for example, tent → "temporary outhouse"; torch → "hand held light"). In contrast, the second patient (VER) had more difficulty with the processing of man-made objects (see also Warrington & McCarthy, 1983). VER had a severe aphasia, resulting from a stroke to the left frontoparietal cortex, and was virtually unable to name objects. For this reason, her knowledge of objects was tested using spoken word-picture matching tasks.[6] In a series of repeated tests, VER matched small sets of flower

---

[5]The visual questions asked by Coltheart, Inglis, Cupples, and colleagues (1998) about ownership of legs, or wheels, appear to be more specific than the more general questions asked about objects, such as "Does it make a noise?" "Does it have a smell?" Equivalent general questions in the visual domain might have been "Does it move?" Specific questions in the auditory and olfactory domains might be "Does it make a high sound?" "Does it have a sweet smell?" General questions were asked about color—"Is it colored or not?"—and were answered at chance level. This test requires a distinction between black/white and color. However, it is not clear that contrast and brightness might not have contributed to decisions about animals such as frog, parrot, panda, and crow, in the examples provided.

[6]VER's performance was affected by the length of the interval between her pointing response and the next stimulus. At intervals of 2 seconds her performance was significantly inferior to that given longer intervals of 10 seconds or more. Warrington and McCarthy (1983) argue that this indicates a deficit in semantic access from vision. It could also reflect an interaction between visual attention and the sensory properties of the multiple stimulus arrays.

and animal names to pairs of pictures more successfully than names of man-made objects.[7]

As further studies made clear, the distinction between performance on living and nonliving things is not always absolute. JBR was later shown by Warrington and Shallice (1984), to perform well with body parts (a member of the living things category on which he should do badly), and badly on musical instruments (man-made objects on which he should do well). Likewise, a further patient, YOT (Warrington & McCarthy, 1987), with a deficit to man-made objects similar to VER, found some man-made objects more difficult than others. In a spoken-to-written word matching task, YOT had more problems with categories of objects that are small enough to handle (specifically furniture and kitchen utensils) compared with categories of nonmanipulable objects (such a buildings and vehicles).[8] However, this distinction was not fully consistent, for her responses to clothing, a manipulable category, were equivalent to responses to vehicles, a nonmanipulable category.

Hillis and Caramazza (1991) argued that brain damage can affect individual categories of objects. JJ, who had a stroke affecting the left temporal lobe and the left basal ganglia, had superior oral naming for pictures of land and water animals and birds, although his naming of fruit, foods, body parts, clothing, and furniture was close to zero. His performance contrasted sharply with a second patient, PS, given the same materials under the same conditions. PS had lesions resulting from a head injury that affected the left temporal lobe and smaller areas in the right temporal and frontal lobes. PS had virtually intact naming of the categories at which JJ failed, namely man-made objects, body parts, and fruit, but was clearly impaired at naming land and water animals and birds, categories at which JJ excelled. Differences in personal familiarity with animals and birds did not appear to account for these contrasting patterns in the performance of JJ and PS, since it was PS, who had a specific interest in birds and animals, who was impaired with these categories. Nevertheless, there is some evidence that personal familiarity can spare categories that might otherwise be expected to be impaired. For example, CW, an accomplished musician with a deficit for living things, did not show the usually accompanying deficit for musical instruments (Wilson & Wearing, 1995), presumably because for him these were highly familiar objects.

Differences in personal familiarity are difficult to assess, but when measures of the general familiarity of objects within a population have been collected, living things turn out to be generally less familiar than man-made objects (Funnell & Sheridan, 1992). Early studies of category-specific performance that were unaware of the importance of familiarity differences failed to control for this factor. Subsequently, some studies have shown that category-specific deficits, reported using uncontrolled materials, disappear once concept familiarity is controlled (Stewart, Parkin, & Hunkin, 1992; Funnell & Sheridan, 1992; Sartori, Coltheart, Miozzo, & Job, 1994, cases 1 and 2). In other studies, the category effect has remained but at a considerably reduced level, and confined to items of low familiarity (Sartori, Coltheart, Miozzo, & Job, 1994 case 3; Sartori, Job, Miozzo, Zago, & Marchiori, 1993; Gainotti & Silveri, 1996; Funnell & De Mornay Davies, 1996). Thus, uncontrolled differences in familiarity clearly contribute to the category-specific deficit for living things, but do not account for it entirely in all cases.

Category-specific disorders are assumed to be semantic in origin (McCarthy & Warrington, 1988), yet there is good evidence that the visual properties of objects can also affect the recognition of objects in particular categories. Using a standard set of object drawings, Gaffan and Heywood (1993) found that five normal control subjects made significantly more errors when naming living things than man-made objects (when all drawings were presented at short exposure and low contrast). Moreover, within the man-made object domain, the controls made

---

[7]A significant effect of category was reported using chi square, but the use of combined data from repeated tests violates the assumptions of the chi square test (Seigel, 1956).

[8]YOT's category-specific deficit was reported only at fast response interval rates of 2 seconds (see note 6).

significantly more errors with musical instruments than tools. Thus, normal subjects produce a pattern similar to JBR when the materials are presented in visually degraded form.

The fact that visual degradation can effect category-specific naming in normal subjects suggests that patients with early visual processing problems might also show category-specific errors of visual identification. This was demonstrated in a patient (NA) with an apperceptive agnosia, affecting the visual processes that precede access to the structural descriptions (Funnell, 2000a). Categories with very close structural similarity, such as insects, produced visual coordinate errors. Objects with few distinctive features (such as fruit and vegetables) produced visual coordinate errors (for example, pear → apple) but also unrelated visual errors (for example, potato → footprint). Unrelated visual errors were also typical of body parts (for example, hair → onion) and man-made objects that were prone to visual segmentation of their parts (for example, whip → spring). There was no effect of concept familiarity on her performance, and her understanding of object names was not impaired.

Category-specific impairments can also be found in visual associative agnosia. For example, Humphreys, Riddoch, and Quinlan (1988) reported that HJA, who was thought to have damage to the processes that link structural descriptions with the semantic system, had particular problems with objects from categories with many structurally similar objects (for example, animals, birds, and insects). Structurally dissimilar categories (such as body parts and man-made objects) created few difficulties. His performance showed strong effects of concept familiarity and a slightly different pattern of category-specific disorders from NA (reported above), suggesting that category-specific disorders can vary according to the nature of the visual input problem.

In summary, what is clear from these studies is that a simple dichotomy between disorders affecting either living or nonliving things will not suffice. Disorders affecting living things are often associated with disorders affecting particular categories of man-made objects, such as musical instruments, while body parts, a category of living things, is usually spared. Moreover, categories themselves show further fractionations: animals and birds may be spared independently of fruit and vegetables (Hillis & Caramazza, 1991); large, nonmanipulable objects may be spared relative to small, usable objects (Warrington & McCarthy, 1987). When semantic memory is unimpaired, early visual processing deficits, and deficits to the links between visual structural descriptions and semantics can also show category-specific effects. Theories of the structural organization of categories based upon category-specific disorders need to take the role of visual processing factors into account. Various theoretical accounts of category-specific deficits, such as OUCH, are described in chapter 7 of this volume, and neuroanatomical bases of category-specific deficits are described in chapter 11. All of the theories that are supported by empirical evidence assume that semantic representations are composed of features, and that either the semantic representation in its entirety, or its component features, is stored or processed in separate brain regions. The proposals differ as to whether the organization is based on the properties that distinguish items in a category (for example, visual versus functional features), or based on the modality (for example, visual versus linguistic) in which the semantic representation or features are first encountered or learned, or based on evolutionary pressures.

Imageable, Concrete, and Abstract Words: Processing Advantage for Imageable and Concrete Words

Concrete words are processed more readily than abstract words in a variety of laboratory tasks using unrelated words, including free recall, recognition memory, short-term memory, paired associate learning and oral reading (see Paivio, Yuille, & Madigan, 1968; Paivio, 1991). Paivio and colleagues (1968) collected ratings on imagery (the capacity of the word to arouse sensory images) and concreteness (the capacity of the word to refer to objects, materials, or people) for a large set of nouns, and found that the two scales were closely related. A further measure of "meaningfulness" (m), based on the number of associated words produced to the target word in one minute, tended to be high for both abstract words and concrete/imageable words. On the basis of these results, Paivio and colleagues (1968) argued that abstract words obtain meaning largely from verbal experience (measured by m), while concrete/imageable words obtain meaning from both sensory and verbal experience.

Paivio (1978) proposed that all word meanings are represented in a verbal system specialized for processing linguistic information, but concrete and imageable words have access to a nonverbal system that stores representations of the perceptual properties of objects and events (see figure 10.5). The two systems are independent, but richly interconnected. Connections are most direct between concrete/imageable words and become more indirect as words become more abstract.

In the neurological literature, concrete words show a marked advantage in a variety of disorders, most notably in deep dyslexia (Coltheart, Patterson, & Marshall, 1980). Within Paivio's model, the advantage to concrete/imageable words found in deep dyslexia could arise from their representation in more than one system. However, Jones (1985) suggested that concreteness and imageability ratings reflect differences in the quantity of semantic predicates (for example, has legs, is old) in the underlying representation, rather than qualitative differences. Based on ratings of the ease with which subjects judged they could generate predicates,

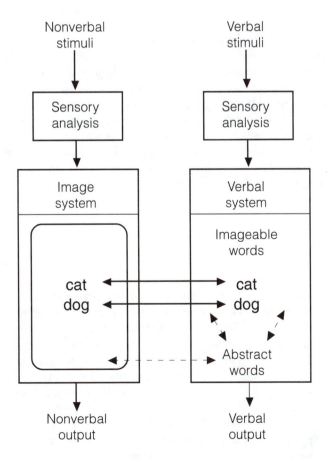

Figure 10.5. Dual coding model of semantic memory (adapted from Paivio, 1978).

Jones proposed that abstract words contain fewer predicates than concrete/imageable words and thus are more vulnerable to brain damage.

Plaut and Shallice (1993b) used ease of predication to simulate the advantage for concrete words found in deep dyslexia. Concrete words in this computer model were assigned more than twice as many features as the abstract words. A few concrete words mapped onto some abstract features, but no abstract words shared concrete features. When the pathway from orthography to meaning was impaired, the phonological output for abstract words was more disturbed than for concrete words. Thus the greater density of semantic features for concrete words gave them an advantage when the semantic pathway was compromised.

Jones's ease of predication measure was based upon judgments rather than the actual production of predicates. When subjects were asked to produce predicates, De Mornay Davies and Funnell (2000) found that, in line with Jones's findings, more predicates were produced overall for concrete than for abstract words, and the numbers correlated highly with Jones's ease of predication ratings for the same words. However, when the sets of concrete and abstract words were considered separately, ease of predication ratings did not correlate significantly with the number of predicates produced, despite the fact that the number of predicates varied quite widely within each word set. Instead, ease of predication completely split the word groups into those with high ratings—all concrete words—and those with low ratings—all abstract words. From this, De Mornay Davies and Funnell argued that ease of predication reflects differences in the nature of the semantic representations rather than the number of associated predicates.

In general, the advantage for concrete/imageable words in deep dyslexia is assumed to reflect semantic processing or semantic access problems. But Newton and Barry (1997) found no evidence of deficits for comprehending abstract words in a study of a young woman (LW) who had developed deep dyslexia as a result of a left hemisphere subarachnoid hemorrhage. Despite equivalent levels of comprehension for concrete and abstract words, LW showed a marked advantage for concrete words in oral reading. Newton and Barry suggested that concrete concepts are more likely to specify a precise word form than abstract concepts, which are more likely to activate a set of related names (for example, idea, concept, notion, thought, hypothesis, and so on), none of which may have a level of activation high enough to trigger a response. Some support for this view is provided by Funnell and Allport (1987), who found that ratings of "concept independence," defined as the ability of a word "to evoke a direct image that can be represented in isolation," correlated highly with the oral reading of two deep dyslexic subjects. Concrete/imageable words were more likely to have high concept independence than were abstract words. Other patients with deep dyslexia, deep dysgraphia, or deep dysphasia have been shown to have *no* semantic deficit, and yet show better performance on concrete words (Hanley & Kay, in press; Hillis, Rapp, & Caramazza, 1999). Hillis and colleagues attributed the advantage for concrete words to the fact that for concrete words there are fewer items that share the majority of features with the target. On the assumption that the features of the semantic representation activate lexical representations to which they correspond, there may be numerous closely semantically related, competing words activated in the lexicon, particularly for abstract words. For example, the semantic representation of a concrete concept like *train* shares a majority of its semantic features with only a few items (van, bus, subway/underground, trolley), whereas the semantic features of an abstract word, say *faith*, shares a majority of its semantic features with many other abstract concepts (belief, credence, creed, tenet, confidence, denomination, hope, reliance, religion, trust, certainty, conviction, doctrine, dogma, persuasion, sect), in various contexts. Consequently, an impairment in accessing the target lexical representation of the word *faith* might result in activation of a large number of competing lexical representations, some of which might have higher activation than the target response (leading to an error in production).

Breedin, Saffran, and Coslett (1994) have proposed that concreteness effects in word processing arise from the activity of brain areas involved in object recognition, and Funnell (2000b) has suggested that the concrete word advantage arises in deep disorders because spoken output is restricted, abnormally, to a system used normally for nominal reference (that is, naming things). Abstract words do not refer to nameable objects in the world and are therefore not called up by naming tasks. Thus, restricted access to a perceptually based lexical system, similar to that described by Paivio (1978), could explain the results.

In summary, deep disorders, such as deep dyslexia, demonstrate a marked advantage for the processing of concrete/imageable words, found to a lesser extent in normal behavior. Attempts to explain this advantage have suggested that concrete words benefit from (1) additional representation in a perceptually based lexical system (Paivio, 1978); (2) from possessing more semantic predicates than abstract words (Jones, 1985); (3) from specifying words with more precision than abstract words (Newton & Barry, 1997); and (4) fewer closely semantically related words in the output lexicon (Hillis et al., 1999). Finally, it has been suggested that the concrete word advantage reflects the properties of a (possibly perceptually based) output system normally used for nominal reference (Funnell, 2000b).

Reverse Concreteness Effect

Although concrete words generally show an advantage in single word processing tasks, this advantage has been reported to disappear, and even to reverse, in some pathological cases. Warrington (1975, 1981) found that AB (the patient with semantic dementia referred to earlier) had a marked deficit for defining concrete words when compared to abstract words, and a similar finding was reported by Warrington and Shallice (1984) for SBY (a patient impaired by herpes simplex encephalitis). The examples provided in these studies show a striking disparity in favor of abstract words (for example, AB: *pact* → "friendly agreement"; *needle* → "I've forgotten"; SBY: *malice* → "To show bad will against somebody"; *frog* → "An animal—not trained"). Warrington (1981) argued that abstract and concrete words are organized by category, each category having different neural substrates. Abstract words are defined in terms of similarity (in the form of synonyms) and in terms of contrast (in the form of antonyms). Concrete words are defined in terms of superordinate category and distinguishing features.

Breedin, Saffran, and Coslett (1994) reported a second patient, DM (a patient with a progressive loss of memory for word meanings), who also showed a reverse concreteness effect. Brain imaging revealed a decrease in perfusion in the inferior temporal lobes bilaterally, consistent with a diagnosis of semantic dementia. DM's definitions generally lacked perceptual information. To explain the reverse concreteness effect, Breedin and colleagues suggested that the linguistic elements of language that support the processing of abstract words were better preserved than the perceptual attribute domains that support the processing of concrete words. They rejected the idea that concrete words benefit from a larger number of semantic features (for example, Jones, 1985; Plaut & Shallice, 1993b) because damage to semantic features should always favor concrete words. They also rejected Paivio's dual coding model because concrete and abstract words should benefit equally from access to verbal codes, following perceptual loss. They argued that the representations for concrete and abstract words are fundamentally different. Concrete word concepts have their basis in information acquired through the five senses, while abstract words have their basis in associations with other concepts—even concrete ones—experienced in the context of language.

Marshall, Pring, Chiat, and Robson (1995/6a) also concluded that concrete words lose their advantage when access to perceptual properties is impaired. They report the case of RG, an elderly man who suffered a left hemisphere stroke and whose speech was affected by semantic jargon. In semantic jargon, a type of expressive aphasia in which anomalous words replace appropriate words in spontaneous speech, there is usually a preponderance of abstract words. For example, RG described a picture of a woman showing a boy a signpost as "The mother is showing the . . . vision aid area to her son who doesn't really know where to go." Tests showed that RG found concrete words more difficult than abstract words. Given pictures of concrete objects (for example, a man riding a donkey with a carrot hanging from a stick), he selected spoken abstract words (for example, *encouragement*) to describe the picture, significantly more successfully than concrete words (for example, *donkey*). He also named objects (for example, *castle*) more successfully when given abstract definitions (for example, "A fortified historic building"), than from concrete definitions (for example, "A building with turrets and a draw-bridge"). Marshall and colleagues argued that RG had well-preserved processing of abstract concepts but had an impaired ability to process the visual aspects of meaning required for concrete concepts. However, they noted that concrete *words* appear to have access to descriptions expressed in both concrete and abstract terms. This differs from a categorical account (for example, Warrington, 1975), in which concrete and abstract words map onto different neural substrates. They suggested that RG's performance fits an account in which individual words have their meaning distributed over a variety of processing domains, in accord with Allport's theory of semantic representations (Allport, 1985).

Actions and Objects: Action Naming Better than Object Naming

Action names are more likely to be impaired than object names in aphasia, but here we will consider first three case reports of patients who show the reverse pattern, since this continues the debate about perceptual properties of concepts. First, AG (one of the patients with optic aphasia reported earlier) had better preserved naming of pictured actions than objects (Campbell & Manning, 1996). For example, he named correctly only one-quarter of a set of objects pictured without actions. In contrast, he named correctly all actions pictured without objects (for example, three men sitting without a visible seat). AG's naming of objects increased significantly when the objects were presented in pictures demonstrating object use. His object naming also improved when he was asked "What would you need to do that?" to pictures of *objectless* actions. Thus, RG was actually better at naming objects when given only relevant pictured actions than when given only pictured objects. However, while pictured actions facilitated the naming of objects, the reverse was not true: pictured objects failed to facilitate the naming of actions. The second patient, DM, reported above (Breedin et al., 1994), was able to spot, almost perfectly, the odd word out in triplets of written verbs (for example, *to allow, to encourage, to permit*), but was significantly impaired at spotting the odd word out given triplets of written nouns (for example, *automobile, train, car*). Finally, RG (the patient with semantic jargon aphasia reported earlier) made fewer errors when producing verbs than nouns in spontaneous speech (Marshall, Chiat, Robson, & Pring, 1995/6a, 1995/6b). He also named pictures of actions significantly more successfully than nouns, matched for word frequency.

Campbell and Manning (1996) propose three speculative accounts for AG's better naming of actions compared with objects. First, they suggest that objects possess unique, defining, perceptual characteristics that might make them more vulnerable to visual access deficits than actions, that are argued to possess more general characteristics. Second, they speculate that there may exist multiple routes from vision to semantics, with a route dedicated to actions spared in optic aphasia. Finally, they suggest that perceived actions may have a variety of resources for accessing names.

Jackendoff (1987) points out that subtle perceptual differences are required to distinguish between some structurally similar categorically related objects, such as goose, duck, and swan, and between physical actions, such as run, jog, lope. Both Breedin and colleagues (1994) and Marshall, Chiat, and colleagues (1995/6) report differences in performance within verb sets according to their possession of perceptual properties. For example, DM (Breedin et al., 1994) was slower, and significantly less accurate, at selecting triplets of verbs of manner (for example, *to gnaw, to gobble, to gulp*), for which knowledge of subtle differences in perceptual properties are required, than triplets of relational verbs (for example, *to remind, to remember, to recall*) that do not posses perceptual properties. Likewise, RG was impressively good at distinguishing thematic verbs (for example, *buy* and *sell, give* and *take*), which specify the relationship between role players, but had difficulty distinguishing between action verbs (for example, *slide, crawl, swim*). Both studies conclude that distinctions in the meaning of action verbs are dependent upon perceptual information, while knowledge of the thematic roles of verbs is represented in a nonperceptual domain concerned with abstract verb structures. In the cases of DM and RG, the perceptual aspects of action verbs appear to have been lost, but the relational aspects of verbs, which capture psychological events represented in their functional argument structure, have been retained. The advantage of actions compared to nouns arises from the fact that some actions do not possess perceptual features.

Breedin, Saffran, and Schwartz (1998) argue that verbs with complex semantic representations are retrieved most successfully in aphasia. Thus "heavy" verbs (such as *run, grab*), which address information about the manner of the action, were retrieved more successfully than "light" verbs (such as *go, get*), which, although more frequent, are less complex. They suggest that a heavy verb is more constrained by context, and so more likely to activate one meaning, than is a light verb, which may generate a number of meanings, making selection of the most appropriate meaning for the context more difficult. However, Breedin and colleagues note also that heavy verbs may be facilitated by the presence of perceptual features.

Black and Chiat (2000) argue that differences in the processing of nouns and verbs cannot be explained entirely, either in terms of differences in perceptibility or in terms of the degree to which words specify particular meanings. Even when objects and actions are both well endowed with perceptual features, and have clearly specified meanings, a difference in naming can be observed. For example, Byng (1988; Byng, Nickels, & Black, 1994) asked a group of aphasic patients—this time with more difficulty producing action than object names—to name pictured concrete objects (for example, *iron*) and pictured actions (for example, *to iron*) that were associated with the objects, and shared the same root morpheme. Despite the high perceptual content of both objects and actions, the objects were named significantly more successfully than the actions. Black and Chiat (2000) suggested that other aspects of meaning, besides concreteness, must account for the discrepancy between action and object naming in these patients. They observed that while nouns refer to entities, verbs specify relationships between entities: they implicitly refer to "scene schemas." Relationships may not be more difficult to process than entities; rather, there may be different mechanisms involved. Other cases of dissociations between nouns and verbs in naming do not occur at the level of semantics, but at the level of the phonological or orthographic output lexicon, as discussed by Chialant and colleagues in chapter 7 of this book.

SEMANTIC MEMORY AND EVENT SCRIPTS

Scene schemas, and the role of actions in constructing the representations of events, tend to be viewed as aspects of meaning lying outside the domain of semantic memory, as episodic knowledge (Tulving, 1972) or as general event scripts (Schank & Abelson, 1977; Schank, 1982). However, Kintsch (1980) has argued that episodic knowledge and semantic knowledge form a continuum of knowledge, while Allport (1985) suggests that semantic knowledge is embedded within episodic knowledge. Recent studies of semantic dementia have indicated that the processing of current personal events plays a central role in the composition, updating, and maintenance of semantic memory, making it difficult to disconnect semantic memory entirely from wider sources of meaning.

Snowden, Griffiths, and Neary (1994) claimed that episodic memory supported the semantic processing in four patients with semantic dementia who had better preserved knowledge for personally known people and places in current experience than people and places personally known to them in their past. Further study of one of these patients showed that her recognition and use of objects was also better preserved for her own possessions than someone else's objects of the same type. In addition, her own objects were recognized more reliably when placed in their usual location in her home than when located out of context. The familiar physical properties of personal possessions and their familiar physical location appear to provide important clues to the recognition of object identity and use in these patients. Having a goal also appears to provide a context for the identification and use of objects. A patient (EP), with a well-preserved memory for the use of objects in the context of daily routines, was able to use objects appropriately as part of a goal-related task—for example, she used a needle appropriately when she was asked to sew a button on a shirt—but she was unable to demonstrate reliably the use of objects presented out of context (Funnell, 2001).

Goals, and the physical properties and location of objects, are proposed to be essential components of physical scripts that connect knowledge of physical properties of the environment with memories of the purposeful activities in which objects are used (Schank & Abelson, 1977; Schank, 1982). Scripts—and there are also personal and social scripts—form the basic level of a dynamic memory system that learns from personal experience. They are organized by structures operating at higher levels of processing, containing increasingly generalizable levels of information. In semantic dementia, it appears that these higher processing levels of information, which would enable the processing of concepts out of context, deteriorate to such an extent that information becomes progressively tied to scripts based in current experience.

Allport (1985) describes a dynamic distributed processing model that combines real-world, episodic information with object concepts. In this model, semantic memory is extracted automatically as a by-product of the encoding of many related, episodic experiences. Object concepts are stored in the episodes in which they are experienced, but also emerge from these episodes as prototypical patterns of the most common sensory and motor features experienced across episodes. These object concepts also contain scripts that encode common interactions with objects. The model predicts that semantic memory should not be lost without a corresponding loss of episodic memory entailing these semantic memories. Yet, in semantic dementia, this is what appears to occur: patients can demonstrate knowledge of the function of objects in everyday situations that they are unable to identify in semantic memory tasks.

Levels of Meaning

According to script theory, meaning is represented at different levels: as decontextualized meaning, as meaning embedded in generalizable contexts, and as meaning embedded in specific physical scripts. Figure 10.6 depicts an attempt to model these different levels of meaning (Funnell, 2001) using evidence from semantic memory and the development of object concepts. The first level, specific event knowledge, represents information regarding specific but recurring events, entailing the physical properties of the particular objects, people, and actions occurring in a particular place and time (for example, breakfast time at home). This is the level most likely to drive personal physical and linguistic routines carried out during, or in reference to, familiar events. The second level, general event knowledge, abstracts from the physical properties of specific scenes, and now the representation reflects the typical properties and activities associated with an activity. It is likely that this is the level at which associated concepts can be accessed. At the third level, concepts (or referential level), information is represented as isolated concepts stripped of context. This is the level, captured by most current models of semantic memory, that enables isolated objects and object names to be processed out of context. Here, different categories of concepts are represented, differentiated according to the degree of specificity. Clinical tests of referential meaning, such as object naming and word-object matching, are likely to be processed at this level of meaning.

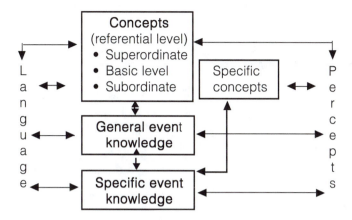

Figure I0.6. Levels of meaning model (redrawn from Funnell, 2001).

Words, pictorial materials, and other sensory information can call up meanings at each level. Names and pictures of isolated objects and actions will call up meanings at the referential level. Names and visual depictions of actions (for example, *push, buy*) and abstract words (for example, *steal, deny*) that capture relationships between objects, locations, and role players, will call up meaning at the level of general events, while names and pictures specifying particular objects, people, and places will call up specific scripts. In semantic dementia, the ability to recall and understand words appears to become increasingly tied to this level of specific event scripts.

The levels of meaning model can provide preliminary accounts for the phenomena reported in this chapter. Optic aphasia might arise from impaired access from visual input to the referential level of meaning, but retained access to associated aspects of meaning (including the ability to gesture object use) and frequently access to knowledge of actions represented at the general event level. Advantages for concrete/imageable words are presumed to arise at the referential level, which represents, in particular, concepts of concrete/imageable nouns. Their representation at this level may depend upon the fact that the physical properties that are confined to these items allows them to be abstracted from their context. Thus, it may be their abstractability rather than their sensory properties per se that is special. Brain damage that restricts processing to the referential level, perhaps by sparing access to names at this level, would be expected to produce concreteness effects for both nouns and verbs. In contrast, reverse concreteness effects could be argued to arise when processing at the referential level is impaired. Abstract nouns and thememtic properties of verbs that capture relationships would benefit (relative to entities) from processing at the level of general event representations.

CONCLUDING REMARKS

Most current models of semantic memory are constrained by the need to account for all aspects of meaning within a single memory system that captures the encyclopedic properties of word meanings. As Kintsch (1980, p. 506) has pointed out, this type of information is just one end of "a continuum reaching from completely context-dependent episodes to truly general knowledge." Kintsch bemoaned the fact that a concentration upon sentence verification tasks had seriously limited the development and scope of semantic memory. The same might be said of the current concentration on semantic tasks that seek to isolate concepts from context.

REFERENCES

Allport, D. A. (1985). Distributed memory, modular systems and dysphasia. In S. K. Newman & R. Epstein (Eds.), *Current perspectives in dysphasia*. Edinburgh: Churchill Livingstone.

Arguin, M., Bub, D., & Dudek, G. (1996). Shape integration for visual object recognition and its implication in category-specific visual agnosia. *Visual Cognition, 3*, 193–220.

Beauvois, M. F. (1982). Optic aphasia: A process of interaction between vision and language. *Philosophical Transactions of the Royal Society of London, B, 298*, 35–47.

Beauvois, M. F., & Saillant, B. (1985). Optic aphasia for colors and color agnosia: A distinction between visual and visuo-verbal impairments in the processing of colors. *Cognitive Neuropsychology, 2*, 1–48.

Black, M., & Chiat, S. (2000). Putting thoughts into verbs: Developmental and acquired impairments. In W. Best, K. Bryan, & J. Maxim (Eds.), *Semantic processing: Theory and practice*. London: Whurr Publishers.

Breedin, S. D., Saffran, E. M., & Coslett, H. B. (1994). Reversal of the concreteness effect in a patient with semantic dementia. *Cognitive Neuropsychology, 11*, 617–660.

Breedin, S. D., Saffran, E. M. & Schwartz, M. F. (1998). Semantic factors in verb retrieval: An effect of complexity. *Brain and Language, 63*, 1–31.

Byng, S. (1988). Sentence processing deficits: Theory and therapy. *Cognitive Neuropsychology, 5*, 629–676.

Byng, S., Nickels, L., & Black, M. (1994). Replicating therapy for mapping deficits in agrammatism: Remapping the deficit? *Aphasiology, 8*, 315–341.

Campbell, R., & Manning, L. (1996). Optic aphasia: A case with spared action naming and associated disorders. *Brain and Language, 53*, 183–221.

Caramazza, A., Hillis, A. E., Rapp, B. C., & Romani, C. (1990). The multiple semantics hypothesis: Multiple confusions? *Cognitive Neuropsychology, 7*, 161–190.

Chertkow, H., & Bub, D. (1990). Semantic memory loss in dementia of the Alzheimer type: What do various measures mean? *Brain, 113*, 397–417.

Coltheart, M., Inglis, L., Cupples, L., Michie, P., Bates, A., & Budd, B. (1998). A semantic subsystem of visual attributes. *Neurocase, 4*, 353–370.

Coltheart, M., Patterson, K., & Marshall, J. C. (1980). *Deep dyslexia*. London: Routledge and Kegan Paul.

Coslett, H. B., & Saffran, E. M. (1989). Preserved object recognition and reading comprehension in optic aphasia. *Brain, 112*, 1091–1110.

De Mornay Davies, P., & Funnell, E. (2000). Semantic representation and ease of predication. *Brain and Language, 73*, 92–119.

DeRenzi, E., & Saetti, M. C. (1997). Associative agnosia and optic aphasia: Qualitative or quantitative difference? *Cortex, 33*, 115–130.

Farah, M. J. (1990). *Visual agnosia*. Cambridge, MA: MIT Press.

Funnell, E. (2000a). Apperceptive agnosia and the visual recognition of object categories in dementia of the Alzheimer type. *Neurocase, 6*, 451–463.

Funnell, E. (2000b). Deep dyslexia. In E. Funnell (Ed.), *Case studies in the neuropsychology of reading*. Hove, England: Psychology Press.

Funnell, E. (2001). Evidence for scripts in semantic dementia: Implications for theories of semantic memory. *Cognitive Neuropsychology, 18*, 323–341.

Funnell, E., & Allport, D. A. (1987). Non-linguistic cognition and word meanings: Neuropsychological exploration of common mechanisms. In A. Allport, D. MacKay, W. Printz, & E. Scheerer (Eds.), *Language perception and production: Relationships between listening, speaking, reading, and writing*. London: Academic Press.

Funnell, E., & De Mornay Davies, P. (1996). JBR: A reassessment of concept familiarity and a category-specific disorder for living things. *Neurocase, 2*, 461–474.

Funnell, E., & Sheridan, J. (1992). Categories of knowledge? Unfamiliar aspects of living and nonliving things. *Cognitive Neuropsychology, 9*, 135–153.

Gaffan, D., & Heywood, C. A. (1993). A spurious category-specific visual agnosia for living things in normal human and nonhuman primates. *Journal of Cognitive Neuroscience, 5*, 118–128.

Gainotti, G., & Silveri, M. C. (1996). Cognitive and anatomical locus of lesion in a patient with a category-specific semantic impairment for living beings. *Cognitive Neuropsychology, 13*, 357–390.

Hanley, J. R., & Kay, J. (In press). Imageability effects and phonological errors: Implications for models of auditory repetition. *Cognitive Neuropsychology*.

Hillis, A., & Caramazza, A. (1991). Category-specific naming and comprehension impairment: A double dissociation. *Brain, 114*, 2081–2094.

Hillis, A. E., & Caramazza, A. (1995). Cognitive and neural mechanisms underlying visual and semantic processing. *Journal of Cognitive Neuroscience, 7*, 457–478.

Hillis, A. E., Rapp, B. C., & Caramazza, A. (1999). When a rose is a rose in speaking but a tulip in writing. *Cortex, 35*, 337–356.

Hillis, A. E., Rapp, B. C., Romani, C., & Caramazza, A. (1990). Selective impairment of semantics in lexical processing. *Cognitive Neuropsychology, 7*, 191–244.

Humphreys, G. W., Riddoch, M. J., & Quinlan, P. T. (1988). Cascade processes in picture identification. *Cognitive Neuropsychology, 5*, 67–104.

Jackendoff, R. (1987). On beyond the zebra: The relation of linguistic and visual information. *Cognition, 26*, 89–114.

Jones, G. V. (1985). Deep dyslexia, imageability, and ease of predication. *Brain and Language, 24*, 1–19.

Kintsch, W. (1980). Semantic memory: A tutorial. In R. S. Nickerson (Ed.), *Attention and performance VIII*. Cambridge, MA: Bolt Beranek and Newman.

McCarthy, R., & Warrington, E. K. (1988). Evidence for modality-specific meaning systems in the brain. *Nature, 207*, 142–175.

Marshall, J., Pring, T., Chiat, S., & Robson, J. (1995/6a). Calling a salad a federation: An investigation of semantic jargon. Part 1: Nouns. *Journal of Neurolinguistics, 9*, 237–250.

Marshall, J., Chiat, S., Robson, J., & Pring, T. (1995/6b). Calling a salad a federation: An investigation of semantic jargon. Part 2: Verbs. *Journal of Neurolinguistics, 4*, 251–260.

Newton, P. K., & Barry, C. (1997). Concreteness effects in word production but not word comprehension in deep dyslexia. *Cognitive Neuropsychology, 14*, 481–509.

Paivio, A. (1978). The relationship between verbal and perceptual codes. In E. C. Carterette & M. P. Friedman (Eds.), *Handbook of Perception, Vol. 8. Perceptual coding*. London: Academic Press.

Paivio, A. (1991). Dual coding theory: Retrospect and

current status. *Canadian Journal of Psychology, 45*, 255-287.

Paivio, A., Yuille, J. C., & Madigan, S. A. (1968). Concreteness, imagery, and meaningfulness values for 925 nouns. *Journal of Experimental Psychology Monograph Supplement, 76*, 1-25.

Plaut, D., & Shallice, T. (1993). Perseverative and semantic influences on visual object naming errors in optic aphasia: A semantic access account. *Journal of Cognitive Neuroscience, 5*, 89-117.

Plaut, D., & Shallice, T. (1993). Deep dyslexia: A case study of connectionist neuropsychology. *Cognitive Neuropsychology, 10*, 377-500.

Rapp, B. C., & Caramazza, A. (1993). The role of representations in cognitive theory: More on multiple semantics and the agnosia. *Cognitive Neuropsychology, 10*, 235-250.

Ratcliff, G., & Newcombe, F. (1982). Object recognition: Some deductions from the clinical evidence. In A. E. Ellis (Ed.), *Normality and pathology in cognitive functions*. London: Academic Press.

Riddoch, M. J., & Humphreys, H. W. (1987). Visual object processing in optic aphasia: A case of semantic access agnosia. *Cognitive Neuropsychology, 4*, 131-185.

Riddoch, M. J., Humprehys, G. W., Coltheart, M., & Funnell, E. (1988). Semantic systems or system? Neuropsychological evidence re-examined. *Cognitive Neuropsychology, 5*, 3-26.

Saffran, E., & Schwartz, M. (1994). Of cabbages and things: Semantic memory from neuropsychological perspective: A tutorial review. In C. Umilta & M. Moscovitch (Eds.), *Attention and performance XV*. Cambridge MA: MIT Books.

Sartori, G., Coltheart, M., Miozzo, M., & Job, R. (1994). Category specificity in neuropsychological impairment of semantic memory. In: C. Umilta & M. Moscovitch (Eds.), *Attention and performance XV: Conscious and nonvonscious information processing*. Cambridge, MA: MIT Press.

Sartori, G., Job, R., Miozzo, M., Zago, S., & Marchiori, G. (1993). Category-specific form-knowledge deficit in a patient with herpes simplex virus encephalitis. *Journal of clinical and Experimental Neuropsychology, 15*, 280-299.

Schank, R. C. (1982). *Dynamic memory*. Cambridge: Cambridge University Press.

Schank, R. C., & Abelson, R. (1977). *Scripts, plans, goals, and understanding*. Hillsdale, NJ: Lawrence Erlbaum.

Siegel, S. (1956). *Nonparametric statistics for the behavioural sciences*. Tokyo: McGraw-Hill.

Shallice, T. (1988a). *From neuropsychology to mental structure*. Cambridge: Cambridge University Press.

Shallice, T. (1988b). Specialisation within the semantic system. *Cognitive Neuropsychology, 5*, 133-142.

Shallice, T. (1993). Multiple semantics: Whose confusions? *Cognitive Neuropsychology, 10*, 251-262.

Snowden, J., Griffiths, H., & Neary, D. (1994). Semantic dementia: Autobiographical contribution to preservation of menaing. *Cognitive Neuropsychology, 11*, 265-288.

Stewart, F., Parkin, A. J., & Hunkin, N. M. (1992). Naming impairments following recovery from herpes simplex encephalitis: Category-specific? *Quarterly Journal of Experimental Psychology, 44A*, 261-284.

Tulving, E. (1972). Episodic and semantic memory. In E. Tulving & W. Donaldson (Eds.), *Organization of memory*. New York: Academic Press.

Warrington, E. K. (1975). The selective impairment of semantic memory. *Quarterly Journal of Experimental Psychology, 27*, 635-657.

Warrington, E. K. (1981). Neuropsychological studies of verbal semantic systems. *Philosophical Transactions of the Royal Society of London, B295*, 411-423.

Warrington, E. K., & McCarthy, R. (1983). Category specific access dysphasia. *Brain, 106*, 859-878.

Warrington, E. K., & McCarthy, R. (1987). Categories of knowledge: Further fractionations and an attempted integration. *Brain, 110*, 1273-1296.

Warrington, E. K., & Shallice, T. (1984). Category specific semantic impairments. *Brain, 107*, 829-854.

Wilson, B. A., & Wearing, D. (1995). Prisoner of consciousness: A state of just awakening from herpes simplex encephalitis. In R. Campbell & M. A. Conway (Eds), *Broken memories*. Hove, England: Lawrence Erlbaum.

11

Neural Substrates
of Semantics

John Hart, Jr.
Lauren R. Moo
Jessica B. Segal
Ellen Adkins
Michael A. Kraut

Delineating the neural bases of semantics, even for single entities (objects, features of objects, categories, actions, and so on) has been fraught with numerous difficulties, including variable definitions of semantic terms and several different models of the functional organization of semantics (see Elaine Funnell, chapter 10 of this book). In addition, while the advent of new investigative techniques has been a major asset in detecting brain regions associated with semantics, this variety of investigative techniques and their frequently incongruent results have confused, perhaps as often as clarified, previous experimental findings. For example, the results of activation studies (PET, fMRI, ERP, and so on), which demonstrate regions "involved" in performing a task, have yet to be fully integrated with the results of lesion-based studies that show regions "essential" for performing a task. A complete account of the complex mechanisms involved in semantics will almost certainly be predicated on the results of such an integration.

We can most profitably focus our attempts to understand the neural bases of semantics by adopting a general framework on which to interpret the studies in the literature. First, we will attempt an interpretation and integration of lesion and activation studies. Second, we will assess the studies in terms of whether the question investigated can be adequately resolved within the scope of the technique used (for example, the limited spatial resolution of ERP, the limited temporal resolution of PET, and so on). Third, due to the complexity of interpreting neural processing for the semantic interpretation of sentences, we have chosen to focus on studies of single semantic entities—features, objects, and categories—as they are the basic units upon which more complex semantic structures (for example, sentences, paragraphs, humor, analogy) likely rely. Largely because of their fundamental roles, they are also the most investigated in terms of anatomic substrates. There are other "single unit" semantic structures (for example, those underlying verbs, adjectives, adverbs) that we will not focus on, due both to a lack of anatomic-based studies and the targeted scope of this chapter.

Fourth, it is clear that interpretation of the anatomic substrates of semantics needs to be considered within the theoretical framework of behavioral-anatomic models of semantics. While both the distributed representation models (see McClelland & Rumelhart, 1985, and Hinton, 1981, for reference to these models) and models of cognitive domain "centers" (Geschwind, 1965) have been much debated, it is clear that neither, in its pure form, is consistent with the current body of both functional and anatomic studies. In other words, the brain is neither homogeneous nor made up only of circumscribed processing centers. In addition, the distributed model has not been described in enough detail to allow for predictions of the anatomic specifications of proposed semantic components. Consequently, we will interpret previously reported studies without constraining ourselves within a specific model. We review studies that address neural organization of semantic *representations* and the neural basis of semantic *processing*.

ORGANIZATION OF SEMANTIC REPRESENTATIONS

One proposed scheme for organization of representations in the semantic system is of a hierarchical organization—categories made up of objects with component features (Hinton, 1981; Sloman & Rips, 1998). For example, such a hierarchical scheme eliminates the need to store redundant information about apples, oranges, and peaches; their commonalties can be indicated by a single pointer, "fruit." Because of this efficiency advantage, it is perhaps not surprising that such hierarchical schema have also been postulated for many different perceptual modalities, including auditory perception (deCharms, Blake, & Merzenich, 1998); olfaction (Skarda & Freeman, 1987), tactile perception (Johnson & Hsiao, 1993), and vision (Livingstone & Hubel, 1988). These examples provide some corroborative evidence for the universality of this conceptual organization in human and nonhuman primate brains. But separate from this evidence from other domains, there has been broad agreement that the concepts underlying language seem to be organized in terms of features, items, and categories (for example, Lamberts & Shanks, 1997). The psychologic and neurologic literatures concerning features, items, and categories have been reviewed recently (Lambert & Shanks, 1997; Millikan, 1998; Schyns, Goldstone, & Thibaut, 1998; Saffran & Schwartz, 1994) and overall support this general organizational schema.

There have been some objections to this hierarchical view, with the main objection being the implied need for a higher-level representation, such as categories. That is, once some "basic" level of representation has been explained, some theorists have argued that it is not necessary to posit separate "higher" levels. Instead, what appear to be "higher levels" of representation may emerge because of a correlational relationship connecting the "basic" levels of representation. Since all living things share certain properties, and all tools share other properties, their "livingness" or "toolness" can be identified without explicit reference to a higher-order categorical representation of "living thing" or "tool." Neural network models in particular can capitalize on these correlations, and endow items with "category" characteristics that are not explicitly represented in the network (Farah & McClelland, 1991; Devlin, Gonnerman, Anderson, & Seidenberg, 1998). The other related objection to the explicit representation of category-level information is based on experimental research. Because of the experimental design of the tasks and the interdependence between features and categories, it has been difficult to separate actual category-level information from correlated featural information. This is particularly true when considering items from less standard categories. Less structured categories, such as "office items," are subject to more individual differences in experience and representation. Therefore, the psychologic investigation of possible hierarchical organizations of featural-, item-, and category-level information is particularly difficult. Nonetheless, the issue of whether such levels exist, and how they are represented, is clearly critical to our understanding of how language represents the world. The manner in which semantic information is represented in the brain is a related and similarly critical issue.

Evidence from focal brain lesions and from degenerative brain conditions supports the conclusion that information from different categories is in some ways distinct within the nervous system, because categories can be differentially affected by these neural injuries. Nielsen (1946) was the first to describe a double dissociation between the ability to name living things and nonliving things (with opposite patterns of preservation or impairment across different patients). Since then, there have been many individual and group reports of such dissociations (Semenza & Zettin, 1988; 1989; Goodglass et al., 1986; Funnell & Sheridan, 1992; Hillis & Caramazza, 1991; Goodglass et al., 1966; Farah et al., 1991; Silveri et al., 1991; Damasio et al., 1990; Farah & Wallace, 1992; Farah, 1989; Temple, 1986; Warrington & Shallice, 1984; Rapcsak et al., 1989; Rapcsak et al., 1993; McCarthy & Warrington, 1988; Berndt, 1988; Humphreys & Riddoch, 1987; Damasio, 1990; Silveri & Gainotti, 1988; Warrington & McCarthy, 1987; Farah et al., 1996; Sartori et al., 1993; Robinson et al., 1996; Warrington & McCarthy, 1983; Gainotti et al., 1995; Mauri et al., 1994; Tippett et al., 1996; Sartori & Job, 1988; Sacchett & Humphreys, 1992; see Grossman et al., 1998, for similar dissociations in degenerative conditions). The living/nonliving distinction, broadly characterized, has been the one reported most often (Damasio et al., 1996; Cappa et al., 1998; Garrard et al., 1998; Ferreira et al., 1997). It should be noted, however, that the specific categories that have most often been studied are animals (representing living things) and tools (representing nonliving artifacts). These categories seem to have the greatest contrasts in terms of their features (for example, tools such as hammers and saws are typically hard, smooth, straight-edged, dry, devoid of their own intention, and put to use by humans; animals are almost the exact opposite). In addition, there are enough familiar items that fall under the categories of "animals" and "tools" to make them useful for experimentation. So, for a combination of theoretical and practical reasons, these are the categories of items most studied in patient populations and neuroimaging studies.

The explanation for the existence of these observable dissociations between categories can be central or peripheral. A central explanation is that there are true, neuroanatomic differences in the representation of different categories such that they are differentially susceptible to disruption. An alternate, relatively peripheral theory would explain category dissociations as accidents of the correlational structure of the items and item properties. Adherents to the latter point of view include several recent investigators who have argued that patients with focal lesions (Moss et al., 1998; Gerrard et al., 1998) or with degenerative conditions (Devlin et al., 1998) showed dissociations because of differences in the degree to which features are correlated among items within each "category." However, many investigators have been careful to control for such confounds, and conclude that their cases reflect true category-level deficits (Caramazza & Shelton, 1998; Samson et al., 1998). A useful product of this debate has been a sharpening of criteria for category-level deficits, and the recognition that some apparent cases of category-level deficits may result from differences in the visual similarity among items in a category, differences in familiarity across categories, and so on. Nevertheless, on careful examination there do appear to be true cases of category-level deficits (Caramazza, 1998; Caramazza & Shelton, 1998; Coltheart et al., 1998).

Neural Substrates of Semantic Categories

From an anatomic basis, it must be pointed out that a large number of these category-specific deficits follow from herpes simplex encephalitis (HSE) (see table 11.1). There are several difficulties with interpreting these lesion data. Most important, it is not clear that imaging of HSE lesions on MRI is adequate to assess the damage from HSE. HSE spreads throughout the central nervous system via two mechanisms: contiguous and transynaptic dissemination. Neuroimaging techniques can capture pathology of the contiguous spread as long as the size of the area of pathologic change is within the resolution of MRI. However, transynaptic spread of the virus is on a microscopic level, typically below the resolution of standard imaging tech-

Table 11.1

Select Studies of Category Organization

Citation	Patients or subjects	Impaired categories or task	Location of pathology or activation	Type of pathology or activation and etiology
Yamadori & Albert, 1973	54 y.o. male	Common objects and body parts	Left FTP lacerations noted during surgery; left posterior TP	Focal; trauma
Dennis, 1976	DLA; 17 y.o. female	Body parts	Left anterior 5 cm resection;	Focal; mesial temporal sclerosis & resection
McKenna & Warrington, 1978	FC; 53 y.o. male	Naming 5 categories—naming countries > color, objects, body parts, & animals	Left temporal extending to inferior parietal	Focal; tumor
Warrington & McCarthy, 1983	VER.; 68 y.o. female	Common household objects, shapes, colors, body parts	Left FTP	Focal; stroke
Warrington & Shallice, 1984	JBR.; 23 y.o. male	Animals, plants, & food	Bilateral temporal	Diffuse; HSE
Warrington & Shallice, 1984	SBY; 48 y.o. male	Animals, plants, food, & concrete words	Bilateral temporal	Diffuse; HSE
Warrington & Shallice, 1984	ING; 44 y.o. female	Food & animals	Lesion deep in right hemisphere; bilateral temporal	Diffuse; HSE
Hart et al., 1985	MD; 34 y.o. male	Fruits & vegetables	Left frontal lobe & basal ganglia by CT	Multifocal; stroke
McCarthy & Warrington, 1985	ROX; 42 y.o. male	Action names, verbs, tense, case, prepositions	Bilateral cortical atrophy	Diffuse; degenerative
Goodglass et al., 1986	Subject 6; 60 y.o. female	Letters	Left MCA distribution	Focal; stroke
Goodglass et al., 1986	Subject 11; 33 y.o. male	Colors	Left inferior posterior frontal; superior posterior temporal sensory & motor strips	Focal; stroke
Temple, 1986	John; 12 y.o. male	Animals, insects, birds, sea creatures	Left midtemporal focus by EEG; normal CT	Diffuse; seizure
Warrington & McCarthy, 1987	YOT; 50 y.o. female	Small, manipulable objects; proper names	Left MCA occlusion by angiography; left TP by CT	Focal; stroke
Basso, Capitani, & Laiacona, 1988	NV; 73 y.o. male	Fruit, vegetables, & animals	Bilateral diffuse atrophy & focal lesion of left caudate	Diffuse; degenerative & focal; stroke

Study	Patient	Category	Lesion location	Etiology
Goodglass & Budin, 1988	AA; 62 y.o.	Body parts, colors, letters, & numbers	Left middle to posterior superior & middle temporal; motor & sensory cortices; angular & supramarginal	Focal; stroke
McCarthy & Warrington, 1988; Tyrrell et al., 1990	TOB; 63 y.o. male	Living things (animals & plants)	Left temporal & perisylvian atrophy	Focal; degenerative
Pietrini et al., 1988	RM; 23 y.o. male	Animals & plants	Left temporal to left basal frontal	Diffuse; HSE
Pietrini et al., 1988	JV; 47 y.o. male	Inanimate objects, animals, & plants	Left medial & basal temporal extending to left frontal	Diffuse; HSE
Sartori & Job, 1988	Michelangelo; 38 y.o. male	Animals, fruit, & vegetables	Bilateral anterior temporal	Focal; HSE
Semenza & Zettin, 1988	PC; 62 male	Family & friends, famous people, cities, rivers, countries, mountains	Left PO	Focal; stroke
Silveri & Gainotti, 1988	LA; 56 y.o. female	Living things & food	Bilateral FT of both deep & superficial structures (L > R)	Diffuse; HSE
Rapcsak, Kaszniak, & Rubens, 1989	65 y.o. male	Emotional facial expressions	Right temporal tip & anterior to midportions of inferior & middle temporal gyri	Focal; trauma (subdural hematoma)
Semenza & Zettin, 1989	LS; 41 y.o. male	Proper names	Left FT	Focal; trauma
Damasio et al., 1990	bilateral (n=4), left (n=11), or right (n=8) hemisphere	Naming & recognizing animals, but not tools or utensils	Bilateral or unilateral (less severe in the left) lesion involving inferotemporal region	Variety of lesions & locations
Hillis & Caramazza, 1991	JJ; 67 y.o. male & PS; 45 y.o. male	JJ: intact production & comprehension of animal names & not other categories PS: impaired production & comprehension of animal names	JJ: left temporal, head of the caudate, anterior internal capsule; putamen PS: large left temporal lobe & small right temporal & frontal	JJ: focal; stroke PS: multifocal; trauma
Farah, McMullen, & Meyer, 1991	2 visual agnostic patients: LH; 36 y.o. male & MB; 30 y.o. female	Both impaired on recognition of line drawings of living stimuli compared to nonliving stimuli	LH: bilateral inferior to right temporal & right frontal MB: left temporal edema but no focal damage by CT	Multifocal; trauma

Continued

Table 11.1
Continued

Citation	Patients or subjects	Impaired categories or task	Location of pathology or activation	Type of pathology or activation and etiology
Silveri et al., 1991	15 subjects diagnosed with Alzheimer's disease	Naming & verbal associates recognition task–worse for living items than nonliving items	Atrophy	Diffuse; degenerative (AD)
Farah & Wallace, 1992	TU; 50 y.o. male	Fruits & vegetables	Left occipital	Focal; AVM
Hart & Gordon, 1992	KR; 70 y.o. female	Animals	Cerebral cortex, including bilateral temporal lobes	Diffuse; paraneoplastic
Hart, Lesser, & Gordon, 1992	39 y.o. female	Access from the verbal to visual system for size knowledge	1 cm region in posterior aspect of left middle temporal gyrus	Focal; cortical interference
Sacchett & Humphreys, 1992	CW; 41 y.o. male	Artifactual objects & body parts	Left FP	Diffuse; stroke
Damasio & Tranel, 1993	3 patients: AN-133, Boswell, & KJ-1033	AN-1033 & Boswell impaired at naming nouns KJ-1360 impaired at naming verbs	Boswell: bilateral amygdala, entorhinal cortex, hippocampus, lateral temporal, basal forebrain, anterior cingulate, & internal capsule AN-1033: left mesial & lateral anterior temporal KJ-1360: left posterior inferior frontal & anterior precentral gyrus	AN: focal; trauma
Rapcsak, Comer, & Rubens, 1993	OK; 72 y.o. male	Naming & pointing to emotional facial expressions	Right inferior & middle temporal gyri & underlying white matter	Focal; stroke
Sartori et al., 1993	Giulietta; 55 y.o. female	Animals & vegetables	Bilateral temporal including hippocampal	Diffuse; HSE
Mauri et al., 1994	Helga; 60 y.o. female & Michelangelo; 38 y.o. male	Animals & vegetables	Helga: atrophy with widespread cortical & temporal lobe involvement Michelangelo: bilateral anterior temporal	Helga: diffuse; degenerative (AD) Michelangelo: diffuse; HSE
Dehaene, 1995	12 normal (all male) volunteers; mean age 20.9	Subjects monitored lists for words in given categories: animal names, verbs, numerals, proper names, & meaningless consonant strings	Left TP negativity for animal names & verbs; left inferior temporal negativity for proper names; bilateral positivity for numerals	ERP; normals

Study	Subjects	Task	Results	Method
Spitzer et al., 1995	5 normal volunteers	Naming of items from four categories	Focal left frontal & temporal of category specific activation	fMRI; normals
Damasio et al., 1996	127 patients with single & focal lesions	Naming pictures of faces of famous people, animals, &/or tools	Naming deficit for: people correlated with left temporal pole (TP) damage; for animals, left inferotemporal (IT) lesions; for tools, posterolateral IT+ lateral TPO	Focal; variety of lesions
Damasio et al., 1996	9 normal volunteers (7 women, aged 22–49).	PET scans while naming famous people, animals, & tools	Naming people → increased activity in left ventrolateral TP & right TP; naming both animals & tools → activation in left posterior IT & TP; tool naming → activation in posterior middle & inferior temporal gyri	PET; normals
Martin et al., 1996	16 subjects (8 male, 8 female)	Naming pictures of animals & tools	Both animals & tools → bilateral ventral temporal & Broca's area activation; animals → left medial occipital also; tools → left premotor & left middle temporal gyrus also	PET; normals
Tippett, Glosser, & Farah, 1996	temporal lobectomy: 17 left & 14 right	Naming line drawings from living & nonliving categories	Left temporal lobectomy patients impaired at living things	Focal; seizures & temporal resection
Ferreira, Giusiano, & Poncet, 1997	MC; 59 y.o. male; PR; 69 y.o. male; VG; 48 y.o. female	MC & VG: tool naming, action verb naming > object naming; All 3: recognition of tools > animals; defining tools > animals; MC only: picture-word matching of tools > animals	Left medial infero-temporal lesion in all 3 patients; PR also had right inferior temporal lesion	MC: focal; stroke PR: focal; HSE VG: focal; HSE
Grafton, Fadiga, Arbib, & Rizzolatti, 1997	8 adult subjects (4 female); mean age 23	1. Tool observation; 2. Silent tool naming; 3. Silent naming of tool use	1. Tool observation—left dorsal premotor cortex; 2. Silent tool naming—Broca's area without additional activity in the dorsal premotor cortex; 3. Silent naming of tool use—left dorsal premotor cortex, left ventral premotor cortex, & left SMA	fMRI; normals

Continued

213

Table 11.1
Continued

Citation	Patients or subjects	Impaired categories or task	Location of pathology or activation	Type of pathology or activation and etiology
Cappa et al., 1998	13 normal males; aged 22–26	6 tasks: (1) rest; (2) baseline: letter detection in pseudowords; (3) animal–long or short tail? (4) animal–typically found in Italy? (5) tool–longer than wider? (6) tool–typically used in kitchen?	Nonliving: the left TO junction, left supramarginal gyrus, right superior temporal gyrus, & right thalamus Living: right middle frontal gyrus & right fusiform gyrus	PET; normals
Jokeit et al., 1998	53 patients with left or right temporal lesion/seizures (nonaphasic)	Verbal fluency for 6 categories: (1) words starting with letters B, F, & L; (2) animals; (3) tools; (4) goods available in supermarket; (5) interior of a flat; (6) visual attributes	Left temporal lesions: impaired for animals; right temporal lesions: impaired tools & words referring to specific visual attributes	Unilateral temporal lobe damage & hippocampal atrophy in all patients
Mummery, Patterson, Hodges, & Price, 1998	10 (all male) normal volunteers	Viewed triads of object names & selected response most similar to the target on either (a) perceptual attribute (color) or (b) associative attribute (typical location) Control task–number of syllables in target & response words.	Semantic tasks → left TPO to posterior middle temporal gyrus & inferolateral & inferomedial temporal; associative judgments → left TPO posterior cingulate, medial temporal; perceptual judgments → antero-medial left temporal lobe & caudate; artifacts → left posterior middle temporal & parahippocampal gyrus	PET; normals
Ishai et al., 1999	12 normal healthy adults (6 female, age 26, plus or minus 3 years)	Passive viewing & delayed match to sample of photographs of houses, faces, & chairs	Houses: medial fusiform gyrus, including collateral sulcus; faces: lateral fusiform gyrus & occipitotemporal sulcus; chairs: inferior temporal gyrus & a small portion of medial fusiform	fMRI; normals
Moore & Price, 1999	Experiment 1: 8 normals; mean age 38 Experiment 2: 6 normals all male; mean age 28.6	Experiment 1. naming objects from (1) animals; (2) vehicles; (3) fruit; (4) tools (matched for visual complexity) Experiment 2. picture matching task with the same categories as in experiment 1	Vehicles → bilateral anterior temporal & right posterior middle (black-&-white line drawings only); animals → right TO & fusiform cortices, the right posterior temporal; tools → left posterior middle temporal; fruit → left anterior temporal/insula	fMRI; normals

Study	Participants	Stimuli / Task	Results	Method
Perani et al., 1999	Experiment 1: 11 (24–32 y.o.) normals Experiment 2: 8 (22–26 y.o.) normals	1a. Living objects vs. shape recognition 1b. Nonliving objects vs. shape recognition 2. Animate words vs. pseudowords	1a. Left hippocampus, ventral inferior frontal, & bilateral lingual 1b. Left dorsolateral prefrontal, middle, & inferior temporal gyrus 2. Bilateral anterior cingulate, right lingual, & inferior temporal gyrus	PET; normals
Thompson-Schill, Aguirre, D'Esposito, & Farah, 1999	5 (1 female) normal volunteers	Yes/no questions re: visual or nonvisual characteristics about living (e.g., animals, vegetables) & nonliving things (e.g., clothing, furniture)	All conditions: ventral occipito-temporal cortex, left middle temporal, visual questions about living & nonliving things & non-visual questions about living things → left fusiform	fMRI; normals
Gorno-Tempini, Cipolotti, & Price, 2000	8 (4 female) normal volunteers, aged 42–60	Pictorial stimuli presented either with or without written name of picture; categories: animals, famous faces, maps of countries, objects, body parts, & colors Task: silently read word or name picture	Naming & reading activation for: maps → increase in right middle & superior occipital gyri (BA 19) + decrease in left putamen; famous faces → increase in left anterior middle temporal (BA 21); faces, animals + maps → increase in left extrastriate visual cortex (BA 18/19)—most extensive for maps; objects + body parts → posterior middle/inferior temporal (BA 21/37)	PET; normals
Moss & Tyler, 2000	ES; 67 y.o. female	Artifacts	Bilateral inferior temporal lobes (L > R)	Diffuse; degenerative

215

niques, and can extend far beyond the scope of the primary imageable lesion. In the case of semantics, this can lead to "false localization." One proposed explanation of categorical organization is via a hierarchical ordering of objects and features under an anatomically distinct categorical node. Thus, transynaptic spread to a neuron or group of neurons encoding a hierarchical node could both impair a specific category and not be detected on MRI.

With these caveats in mind, the key anatomic findings that are cited across these lesion studies are that impairments of animal-specific semantic knowledge in particular, and possibly all animate items, are generally associated with left temporal lobe pathology. (See table 11.1 for a summary of select lesion and imaging studies related to category-specific deficits.) There are few cases of patients with inanimate object deficits. Some have inferred, based on the association of impaired verb naming and lesions in the left premotor area (Damasio & Tranel, 1993), that semantic knowledge of inanimate objects, with their associated motor actions, are related to disruption is this area. (The lesion data supporting this finding are rare, but see the activation studies below.) While the animate-left temporal lobe generalization on the surface appears to hold across lesion studies, there are several questions left unanswered. First, the pathologic changes associated with these lesions are not usually focal (but from HSE or degenerative disease), and thus it is difficult to make precise anatomic localizations. Second, on review of the experimental design and data from these studies, it is not clear what aspects of animals are being associated with a given brain region. Is it: (1) the category label "animal"? (2) some conceptual node for animals? (3) features common to animals? (4) the names of all the "items" in the animal category? (5) the processing regions required to access the "animal" category? and so on. The ambiguity of exactly what was being "lesioned" from a behavioral perspective further compounds the difficulties in identifying the anatomic loci associated with these categories. Second, there are so few unambiguous cases of category-level distinctions on a behavioral level that also have clear lesion localization information available that drawing generalizable conclusions is difficult.

Functional neuroimaging studies have also shown evidence for category-level differences. The animals versus tools distinction has been examined in normal subjects, using PET and most recently fMRI. The picture naming task was used by both Martin and colleagues (1996) and Damasio and colleagues (1996) in PET studies to explore category-level differences. Both sets of investigators found that the different categories elicited different regions of activation, many of which were in left temporal lobe. In this respect, these studies agreed with the data from patients with focal lesions and degenerative conditions reviewed above. However, the specific regions found by the two groups were not in agreement. Martin and colleagues (1996) found that both types of stimuli led to activation of the bilateral ventral temporal lobes and Broca's area. In addition, in the Martin et al. (1996) study, animals selectively activated the left medial occipital lobe. Tools selectively activated the left middle temporal gyrus and the left premotor region. (They also pointed out that the two areas selectively activated by tools were the same regions selectively activated by generation of action words and by imagined hand movements, respectively.) In contrast, Damasio and colleagues (1996) found that naming animals was associated with activation of the left third (inferior) and fourth temporal gyri, while naming of tools was associated with activation of the left middle and inferior temporal gyri.

Spitzer and colleagues (1995) also used naming of pictures to explore differences in category representation, but used fMRI, with its intrinsically higher spatial resolution than PET. The objects in the Spitzer et al. study represented the categories of animals, tools, furniture, and fruit. Spitzer and colleagues reported finding activations for all categories that were generally within left superior temporal, left medial temporal, and left lateral frontal regions. These data are consistent with both the other functional imaging studies reviewed above, and the conclusions from focal lesions and degenerative cases. Furthermore, like the PET studies, this fMRI study found, within these regions, different specific loci of activation for items from different categories. These results were interpreted as evidence for differences in the spatial representation of different categories of information in the dominant temporal lobe. However, the authors did not pinpoint the localization of these differences within left temporal and frontal lobes as other studies had.

What can be concluded at this point is that there is behavioral evidence from patients for neural organization of semantic representations that reflects categorical distinctions, but lesion-based evidence for discrete, category-specific localization is not overwhelming. There is substantial, but partially contradictory, evidence for neuroanatomic differences associated with category-level distinctions from the functional neuroimaging literature. Unfortunately, functional imaging studies do not clarify distinctions between lexical and conceptual representations nor between feature-, item-, or category-level activation. These latter distinctions must be addressed in future functional imaging studies that attempt to better isolate these levels of representation.

SEMANTIC PROCESSING

Even if we accept that semantic representations are organized in the brain by semantic category, a key issue typically left unaddressed is what parts of the brain are used to perform various semantic operations or tasks. There have been several recent studies that have examined the activation patterns associated with different semantic processing tasks. Perani and colleagues (1995) had their subjects push a button if the two pictured items were from the same basic category (for example, on being shown pictures of individual dogs, push the button if they were both pictures of dogs). They used pictures of both animals and artifacts. Categorization of animals in this fashion activated the inferior temporal regions bilaterally. Categorization of artifacts activated the left dorsolateral frontal region. Mummery and colleagues (1998) used printed words rather than pictures. The task they gave subjects was considerably different than that used in the Perani et al. study, in that subjects not only had to make similarity judgments, but also had to consider either the color of the items, or whether items were found in specific locations. Compared to a control condition (judgments of the number of syllables), Mummery and colleagues found that similarity judgments activated the temporo-parietal-occipital (TPO) junction, the posterior midtemporal gyrus, the inferomedial and inferolateral temporal lobe, and the inferior frontal lobe, all on the left. Selection by the color attribute activated the left anteromedial temporal lobe and the left caudate nucleus. Selection by location, in contrast, activated the left TPO junction, the left medial parietal lobe, and the posterior cingulate.

The multiple regions activated during categorization tasks may be associated with a variety of roles, including semantic processing, access to semantic representations, or the semantic representations themselves. It has been suggested, for example, that primary information about the sensory or motor properties of objects are stored in their original processing areas, such that tactile information would be stored in somatosensory areas, visual information stored in visual areas, and so on. These properties would then be accessed by pointers from the language system; the language system may not keep such information within its own confines. Grafton and colleagues (1997) showed that there is different activation for the word for a tool (for example, the lexical referent *hammer*) versus the motor memory for the same tool (for example, the memory of how to hold and swing a hammer to hit a nail). In related studies, some investigators have claimed that they have isolated lexicons in discrete cortical regions (Petersen et al., 1988). Others have implied that the representations of the lexical units in a visual orthographic lexicon are represented in a neurally, spatially distributed fashion,[1] with

---

[1]By the term *neurally distributed*, we mean that a given representation is not encoded by a single neuron, or even a group of neighboring neurons (or even all transynaptically connected neurons). A representation in this schema is encoded by multiple neurons, in different locations, whose firing patterns uniquely designate that representation (for example, coarse coding neural model; see Hinton, 1981). A given neuron may be paired in multiple other neuron groups, with the firing pattern of each group designating a different representation.

the regions isolated during activation studies representing processing centers necessary to access the word representations (Hart et al., 2000b). Consequently, interpretations of activations during semantic processing tasks should always keep in mind the context of the specific task instructions, mode of presentation of the semantic representations, and lexical correlates.

Overall, lesion studies have been productive in localizing regions involved in semantic processing and its associated correlates, but are limited by the accidental nature of where the lesions occur, their variable locations, size, and extent of involvement of underlying white matter. In a study of eighteen aphasic subjects (Hart & Gordon, 1990), three demonstrated isolated deficits in generalized semantic processing for multiple modalities of stimuli. All three patients were impaired, compared to the other aphasic subjects, in category, property, and synonym judgment and naming to definition with multiple modalities of stimulus presentation. In all three patients, the lesion site associated with these auditory-visual multimodality semantic deficits was the left inferior parietal-superior temporal region, which is anatomically ideally situated to integrate auditory- and visual-based semantic knowledge. From these and other findings we can advance the notion that the functions subsumed by a given processing area can be segregated not by function type alone but by the relative proximity to specific verbal and sensorimotor representation systems. However, the anatomic resolution in this study was too coarse for finer localization.

One exploration of how communication within the semantic system occurs between two modalities—visual and verbal—has been conducted with direct electrical cortical interference (Hart, Lesser, & Gordon, 1992). Direct electrical interference can create temporary, electrical lesions that are on the order of approximately 1 cm^3 via subdural electrode arrays placed for the presurgical evaluation of patients with medically intractable epilepsy. While asking relative size questions such as, "Which is larger, an apple or an airplane?" one patient could not answer correctly with interference at the posterior aspect of the left middle temporal gyrus. She was not impaired when similarly questioned without electrical interference or when stimuli were presented as pictures (including size-matched pictures) with interference at the same site. Also, with interference at that site, there was no interference with other verbal-to-visual judgments such as color, shape, orientation, movement, and texture. We interpreted these findings as evidence for a verbal-to-visual disconnection for size judgments, with sparing of other visual categories such as color, demonstrating possible category-based connections between the verbal and visual systems. Given that the posterior aspect of the left middle temporal gyrus is located between traditional language and higher-order visual processing regions, this location is well situated for this type of communication system.

The isolation of regions associated with specific semantic operations has been greatly enhanced by the advent of functional neuroimaging, which allows for study of semantic processes in vivo in normal individuals. This was clearly demonstrated in studies attempting to isolate the semantic functions associated with the dorsolateral prefrontal cortex (DLPFC). Since Posner and colleagues (1988) first reported the DLPFC involvement with the process of producing a semantically associated verb for a presented noun, the DLPFC has been associated with a variety of cognitive tasks in general, and semantic tasks in particular (Posner et al., 1988; Petersen et al., 1988; Petersen et al., 1990; Demb et al., 1995; Kapur et al., 1994; Demonet et al., 1992; Ricci et al., 1999). Thompson-Schill and colleagues (1997) have tried to specifically delineate which semantic operations or functions are associated with the DLPFC. Using sets of semantic judgment tasks that differed in the number of possible correct choices, they suggested that the inferior frontal gyrus was involved in the *selection* of semantic knowledge among alternative choices. This selection role is likely a component in the manipulations necessary to perform in a variety of semantic tasks (Thompson-Schill et al., 1997, 1998), explaining its involvement during various activation studies.

Electrophysiologic examination of the temporal dynamics of processing at a given brain region is an additional method that can help to decipher the role that region plays in semantic processing. Our group used electrocorticography (ECoG) in a patient with subdural electrode arrays to determine the time of onset of activation at an electrode site (Hart et al., 1998). We also developed the technique of timeslicing, an adaptation of the electrical cortical interference technique, by varying the onset latency of electrical interference relative to the presentation of the behavioral stimulus. This provides for interference with semantic processing at different times during the performance of a task, and thus allows for determination of the duration of a cognitive function at an electrode site. In a twenty-two-year-old with a subdural array of 174 electrodes, we used cortical interference to identify a pair of electrodes overlying the left fusiform gyrus that was involved in amodal semantic processing. Interference at this site affected both visual confrontation naming and comprehension tasks (including naming to definition and categorization). To determine the onset of this semantic processing, changes in the power spectrum of ECoG recordings were evaluated while the subject performed the picture naming task (Crone, Miglioretti, Gordon, Sieracki, Wilson, Vematsu, & Lesser, 1998; Crone, Miglioretti, Gordon, & Lesser, 1998). The onset of neural activation at this site was 250 to 300 msec after stimulus presentation, thus indicating the onset of semantic processing at this location. Using the timeslicing technique with the picture naming task, we determined that for some stimuli, processing for semantics became resistant to interference at that electrode site as early as 450 msec after picture presentation, while for others it remained vulnerable up to 750 msec after picture onset. Further analysis revealed that the processing of items with high subjective familiarity was completed sooner than for low-familiarity ones. These findings indicate that neural activity at this site on the left fusiform gyrus begins approximately 250 to 300 msec after stimulus presentation. This is convergent with evidence from other investigators as to the time course of semantic processing as measure by ERP and intracranial recording (Abdullaev & Posner, 1998; Nobre, McCarthy, & Allison, 1994). The next 200 msec, we infer, are involved in semantic processing for all items (250 to 450 msec), and semantic processing is then completed for items at this site from 450 to 750 msec after stimulus onset; those that are familiar have processing completed earlier than those subjectively unfamiliar to the patient. Application of this technique and other event-related electrophysiological measures (for example, ERP [Kutas & Van Petten, 1994; Friederici, 1997]) to determine the timing of processing at a specific region or to delineate one type of processing from another may lead to better isolation of behavioral-anatomic correlates of semantic functions.

Overall, there are several distinct brain regions that are consistently associated with semantic processing, irrespective of the items used in the task: left inferior parietal, left posterior superior temporal, left fusiform, and bilateral inferior (ventral) temporo-occipital region. (See table 11.2 for a summary of select lesion and imaging studies related to semantic processing deficits.) Additional evidence for the crucial role of the left posterior, superior temporal gyrus (Brodmann's area 22) in semantic processing is discussed in chapter 2.

NEURAL "HYBRID" MODEL OF SEMANTICS

To best view the behavioral-anatomic findings to date, we propose an alternative framework that we term a "hybrid" model of the neural organization of the semantic system. It shares features of both a distributed neural and a processing center model. In this "hybrid" model, there are two basic (not necessarily exclusive) components to the system in terms of both neural configuration and function. The major components are: (1) sensorimotor and language-based representations within semantic memory and (2) processing centers.

Basic sensorimotor memory representations (akin to the "structural descriptions" in the models illustrated by Elaine Funnell in chapter 10 of this volume) are likely stored or computed near their related sensorimotor cortices. For example, the motor memory of a hammering motion would be represented near the motor strip, the sensation of holding a heavy object

Table 11.2

Select Studies of Semantic Processing

Citation	Patients or subjects	Impaired semantic processing or task	Location of pathology or activation	Type of pathology or activation and etiology
Coughlan & Warrington, 1981	EM; 67 y.o. female	Impaired definition of spoken words–41 nouns, 38 verbs, & 42 adjectives	Diffuse cortical atrophy	Diffuse; atrophy
Petersen et al., 1988	17 (11 female) normals	Semantic association task	Left inferior frontal area & anterior cingulate gyrus	PET; normals
Hart & Gordon, 1990	Two anomic aphasics & one TSA	Category judgment & property judgment for pictures & words; visual & auditory word synonym judgment; naming to definition	Left inferior parietal–posterior superior temporal region	Focal; stroke
Demonet et al., 1992	9 normal volunteers (all male), mean age 35.7	3 auditory tasks: (1) baseline, tone task; (2) phoneme monitoring task; & (3) word task–monitor for names of small animals with "positive" attributes in attribute-noun pairs	Phonological processing → left superior temporal gyrus (mainly Wernicke's area) & Broca's area & right superior temporal regions; lexico-semantic task → left middle & inferior & superior temporal, inferior parietal & superior prefrontal	PET; normals
Nobre, Allison, & McCarthy, 1994	27 intractable seizure patients	Words with semantic content elicited larger P400	Anterior fusiform gyrus	ERP; seizure patients
Demb et al., 1995	10 (9 male) right-handed normals	Semantic encoding task (abstract or concrete word?) compared with two nonsemantic encoding tasks	Left inferior prefrontal cortex (LIPC) during semantic encoding compared to nonsemantic encoding	fMRI; normals
Nobre & McCarthy, 1995	10 patients with intracranial electrodes placed in the temporal lobe	1. Detect words belonging to a specific semantic category 2. Semantic priming task–exemplar words were from category "body parts" with primes being semantically related	AMTL negative field potential was diminished by semantic priming & was larger for words with semantic content than for function words; unpronounceable nonwords did not elicit the AMTL	ERP; seizure patients
Shaywitz et al., 1995	9 males; aged 22–24	Silent generation: (1) rhyming word to target; (2) exemplar to target category	Semantic task → bilateral inferior frontal & left posterior temporal	fMRI; normals

Study	Subjects	Task	Findings	Method
Vandenberghe et al., 1996	6 (all male) normals	Matching-to-sample tasks either with pictures or words. Match stimuli closest in (1) meaning; and (2) real-life size. In the baseline task, they performed a matching-to-sample for physical size on the screen	Semantic processing words & pictures → left TP junction, middle temporal gyrus, & inferior frontal + semantic processing of pictures → left posterior inferior temporal sulcus; words → left superior temporal sulcus, left anterior middle temporal gyrus, & left inferior frontal sulcus	fMRI; normals
Grafton, Fadiga, Arbib, & Rizzolatti, 1997	8 adult subjects (4 female)	1. Tool observation 2. Silent tool naming 3. Silent naming of tool use	Tool observation → left dorsal premotor; Silent tool naming → Broca's area; silent naming of tool use → left dorsal premotor cortex & ventral premotor cortex & the left SMA	fMRI; normals
Thompson-Schill, D'Esposito, Aguirre, & Farah, 1997	5 normal volunteers	1. Generation task—verb related to a visually presented noun 1a. High selection condition: nouns with many appropriate responses 1b. Low selection condition: nouns with few associated responses or with a dominant response 2. Classification task—classified line drawings of common objects 2a. High selection condition: pictures classified according to one attribute 2b. Low selection condition: pictures classified by basic level object names 3. Comparison task—compared a target word to several probe words 3a. High selection condition: based on specific attributes or features 3b. Low selection condition: based on global attributes	1a, 1b. Generation → Left inferior frontal gyrus (IFG)—greater in high deletion condition; high selection condition → SMA & anterior cingulate gyrus 2. Classification, high selection condition → left IFG, SMA, anterior cingulate gyrus, & left fusiform gyrus 3. Comparison, high selection condition → left IFG Comparing 4-choice & 2-choice low selection conditions → no IFG activity, indicating that it is not increases in the amount or duration of semantic processing that is associated with increases in left IFG activity	fMRI; normals
Hart et al., 1998	22 y.o. male trilingual (Farsi, English, French)	Impaired synonym judgment; property judgment; category judgment; & naming to definition	Circumscribed 1 cm reversible electrical "lesion" in the left fusiform gyrus	Focal; cortical stimulation in seizure patients

Continued

Table 11.2
Continued

Citation	Patients or subjects	Impaired semantic processing or task	Location of pathology or activation	Type of pathology or activation and etiology
Mummery, Patterson, Hodges, & Price, 1998	10 (all male) normals, aged 25–31	Tasks with word triads, of living things vs. artifacts: (1) syllable judgments; (2) color similarity; (3) location similarity judgments	Semantic compared to syllable tasks → left TPO, posterior middle temporal gyrus, & inferior temporal lobe; color similarity → left TPO, posterior cingulate, & medial temporal lobe; location similarity → left anteromedial temporal lobe & caudate nucleus	PET; normals
Thompson-Schill et al., 1998	14 patients with focal frontal cortex lesions & 16 control subjects	Asked to generate a verb from a concrete noun. There were two types of nouns: high selection (many competing responses) or low selection (few competing responses)	Lesions in the left IFG → impairment in generating semantically appropriate verbs for concrete nouns with high selection among competing responses only	Focal; variety of etiologies
Bayles, Tomoeda, & Cruz, 1999	60 probable AD patients & 48 normal elders	Making judgments about the relatedness of concepts deteriorates & reflects severity of dementia	Diffuse cortical atrophy	Diffuse; degenerative (AD)
Dapretto & Bookheimer, 1999	8 (4 female) normals	Listening to syntactically or semantically correct/incorrect sentences	Semantic condition → Lower aspect of left inferior frontal gyrus (BA 47)	fMRI; normals
Perani et al., 1999	14 (all males) normal, aged 22–26	Reading of concrete & abstract nouns & verbs for lexical decision	Verbs vs. nouns → left dorsolateral frontal cortex, superior parietal, anterior & middle temporal, & occipital; abstract vs. concrete words → bilateral lateral ventral frontal; right temporal pole, PO junction, anterior cingulate gyrus, & amygdala	PET; normals
Price et al., 1999 (Continued next row)	SW, 50 y.o. male	Tasks with word & picture triads: semantic association; visual similarity	Left inferior frontal, anterior superior temporal, & anterior parietal lesion fMRI: semantics → left posterior basal temporal, posterior inferior parietal, & anterior middle temporal; right anterior middle temporal & medial superior frontal (not in normals)	Focal; stroke fMRI

Study	Subjects	Tasks	Findings	Method
Price et al., 1999	6 control subjects, mean age 57	Tasks with word & picture triads: semantic association; visual similarity	Semantics → left posterior basal temporal, posterior inferior parietal, & anterior middle temporal, left inferior frontal (BA 47) & right cerebellum (not in SW)	fMRI; normals
Ricci et al., 1999	8 (3 female) normals	Tasks: baseline (visual noise), figure matching (nonsense objects), size matching, group matching (e.g., 2 types of telephones), & semantic object matching	All tasks relative to the baseline → inferior occipital & temporal cortices; parahippocampal gyrus & BA 47 of the inferior frontal cortex	PET; normals
Thompson-Schill, Aguirre, D'Esposito, & Farah, 1999	5 (1 female) normals	1. Yes/no questions re: visual or nonvisual characteristics about living (e.g., animals, vegetables) & nonliving (e.g., clothing, furniture) things	All conditions → ventral occipito-temporal cortex, left middle temporal; visual questions about living & nonliving things & nonvisual questions about living things → left fusiform	fMRI; normals
Friederici, Opitz, & von Cramon, 2000	14 (6 female), right-handed normals	Categorization tasks: (1) baseline-physical characterization; (2) syntactic-identify word as noun or function word; (3) semantic- identify word as abstract or concrete	Semantic task → left pars triangularis (inferior frontal & posterior middle/superior temporal); syntactic task → inferior tip of left frontal operculum & cortex ling junction of inferior frontal & inferior precentral sulcus	fMRI; normals
Gold & Kertesz, 2000	Patient GP, 52 y.o. male & RT, 54 y.o. male normal control subject	Semantic association task Orthographic task—decide whether all words in the triad were spelled correctly	GP: left TP, posterior frontal & lateral occipital lesion. semantic task → right middle frontal, superior temporal, supramarginal angular, & precuneate for GP only	Focal: hemorhagic infarct of GP & fMRI (patient & control)
Mummery et al., 2000	6 (5 female, mean age 60.5) with semantic dementia; 14 controls (9 female, mean age 62)	Anomia & loss of meaning for words & objects	Degree of atrophy in left anterior temporal lobe correlated with semantic performance, while degree of atrophy in the ventromedial frontal region was not significantly correlated with performance	Morphometric analysis of MRI for patients with semantic controls

223

and the coolness of the metal head of a hammer would be near the sensory strip, and the visual image of a hammer would be represented in visual cortices. Whether these representations are stored in a focal circumscribed neural region or are distributed throughout neural elements is unknown at present.

Another form of representation is lexical-semantic (the meaning of the word *hammer*) and the associated connections between semantically related lexical referents to that item (the meaning of words for "tool," "nail," "repair," and so on). These lexical-semantic representations may also serve as pointers to some of the sensorimotor ones by triggering, lowering the activation threshold, or activating select sensorimotor representations. The extent or presence of such triggering may differ, depending upon the specific item or task. While the neural substrates of these lexical-semantic representations has been debated, we believe that the regions isolated during previous activation studies (left inferior parietal, left posterior superior temporal, left fusiform, and bilateral inferior temporo-occipital regions) are essential for accessing these lexical-semantic representations. It is likely that some of these regions are crucial for accessing all lexical-semantic representations, whereas others are crucial for accessing only certain types of lexical-semantic representations (for example, animals versus actions).

The modal, amodal, or multimodal semantic processing centers appear as distinct, relatively circumscribed regions in the brain that perform specific operations or functions involving semantic representations. Our review demonstrates that these regions include, but are not limited to the following: left inferior prefrontal frontal lobe, left inferior parietal-posterior superior temporal, left fusiform. The exact functions performed within these areas will need to be further delineated in the future. Some of the proposed operations include selection between choices of stimuli, visual-verbal integration, feature-object correlation, noun-verb association, feature binding (Hart et al., 2000a; Kraut, et al., 2002), and so on.

Thus, the semantic memory of an object may involve activation of representations from multiple regions (for example, sensorimotor representations, lexical semantic representations, amodal/multimodal semantic processing centers, and so on). The number and/or strength of the activated representations likely depend on the object being activated, the critical representations necessary to uniquely distinguish the object from other stimuli eliciting the conceptual activation, and/or the task to be performed with the object. Focal, circumscribed processing centers access and integrate these representations to form semantic memories. Further refinements in this model will occur as improved spatial and temporal resolution develops in neuroinvestigative techniques.

REFERENCES

Abdullaev, Y. G., & Posner, M. I. (1998). Event-related brain potential imaging of semantic encoding during processing single words. *Neuroimage, 7,* 1–13.

Basso, A., Capitani, E., & Laiacona, L. (1988). Progressive language impairment without dementia: A case with isolated category specific semantic defect. *Journal of Neurology, Neurosurgery and Psychiatry, 51,* 1201–1207.

Bayles, K. A., Tomoeda, C. K., & Cruz, R. F. (1999). Performance of Alzheimer's disease patients in judging word relatedness. *Journal of the International Neuropsychological Society, 5,* 668–675.

Berndt, R. S. (1988). Category-specific deficits in aphasia. *Aphasiology, 2,* 237–240.

Cappa, S. F., Frugoni, M., Pasquali, P., Perani, D., & Zorat, F. (1998). Category-specific naming impairment for artefacts: A new case. *Neurocase, 4/5,* 391–398.

Caramazza, A. (1998). The interpretation of semantic category-specific deficits: What do they reveal about the organization of conceptual knowledge in the brain? *Neurocase, 4,* 265–272.

Caramazza, A., & Shelton, J. R. (1998). Domain-specific knowledge systems in the brain: The animate-inanimate distinction. *Journal of Cognitive Neuroscience, 10,* 1–34.

Coltheart, M., Inglis, L., Cupples, L., Michie, P., Bates, A., & Budd, W. (1998). A semantic subsystem of visual attributes. *Neurocase, 4,* 353–370.

Coughlan, A. K., & Warrington, E. K. (1981). The impairment of verbal semantic memory: A single case study. *Journal of Neurology, Neurosurgery and Psychiatry, 44,* 1079–1083.

Crone, N. E., Miglioretti, D. L., Gordon, B., & Lesser, R. P. (1998) Functional mapping of human sensorimotor cortex with electrocorticographic spectral analysis II: Event-related synchronization in the gamma band. *Brain, 121,* 2301–2315.

Crone, N. E., Miglioretti, D. L., Gordon, B., Sieracki, J.,

Wilson, M. T., Uematsu, S., & Lesser, R. P. (1998) Functional mapping of human sensorimotor cortex with electrocorticographic spectral analysis I: Alpha and beta event-related desynchronization. *Brain, 121,* 2271–2299.

Damasio, A. R. (1990). Category-related recognition defects as a clue to the neural substrates of knowledge. *Trends in Neuroscience, 13,* 95–98.

Damasio, A. R., Damasio, H., Tranel, D., & Brandt, J. P. (1990). Neural regionalization of knowledge access: Preliminary evidence. *Cold Spring Harbor Symposia on Quantitative Biology, 55,* 1039–1047.

Damasio, H., Grabowski, T. J., Tranel, D., Hichwa, R. D., & Damasio, A. R. (1996). A neural basis for lexical retrieval. *Nature, 380,* 499–505.

Damasio, A. R., & Tranel, D. (1993). Nouns and verbs are retrieved with differently distributed neural systems. *Proceedings of the National Academy of Sciences USA, 90,* 4957–4960.

Dapretto, M., & Bookheimer, S. Y. (1999). Form and content: dissociating syntax and semantics in sentence comprehension. *Neuron, 24,* 427–432.

Dehaene, S. (1995). Electrophysiological evidence for category-specific word processing in the normal human brain. *Neuroreport, 6,* 2153–2157.

deCharms, R. C., Blake, D. T., & Merzenich, M. M. (1998). Optimizing sound features for cortical neurons. *Science, 280,* 1439–1443.

Demb, J. B., Desmond, J. E., Wagner, A. D., Vaidya, C. J., Glover, G. H., & Gabrieli, J. D. (1995). Semantic encoding and retrieval in the left inferior prefrontal cortex: A functional MRI study of task difficulty and process specificity. *Journal of Neuroscience, 15,* 5870–5878.

Demonet, J. F., Chollet, F., Ramsay, S., Cardebat, D., Nespoulous, J., Wise, R., Rascol, A., & Frackowiak, R. (1992). The anatomy of phonological and semantic processing in normal subjects. *Brain, 115,* 1753–1768.

Dennis, M. (1976). Dissociated naming and locating of body parts after left anteriortemporal lobe resection: An experimental case study. *Brain and Language, 3,* 147–163.

Devlin, J. T., Gonnerman, L. M., Anderson, E. S., & Seidenberg, M. S. (1998). Category-specific semantic deficits in focal and widespread brain damage: A computational account. *Journal of Cognitive Neuroscience, 10,* 77–94.

Farah, M. J. (1989). The neuropsychology of mental imagery. In J. W. Brown (Ed.), *Neuropsychology of visual perception.* Hillsdale, NJ: Lawrence Erlbaum.

Farah, M. J., & McClelland, J. L. (1991). A computational model of semantic memory impairment: Modality specificity and emergent category specificity. *Journal of Experimental Psychology: General, 120,* 339–357.

Farah, M. J., McMullen, P., & Meyer, M. (1991). Can recognition of living things be selectively impaired? *Neuropsychologia, 29,* 185–193.

Farah, M. J., Meyer, M. M., & McMullen, P. A. (1996). The living/nonliving dissociation is not an artifact: Giving an a priori implausible hypothesis a strong test. *Cognitive Neuropsychology, 13,* 137–154.

Farah, M. J., & Wallace, M. A. (1992). Semantically-bounded anomia: Implications for the neural implementation of naming. *Neuropsychologia, 30,* 609–622.

Ferreira, C. T., Giusiano, B., & Poncet, M. (1997). Category-specific anomia: Implication of different neural networks in naming. *Neuroreport, 8,* 1595–1602.

Friederici, A. D. (1997). Neurophysiological aspects of language processing. *Clinical Neuroscience, 4,* 64–72.

Friederici, A. D., Opitz, B., & von Cramon, D. Y. (2000). Segregating semantic and syntactic aspects of processing in the human brain: An fMRI investigation of different word types. *Cerebral Cortex, 10,* 698–705.

Funnell, E., & Sheridan, J. (1992). Categories of knowledge? Unfamiliar aspects of living and nonliving things. *Cognitive Neuropsychology, 9,* 135–153.

Gainotti, G., Silveri, M., Daniele, A., & Giustolisi, L. (1995). Neuroanatomical correlates of category-specific semantic disorders: A critical survey. *Memory, 3/4,* 247–264.

Garrard, P., Patterson, K., Watson, P. C., & Hodges, J. R. (1998). Category-specific semantic loss in dementia of Alzheimer's type: Functional-anatomical correlations form cross-sectional analyses. *Brain, 121,* 633–646.

Geschwind, N. (1965). Disconnexion syndromes in animals and man. *Brain, 88,* 237–297, 585–644.

Gold, B. T., & Kertesz, A. (2000). Right hemisphere semantic processing of visual words in an aphasic patient: An fMRI study. *Brain and Language, 73,* 456–465.

Goodglass, H., & Budin, C. (1988). Category and modality specific dissociations in word comprehension and concurrent phonological dyslexia. *Neuropsychologia, 26,* 67–78.

Goodglass, H., Wingfield, A., Hyde, M., & Theurkauf, J. C. (1986). Category specific dissociations in naming and recognition by aphasic patients. *Cortex, 22,* 87–102.

Gorno-Tempini, M. L., Cipolotti, L., & Price, C. J. (2000). Category differences in brain activation studies: Where do they come from? *Proc R Soc Lond B Biol Sci, 267,* 1253–1258.

Grafton, S. T., Fadiga, L., Arbib, M. A., & Rizzolatti, G. (1997). Premotor cortex activation during observation and naming of familiar tools. *Neuroimage, 6,* 231–236.

Grossman, M., Robinson, K., Biassou, N., White-Devine, T., & D'Esposito, M. (1998). Semantic memory in Alzheimer's disease: Representativeness, ontologic category, and material. *Neuropsychology, 12,* 34–42.

Hart, J., Berndt, R. S., & Caramazza, A. (1985). Category-specific naming deficit following cerebral infarction. *Nature, 316,* 439–440.

Hart, J., Crone, N. E., Lesser, R. P., Sieracki, J., Miglioretti, D. L., Hall, C., Sherman, D., & Gordon, B. (1998). Temporal dynamics of verbal object comprehension. *Proceedings of the National Academy of Sciences USA, 95,* 6498–6503.

Hart, J., & Gordon, B. (1990). Delineation of single-word semantic comprehension deficits in aphasia, with anatomical correlation. *Annals of Neurology, 3,* 226–231.

Hart, J., & Gordon, B. (1992). Neural subsystems for object knowledge. *Nature, 359,* 60–64.

Hart, J., Kremen, S., Segal, J., & Kraut, M. (2000a). *Object activation via feature binding in the semantic system using fMRI.* Platform presentation at the meeting of the American Academy of Neurology, San Diego. (*Neurology, 54,* A398).

Hart, J., Lesser, R. P., & Gordon, B. (1992). Selective interference with the representation of size in the human by direct cortical stimulation. *Journal of Cognitive Neuroscience, 4,* 337–344.

Hart, J., Kraut, M. A., Kremen, S., Soher, B., & Gordon, B. (2000b). Neural substrates of orthographic lexical access as demonstrated by functional brain imaging.

Neuropsychiatry, Neuropsychology and Behavioral Neurology, 13, 1-7.

Hillis, A., & Caramazza, A. (1991). Category-specific naming and comprehension impairment: A double dissociation. *Brain, 114,* 2081-94.

Hinton, G. E. (1981). Implementing semantic networks in parallel hardware. In G. E. Hinton & J. A. Anderson (Eds.), *Parallel models of associative memory.* Hillsdale, NJ: Erlbaum.

Humphreys, G. W., & Riddoch, M. J. (1987). On telling your fruits from your vegetables: A consideration of category-specific deficits after brain damage. *Trends in Neuroscience, 10,* 145-148.

Ishai, A., Ungerleider, L. G., Martin, A., Schouten, J. L., & Haxby, J. V. (1999). Distributed representation of objects in the human ventral visual pathway. *Proceedings of the National Academy of Sciences USA, 96,* 9379-9384.

Johnson, K. O., & Hsiao, S. S. (1992). Neural mechanisms of tactile form and texture perception. *Annual Review of Neuroscience, 15,* 227-250.

Jokeit, H., Heger, R., Ebner, A., & Markowitsch, H. J. (1998). Hemispheric asymmetries in category-specific word retrieval. *Neuroreport, 9,* 2371-2373.

Kapur, S., Rose, R., Liddle, P. F., Zipursky, R. B., Brown, G. M., Stuss, D., Houle, S., & Tulving, E. (1994). The role of the left prefrontal cortex in verbal processing: Semantic processing or willed action? *Neuroreport, 5,* 2193-2196.

Kraut, M. A., Kremen, S., Segal, J. B., Calhoun, V., Moo, L., & Hart, J. (2002). Object activation from features in the semantic system. *Journal of Cognitive Neuroscience, 14,* 24-36.

Kutas, M., & Van Petten, C. K. (1994). Psycholinguistics electrified: Event-related brain potential investigations. In M. A. Gernsbacher (Ed.), *Handbook of psycholinguistics.* San Diego: Academic Press.

Lamberts, K., & Shanks, D. (Eds.). (1997). *Knowledge, concepts, and categories.* Cambridge, MA: MIT Press.

Livingstone, M. S., & Hubel, D. H. (1988). Psychophysical evidence for separate channels for the perception of form, color, movement, and depth. *Journal of Neuroscience, 7,* 3416-3468.

Martin, A., Wiggs, C. L., Ungerleider, L. G., & Haxby, J. V. (1996). Neural correlates of category-specific knowledge. *Nature, 379,* 649-652.

Mauri, A., Daum, I., Sartori, G., Riesch, G., & Birbaumer, N. (1994). Category-specific semantic impairment in Alzheimer's disease and temporal lobe dysfunction: A comparative study. *Journal of Clinical and Experimental Neuropsychology, 16,* 689-701.

McCarthy, R. A., & Warrington, E. K. (1985). Category specificity in an agrammatic patient: The relative impairment of verb retrieval and comprehension. *Neuropsychologia, 23,* 709-727.

McCarthy, R. A., & Warrington, E. K. (1988). Evidence for modality-specific meaning systems in the brain. *Nature, 334,* 428-430.

McClelland, J. L., & Rumelhart, D. E. (1985). Distributed memory and the representation of general and specific information. *Journal of Experimental Psychology: General, 114,* 159-188.

McKenna, P., & Warrington, E. K. (1978). Category-specific naming preservation: A single case study. *Journal of Neurology Neurosurgery and Psychiatry, 41,* 571-574.

Millikan, R. G. (1988). A common structure for concepts of individuals, stuffs, and real kinds: More mama, more milk, and more mouse. *Behavioral Brain Science, 21,* 55-66.

Moore, C. J., & Price, C. J. (1999). A functional neuroimaging study of the variables that generate category-specific object processing differences. *Brain, 122,* 943-962.

Moss, H. E., & Tyler, L. K. (2000). A progressive category-specific semantic deficit for non-living things. *Neuropsychologia, 38,* 60-82.

Moss, H. E., Tyler, L. K., Durrant-Peatfield, M., & Bunn, E. M. (1998). "Two eyes of a see-through": Impaired semantic knowledge in a case of selective deficit for living things. *Neurocase, 4,* 291-310.

Mummery, C. J., Patterson, K., Hodges, J. R., & Price, C. J. (1998). Functional neuroanatomy of the semantic system: Divisible by what? *Journal of Cognitive Neuroscience, 10,* 766-777.

Mummery, C .J., Patterson, K., Price, C. J., Ashburner, J., Frackowiak, R. S., & Hodges, J. R. (2000). A voxel-based morphometry study of semantic dementia: Relationship between temporal lobe atrophy and semantic memory. *Annals of Neurology, 47,* 36-45.

Nielsen, J. M. (1946). *Agnosia, apraxia, aphasia: Their value in cerebral localization* (2nd ed.). New York: Paul B. Hoeber.

Nobre, A. C., Allison, T., & McCarthy, G. (1994). Word recognition in the human inferior temporal lobe. *Nature, 372,* 260-263.

Nobre, A.C., & McCarthy, G. (1995). Language-related field potentials in the anterior-medial temporal lobe II: Effects of word type and semantic priming. *Journal of Neuroscience, 15,* 1090-1098.

Perani, D., Cappa, S., Bettinardi, V., Bressi, S., Gorno-Tempini, M., Matarrese, M., & Fazio, F. (1995). Different neural systems for the recognition of animals and man-made tools. *Neuroreport, 6,* 1637-1639.

Perani, D., Schnur, T., Tettamanti, M., Gorno-Tempini, M., Cappa, S. F., & Fazio, F. (1999). Word and picture matching: A PET study of semantic category effects. *Neuropsychologia, 37,* 293-306.

Petersen, S. E., Fox, P. T., Posner, M. I., Mintun, M., & Raichle, M. E. (1988). Positron emission tomographic studies of the cortical anatomy of single-word processing. *Nature, 331,* 585-589.

Petersen, S. E., Fox, P. T., Snyder, A. Z., & Raichle, M. E. (1990). Specific extrastriate and frontal cortical areas are activated by visual words and word-like stimuli. *Science, 249,* 1041-1044.

Pietrini, V., Nertempi, P., Vaglia, A., Revello, M. G., & Pinna, V. (1988). Recovery from herpes simplex encephalitis: Selective impairment of specific semantic categories with neuroradiological correlation. *Journal of Neurology, Neurosurgery, and Psychiatry, 51,* 1284-1293.

Posner, M. I., Petersen, S. E., Fox, P. T., & Raichle, M. E. (1988). Localization of cognitive operations in the human brain. *Science, 240,* 1627-1631.

Price, C. J., Mummery, C. J., Moore, C. J., Frackowiak, R. S., & Friston, K. J. (1999). Delineating necessary and sufficient neural systems with functional imaging studies of neuropsychological patients. *Journal of Cognitive Neuroscience, 11,* 371-382.

Rapcsak, S. Z., Comer, J. F., & Rubens, A. B. (1993). Anomia for facial expressions: Neuropsychological mechanisms and anatomical correlates. *Brain and Language, 45,* 233-252.

Rapcsak, S. Z., Kaszniak, A. W., & Rubens, A. B. (1989). Anomia for facial expressions: Evidence for a category specific visual-verbal disconnection syndrome. *Neuropsychologia, 27,* 1031–1041.

Ricci, P. T., Zelkowicz, B. J., Nebes, R. D., Meltzer, C. C., Mintun, M. A., and Becker, J. T. (1999). Functional neuroanatomy of semantic memory: Recognition of semantic associations. *Neuroimage, 9,* 88–96.

Robinson, K. M., Grossman, M., White-Devine, T., & D'Esposito, M. (1996). Category-specific difficulty naming with verbs in Alzheimer's disease. *Neurology, 47,* 178–182.

Sacchett, C., & Humphreys, G. W. (1992). Calling a squirrel a squirrel but a canoe a wigwam: A category-specific deficit for artefactual objects and body parts. *Cognitive Neuropsychology, 9,* 73–86.

Samson, D., Pillon, A., & De Wilde, V. (1998). Impaired knowledge of visual and non-visual attributes in a patient with a semantic impairment for living entities: A case of a true category-specific deficit. *Neurocase, 4,* 273–290.

Sartori, G., & Job, R. (1988). The oyster with four legs: a neuropsychological study on the interaction of visual and semantic information. *Cognitive Neuropsychology, 5,* 105–132.

Sartori, G., Job, R., Miozzo, M., Zago, S., & Marchiori, G. (1993). Category-specific form-knowledge deficit in a patient with herpes simplex virus encephalitis. *Journal of Clinical and Experimental Neuropsychology, 15,* 280–299.

Semenza, C., & Zettin, M. (1988). Generating proper names: A case of selective inability. *Cognitive Neuropsychology, 5,* 711–721.

Semenza, C., & Zettin, M. (1989). Evidence from aphasia for the role of proper names as pure referring expressions. *Nature, 342,* 678–679.

Shaywitz, B. A., Pugh, K. R., Constable, T., Shaywitz, S. E., Bronen, R. A., Fulbright, R. K., Shankweiler, D. P., Katz, L., Fletcher, J. M., Skudlarski, P., & Gore, J. C. (1995). Localization of semantic processing using functional magnetic resonance imaging. *Human Brain Mapping, 2,* 149–158.

Silveri, M. C., Daniele, A., Giustolisi, L., & Gainotti, G. (1991). Dissociation between knowledge of living and nonliving things in dementia of the Alzheimer type. *Neurology, 41,* 545–546.

Silveri, M. C., & Gainotti, G. (1988). Interaction between vision and language in category-specific semantic impairment. *Cognitive Neuropsychology, 5,* 677–709.

Skarda, C. A., & Freeman, W. J. (1987). How brains make chaos in order to make sense of the world. *Behavioral Brain Science, 10,* 161–195.

Sloman, S. A., & Rips, L. J. (Eds.). (1998). *Similarity and symbols in human thinking.* Cambridge, MA: MIT Press.

Spitzer, M., Kwong, K. K., Kennedy, W., Rosen, B. R., & Bellivean, J. W., (1995). Category-specific brain activation in fMRI during picture naming. *Neuroreport, 6,* 2109–2112.

Temple, C. (1986). Anomia for animals in a child. *Brain, 109,* 1225–1242.

Tippett, L. J., Glosser, G., & Farah, M. J. (1996). A category-specific naming impairment after temporal lobectomy. *Neuropsychologia, 34,* 139–146.

Thompson-Schill, S. L, Aguirre, G. K., D'Esposito, M., & Farah, M. J. (1999). A neural basis for category and modality specificity of semantic knowledge. *Neuropsychologia, 37,* 671–676.

Thompson-Schill, S. L., D'Esposito, M., Aguirre, G. K., & Farah, M. J. (1997). Role of left inferior prefrontal cortex in retrieval of semantic knowledge: A reevaluation. *Proceedings of the National Academy of Sciences USA, 94,* 14792–14797.

Thompson-Schill, S. L., Swick, D., Farah, M. J., D'Esposito, M., & Kan, I. P. (1998). Verb generation in patients with focal frontal lesions: A neuropsychological test of neuroimaging findings. *Proceedings of the National Academy of Sciences USA, 95,* 15855–15860.

Tyrrell, P. J., Warrington, E. K., Frackowiak, R. S. J. & Rossor, M. N. (1990). Heterogeneity in progressive aphasia due to focal cortical atrophy. *Brain, 113,* 1321–1336.

Vandenberghe, R., Price, C., Wise, R., Josephs, O., & Frackowiak, R. S. (1996). Functional anatomy of a common semantic system for words and pictures. *Nature, 383,* 254–256.

Warrington, E. K., & McCarthy, R. A. (1983). Category specific access dysphasia. *Brain, 106,* 859–878.

Warrington, E. K., & McCarthy, R. A. (1987). Categories of knowledge: Further fractionation and an attempted integration. *Brain, 110,* 1273–1296.

Warrington, E. K., & Shallice, T. (1984). Category specific semantic impairments. *Brain, 107,* 829–854.

Yamadori, A., & Albert, M. L. (1973). Word category aphasia. *Cortex, 9,* 112–125.

12

"Semantic Therapy" in Day-to-Day Clinical Practice: Perspectives on Diagnosis and Therapy Related to Semantic Impairments in Aphasia

Simon Horton
Sally Byng

INTRODUCTION

"Semantic therapy" has become a convenient shorthand for a number of different therapy interventions all of which involve various aspects of semantic processing. Nickels (2000) points out the importance of distinguishing between the nature of the tasks used and the nature of the deficit that is to be remediated. Many "semantic therapy" tasks described in the literature rely on semantic processing, but do not necessarily have the remediation of semantics as their core aim, mostly being concerned with improving word finding. We will use "semantic therapy" in this chapter with a deliberately broad definition—simply, therapy that targets processing of semantic representations as a means of achieving a variety of goals.

However, one relatively extensive inventory and classification of various language therapy methods (Methé, Haber, & Paradis, 1993), did not mention "semantic therapy" per se at all, although not surprisingly many of the therapy approaches reviewed entailed at least an element of semantic processing. In another review of treatment for aphasia, Horner and colleagues (1994) looked at the prevalence of explicit model-driven aphasia therapy research in five major journals. Although the authors used a "processing model" as one of their categories, cognitive neuropsychological models are not referred to explicitly, and neither is "semantic therapy," the latter probably falling between the stools of "linguistic model" and "processing model." We will address other possible cultural differences when we come to consider the process of assessment and remediation in more detail.

Most studies of semantic therapy—and there have been many over the last fifteen years or so—have been single-case or small-group studies. Without exception these are efficacy studies— studies that evaluate the effects of a specific method used in therapy—rather than ones that seek to show that therapy works in clinical practice (Marshall, Pound, White-Thomson, & Pring, 1990). We are not aware of any published randomized-controlled trials of semantic therapy, although there is a multicenter study of the effectiveness of BOX, a lexical semantic therapy (Visch-Brink, Bajema, & Van de Sandt-Koenderman, 1997) currently under way in the Netherlands.

The emphasis on model-guided treatments is almost universal, and Seron and Deloche's (1989) injunction that treatments should be theoretically motivated has echoed down the years. Furthermore, "semantic therapy" has become very closely associated with a cognitive neuropsychological approach to the study of aphasia, as embodied in modular models of language processing such as that of Patterson and Shewell (1987). We will be mostly considering therapies driven by such psycholinguistic models, but recognize of course that there is a range of other therapies or therapy approaches that clearly address semantic processing. However, it is worth noting that Wilson and Patterson (1990) came to rather pessimistic conclusions on the value of theory as a guidance to choice of treatments, pointing out that beneficial treatment certainly does occur in the absence of input from theoretical cognitive psychology (p. 257). Pring and colleagues (1993) also came to rather gloomy conclusions in their review of therapies for word finding difficulties. Pointing out that while the ambiguity arising from many studies is the stuff on which theoreticians thrive, they note that *clinicians* need clear recommendations on the effectiveness of different treatment regimes, and as such these were not yet available. However, as Pring and colleagues (1993) also point out, the findings of early work on the benefits of semantic activation (for example, Howard, Patterson, Franklin, Orchard-Lisle, & Morton, 1985a) have been influential. Many therapists are familiar with the view that semantic therapy tasks assist naming, whatever the theory or imputed mechanisms behind these interventions. Therapists have not been slow to take up and use semantic therapy tasks in everyday clinical practice.

In this chapter, we will briefly discuss methodologies used in semantic therapy and provide some examples from the literature on assessment, development of a working hypothesis, stimulus selection, treatment planning, and treatment strategies. The chapter is not intended to be a comprehensive review of the literature on semantic therapy interventions (for a recent review see Nickels 2000, among others), but to present a variety of perspectives. We then will summarize results from a study of semantic therapy in day-to-day clinical practice as a means of illustrating and illuminating a variety of aspects of treating impairments related to semantic problems in aphasia. We will outline the framework we have developed for structuring therapy data, and present some analysis using this framework.

Methodology

Single-case methodology has been advocated as a useful means of exploring the effects of a particular aphasia therapy.[1] The question of whether aphasia therapy per se is effective has been judged to be inappropriate and probably unanswerable (Howard, 1986). Best and Nickels (2000) argue that we need to address the question of whether a particular therapy can be shown to be effective in addressing an individual person's aphasia (or aphasic symptoms). This question has been addressed in numerous single-case studies of semantic therapy (for example, Behrmann & Lieberthal, 1989; Hillis, 1989; Nickels & Best, 1996b; Coelho, McHugh, & Boyle, 2000). Pring (1986) points out that replication of single cases is a necessary step toward establishing that the effects of treatment generalize to other patients with similar problems. Replications have taken various forms, including replicating treatment used in single-case studies in a small-group design (for example, Marshall et al., 1990).

There have been many encouraging results of single case studies. For example, Pring and colleagues (1993) point out the very long lasting effects of treatments for word finding difficulties, with some generalization of naming. However, they point out that the conditions under

---

[1]For wide-ranging reviews and overviews of single-case approaches see: Coltheart, 1983; Franklin, 1993; Howard, 1986; Pring, 1986; Wertz, 1995; Willmes, 1995.

which it occurs remain uncertain. Nickels and Best (1996a, 1996b) concluded from the research on treatment of anomia that it was difficult to draw any clear conclusions about *which* people with *which* particular levels of breakdown in word production would benefit from *which* task.

Single-case approaches have certainly ensured that clinicians are in a much better position to be aware of treatment effects at a "local level." However, the issues around treatment "dosage"—intensity, duration, and timing of treatment—have barely begun to be addressed (but see Hillis, 1998). In clinical practice these issues are probably dictated by factors outside the control of the individual clinician, as is suggested by the data from our study, where treatment frequency is related to the type of facility where therapy takes place. The relative needs of different people with aphasia or their ability to make use of therapy do not seem to be the critical issues in determining how much therapy they receive, for how long.

Because of the almost exclusive inclusion of "chronic aphasic" patients in studies of semantic therapy, we know very little about the relative benefits of the application of semantic therapy applied at different time points in the natural course of recovery from aphasia. As Wertz (1995) points out, clinicians need to know at which point postonset their efforts are most efficacious (p. 332). There have been studies on the differential effects of treatment at different time points (for example, Basso, Capitani, & Vignolo, 1979, Wertz et al., 1986), but nothing that we are aware of in relation to semantic therapy specifically.[2]

ASSESSMENT

Formal Assessment

In a study on semantic therapy described later, we asked therapists to give us background data on assessments they (or previous therapists) had carried out. Table 12.1 gives an overview of the assessments reported in the study. One must be cautious about drawing any firm conclusions about the use of assessments in day-to-day practice generally on the basis of the type of assessments reported in this study. It is likely that therapists tended to report only those assessments they thought were relevant to the "semantic" element of the project. However, the large proportion of mentions of the use of the Psycholinguistic Assessment of Language Processing in Aphasia (PALPA) (63 percent of formal assessments here) echoes the findings of a recent survey of aphasia management practices (Katz et al., 2000). In their study, the PALPA was reported as joint equal with the Boston Naming Test (BNT) (Kaplan, Goodglass, & Weintraub, 1983) as the UK's most frequently administered test in the assessment of acute aphasic in-patients. It was also the most frequently administered test for people with chronic aphasia who were seen as out-patients in the UK. In their study, 22 percent of respondents in the UK reported using Pyramids and Palm Trees (Howard & Patterson, 1992) with people with chronic aphasia who were seen as out-patients. This is the same proportion as our study (22 percent of formal assessments), although our study covers in- and out-patient groups.

Katz and colleagues' (2000) study is interesting in that there are clear cultural differences in the use of certain types of assessment in whatever settings. For example, there is no reported use of the PALPA or Pyramids and Palm Trees in the United States or Canada (although due to the relatively small numbers in the survey one has to question how representative the findings are, a point the authors also make). This suggests that the taste for psycholinguistic assessment in day-to-day practice may not be shared across the Atlantic[3] (although it finds some favor in Australia).

---

[2]But see Raymer, Maher, Foundas, Gonzalez Rothi, & Heilman, 2000, for an overview of investigations of recovery of lexical impairments with respect to models of lexical processing, and a single-case study of recovery patterns in relation to semantic deficits.
[3]This is clearly not the case for academic studies and published papers. See also Raymer et al. (1990) for a further semantic assessment.

Table 12.1

Assessments Reported in the Study of Semantic Therapy in Clinical Practice

Assessment	Sections/specification	Number of mentions
PALPA[a]	Written or spoken naming	4
	Written or spoken word-picture matching	17
	Lexical decision	1
	Repetition (imageability and frequency)	1
	Naming (spoken, written); reading aloud; repetition; spelling to dictation (same stimuli)	5
	Word semantic association	1
	Spelling to dictation	1
	Spelling to dictation (nonwords)	1
TROG[b]	Assesses receptive grammatical abilities using a variety of different sentence constructions (standardized on children)	4
"Kay's test"[c]	Spoken word-picture matching (with distracters)	1
The Pyramids and Palm Trees Test[d]	Unspecified format	5
	Three-picture version	1
	Three-word version	5
Mt Wilja[e]	Not specified	1
BDAE[f]	Cookie Theft picture description	1
Informal assessments	Verb judgment and comprehension	2
	Verb naming	1
	Object naming	1
	Odd one out (two levels of difficulty)	1
	Drawing to spoken and written word stimuli	1
	Word repetition	1
	Three letter tile sort to picture stimulus	1

[a]Psycholinguistic Assessments of Language Processing in Aphasia (PALPA; Kay et al., 1996)
[b]Test for Reception of Grammar (TROG; Bishop, 1982)
[d]Kay's test (Kay, unpublished)
[d]The Pyramids and Palm Trees Test (Howard & Patterson, 1992)
[e]Mt Wilja—a nonstandardized, unpublished test of high-level language, from Australia
[f]Boston Diagnostic Aphasia Examination (Goodglass & Kaplan, 1983)

The need for assessments of various kinds in the treatment and monitoring of progress in aphasia is undisputed. What is more in dispute is the nature of the assessments used, and to what ends they are used.[4] In terms of language impairments, clinicians who are alerted to semantic deficits in aphasia through presentation of surface symptoms such as omissions, circumlocutions, or semantic paraphasias in conversational speech may carry out formal testing using any, or parts of any of the aphasia assessment batteries, such as the Boston Diagnostic Aphasia Examination (Goodglass & Kaplan 1983) or the Western Aphasia Battery (Kertesz, 1982), or their non-English-language equivalents.[5] This type of assessment is clearly very popular in day-to-day clinical practice throughout the world (Katz et al., 2000). However, much criticism has been levelled at these syndrome-based approaches to assessment in aphasia for grouping together people who present highly heterogeneous deficits at the level of psycholinguistic processing. Consequently they have been seen to fail to "inspire therapeutic strategies based

[4]For a variety of perspectives and general discussion see: *Aphasiology*, *4*(1), 67–122, Clinical Forum; *Aphasiology*, *10*(2) 159–215, Clinical Forum.
[5]For example: French—Protocole Montréal-Toulouse d'Examen Linguistique de l'Aphasie (PMTELA) (Nespoulous et al., 1986); German (and translations into Italian, Dutch, and Thai)—Aachener Aphasie Test (Huber, Poeck, Weniger, & Willmes, 1983).

on a psychological interpretation of the disorders" (Seron & Deloche, 1989, p. 3). Driving the use of assessments that are based on psycholinguistic models of language processing (for example, PALPA) has been the hope that in providing more precise, theoretically motivated explanations of strengths and difficulties (Byng, Kay, Edmundson, & Scott, 1990), such explanations could be used to devise rational therapies and rehabilitation programs. These should then be based on a theoretical analysis of the disorder to be treated (Coltheart, 1984).

The PALPA was developed in order to meet the need for a convenient, "off the peg" battery of tests for a variety of language disorders (Kay, Lesser, & Coltheart, 1996), and is based on a modular model of cognitive processes that can be selectively impaired by brain damage. As such it distinguishes between language processing as a mental activity and language as a means of communication in everyday life. The PALPA is neither fully standardized, nor reliability tested, although there are normative data from non–brain-damaged subjects. This can make interpretation of test scores problematic. Marshall (1996) takes two of the PALPA subtests as examples of the relative lack of specificity of the language model. Tests 47 and 48 explore the ability to match a spoken or written word to a target picture in the presence of semantic, visual, and unrelated distracters. The semantic distracters hold a variety of relationships to the targets, and poor patterns of performance on these assessments would suggest a "semantic deficit," but the precise nature of the deficit remains a mystery. We have only a relatively tenuous understanding of the normal workings of the semantic system, and the diverse range of semantic associations tapped by these PALPA subtests reflect this lack of understanding. On the positive side, the PALPA is organized in a way that allows the therapist to tailor his or her investigation using assessments that are appropriate to the hypothesis under investigation, and to test for the effects of a number of linguistic variables (for example, word frequency, imageability, syllable length). The authors point out that it is important to examine type of errors, with evidence being accumulated on a number of tasks that are designed to address different levels of processing.

The PALPA assumes a common semantic system for words and pictures/objects, and incorporates a visual object recognition system analogous to the orthographic and phonological input lexicons for written and spoken words, respectively. In this respect it differs from Pyramids and Palm Trees, which is based on a view of semantic knowledge organization that postulates partially independent representational systems for words and objects, while also including a picture recognition system. In this test, a triad of pictures, words, or picture/word combinations are presented, and the subject is asked to select one of two pictures or words that is most closely associated with a stimulus picture or word. For example, the person must select a palm tree or a pine tree to match a pyramid. Kay and colleagues (1996) and Howard and Patterson (1992) acknowledge that their particular view of the organization of the semantic system is not universally accepted. As Funnell (2000) points out, no current model of semantic memory can be applied to all data and all relevant theoretical questions in an even partially satisfactory way.

Howard and Patterson (1992) argue that Pyramids and Palm Trees, with its combination of different modalities of presentation—three pictures, three words, written or spoken words and pictures—allows the therapist to build up a picture of a patient's ability to access conceptual and semantic information from words and pictures, and to test hypotheses about the levels of impairment in an individual person. Pyramids and Palm Trees was pretested with groups of non–brain-damaged adults, and the authors claim that someone who scores 90 percent or better (on any particular presentation) does not have a clinically significant impairment. However, they describe patterns of performance that "look" the same on the test, but that could arise from different loci of impairment. For example, impaired performance on the three-picture version could arise from impairment in picture recognition, impairment in access to object semantics from the picture stimuli, or impairments in the object semantic system itself.

For both the PALPA and Pyramids and Palm Trees, it is obviously vital for the therapist to have a good understanding of the language processing models on which the tests are founded. Neither test assumes that it can provide a complete picture of an individual's language processing deficits, and both probably require further testing at some level before the clinician can proceed to planning treatment. As Marshall (1996) points out, the PALPA—or any cognitive processing model of assessment—asks the clinician to adopt an experimental approach to the assessment of people with aphasia. The clinician must choose the assessments to test his or her hypotheses, and understand how to interpret the resulting data.

Informal Assessment

The data from our treatment study also show that, in common with many research studies, informal language assessment is used (see table 12.1), very often to refine the hypothesis testing described above. Many different tasks are described in the literature—for example, semantic verification and verbal fluency by category tasks (Funnell & Hodges, 1996); category-specific naming and object reality decision tasks (Basso, 1993). Materials used for testing are sometimes idiosyncratic or personal to the aphasic person (for example, Robson & Horton, in press), sometimes drawn from picture sets (for example, Snodgrass & Vanderwart, 1980), and use word frequency or familiarity norms (Kucera & Francis, 1967). Informal assessment also includes what has been called "diagnostic therapy" by various authors. This entails taking evidence from the person's performance on a variety of tasks, including the types of errors and error patterns and observations of the manner in which someone goes about the task (Byng et al., 1990).

DEVELOPING A WORKING HYPOTHESIS

The purpose of assessment is to formulate a working hypothesis (a "diagnosis") about what is impaired in the individual who is tested. There is no doubt that a cognitive neuropsychological approach to the assessment of semantic and other language processing deficits places high demands on the practicing clinician. Nevertheless, clinicians appear to be meeting the investigative challenges, and are quite prepared to form working hypotheses about the nature of someone's language difficulties, often using psycholinguistic models as a basis for their observations. Remarks recorded in the data from our study of semantic therapy (described later; see also Byng, Swinburn, & Pound, 1999) include such comments as:

- "Breakdown of central semantic system causing lack of specificity when accessing phonological output lexicon";
- "Central semantic and phonological output problems . . . good auditory comprehension of concrete high-frequency nouns, more variable with verbs"; and
- "Semantic errors in input and output tasks (mainly close semantic errors). Suspect reduced semantic drive to phonological output lexicon and orthographic output lexicon (as well as some central semantic impairment)."

STIMULUS SELECTION FOR THERAPY

Many therapists use photographic picture materials readily available on the market in semantic therapy. These materials are often systematically organized along "semantic category" lines, and are therefore extremely convenient for the hard-pressed clinician. There is no doubt that materials thus organized have been developed by publishers to meet needs expressed by the market. However, there is no getting away from the feeling that there is something rather sterile and uninspiring about the use of pictures of food (fruit, vegetables), animals (wild, domestic) or household items (electrical goods, things you find in various rooms). Some therapists make up their own materials based on the specific aims of the therapy (for example: written sentences and paragraphs; particular combinations of nouns or verbs), or use items that were personal to and are chosen by the aphasic person, and work the semantic therapy around these items.

Many therapy tasks require selecting a target from semantically related words or semantically related pictures. The whole subject of semantic relatedness is extremely cloudy, not only because relatedness could be considered to be in part a matter of individual difference in perception and experience, but also because there are so many different levels of relatedness just within proposed models of lexical semantics alone (see Elaine Funnell, chapter 10 in this volume, and Funnell, 2000). Nickels (2000) questions the assumption that the notion of "graded difficulty" of tasks (for example, the use of ever more "closely related" semantic distracters) is valid for all aphasic people. She cites a study by Morris (1997), where rated similarity of target and distracter affected the performance of only one of two aphasic people on a word-picture verification task. Furthermore, she cites studies of the facilitation of naming for people with aphasia (Barry & McHattie, 1991; Howard et al., 1985), where no effect has been found on the "depth of semantic processing."

In designing semantic therapy, the clinician must also choose whether to train stimuli that are "typical" for members of a category (for example, robin is a "typical" exemplar of bird), or items that are "atypical" (for example, ostrich is an "atypical" exemplar of bird). In a recent study of semantic therapy involving teaching of semantic features (for example, a robin flies, lays eggs, eats worms, and so on), Kiran and Thompson (in press) found that patients with semantic deficits showed faster improvement on trained items and more generalization to untrained, semantically related items when atypical exemplars were trained than when typical exemplars were trained.

PLANNING TREATMENT: MODEL GUIDED?

There has been a considerable amount of pessimism and scepticism about how much psycholinguistic models of language processing can offer the practicing clinician in planning appropriate treatments. These models were not developed in order to plan or explain treatments for disordered processes, but rather to model intact systems in a particular way. There is an appealing logic to some of the treatments based on the use of such models. For example, Marshall and colleagues (1990) demonstrate the use of word-picture matching plus reading aloud in therapy, thus "reinforcing links between semantics and phonology" (p. 175). However, critics have argued that theory itself has played very little part in treatment programs (Wilson & Patterson, 1990). Even though many authors allude to information processing models as the basis of their treatment planning, it is not clear how the models have contributed in terms of treatment design (Hillis, 1993). Hillis and others have pointed out that the only reasonable starting point for any intervention should be the careful identification of impaired and intact cognitive functions. But Howard and Hatfield (1987) observed that "too often . . . the relationship between deficit and treatment is based on some implicit idea of how treatment has its effects, which has no good justification or scientific support" (p. 106). Should clinicians lose all hope of having theoretical models to guide therapy? Aphasia therapy down the years has been guided by a variety of different models—what have we gained particularly from models of language processing, and have models of semantic memory contributed significantly to our practice?

It is probably fair to say that clinicians, researchers, and test developers have used a "pick-and-mix" approach to theories of semantic memory and organization. Elements from a variety of models (for example: single semantic system, or separable verbal and visual semantic systems; category membership and feature models of semantic memory; spreading activation model) have been incorporated in assessments and, as we will see in the next section, treatment approaches.

For all the limitations of cognitive neuropsychological models, they have contributed to a deeper and more detailed understanding of cognitive processes underlying surface symptoms that often present in apparently mystifying combinations. This has allowed clinicians to offer much clearer explanations to people with aphasia and relatives (see for example, Lesser & Algar, 1995), although not offering them the certainty of precise predictions (Best & Nickels, 2000). We cannot wait for new and more precise models; we cannot wait for a definitive theory of rehabilitation.

As we will discuss in the next section on semantic therapy treatments themselves, there are numerous studies that have reported successful treatments. We would endorse Helm Estabrooks and Holland (1997) and Best and Nickels (2000) in their call for careful and detailed analyses of linguistic strengths as well as weaknesses in the planning of treatments. This will of necessity entail taking a stance on some kind of model of language processing as a basis for understanding the language impairment, using existing assessments, but will also call for imagination, creativity, systematic observation, and a willingness to engage in targeted informal assessment and diagnostic therapy.

Semantic Therapy Treatment in the Literature

Despite the pessimistic views about the contribution of theory to therapy mentioned above, a large number of successful treatments have been reported over the last decade or so. Although there is a lack of specificity about what is meant by facilitating semantic processing (Weniger, 1990), it is also true to say that much of any sort of treatment for aphasic language impairment actually involves semantic processing because of the pivotal role semantics plays in language (Nickels, 2000). As we outlined in the introduction, we are taking a broad view of semantic therapy. We will review studies that have had a variety of aims, and look particularly at the tasks and materials involved in the treatment.

In this section, we examine reported semantic therapy tasks, to determine what aphasic people are being asked to do and how they do it. In our quest to try and pin down what *actually* happens in semantic therapy, we briefly review some of the studies in the literature that report on the process of the therapy as it was carried out. We address issues such as whether the tasks were performed effortlessly or whether there was a great deal of variability, whether the aphasic people were asked to do things they couldn't do, and whether actual performance during therapy had any bearing on the outcome of the therapy. While it is clearly not reasonable to expect published studies to contain blow-by-blow accounts of the therapy as it was carried out, we believe that for various reasons a proper compromise between brevity and loss of critical information, especially about process, has not yet been reached. We also examine the relationship between use (or not) of theoretical models (of semantics or language processing) in treatment planning and observations of the aphasic person's behavior in informing the choice of therapy task. We examine a few studies in detail to exemplify issues that are typically left unaddressed in descriptions of therapy. We emphasize that we know of no therapy studies that do include an adequate and complete discussion of therapy process issues.

It is interesting to note that among the many tasks that have appeared in studies of semantic therapy over the years, time as a factor or therapy resource (or as a measure of outcome) does not get much of a mention. Howard and colleagues (1985), citing studies by Marshall (1976) and Farmer (1977), note that additional time for lexical search is the most effective method that aphasic people use to aid word finding in speech production. In a study of facilitative techniques, Patterson and colleagues (1983) found that given a second opportunity to name a failed item the aphasic people tested were successful on about 25 percent of occasions. It is these types of observations—essentially atheoretical observations of behavior—that sometimes form the basis of a therapy treatment in studies that have been reported in the literature.

Hillis (1989) reports on therapy for two patients with impaired naming. One patient's performance across tasks indicated a semantic impairment, while the other patient's performance across tasks indicated an impairment in accessing the phonological representations of words for output, and an impairment at the level of the graphemic buffer in writing (see Brenda Rapp, chapter 4 of this volume, for an explanation of the role of the graphemic buffer in spelling). The author remarked that "Since there is currently no theory regarding how (or if) the hypothesized underlying cause/s of naming errors in each patient might be treated, a behavioral approach to remediation was taken" (p. 634). The treatment for written and verbal picture naming made use of a cueing hierarchy devised through observation of the sorts of stimuli that sometimes elicited the correct names, in conjunction with an observation that both patients were able to write picture names when given anagrams to work from. The same treatment was carried out with both patients even though they had different underlying deficits.

Nothing is noted about the therapist's input except as laid out in the cueing hierarchy, which is given in some detail. The patients' performance as reported is not linked to stages in either cueing hierarchy in any way. However, despite different underlying deficits, and receiving the same treatment regime, both people benefited from the treatment—but in different ways. For both people, written naming improved, but only the patient who had the semantic impairment showed generalization across modalities and to untrained nouns.

The point of Hillis's study was not to describe how therapy should be done in patients with semantic or other deficits, but to show that the identical therapy, particularly one in which the target word response is paired with a picture or object, can benefit individuals with *either* semantic or output deficits. Hillis argues that therapy "worked" for the two patients for different reasons. For the patient with intact semantics but an impairment in written (and spoken) output, the pairing of the picture and the cued production of the written word improved her written word, but not spoken word, production, probably because it influenced written output processes. But for the patient whose deficit in spoken and written naming was at the level of semantics (not output), pairing the picture with the written word response seemed to "work" by increasing the meaningfulness or semantics of trained words. The improved access to the semantics of trained words was reflected in improved written and spoken output (that is, there was generalization across modalities).

In later studies, Hillis reported that other therapies work differentially for patients with deficits at different levels of the lexical system. For example, a task of written word to picture matching (but not cued oral reading practice) improved naming of trained words in a patient with a selective deficit in semantics. In contrast, a task of cued oral reading practice, but not the written word-picture matching task, improved naming in a patient with impaired access to the phonological representations of words for output (Hillis & Caramazza, 1994). Furthermore, in a patient with deficits both at the level of semantics and at the level of accessing phonological representations of words, two separate treatments affected processing at the two different levels. That is, a "semantic therapy" (teaching semantic distinctions between the target and any semantically related word produced by the patient) reduced semantic errors in spoken and written word comprehension and in written naming, but did not improve spoken production of the words. In contrast, a "phonological therapy" (teaching pronunciations of trained words by spelling them phonetically for the patient to "sound out") improved spoken production of the same words (Hillis, 1991).

Basso (1993) described therapy provided to BA, who was fluently aphasic and whose main deficit was semantic-lexical, including a semantic category effect. A decision was made that, as the main deficit was "damage to the semantic system," therapy had to be directed toward its restoration. This appears to be a version of the "if-they-can't-do-it-get-them-to-do-it" approach to therapy, and this is perhaps confirmed by the author's note that one of the categories used in the semantic categorization tasks, which BA was able to perform correctly, was soon abandoned. In other categories BA had a lot of difficulties—"nothing that the therapist could do helped the patient" (p. 260)—but we do not know *what* the therapist *did*.

In odd-one-out tasks, BA was given five pictures, four of which belonged to the same semantic category, but he could not pinpoint the odd one out. We do not know how closely the odd one out related to the other items, or the nature of the relationship. We do not know if the therapist attempted to modify the task in any way, perhaps reducing the cognitive processing load by reducing the numbers of items and so on. Therapy was stopped after five months. Some time later–nineteen months after the original injury–BA returned for advice, and an entirely different treatment regime was instigated. This time he showed some improvement. One of Basso's conclusions is that "identification of the functional level of impairment is obviously necessary for a rational therapeutic intervention but . . . provides no specific guidance as to how an effective therapeutic program must be accomplished." This study demonstrates that identification of the "functional locus" in the semantic system clearly does not, as Basso points out, necessarily help therapy planning at all.

Behrmann and Lieberthal (1989) reported a study of treatment that aimed to improve the comprehension of single items in an aphasic person who had a central semantic deficit. As they state, clinicians who wish to rely on a clearly articulated model of semantics will either have to wait until such a model exists, or "to capitalise on existing theory, treading cautiously through the theoretical minefield" (p. 282). They point out that contrasting theories of semantics may have implications for treatment–for example, if meanings are represented separately for visual and verbal material, therapy will have to be carried out differently than if the view is taken that representations are stored in a single system. Theories about the organization of knowledge within the semantic system may also be critical factors in designing therapy. Behrmann and Lieberthal base their treatment on the assumption that meaning is organized in a category-specific, hierarchical fashion, and are neutral on the unitary versus multiple semantic systems' hypotheses, assessing and treating both visual and verbal semantics.

The treatment was in two major stages: the first aimed at teaching meaning at a general level of description (the superordinate features of each category); the second aimed at teaching specific details of items, leading to the precise identification of these items. The treatment was successful in several respects–better performance on treated items in treated categories, and carryover to untreated items within the same categories, for example.

However, one of the difficulties here–certainly for clinicians who might wish to use this particular approach to treatment–is the lack of specificity entailed in the term *teaching*. On the basis of this report, it is generally very hard to know exactly how the authors went about the process of "teaching." To be fair, they do go into some detail as regards progression through the hierarchy of different tasks, and give an example of how semantic features "distinctive to each category" might be explained–for example, by actual manipulation of physical objects, identifying the parts as fulfilling certain concepts. Despite this, it is very hard to see how this study could actually be replicated, and this illustrates one of the major problems with lack of specificity in reporting the therapy as it was actually carried out.

We would argue that one plank in the bridge that will link theoretical concepts entailed in language processing models or theories of semantic memory to the treatment of impairments related to semantic deficits must be a more precise specification of what is entailed in "teaching." The issues raised in this section are not specific to the studies described here, but rather illustrate the fact that there seems to be no well-articulated, explicit framework of the information that needs to be provided to understand how therapy might have worked. There seems to be no baseline set of descriptions to enable sharing of information and the development of theories about how therapy works.

One clear reason for the underreporting of the therapy as it was carried out is that there is an inadequate vocabulary and structure for doing this in anything other than a rather anecdotal way. To be fair, there are a number of studies where there is a clear treatment protocol that is adhered to, with little or no divergence on the part of the clinician–or so it would appear. But in our experience, few therapists adhere absolutely to a pre-prepared therapeutic script, but rather engage in discussion and debate with people with aphasia during the enact-ment of any therapy. The potential importance of that discussion to the aphasic person's understanding of the therapy should not be underestimated. It also must be said that there does have to be a clear schema for the treatment carried out in experimental studies; otherwise they would be meaningless and uninterpretable. However, as Byng (1995) points out, therapy is not synonymous with the task—it takes place at the interaction between the aphasic person and the clinician. There is a continuous adaptation of behavior on the part of both participants according to what the other does or says. This issue formed the basis for our study of semantic therapy in day-to-day clinical practice.

Semantic Therapy Study: Developing a Framework for Describing Interactions in Therapy

The primary motivation for our study of day-to-day language therapy in clinical practice was the fact that many descriptions of semantic therapy in the literature focus primarily on de-scribing the assessments, tasks, and materials to be used. There is passing reference to routines for presentation and feedback, but it is probably true to say that the treatment *as it was actually carried out*—the independent variable—is almost universally underspecified. Therapy as it is carried out in the clinic usually represents a flexible interaction, which evolves between therapist, aphasic person, and any materials that they are using. The therapy for language impairments that is described in the literature is usually different from clinical practice in that it does not account for this flexible interaction. This suggests that there is a fundamentally important element missing from description and analysis of therapeutic interventions. Our study aimed to develop a way of examining the everyday practice of therapy. We sought to determine whether, by looking at this practice in detail, we could use our observations to develop a means of defining and describing therapy intervention. We wanted this means to be practical and useable in enabling clinicians to communicate with each other in more depth about the content and process of therapy. We also hoped to develop a tool to be used in clinical research in the future, to facilitate a vocabulary for describing the process of therapy—all too often the missing, but not the weakest, link in the detail of a therapy study.

Background to the Study

This study was intended to provide data comprising real-life semantic therapy, carried out in everyday clinical practice, from a reasonable cross section of experienced therapists working in a variety of settings. Thirteen therapist–aphasic person dyads participated in this study. Therapist participants had to have at least three years' experience in aphasia therapy treatment, be members of the professional body for speech and language therapists in the UK, and be members of the British Aphasiology Society. Aphasic participants had to have a left hemi-sphere stroke, had to be at least one month post onset of aphasia, and had to be neurologically stable, with evidence of lexical semantic impairment. Aphasic people who had significant nonlinguistic cognitive difficulties, severe comprehension difficulties, hearing impairment, or concurrent psychiatric difficulties were not included. The time post onset of aphasia ranged from three to sixty months, with a mean of just over eighteen months. Six of the participants were under a year post onset of aphasia, the rest between one and a half and five years.

The sessions took place in a variety of locations—hospital and rehabilitation unit out-patient clinics, in-patient rehabilitation, and domiciliary visits. Frequency of therapy varied from two to three times a month to five times weekly (in-patient rehabilitation), with a mean of just over twice weekly. The different locations suggest different types of work and different expectations from the therapy.

We asked the participants to video- and tape-record three sessions of therapy. Therapy sessions were based on therapists' own assessments and choice of tasks, being representative of what they would normally carry out at that particular stage in their client's treatment. Therapy tasks could be based on principles of semantic intervention, designed to address the semantic system but could be in any modality, and could be input or production tasks. We asked that sessions should be relatively close together (for example, once weekly over three weeks). In addition to the videotapes and audiotapes submitted by the participants, therapists were asked to provide background information about the aphasic person (type of lesion, assessment results, and so on), and details of tasks and materials used for each of the three recorded sessions.

Thus, the raw data of actual therapy from our study consisted of thirty-nine videotapes and thirty-two audiotapes submitted by the participants. Analysis of the tapes proceeded using a qualitative methodology, allowing the issues of interest to emerge from the data, rather than fitting the data into a preexisting schema. Audiotapes were transcribed according to an agreed protocol. The researchers viewed all videotapes, annotating the transcripts for nonverbal behavior and correcting errors of transcription. Our first step in trying to make sense of this large body of interactions was to develop a framework for structuring the data in terms of the discourse, rather than in terms of the tasks and materials. We were looking to develop a structure that allowed us to isolate comparable "events" within and across therapy sessions. We developed a discourse framework, which is not dissimilar to ones developed by other investigators looking at child language and other related therapies (for example, Panagos, 1996).

Results

The types of semantic therapy tasks and their relative numbers are summarized in figure 12.1. A little over 71 percent of all tasks were either category sorting, odd-one-out, or word to picture matching tasks. Of the category sorting tasks, the most common task involved sorting pictures into two (or, less frequently, three) different categories, and the next most common task involved sorting written words into two (or more) categories. Odd-one-out tasks used pictures as often as written words, and more commonly than spoken words. Word-picture matching tasks most frequently involved matching one stimulus picture to one of two or more pictures in an array, or one spoken or written word stimulus to one of two or more pictures in an array. Occasionally, the aphasic person was given two or more written words to match to two or more pictures.

It would be misleading to characterize all of the treatment data as "semantic therapy" in the sense that "semantic therapy" is reported in the literature. A certain proportion of the tasks described here appeared to be central to a particular session; that is, the session's primary therapeutic aim was to address the semantic system in a particular way. Other semantic tasks, however, could be seen to form part of a therapy that was primarily aimed at addressing other systems. For example, word-picture matching tasks were used as "precursors" both to therapy aimed at improving written naming, and to therapy aimed at improving verb finding and sentence-level fluency.

We have only mentioned the tasks so far that might be considered in the mainstream of semantic therapy. However, there were also sessions devoted to clause-level production tasks, story-level writing using picture sequencing prompts with help from a synonym-antonym dictionary, and sessions where the aphasic person's own output in response to picture stimuli was used as a resource for semantic decision tasks.

The framework of our analysis of the therapy sessions consisted of structures that we have called "enactment processes." These are defined as sets of interactions that can be isolated in

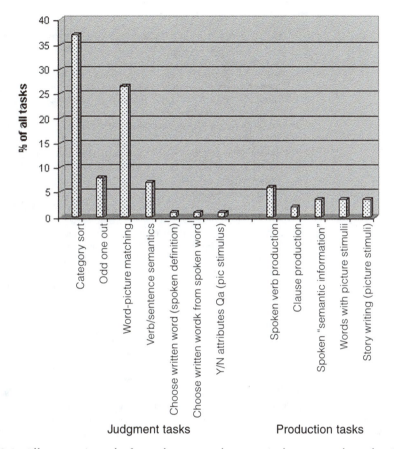

Figure 12.1. All semantic tasks from the corpus by type: judgment and production tasks.

terms of: (1) topical uniformity, (2) interactional structure, (3) use of particular vocabulary and materials, and (4) those that may be identified by their sequential position in the interaction. The framework focuses on the "technical" aspects of doing therapy and does not attempt to address the affective relationship, or the social dynamics of the relationship between therapist and client. *Technical* therefore means those features of the therapist-client interaction that specifically address the *language work together*. Table 12.2 outlines the enactment process framework.

Space does not allow a detailed discussion of all the features of this framework and its development. Suffice to say that it was developed through examination and reexamination of the data, but that, in common with any categorical framework, it is open to criticism from many points of view. While we have made use of this framework and the structures within it to help take forward description and analysis of "therapy enactment," it cannot be claimed to be a definitive account of how therapy is carried out.

We will continue by isolating just one enactment process and describe a set of observations related to this process, which we hope will begin to shed light on some of the difficulties outlined above in relation to how "doing therapy" has been reported in the literature.

Response Management Process. We chose to use the response management process as one "window" on the data. We saw this particular process as the most fruitful starting point for our purpose, including as it does many of the therapeutic techniques such as cues and feedback

Table 12.2
Describing Therapy Interactions: A Preliminary Framework of Enactment Processes

Enactment processes	Typical features
Greetings	• The very start of the session (and therefore not often on camera)
Openings	• Pretask introductions and preamble to the task—the period after "Greetings" but before 'Elicitation'
Elicitation	• Verbal or nonverbal moves to initiate the client's task-related responses
	• "Empty" opening move—client makes task-related response without obvious elicitation—elicitation is implicit in the structure of the session
Response management	• Follows "Elicitation"
	• Response-to-the-task entails management routines by both aphasic person and therapist
	• Requests for clarification on part of therapist or aphasic person
	• Misunderstandings; i.e., the aphasic person carries out a different task from the one the therapist thought they had elicited
	• Evaluative routines
Summaries	• Posttask information from therapist on aphasic person's performance
	• Aphasic person does own "summary" by redoing the task
	• Aphasic person comments on the task or on own performance
Off-task	• Asides of various sorts, not directly related to the task
	• Conversations and quasiconversations
Transitions	• Boundaries between items or tasks (or enactment processes), which may be informative or quasiconversational
	• Often characterized by discourse markers (such as "OK," "so," etc.)
Clarification	• Therapist or client asks for information
	• Therapist or client states own state of understanding

that are commonly referred to in the literature, but that are underspecified. We consider response management to be critical for getting inside the process of therapy because it is the interaction between therapist and aphasic person through which specific problems are addressed, progressed, clarified, or resolved. This means that it is at the heart of the therapy process, and could be said to represent the core of the therapy itself.

The response management process begins after elicitation, and includes the interaction during and after the aphasic person's response or responses, until the particular task resolves. It includes contributions from both the therapist and the aphasic person. To illustrate:

1. T: any idea which is the odd one out?
2. A: mm what about that ((points)) no that ((points))
3. T: okay (.) any idea why?
4. A: um

Response management. T = therapist, A = aphasic person. (( )) = transcriber's observations. (.) = micropause. Numbers 1, 2, etc. refer to turns.

This example of response management includes the starting point of the process (turn 2), and repairs on the aphasic person's behalf (turn 2: self-initiated self-repair). It usually includes the therapist's response to the aphasic person's response, where they either draw the task to a conclusion, or invite further consideration (turn 3). The response management process may take up very little time, or may be a protracted affair involving many turns and repairs.

We believe that the essential purpose of the interactions between therapist, aphasic person, and the therapy materials that take place during the response management process is to *sustain the work on language and cognitive processing,* which was the primary goal of the treatment. That is, the specific aims of the work on language and cognitive processing need to be reflected in the way that therapist and aphasic person work together. Table 12.3 outlines the set of factors that are entailed in this purpose. Language and cognitive processing goals are realized through the way the task is set up. Treatments that incorporate a hierarchy of task difficulty (and this notion is just as prevalent in day-to-day clinical practice as it is in the literature) clearly begin with the "easy to complete" task. To take an example from our data, one dyad was engaged in a series of categorization tasks using pictures. At the first level of difficulty the aphasic person was asked to sort all the pictures into two categories—animals and transport. The next stage was to sort the transport pictures into land, sea, and air transport. Then land transport was to be sorted into private and commercial vehicles.

Now the logic of this task hierarchy is reasonably clear. The tasks seem and are straightforward. What was interesting to us was how exactly they were put into operation, given their inherent structure. For example, in a two-choice sorting task with a 50 percent chance of error, how does the therapist structure the enactment of the task to ensure that the language and cognitive processing goals inherent in the purpose of the task are sustained in the event of an error? There are several possibilities, of course, and they relate both to timing and information exchange factors. However, it becomes clear from a detailed examination of the videotaped data that sustaining language and cognitive processing goals relies heavily on *consistent* implementation by the therapist. Any, even very small, changes to the usual patterns of the type and timing of therapist contributions alter the "learning" structure inherent in the task. By this we mean that the aphasic person—as any person in a "learning" environment—becomes extremely good at picking up cues from the person in the "dominant" or "teacher" role. Of course this only becomes an issue in the event of trouble completing the task. The majority of aphasic people who were engaged in two-category picture sorting tasks completed the tasks with very little difficulty (on average about 87 percent correct on 17 sets of such tasks).

Table 12.3
Factors Entailed in the Response Management Process

Factors	Entails
Time and timing	• Time "allowed" for the aphasic person to respond • Time "allowed" for the aphasic person to consider response • Timing of therapist's follow-up contribution
Information exchange (what each participant says or does that, consciously or unconsciously, informs the other person)	Therapist ➢ information given about the response itself ➢ information given about the stimuli ➢ information given about the target ➢ information about the process of responding ➢ nature of information (and modality) • Aphasic person ➢ information about a stance toward their response (i.e., uncertainty, etc.) ➢ information about the process of responding ➢ information about the stimuli or target ➢ nature of information

Characterizing "Doing Therapy" Data

We have presented the broad outline of a framework that might lead to the more precise specification of the way in which therapy is enacted. How could this be implemented to reveal more about the process of therapy? There are two broad ideas we would like to propose, although it has to be emphasized that these are largely untested propositions.

1. Using the enactment process framework. Let us take the response management process as an example to compare the way an aphasic person or therapist responds during the treatment in question both within and across sessions. Given the set of factors entailed in the response management process outlined above, variations in the aphasic person's response to items, tasks, or therapist input variation can be studied in some detail. The therapist would be able deliberately to alter their own response management routine according to a set of factors that are reasonably clear-cut and that are laid out in a systematic way. That being said, in order really to flesh out the significant distinctions between different instances of the response management process there needs to be considerably more detail than that outlined in table 12.3. One option would be to use a system such as the Aphasia Therapy Interaction Coding System (ATICS; Horton & Byng, 2000) to code the interactions across a sample of response management processes.

2. Coding response management categories. Another possibility would be to use a different type of codification, which, although it would not yield sequential data, might provide a useful tally analysis of behaviors across conditions. For example, we could tally the number of actions, such as "initiates repairs," "highlights a trouble source," "elicits repair help," "allows time for self-correction," observed in the therapist and the aphasic person. The set of such categories could be as small or large as was necessary for the purpose, and therefore tailored to the particular therapy under scrutiny.

Macro and Micro-Learning Goals

Due to the huge number of flexible interactions that evolve during the response management process, it was very difficult to find any basis for making comparisons across the data with regard to goals. In order to address this issue we decided to analyze the therapy in terms of: (1) *What* the therapy is aiming to achieve overall—we have dubbed these "macro goals"—and (2) *How* this will be achieved—what a therapy intervention aims to convey, which we have dubbed "micro-learning goals."

Examples of macro goals might be: "To improve picture naming through the use of word-picture matching tasks," or "To improve comprehension of single lexical items through category-specific rehabilitation." An example of a micro-learning goal might be might be: "Facilitation of the processing of semantic representations through increased awareness of differences in meaning." These are called "micro," to focus attention on the way in which therapy targets very small systems, and "learning" to acknowledge the "internal state changes" or "changes to internal representations" that therapy intervention is aiming to bring about.

We then analyzed the interactions within the response management process in relation to micro-learning goals (what the therapy was aiming to convey). That is, we studied how the interaction between therapist and aphasic person achieved enactment of the micro-learning goals. This analysis permitted development of a set of "interaction profiles" that could be used as a basis for comparisons across the data. These interaction profiles can be summarized as:

1. Correct response [correct];
2. Self-initiated self-repair [profile 1];

Following an error response/s:

3. A descriptive profile of the process in which a response is given by the aphasic person followed (immediately or after a time interval) by a new and correct response. The process involves an interaction between the aphasic person, the materials, and the task demands—that is, the micro-learning goals [Profile 2];

4. A descriptive profile of the process in which the materials-task demands-response management constellation has exhausted its capacity to provide the foreseen challenge to the aphasic person (that is, exhausted its capacity to be the vehicle for the envisaged micro-learning goals) [profile 3].

More precise definitions are given by Horton and Byng (2000).

We now go on to give one example of how we have used interaction profiles to characterize some of the data from our study.

As we mentioned above, category sorting, odd-one-out, and word-picture matching tasks constituted just over 71 percent of all tasks in the data. Figure 12.2 shows a comparison of interaction profiles from two different dyads carrying out what are essentially comparable tasks, although they are not exactly the same tasks. Some modalities are used by one dyad but not the other (for example, odd one out task involved pictures in dyad A, but only written words in dyad B). Other tasks appear in the data for one dyad but not the other (for example, dyad A has no word-picture matching tasks, while dyad B does).

This analysis illustrates how interaction profiles can be used to draw comparisons within or between dyads. For example, in dyad A there is a clear difference in the number of instances of profile 3 according to the type of task. Not only did the aphasic person generally make more errors on odd-one-out tasks, but the therapist also made more of the opportunities for facilitated problem-solving than in written word sorting tasks for example. In order to get a clearer understanding of the implications and meaning of the different configuration of profiles across tasks, one would of course have to have information about the materials and task demands. For example, in the comparison of profiles here, we have not distinguished between numbers of items in each task, nor whether the names of the pictured objects in odd one out tasks were the same as those used in the written odd one out tasks.

Similar comments can be made in a comparison between dyad A and dyad B, quite apart from the fact that the numbers of tasks of a comparable type are not the same. What is striking, though, is that there are very few instances of profile 3 in dyad B. The correct profile predominates, but where there are errors, it generally results in profile 2, where the therapist response management strategies do not sustain the micro-learning goals.

These examples are not intended to be the basis for an exhaustive discussion of the therapies we have studied—this was not the purpose of our study. However, in working toward and outlining possible methods for the description and analysis of therapy enactment, both at a relatively microscopic and at a broader level, we hope to have shown the potential contribution to an understanding of aphasia treatment that this field of study could make.

CONCLUSION

Why should we bother particularly with a more precise structural specification of therapy—semantic or otherwise? It seems, in the light of a considerable body of evidence from the literature, that semantic therapy of various types can effect changes in aphasic peoples' naming and other abilities. Is there any compelling reason then for therapists to adopt anything other than a sort of scattergun approach to semantic stimulation, as long as it also includes word forms, too? Our feeling is that, on some of the evidence from our study, as far as day-to-day clinical practice is concerned, a more ordered and precise approach to description of therapy enactment is called for. The purpose would be to increase awareness by therapists of

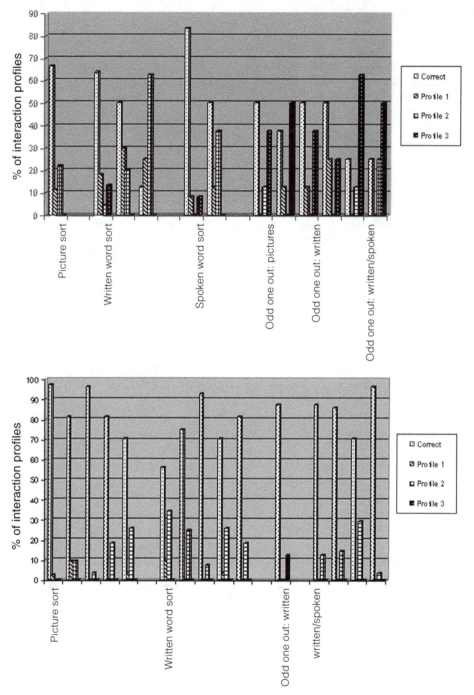

Figure 12.2. Comparison of interaction profiles across therapist-aphasic person dyads. Task profiles for dyad A are shown in the top graph. Task profiles for dyad B are shown in the lower graph.

the parameters of therapy that can be modified and the consistency of interventions, thus leading (we assume) to more efficient and possibly more effective therapy.

To the research community, the benefits will be in terms of: (1) more precise specification of therapies to be delivered (that is, protocols set out in terms of response management routines and so on); and (2) a much greater facility to hold therapies (successful or otherwise) up to the microscope, informing not only the interpretation of outcome, but also contributing to the body of knowledge around models of language processing.

ACKNOWLEDGMENT

The semantic therapy study was funded by a grant from the Stroke Association (Research Grant 18/98) awarded to Sally Byng and Simon Horton. We are greatly indebted to all the therapists and people with aphasia who agreed to take part in our study of semantic therapy and comment on some of our findings.

Our thoughts on therapy enactment have been nurtured and honed through discussion with many supportive colleagues, both clinical and academic, but special thanks go to Eirian Jones, Dr. Nina Simmons-Mackie, and Dr. Judy Duchan.

REFERENCES

Barry, C., & McHattie, J. (1991). Depth of semantic processing in picture naming facilitation in aphasic patients. Paper presented at the British Aphasiology Society Conference, Sheffield. September.

Basso, A. (1993). Two cases of lexical-semantic rehabilitation. In F. J. Stachowiak, R. De Bleser, G. Deloche, R. Kaschel, H. Kremin, P. North, L. Pizzamiglio, I. Robertson, & B. Wilson, (Eds.), *Developments in the assessment and rehabilitation of brain-damaged patients.* Tübingen: Gunter Narr Verlag.

Basso, A., Capitani, E., & Vignolo, L. (1979). Influence of rehabilitation of language skills in aphasic patients: a controlled study. *Archives of Neurology, 36,* 190–196.

Behrmann, M., & Lieberthal, T. (1989). Category-specific treatment of a lexical-semantic deficit: A single case study of global aphasia. *British Journal of Disorders of Communication, 24*(3), 281–299.

Best, W., & Nickels, L. (2000). From theory to therapy in aphasia: Where are we now and where to next? *Neuropsychological Rehabilitation, 10*(3), 231–247.

Bishop, D. (1982). *Test for reception of grammar.* Oxford: MRC and Thomas Leach.

Byng, S. (1995). What is aphasia therapy? In C. Code & D. Muller (Eds.), *The treatment of aphasia.* London: Whurr Publishers.

Byng, S., & Black, M. (1996) What makes a therapy? Some parameters of therapeutic intervention in aphasia. *European Journal of Disorders of Communication, 30,* 303–316

Byng, S., Kay, J., Edmundson, A., & Scott, C. (1990). Aphasia tests reconsidered. *Aphasiology, 4*(1), 67–91.

Byng, S., Swinburn, K., & Pound, C. (1999). *The aphasia therapy file.* Hove, England: Psychology Press.

Coelho, C. A., McHugh, R. E., & Boyle, M. (2000). Semantic feature analysis as a treatment for aphasic dysnomia: A replication. *Aphasiology, 14*(2), 133–142.

Coltheart, M. (1983). Aphasia therapy research: A single case study approach. In C. Code, & D. Müller (Eds.), *Aphasia therapy.* London: Edward Arnold.

Farmer, A. (1977). Self-correctional strategies in the con-

versational speech of aphasic and non-aphasic brain damaged adults. *Cortex, 13,* 327–334.

Franklin, S. (1993). Researching the treatment of anomia: The case for single cases. In F. J. Stachowiak, R. De Bleser, G. Deloche, R. Kaschel, H. Kremin, P. North, L. Pizzamiglio, I. Robertson, & B. Wilson (Eds.), *Developments in the assessment and rehabilitation of brain-damaged patients.* Tübingen: Gunter Narr Verlag.

Funnell, E. (2000). Models of semantic memory. In W. Best, K. Bryan, & J. Maxim (Eds.), *Semantic processing, theory and practice.* London: Whurr Publishers.

Funnell, E., & Hodges, J. R. (1996). Deficits of semantic memory and executive control: Evidence for differing effects upon naming in dementia. *Aphasiology, 10*(7), 687–709.

Goodglass, H., & Kaplan, E. (1983). *Boston diagnostic aphasia examination.* Philadelphia: Lea and Febiger.

Helm Estabrooks, N., & Holland, A. (1997) *The treatment of aphasia.* San Diego, CA: Singular Press

Hillis, A. E. (1989). Efficacy and generalization of treatment for aphasic naming errors. *Archives of Physical Medicine and Rehabilitation, 70,* 632–636.

Hillis, A. E. (1991). Effects of separate treatments for distinct impairments within the naming process. In T. Prescott (Ed.), *Clinical aphasiology, Vol. 19.* Austin, TX: Pro-Ed.

Hillis, A. E. (1993). The role of models of language processing in rehabilitation of language impairments. *Aphasiology, 7*(1), 5–26.

Hillis, A. E. (1998). Treatment of naming disorders: New issues regarding old therapies. *Journal of the International Neuropsychological Society, 4,* 648–660.

Hillis, A. E., & Caramazza, A. (1994). Theories of lexical processing and theories of rehabilitation. In G. Humphreys & M. J. Riddoch (Eds.), *Cognitive neuropsychology and cognitive rehabilitation.* Hillsdale, NJ: Lawrence Erlbaum.

Horner, J., Loverso, F. L., & Gonzalez Rothi, L. (1994). Models of aphasia treatment. In R. Chapey (Ed.), *Language intervention strategies in adult aphasia.* Baltimore, MD: Williams and Wilkins.

Horton, S., & Byng, S. (2000). Examining interaction in language therapy. *International Journal of Language and Communication Disorders, 35*(3), 355–375.

Howard, D. (1986). Beyond randomised controlled trials: The case for effective case studies of the effects of treatment in aphasia. *British Journal of Disorders of Communication, 21*, 89–102.

Howard, D., & Hatfield, F. (1987). *Aphasia therapy: Historical and contemporary issues.* Hove, UK: Psychology Press.

Howard, D., & Patterson, K. E. (1992). *The pyramids and palm trees test.* Bury St. Edmunds: Thames Valley Test Company.

Howard, D., Patterson, K., Franklin, S., Orchard-Lisle, V., & Morton, J. (1985a). The facilitation of picture naming in aphasia. *Cognitive Neuropsychology, 2*(1), 49–80.

Huber, W., Poeck, K., Weniger, D., & Willmes, K. (1983). *Aachener aphasie test.* Goettingen: Hogrefe.

Kaplan, E., Goodglass, H., & Weintraub, S. (1983). *The Boston naming yest.* Media: Williams and Wilkins.

Katz, R. C., Hallowell, B., Code, C., Armstrong, E., Roberts, P., Pound, C., & Katz, L. (2000). A multinational comparison of aphasia management practices. *International Journal of Language and Communication Disorders, 35*(2), 303–314.

Kay, J., Lesser, R., & Coltheart, M. (1996). *Psycholinguistic assessments of language processing in aphasia.* London: Lawrence Erlbaum.

Kertesz, A. (1982). *The Western aphasia battery.* New York: Grune & Stratton.

Kiran, S., & Thompson, C. K. (In press). Effects of exemplar typicality on naming deficits in fluent aphasia. *Aphasiology.*

Kucera, H., & Francis, W. N. (1967). *Computational analysis of present-day English.* Providence, RI: Brown University Press.

Lesser, R., & Algar, L. (1995). Towards combining the cognitive neuropsychological and the pragmatic in aphasia therapy. *Neuropsychological Rehabiliation, 5*(1/2), 67–92.

Marshall, J. (1996). The PALPA: a commentary and consideration of the clinical implications. *Aphasiology, 10*(2), 197–202.

Marshall, J., Pound, C., White-Thomson, M., & Pring, T. (1990). The use of picture/word matching tasks to assist word retrieval in aphasic patients. *Aphasiology, 4*(2), 167–184.

Marshall, R. C. (1976). Word retrieval behaviour of aphasic adults. *Journal of Speech and Hearing Disorders, 41*, 444-451.

Methe, S., Huber, W., & Paradis, M. (1993). Inventory and classification of rehabilitation methods. In M. Paradis (Ed.), *Foundations of aphasia rehabilitation.* Oxford, UK: Pergamon Press.

Morris, J. (1997). Word deafness: A comparison of auditory and semantic treatments. Unpublished Ph.D. thesis, University of York.

Nespoulous, J.-L., Lecours, A. R., Lafond, D., Lemay, A., Puel, M., Joanette, Y., Cot, F., & Rascol, A. (1986). *Protocole Montréal-Toulouse d'examen linguistique de l'aphasie.* Montréal: Centre Hospitalier Côtes-des-Neiges.

Nickels, L. (1992). The autocue? Self-generated phonemic cues in the treatment of a disorder of reading and naming. *Cognitive Neuropsychology, 9*(2), 155–182.

Nickels, L. (2000) Semantics and therapy in aphasia. In

W. Best, K. Bryan, & J. Maxim (Eds.), *Semantic processing, theory, and practice.* London: Whurr Publishers.

Nickels, L., & Best, W. (1996a). Therapy for naming disorders (Part I): Principles, puzzles, and progress. *Aphasiology, 10*(1), 21-47.

Nickels, L., & Best, W. (1996b). Therapy for naming disorders (Part II): Specifics, surprises, and suggestions. *Aphasiology, 10*(2), 109–136.

Panagos, J. M. (1996). Speech therapy discourse. The input to learning. In M. D. Smith & J. S. Damico (Eds.), *Childhood language disorders.* New York: Thieme Medical Publishers.

Patterson, K. E., Purell, C., & Morton, J. (1983). Facilitation of word retrieval in aphasia. In C. Code & D. J. Müller (Eds.), *Aphasia therapy.* London: Arnold.

Patterson, K. E., & Shewell, C. (1987) Speak and spell: Dissociation and word-class effects. In M. Coltheart, R. Job, & G. Sartori (Eds.), *The cognitive neuropsychology of language.* Hillsdale, NJ: Lawrence Erlbaum.

Pring, T. (1986). Evaluating the effects of speech therapy for aphasics: Developing the single case methodology. *British Journal of Disorders of Communication, 21*, 103–115.

Pring, T., Davis, A., & Marshall, J. (1993). Therapy for word finding ceficits: Can experimental findings inform clinical work? In F. J. Stachowiak, R. De Bleser, G. Deloche, R. Kaschel, H. Kremin, P. North, L. Pizzamiglio, I. Robertson, & B. Wilson, (Eds.), *Developments in the assessment and rehabilitation of brain-damaged patients.* Tübingen: Gunter Narr Verlag.

Raymer, A., Maher, L., Foundas, A. L., Gonzalez Rothi, L. J., & Heilman, K. M. (2000). Analysis of lexical recovery in an individual with acute anomia. *Aphasiology, 14*(9), 901–910.

Raymer, A. M., Maher, L. M., Greenwal, M. L., Morris, M., Rothi, L. J. G., & Heilman, K. M. (1990). *The Florida semantics battery.* Unpublished test.

Robson, J., & Horton, S. (In press). Replicating therapy: More than just more of the same? In S. Byng, K. Swinburn, & C. Pound (Eds.), *The aphasia therapy file.* London, UK: Psychology Press.

Seron, X., & Deloche, G. (1989). Introduction. In X. Seron & G. Deloche (Eds.), *Cognitive approaches in neuropsychological rehabilitation.* London: Lawrence Erlbaum.

Snodgrass, J. G., & Vanderwart, M. (1980). A standardized set of 260 pictures: Norms for name agreement, image agreement, familiarity, and visual complexity. *Journal of Experimental Psychology, Human Memory, and Learning, 6*, 174–215.

Visch-Brink, E. G., Bajema, I. M., & Van de Sandt-Koenderman, M. E. (1997). Lexical semantic therapy: BOX. *Aphasiology, 11*(11), 1057–1078.

Weniger, D. (1990). Diagnostic tests as tools of assessment and models of information processing: A gap to bridge. *Aphasiology, 4*(1), 109–113.

Wertz, R. T. (1995). Efficacy. In C. Code & D. Müller (Eds.), *Treatment of aphasia: From theory to practice.* London: Whurr Publishers.

Wertz, R. T., Weiss, D. G., Aden, J., Brookshire, R. H., Garcia-Bunuel, L., Holland, A. L., Kurtzke, J. F., Lapointe, L. L., Milianti, F. J., Brannegan, R., Greenbaum, H., Marshall, R. C., Vogel, D., Carter, J., Barnes, N. S., & Goodman, R. (1986). Comparison of clinic, home, and deferred language treatment for aphasia: A Veterans Administration co-operative study. *Archives of Neurology, 43*, 653–658.

Willmes, K. (1995). Aphasia therapy research: Some psychometric considerations and statistical methods of the single-case study approach. In C. Code & D. Müller (Eds.), *Treatment of aphasia: From theory to practice.* London: Whurr Publishers.

Wilson, B., & Patterson, K. (1990). Rehabilitation for cognitive impairment: Does cognitive psychology apply? *Applied Psychology, 4,* 247–260.

Part 5

Auditory Discrimination and Recognition

13

Models of Speech Processing

Martha W. Burton
Steven L. Small

INTRODUCTION

One of the fundamental questions of language is how listeners map the acoustic signal onto syllables, words, and sentences, resulting in understanding of spoken language. For normal listeners, this mapping is fast and effortless, taking place so automatically that in everyday conversation we rarely think about how it might occur. Studies of the speech signal have provided much evidence that, in fact, the system contains a great deal of underlying complexity that is not evident to the casual listener. Several different models are currently competing to explain how these intricate speech processes work (Klatt, 1979; Marslen-Wilson & Warren, 1994; McClelland & Elman, 1986; Norris, McQueen, & Cutler, 2000). These models have narrowed the problem to mapping the complex speech signal onto isolated words, setting aside the complexity of segmenting continuous speech. Continuous speech remains a major challenge for most models because of the increased variability of the signal and known difficulties segmenting speech into words.

The importance of understanding speech becomes readily apparent when neurological disease affects such a fundamental ability as language. Lesion studies have explored impairments of speech sound processing to determine whether deficits occur in perceptual analysis of acoustic-phonetic information or in the stored abstract phonological representations of the signal (for example, Basso, Casati, & Vignolo, 1977; Blumstein, Cooper, Zurif, & Caramazza, 1977). Furthermore, researchers have attempted to determine in what ways underlying phonological/phonetic impairments may contribute to auditory comprehension deficits (Blumstein, Baker, & Goodglass, 1977).

In this chapter, we will outline a framework for word recognition (the process of how the speech signal is mapped onto the lexical level), and discuss how such a model corresponds to the functional anatomy of the brain. This framework encompasses two stages, perceptual analysis of the speech signal into sublexical units (speech perception) and mapping of those units onto the word level. We will relate evidence from brain lesion and brain activation studies to components of models of speech processing.

MODELS OF WORD RECOGNITION

The speech signal contains well-known characteristics that provide constraints on models of word recognition (Frauenfelder & Floccia, 1998; Jusczyk, 1986). First, the fine acoustic details of every utterance differ each time that it is produced. Thus, the challenge for models of word recognition is to take acoustically different tokens of a word that may vary as a function of the talker (for example, pitch of voice), word (for example, speech sound content) and context (for example, neighboring sounds), and determine what single word (of which there may be a number of similar words) corresponds to that speech token. In addition, the speech signal is continuous, lacking easily discernible discrete boundaries between sounds or words. Thus, any model must account for how diverse phonetic tokens that are part of a continuous signal can be mapped onto discrete units that can be recognized as sounds and words.

Currently, while models of word recognition disagree on particular details, especially with regard to the nature of intermediate representations, there does appear to be a growing consensus on the components of a general model of word recognition (Frauenfelder & Floccia, 1998) that will account for a wide range of experimental results from the psycholinguistic literature.[1] Most models consist of processes by which sublexical units, such as phonetic features or phonemes, are extracted from the acoustic signal and then matched with the appropriate lexical entry. Figure 13.1 shows a schematic model of speech perception. Sublexical units have been postulated in most models of word recognition, including TRACE (McClelland & Elman, 1986), Cohort (Marslen-Wilson & Warren, 1994), and Merge (Norris et al., 2000), to provide a less variable, more abstract form of the acoustic signal to simplify the matching sublexical information to the lexical level.

The main point of difference among current models is over the nature of these input representations. Some models rely on relatively small units, such as phonetic features that correspond to either acoustic or articulatory characteristics as in the Cohort model (for example, the timing of vocal cord vibration in voicing contrasts between /t/ versus /d/) (Lahiri & Marslen-Wilson, 1991; Marslen-Wilson & Warren, 1994). Other models, such as TRACE, proposed by McClelland and Elman (1986), rely on sets of phonetic features that make up the identity of more abstract units (segment or phoneme) that are considered the minimal units of sound that distinguish the meaning of words. For example, the initial phonemes, /p/ versus /b/, which share the same place and manner of articulation features, but contrast in phonetic voicing characteristics, differentiate the words *pear* and *bear*. At the phonemic level, the detailed physical characteristics of the speech signal are not relevant, whereas at the phonetic level, low-level properties of the signal are distinct. For example, in English, the same phoneme, /p/, is produced with different phonetic realizations, depending on where it occurs (for example, with aspiration noise in initial position, as in "pill," and without aspiration after /s/, as in "spill").

The nature of these abstract representations remains controversial. Early evidence found that listeners show poor discrimination between acoustically different members of the same phonetic category (for example, acoustically different exemplars of /d/ as in the classic categorical perception experiments of Liberman, Harris, Hoffman, & Griffith [1957]), suggesting that listeners perceive speech sounds using abstract phoneme category information and discard much of the fine acoustic detail.

More recent studies have indicated that listeners retain more acoustic detail in stored

---

[1]In addition to psycholinguistic models, a number of computational models have been developed to perform automatic speech recognition in many cases using hidden Markov models (Deng & Erler, 1992; Krogh & Riis, 1999; Watrous, 1990). Many of these neural network models employ the same types of subphonetic (for example, features) and phonemic representations to achieve high levels of success in recognizing isolated words. However, because these models typically have not attempted to account for a wide range of psycholinguistic data, we will not discuss them further.

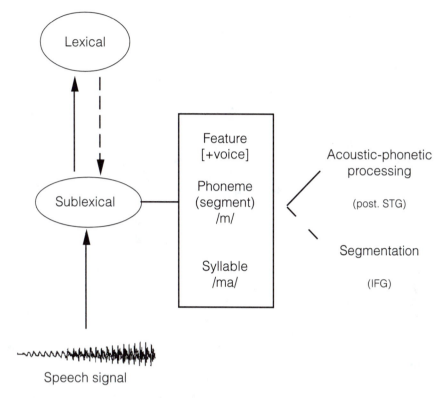

Figure 13.1. Schematic model of speech processing. Levels of processing are circled. Arrows indicate direction of processing. The box contains possible sublexical representations of speech with examples. Sublexical processes and their hypothesized locations are at right. Solid lines indicate obligatory processing, dotted lines are possible routes of processing.

representations of speech than originally thought (Kuhl, 1991; Pisoni, 1993). Kuhl and colleagues have argued that listeners maintain internal structure within categories for speech sounds such as vowels. Some speech sounds within the same speech category (for example, /i/) are rated by listeners as better exemplars of the category than others or, in other words, are considered to be more prototypical. Furthermore, these prototypical sounds serve as perceptual magnets, affecting the perception of other similar speech stimuli, whereas nonprototypical sounds do not show such effects. Thus, Kuhl (1991) has provided evidence that listeners are sensitive to some within-category acoustic detail, and that speech prototypes may serve to organize categories of sounds during perception.

Pisoni (1993) has further challenged traditional views of speech perception, arguing that even more acoustic information (including variability from utterances of individual talkers and context effects, such as rate) is preserved from initial perceptual analysis of the speech signal, and furthermore provides important information for later recognition of specific talkers (Nygaard, Sommers, & Pisoni, 1995). According to Pisoni (1993), information about specific acoustic characteristics of the talker is stored in long-term memory.

Despite these challenges suggesting that more acoustic detail than originally believed is maintained in memory, models of speech perception continue to assume that during perceptual analysis of the signal listeners are able to "normalize" variability in the signal and map acoustic input onto representations, such as features (Marslen-Wilson & Warren, 1994) and phonemes (Norris et al., 2000). Some models of speech perception, such as the connectionist model of McClelland and Elman (1986) (TRACE), incorporate both more abstract segmental units as well as phonetic features, whereas other models map spectral properties of the acoustic signal directly onto syllables (Klatt, 1979). The motor theory of speech claims that these intermediate units correspond to articulatory gestures (Liberman & Mattingly, 1985).

The mapping of these input representations onto the word level characteristically involves activation of lexical entries in which the goodness of fit between the input representation and the lexical representation determines the level of activation. Typically, once a threshold of activation has been reached, a word is recognized. An example of such a model implemented using the connectionist framework is TRACE (McClelland & Elman, 1986), which has been used to account for a number of effects of lexical influence on phonetic categorization (for example, Pitt & Samuel, 1993).

Despite the common use of an activation mechanism to encode how words are recognized, models differ in the mechanistic details of the activation process per se (for example, the amount of top-down processing that is permitted from higher levels to lower levels, the degree to which inhibition between competing representations plays a role). For example, the Merge model maintains that top-down (lexical) information does not influence categorization of lower-level phonetic information (Norris et al., 2000), whereas connectionist models such as TRACE allow such feedback (McClelland & Elman, 1986). Other models, such as the Neighborhood Activation Model, emphasize the role of competition between lexical entries in facilitating word recognition (Luce & Pisoni, 1998). In this model, the number of similar words, their phonetic similarity, and frequency of occurrence in a language (similarity-neighborhood) affects the speed and accuracy of word recognition.

Nonetheless, the generally accepted view that the speech signal is analyzed into sublexical units that activate word entries provides a framework for how the most basic processes of word recognition proceed (Frauenfelder & Floccia, 1998). Although early lesion studies have been confusing as to the physical locus of these processes in the brain, the combination of evidence from a variety of experimental tasks in neuropsychological studies and from functional neuroimaging of normal adults has yielded promising results. The results of these studies reveal a network of regions of the brain that appears to correspond to specific functions postulated in models of speech processing. Below we will consider what specific areas of the brain may be involved in the analysis and mapping of the speech signal onto lexical information. We will argue that although listeners have access to different sublexical representations, their use depends critically on task demands, and the effects of such task demands are reflected in activation patterns seen in neuroimaging studies.

EVIDENCE FROM APHASIA

Experiments exploring speech perception in stroke patients with aphasia have focused a great deal of attention on segmental contrasts within words (for example, /p/ versus /b/ in pear/ bear) or in nonsense syllables (for example, pa/ba) (Basso et al., 1977; Benson, 1988; Blumstein, Cooper, et al., 1977; Carpenter & Rutherford, 1973; Miceli, Caltagirone, Gainotti, & Payer-Rigo, 1978; Oscar-Berman, Zurif, & Blumstein, 1975; Riedel & Studdert-Kennedy, 1985). Nearly all patients show some impairments in discrimination ("same-different" judgments), and/or labeling or identification (for example, is the first sound a p or a b?) (Blumstein, 1998). Patterns of errors on these tasks follow those seen in speech production errors. For example, more errors occur in medial or final position in the syllable than in initial position (Blumstein, 1998). Patients with lesions in the temporal lobe might be expected to show speech discrimination deficits because primary auditory areas are located in the temporal lobe and have direct connections to the auditory association areas. However, patients with anterior lesions also manifest such impairments. These data challenge the traditional but increasingly suspect association between speech perception impairments and solely posterior lesions in aphasic patients.

Several types of evidence suggest that speech perception impairments in aphasic patients do not occur at the stage of extracting sublexical information from the acoustic signal. Patients' performance is generally better on discrimination tasks than on identification tasks, indicating that they are sensitive to acoustic-phonetic differences in the stimuli, but may have difficulty providing accurate responses based on segmental information (Gow & Caplan, 1996). Furthermore, patterns of results in discrimination tasks are similar to those of normals in the location of boundaries between phonetic categories and in the overall shape of the discrimination functions, even in cases where patients cannot label the stimuli (Blumstein, 1998).

More recent evidence testing effects of phonetic/phonological priming further suggests that patients are able to extract acoustic properties from the signal (Blumstein et al., 2000). In a set of priming tasks, patients presented with pairs of words or nonwords performed a lexical decision on the second member of the pair. The phonetic/phonological properties of the first member of the pair were systematically varied, for example, producing either rhyming or unrelated pairs (for example, "pear-bear," "pen-bear").

Both Broca's and Wernicke's aphasics show the effects of rhyming primes on lexical decision times, suggesting that both types of patients are sensitive to phonological similarity (Blumstein et al., 2000; see also Gordon & Baum, 1994). However, the patterns of reaction times differed between aphasic groups. Wernicke's aphasics showed faster reaction times for rhyming pairs relative to unrelated pairs. This facilitation indicates that impairments in these patients are not in mapping of sound information onto the lexicon. Rather, impairments shown in semantic priming tasks that are phonologically mediated (for example, "gat-dog"), may be due to inappropriate activation at the lexical level (Blumstein & Milberg, 1999; Milberg, Blumstein, & Dworetzky, 1988). In contrast, Broca's aphasics showed slower reaction times for rhyming pairs relative to unrelated control pairs. As in the Wernicke's patients, these results indicate that these patients are sensitive to phonological relationships, but by contrast with the Wernicke's patients, Broca's patients may have reduced activation within the lexical network, resulting in slowed responses.

A second experiment in the Blumstein et al. (2000) study tested repetition priming with these same patients using lexical decision on repeated words occurring at different intervals (that is, presentation of the same word immediately following the prime, two words following the prime, eight words following the prime, and so on). The results suggested the presence of a second impairment in these patients, namely, maintaining an acoustic form in short-term memory. Unlike normals, the patients showed neither increased repetition effects at shorter intervals compared to longer intervals nor any repetition effects for nonwords. As long as the lexicon was activated by a real word, patients showed priming effects. However, the lack of increased repetition effects at shorter intervals suggests that the patients were "matching" the meaning of the stimulus, not its phonetic form, which may have dissipated in working memory faster for the patients than for controls. The lack of increased repetition effects at longer intervals and nonword effects was consistent across all patients.

These findings are also in agreement with other patterns of deficits described in single-case studies. For example, Martin, Bredin, and Damian (1999) report a patient able to perform phoneme discrimination at a level similar to that of normals, yet speech discrimination declined with increased interstimulus interval, suggesting a short-term memory deficit. Such short-term memory impairments of maintaining information over time may contribute to auditory language comprehension deficits, such as those in which listeners must actively retrieve specific pieces of information over the longer periods of time required by sentence processing (Caplan & Waters, 1995; Martin & Romani, 1994; Miyake, Carpenter, & Just, 1994). In contrast, low-level speech perception impairments may have some limited role in higher-level language comprehension, but do not appear to account for severe auditory language comprehension difficulties (Blumstein, Baker, et al., 1977). Blumstein and colleagues found that the level of performance on identification and discrimination of consonant-vowel syllables that do not require maintenance over long intervals was a poor predictor of auditory comprehension as measured by standard clinical diagnostic tests.

In summary, a number of studies have extensively investigated speech perception in aphasic patients using several different experimental tasks. The results have generally demonstrated that impairments are not due to initial acoustic analysis of the speech signal. Because lesions in these patients are in the left hemisphere, this spared speech discrimination ability is likely due to some right hemisphere mechanism, possibly in the right posterior temporal regions (Hickok & Poeppel, 2000).

There is less of a theoretical framework to explain the pattern of speech perception impairments that do exist in these patients. Because the patterns of impairment have not clearly corresponded to particular levels of representation in speech perception models and have had unclear localization, they have not played a significant role in models of normal speech perception. Nonetheless, there have been general findings that with the advent of sophisticated neuroimaging techniques may now become more coherent. For example, why do both anterior and posterior patients have greater difficulty with identification tasks than discrimination tasks? An account for such phenomena that cuts across different lesion locations and a wide range of behavioral data may lead to anatomical commonalities that do not necessarily correspond to damage to a single structure, but do coincide with shared behavioral patterns among aphasic groups. Anatomically, the effects of hypometabolism in temporal regions have been found for patients with clinical diagnoses of Broca's, Wernicke's, and conduction aphasia and thus may provide a potential common neural substrate (Metter et al., 1989). Behaviorally, many aphasic patients have problems with auditory working memory that may play a greater role in speech identification (comparison of stimulus to a stored representation) than speech discrimination (comparison between two exemplars).

However, basing our understanding of the underlying neuroanatomy of speech perception on lesion studies alone leaves a number of unanswered questions. The common finding that inferior frontal cortex is activated in phonological tasks and in tasks that are designed to require verbal working memory suggests that the role of working memory requires more attention in explaining impaired performance on certain speech perception tasks and is discussed in further detail below.

FUNCTIONAL NEUROANATOMY OF SPEECH PERCEPTION

In contrast to the lesion data, recent neuroimaging studies of normal subjects have been converging on a network of regions involved in specific functional components of speech perception. From these studies, it is possible to gain insight into why some aphasic patients may have difficulty with particular tasks, such as phoneme identification, and to determine whether processing of different types of sublexical information (for example, acoustic-phonetic features and phonemes) produces distinct patterns of brain behavior (for example, patterns of activation, electromagnetic responses). Evidence that listeners are sensitive to sublexical information (acoustic-phonetic features and/or phonemic category information) as demonstrated through neurobiological responses will help to clarify what role sublexical information may play in models of speech perception.

Functional neuroimaging studies of speech perception often rely on one of two task-dependent imaging methods, either PET (positron emission tomography) or fMRI (functional magnetic resonance imaging), to reveal areas of the brain that participate in a task yet when damaged may not necessarily impair performance of language functions. Although PET and fMRI differ in a number of aspects of experimental design and analysis, and have different spatial and temporal properties, both methods involve imaging some (presumed) correlate of neural activity during performance of a cognitive task. These methods allow observation of the particular areas of the brain that participate in a cognitive task (see Burton & Small, 1999, for a review of neuroimaging methods). Magnetoencephalography (MEG) provides highly accurate information about the time course of processing for relatively small areas of cortex by measuring neuromagnetic responses to stimulation. For that reason, MEG has been used to study speech perception, which takes place within milliseconds in the temporal lobe. Other methods, such as event-related potentials (ERP), that provide highly accurate time course information but not spatial localization, have also been used to identify stages of speech processing.

Current evidence supports the view, discussed below, that three main areas of activity, posterior superior temporal gyrus, inferior parietal lobule, and inferior frontal gyrus, each perform unique functions during the processing of speech. Figure 13.2 shows the approximate location of these areas on a structural image of the left lateral cortex of a normal subject. We will then discuss how speech perception functions correspond to the theoretical framework outlined at the outset of the chapter.

Posterior Temporal Cortex

Some of the most compelling evidence for the role of posterior superior temporal gyrus in early speech analysis is the consistent pattern of activation when passive speech is compared to rest. Activation of primary auditory cortex and auditory association areas appear to be due to initial acoustic/phonetic analysis in which phonetic/phonemic information is extracted from the acoustic signal (Binder et al., 1994; Dhankhar et al., 1997; Gage, Poeppel, Roberts, & Hickok, 1998; Kuriki, Okita, & Hirata, 1995; Petersen, Fox, Posner, Mintun, & Raichle, 1988; Poeppel et al., 1996; Price et al., 1992; Wise et al., 1991; Zatorre, Meyer, Gjedde, & Evans, 1996). Some studies comparing speech tasks to tone have shown increased temporal activity for the speech stimuli, particularly in the left hemisphere, which might suggest specialized mechanisms for speech tasks (Burton, Blumstein, & Small, 2000; Mummery, Ashburner, Scott, & Wise, 1999). However, at least some of this activity may be due to the increased complexity of the speech syllables compared to the tone stimuli in these studies. Celsis and colleagues (1999) specifically

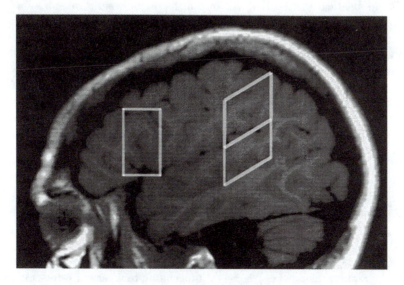

Figure 31.2. Sagittal view of left lateral cortex acquired using structural magnetic resonance imaging. White boxes highlight areas involved in components of speech processing, including posterior two-thirds of inferior frontal gyrus (Broca's area), posterior superior temporal gyrus including primary auditory cortex, and inferior parietal lobe.

tested syllable versus tone conditions using fMRI in a habituation recovery paradigm in which subjects listened to a series of four identical stimuli compared to a series of stimuli in which the fourth member of the sequence was deviant. The left posterior temporal region was implicated in the detection of changes in both the speech as well as the nonspeech stimuli.

Patterns of cortical responses in ERP data have provided an index of the type of acoustic changes that are discriminable in sequences of repetitive auditory stimuli early in processing. When a change (deviant) in speech or nonspeech is detected, it is reflected by the generation of an event-related brain potential that peaks 100 to 200 msec after stimulus onset (referred to as mismatch negativity). Collectively, these studies have confirmed that speech analysis takes place in left hemisphere regions at a very early (preattentive) stage of processing (Rinne et al., 1999). This preattentive or automatic response occurs without any overt response from the subject or the subjects' attention even directed toward the auditory stimulus. Although ERP studies do not provide detailed information on spatial location, the source of auditory mismatched negativity has been reported to originate in the auditory cortex (Naatanen et al., 1997), consistent with MEG studies that have indicated that the electromagnetic response is localized to the STG (Gage et al., 1998).

In contrast to imaging studies, which have not provided a clear answer to whether there are regions specialized for speech, several ERP studies have suggested that some of these preattentive processes may be specific to language (Dehaene-Lambertz, 1997; Jaramillo, Alku, & Paavilainen, 1999; Naatanen et al., 1997). Naatanen and colleagues, in a series of studies, have examined mismatch negativity responses of subjects in their native and non-native language and found language-specific responses to speech stimuli, such as vowels, in the left auditory cortex (Naatanen et al., 1997; Winkler et al., 1999). Crucially, the mismatch negativity response from speech stimuli with the same acoustic variation was elicited in native speakers, for whom the sounds corresponded to different phonemic categories (for example, /e/ and /æ/), but not from non-native speakers for whom the speech stimuli corresponded to only one phonemic category (for example, /ɛ/). Although some studies of normal speech perception have questioned whether listeners use abstract phonemic representations (for example, Marslen-Wilson & Warren, 1994), such as the vowel categories tested in these ERP studies during word recognition, evidence that acoustically identical stimuli that fall into different phonemic categories depending on native language elicit different responses suggests that listeners are indeed sensitive to phonemic representations even at early preattentive stages of processing.

Despite the tendency in some studies for greater left temporal activation than right, and the predilection to discuss more fully the left hemisphere findings, the activation across neuroscientific studies of speech perception has been consistently bilateral (Hickok & Poeppel, 2000). Further evidence for bilateral activation comes from fMRI studies of speech perception in normals and two aphasic patients listening to speech presented at varying rates (Mummery et al., 1999). In normal subjects, increasing rates of speech correlate with bilateral superior temporal activation to speech stimuli. Patients with left temporal infarction, who perform well on single-word comprehension tests, have right superior temporal activity correlated with the rate of speech presentation, but no significant left temporal activity. Thus, their spared speech comprehension ability may be due to the involvement of the right hemisphere, which, in normals, is more characteristically involved in prelexical processing of speech.

Based on patterns of bilaterality, several groups of researchers have postulated different roles for the left and right superior temporal cortices in speech signal analysis. One such hypothesis claims that left hemisphere is specialized for processing rapid temporal information, such as the rapid transitions of frequency information that occur in stop consonants, such as /p t k b d g/ (see Hickok & Poeppel, 2000; Nicholls, 1996, for a review). For example, Belin and colleagues (1998) showed significantly greater activation for left auditory cortex than right when subjects were presented with speech-like rapid acoustic changes (for example, 40 msec) that had identical temporal structure to frequency transitions between consonants and vowels.

In contrast, the right hemisphere has been associated with processing of slower temporal information found in some speech sounds, such as fricatives and nasals, compared to the rapid frequency transitions found in stops (Allard & Scott, 1975; Gage et al., 1998) or spectral information (Zatorre, 1997). Slower information may be useful for processing that occurs over longer windows of time, such as prosody or the melody of a sentence.

An alternative view (double filtering by frequency) has attempted to draw together a number of sources of evidence to suggest that an attentional filter determines the relevant frequency properties for analysis of the signal (Ivry & Robertson, 1998). Relatively high-frequency components compared to an anchoring point are processed in the left hemisphere, whereas relatively low-frequency components are processed on the right. Thus, there are a number of active proposals currently being pursued to determine the role of the left and right hemispheres in early acoustic/phonetic analysis. Whether these processes are speech-specific remains to be determined. It may be possible for the same temporal and spectral processing mechanisms to apply to speech as well as nonspeech, but phonemic effects at early stages of processing in ERP studies will still require explanation. It may be possible for the contralateral hemisphere to compensate for loss when damage occurs. Thus, it may be difficult to see evidence of hemispheric differences in aphasia.

Inferior Parietal Cortex

Once the initial acoustic analysis is performed, the resulting sound representation must make contact with lexical-semantic information. Hickok and Poeppel (2000) have argued that the vicinity of the temporal-parietal-occipital junction is a likely locus for such processes, which then may interface with those involved in auditory comprehension. In addition, the inferior parietal and frontal areas may be involved in tasks that require access to sublexical information (for example, segments). According to this view, the inferior parietal region forms part of a network of areas involved in mediating between the auditory and articulatory representations. Recently, this area has been associated with tasks requiring short-term storage of phonological information (Awh, Smith, & Jonides, 1995; Jonides et al., 1998; Paulesu, Frith, & Frackowiak, 1993; Paulesu et al., 1996). This activation appears more consistently with tasks that involve stimuli that require more extensive phonological coding (for example, nonwords) than with word tasks in which subjects may use a combination of semantic and phonological coding to store verbal material (Jonides et al., 1998). One method of maintaining information in a phonological store is through rehearsal. If this area were part of an auditory-motor (articulatory) integration network that includes inferior frontal regions, the concomitant activity in the inferior frontal lobe due to rehearsal and inferior parietal lobe due to temporary storage could be explained as a single network of regions that participate in speech processing (Hickok & Poeppel, 2000).

Inferior Frontal Cortex

Activation of the inferior frontal gyrus has often been attributed to phonological processing in auditory tasks (Demonet et al., 1992; Demonet, Price, Wise, & Frackowiak, 1994; Zatorre, Evans, Meyer, & Gjedde, 1992; Zatorre et al., 1996). However, reviews of early PET evidence found that the patterns of activation, particularly within the inferior frontal regions, did not converge as expected (compare Poeppel, 1996, and Demonet, Fiez, Paulesu, Petersen, & Zatorre, 1996). More recent studies, which have tested phonological processing with increasingly specific cognitive tasks, have suggested that there are indeed common underlying speech processes that may specifically activate the inferior frontal gyrus.

Previous PET studies have argued that inferior frontal activation is due to segmentation processes in which listeners must separate speech sounds contained within syllables (Zatorre et al., 1992, 1996). For example, in pairs of spoken consonant-vowel-consonant sequences, such as "fat-tid," where the vowels were always different, subjects must separate out the final consonant from a continuous acoustic signal to make a "same/different" judgment. By creating stimuli in which different vowels precede the consonant within the pairs, the need for segmentation is ensured because the consonant transitions vary as a function of preceding vowel context. Furthermore, in performing this segmentation, Zatorre and colleagues (1992, 1996) have argued that listeners are required to access articulatory representations. Such recoding of acoustic information to articulatory gestures is said to require Broca's area involvement because of its traditional association with articulatory deficits in neuropsychological studies of aphasic patients. Results of experiments comparing speech discrimination to either pitch discrimination or passive listening have shown activation of the left frontal cortex in the phonetic discrimination task. However, there was no such activation in Broca's area under passive listening conditions to the same stimuli (Zatorre et al., 1992, 1996).

The location of activation in the speech discrimination tasks was in the most posterior and superior aspect of Broca's area. This subregion of Broca's area is similar to that reported in several other studies of auditory phonological processing that involve segmentation of speech sounds and comparison of stimuli for a decision (either between two consonants in a pair of syllables or between a consonant and a target phoneme) (Burton et al., 2000; Demonet et al., 1992; Demonet et al., 1994; Zatorre et al., 1992, 1996). These studies have compared phoneme monitoring for sequences of sounds or consonant segmentation to passive or sensory tasks. This area contrasts with the regions cited in studies of semantic tasks that have argued for Broca's area activation (Poldrack et al., 1999). The postulation of subregions for Broca's area may help explain why multiple functions have been attributed to Broca's area (Dronkers, 1998).

A remaining question is whether listeners are always required to access segmental information in speech discrimination tasks. In a recent study, we investigated whether listeners would show inferior frontal activation in an overt speech discrimination task in which subjects were required to make a same/different judgment about phonetic segments in initial position (Burton et al., 2000). We expected that Broca's area would be involved only when the subject must perform a task that requires articulatory recoding. In segmentation tasks, such as those of Zatorre and colleagues (1992, 1996), in which there are a number of differences in the segments in the stimuli, it appears likely that the subject must overtly identify the initial segments of each member of the pair and then compare these segments in order to make a same/different judgment. In contrast, if there is a difference in only one phonetic feature, such as voicing, there may be no need for segmentation, since the subject only has to perceive a single phonetic difference between the stimulus pairs to make a decision.

Thus, with two groups of subjects, we used functional MRI to investigate activation patterns during the discrimination of voicing in stop consonants (for example, "t-d, k-g") in two conditions, one that required segmentation (for example, "dip-doom") and one that did not require overt segmentation (for example, "dip-tip"). These speech conditions were compared to a tone control task where subjects discriminated between pairs of tones with either same or different pitch. The imaging data showed significantly more frontal activation in the group of subjects that discriminated pairs that required overt segmentation (for example, "dip-doom" pairs) compared to the group that did not (for example, "dip-tip" pairs). Thus, phonetic judgments may invoke different neural mechanisms depending on task demands. More specifically, inferior frontal activation emerges in tasks that invoke segmentation, whereas it does not appear in those that do not require such processes (for example, discrimination of "dip-tip").

Importantly, significant superior temporal gyrus activation (with a trend toward left-lateralization) was evident in all subjects, regardless of whether or not the speech task required segmentation. Thus, posterior brain structures may participate in perceptual analysis of the signal that is necessary for mapping acoustic/phonetic patterns onto higher levels of language, such as meaning. The results of Burton and colleagues (2000) further suggest that frontal areas may not typically be recruited in the processing of speech for purposes of at least some speech discrimination tasks (that is, those that do not require segmentation) and may not necessarily be invoked on a more global level for auditory language comprehension, a situation in which listeners may not need to identify individual sounds to accomplish word recognition.

Although neuroimaging studies of speech focusing on frontal activity have typically concentrated on segmental phonological tasks, recent PET studies have suggested that suprasegmental information such as pitch contour may also activate inferior frontal cortex in discrimination tasks (Gandour et al., 2000; Gandour, Wong, & Hutchins, 1998). Pitch cues can be used to distinguish lexical meaning in tone languages, such as Thai. Cross-linguistic studies provide the opportunity to compare perception of the same pitch contrasts under circumstances in which the pairs of speech stimuli are linguistically distinctive (for example, two Thai words varying in lexical tones that have different meanings) to cases where they are not (for example, English). When the pitch discrimination condition was compared to a filtered speech control task in which semantic and phonological information was eliminated but other suprasegmental information was preserved, the results showed that only Thai speakers showed inferior frontal activation. Similar to English speakers, Chinese listeners who had experience with tone languages, but not the particular tone distinctions in Thai, did not activate Broca's area. These findings were interpreted as indicating that Broca's area subserves not only segmental, but also suprasegmental processing.

The location of activity within the inferior frontal cortex for the Thai speakers is close to one of the foci of activation reported by Zatorre and colleagues (1996) for phonetic discrimination, but is more anterior and somewhat inferior to where activity in most of the auditory segmental tasks has clustered (Burton et al., 2000; Demonet et al., 1992, 1994; Zatorre et al., 1992, 1996). The location reported by Gandour and colleagues (2000, 1998) is closer to the frontal opercular activity reported in auditory detection tasks by Fiez and colleagues (1995). It is possible that the differences that have emerged across experiments reflect the different task demands made on the subjects, and in particular the extent to which the tasks require verbal rehearsal to perform discrimination or detection tasks. Although discrimination tasks require subjects to hold stimuli in memory for comparison prior to making a linguistic decision, it is not clear whether retention of different types of information may affect the amount of verbal rehearsal needed to perform the task. Because the tasks are difficult to compare in terms of the degree to which processing of stimuli requires verbal rehearsal, further research is necessary to settle this issue.

CONCLUSIONS

Currently competing speech models, although differing in some details, particularly with regard to the nature of sublexical representation, are converging in overall structure; that is, sublexical information is extracted from the speech signal and mapped onto a lexical level encoded using an activation method. Because of the similarities of the models, they are often difficult to separate on the basis of psycholinguistic evidence. Nevertheless, neuroimaging evidence suggests that the recruitment of different brain areas for different types of sublexical information provides evidence for the basic framework of these models. More specifically, functional neuroimaging studies of normal subjects are converging upon several brain regions associated with different components of speech processing. Posterior superior temporal activation has been attributed to sublexical perceptual analysis of the speech signal. Inferior frontal activation appears to occur in phonological tasks that require articulatory recoding of the signal in order to perform segmentation of the speech signal. The inferior parietal lobe has been associated with temporary storage of phonological information. These three areas work together to form a network of regions involved in processing of speech.

Although one might hypothesize that components of sublexical processing could be selectively impaired (for example, perceptual analysis of the signal or segmentation), neuropsychological studies have shown that nearly all aphasic patients display some impairments in speech perception. These difficulties performing a range of tasks do not appear to be due to early stages of sublexical speech processing in which the acoustic information, such as temporal or spectral properties, are extracted from the signal. Thus, even if patients have left temporal damage, they may be able to perform some speech discrimination tasks because of spared right hemisphere structures.

Knowledge about the function of brain regions in components of normal speech processing can now contribute to understanding the nature of some aphasic deficits. Specifically, patients with damage to anterior structures may have difficulty with tasks that require explicit segmentation of the speech signal. Thus, they may have trouble with phoneme identification tasks, which require such segmentation. However, because other auditory speech comprehension tasks may not require explicit segmentation of speech information, these patients may have relatively good speech comprehension. In contrast, patients with damage in the posterior temporo-parietal junction may have difficulty performing an identification task because of difficulty with intergrating the auditory and articulatory information in the inferior parietal component of the network. Thus, both types of patients may do poorly on tasks involving explicit identification of speech sounds, but for different reasons, which are congruent with evidence from neuroimaging studies of control subjects and are consistent with the framework of models of word recognition.

Patients may show some impairments in discrimination tasks as well as identification tasks. It remains unclear to what extent hemispheric differences in the posterior temporal lobe play a role in speech perception impairments. However, theories that postulate hemispheric asymmetries predict difficulties on those speech contrasts that rely on high-frequency or rapid temporal information. Such a theory could explain why some adults with focal brain lesions in the left hemisphere have difficulties with rapid formant transitions in stop consonants (Ivry & Robertson, 1998).

While the role of the posterior superior temporal gyrus in performing acoustic analysis of the auditory signal has been clarified by recent neuropsychological and neuroimaging evidence, the extent to which this region processes phonemic information is less certain. ERP studies suggest language-specific processing of more abstract phonological information. This region may play a role in extracting such information, resulting in fMRI, MEG, and ERP studies showing phonemic effects for speech stimuli. However, recoding of the information may take place in the network of the inferior frontal gyrus and inferior parietal lobule, thus accounting for impairments in some speech perception tasks for aphasic patients and activity seen in functional neuroimaging studies of normal subjects.

Several challenges remain in understanding the nature of breakdown of speech processing in aphasia. It is unlikely that an aphasic patient would have damage only affecting as specific an area as described by the functional neuroimaging studies. For example, in the frontal lobe, few patients have damage only affecting Broca's area (Dronkers, 2000) and it is even less likely that the lesion would only damage a subregion of Broca's area. Thus, understanding other functions, such as the role of verbal working memory, will be crucial to understanding how damage in a particular area contributes to language comprehension. In addition, further research using recent structural and functional imaging techniques that link the location of lesions with specific types of impairments in aphasia may provide additional information about the neural underpinnings of impairments.

ACKNOWLEDGMENTS

This research was supported in part by the National Institutes of Health under grants NIH DC R01-3378 to the University of Chicago and by NIH DC R01-4202 to the University of Maryland, Baltimore.

REFERENCES

Allard, F., & Scott, B. L. (1975). Burst cues, transition cues, and hemispheric specialization with real speech sounds. *Quarterly Journal of Experimental Psychology, 27,* 487–497.

Awh, E., Smith, E. E., & Jonides, J. (1995). Human rehearsal processes and the frontal lobes: PET evidence. *Annals of the New York Academy of Sciences, 769,* 97–117.

Basso, A., Casati, G., & Vignolo, L. (1977). Phonemic identification defect in aphasia. *Cortex, 13,* 85–95.

Belin, P., Zilbovicius, M., Crozier, S., Thivard, L., Fontaine, A., Masure, M. C., & Samson, Y. (1998). Lateralization of speech and auditory temporal processing. *Journal of Cognitive Neuroscience, 10,* 536–540.

Benson, D. (1988). Classical syndromes of aphasia. In F. Boller & J. Grafman (Eds.), *Handbook of Neuropsychology.* New York: Elsevier.

Binder, J. R., Rao, S. M., Hammeke, T. A., Yetkin, F. Z., Jesmanowicz, A., Bandettini, P. A., Wong, E. C., Estkowski, L. D., Goldstein, M. D., Haughton, V. M., et al. (1994). Functional magnetic resonance imaging of human auditory cortex. *Annals of Neurology, 35,* 662–672.

Blumstein, S. E. (1998). Phonological aspects of aphasia. In M. Sarno (Ed.), *Acquired aphasia.* New York: Academic Press.

Blumstein, S. E., Baker, E., & Goodglass, H. (1977). Phonological factors in auditory comprehension in aphasia. *Neuropsychologia, 15,* 19–30.

Blumstein, S. E., Cooper, W., Zurif, E., & Caramazza, A. (1977). The perception and production of voice-onset time in aphasia. *Neuropsychologia, 15,* 371-383.

Blumstein, S. E., Milberg, W., Brown, T., Hutchinson, A., Kurowski, K., & Burton, M. W. (2000). The mapping from sound structure to the lexicon in aphasia: evidence from rhyme and repetition priming. *Brain and Language, 72,* 75–99.

Blumstein, S. E., & Milberg, W. P. (1999). Language deficits in Broca's and Wernicke's aphasia: A singular impairment. In Y. Grodzinsky, L. Shapiro, & D. Swinney (Eds.), *Language and the brain: Representation and processing.* New York: Academic Press.

Burton, M., Blumstein, S., & Small, S. (2000). The role of segmentation in phonological processing: An fMRI investigation. *Journal of Cognitive Neuroscience, 12,* 679–690.

Burton, M. W., & Small, S. L. (1999). An introduction to fMRI. *The Neurologist, 5,* 145–158.

Caplan, D., & Waters, G. S. (1995). Aphasic disorders of syntactic comprehension and working memory capacity. *Cognitive Neuropsychology, 12,* 637–649.

Carpenter, R., & Rutherford, D. (1973). Acoustic cue discrimination in adult aphasia. *Journal of Speech and Hearing Research, 16,* 534–544.

Celsis, P., Boulanouar, K., Doyon, B., Ranjeva, J. P., Berry, I., Nespoulous, J. L., & Chollet, F. (1999). Differential fMRI responses in the left posterior superior temporal gyrus and left supramarginal gyrus to habituation and change detection in syllables and tones. *Neuroimage, 9,* 135–144.

Dehaene-Lambertz, G. (1997). Electrophysiological correlates of categorical phoneme perception in adults. *Neuroreport, 8,* 919–924.

Demonet, J.-F., Chollet, F., Ramsay, S., Cardebat, D., Nespoulous, J.-L., Wise, R., Rascol, A., & Frackowiak, R. (1992). The anatomy of phonological and semantic processing in normal subjects. *Brain, 115,* 1753-1768.

Demonet, J.-F., Fiez, J. A., Paulesu, E., Petersen, S. E., & Zatorre, R. J. (1996). PET Studies of phonological processing: A critical reply to Poeppel. *Brain and Language, 55,* 352–379.

Demonet, J.-F., Price, C., Wise, R., & Frackowiak, R. J. (1994). A PET study of cognitive strategies in normal subjects during language tasks: Influence of phonetic ambiguity and sequence processing on phoneme monitoring. *Brain, 117,* 671–682.

Deng, L., & Erler, K. (1992). Structural design of hidden Markov model speech recognizer using multivalued phonetic features: Comparison with segmental speech units. *Journal of the Acoustical Society of America, 92,* 3058–3067.

Dhankhar, A., Wexler, B. E., Fulbright, R. K., Halwes, T., Blamire, A. M., & Shulman, R. G. (1997). Functional magnetic resonance imaging assessment of the human brain auditory cortex response to increasing word presentation rates. *Journal of Neurophysiology, 77,* 476–483.

Dronkers, N. (1998). Symposium: The role of Broca's area in language. *Brain and Language, 65,* 71–72.

Dronkers, N. F. (2000). The pursuit of brain-language relationships. *Brain and Language, 71,* 59–61.

Fiez, J., Raichle, M., Miezen, F., Petersen, S., Tallal, P., & Katz, W. (1995). PET studies of auditory and phonological processing: Effects of stimulus characteristics and task demands. *Journal of Cognitive Neuroscience, 7,* 357–375.

Frauenfelder, U., & Floccia, C. (1998). The recognition of spoken word. In A. Friederici (Ed.), *Language comprehension.* New York: Springer.

Gage, N., Poeppel, D., Roberts, T. P. L., & Hickok, G. (1998). Auditory evoked M100 reflects onset acoustics of speech sounds. *Brain Research, 814,* 236–239.

Gandour, J., Wong, D., Hsieh, L., Weinzapfel, B., Van Lancker, D., & Hutchins, G. D. (2000). A crosslinguistic PET study of tone perception. *Journal of Cognitive Neuroscience, 12,* 207–222.

Gandour, J., Wong, D., & Hutchins, G. (1998). Pitch processing in the human brain is influenced by language experience. *Neuroreport, 9,* 2115–2119.

Gordon, J., & Baum, S. (1994). Rhyme priming in aphasia: The role of phonology in lexical access. *Brain and Language, 47,* 661–683.

Gow, D. W., & Caplan, D. (1996). An examination of impaired acoustic-phonetic processing in aphasia. *Brain and Language, 52,* 386–407.

Hickok, G., & Poeppel, D. (2000). Towards a functional neuroanatomy of speech perception. *Trends in Cognitive Sciences, 4,* 131-138.

Ivry, R., & Robertson, L. (1998). *The two sides of perception.* Cambridge, MA: MIT Press.

Jaramillo, M., Alku, P., & Paavilainen, P. (1999). An event-related potential (ERP) study of duration changes in speech and non-speech sounds. *Neuroreport, 10,* 3301–3305.

Jonides, J., Schumacher, E. H., Smith, E. E., Koeppe, R. A., Awh, E., Reuter-Lorenz, P. A., Marshuetz, C., & Willis, C. R. (1998). The role of parietal cortex in verbal working memory. *Journal of Neuroscience, 18,* 5026–5034.

Jusczyk, P. (1986). Speech perception. In K. Boff, K.

Kaufman, & J. Thomas (Eds.), *Handbook of perception and human performance: Cognitive processes and performance* (Vol. 2). New York: Wiley.

Klatt, D. (1979). Speech perception: A model of acoustic-phonetic analysis and lexical access. In R. Cole (Ed.), *Perception and production of fluent speech.* Hillsdale, NJ: Lawrence Erlbaum.

Krogh, A., & Riis, S. (1999). Hidden neural networks. *Neural Computation, 11*, 541–563.

Kuhl, P. K. (1991). Human adults and human infants show a "perceptual magnet effect" for the prototypes of speech categories, monkeys do not. *Perception and Psychophysics, 50*, 93–107.

Kuriki, S., Okita, Y., & Hirata, Y. (1995). Source analysis of magnetic field responses from the human auditory cortex elicited by short speech sounds. *Experimental Brain Research, 104*, 144–152.

Lahiri, A., & Marslen-Wilson, W. (1991). The mental representation of lexical form: A phonological approach to the recognition lexicon. *Cognition, 38*, 245–294.

Liberman, A. L., & Mattingly, I. G. (1985). The motor theory of speech revised. *Cognition, 21*, 1-36.

Liberman, A. M., Harris, K. S., Hoffman, H. S., & Griffith, B. C. (1957). The discrimination of speech sounds within and across phoneme boundaries. *Journal of Experimental Psychology, 54*, 358–368.

Luce, P. A., & Pisoni, D. B. (1998). Recognizing spoken words: The neighborhood activation model. *Ear and Hearing, 19*, 1–36.

Marslen-Wilson, W., & Warren, P. (1994). Levels of perceptual representation and process in lexical access: Words, phonemes, and features. *Psychological Review, 101*, 653–675.

Martin, R. C., Breedin, S. D., & Damian, M. F. (1999). The relation of phoneme discrimination, lexical access, and short-term memory: A case study and interactive activation account. *Brain and Language, 70*, 437–482.

Martin, R., & Romani, C. (1994). Verbal working memory and sentence comprehension: A multiple-components view. *Neuropsychology, 8*, 506–523.

McClelland, J. L., & Elman, J. L. (1986). The TRACE model of speech perception. *Cognitive Psychology, 18*, 1–86.

Metter, E. J., Kempler, D., Jackson, C., Hanson, W. R., Mazziotta, J. C., & Phelps, M. E. (1989). Cerebral glucose metabolism in Wernicke's, Broca's, and conduction aphasia. *Archives of Neurology, 46*, 27–34.

Miceli, G., Caltagirone, C., Gainotti, G., & Payer-Rigo, P. (1978). Discrimination of voice versus place contrasts in aphasia. *Brain and Language, 6*, 47–51.

Milberg, W., Blumstein, S., & Dworetzky, B. (1988). Phonological processing and lexical access in aphasia. *Brain and Language, 34*, 279–293.

Miyake, A., Carpenter, P., & Just, M. (1994). A capacity approach to syntactic comprehension disorders: Making normal adults perform like aphasic patients. *Cognitive Neuropsychology, 11*, 671–717.

Mummery, C. J., Ashburner, J., Scott, S. K., & Wise, R. J. (1999). Functional neuroimaging of speech perception in six normal and two aphasic subjects. *Journal of the Acoustical Society of America, 106*, 449–457.

Naatanen, R., Lehtokoski, A., Lennes, M., Cheour, M., Huotilainen, M., Iivonen, A., Vainio, M., Alku, P., Ilmoniemi, R. J., Luuk, A., Allik, J., Sinkkonen, J., & Alho, K. (1997). Language-specific phoneme representations revealed by electric and magnetic brain responses. *Nature, 385*, 432–434.

Nicholls, M. (1996). Temporal processing asymmetries between the cerebral hemispheres: evidence and implications. *Laterality, 1*, 97–137.

Norris, D., McQueen, J. M., & Cutler, A. (2000). Merging phonetic and lexical information in phonetic decision-making. *Behavioral and Brain Sciences, 23*, 299–325.

Nygaard, L. C., Sommers, M. S., & Pisoni, D. B. (1995). Effects of stimulus variability on perception and representation of spoken words in memory. *Perception and Psychophysics, 57*, 989–1001.

Oscar-Berman, M., Zurif, E., & Blumstein, S. (1975). Effects of unilateral brain damage on the processing of speech sounds. *Brain and Language, 2*, 345–355.

Paulesu, E., Frith, C. D., & Frackowiak, R. J. (1993). The neural correlates of the verbal component of working memory. *Nature, 362*, 342–345.

Paulesu, E., Frith, U., Snowling, M., Gallagher, A., Morton, J., Frackowiak, R. S. J., & Frith, C. D. (1996). Is developmental dyslexia a disconnection syndrome? Evidence from PET scanning. *Brain, 199*, 143–157.

Petersen, S. E., Fox, P. T., Posner, M. I., Mintun, M. A., & Raichle, M. E. (1988). Positron emission tomographic studies of the cortical anatomy of single-word processing. *Nature, 331*, 585–589.

Pisoni, D. B. (1993). Long-term memory in speech perception: Some new findings on talker-variability, speaking rate, and perceptual learning. *Speech Communication, 13*, 109–125.

Pitt, M. A., & Samuel, A. G. (1993). An empirical and meta-analytic evaluation of the phoneme identification task. *Journal of Experimental Psychology: Human Perception and Performance, 19*, 699–725.

Poeppel, D. (1996). A critical review of PET studies of phonological processing. *Brain and Language, 55*, 317–351.

Poeppel, D., Yellin, E., Phillips, C., Roberts, T. P., Rowley, H. A., Wexler, K., & Marantz, A. (1996). Task-induced asymmetry of the auditory evoked M100 neuromagnetic field elicited by speech sounds. *Brain Research: Cognitive Brain Research, 4*, 231–242.

Poldrack, R. A., Wagner, A. D., Prull, M. W., Desmond, J. E., Glover, G. H., & Gabrieli, J. D. (1999). Functional specialization for semantic and phonological processing in the left inferior prefrontal cortex. *Neuroimage, 10*, 15–35.

Price, C., Wise, R., Ramsey, S., Friston, K., Howard, D., & Patterson, K. (1992). Regional response differences within the human auditory cortex when listening to words. *Neuroscience Letters, 146*, 179–182.

Riedel, K., & Studdert-Kennedy, M. (1985). Extending formant transitions may not improve aphasics' perception of stop consonant place of articulation. *Brain and Language, 24*, 223–232.

Rinne, T., Alho, K., Alku, P., Holi, M., Sinkkonen, J., Virtanen, J., Bertrand, O., & Naatanen, R. (1999). Analysis of speech sounds is left-hemisphere predominant at 100-150ms after sound onset. *Neuroreport, 10*, 1113–1117.

Watrous, R. L. (1990). Phoneme discrimination using connectionist networks. *Journal of the Acoustical Society of America, 87*, 1753–1772.

Winkler, I., Lehtokoski, A., Alku, P., Vainio, M., Czigler, I., Csepe, V., Aaltonen, O., Raimo, I., Alho, K., Lang, H., Iivonen, A., & Naatanen, R. (1999). Pre-attentive detection of vowel contrasts utilizes both phonetic and auditory memory representations. *Brain Research: Cognitive Brain Research, 7*, 357–369.

Wise, R., Chollet, F., Hadar, U., Friston, K., Hoffner, E.,

& Frackowiak, R. (1991). Distribution of cortical neural networks involved in word comprehension and word retrieval. *Brain, 114*, 1803-1817.

Zatorre, R. (1997). Cerebral correlates of human auditory processing: Perception of speech and musical sounds. In J. Syka (Ed.), *Acoustical signal processing in the central auditory system*. New York: Plenum Press.

Zatorre, R., Evans, A., Meyer, E., & Gjedde, A. (1992). Lateralization of phonetic and pitch in auditory short-term memory. *Science, 256*, 846–849.

Zatorre, R., Meyer, E., Gjedde, A., & Evans, A. (1996). PET studies of phonetic processing of speech: Review, replication, and reanalysis. *Cerebral Cortex, 6*, 21–30.

14

Neurobiological Bases of Auditory Speech Processing

Dana Boatman

The human auditory system is capable of transforming a continuous acoustic signal into neural representations that, ultimately, provide access to word meaning information. Exactly how this is accomplished has yet to be fully determined, although recent technological advances have greatly enhanced our understanding of this complex phenomenon. In this chapter, we will review the neuroanatomy and neurophysiology of the human auditory system, as they pertain to the processing of spoken speech.

The auditory system is divided conceptually into *peripheral* and *central* systems. The peripheral auditory system is associated with our ability to detect sound and includes structures that we typically associate with "hearing," namely the outer ear, middle ear, and inner ear. The central auditory system enables us to identify sounds, recognize words, and understand spoken speech. This is accomplished by transmitting nerve impulses from the auditory nerve to the brain where sound is decoded, analyzed, and processed. In this chapter, we will focus on central auditory mechanisms associated with speech perception, especially at the cortex. Although a detailed discussion of the peripheral auditory system is beyond the scope of this chapter, a brief overview (figure 14.1) is provided of the system where auditory processing begins.

PERIPHERAL AUDITORY SYSTEM

Outer Ear

Sound perception begins at the outer ear, which is optimized by its shape and position on the head to capture sound waves from the environment. The outer ear, also known as the pinna or auricle, is one of the first structures to develop in the auditory system, being fully formed by seven to eight weeks' gestation. Sound waves are captured by the pinna and funneled down the ear canal. The adult ear canal is approximately 1 inch long. The outer one-third of the canal is composed of cartiledge, the inner two-thirds of bone. Coupled with the head, the ear canal plays an important role in localizing sounds, based on differences in time and intensity of stimuli arriving at each ear. Because of its particular shape and length, the ear canal responds best to frequencies in the range of 2500 to 3000 Hz. By resonating at these frequencies, the ear canal serves as a natural amplifier for speech sounds, especially consonants.

Gross division	Outer ear	Middle ear	Inner ear	Central auditory nervous system
Anatomy	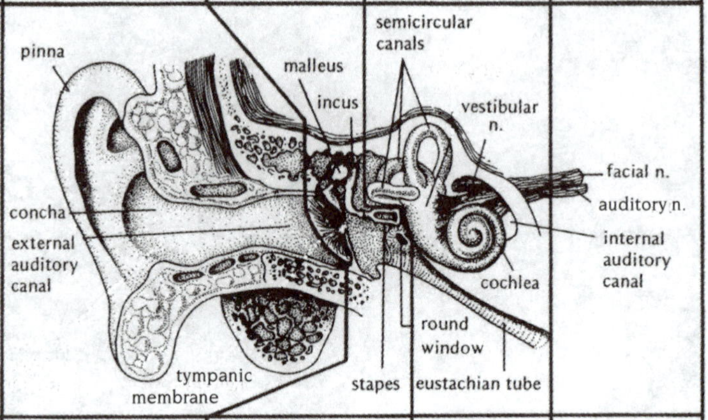			
Mode of operation	Air vibration	Mechanical vibration	Mechanical, Hydrodynamic, Electrochemical	Electrochemical
Function	Protection, Amplification, Localization	Impedance matching, Selective oval window stimulation, Pressure equalization	Filtering distribution, Transduction	Information processing

Figure 14.1. Schematic showing cross-section of human peripheral auditory system, with divisions into outer, middle, and inner ear, and auditory nerve. Adapted from *Fundamentals of Hearing: An Introduction*, Fourth Edition, by William A. Yost, copyright © 2000 by Academic Press. Reproduced by permission of the publisher.

Middle Ear

The ear drum, or tympanic membrane, separates the outer ear from the middle ear. It is oval in shape and composed of three fibrous layers. At birth, the tympanic membrane lies horizontally in the ear canal. As the canal lengthens with age, the tympanic membrane gradually erects to the 40-degree angle seen in the adult ear.

Sound waves travel down the ear canal and impinge on the ear drum, causing it to vibrate. The characteristics of the vibrations are determined by the particular frequency and intensity features of the sound waves. The vibratory motion of the ear drum is transferred to a series of three small bones, called ossicles, that extend in a chain from the ear drum through the middle ear cavity to the oval window of the inner ear. The three ossicles are called the malleus, incus, and stapes, and are the smallest bones in the body. Sound is transmitted by the motion of the ossicles, which vibrate optimally in the normally air-filled middle ear. In the event that the air supply to the middle ear is restricted, as when the Eustachian tube swells shut, increased negative pressure causes fluid to build up in the middle ear. The presence of fluid attenuates the vibratory motion of the ossicles, causing a temporary hearing loss. Abnormalities in the structure or mobility of the ossicles, or a disconnection between them, can also affect the transmission of sound. Hearing losses associated with such middle ear disorders are termed "conductive" because they result from decreased hearing of sound conducted through air. Conductive hearing loss results in decreased speech perception, especially of consonant sound, which are typically less intense than vowel sounds.

Inner Ear

The inner ear is housed in the temporal bone and contains structures associated with both hearing and balance. The inner ear structure associated with hearing is the cochlea, which is a snail-shaped structure, with three spiral fluid-filled chambers. The floor of the middle chamber is the basilar membrane, embedded in which are approximately 30,000 hair cells that are responsible for encoding sound into neural impulses that are then transmitted to the brain. The basilar membrane is tonotopically organized, with high frequencies represented at the basal end and lower frequencies represented at the apical end. Mechanical vibrations, generated by the movement of the stapes in the oval window, cause a pressure gradient in the cochlear fluid, which, in turn, displaces the basilar membrane. The extent and location of displacement along the basilar membrane is determined by frequency and intensity of the vibratory motion of the stapes in the oval window (Bekesey, 1960).

Hearing losses associated with disorders of the cochlea are classified as sensorineural in nature and are distinguished from conductive hearing losses associated with middle ear pathologies. Aging, noise exposure, and ototoxic drugs are all causes of sensorineural hearing loss because they affect the functionality of hair cells, especially at the basal end of the cochlea. This accounts for the high-frequency sensorineural hearing losses seen in the elderly and in individuals with a history of noise exposure or ototoxicity. Congenital malformations of the cochlea, termed aplasias, also cause hearing loss. Incomplete formation of the basal (high-frequency) end of the cochlea is known as Mondini's syndrome, while incomplete formation of the apical (low-frequency) region is called Michael's syndrome. Congenital aplasias typically result in significant sensorineural hearing loss.

Auditory Nerve

The shearing motion of the basilar membrane across the auditory hair cells causes them to depolarize, generating an electrical potential that is propagated along the innervating neuronal fibers of the eighth cranial nerve, also called the auditory nerve. The particular population of auditory nerve fibers that fire and their rate of firing serve to encode the frequency and intensity characteristics of the sound stimulus (Viemeister, 1988). The cell bodies of the neurons innervating the cochlear are contained in the spiral ganglion. Their axons relay neuronal impulses from the peripheral to the central auditory system. There is growing evidence that excitatory neurotransmitters such as glutamate and aspartate play an important role in transmission of neural impulses along the auditory nerve. Damage to these auditory nerve fibers can result in sensorineural hearing loss.

CENTRAL AUDITORY SYSTEM

The central auditory system begins where the auditory nerve fibers synapse in the cochlear nucleus of the brainstem and ends at the cortex. Ascending auditory pathways project from the lower brainstem to auditory cortex in a complex system of parallel and crossing fiber tracts. These pathways are represented schematically in figure 14.2.

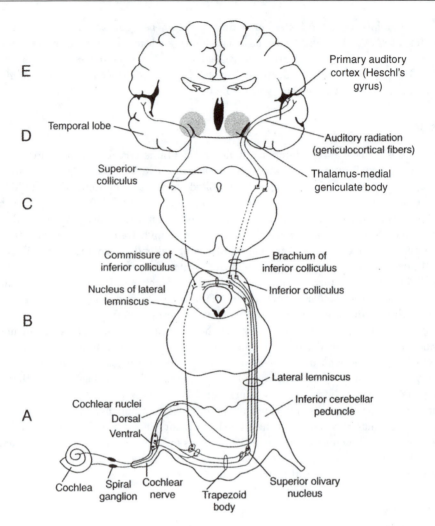

E

D   Temporal lobe

C   Superior colliculus

Primary auditory cortex (Heschl's gyrus)

Auditory radiation (geniculocortical fibers)

Thalamus-medial geniculate body

Commissure of inferior colliculus

Brachium of inferior colliculus

Nucleus of lateral lemniscus

Inferior colliculus

B

Lateral lemniscus

Inferior cerebellar peduncle

Cochlear nuclei
Dorsal
Ventral

A

Cochlea   Spiral ganglion   Cochlear nerve   Trapezoid body   Superior olivary nucleus

Figure 14.2. Schematic of human central auditory pathways, beginning with auditory nerve fiber synapse on cochlear nuclei. A. Medulla. B. Pons. C. Inferior Colliculus. D. Thalamus. E. Transverse temporal plane. Adapted from *Neuroscience: Communicative Disorders*, by Subhash C. Bhatnagar and Orlando J. Andy, copyright © 1995 by Lippincott Williams & Wilkins. Reproduced by permission of the publisher.

Ascending Auditory Pathways

Cochlear Nucleus

The CN is the first major structure in the central auditory system and an obligatory synapse for all auditory nerve fibers. The CN is a group of three nuclei located bilaterally on the posterolateral surface of the brainstem, where the pons and medulla intersect. Eighth cranial nerve fibers entering the CN branch to all three major divisions. The CN is the only structure in the central auditory system that does not receive binaural input. It is tonotopically organized, with tuning curves similar to those of auditory nerve fibers when stimulated with tone bursts of different frequencies. This allows the CN to preserve the frequency resolution of auditory information encoded in the cochlea. In addition to preserving frequency information, the CN is responsible for preserving and transmitting stimulus timing and intensity information to the superior olivary complex, which, in turn, uses that information for sound localization (Young, Shofner, White, Robert, & Voight, 1988). There is also evidence that the CN is responsible for encoding many acoustic features necessary for vowel discrimination and identification, including formant frequencies, duration, and vowel intensity (Sachs & Young, 1979; Delgutte, 1980). Damage to the CN can result in ipsilateral pure tone deficits. Although there are CN fibers that project ipsilaterally in the afferent auditory pathway, the majority of fibers project contralaterally. There are three major contralateral fiber tracts projecting from the CN to higher auditory structures. The largest of the three is the ventral acoustic stria, which arises from the anterior ventral CN and projects to the contralateral superior olivary complex via the trapezoid body. A second fiber tract is the intermediate acoustic stria, which projects contralaterally from the posterior ventral CN to the lateral lemniscus and inferior colliculus. The third CN projection is the dorsal acoustic stria, arising from the dorsal CN and terminating in the contralateral superior olivary complex, lateral lemniscus, inferior colliculus, and cerebellum. The majority of auditory fibers from the CN project contralaterally.

Superior Olivary Complex

The SOC is the first major binaural relay station in the central auditory system. The SOC is located medial to the CN in the brainstem, in the caudal portion of the pons. The SOC also has three major nuclei: medial nucleus of the trapezoid body, medial superior olivary nucleus, and lateral superior olivary nucleus. All three divisions of the SOC are tonotopically organized and bilaterally innervated. Because it is a major center for processing binaural information, the SOC is thought to play a major role in sound localization. The SOC uses interaural timing differences to localize low-frequency sounds, whereas high-frequency sound localization is accomplished by encoding interaural stimulus intensity differences. It is not currently known what role the SOC plays, if any, in speech perception.

Lateral Lemniscus

The LL is a fiber tract projecting from the rostral portion of the pons in the brainstem to the inferior colliculus. It contains both ascending and descending auditory fibers. The primary source of input to the LL is from the contralateral dorsal CN and from both the SOC and the ipsilateral and contralateral ventral CN. Communication between the lateral lemnisci occurs via the commissure of Probst, enabling the nuclei of the LL to be activated bilaterally or contralaterally. The LL appears to serve primarily as a relay station between the CN and SOC and the inferior colliculus. It has also been suggested that the three morphologically distinct nuclei of the LL may play different roles in auditory processing (Helfert, Snead, & Altschuler, 1991). Additional studies are needed to better understand the function and organization of the LL.

Inferior Colliculus

The IC is located on the dorsal side of the midbrain and is the largest auditory structure in the brainstem. Although a small number of fibers originating in the LL may bypass the IC and project directly to the thalamus, most fibers in the ascending auditory pathway synapse in the IC. The core of the IC contains only auditory fibers and is highly tonotopically organized. Indeed, unit recordings from this area show very sharp tuning curves, suggesting that the IC plays a role in enhancing frequecy resolution. IC neurons also respond to temporal and spatial distinctions, as well as to binaural stimulation (Ehret, 1997). The belt areas of the IC contain both auditory and somatosensory fibers. IC auditory fibers project tonotopically to medial geniculate body, both ipsilaterally and contralaterally.

Medial Geniculate Body

The MGB is the auditory division of the thalamus, located on its dorsolateral surface approximately 1 cm from the IC. The MGB is an obligatory relay station between the IC and auditory cortex (Ribaupierre, 1997). It is further subdivided into ventral, dorsal, and medial divisions. The ventral division is the most tonotopically organized, with the largest number of inputs, and projects directly to primary auditory cortex. Neurons in the ventral MGB are also selectively responsive to binaural stimulation and interaural intensity differences. Conversely, the medial and dorsal divisions of the MGB do not appear to be tonotopically organized, with neurons responding equally well to simple and complex acoustic stimuli or just to complex acoustic stimuli (Ribaupierre, 1997). The medial MGB projects to both primary and nonprimary auditory cortices, while the dorsal MGB projects only to nonprimary auditory cortex. It has recently been suggested that the medial division of the MGB plays a role in awakening auditory cortex (Ribaupierre, 1997). We are just beginning to understand the role of the MGB in speech perception. It is now known that the MGB is one of the generators of late auditory potentials reflecting detection of acoustic-phonetic change (Giard, Perrin, Pernier, & Bouchet, 1990; Kraus, McGee, Littman, Nichel, & King, 1994). While auditory radiations from the ventral MGB project only to primary auditory cortex, the dorsal and medial divisions of the MGB project to both primary and nonprimary auditory cortices.

Auditory Cortex

Auditory cortex has been the subject of considerable recent interest. Although much of what is known about the organization and function of auditory cortex derives from neuroanatomical and neurophysiological studies of animal models, recent application of in vivo neuroimaging techniques, including positron emission tomography (PET) and functional MRI (fMRI), now enables researchers to study the human auditory cortex directly. We will first discuss the organization of auditory cortex, followed by a review of recent developments in our understanding of auditory cortical connectivity (figure 14.3).

Cortical areas involved in the processing of auditory information are located in the transverse temporal planes of both hemispheres. Although both the left and right hemispheres have areas devoted to auditory processing, there are morphological and functional differences between them. Volumetric studies showed that auditory cortex is typically larger in the language-dominant (left) hemisphere than in the right hemisphere (Geschwind & Levitsky, 1968; Steinmetz et al., 1991; Foundas, Leonard, & Heilman, 1995). This morphological asymmetry is thought to reflect left hemisphere dominance for language.

A right-ear advantage for speech on tests of dichotic listening is also thought to reflect left hemisphere language dominance. The term *dichotic* refers to the simultaneous presentation of two different stimuli to each ear. Stimuli presented to the right ear are typically repeated with greater accuracy than stimuli presented to the left ear. This is attributed to the greater efficiency of contralateral pathways in the auditory system and to the lateralization of language to the left hemisphere in most individuals (Kimura, 1961; Studdert-Kennedy & Shankweiler, 1970).

Histochemical and neurophysiolgical studies of animals have shown that auditory cortex is divided into three major areas: a core or primary auditory area, a belt or secondary auditory area, and a parabelt or association auditory area (Hackett, Stepniewaska, & Kaas, 1998; Rauschecker, 1995; Kaas, 1999).

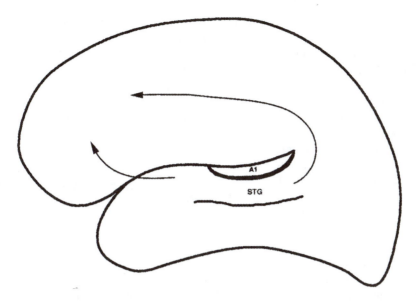

Figure 14.3. Schematic of auditory cortex and associated pathways. AI refers to primary auditory cortex, with the darker auditory parabelt contour. STG refers to superior temporal gyrus, including auditory association cortex within Wernicke's area (BA 22). Ventral and dorsal pathways connect auditory association cortex to frontal areas.

Primary Auditory Cortex

The auditory core area is most closely associated with what has traditionally been referred to as primary auditory cortex, also known as areas 41 and 42 in Brodmann's system. It is located inside the sylvian fissure on the posterior portion of the transverse plane of the temporal lobe, cutting across Heschl's gyrus. The auditory core is a cone-shaped region, approximately 14 mm long, that is wider at the posterior end and narrows more anteriorly (Hackett et al., 1998). This core area is further subdivided into two to three areas, the largest of which is AI, located at the posterior end of the core. Neurophysiological studies have shown that AI most closely resembles what has traditionally been referred to as primary auditory cortex: it contains the full tonotopic representation of the cochlea, with higher frequencies located medially and lower frequencies located more laterally (Merzenich & Brugge, 1973). Immediately adjacent and anterior to AI is another primary auditory area, labeled "Rostral core" or just "R," that is somewhat less tonotopically organized than AI and with high to low frequencies oriented in reverse direction, with high frequencies located more laterally and low frequencies located medially. Consequently, AI and R share a low-frequency border. A third more anterior core subdivision has been recently proposed, called RT, and remains to be further characterized (Morel & Kaas, 1992). In addition to frequency information, the core area also appears to be involved in the coding of temporal acoustic information. Auditory neurons in this area appear sensitive to voice onset timing differences (Steinschneider, Schroeder, Arezzo, & Vaughan, 1995). Although primary auditory cortex maintains information extracted earlier, this area is not thought to do much new processing.

Each subdivision of the auditory core receives separate input from the ventral division of the medial geniculate body of the thalamus, suggesting that the core areas process auditory information in parallel (Hackett et al., 1998; Kaas, Hatchett, & Tramo, 1999). The core area also receives input from contralateral primary auditory cortex through the posterior portion of the body of the corpus callosum.

Posterior to the core area on the supratemporal plane is another auditory structure that is roughly triangular in shape and known as the planum temporale. There is considerable speculation that it is associated with language processing since it is generally larger in the language-dominant (left) hemisphere than in the nondominant hemisphere (Geschwind & Levitsky, 1968; Steinmetz et al., 1991; Foundas et al., 1995). This view was supported by a study of adult dyslexic patients who did not show the same degree of asymmetry of the planum temporale as did normal control subjects (Galaburda, Sherman, Rosen, Abritiz, & Geschwind, 1985). However, the precise function of the planum temporale is not yet known. A recent fMRI study showed activation of this area in both tone and word listening conditions, suggesting that the planum temporal may be involved in early (for example, prelinguistic) auditory processing, while other areas of the left temporal lobe are involved in the processing of specifically linguistic stimuli (Binder, Frost, Hammeke, Rao, & Cox, 1996).

Auditory Belt

Surrounding the core area, both medially and laterally, there is a narrow belt of secondary auditory cortex, also referred to as secondary auditory cortex. This belt area is approximately 2 to 4 mm wide and surrounds the core both medially and laterally. On the medial side the belt region abuts the insula. There is general agreement that the belt region does not extend significantly onto the lateral surface of the superior temporal gyrus. The belt area receives input from the core area and from the dorsal and medial divisions of the MGB (Kaas et al., 1999). The function of the belt region is not well understood. However, one of its primary functions appears to be serving as an intermediary relay station for connections from adjacent areas of the auditory core to the more lateral parabelt areas (Morel & Kaas, 1992).

Auditory Parabelt

The auditory parabelt, also known as auditory association cortex or Brodmann's area 22, is located along the lateral posterior portion of the belt region, extending onto the surface of the superior temporal gyrus. The auditory parabelt receives projections from the belt area and from the medial and dorsal divisions of the MGB (Kaas et al., 1999). In contrast to the auditory core areas, the parabelt area does not appear to be tonotopically organized. The functional properties of this region have yet to be fully specified. This is, in part, because most animal models do not have a homologue for this area. Instead, much of what is known about this region comes from studies of patients with lesions in this area and from recent neuroimaging studies. The parabelt area forms part of what has traditionally been referred to as Wernicke's area in the aphasia literature. This area is associated with phonological processing and comprehension of spoken speech.

It has long been known that lesions involving the parabelt area are associated with impaired auditory comprehension (Wernicke, 1874; Luria, 1976). A series of seminal studies in the late 1970s and early 1980s by Sheila Blumstein and others confirmed the role of this area in phonological processing (Blumstein, Cooper, Zurif, & Caramazza, 1977; Miceli, Caltagirone, Gainotti, & Payer-Rigo, 1978). Because posterior lesions often extend into primary auditory areas as well as subcortically, it has been difficult, however, to define the precise role of auditory association cortex in this patient population. This issue has recently been addressed using the technique of cortical electrical interference, used to map speech and language functions in epilepsy patients. Cortical electrical interference, also known as cortical stimulation, involves generating a low-level (15 mA) electrical current between adjacent pairs of electrodes that are surgically implanted directly over the cortical surface. The electrical current disrupts the processing associated with the underlying brain tissue. Language functions are mapped to those sites where they are impaired by electrical interference. This technique can be used to map multiple language functions at multiple sites in the same patient. An advantage of this technique is that the current distribution is restricted to cortical gray matter and to a relatively circumscribed region (~1 cm^2). Consequently, it is possible to restrict the site of testing to auditory association cortex. A series of speech perception studies using this technique confirmed the role of auditory association cortex in phonological processing and in accessing lexical-semantic information (Boatman, Lesser, & Gordon, 1995; Boatman, Hall, Goldstein, Lesser, & Gordon, 1997).

The role of auditory association cortex in phonological processing and lexical-semantic access has been confirmed by neuroimaging studies using PET and, more recently, fMRI. PET studies of word comprehension and retrieval showed selective activation of auditory association cortex (Wise et al., 1991; Demonet et al., 1992; Zatorre, Evans, Meyer, & Gjedde, 1992). Similarly, activation of the same lateral posterior temporal lobe area has been identified by fMRI studies using both active and passive listening conditions (Binder et al., 1994).

Current understanding of the organization of auditory cortex has engendered a hierarchical view of cortical auditory processing (Boatman et al., 1995; Rauschecker, 1998; Kaas et al., 1999). Specifically, there appears to be a medial-to-lateral progression in selectivity of cortical areas for processing increasingly complex acoustic stimuli. Rauschecker (1998) showed that neurons in primary auditory areas of monkeys are selectively responsive to different frequencies, while neurons in more lateral auditory areas of the superior temporal gyrus are selectively responsive to complex acoustic stimuli, including species-specific calls. In our own studies, we have found that homologous areas of human auditory association (parabelt) cortex are critically involved in phoneme processing, but not in pitch discrimination (Boatman et al., 1997). There is also growing evidence that the hierarchical organization of auditory cortex for acoustic-to-phonological processing is evident as early as three months of age, suggesting that a dedicated neural network for auditory language processing may be present in the human brain from birth (Dehaene-Lambertz & Baillet, 1998).

Connectivity of Auditory Cortex

Ipsilateral Connections

Recently, researchers have turned their attention to the issue of how auditory cortex is connected to other areas of the brain. In animal models, retrograde tracer studies have been particularly useful for identifying anatomical connections. Previous studies have shown that the core auditory areas project largely to adjacent areas of the medial and lateral belt region, which in turn projects to the auditory parabelt area (Hackett et al., 1998). A dense network of pathways then connects the parabelt, or auditory association area, to other areas of the brain, suggesting that this region is a gateway to higher-level language processing. More recently, connections between auditory association cortex and the frontal lobe have been identified (Hackett et al., 1998; Romanski, Bates, & Goldman-Rakic, 1999). These connections appear to form two processing streams: one that projects from the posterior temporal lobe through the parietal lobe to the frontal areas and a second stream that projects between the anterior portion of the temporal lobe and the inferior frontal and prefrontal areas. Although the precise role of the multiple auditory projections to the frontal lobe has yet to be fully determined, it is speculated that these two auditory pathways diverge in function, as in the visual system, with the ventral stream for the processing of auditory pattern information, including speech, and the dorsal stream for processing auditory spatial information (Rauschecker, 1998; Romanski et al., 1999).

Contralateral Connections

Primary auditory cortex receives input from contralateral auditory cortex through the posterior section of the body of the corpus callosum. Despite the traditional view that speech perception is strongly left hemisphere lateralized, there is evidence that the nondominant (right) hemisphere can support auditory language processing. A small number of studies report impaired speech perception in patients with bilateral or unilateral right hemisphere lesions (Eustache, Lechevalier, Viader, & Lambert, 1990; Coslett, Brashear, & Heilman, 1984). Likewise, numerous studies invoke right hemisphere recruitment in recovery from aphasia (Cummings, Benson, Walsh, & Levine, 1979; Coslett & Monsul, 1994). Furthermore, most neuroimaging studies report bilateral activation during speech perception (Wise et al., 1991; Binder et al., 1994; Zatorre et al., 1992). Recent intracarotid sodium amobarbital studies have shown evidence of right hemisphere auditory language capabilities (McGlone, 1984; Boatman et al., 1998). More recently, a study of auditory language function after left hemispherectomy in children up to fourteen years of age showed evidence of intrinsic right hemisphere receptive language abilities (Boatman et al., 1999). These studies suggest that we may have previously underestimated the receptive language abilities of the right hemisphere. Future studies will help delineate the scope of right hemisphere auditory language processing abilities.

Efferent Auditory Pathways

Until recently, relatively little has been known about the efferent auditory system. Although the anatomy of the efferent system is well established, the functional role of this system is still poorly understood. Efferent connections begin at the level of the cortex and extend down to the cochlea, involving many of the same relay stations as the ascending pathways, and maintaining a tonotopic organization. Efferent connections project both ipsilaterally and contralaterally (Imig & Morel, 1983), with the thalamus receiving as many efferent as afferent inputs (Ribaupierre, 1997). The primary function of the efferent pathways is thought to be inhibitory, especially at the level of the thalamus and the olivocochlear bundle. Examples of the inhibitory, or feedback, function of the efferent system include decreasing the neuronal response to background noise, thereby increasing the signal-noise ratio and optimizing the neuronal response to biologically significant signals, including speech (Musiek & Lamb, 1992; Ribaupierre, 1997).

REFERENCES

Binder, J. R., Frost, J. A., Hammeke, T. A., Rao, S. M., & Cox, R. W. (1996). Function of the left planum temporale in auditory and linguistic processing. *Brain, 119*, 1239–1247.

Binder, J. R., Rao, S. M., Hammeke, T. A., Yetkin, F. Z., Jesmanowicz, A., Bandettini, P. A., Wong, E. C., Estkowski, L. D., Goldstein, M. D., Haughton, V. M., & Hyde, J. S. (1994). Functional magnetic resonance imaging of human auditory cortex. *Annals of Neurology, 35*, 637–638.

Blumstein, S., Cooper, W., Zurif, E., & Caramazza, A. (1977). The perception and production of voice onset time in aphasia. *Neuropsychologia, 36*, 371–383.

Boatman, D., Hall, C., Goldstein, M., Lesser, R., & Gordon, B. (1997). Neuroperceptual differences in consonant and vowel discrimination: As revealed by direct cortical electrical interference. *Cortex, 33*(1), 83–98.

Boatman D, Hart J, Lesser R, Honeycutt N, Anderson N, Miglioretti D, & Gordon B. (1998). Right hemisphere speech perception revealed by amobarbital injection and electrical interference. *Neurology, 51*, 458–464.

Boatman, D., Freeman, J., Vining, E., Pulsifer, M., Miglioretti, D., Minahan, R., Carson, B., Brandt, J., & McKhann, G. (1999). Language recovery after left hemispherectomy in children with late onset seizures. *Annals of Neurology, 46*(4), 579–586

Boatman, D., Lesser, R., & Gordon, B. (1995). Auditory speech processing in the left temporal cortex: An electrical interference study. *Brain and Language, 51*, 269–290.

Coslett, B., Brashear, H., & Heilman, K. (1984). Pure word deafness after bilateral primary auditory cortex infarcts. *Neurology, 34*, 347–352.

Coslett, B., & Monsul, N. (1994). Reading with the right hemisphere: Evidence from transcranial magnetic stimulation. *Brain and Language, 46*, 198–211.

Cummings, J., Benson, D., Walsh, M., & Levine, H. (1979). Left-to-right transfer of language dominance: A case study. *Neurology, 29*, 1547–1550.

Dehaene-Lambertz, G., & Baillet, S. (1998). A phonological representation in the infant brain. *Neuroreport, 9*, 1885–1888.

Delgutte, B. (1980). Representation of speech-like sounds in the discharge patterns of auditory-nerve fibers. *Journal of the Acoustical Society of America, 68*(3), 843–857.

Demonet, J., Chollet, F., Ramsay, S., Cadebat, D., Nesoulous, J., Wise, R., Rascol, A., & Frackowiak, R. (1992). The anatomy of phonological and semantic processing in normal subjects. *Brain, 115,* 1753–1768.

Ehert, G. (1997). The auditory midbrain, a "shunting yard" of acoustical information processing. In G. Ehret & R. Romand (Eds.), *The central auditory system.* Oxford: Oxford University Press.

Eustache, F., Lechevalier, B., Viader, F., & Lambert, J. (1990). Identification and discrimination disorders in auditory perception: A report on two cases. *Neuropsychologia, 28,* 257–270.

Foundas, A., Leonard, C., & Heilman, K. (1995). Morphologic cerebral asymmetries and handedness. *Archives of Neurology, 52,* 501–508.

Galaburda, A., Sherman, G., Rosen, G., Aboitiz, F., & Geschwind, N. (1985). Developmental dyslexia: Four consecutive patients with cortical anomalies. *Annals of Neurology, 18,* 222–233.

Geschwind, N., & Levitsky, W. (1968). Human brain: Left-right asymmetries in temporal speech region. *Science, 161,* 186–187.

Giard, M., Perrin, F., Pernier, J., & Bouchet, P. (1990). Brain generators implicated in the processing of auditory stimulus deviance: A topographic event-related potential study. *Psychophysiology, 27*(6), 627–640.

Hackett, T., Stepniewaska, I., & Kaas, J. (1998). Subdivisions of auditory cortex and ipsilateral cortical connections of the parabelt auditory cortex in macaque monkeys. *Journal of Comparative Neurology, 394,* 475–495.

Helfert, R., Snead, C., & Altschuler, R. (1991). The ascending auditory pathways. In R. Altschuler, R. Boobin, B. Clopton, & D. Hoffman (Eds.), *Neurobiology of hearing: The central auditory system.* New York: Raven Press.

Imig, T., & Morel, A. (1983). Organzation of the thalamocortical auditory system in the cat. *Annual Review of Neuroscience, 6,* 95–120.

Jäncke, L., & Steinmetz, H. (1993). Auditory lateralization and planum temporale asymmetry. *Neuroreport, 5,* 169–172.

Kaas, J. H., Hackett, T. A., & Tramo, M. J. (1999). Auditory processing in primate cerebral cortex. *Current Opinion in Neurobiology, 9,* 164–170.

Kimura, D. (1961). Cerebral dominance and perception of verbal stimuli. *Canadian Journal of Psychology, 15,* 166–171.

Kraus, N., McGee, T., Ferre, J., Hoeppner, J., Carrell, T., Sharma, A., & Nicol, T. (1993). Mismatch negativity in the neurophysiologic/behavioral evaluation of auditory processing deficits: A case study. *Ear and Hearing, 14,* 223–234.

Kraus, N., McGee, T., Littman, T., Nicol, T., & King, C. (1994). Nonprimary auditory thalamic representation of acoustic change. *Journal of Neurophysiology, 72*(3), 1270–1277.

Luria, A. (1976). *Basic problems of neurolinguistics.* Paris: Mouton.

McGlone, J. (1984). Speech comprehension after unilateral injection of sodium amytal. *Brain & Language, 22,* 150–157.

Merzenich, M., & Brugge, J. (1973). Representation of the cochlear partition on the superior temporal plane of the macaque monkey. *Brain Research, 50,* 275–296.

Miceli, G., Caltagirone, C., Gainotti, G., & Payer-Rigo, P. (1978). Discrimination of voice versus place contrasts in aphasia. *Brain & Language, 6,* 47–51.

Morel, A, & Kaas, J. (1992). Subdivisions and connections of auditoyr cotex in owl monkeys. *Journal of Comparative Neurology, 318,* 437–459.

Musiek, F., & Lamb, L. (1992). Neuroanatomy and neurophysiology of central auditory processing. In J. Katz, N. Stecker, & D. Henderson (Eds.), *Central auditory processing: A transdisciplinary view.* St. Louis: Mosby Year Book.

Rauschecker, J., Tian, B., & Hauser, M. (1995). Processing of complex sounds in macaque nonprimary auditory cortex. *Science, 268,* 111–114.

Rauschecker, J. (1998). Parallel processing in the auditory cortex of primates. *Audiology Neuro-Otology, 3,* 86–103.

Ribaupierre, F. (1997). Acoustical information processing in the auditory thalamus and cerebral cortex. In G. Ehret & R. Romand R. (Eds.), *The central auditory system.* Oxford: Oxford University Press.

Romanski, L. M., Bates, J. F., & Goldman-Rakic, P. S. (1999). Auditory belt and parabelt projections to the prefrontal cortex in the rhesus monkey. *Journal of Comparative Neurology, 403,* 141–157.

Sachs, M. B., Voigt, H. F., & Young, E. D. (1983). Auditory nerve representation of vowels in background noise. *Journal of Neurophysiology, 50,* 27–45.

Sachs, M., & Young, E. (1979). Representation of steady-state vowels in the temporal aspects of the discharge patterns of populations of auditory-nerve fibers. *Journal of the Acoustical Society of America, 66,* 1381–1403.

Steinmetz, H., Volmann, J., Jancke, L., & Freund, H. J. (1991). Anatomic left-right asymmetry of language-related temporal cortex is different in left- and right-handers. *Annals of Neurology, 29*(3), 315–319.

Steinschneider, M., Schroeder, C., Arezzo, J., &Vaughan, H. (1995). Physiological correlates of voice onset time in primary auditory cortex (A1) of the awake monkey: Temporal response patterns. *Brain and Language, 48,* 326–340.

Studdert-Kennedy, M., & Shankweiler, D. (1970). Hemispheric specialization for speech perception. *Journal of the Acoustical Society of America, 48,* 579–594.

Tian, B., & Rauschecker, J. (1995). FM-selectivity of neurons in the lateral areas of rhesus monkey auditory cortex. *Society for Neuroscience Abstracts, 21,* 269.17.

Viemeister, N. (1988). Psychophysical aspects of auditory intensity coding. In G. Edelman, W. Gall, & W. Cowan (Eds.), *Auditory function: Neurobiological bases of hearing.* New York: Wiley.

von Bekesy, G. (1960). *Experiments in hearing.* New York: McGraw-Hill.

Wernicke, C. (1977). Der aphasische symptomenkamplex: Eine psychologische studie auf anatomomischer basis. In G. H. Eggert (Ed.), *Wernike's work on aphasia.* The Hague: Mouton. (Original work published 1874.)

Wise, R., Chollet, F., Hadar, U., Friston, K., Hoffner, E., & Frackowiak, R. (1991). Distribution of cortical neural networks involved in word comprehension and word retrieval. *Brain, 114,* 1803–1817.

Young, E., Shofner, W., White, J., Robert, J., & Voigt, H. (1988). Response properties of cochlear nucleus neurons in relationship to physiological mechanisms. In

G. Edelman, W. Gall, &W. Cowan (Eds.), *Auditory function: Neurobiological bases of hearing.* New York: Wiley.

Zatorre, R., Evans, A., Meyer, E., & Gjedde, A. (1992). Lateralization of phonetic and pitch discrimination in speech processing. *Science, 256,* 846–849.

15

Diagnosis and Treatment
of Auditory Disorders

Dana Boatman

Disorders of the auditory system can be classified broadly as one of two general types: those affecting the peripheral auditory system and those affecting the central auditory system. Disorders of the peripheral auditory system affect the listener's ability to detect sound, resulting in hearing loss. Conversely, a central auditory processing disorder typically does not affect sound detection, but rather subsequent processing of what is heard, including analysis of the phonological and lexical-semantic content of the signal. Disorders of the central auditory system may be developmental or acquired, as in the case of a stroke patient with a receptive aphasia. Developmental central auditory disorders often have no known neurological basis and may be subtle enough to go undetected in normal conversation, unless the acoustic signal or the listening environment is degraded. In contrast, a brief conversational exchange with a patient who has suffered a left hemisphere stroke is often sufficient to identify the presence of an auditory comprehension deficit. We will focus here on adults with acquired central auditory disorders and, in particular, auditory disorders that are associated with the disruption of cortical function. Because of the physical contiguity of the peripheral and central auditory systems, disorders of the peripheral auditory system directly affect central auditory processing. Consequently, a comprehensive auditory evaluation includes a hearing assessment. This is especially important in the evaluation of elderly stroke patients who, in addition to speech understanding difficulties, may also have peripheral hearing loss. For this reason, we begin with a review of peripheral hearing loss.

DIAGNOSIS AND TREATMENT OF HEARING LOSS

Hearing loss is defined as an increase in hearing thresholds above normal sensitivity. Hearing loss is diagnosed by a hearing test, or audiological evaluation, using acoustically calibrated equipment in a sound-treated booth (for more detailed discussion, see Martin, 1994). Frequency-specific (250 to 8000 Hz) thresholds are elicited by both air and bone conduction for each ear separately. Sound transmitted from the outer ear through the middle and inner ear is heard by air conduction. In bone conduction testing, the outer ear and middle ear are bypassed by directly stimulating the inner ear using a bone conduction vibrator. In addition to pure tone testing, routine audiological evaluation includes word recognition testing at suprathreshold levels and evaluation of middle ear function by tympanometry. Hearing thresholds worse (that is, greater) than 25 dB at two or more frequencies suggest a hearing loss. Comparison of air and bone conduction thresholds permits further classification of the hearing loss. There are three types of hearing loss: conductive, sensorineural, and mixed.

Conductive Hearing Loss

Conductive hearing loss refers to decreased air conduction thresholds in the presence of normal bone conduction thresholds. When air conduction thresholds are greater than or equal to 15 dB worse than bone conduction thresholds at two or more frequencies, a conductive hearing loss is present. The main feature of a conductive hearing loss is sound attenuation. If the presentation level is sufficiently high, the patient with a conductive hearing loss often performs within normal limits on word recognition tests. Conductive hearing losses do not usually exceed 65 dB (moderate-severe) and are often temporary. The poorer air than bone conduction thresholds typically reflect middle ear pathologies. The most common middle ear pathology is otitis media, which results in a build-up of fluid in the middle ear. The attenuation of sound through middle ear fluid is responsible for the poorer air versus bone conduction hearing thresholds. A flat tympanogram or one with a negatively skewed compliance peak confirms the presence of middle ear fluid. Otitis media typically affects school-age children more than adults and can result in a fluctuating conductive hearing loss.

A common middle ear pathology in adults is otosclerosis, which is often hereditary and has a higher incidence in women (Morrison & Bundey, 1970). Otosclerosis is a progressive, unilateral or bilateral disease resulting in new growth of spongy bone on the middle ear ossicles, especially the stapes footplate. Fixation of the stapes footplate in the oval window damps the amplitude of sound transmitted to the inner ear. Early signs of otosclerosis on the hearing test include a low-frequency conductive hearing loss and a notch in the audiogram around 2000 Hz where bone conduction thresholds are 10 to 15 dB worse than air conduction thresholds. This anomalous bone conduction pattern is referred to as Carhart's notch. In contrast to patients with otitis media, the patient with otosclerosis typically has a normal tympanogram, although there may be reduction in peak compliance.

Other middle ear pathologies include dysarticulation of the ossicles, as can occur with head trauma, congenital malformations of the middle and outer ear, and middle ear tumors. Glomus tumors arise in the middle ear and are associated with glomus bodies in the tympanic branches of the ninth and tenth cranial nerves. Patients' presenting symptoms often include pulsatile tinnitus as well as conductive hearing loss.

Treatment of conductive hearing loss aims to reduce the gap between the patient's air and bone conduction thresholds. This is usually accomplished by medical treatment of the underlying middle ear pathology. Otitis media is usually treated with a course of antibiotics. For patients who suffer from chronic otitis media, pressure-equalizing (PE) tubes can be surgically inserted into the tympanic membrane to permit drainage of middle ear fluid. If left untreated, the tympanic membrane can rupture, which is painful and often takes considerable time to heal. Because school-age children with conductive hearing losses are at risk for speech, language, and auditory processing disorders, preferential classroom seating is usually recommended. If the conductive hearing loss is relatively stable, a hearing aid may be helpful in compensating for sound attenuation in the middle ear. Most other middle ear pathologies are treated surgically. Stapedectomy remains the surgical procedure of choice for treatment of otosclerosis. This involves prosthetic replacement of the stapes, which can help restore hearing thresholds. Fractures or interruptions of the ossicular chain, resulting from head trauma, can also be corrected surgically. Surgery is invariably indicated for removal of middle ear tumors.

Sensorineural Hearing Loss

Sensorineural hearing loss refers to a corresponding decrease in both air and bone conduction thresholds and can be *sensory* (for example, cochlear) or *neural* (eighth cranial nerve) in nature. Sensory hearing loss is often associated with damage to the sensory hair cells in the cochlea. This can be caused by noise exposure, ototoxic drugs (for example, aminoglycosides), or normal aging. Because of their location at the basal end of the cochlea, hair cells associated with high-frequency hearing are more vulnerable to impairment. Consequently, sensorineural hearing loss from cochlear pathologies often affects high-frequency hearing (for example, greater than 1000 Hz) more than low-frequency hearing. The elderly individual with a high-frequency sensorineural hearing loss, known as presbycusis, will frequently report difficulty hearing consonant sounds, especially in the presence of background noise. This is because consonant sounds contain high-frequency information, which is typically less intense than low-frequency vowel sounds and more likely to be masked in the presence of background noise. Because the hearing test does not distinguish between sensory and neural contributors to a sensorineural hearing loss, clinicians may use other tests, including otoacoustic emissions (OAE), which assess the integrity of outer hair cell motility. Absence of OAEs is consistent with a cochlear (sensory) hearing loss. Other sources of cochlear pathology resulting in unilateral and/or bilateral sensorineural hearing loss include childhood illnesses, such as mumps and meningitis, as well as congenital malformations of the cochlea.

Patients presenting with sensorineural hearing loss accompanied by other clinical symptoms such as unilateral tinnitus, dizziness, and/or aural fullness require further evaluation to rule out retrocochlear pathologies or other underlying medical conditions. Retrocochlear pathologies include tumors of the eighth cranial nerve, referred to as acoustic neuromas. Most acoustic neuromas are unilateral and arise from schwann cells in the sheath covering the vestibular branch of the eighth nerve and, therefore, are more accurately termed vestibular schwannomas. As these tumors grow, they expand into the cerebellopontine angle, exerting pressure on the eighth nerve and other cranial nerves, including the trigeminal nerve (Vth cranial nerve). Although brainstem auditory evoked response (BAER, ABR) testing was used formerly to identify cerebellopontine tumors, clinical diagnosis is now largely based on results of MRI studies. It has been suggested that both techniques be used in combination for the most effective early diagnosis of eighth nerve tumors (Josey, Glasscock, & Musiek, 1988). Because cochlear function should not be affected, OAEs can be also useful for differential diagnosis of retrocochlear pathology. Surgical treatment is indicated for most patients with eighth nerve tumors.

In the event of a sudden-onset sensorineural hearing loss, immediate medical evaluation is indicated to rule out retrocochlear pathology, thrombosis of the internal auditory artery, or vascular occlusion resulting in reduction of the arterial blood supply to the common cochlear artery or auditory nerve. If MRI studies rule out a retrocochlear pathology, Meniere's disease may be suspected. In addition to unilateral hearing loss, Meniere's disease is characterized by sudden attacks of vertigo, tinnitus, and vomiting. Meniere's disease is a cochlear pathology resulting in endolymphatic hydrops, the overgeneration of endolymph fluid in the cochlear duct. In contrast to other sensorineural hearing losses, patients with Meniere's disease often have fluctuating low-frequency sensorineural hearing losses. A definitive diagnosis of Meniere's disease can be made by electrocochleography (ECoG), whereby abnormal electrical responses from the cochlea confirm the presence of increased inner ear fluid pressure. In some patients with sudden-onset hearing loss, no known cause is identified although a viral etiology may be suspected. In such cases, early treatment with steroids (within forty-eight hours of onset) can sometimes restore patients' hearing.

Treatment of sensorineural hearing loss depends largely on the underlying etiology. The patient with presbycusis and no other medical complications is a likely candidate for hearing aids. Over the past five years, enormous advances have been made in hearing aid technology, including development of digital hearing aids with noise suppression algorithms. Patients with bilateral hearing loss benefit from binaural amplification, even if hearing in one ear is better than in the other ear. Studies have found that when only the poor ear is amplified, hearing thresholds in the better ear continue to worsen, whereas this pattern was not seen when both ears were amplified. Furthermore, sound localization is dependent, in part, on detection of interaural intensity differences that can be distorted by monaural amplification. Despite amplification, there are some patients with sensorineural hearing loss who continue to demonstrate poor speech recognition abilities. In such cases, a central auditory processing disorder may also be present. Patients with severe-profound unilateral sensorineural hearing loss and intact eighth nerve function, who have shown no measurable benefit from hearing aids, may be candidates for a cochlear implant. Cochlear implants are surgically implanted electrodes in the cochlea that electrically stimulate the auditory nerve to transmit auditory information to the brain.

There are multiple treatment options for patients with Meniere's disease, including medications, low-sodium diet, surgery, and gentamycin injection. For patients with retrocochlear pathologies, surgery is almost always the treatment of choice. A potential complication of such surgery is damage to the auditory and/or facial nerve. The likelihood of this occurring is largely a function of the size and placement of the tumor.

Mixed Hearing Loss

The combination of a conductive and sensorineural hearing loss is referred to as mixed hearing loss. In this case, air conduction thresholds are greater than bone conduction thresholds, and both are increased relative to normal thresholds. This pattern can be seen in the elderly patient with an established sensorineural hearing loss who then develops an ear infection that further decreases their air conduction thresholds. In general, the conductive portion of a mixed hearing loss is treated first (as described above). Once the air-bone gap has closed and thresholds are stable, the degree of sensorineural hearing loss can be reevaluated and remediation options determined.

Patients' hearing can be screened at bedside or in the physician's exam room using a portable audiometer or tuning fork tests. Tuning fork tests have long been used by neurologists to screen patients for hearing loss and are part of the neurological exam. Tuning forks generate tones of a single frequency. Three tuning fork tests are commonly used: the Rinne, the Weber, and the Schwabach. The Rinne test compares patients' hearing sensitivity by air and bone conduction to identify a sensorineural hearing loss (positive Rinne) or conductive hearing loss (negative Rinne). This is accomplished by asking patients to report whether the tone is louder when the tuning fork is held up to the outer ear as compared with when it is held against the bone (mastoid) behind the same ear. If patients judge the tone emitted by bone conduction to be the louder of the two (negative Rinne) this is consistent with a conductive hearing loss. A positive Rinne occurs in patients with normal hearing as well as patients with sensorineural hearing loss.

The Schwabach test is a bone conduction test that compares the hearing of the patient with that of the clinician. The patient responds by signaling when the tone is no longer audible. The clinician then places the tuning fork against his/her own mastoid and notes the length of time (seconds) the sound remains audible. A normal Schwabach is when both patient and clinician stop hearing the tone at the same time. A diminished Schwabach is when the patient stops hearing the tone before the clinician and is suggestive of a sensorineural hearing loss. An obvious limitation of this particular tuning fork test is the assumption that the clinician has normal hearing.

The Weber test is a lateralization test in which the patient determines whether the tone is heard in either ear or at midline. The tuning fork stem is placed at midline on the patient's forehead. Patients with normal hearing or a symmetrical hearing loss of the same type will hear the tone at midline. The tone will lateralize to the ear with a unilateral conductive hearing loss. In the case of a unilateral sensorineural hearing loss, the tone will lateralize to the good ear. Tuning fork tests are useful for screening patients with possible hearing loss. However, they should not be substituted for a hearing test since they cannot provide information about the degree of hearing loss. Moreover, tuning forks only test a single, usually low, frequency, thereby potentially missing hearing losses at other frequencies. Furthermore, the interpretation of tuning fork tests can be confounded by a number of factors, including the presence of a mixed hearing loss and lack of standardized test instructions.

DIAGNOSIS AND TREATMENT OF ACQUIRED AUDITORY PROCESSING DISORDERS

Acquired auditory processing disorders are associated with the disruption of central auditory function. Although this can occur at any level of the central auditory system, it is perhaps most clearly seen in left hemisphere stroke (lesion) patients. Two types of auditory disorder are associated with focal cortical dysfunction: receptive aphasia and auditory agnosia.

Receptive (Auditory) Aphasias

The hallmark of receptive aphasia is the impairment of language comprehension—in particular, spoken language comprehension. Receptive aphasia has traditionally been associated with lesions of the posterior perisylvian region, including the temporal and parietal lobes. We will discuss three types of receptive aphasia: Wernicke's aphasia, transcortical sensory aphasia, and the receptive component of global aphasia.

Wernicke's Aphasia

Wernicke's aphasia is characterized by the severe impairment of spoken and written language comprehension, with fluent speech output. In addition to poor comprehension, Wernicke's aphasics also have impaired repetition and naming. Although their speech output is fluent, the productions of Wernicke's aphasics are usually meaningless, with numerous phonological and semantic paraphasias. Patients with Wernicke's aphasia cannot monitor their own speech output for meaning or phonological accuracy. As a result, they may incorporate neologisms (invented words) into their spoken speech. Traditionally, Wernicke's aphasia has been associated with lesions of the posterior perisylvian region, including the temporal and parietal lobes. In most cases, Wernicke's area (Brodmann's area 22) in the posterior temporal lobe is implicated (Naeser & Hayward, 1978). Auditory association cortex forms part of Wernicke's area, thereby accounting for the presence of phoneme decoding disorders seen in many patients with Wernicke's aphasia. Not all Wernicke's aphasics, however, have impaired phonological abilities, as reported by Blumstein and colleagues (1977). Wernicke's aphasia has also been associated with subcortical lesions (Naeser et al., 1982).

Clinical diagnosis of Wernicke's aphasia is based on patients' performance on receptive language tests or on subtests of standardized aphasia test batteries, such as the Boston Diagnostic Aphasia Examination (Goodglass & Kaplan, 1972), the Western Aphasia Battery (Kertesz, 1982), or the European Aachen Aphasia Test (Huber, Poeck, Weniger, & Willmes,

1983). In addition to testing patients' language comprehension abilities, it is important to evaluate patients' phonological processing abilities, since this lower-level auditory language processing ability may also be compromised. There are numerous clinical tests designed to evaluate phonological processing. Most of these tests require the listener to discriminate pairs of words that are phonologically contrasted (for example, *pat-bat*) or to identify auditory stimuli by repetition, orthographic matching, or picture matching. It is also important to assess the auditory processing abilities of most aphasic patients, not just receptive aphasics, since more subtle auditory processing disorders, including phonological deficits, may be present (Blumstein et al., 1977).

Transcortical Sensory Aphasia

This rare form of receptive aphasia is characterized by impaired auditory comprehension, with intact repetition and fluent speech. Comprehension of written and spoken speech is usually severely impaired, and patients may also be echolalic. The sparing of repetition distinguishes transcortical sensory aphasia from other receptive language aphasias and is thought to reflect the disruption of access from intact phonology to otherwise intact lexical-semantic processing. This view is supported by patients' relatively intact performance on phonological tasks, despite poor auditory comprehension. Although patients' speech output is typically fluent, it is often characterized by paraphasias. Likewise, patients' ability to read aloud may be relatively spared despite poor reading comprehension. This rare receptive aphasia has traditionally been associated with relatively circumscribed lesions that spare Wernicke's area and isolate it from more posterior language areas (Geschwind, Quadfasel, & Segarra, 1968; Kertesz, Sheppard, & MacKenzie, 1982). However, recent studies have also identified transcortical sensory aphasia in patients with frontal lobe lesions and/or lesions of Wernicke's area (Otsuki et al., 1998; Boatman, Gordon, Hart, Selnes, & Miglioretti, 2000). The differential diagnosis of transcortical sensory aphasia from other receptive aphasias is based largely on the sparing of repetition. Transcortical sensory aphasia is further distinguished from other transcortical aphasias by the combination of impaired auditory comprehension and fluent speech output.

Global Aphasia

The patient with global aphasia has both receptive and expressive language disorders. The receptive component of global aphasia is similar to a Wernicke's aphasia. The language comprehension deficits of patients with global aphasia may be less severe than their expressive deficits. In most cases phonological processing is also compromised. Traditionally, global aphasia has been associated with damage to the anterior and posterior language areas (Hayward, Naeser, & Zatz, 1977; Kertesz, Harlock, & Coates, 1979). However, there are also reports of global aphasia with sparing of Wernicke's area (Mazzochi & Vignolo, 1979; Basso, Lecours, Moreshini, & Vanier, 1985; Vignolo, Boccardi, & Caverni, 1986). In a number of these cases, subcortical involvement was documented, suggesting that receptive aphasia is not exclusively associated with posterior cortical lesions.

Current aural rehabilitation therapies designed for patients with receptive aphasia focus largely on the recovery of lexical-semantic information. Aural rehabilitation is usually implemented by a speech pathologist or audiologist. Rehabilitation therapy for patients with Wernicke's aphasia may begin with common semantic categories, such as those involved in everyday activities. The initial goal is often improvement of patient's single-word comprehension, followed by introduction of increasingly more complex spoken language structures (phrases). Examples of therapies for semantic impairments are described in chapters 9 and 12 in this volume. Because transcortical sensory aphasia is usually transient in nature, aural rehabilitation therapy may not be particularly useful. For patients who also have phonological processing disorders, therapies designed to improve their phoneme decoding skills can be incorporated. There are now a number of aural therapy programs, including software programs, designed to improve patients' phonological processing skills. Typically these programs focus on improving the listener's ability to decode speech sounds (phonemes) from the incoming acoustic signal, to discriminate them from other similar phonemes, and to identify them by their corresponding orthographic representations or by use of pictures. For example, the listener hears a "b" sound and is then asked to point to a picture of an object beginning with that sound (for example, bat) from among several phonological foils (for example, cat). With recent improvements in signal processing algorithms, most aural rehabilitation programs that are available for computer have audio capabilities. Speech reading (lip reading) may also be helpful for the patient with phonological processing disorders. In contrast to patients with auditory agnosias, modified speech rates have not been found to be particularly useful for improving the speech understanding abilities of receptive aphasics (Blumstein, Katz, Goodglass, Shrier, & Dworetsky, 1985). Although the potentially confounding effects of spontaneous recovery make it difficult to assess the effect of rehabilitation programs during the early stages of language recovery, continued functional recovery after the first year of onset has been attributed, in large part, to the effects of therapy (Kertesz, 1997). It is important that the therapies be individualized to each patient to capitalize on their strengths and to focus on their particular areas of impairment.

Auditory Agnosia

Auditory agnosia is characterized by the impaired ability to recognize sound, despite otherwise normal peripheral hearing. Three forms of auditory agnosia have been identified: auditory verbal agnosia (pure word deafness), auditory sound agnosia (nonverbal agnosia), and cortical deafness.

Auditory Verbal Agnosia

Also called pure word deafness, auditory verbal agnosia refers to a selective impairment in the ability to recognize or understand spoken speech. In contrast to transcortical sensory aphasia, repetition and phonological processing are always severely impaired in patients with pure word deafness. Although most patients can differentiate speech from nonspeech or environmental sounds, they often report that speech, including their own, sounds like a foreign language (Albert & Bear, 1974). In contrast, the ability to interpret intonation and other affective aspects of speech may be spared in pure word deafness (Coslett, Brashear, & Heilman, 1984). Despite impaired auditory comprehension, written comprehension and oral reading usually remain intact. Sparing of written language comprehension distinguishes pure word deafness from Wernicke's aphasia and points to an underlying auditory processing disorder rather than a language disorder (aphasia). However, because many of these patients also demonstrate aspects of Wernicke's aphasia, there is disagreement as to whether pure word deafness is a separate syndrome or a component of Wernicke's aphasia.

Pure word deafness is usually associated with bilateral lesions of auditory cortex, with some sparing of primary cortex, or with deep unilateral left hemisphere lesions that disrupt auditory radiations from the thalamus and contralateral auditory cortex. Auditory evoked potentials (BAER, ABR) are typically normal (but see also Auerbach, Allard, Naeser, Alexander, & Albert, 1982), although results of late auditory potentials are variable.

Studies of the auditory processing disorders associated with pure word deafness have revealed two subtypes: a phonological decoding deficit or a deficit in earlier (prephonologic) auditory temporal processing (Chocholle, Chedru, Bolte, Chain, & Lhermitte, 1975; Auerbach et al., 1982). Pure word deafness patients with unilateral left hemisphere lesions appear to have the phonological decoding deficits as evidenced by their reported difficulty discriminating consonant contrasts but not vowel contrasts (Saffran, Marin, & Yeni-Komshan, 1976; Denes & Semenza, 1975). Conversely, a detailed case study of a patient with consecutive bilateral temporal lobe lesions revealed a more general impairment of auditory temporal acuity, including inability to detect rapidly sequenced auditory events (Auerbach et al., 1982). It is important to note that although patients with pure word deafness show severe impairments in the processing of spoken language, their ability to process other sounds, including environmental sounds, may also be affected, just to a lesser degree.

Auditory Sound Agnosia (Nonverbal Auditory Agnosia)

Nonverbal agnosia refers to the inability to recognize previously familiar environmental sounds despite normal peripheral hearing and no evidence of aphasia. This disorder is more rare than pure word deafness, but may also be underreported since speech comprehension remains intact and recognition of environmental sounds is not routinely evaluated. In addition to impairments in recognition of environmental sounds, patients with auditory sound agnosia may also have impaired pitch discrimination (Spreen, Benton, & Fincham, 1965). When patients show a selective impairment in the processing of musical information (for example, pitch, prosody), it is referred to as auditory amusia. A recent study of two such patients revealed normal performance on receptive language tasks, phonological decoding tasks, and tests of environmental sound identification, with selective impairment of melody and musical instrument identification (Peretz, Kolinsky, & Tramo, 1994). Although most cases of auditory sound agnosia are associated with bilateral involvement (Albert, Sparks, von Stockert, & Sax, 1972), it may also occur with a deep unilateral right hemisphere lesion (Spreen et al., 1965). Despite normal auditory comprehension, some patients with auditory sound agnosia have difficulty on phoneme decoding tasks, suggesting that a less severe auditory verbal processing deficit may also be present (Bauer & Rubens, 1979).

Cortical Deafness

Cortical deafness refers to the severe impairment in the ability to recognize sounds, whether verbal or nonverbal, despite normal peripheral hearing abilities and otherwise normal language abilities (Vignolo, 1969). The patient with cortical deafness can understand written speech and has intact speech output. These patients typically exhibit indifference to sound, and may report that they are deaf (Michel, Peronnet, & Schott, 1980). Cortical deafness is commonly associated with bilateral lesions of the temporal lobes, including Heschl's gyrus, and/or bilateral damage to auditory radiations. Cortical auditory evoked potentials are usually significantly abnormal or absent, while BAER (ABR) testing may yield largely normal results, indicating normal transmission of auditory information up through the lower brainstem. It has been suggested that bilateral absence of late auditory potentials serve as a clinical criterion for diagnosis of cortical deafness (Michael et al., 1980).

Because there is often spontaneous recovery from auditory agnosia, especially pure word deafness (Kertesz, 1997), long-term aural rehabilitation therapy may not be indicated. In such cases where rehabilitation is indicated, a language-based therapy is likely not to be as useful as a program that focuses more directly on lower-level auditory processing abilities. For example, if these patients have difficulty processing frequency information, they may benefit from pitch discrimination training using steady state and frequency-modulated tones. Similarly, patients who have difficulty detecting auditory events that occur in rapid succession (a feature of spoken speech) may benefit from a number of recent software programs that train patients to detect auditory stimuli that are systematically sequenced at shorter and shorter intervals. Patients with auditory agnosia have also shown improved auditory comprehension at slower speech rates (Neisser, 1976). Emphasis on speech reading (lip reading) skills may further supplement information lost during auditory processing by exploiting visual articulatory cues (Auerbach et al. 1982). Because written language comprehension is usually spared, this modality can be used for communication as well as for reestablishing access to lexical-semantic information from audition. Finally, auditory comprehension can often be improved in patients with auditory agnosia by increasing reliance on contextual information.

In addition to focal cortical dysfunction, auditory processing disorders have been associated with more diffuse cortical neuropathologies, such as Alzheimer's disease. The main pathological changes associated with Alzheimer's disease include accumulation of microscopic neurofibrillary tangles and amyloid plaques, which tend to involve primarily the temporal lobe and hippocampus. It is not surprising, therefore, that patients with Alzheimer's disease show evidence of impaired spoken language comprehension relatively early in the course of the disease. It has been suggested that the language comprehension deficits of Alzheimer's patients resemble those of patients with transcortical sensory aphasia or, in the later stages, Wernicke's aphasia (Murdoch, Chenery, Wilks, & Boyle, 1987; Cummings, Benson, Hill, & Read, 1985). Impaired auditory comprehension coupled with evidence of phonological paraphasias in the speech productions of Alzheimer's patients raise the question of an underlying receptive phonological processing deficit. This issue was addressed in a study of Alzheimer's patients by Biassou and colleagues (1995), who found no clear evidence of phoneme discrimination/perception deficits.

Another source of cortical dysfunction associated with auditory processing disorders is epilepsy. Landau-Kleffner, while largely a childhood epilepsy syndrome, is characterized initially by the disproportionate impairment of language comprehension as compared with expressive language abilities (Landau & Kleffner, 1957; Rapin, Mattis, Rowan, & Golden, 1977). Phoneme decoding disorders are frequently exhibited in adult patients with temporal lobe epilepsy. Furthermore, while their auditory language comprehension may be largely normal in good listening conditions, studies have shown evidence of central auditory processing disorders when the listening environment or acoustic signal is degraded. It may be that the presence of abnormal cortical electrical activity adds "noise" to the system, rendering it less capable of compensating, as normal subjects readily do, for the additional loss of redundancy in the acoustic signal.

NEURAL PLASTICITY IN THE ADULT AUDITORY SYSTEM

Traditionally, neural plasticity was associated with the developing nervous system and thought to decrease inversely with age (Lenneberg, 1967; Krashen & Harshman, 1972). Recent studies, however, have demonstrated that neural plasticity continues to be evident in the mature auditory system. Changes in the organization of auditory cortex following cochlear hearing loss have been documented in the adult cat and primate systems (Rajan, Irvine, Wise, & Heil, 1993; Schwaber, Garraghty, & Kaas, 1993). In such cases, auditory cortex reorganizes to become maximally responsive to the remaining intact cochlear frequencies.

The organization of adult auditory cortex also appears to be responsive to the effects of auditory training. A study of adult owl monkeys showed that auditory training resulted in modifying the tonotopic organization of auditory cortex (Recanzone, Schreiner, & Merzenich, 1993). Subsequent studies of auditory training effects have been conducted in humans. In one such study, normal hearing adult subjects underwent six hours of discrimination training on two normally indistinguishable variants of /da/ (Kraus et al., 1995). Using a cortical auditory potential known as mismatch negativity (MMN), subjects were tested before and after exposure to auditory training. Upon completion of training, subjects were able to reliably discriminate between the two variants of /da/ on behavioral tests. Pre- versus post-training comparisons of the MMN latencies and amplitudes showed a decreased latency and increased amplitude as a function of training suggesting modification of the auditory neural response system.

A recent functional MRI (fMRI) study of an adult right-handed patient with acute unilateral right-ear hearing loss showed evidence of increased fMRI activation of the contralateral auditory cortex within one year of onset (Bilecen et al., 2000). This suggests that the entire central auditory system can be reorganized in the event that one of the major auditory input pathways is disrupted.

These studies suggest that neural plasticity in the auditory system extends into adulthood. Moreover, sustained neural plasticity allows modification of the adult auditory system by training and aural rehabilitation.

REFERENCES

Albert, M. L., & Bear, D. (1974). Time to understand: a case study of word deafness with reference to the role of time in auditory comprehension. Brain, 97, 373-384.

Albert, M. L., Sparks, R., von Stockert, T., & Sax, D. (1972). A case study of auditory agnosia: Linguistic and non-linguistic processing. Cortex, 8, 427-433.

Auerbach, S. H., Allard, T., Naeser, M., Alexander, M. P., & Albert, M. L. (1982). Pure word deafness: Analysis of a case with bilateral lesions and a defect at the prephonemic level. Brain, 105, 271-300.

Basso, A., Lecours, A. R., Morashini, S., & Vanier, M. (1985). Anatomoclinical correlations of the aphasias as defined through computerized tomography: Exceptions. Brain and Language, 26, 201-229.

Bauer, R. M., & Reubens, A. B. (1979). Clinical neuropsychology. New York: Oxford University Press.

Biassou, N., Grossman, M., Onishi, K., Mickanin, J., Hughes E., et al. (1995). Phonologic processing deficits in Alzheimer's disease. Neurology, 45, 2165-2169.

Bilecen, D., Seifritz, E., Radu, E. W., Schmid, N., Wetzel, S., et al. (2000). Cortical reorganization after acute unilateral hearing loss traced by fMRI. Neurology, 54, 765-767.

Blumstein, S. E., Baker, E., & Goodglass, H. (1977). Phonological factors in auditory comprehension in aphasia. Neuropsychologia, 15, 19-30.

Blumstein, S. E., Katz, B., Goodglass, H., Shrier, R., & Dworetsky, B. (1985). The effects of slowed speech on auditory comprehension in aphasia. Brain and Language, 24, 246-265.

Boatman, D., Gordon, B., Hart, J., Selnes, O., Miglioretti, D., et al. (2000). Transcortical sensory aphasia: Revised and revisited. Brain, 123, 1634-1642.

Chocholle, R., Chedru, F., Bolte, M. C., Chain, F., & Lhermitte, F. (1975). Etude psychoacoustique d'un cas de "surdite corticale." Neuropsychologia, 13, 163-172.

Coslett, H. B., Brashear, H. R., & Heilman, K. M. (1984). Pure word deafness after bilateral primary auditory cortex infarcts. Neurology, 34, 347-352.

Cummings, J. L., Benson, D. F., Hill, M. A., & Read, S. (1985). Aphasia in dementia of the Alzheimer type. Neurology, 35, 394-397.

Denes, G., & Semenza, C. (1975). Auditory modality-specific anomia: Evidence from a case of pure word deafness. Cortex, 11, 401-411.

Geschwind, N., Quadfasel, F. A., & Segarra, J. M. (1968). Isolation of the speech area. Neuropsychologia, 6, 327-340.

Goodglass, H., & Kaplan, E. (1992). Assessment of aphasia and related disorders. Philadelphia: Lea and Febiger.

Hayward, R. W., Naeser, M. A., & Zatz, L. M. (1977). Cranial computed tomography in aphasia. Radiology, 123, 653-660.

Huber, W., Poeck, K., Weniger, D., & Willmes, K. (1983). Aachener-aphasie test. Gottingen: Hogrefe.

Josey, A. F., Glasscock, M. E., & Musiek, F. E. (1988). Correlation of ABR and medical imaging in patients with cerebellopontine angle tumors. The American Journal of Otology, 9, 12-16.

Kertesz, A., Harlock, W., & Coates, R. (1979). Computer tomographic localization of lesion size and prognosis in aphasia and nonverbal impairment. Brain and Language, 8, 34-50.

Kertesz, A. (1982). The Western aphasia battery. New York: Grune and Stratton.

Kertesz, A. (1997). Recovery of aphasia. In T. E. Feinburg & M. J. Farah (Eds.), Behavioral neurology and neuropsychology. New York: McGraw-Hill.

Kertesz, A., Sheppard, M. A., & MacKenzie, R. (1982). Localization in transcortical sensory aphasia. Archives of Neurology, 39, 475-478.

Krashen, S., & Harshman, R. (1972). Lateralization and the critical period. UCLA Work Papers Phonetics, 23, 13-21.

Kraus, N., McGee, T., Carrell, T. D., King, C., Tremblay, K., & Nicol, T. (1995). Central auditory system plasticity associated with speech discrimination training. Journal of Cognitive Neuroscience, 7, 25-32.

Landau, W. M., & Kleffner, F. R. (1957). Syndrome of acquired aphasia with convulsive disorder in children. Neurology, 10, 915-921.

Lenneberg, E. H. (1967). Biological foundations of language. New York: Wiley.

Martin, F. N. (1994). Introduction to audiology. Englewood Cliffs, NJ: Prentice Hall.

Mazzochi, F., & Vignolo, L. A. (1979). Localizations of lesions in aphasia: Clinical-CT correlations in stroke patients. Cortex, 15, 627-654.

Michel, J., Peronnet, F., & Schott, B. (1980). A case of cortical deafness: Clinical and electrophysiological data. Brain and Language, 10, 367-377.

Morrison, A. W., & Bundey, S. E. (1970). The inheritance of otosclerosis. *Journal of Laryngology and Otology, 84,* 921-932.

Murdoch, B. E., Chenery, H. J., Wilks, V., & Boyle, R. (1987). Language disorders in dementia of the Alzheimer type. *Brain and Language,* 31, 122-137.

Naeser, M. A, Alexander, M. P., Helm-Estabrooks, N., Levine, H. L., Laughlin, M. A., et al. (1982). Aphasia with predominantly subcortical lesion sites: Description of three capsular/putaminal aphasia syndromes. *Archives of Neurology, 39,* 2-14.

Naeser, M. A, & Hayward, R. W. (1978). Lesion localization in aphasia with cranial computed tomography and the B.D.A.E. *Neurology, 28,* 545-551.

Neisser, U. (1976). *Cognition and reality.* San Francisco: Freeman.

Otsuki, M., Soma, Y., Koyama, A., Yoshimura, N., Furkawa, H., & Tsuji, S. (1998). Transcortical sensory aphasia following left frontal infraction. *Journal of Neurology, 245,* 69-76.

Peretz, I., Kolinsky, R., Tramo, M., et al. (1994). Functional dissociations following bilateral lesions of auditory cortex. *Brain, 117,* 1283-1301.

Rajan, R., Irvine, D. R. F., Wise, L. Z., & Heil, P. (1993). Effect of unilateral partial cochlear lesions in adult cats on the representation of lesioned and unlesioned cochleas in primary auditory cortex. *Journal of Comparative Neurology, 338,* 17-49.

Rapin, I., Mattis, S., Rowan, A. J., & Golden, G. G. (1977). Verbal auditory agnosia in children. *Developmental Medicine and Child Neurology, 19,* 192-207.

Recanzone, G. H., Schreiner, C. E., & Merzenich, M. M. (1993). Plasticity in the frequency representation of primary auditory cortex following discrimination training in adult owl monkeys. *Journal of Neuroscience, 13,* 87-103.

Saffran, R., Marin, O., & Yeni-Komshan, G. (1976). An analysis of speech perception in word deafness. *Brain and Language, 3,* 209-228.

Schwaber, M. K., Garraghty, P. E., & Kaas, J. H. (1993). Neuroplasticity of the adult primate auditory cortex following cochlear hearing loss. *American Journal of Otology, 14,* 252-258.

Spreen, O., Benton, A. L., & Fincham, R. (1965). Auditory agnosia without aphasia. *Archives of Neurology, 13,* 84-92.

Vignolo, L. A. (1969). Auditory agnosia: a review and report of recent evidence. In A. L. Benton (Ed.), *Contributions to clinical neuropsychology.* Chicago: Aldine.

Vignolo, L. A., Boccardi, E., & Caverni, L. (1986). Unexpected CT-scan finding in global aphasia. *Cortex, 22,* 55-69.

Part 6

—

Sentence Processing

—

Sentence Comprehension Deficits: Independence and Interaction of Syntax, Semantics, and Working Memory

Randi C. Martin
Michelle Miller

Findings during the 1970s demonstrated impaired sentence comprehension in aphasic patients who had good single word comprehension (for example, Caramazza & Zurif, 1976; von Stockert & Bader, 1976). For example, a patient might understand the meanings of *girl, boy, kiss, red,* and *hair,* but be unable to determine for a sentence such as "The boy that the girl kissed had red hair" who is doing the kissing and who has red hair. Difficulties in establishing the roles played by nouns based on syntactic structure were found even for simple active and passive sentences such as "The cat was chasing the dog" or "The dog was chased by the cat" (Schwartz, Saffran, & Marin, 1980). These sentences are termed reversible, since either noun can play the role of agent (that is, person carrying out the action) or theme (that is, person or object being acted upon). The same patients did not have difficulty understanding sentences with similar structures that were nonreversible, such as "The car that the woman drove was an import" or "The apple was eaten by the boy." Thus, the patients were able to integrate word meanings into a sentence meaning when such could be done on the basis of semantic plausibility but were impaired when they had to use syntactic structure to understand the relations in the sentence. These findings generated a good deal of excitement among researchers in and outside the field of aphasia because they seemed to provide strong evidence for the disruption of a syntactic processing module that was independent of semantics (for example, see Caramazza & Berndt, 1978, Jackendoff, 1993, chap. 11). However, since these early studies, additional results have complicated the interpretation of these findings and their implications for sentence processing.

The early findings on sentence comprehension deficits seemed in tune with psycholinguistic theories of sentence processing from the 1960s that assumed a deterministic set of rules for parsing; that is, a set of rules such as phrase structure rules and transformations for assigning the syntactic structure to a sentence (for example, Fodor & Garrett, 1967). These rules were assumed to be purely syntactic in nature and were applied to a sequence of words on the basis of the syntactic category of the words (for example, noun, verb, adjective) and not on the basis of the meaning of the words. If the entire set of rules were disrupted due to brain damage, one would expect patients with such a deficit to perform poorly on any task involving syntactic processing. One influential paper hypothesized that Broca's aphasics demonstrated such a deficit in all aspects of syntactic processing, attributing both their agrammatic speech and difficulties understanding reversible sentences to a global deficit in syntactic parsing (Berndt & Caramazza, 1980). However, this proposal has encountered numerous difficulties. For one, dissociations have been found between agrammatic speech and syntactic comprehension difficulties (Miceli, Mazzucchi, Menn, & Goodglass, 1983). Also, several studies reported that aphasic patients showed a graded degree of disruption on sentence comprehension tasks depending on the difficulty of the syntactic structure, with patients generally performing much better on simple passive sentences than on more complex relative clause sentences (Caplan & Hildebrandt, 1988). Such findings might still be accounted for in terms of a syntactic deficit if it were hypothesized that different syntactic rules might be selectively affected by brain damage—with different patients having disruptions of different rules. Thus, good performance should be found on sentences not tapping these rules and chance performance on sentences involving these rules. However, other findings demonstrated that even for a given syntactic construction (for example, passive) a graded level of performance could be obtained across patients, with scores falling on a continuum between 100 percent performance and chance (Kolk & van Grunsven, 1985).

Other findings demonstrated that patients' apparent syntactic processing abilities might vary depending on the nature of the task. Linebarger, Schwartz, and Saffran (1983) showed that aphasic patients with near chance performance on reversible passive sentences using a sentence-picture matching paradigm might perform at a much higher level when asked to make grammaticality judgments (that is, judge whether a sentence was grammatically acceptable). These authors hypothesized that the patients' difficulties were not with syntactic parsing at all, but rather with the mapping between the grammatical roles that entities played in a sentence and their thematic roles with respect to the verb (that is, roles such as agent, theme, and recipient). For example, for a sentence such as "The car that the truck splashed was green," the patient might be able to parse this sentence into the main and subordinate clauses and identify *truck* as the grammatical subject of *splash* and *car* as the grammatical object of *splash*. However, he or she would be unable to map *car* onto the thematic role of agent and *truck* onto the grammatical role of theme. (See further discussion of mapping deficit hypothesis below.)

In contrast to the early emphasis on purely syntactic factors in sentence parsing, more recent linguistic and psycholinguistic research has uncovered the importance of lexical and semantic factors. For example, Spivey-Knowlton and Sedivy (1995) showed that preferences for attachment of a prepositional phrase to a verb or to a noun (as in the ambiguous "He saw the girl with the binoculars") depended on whether the verb was a perception verb (*saw*) or an action verb (for example, *hit*). Other recent findings indicate that lexical-semantic and even discourse-level semantics can influence initial parsing decisions (Trueswell, Tanenhaus, & Garnsey, 1994; Spivey & Tanenhaus, 1998; van Berkum, Brown, & Hagoort, 1999). For example, consider sentences beginning with "The evidence examined . . . ," versus "The woman examined . . . " In both cases, *examined* could be either the main verb or part of a reduced relative clause construction (for example, "The evidence examined by the lawyer . . . ," or "The woman examined by the lawyer . . . " Trueswell and colleagues (1994) found that both the likelihood of the initial noun as an agent and its likelihood as a theme of the verb influenced whether initial parsing decisions favored the main verb versus reduced relative interpretation of the verb. Thus, in these examples, *examined* would be more likely to be given the reduced relative interpretation when *evidence* is the head noun compared to when *woman* is the head noun, since *evidence* is unlikely as an agent of *examine*. The emerging consensus is that syntactic and semantic systems generate constraints independently (Boland & Cutler, 1996; Trueswell & Tanenhaus, 1994; but see MacDonald, Pearlmutter, & Seidenberg, 1994) but that many constraints (syntactic, lexical, semantic, and discourse) act simultaneously to determine initial sentence interpretation.

These findings on the influence of nonsyntactic factors on syntactic parsing do not rule out the possibility that *knowledge* of general syntactic constraints is represented autonomously from lexically specific syntactic information and semantic information. However, they do indicate that during sentence *processing*, syntactically based rules do not play some overriding role that is unaffected by other sources of information. The findings also suggest that at points of ambiguity, different possible structures may be activated in parallel with different strengths, with the strength being determined by several factors. One example of a model assuming representational independence but processing interaction is Boland's (1997) concurrent model. (See figure 16.1) This model assumes that all of the syntactic structures consistent with the input are generated in parallel as each word is processed, with the strength of the different structures varying based on frequencies associated with lexically specific information. Semantic interpretations are constructed concurrently, assigning noun constituents to likely roles based on lexical and pragmatic information. The output of the syntactic system also feeds into the semantic system. When more than one syntactic structure is possible, semantic information is used immediately to select the most likely syntactic structure. In the example above of a sentence beginning with "The evidence examined . . . ," the syntactic system would generate both the main verb and reduced relative interpretation of *examined* with greater weight given to the main verb reading because of the infrequency of reduced relative constructions. Simultaneously, the semantic system would be generating plausible relations among *evidence* and *examined*, with much greater weight given to *evidence* as theme than as an agent. After the two possible syntactic analyses feed into the semantic system, the reduced relative interpretation would be selected; that is, the interpretation allowing for the "theme" interpretation of *evidence*. The selection of the reduced elative interpretation in this example reflects the greater strength of the theme interpretation of *evidence* generated by the semantic system, which allows it to override the main verb interpretation of *examined* generated by the syntactic system. In contrast, for the sentence beginning with "The woman examined . . . ," the main verb interpretation would be favored because the greater strength given to the main verb interpretation of *examined* by the syntactic system allows it to override the relatively weak interpretation of *woman* as theme generated by the semantic system (relatively weak, because the theme and agent roles are approximately equally likely for *woman*). Thus, in this model, syntactic and semantic information *are* represented independently, but the products of these different analyses are integrated as each word is processed.

A similar approach has been advocated by Spivey and Tanenhaus (1998). In their model of the interpretation of these main verb/reduced relative ambiguities, they have proposed a

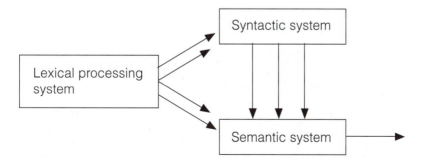

Figure 16.1. Boland's (1997) concurrent model.

competitive integration model. (See figure 16.2). Input from several different domains feeds into the interpretation of the ambiguity (that is, verb tense, syntactic bias for main clause, discourse information, and, in the case of reading, parafoveal information). (Presumably, thematic role information would also contribute, but this was not the focus of this study.) Within each domain, the different alternatives compete with each other, with activation of one leading to inhibition of the other. The strength of the influence of different domains on the syntactic interpretation would depend on previous experience (for example, the frequency with which *examined* is the past tense in an active construction versus a past participle in a passive construction).

These recent approaches to sentence parsing are termed "constraint-based" because they allow for several different types of constraints to be integrated in determining a syntactic interpretation. Both of the models allow for variation in the strength of the outputs of different modules or domains. As has been assumed in other areas of cognitive processing, brain damage might be assumed to weaken the output from one or more modules, or equivalently decrease the connection strength between different nodes in an interactive activation framework. That is, within each domain, processing may be disrupted in such a way that rather than failing to produce any output, the system instead produces weakened output. Thus, within Boland's model, if one assumed a weakening of the syntactic processing system, then the

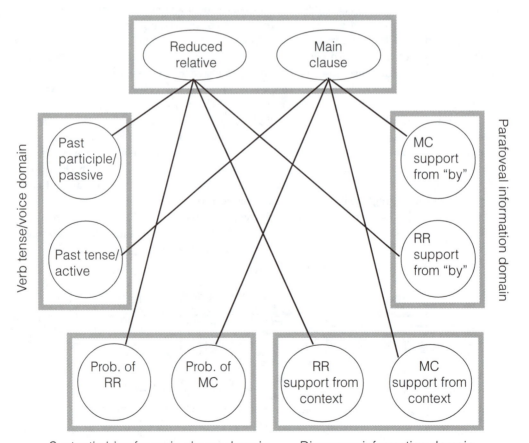

Figure 16.2. Spivey and Tanenhaus's (1998) constraint-based model of comprehension.

correct syntactic alternatives might still be generated but with reduced strengths for each. According to these approaches it should be possible to find patients who have selective deficits in different domains of sentence processing; for example, in generating syntactic structures or in using semantic information in computing thematic roles. However, within each of these domains, one would not necessarily expect to find either complete preservation or complete disruption of processing, given that a weakening of the output of one system should be possible. Also, these approaches imply that the influence of the weakened system on sentence interpretation would depend on the strength of the outputs of other systems. For sentences with strong constraints coming from other *systems*, the output of the weakened system *would likely* be completely overridden, while in the absence of such strong constraints, the output of the weakened system might have some influence on the sentence interpretation.

INDEPENDENCE OF SYNTAX AND SEMANTICS

Preserved Syntax and Disrupted Semantics

Evidence for selective preservation of syntax in the presence of semantic disruptions comes from a number of studies of patients with Alzheimer's dementia or progressive aphasia (Breedin & Saffran, 1999; Hodges, Patterson, & Tyler, 1994; Kempler, Curtiss, & Jackson, 1987; Schwartz & Chawluk, 1990; Schwartz, Marin, & Saffran, 1979). One example of this dissociation comes from a study by Hodges and colleagues (1994) of patient PP, a semantic dementia case who showed impaired performance on a variety of semantic tasks, including picture naming, picture-word matching, and attribute judgments. PP's syntactic abilities were assessed in a word monitoring paradigm, which has been used extensively by Tyler (see Tyler, 1992). In this paradigm, subjects are given a target word followed by a sentence and asked to respond as soon as they hear the target word in the sentence. A number of studies by Tyler and colleagues have demonstrated that subjects' times to detect the target words depend on the semantic and syntactic well formedness of the sentence materials. PP's times to detect a target word were faster for grammatically well formed sentences compared to sentences with scrambled word order, consistent with previous findings from normal subjects (Tyler, 1992). However, unlike normal subjects, PP showed no such reaction time advantage for semantically and grammatically well formed prose relative to grammatically well formed but semantically anomalous prose; that is, she failed to benefit from semantic meaningfulness. This pattern of findings, in which there is an effect of grammatical structure but not of semantic meaningfulness, suggests that PP's deficit selectively affected her ability to process semantic information during sentence comprehension while sparing her ability to process syntax.

The evidence from Hodges and colleagues indicates that patients with severe semantic deficits may be able to access the syntactic properties of individual words (for example, word class) and may be able to process phrase structure. Work by Schwartz and colleagues (1979) and Breedin and Saffran (1999) further suggests that such patients can also carry out thematic role assignments based on sentence structures and verb argument structure. They used modified versions of standard sentence-picture matching tasks in which patients saw two animals involved in some semantically reversible action (for example, a tiger chasing a lion), then heard a sentence describing the action and were asked to point to one of the animals in the sentence, either the agent or the theme (for example, "The lion was chased by the tiger. Show me lion"). Patients in these studies showed a preserved ability to indicate the correct animal when the sentence correctly described the action, but routinely chose the wrong animal when the sentence reversed the roles of the animals. For example, for the stimulus "The tiger was bitten by the lion. Show me lion" paired with a picture of a tiger biting a lion, the patient chose the tiger. Thus, these patients were not making their choices based on lexical-semantics, but instead based on the thematic role that the named entity played in the sentence. In this sentence, *lion* is the grammatical object of the *by* phrase, but plays the thematic role of agent. The patient chose the entity in the picture that appeared to be the agent of the verb. This ability to determine grammatical and thematic roles for noun entities was demonstrated for complex sentence structures including passive, subject cleft, and object cleft sentences. These results provide a dramatic demonstration that some patients with severe semantic deficits can process grammatical structure, including mapping of grammatical structure onto thematic roles, even when the semantics of single words *are* severely disrupted.

Other studies reported dissociations in the opposite direction—that is, with patients showing preserved semantic processing but impaired syntactic processing. Ostrin and Tyler (1995) reported a case (JG) who showed a marked disruption of all syntactic abilities together with relatively preserved lexical-semantic abilities. In a standard sentence-picture matching paradigm, he showed an asyntactic comprehension pattern with poor performance when the distracter picture depicted a reversal of agent and object, but good performance when the distracter picture included a lexical substitution. Unlike the patients reported in Linebarger et al. (1983), he performed poorly on a grammaticality judgment task. In on-line word and sentence processing tasks he also showed a dissociation between disrupted syntactic *and* preserved semantic processing. In a series of word monitoring tasks involving the processing of words in sentence contexts, he showed an insensitivity to a variety of grammatical violations—violations of subcategorization frame, violations of inflectional and derivational morphology, and, in a previous study, violations of word order (Tyler, 1992). However, like normal subjects he showed semantic priming in a lexical decision task. This case thus showed the reverse pattern as the case reported by Hodges and colleagues (1994) (described above) on a similar set of tasks.

Interactions between Syntax and Semantics

The data from brain-damaged patients suggest that at least some aspects of semantic and syntactic information are represented independently. However, as discussed earlier, such a conclusion does not imply that semantic and syntactic constraints do not interact during sentence processing. One might surmise that for some patients syntactic knowledge is weakened though not completely disrupted. Within Boland's (1997) model, brain injury might lessen the strength of all syntactic structures, with the result that the least frequent structures are most affected. If one assumes that the processes involved in assigning thematic roles based on semantic and pragmatic information are preserved in these patients, one might see that semantic factors override syntactic information in role assignment, particularly for less frequent syntactic structures. When semantic information provides weaker constraints, the influence of syntactic structure may appear.

Consistent with this idea, Saffran, Schwartz, and Linebarger (1998) report that aphasic patients (five Broca's, one conduction aphasic, and one transcortical motor aphasic) with asyntactic comprehension patterns on sentence-picture matching tasks also showed an exaggerated effect of semantic constraints on thematic role mapping in a sentence anomaly task. Two types of sentences were used: (1) verb constrained and (2) proposition based. In the verb-constrained sentences, one of the nouns was implausible as a filler of one thematic role of the verb but the other noun was plausible in either role. For example, in the implausible sentence "The cat barked at the puppy," a puppy can bark or be barked at, but a cat can only be barked at. In the proposition-based sentences, both nouns could fill either role; however, for the implausible versions, the overall proposition was implausible. For example, in the implausible sentence "The insect ate the robin," both robins and insects can eat and be eaten, but it is implausible for something as small as an insect to eat a robin. Normal controls were less accurate at detecting implausible sentences in the verb-constrained relative to the proposition-based condition (4.7 percent errors versus 1.3 percent errors, respectively), reflecting some tendency to interpret the implausible verb-constrained sentences by assigning nouns to their most semantically plausible slot, even though the syntax indicated otherwise. The patients showed an exaggeration of this disparity between the verb-constrained and proposition-based conditions (45.7 percent errors versus 22.9 percent errors, respectively), reflecting a large effect of thematic role plausibility on assignment of nouns to roles. Thus, for even a simple active sentence such as "The deer shot the hunter" the patients often said that the sentence was plausible, presumably because role assignments had been made on the basis of semantic constraints rather than on the basis of syntactic structure of the sentence. However, their relatively preserved performance on the proposition-based sentences indicates that these patients were not completely insensitive to syntactic structure. The results imply a weakened, though not totally disrupted, influence of syntactic structure and a stronger role of semantic influences on sentence comprehension, supporting a mapping deficit explanation for these patients.

Other evidence of an interaction between semantic and syntactic influences comes from Tyler's (1989) word monitoring studies of an agrammatic aphasic patient, DE, who had shown evidence in a previous study of difficulty in structuring prose materials syntactically (Tyler, 1985). Tyler's (1989) study showed that DE was sensitive to local syntactic violations (for example, "slow very kitchen") in sentences that were otherwise well formed syntactically, but semantically anomalous. However, for meaningful prose sentences, the patient's sensitivity to the local syntactic violations disappeared. Tyler concluded that for meaningful materials, the patient's analysis focused on the use of word meaning and pragmatic inference to construct an interpretation of the sentence, and made little use of at least some aspects of syntactic structure.

ASPECTS OF SYNTACTIC PROCESSING

Mapping between Grammatical and Thematic Roles

As discussed earlier, some patients demonstrating asyntactic comprehension on sentence-picture matching and enactment tasks have performed well on grammaticality judgment tasks. This dissociation has been attributed to a deficit in mapping between grammatical roles and thematic roles (Linebarger, 1990; Saffran & Schwartz, 1988). However, if patients were completely unable to carry out this mapping process, they should perform poorly on all sentence types, whether or not the sentence had a canonical S-V-O structure. In fact, although aphasic patients often do show some impairment in the comprehension of sentences with canonical word orders they typically show a greater impairment for noncanonical word orders—as in passive sentences and in cleft object and object-extracted relative clause sentences (Schwartz et al., 1980; Berndt, Mitchum, & Haendiges, 1996).

Perhaps some notion of "strength" of a syntactic analysis can be introduced here to help explain this pattern of results. As discussed earlier, recent models of sentence comprehension assume that multiple syntactic interpretations of an ambiguous string may be generated in parallel with different strengths assigned to each that depend on the frequency with which each is encountered. Although these models typically assume that these strengths are lexically specific (for example, Boland, 1997), some researchers have assumed that the frequencies of occurrence of different syntactic structures are encoded independently of particular lexical items, and these frequencies play a role in comprehension (Mitchell, Cuetos, Corley, & Brysbaert, 1996). Under this latter view, in even unambiguous sequences such as "The boy that the girl pushed" the assignment of boy to object position with respect to the embedded verb would have a relatively weak strength (in normal subjects as well as in patients) because of the overall infrequency of this type of object relative construction. One could further surmise that although syntactic analysis is being carried out by the patients, the strengths throughout the system have been weakened due to brain damage, a problem that combines with a mapping deficit to create particular difficulties in mapping for infrequently encountered structures.

This explanation thus assumes that these patients have two deficits rather than one. If, however, syntactic analysis and mapping are independent processes, then one might expect to find some patients who show a deficit only in the mapping process. A case demonstrating this pattern was reported by Breedin and Martin (1996) in their study of verb comprehension deficits. However, this patient's deficit was hypothesized to be due to a disruption in verb-specific information concerning the mapping between grammatical and thematic roles, rather than in an abstract mapping process. Thus, this patient is discussed in the next section, which is concerned with lexical deficits.

The Role of the Verb

Breedin and Martin (1996) reported on the case of LK, who performed at chance in choosing between two pictures to match a verb when the distracter picture depicted a "reverse-role" verb. Reverse-role pairs included verbs like *buy-sell, chase-flee,* and *borrow-lend,* where the thematic roles of the participants were the same but their mapping to grammatical roles with respect to the verb differed for the words within the pair. LK's poor performance on the reverse-role pairs could not be attributed to difficulty with semantically complex verbs, as he performed significantly better (92 percent correct) when asked to discriminate one of the reverse-role verbs from a semantically related verb that was equally complex. LK's difficulty seemed to be specifically in discriminating between verbs that had very similar semantic representations but different mappings between grammatical and thematic roles, which Breedin and Martin attributed to disruptions affecting the representations of particular verbs. In the case of the verbs *lend* and *borrow,* for example, LK appears to know that these verbs imply that someone owns some object and that this owner allows someone else to temporarily take possession, but lacks the knowledge that in the case of *lend* the agent role is assigned to the permanent owner, whereas in *borrow* the agent is the person temporarily taking possession. (See also Byng, 1988; Jones, 1984.)

Berndt, Haendiges, Mitchum, and Sandson (1997) have provided evidence that difficulties with verb representation may underlie some patients' difficulty in comprehending reversible sentences. In their study, aphasic patients who showed worse verb than noun retrieval in single word and sentence production also showed comprehension deficits for reversible relative to nonreversible sentences. Patients who showed better verb than noun retrieval or equivalent noun and verb retrieval performed well on comprehension of both reversible and nonreversible sentences.

Disruptions of Specific Aspects of Syntactic Parsing

Few of the case studies in aphasia to date begin with linguistic theory and a specific processing model as the basis for documenting possible dissociations between knowledge of different types of linguistic rules or categories.[1] An exception in this regard are the cases reported by Caplan and Hildebrandt (1988) and Caplan, Hildebrandt, and Evans (1987). These researchers examined sentence processing deficits from the point of view of Chomsky's (1982) government and binding theory, comparing patients' comprehension of sentences with and without referential dependencies. In their studies, referential dependencies refer to noun phrases that depend on the linkage with another noun phrase for their interpretation—such as the linkage between a

---

[1]It has been more often the case that group studies on agrammatism have used linguistic theory to generate hypotheses about the locus of deficits (for example, Grodzinsky, 1995; Kean, 1977).

reflexive and its referent or between a "trace" and the noun phrase that was moved from that position. (A "trace" is a construct from linguistic theory that indicates the position that a noun phrase has been moved from during a transformation. For instance, in a sentence such as "That's the boy that the girl liked," it is assumed that *boy* plays the role of object with respect to the verb *liked* in the relative clause, but has been moved out of this deep structure position to its surface structure position in the main clause. This movement is hypothesized to leave behind a trace that links it from its position in the main clause to this empty position in the relative clause.)

In the Caplan et al. (1987) study, patient KG was tested on a wide range of sentence types in order to assess his ability to process sentences with moved elements (and traces) and sentences with other types of referential dependencies. KG showed a striking deficit on an enactment task for many of the structures involving moved elements. However, his performance was affected by the complexity of the sentence involving moved elements—with good performance for cleft object sentences with transitive verbs and two nouns and poorer performance for cleft object sentences with dative verbs and three nouns and subject-object relative clauses. Also, he performed well on simple sentences involving either missing subjects (termed PRO) or reflexives, but he performed poorly on sentences combining both. (PRO, like trace, is a hypothetical empty element. It differs from a trace in that no movement from a deep structure position is presumed to be involved with PRO. The term *PRO* is used because the empty element acts like a pronoun referring back to an entity earlier in the sentence.) This effect of complexity rules out the possibility that KG has a complete disruption of knowledge of, for instance, the processing of empty noun phrases. Caplan and colleagues thus interpreted this pattern of results as indicating a capacity limitation specific to syntactic parsing, hypothesizing that several factors contribute to capacity demands during parsing, including: (1) having to postulate empty noun phrases (relative to the processing of overt noun phrases), (2) having to hold a noun phrase without a thematic roles assignment while assigning thematic roles to other noun phrases, and (3) searching over a long distance in the syntactic structure to determine the mapping of referential dependencies. Although KG could handle one of these capacity demands, when two or more combined, his performance broke down. It should be noted that KG's capacity constraint for syntactic parsing could not be attributed to a general verbal memory span deficit, as his performance on a variety of span tasks was within normal range.

Caplan and Hildebrandt (1988) reported several other case studies of patients with mild or more severe deficits on their syntactic comprehension battery. Among the mildly impaired patients, the pattern of deficits across sentence types differed. For instance, patient GS had difficulty with a variety of relative clause constructions involving object movement, but not with sentences termed NP-raising constructions (for example, "Joe seems to Patrick to be praying") where the subject of the main verb (*Joe*) must be interpreted as the subject of the embedded verb phrase (*to be praying*). Patient JV showed the opposite dissociation. The highly specific deficits demonstrated in these patients suggest that there are different parsing operations associated with comprehending these various linguistic constructions that may be selectively affected by brain damage. Caplan and Hildebrandt (1988) make suggestions regarding what these operations might be (see pp. 198-199 for a summary), but they imply that parsing theories are not well specified enough to accommodate all of their findings, a state of affairs that persists even a decade after these papers appeared. Much of the psycholinguistic literature has focused on an analysis of a few sentence types with ambiguous structures in order to determine the role of lexical and semantic information in resolving these ambiguities. However, findings like those of Caplan and Hildebrandt (1988) would be very useful in helping to delineate different aspects of parsing. It should be noted, though, that some researchers have found that patient performance may vary substantially across different tasks (grammaticality judgment, sentence anomaly judgment, and word sentence-picture matching) (Linebarger et al., 1983; Cupples & Inglis, 1993). Thus, it would be important to determine if the results found by Caplan and Hildebrandt on a single task (that is, enactment) would generalize to other tasks.

WORKING MEMORY AND SENTENCE COMPREHENSION

The graded nature of syntactic processing deficits and the influence of semantic context on syntactic parsing has led some researchers to hypothesize that aphasic patients' comprehension deficits are not due to specific disruptions of parsing or other sentence processing mechanisms, but rather due to restrictions in working memory capacity (Kolk & van Grunsven, 1985; Miyake, Carpenter, & Just, 1994). However, as discussed previously, if one assumes that syntactic processing deficits are not all or none, these findings can be explained in terms of a syntactic deficit, but one which reflects a reduction in strength of syntactic contributions to sentence interpretation.

It is certainly the case, however, that some aphasic patients have restricted verbal short-term memory spans (De Renzi & Nichelli, 1975; Martin, 1987; N. Martin & Saffran, 1997). Whereas a normal subject might be able to retain a list of five or six words and seven or eight digits, aphasic patients often have spans that range from one to three words. Given that span tasks do not require syntactic processing, it is possible that the patients' restricted spans reflect a deficit independent of any syntactic deficit that could contribute to difficulties in sentence comprehension. A large body of data from normal subjects indicates that memory span performance relies heavily on the retention of phonological codes (Baddeley, Gathercole, & Papagno, 1998; Schweickert, Guentert, & Hersberger, 1990). At least some patients' restricted spans result from a specific deficit in retaining phonological codes. Arguments have been put forward that difficulty in retaining phonological codes could cause difficulties in syntactic processing. For instance, function words and grammatical markers often carry little in the way of semantic information, and consequently retaining such words during sentence comprehension may depend heavily on retaining phonological codes. In addition, it has been suggested that for certain sentence constructions, such as object-relative forms (for example, "The boy that the girl liked had red hair"), the role of certain entities in the sentence (for example, *boy*) cannot be determined until several subsequent words have been processed. Consequently, it might be necessary to hold these words in a phonological form until the role can be determined.

Despite the intuitive plausibility of such arguments, a number of findings have demonstrated that a phonological retention deficit does not appear to cause difficulties with processing syntactically complex sentences (see Martin, 1993; Martin & Romani, 1994, for discussion). Recently, Waters and Caplan (1999) have provided an overview of work from their lab and others that reinforces this view. These findings can be understood in terms of "immediacy of processing" during sentence processing. That is, when understanding a sentence, individuals access the syntactic and semantic specifications of each word as they hear them and construct syntactic and semantic interpretations of the sentence on a word-by-word basis, to the extent possible. What is important for sentence comprehension is that these semantic and syntactic interpretations be retained, not the phonological forms that gave rise to them. Thus, for example, for a sentence such as "The dog was chased by the cat," the listener would encode the function word *was* as a past auxiliary verb of a certain type, and upon hearing *chased* would know that a passive structure was being presented. Thus, there would be no need to maintain *was* in some uninterpreted phonological fashion for a long period before determining its role in a sentence. In the case of an object-relative sentence such as "The boy that the girl carried had red hair," it might be true that the role of the boy would remain indeterminate for a longer time, but the listener could retain *boy* in terms of its semantic and syntactic specifications rather than in terms of its phonological form.

Martin and colleagues have provided evidence that some types of span deficits do cause sentence comprehension difficulties for patients. However, these are deficits in retaining lexical-semantic information rather than in retaining phonological information. Patients with difficulty retaining lexical-semantic information have difficulty comprehending sentences in which the integration of individual word meanings into propositional representations is delayed. For instance, in a sentence with several prenominal adjectives such as "the rusty old red pail," the integration of the first adjective with the noun (*rusty* with *pail*) is delayed in comparison to a sentence in which the adjectives appear postnominally (for example, "The pail was old, red, and rusty . . . "). Thus, the meaning of the adjectives in the prenominal case must be maintained in a lexical-semantic form for some time prior to integration. Similar arguments can be made for sentences in which several nouns precede (for example, "The vase, the mirror, and the platter cracked") or follow a verb (for example, "The movers cracked the platter, the mirror, and the vase"). When the nouns precede the verb, their assignment to roles with respect to the verb is delayed in comparison to when the nouns appear after the verb. Martin and Romani (1994; Martin, 1995) reported that two patients whose span deficits appeared to be due to lexical-semantic retention deficits (ML and AB) scored near chance on a sentence anomaly task when two or three adjectives preceded a noun or two or three nouns preceded the verb, but performed at a much higher level when the adjectives followed the noun or the nouns followed the verb. (See table 16.1 for example stimuli and figure 16.3 for results.) A patient with a phonological retention deficit (EA) did not show this pattern, instead showing a pattern within the range of controls for the before/after manipulation.

An interesting contrast between retention of lexical-semantic information and syntactic information during sentence processing was uncovered in the Martin and Romani (1994) and Martin (1995a) studies. The patients with the lexical-semantic retention deficits were unaffected by the distance between two words that signaled that a sentence was ungrammatical (for example, near condition: "Susan didn't leave and neither was Mary" versus far condition: "Susan didn't leave, despite many hints from her tired hosts, and neither was Mary"). In

Table 16.1

Examples of Distance 1 and Distance 3 Sentences from Anomaly Judgment Task of Martin & Romani (1994)

	Sensible	Anomalous
Distance 1		
Adj-N		
Before	The rusty pail was lying on the beach.	The rusty swimsuit was lying on the beach.
After	The pail was rusty but she took it to the beach anyway.	The swimsuit was rusty by she took it to the beach anyway.
N-V		
Before	The platter cracked during the move.	The cloth cracked during the move.
After	The movers cracked the platter.	The movers cracked the cloth.
Distance 3		
Adj-N		
Before	The rusty, old, red pail was lying on the beach.	The rusty, old, red swimsuit was lying on the beach.
After	The pail was old, red, and rusty but she took it to the beach anyway.	The swimsuit was old, red, and rusty by she took it to the beach anyway.
N-V		
Before	The platter, the vase, and the mirror cracked during the move.	The cloth, the vase, and the mirror cracked during the move.
After	The movers cracked the vase, the mirror, and the platter.	The movers cracked the vase, the mirror, and the cloth.

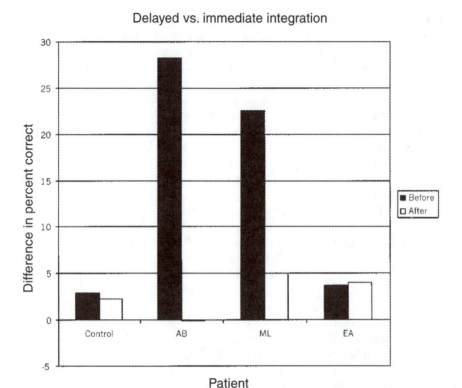

Figure 16.3. Difference in percent errors for |(mean of distance 2 and 3)—distance 1| on sentence anomaly judgments. "After" condition allows for immediate integration, whereas "before" condition involves delayed integration. Patients AB and ML show a semantic STM deficit, whereas patient EA shows a phonological STM deficit.

contrast, one patient (MW), who had not shown the interaction between before/after and distance in the sentence anomaly task, did perform significantly worse in the far than near condition in the grammaticality judgments. (See table 16.2.) Thus, these findings suggest a further dissociation between the capacities involved in retaining syntactic information and those involved in retaining lexical-semantic and phonological information.

Recently, Gibson (1998) has put forward a model of sentence comprehension that specifically deals with the working memory demands involved in maintaining and integrating syntactic and semantic information. His proposal is consistent with the delayed versus immediate integration findings reported by Martin and Romani (1994). According to his view, when a new discourse entity is processed that must be integrated with previous lexical-semantic information, these prior lexical representations have to be reactivated. The farther back in the sentence, in terms of intervening content information, the weaker the persisting activation, and the more difficult the reactivation and integration. Consequently, the model correctly predicts comprehension difficulty in the delayed integration conditions in Martin and Romani (1994). (For example, encountering the head noun after processing the preceding adjectives would require that these preceding adjectives be reactivated.) However, according to Gibson's model, if these previous entities have recently been reactivated due to integration with other intervening material, they are in a higher state of activation. Again the model is consistent with the findings indicating that in the immediate integration conditions there was little effect of distance. (For example, although encountering a third postnominal adjective would require

Table 16.2
Comparison of Semantic Anomaly and Grammaticality Judgments
for Patients AB, ML, and MW (Percent Correct)

	Anomaly judgments (distances 2 and 3)		
	Before	After	Difference
AB (semantic)	61	83	22 (p < .01)
ML (semantic)	62	79	17 (p < .01)
MW (normal span)	75	74	−1 (ns)
	Memory-stressed grammaticality judgments		
	Intervening	ATB	Difference
AB (semantic)	87	91	4 (ns)
ML (semantic)	88	91	3 (ns)
MW (normal span)	77	85	8 (p < .01)

reactivation of the preceding noun, it should be in an activated state already after having been recently reactivated in order to be integrated with the second postnominal adjectives.) It should be noted that, in terms of error rate data, this interaction of distance in the delayed versus immediate integration conditions was only obtained in the patient data. The error rates for control subjects showed a main effect of immediate/delayed and distance, but no interaction. However, there was an interaction in the predicted direction in the reaction time data for control subjects. The dissociation between the effects of distance in the lexical-semantic retention task and the effects of intervening material in the grammaticality task was not predicted by Gibson's model. His model assumes a single capacity for maintaining both types of information, whereas the patient data suggest a separation between syntactic and semantic retention capacities.

SUMMARY AND DIRECTIONS FOR FUTURE RESEARCH

Most current sentence processing theories assume that there are separable syntactic parsing and semantic processing components. However, numerous findings indicate that during comprehension, the outputs of these two domains are integrated quickly. For syntactically ambiguous sentences, semantic and discourse information play an immediate role in selecting among different possible syntactic structures. Further, recent findings suggest that the strength with which a particular structure is postulated upon processing a certain word relates to the frequency of that lexical item occurring in that structure. There is also some evidence that frequency of a particular structure irrespective of the particular lexical items in that structure also affects comprehension.

A number of patient studies support the contention that there are separable semantic and syntactic components, with several patients showing a pattern of disrupted syntactic processing but preserved semantic processing or the reverse. However, disruptions in syntactic processing are rarely total. Patients typically display a graded breakdown in performance, with poorer performance on more complex constructions. However, even for the most complex constructions, patients may show above-chance performance on comprehension tasks. Moreover, their success at carrying out syntactic computations may vary depending on the extent to which parsing decisions are supported or contradicted by semantic constraints. These results suggest that the output of syntactic parsing mechanisms may be weakened rather than totally disrupted. This weakening has the greatest effect on structures that are less frequently encountered.

To the extent that there are different mental components involved in different parsing operations localized in different neural tissue, one might expect to see patients with deficits in specific syntactic parsing procedures and not others. These dissociations could go against frequency. That is, even though low-frequency structures would be expected to be the most vulnerable overall, greater deficits in processing other structures might be possible if these have a different neural basis that has been selectively affected by brain damage. Caplan and Hildebrandt (1988) presented some evidence that highly specific disruptions along these lines might be observed, but there has been little other work aimed at investigating specific parsing operations.

With regard to working memory capacities involved in sentence processing, it appears that the capacity involved in lexical-semantic retention, which contributes to word span, plays a critical role in sentence comprehension when integration of word meanings is delayed. However, phonological retention capacity does not appear to play this role in sentence comprehension. Whatever the capacity involved in maintaining a syntactic parse, it appears to be different from that involved in lexical-semantic retention. Previous findings that have been taken as supporting a working memory interpretation of syntactic comprehension deficits could be interpreted instead as related to the degree of vulnerability of different parsing interpretations due to their frequency. At present, there appears to be little evidence that maintaining a syntactic structure per se is a capacity-demanding processing. As proposed by Gibson (1998), one central capacity demand in sentence comprehension involves retrieving prior discourse entities when they must be integrated with new entities. We would assume that the capacity involved maintaining these entities is the capacity involved in lexical-semantic retention. Once lexical-semantic information has been integrated into propositions, it appears that different capacities are involved (see Ericsson and Kintsch, 1995, for discussion)—and capacities that may not typically be affected in aphasic patients (see Martin & Romani, 1994; Romani & Martin, 1999, for a bit of relevant data).

The above claims lead to a number of predictions that could be investigated in future research. In order to investigate issues related to the strength of a hypothesized structure, one would need to have data on the frequency with which particular structures occur in general and the frequency with which these structures occur for particular verbs. This information could be used to construct sentence materials that varied both factors. Although previously used structures (such as actives and cleft subjects versus passives and cleft objects) no doubt tap into this frequency manipulation, a number of other structures could be investigated as well. There appear to be no previous studies that have examined whether patients' success at parsing a particular structure relates to the frequency with which that structure is associated with a particular verb. Such findings would be expected if a strength hypothesis is to be substantiated. In addition, further studies need to be carried out to investigate the interaction between semantic and discourse context and patients' comprehension of various structures. One might expect these factors to have the greatest effect when the output of the syntactic component is weakest.

Further exploration of capacity issues is certainly needed. Currently, the claims regarding the role of a lexical-semantic retention capacity in maintaining unintegrated semantic information are based on the investigation of only a few structures and a few patients. Consequently, replication and extension of these findings are needed. One interesting issue is whether a restriction in capacity specific to syntactic parsing and to maintaining syntactic predictions can be uncovered. Although Martin and Romani (1994) reported one case (MW) who seemed to have specific difficulty in maintaining syntactic information, this case was not investigated extensively. Recently, Martin and Miller (1999) reported that, contrary to predictions based on capacity demands for maintaining syntactic predictions, normal subjects were actually faster and more accurate in detecting grammatical errors when words intervened between the two words signaling an error. Further work is under way investigating whether this counterintuitive finding can be accommodated in terms of strong syntactic expectations causing a top-down filling in of missing grammatical information.

Has neuropsychological research lived up to its early promise in contributing to our understanding of sentence comprehension processes? In many respects, the topics of interest in studies of normal and impaired sentence comprehension have diverged. Studies of normal subjects have concentrated on the relative independence and timing of syntactic and semantic factors in resolving syntactic ambiguities (for example, Spivey & Tanenhaus, 1998), whereas studies of brain-damaged patients have concentrated on the difficulty of various syntactic structures (for example, Caplan & Hildebrandt, 1988). However, the findings from neuropsychological studies have provided converging evidence for conclusions drawn from studies of normal subjects and at other times have provided additional constraints on models of sentence processing. The neuropsychological findings have provided strong support for the independent representation of syntactic and semantic knowledge, but have also provided evidence of the immediate interaction of these different sources of knowledge. The graded nature of syntactic deficits is consistent with proposals assuming that different strengths are associated with different syntactic parsing outcomes. The relative difficulty of different syntactic structures has yet to be given a comprehensive treatment in theories of sentence processing, but there are promising proposals, such as that of Gibson (1998), that could be applied to abundant patient data—with the likely result that while some assumptions of the models are upheld, others must be modified. The results with patients provide strong constraints concerning the role of working memory in sentence comprehension, with patient data indicating multiple capacities, rather than a single capacity, involved in sentence processing. Thus, while researchers are far from coming up with a model of sentence processing that can accommodate all of the findings from normal subjects and brain-damaged patients, much as has been learned. The constraints from the patient research should simplify the task of making progress toward this comprehensive model.

ACKNOWLEDGMENT

Preparation of this mansucript was supported in part by NIH grant DC-00218 to Rice University.

REFERENCES

Baddeley, A., Gathercole, S., & Papagno, C. (1998). The phonological loop as a language learning device. *Psychological Review, 105*, 158–173.

Berndt, R. S., & Caramazza, A. (1980). A redefinition of the syndrome of Broca's aphasia: Implications for a neuropsychological model of language. *Applied Psycholinguistics, 1*, 225–278.

Berndt, R. A., Haendiges, A., Mitchum, C., & Sandson, J. (1997). Verb retrieval in aphasia. 2: Relationship to sentence processing. *Brain and Language, 56*, 107–137.

Berndt, R. S., Mitchum, C., & Haendiges, A. (1996). Comprehension of reversible sentences in "agrammatism": A meta-analysis. *Cognition, 58*, 289–308.

Boland, J. (1997). The relationship between syntactic and semantic processes in sentence comprehension. *Language and Cognitive Processes, 12*, 423–484.

Boland, J., & Cutler, A. (1996). Interaction with autonomy: Multiple output models and the inadequacy of the Great Divide. *Cognition, 58*, 309–320.

Breedin, S., & Martin, R. (1996). Patterns of verb deficits in aphasia: An analysis of four cases. *Cognitive Neuropsychology, 13*, 51-91.

Breedin, S., & Saffran, E. (1999). Sentence processing in the face of semantic loss: A case study. *Journal of Experimental Psychology: General, 128*, 547-562.

Byng, S. (1988). Sentence processing deficits: Theory and therapy. *Cognitive Neuropsychology, 5*, 629–676.

Caplan, D., & Hildebrandt, N. (1988). *Disorders of syntactic comprehension*. Cambridge, MA.: MIT Press.

Caplan, D., Hildebrandt, N., & Evans, K. (1987). The man left without a trace: A case study of aphasic processing of empty categories. *Cognitive Neuropsychology, 4*, 257–302.

Caramazza, A., & Berndt, R. S. (1978). Semantic and syntactic processes in aphasia: A review of the literature. *Psychological Bulletin, 85*, 898–918.

Caramazza, A., & Zurif, E. (1976). Dissociation of algorithmic and heuristic processes in language comprehension: Evidence from aphasia. *Brain and Language, 3*, 572–582.

Chomsky, N. (1982). *Some concepts and consequences of the theory of government and binding*. Cambridge, MA: MIT Press.

Cupples, L., & Inglis, A. L. (1993). When task demands induce "asyntactic" comprehension: A study of sentence interpretation in aphasia. *Cognitive Neuropsychology, 10,* 201–234.

De Renzi, E., & Nichelli, P. (1975). Verbal and nonverbal short term memory impairment following hemispheric damage. *Cortex, 11,* 341–354.

Ericsson, K., & Kintsch, W. (1995). Long-term working memory. *Psychological Review, 102,* 211–245.

Fodor, J., & Garrett, M. (1967). Some syntactic determinants of sentential complexity. *Perception and Psychophysics, 2,* 289–296.

Gibson, E. (1998). Linguistic complexity: Locality of syntactic dependencies. *Cognition, 68,* 1–76.

Grodzinsky, Y. (1995). A restrictive theory of agrammatic comprehension. *Brain and Language, 50,* 27–51.

Hodges, J., Patterson, K., & Tyler, L. (1994). Loss of semantic memory: Implications for the modularity of mind. *Cognitive Neuropsychology, 11,* 505–542.

Jackendoff, R. (1993). *Patterns in the mind.* New York: Harvester Wheatsheaf.

Jones, E. (1984). Word order processing in aphasia: Effect of verb semantics. In F. C. Rose (Ed.), *Advances in neurology, 42: Progress in aphasiology.* New York: Raven.

Kean, M. (1977). The linguistic interpretation of aphasia syndromes: Agrammatism in Broca's aphasia, an example. *Cognition, 5,* 9–46.

Kempler, D., Curtiss, S., & Jackson, C. (1987). Syntactic preservation in Alzheimer's disease. *Journal of Speech and Hearing Research, 30,* 343–350.

Kolk, H., & van Grunsven, M. (1985). Agrammatism as a variable phenomenon. *Cognitive Neuropsychology, 2,* 347–384.

Linebarger, M., Schwartz, M., & Saffran, E. (1983). Sensitivity to grammatical structure in so-called agrammatic aphasics. *Cognition, 13,* 361–392.

MacDonald, M., Pearlmutter, N., & Seidenberg, M. (1994). The lexical nature of syntactic ambiguity resolution. *Psychological Review, 101,* 676–703.

Martin, N., & Saffran, E. M. (1997). Language and auditory-verbal short-term memory impairments: Evidence for common underlying processes. *Cognitive Neuropsychology, 14,* 641–682.

Martin, R. (1995). A multiple capacities view of working memory in language. Paper presented at the Psychonomics Society Meeting. Los Angeles.

Martin, R. C. (1987). Articulatory and phonological deficits in short-term memory and their relation to syntactic processing. *Brain and Language, 32,* 159–192.

Martin, R. C. (1993). Short-term memory and sentence processing: Evidence from neuropsychology. *Memory and Cognition, 21,* 176–183.

Martin, R. C., & Miller, M. D. (1999). Increasing memory load does not reduce detection of grammatical anomalies in sentences. Poster presented at the annual meeting of the Psychonomic Society. Dallas, TX.

Martin, R. C., & Romani, C. (1994). Verbal working memory and sentence processing: A multiple components view. *Neuropsychology, 8,* 506–523.

Miceli, G., Mazzucchi, A., Menn, L., & Goodglass, H. (1983). Contrasting cases of Italian agrammatic aphasia without comprehension disorder. *Brain and Language, 19,* 65–97.

Mitchell, D., Cuetos, F., Corley, M., & Brysbaert, M. (1996). Exposure-based models of human parsing: Evidence for the use of coarse-grained (non-lexical) statistical

records. *Journal of Psycholinguistic Research, 24,* 469–488.

Miyake, A., Carpenter, P , & Just, M.. (1994). A capacity approach to syntactic comprehension disorder: Making normal adults perform like aphasic patients. *Cognitive Neuropsychology, 11,* 671–717.

Ostrin, R., & Tyler, L. (1995). Dissociations of lexical function: Semantics, syntax, and morphology. *Cognitive Neuropsychology, 12,* 345–389.

Romani, C., & Martin, R. C. (1999). A deficit in the short-term retention of lexical-semantic information: Forgetting words but remembering a story. *Journal of Experimental Psychology: General, 128,* 56–77.

Saffran, E., Schwartz, M., & Linebarger, M. (1998). Semantic influences on thematic role assignments: Evidence from normals and aphasics. *Brain and Language, 62,* 255–297.

Schwartz, M., & Chawluk, J. (1990). Deterioration of language in progressive aphasia: A case study. In M. Schwartz (Ed.), *Modular deficits in Alzheimer-type dementia.* Cambridge, MA: MIT Press.

Schwartz, M., Marin, O. S. M., & Saffran, E. (1979). Dissociations of language function in dementia: A case study. *Brain and Language, 7,* 277–306.

Schwartz, M., Saffran, E., & Marin, O. S. M. (1980). The word order problem in agrammatism: I: Comprehension. *Brain and Language, 10,* 249–262.

Schweickert, R., Guentert, L., & Hersberger, L. (1990). Phonological similarity, pronunciation rate, and memory span. *Psychological Science, 1,* 74–77.

Spivey, M., & Tanenhaus, M. (1998). Syntactic ambiguity resolution in discourse: Modeling the effects of referential context and lexical frequency. *Journal of Experimental Psychology: Learning, Memory, and Cognition, 24,* 1521–1543.

Spivey-Knowlton, M., & Sedivy, J. (1995). Resolving attachment ambiguities with multiple constraints. *Cognition, 55,* 226–267.

Trueswell, J., & Tanenhaus, M. (1994). Toward a lexicalist framework of constraint-based syntactic ambiguity resolution. In C. Clifton, L. Frazier, & K. Rayner (Eds.), *Perspectives on sentence processing.* Hillsdale, NJ: Lawrence Erlbaum.

Trueswell, J., Tanenhaus, M., & Garnsey, S. (1994). Semantic influences on parsing: Use of thematic role information in syntactic ambiguity resolution. *Journal of Memory and Language, 33,* 285-318.

Tyler, L. (1985). Real-time comprehension problems in agrammatism: A case study. *Brain and Language, 26,* 259–275.

Tyler, L. (1989). Syntactic deficits and the construction of local phrases in spoken language comprehension. *Cognitive Neuropsychology, 6,* 333–355.

Tyler, L. (1992). *Spoken language comprehension: An experimental approach to disordered and normal processing.* Cambridge, MA: MIT Press.

van Berkum, J., Brown, C., & Hagoort, P. (1999). Early referential context effects in sentence processing: Evidence from event-related brain potentials. *Journal of Memory and Language, 41,* 147–182.

von Stockert, T. ,& Bader, L. (1976). Some relations of grammar and lexicon in aphasia. *Cortex, 12,* 49–60.

Waters, G., & Caplan, D. (1999). Verbal working memory and sentence comprehension. *Behavioral and Brain Sciences, 22,* 77-126.

17

Models of Sentence Production

Cynthia K. Thompson
Yasmeen Faroqi-Shah

The mechanisms underlying sentence production include a number of complex, highly integrated processes. Contemporary models of sentence production place these processes in a largely serial, top-down architecture that proceeds from the speaker's communicative intention to overt speech (Bock & Levelt, 1994; Garrett, 1975, 1980, 1982, 1988; Levelt 1993, 1999). At each level in the model, distinct data sets are examined and certain rules operate in order to construct utterances that convey specific messages that conform to the grammar. The result is a system that is putatively modular, not only in that language processes are separate from general cognitive processes (Fodor, 1983), but also in that there are distinguishable modules within the sentence production system itself.

It is important to point out at the outset that the process of sentence production is not well understood and that the models discussed here are underspecified in terms of how component processes within the model operate and how they interact with one another. The major source of data informing the development of these models comes from speech error data from normal speakers, which provide insights into how language production works (Cutler, 1982; Dell & Reich, 1981; Fay & Cutler, 1977; Fromkin, 1971; Garrett, 1975). The so-called tip-of-the-tongue (TOT) phenomenon also provides evidence about certain aspects of production models such as distinguishable access to semantic, syntactic, and phonological representations (Vigliocco, Antonini, & Garrett, 1997).

While these data provide compelling evidence supporting certain production processes, as pointed out by Bock and Levelt (1994), the underpinnings of speech errors and TOT phenomenon are sometimes ambiguous and are open to alternative interpretations. However, experimental studies serve to validate hypotheses generated based on error data and allow alternative explanations to be ruled out. Experimental studies also allow examination of aspects of sentence production that are seldom involved in errors. In the last decade, a number of experiments have been conducted, the results of which provide insight into the nature of sentence production processing and the component processes involved. In this chapter we summarize existing models of sentence production and discuss their inherent component processes. Where possible, we present data, primarily from normal subjects, that have been used to develop and refine the models. We also present data from brain-damaged patients with aphasia that provide insight into the sentence production process. In discussion of the aphasia data we assume that brain damage results in *focal/discrete* disruption of the normal language production system, even though it is possible that brain damage may lead to modified processing strategies that are fundamentally different from those utilized under non-brain-damaged conditions.

COMPONENT PROCESSES OF SENTENCE PRODUCTION

There is broad agreement across models of sentence production concerning the major compo-nents or stages involved. These conform roughly to those first posed by Garrett (1975, 1980, 1982, 1988), although they have been refined by Bock (1990), Bock and Levelt (1994), Lapointe and Dell (1989), Levelt (1993, 1999), and others. The four levels of processing discussed by Garrett (1975) include: (1) a *message level* involved in generating what is to be said, (2) a *functional level* concerned with selecting major lexical concepts for conveying the intended message and assigning grammatical roles or syntactic functions, (3) a *positional level* involved in assembling phonologically realized words and morphemes into a sentence frame, and (4) a *sound level* involved in programming articulatory processes. The primary focus of this chapter is processes involved in the computation of functional- and positional-level representations.

Bock and Levelt's (1994) model is similar to that proposed by Garrett. One difference is that they consider both functional and positional processing as components of grammatical encod-ing, as shown in figure 17.1. Bock and Levelt (1994) also further specify processes involved at

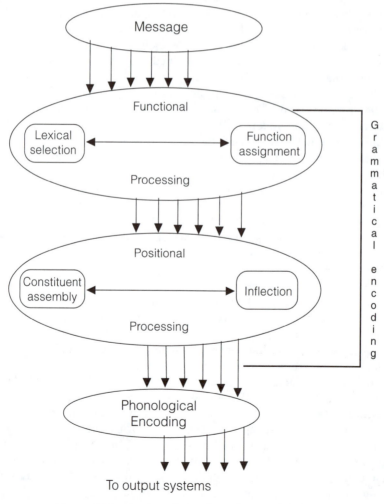

Figure 17.1. Bock and Levelt (1994) model (p. 946).

the positional level, which include constituent assembly and inflectional processes. Levelt (1989) considers grammatical encoding and phonological processing as part of a more general formulator that interacts with the lexicon. Finally, on the basis of evolutionary and ontogenetic patterns, Levelt (1999) provides a blueprint of sentence production with two core systems. The first core includes conceptual preparation and grammatical encoding, which, by interacting with knowledge of the external and internal world and the mental lexicon, serve to generate the surface structure of sentences. The second core includes morpho-phonological encoding, phonetic encoding, and articulatory processes.

Generating the Message

Regardless of which model one embraces, production of all sentences involves generation of a nonlinguistic message. According to Bock (1990), message generation is considered the interface between thought and language. Garrett (1988) discusses the message level as involving both the content and the effect that the speaker wishes to convey. Levelt (1993) places message generation within a larger mechanism termed the "conceptualizer," which involves discourse processing (input) as well as generation of messages based on communicative intention (output). Levelt (1993, 1999) further details conceptual preparation that involves two processes: macroplanning, deciding what to say and in what order, and microplanning, casting the propositional form of the message—for example, specification of referents and predication (that is, who did what to whom), modification (that is, attributes of the referents; such as happy, poor), quantification (for example, some or all), and mood (that is, declarative, imperative, or interrogative). Data generated at this level provide the raw material for subsequent processes.

Functional Processing

Functional processing involves two major components: lexical selection and function assignment (per Garrett, 1988; Bock & Levelt, 1994). Lexical selection involves retrieving specific entries in the lexicon (lemmas) associated with message elements. Grammatical information—for example, the form class of selected items and information about person, number, tense, and aspect—also is accessed during lexical selection. Function assignment, occurring once lexical selection has been accomplished, links lexical items and their syntactic or grammatical functions (for example, subject—nominative, object—accusative). Consider, for example, the sentence "The man followed the dog." In formulation of this sentence, concepts for *man*, *dog*, and *follow* and corresponding form class information are selected from the lexicon. *Man* is then linked to the subject/nominative function, and *dog* is linked to the object/accusative function.

Lexical Selection

The process of lexical selection proceeds once a message is formulated by the speaker. Speech error, TOT, and experimental data suggest that lexical selection is a two-stage process, involving: (1) activation of a lemma (but see chapter 1 in this volume, by Doriana Chialant, Albert Costa, and Alfonso Caramazza, for an alternative view regarding the lemma level) and (2) spreading activation to the phonological form of the word (lexeme) (see figure 17.2).

Lemma Access. At the lemma level, target elements as well as semantically related items are activated. A common type of speech error that likely reflects difficulty at the lemma level is a semantic substitution; for example, *cat* for *dog*. Such errors also are commonly seen in individuals with aphasia and referred to as semantic paraphasias (Schwartz, 1987). Substituted elements typically preserve the general semantic features of the intended word (for example, cat and dog are both four-legged animals). Errors also have been noted in which *blending* of two

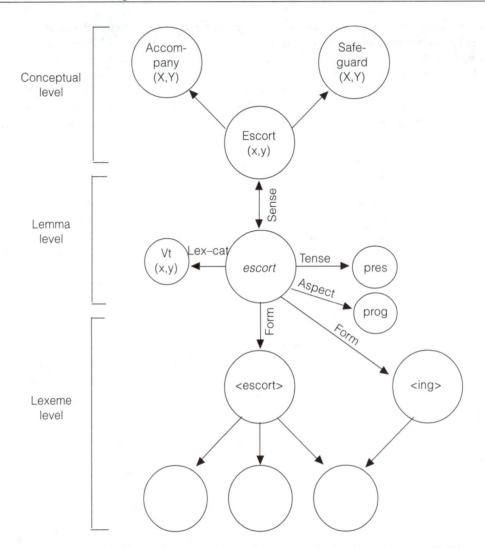

Figure 17.2. Levels of lexical access (adapted from Levelt, Roelofs, & Meyer, 1999).

lexical items occurs. For example, the word string "A *my* offered him some celery" is produced, reflecting a blend of man and guy (Bock, 1995). Such blending errors suggest that two semantically related items are selected simultaneously, and phonologically "blended" in production. These speech error patterns indicate that the mental lexicon is semantically organized and that the process of lexical selection involves accessing not only the intended item, but also items that are semantically related to the targets.

Evidence that the lexicon is organized by semantic class also shows up in the error patterns of brain-damaged individuals. Several researchers have reported patients with category-specific deficits. For example, patients with selective loss of concrete versus abstract categories and animate versus inanimate categories have been reported (Damasio, 1990; Hillis & Caramazza, 1991; Warrington & McCarthy, 1983; Warrington & Shallice, 1984; Young, Newcombe, Hellawell, & DeHaan, 1989; see also discussion in chapters 7, 10, and 11 of this volume). These data suggest that semantic class is a fundamental dimension of lexical organization; thus, it is not surprising that semantic errors are common in both normal and aphasic individuals' sentence production efforts.

Speech error data also suggest that the mental lexicon is organized by form class. Analysis of semantic substitution data indicates that error and target items are typically members of the same grammatical form class; for example, *cat* and *dog* are both nouns. Interestingly, Stemberger (1985a) found that in analysis of a large corpus of error data, 98 percent of all lexical substitutions represented the same form class as the target word. Dissociation between nouns and verbs noted in patients with aphasia also suggest that entries in the lexicon are organized by grammatical class. Patients with agrammatic (Broca's) aphasia often show greater difficulty naming verbs than nouns, while patients with anomic aphasia show the opposite pattern (Berndt, Mitchum, Haendiges, & Sandson, 1997; Kim & Thompson, 2000; Miceli, Silveri, Nocentini, & Caramazza, 1988; Miceli, Silveri, Villa, & Caramazza, 1984; Zingeser & Berndt, 1990). These patterns suggest a deficit in lemma- or lexeme-level access to verbs for some patients and to nouns for others (see chapter 7, for discussion). Such patients typically show good comprehension of failed items, and they show ability to access phonological entries by virtue of relatively intact naming of items in the unimpaired word class.

Word Form Access (Lexeme Selection). The second stage in lexical selection involves accessing the phonological form of chosen items. TOT data are revealing in this regard. During a typical TOT state, normal speakers are unable to access a particular word, although they know the meaning of the word to be expressed (concept) and syntactic information about the word (for example, that it is a noun or a verb). Speakers also are often aware of the first letter of the word, its stress pattern, and the number of syllables. While it has been debated as to whether or not such observations are indicative of a breakdown at the lemma level or the level of word form access, the problem, as argued by Levelt (1989), is in accessing the phonological word form. This postulate has been borne out in experiments with Italian speakers who retain access to the grammatical gender of target nouns (information supplied by the lemma) but are unable to produce target words (Caramaza & Miozzo, 1997; Viggliocco, Antonini, & Garrett, 1997). Badecker, Miozzo, and Zanuttini (1995) reported a similar pattern in a patient with aphasia. Dante, an Italian aphasic patient, was able to retrieve the grammatical gender of nouns that he could not name, but not the number of syllables or the first phoneme. Unimpaired comprehension and grammatical gender information, together with impaired word form information, was taken as evidence of preserved access to word lemmas, and impaired access to lexemes. The converse pattern of impaired lemma access (or impaired semantic representation) was reported by Hillis, Rapp, Romani, and Caramazza (1990). Their aphasic patient KE produced only semantic errors in all modalities.

Individuals with aphasia show characteristic error patterns that can be discussed with regard to components of lexical access that may be disrupted. Kay and Ellis (1987) and Schwartz (1987) attempted to correlate error patterns with disruption of certain components of lexical access. They postulated that impaired lemma access would cause semantic paraphasias and that impaired lexeme access would result in circumlocutory errors and phonological paraphasias (that is, errors involving phonological substitutions, additions, or deletions; for example, *pentil* for *pencil*). Schwartz (1987) explained neologistic paraphasic errors (for example, errors in which the form produced bears no resemblance to the target word form; for example, *flanginlangin* for *hammer*) as involving both lemma and lexeme access; here patients' semantic paraphasias are confounded by superimposed phonological errors. Some support for categorizing errors this way was garnered by Gainnotti, Miceli, Caltagirone, Silveri, and Masullo (1981), who classified 118 aphasic patients according to the type of errors made on confrontation naming tasks and correlated their prevalent error type with performance on semantic-lexical discrimination tests. They found that patients with a prevalence of verbal semantic paraphasias, neologisms, or anomia (no response) were more impaired on semantic-lexical discrimination tests than were subjects who produced phonetic or phonemic errors.

Caramazza and Hillis (1990a) argue, however, that semantic errors could result from selective damage to the phonology, the assumption being that a semantic representation (or lemma) activates all related lexemes in proportion to their similarity, or number of semantic features in common, with the activated semantic representation or lemma. Therefore, damage to the target lexeme would make the lexemes of other related words available, leading to semantic paraphasias. Caramazza and Hillis (1990b) described two subjects (RGB and HW) who produced frequent semantic paraphasias in oral tasks (both reading and naming), but not in written tasks. Further, their subjects demonstrated unimpaired comprehension of the words that they were unable to name. These patterns were interpreted as resulting from damage to lexeme access, and Caramazza and Hillis argued that lexeme representations are either different or accessed differently for oral and written modalities.

Experimental Evidence. Experimental studies examining the lexical selection process involve the use of a picture interference paradigm (Glaser, 1992; Glaser & Dungelhoff, 1984; Roelofs, 1992; Schriefers, Meyer, & Levelt, 1990). Participants are asked to name pictures of objects (nouns) or actions (verbs) presented with either visual or auditory distractor words. Naming reaction times (RTs) are recorded under all conditions. Results of such experiments have shown that when the distractor word is semantically related to the target picture, interference in activation of the target word ensues, resulting in longer RTs as compared to when nonrelated distractor words are presented. This happens, for example, when participants are required to say "chair" when presented with a picture of a chair and ignore a distractor word such as *bed* (semantically related to the target word). Reaction times are longer in this example as compared to a situation requiring the participant to name "chair" when the word *fish* is presented (a semantically unrelated word). This pattern of performance can be explained as follows: when two concepts are activated (that is, a distractor word and a target picture) lemmas for both are activated, reducing the probability of selecting the target (as compared to when no distractor is present). This is called conceptual intrusion (Levelt, 1989). When the distractor and target are semantically related, activation of the two semantically related lemmas creates even greater interference, resulting in slowed activation of the target (associative intrusion).

In their picture naming study, Schriefers and colleagues (1990) not only examined the effects of semantically related distractors as compared to unrelated distractors, but also examined the effects of presenting phonologically related distractor words. They found a phonological facilitation effect when phonological distractors were presented immediately after the picture to be named (that is, +150 msec), or simultaneously with the picture (0 msec). That is, naming ability was enhanced. The phonological facilitation effect, however, was not seen when the phonological distractors were presented prior to the picture to be named (that is, at -150 msec). These findings support the notion that lexical selection involves two stages. In addition, they suggest that lexical selection is a serial process. First the lemma is selected, followed by selection of its phonological form, the lexeme. This ordering of access is intuitively appealing. Lexical selection and phonological encoding are quite different. Lexical selection involves a semantic search through the lexicon, whereas phonological encoding involves the creation of a pronounceable phonetic pattern for each selected word. (See Levelt, Roelofs, & Meyer [1999] for a complete discussion of this theory and experimental data supporting it. See also Chialant et al., chapter 7 of this volume, for an alternative view and supporting data.)

It is important to note, however, that there is not complete agreement in the literature that lexical selection follows a strict order. For example, Dell (1986), Martin, Dell, Saffran, & Schwartz (1994), Stemberger (1995), and others argue that lexical access during sentence production involves interactive activation (IA) between conceptual, lexical, and phonological levels of representation in a feedforward and feedback fashion. In the IA model, targeted and related sets of semantic features, activated by conceptual input, feed forward to lexical and phonological levels to activate the target as well as related nodes. When nodes are primed at each level, feedback is sent back to the source node and related nodes. Errors occurring in normal speech, such as *rat* for *cat,* have been used as evidence supporting IA. These mixed errors have been found to occur more frequently than would be expected based on chance in normal speech (Dell & Reich, 1981). The observation that phonologically erred productions are often real words (that is, the lexical bias effect) also serves to support that interaction occurs between levels of lexical representation. Such errors suggest that feedback from the phonological level to the lexical level occurs, since retrieval of the phonological form, without feedback to the lexical level, would not result in real word productions.

Support for the IA model of lexical access also shows up in experiments such as that by Jescheniak and Schriefers (1998). Using a picture interference paradigm, they tested picture naming using semantic, phonological, and unrelated distractors. As in previous studies, they found phonological facilitation at 0 msec and +150 msec; however, they also noted interference for semantically related distractors presented both prior to the target (at -150 msec) and after the target picture (at +150 msec). These findings provide support for interaction among levels of lexical representation during picture naming.

Whether or not lexical selection is a serial or interactive process also has been discussed in the aphasia literature. Cueing studies in aphasia have shown that aphasic patients who show lack of word form knowledge in TOT states are the ones who benefit most from phonological cues (Pease & Goodglass, 1978). This observation could be taken as evidence of impaired access to the phonological form of words. However, Laine and colleagues (1992) hypothesized (based on IA models of lexical access) that improvement in naming with phonological cues would indicate a lemma-level impairment because feedback to the lemma level, resulting from the sound cue, aids in lexical selection. Laine and colleagues also predicted that sound cues would have little effect if the deficit were at the lexeme level, assuming that word form representations are "lost" in which case no amount of phonologic cueing would help. However, their predictions were not supported by data from their aphasic subjects with lexical-phonological deficits, all three of whom benefited from phonological cues.

Data derived from treatment of lexical access deficits in aphasia also provide some insight into the process of lexical retrieval. For example, Baynes, Share, and Redfern (1995) and Drew and Thompson (1999) reported the outcome of semantic and phonological treatments in subjects whose naming impairments were primarily either meaning based or sound based. Subjects with a semantic source of naming deficit showed greater improvements with a semantic treatment than with a phonological treatment, and vice versa. These data suggest that for patients with lemma-level deficits, treatment focused on lemma access improves naming; for those with lexeme access deficits, treatment focused on activation of the word form is helpful.

Summary of Lexical Selection. In summary, the available data suggest that the lexicon is organized by semantic category and by grammatical class. There also is widespread agreement that lexical selection involves two stages—lemma selection and lexeme selection—although alternative proposals have not been ruled out (see chapter 7 of this book). Whether or not the stages of word selection are discrete, serial, or are interactive is unclear, as is also discussed in chapter 7.

Function Assignment

The process of function assignment involves assigning functional (grammatical) roles to selected lemmas based on the message to be conveyed. Functional roles to be assigned include the instigator of an event (that is, the agent), the entity on whom the action is performed (that is, the theme, recipient, or goal), an experiencer of an event, and so on. In configurational languages such as English, function assignment corresponds with the ordering of words in sentences because agents are more likely to be placed in sentence initial position (that is, the subject position). In contrast, in nonconfigurational languages, functions are denoted by case marking.

Some error patterns noted in normal speech reflect difficulty in assigning the proper grammatical function to selected lexical concepts. A speaker may, for example, produce the sentence "The dog followed the man" rather than "The man followed the dog." In this situation two sentence constituents are exchanged with one another, while the syntax of the sentence is preserved. Importantly, these exchange errors involve constituents of the same type (that is, two noun phrases). Interestingly, phrase exchange errors often are adjusted for case; for example, a speaker produces the sentence "*He* wants *us* to do something else" instead of "*We* want *him* to do something else" (from Bock, 1995). This error is not a simple word exchange error (that is, the error was not "*Us* wants *he* to do something else"). Instead, the exchanged pronouns bear the appropriate case for the position in which they erroneously occur.

Exchange errors also are commonly seen in individuals with aphasia. In the aphasia literature such errors are termed *role-reversal* errors and involve exchanges of the agent and theme. That is, the agent is placed in the object position and the theme is placed in the subject position of the sentence. A classic example is Martin and Blossom-Stach's (1986) Wernicke's aphasic patient who produced sentences with acceptable surface form, but made function assignment errors, such as "The pupil gave her an A+" for the target "She gave the pupil an A+."

Function assignment errors also are found in noncanonical sentence production in aphasic individuals; that is, in sentences not in subject-verb-object (SVO) order in English such as passives (Caramazza & Miceli, 1991; Martin & Blossom-Stach, 1986), although such errors also could arise from difficulty with constituent assembly (see below for a more complete discussion of noncanonical sentence production). It is interesting, however, that individuals who have difficulty producing passive sentences, for example, do not show difficulty accessing passive morphology; errors instead are characterized by improper assignment (or arrangement) of grammatical functions.

Factors Involved in Function Assignment. The process of function assignment is by no means simple, and a number of questions regarding how it is controlled and what precise functions are assigned are currently being debated. Factors that likely play a role in function assignment are the animacy and concreteness of selected items, their prominence in terms of the discourse, and verb selection. The importance of animacy in function assignment has been elucidated in experiments using a sentence-recall paradigm. For example, using this task Bock and Warren (1985) showed that animate and concrete elements are more likely to be assigned to sentence initial position than inanimate or abstract elements. Similarly, McDonald, Bock, and Kelly (1993) noted a tendency for production of animate nouns as subjects in transitive sentences.

The importance of animacy also shows up in the aphasia data. Function assignment deficits in aphasia are more common in semantically reversible sentences (where both nouns are animate) as compared to nonreversible sentences (one noun is animate and the other inanimate) (Martin & Blosom-Stach, 1986; Saffran, Schwartz, & Marin, 1980). This pattern suggests that when two animate nouns are selected from the lexicon, the animacy rule does not assist in assignment of the subject function, resulting in role-reversal errors (see Bock & Warren, 1985).

The prominence of particular elements in the discourse also may affect function assignment in that elements that are more prominent than others may be more likely to be assigned the subject function. This postulate has been tested in experiments using queries about pictures. For example, presented with a scene such as a girl chasing a boy and a query about the boy (for example, "What is going on with the boy?"), participants are likely to assign the subject role to the boy in their answers. When questioned about the girl, the girl receives subject status (Bates & Devescovi, 1989; Bock, 1977).

The Role of the Verb in Function Assignment. Verbs are integrally involved in function assignment in sentence production, in that verb selection heavily influences selection of the participants or event roles in a sentence. Because verbs are acquired together with knowledge that they can (and sometimes must) occur with particular structures, the participant or event roles (that is, argument structure of the verb) are part of the lexical representation of the verb. Thus, in accessing a particular verb for production, the argument structure properties of that verb also are accessed.

There are several different types of verbs determined by the number of participants (that is, arguments) that go into the action described by the verb and the number of different argument structure arrangements that are possible given a certain verb. The transitive verb *hit*, as in "Zack hit the ball," requires two participants; the dative verb *put* requires three participants as in "Zack put the shirt in the closet." Complement verbs such as *know* can occur with an NP internal argument (for example, "Zack knew the answer") or a sentential complement (for example, "Zack knew that the movie would be great," or "Zack knew who won the race."

Another way that verbs vary concerns the type of thematic roles that are assigned. Unaccusative verbs, such as *melt*, within the class of intranstive verbs, differ from unergative intransitives in their thematic roles. Consider the following:

1. The boy $_{\text{AGENT}}$ runs.
2. The ice $_{\text{THEME}}$ melts.

According to linguistic theory (see Levin & Rappaport-Hovav, 1995; Grimshaw, 1990), unaccusatives as in (2) involve movement of the theme from the postverbal object position in d-structure to the subject position in s-structure.

Psychological verbs (psych-verbs) are still different in their thematic roles. Consider the following sentences:

3. The children $_{\text{EXPERIENCER}}$ admired the clown $_{\text{THEME}}$.
4. The clown $_{\text{THEME}}$ amused the children $_{\text{EXPERIENCER}}$.

Psych-verbs such as *admire* and *amuse* involve an experiencer, the individual experiencing the mental state, and a theme, the content or object of the mental state (Belletti & Rizzi, 1988). Traditional linguistic analysis of psych-verbs divides them into two classes. The admire class has an experiencer-theme sequence in active sentences (for example, "The boy $_{\text{EXPERIENCER}}$ admired the spaceship $_{\text{THEME}}$"), whereas the amuse class has a theme-experiencer sequence in active sentences (for example, "The cartoon $_{\text{THEME}}$ amused the boy $_{\text{EXPERIENCER}}$"). Admire verbs are thought to have a d-structure subject (experiencer) and an object (theme), whereas amuse verbs have no d-structure subject; the d-structure object (theme) moves to the subject position at s-structure.

The point here is that the particular verb selected influences selection of other sentence constituents because part of the verb's lexical representation is its argument structure. When certain verbs are selected, so too are its argument structure properties. During functional assignment, the selected argument structure elements are assigned grammatical functions; for example, agents are assigned nominative function, themes are assigned accusative. Experiencers and other aruguments also must be assigned grammatical functions that must be represented in sentences produced.

Interestingly, Ferreira (1994) found that argument structure requirements influence the type of sentence produced. For example, passive sentences were more likely to be produced with amuse-type verbs (theme-experiencer) rather than admire-type verbs (experiencer-theme) or verbs like *attack* (agent-theme) when arguments differ in animacy. That is, subjects showed a tendency to produce sentences like "The boy was amused by the cartoon" rather than "The cartoon amused the boy," indicating a preference for producing animate agruments in the sentence initial position. This finding suggests that verb choice interacts with other factors such as animacy in function assignment. These observations also are consistent with Grimshaw's (1990) thematic hierarchy, a hypothesized ordering of thematic roles by prominence. The agent is the highest in the hierarchy, followed by experiencer. The theme is at the bottom of the hierarchy. Thus, when agents or experiencers compete with the theme for the subject position, the theme is likely to lose.

The role of the verb in sentence production has received recent attention in the aphasia literature. That is, some aphasic patients show more difficulty producing verbs with a greater number of arguments (for example, datives) than verbs with fewer (for example, intransitives) (Kiss, 2000; Thompson, Lange, Schneider, & Shapiro, 1997; Kim & Thompson, 2000; DeBlesser & Kauschke, 2000). Kegl (1995) and Thompson (2000) also showed that agrammatic aphasic individuals, unlike normal controls or patients with anomic aphasia, have difficulty producing unaccusative verbs, perhaps because of the complex argument structure properties of these verbs. Kim and Thompson (2000) also showed that agrammatic aphasic patients with verb production deficits are impaired in their ability to categorize verbs by argument structure and that they are more impaired at categorizing verbs with more arguments than those with fewer. These data indicate impoverished access to verbs and verb argument structure, the latter of which likely interferes with function assignment. That is, if the full array of verb arguments is not accessed, function assignment cannot proceed normally.

The relation between verb and sentence production has been addressed in several studies of aphasia. Marshall, Pring, and Chiat (1998) described a patient who had intact verb semantics and verb argument structure information, but was unable to name verbs or produce well-formed sentences. However, when provided with verbs, his sentence production ability improved. Further, treatment aimed at improving verb naming in isolation resulted in improved sentence production, suggesting that improved access to verbs also improved access to the argument structure of verbs, which, in turn, improved function assignment and sentence production. Marshall and colleagues (1998), however, attributed this patient's deficit to impaired word form (phonological) access to verbs. It is difficult to ascertain, however, how improved access to the phonology of verbs would influence sentence production, unless feedback from the phonology to earlier levels of sentence production occurs. Interestingly, Schneider and Thompson (in press) showed a similar result for patients whose verb deficits were attributed to lemma selection as opposed to phonological access difficulty. That is, like Marshall and colleagues' patient, their patients' sentence production was improved with verb naming treatment.

Summary of Function Assignment. In summary, function assignment involves the assignment of grammatical roles to selected lemmas. Factors that play a role in function assignment include the animacy and concreteness of selected lemmas, their prominence in terms of the discourse, and verb selection. Verbs are central to sentence production because the argument structure of verbs is part of the verbs' lexical representation. The verb, then, is largely responsible for assigning grammatical roles.

It is clear from this discussion that function assignment has a lot to do with the ordering of words in sentences. It is important to point out, however, that current models of sentence production consider these processes to be modular and computationally separate from one another. The results of syntactic priming experiments of Bock and colleagues (Bock & Loebell, 1990; Bock, Loebell, & Morey, 1992), for example, suggest that syntactic construction is separable from the meaning that sentences convey. In these studies subjects were primed by asking them to repeat a sentence of a certain type (for example, active versus passive). Subjects then were asked to describe a picture that was unrelated to the sentence. Results revealed a structural or form priming effect. That is, the likelihood of producing a particular sentence structure during picture description was influenced by the type of sentence used as the prime. Function assignment, then, appears to provide the data to be used for sentence ordering, but sentence structure does not proceed at the functional level. In one view, function assignment can be considered akin to d-structure in linguistic theory (Chomsky, 1986); ordering of words into sentence frames occurs subsequently, at s-structure.

Positional Processing

Models of sentence production are not explicit about the processes that constitute positional processing (Caramazza & Hillis, 1989). Speech error data, however, once again provide some insight into the process, although normal speakers are known to produce few errors in syntactic planning (Stemberger, 1982). Additionally, there are empirical studies examining sentence formulation (Bock et al., 1985, 1990, 1992), although there are fewer in this domain as compared to studies of lexical selection and retrieval. The available data suggest that integration of words into a sentence is controlled by a scheme that represents form class and grammatical relation information within a clause. Thus, positional processing is highly tied to functional processing. A set of lemmas is activated, as are their corresponding syntactic functions, which are linked together by the argument structures of selected lemmas (primarily that of the verb). Positional processing computes the order or sequence in which these elements will appear in the sentence and the relevant grammatical morphemes required to formulate a grammatically acceptable sentence according to the rules of the language. This involves both constituent assembly—the structural mechanism—and morpheme retrieval or inflectional processes (per Bock and Levelt's [1994] model)—a lexical mechanism. In the following sections we address these two processes.

Constituent Assembly

Constituent assembly is concerned with ordering elements of the intended utterance into their sentence positions. Lemmas, selected from the lexicon and coded in terms of their grammatical structure at earlier processing levels, are hierarchically organized into phrasal constituents (for example, noun phrases) and placed in a planning frame that manages the order of constituents. The resulting sentence frame captures dependencies among syntactic functions. Levelt (1999) refers to this process as unification.

Word exchange errors seen in normal speech suggest that sentence planning proceeds in clause-sized units. Generally, word exchanges occur within the same clause, as illustrated in examples cited by Garrett (1982); for example, "Did you stay up late very last night?" was produced rather than "Did you stay up very late last night?" Assuming that exchanges reflect the concurrent activity of the switched elements, this implies that items within clauses are simultaneously available for insertion into the planning frame

Building Phrase Structure

Constituent assembly or generation of a surface structure involves not only sequencing major lexical items but also specifying phrase structures for all lexical items. The traditional notion advanced by Garrett (1982, 1988) is that an algorithm generates a syntactic tree. Lexical items then are inserted into the tree along with elements required for each phrasal node. According to Levelt (1999) a syntactic fragment, not exactly akin to a syntactic tree, but following the phrase structure rules of the language, is generated for each lemma activated. The particular configuration of the fragment depends largely on the form class of the selected lemma. For example, selected verbs generate a fragment containing a slot for the verb and slots for all of the verb's arguments—typically represented by NPs. For example, a phrase fragment for a

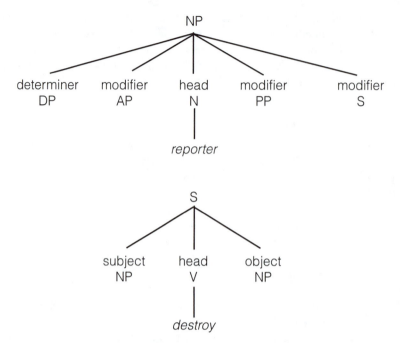

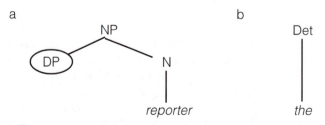

Figure 17.3. Syntactic tree fragments as per Levelt (1999). NP = noun phrase, DP = determiner phrase, AP = adjectival phrase, N = noun, PP = prepositional phrase, S = sentence, V = verb.

transitive verb such as *destroy* would contain two NP slots, one for the agent and one for the patient/theme; a phrase fragment for a dative verb would have three, one for the agent, one for the patient/theme, and one for the goal. Fragments for NPs contain slots for the head of the NP (the selected noun; for example, *reporter*) and a determiner phrase (DP) as shown in figure 17.3. In addition, slots for all potential NP modifiers are generated, including an adjectival phrase (AP), prepositional phrase (PP), and a relative clause (shown as S). At a minimum, the information represented in syntactic surface structure is computed. Any components of phrase fragments that are not filled with lexical items are trimmed and do not undergo unification. The exact configuration of phrasal fragments generated, however, has been debated. Garrett (1980, 1982, 1988) proposed that phrasal fragments contain function words in them. On the other hand, Lapointe and Dell (1989) proposed that phrase fragments (for example, VP and NP fragments) do not contain function words (for example, DPs and auxiliary verbs). Instead, they proposed, based on analysis of error data from English- and Italian-speaking aphasic individuals, that phrasal fragments contain attachment sites for determiners and auxiliaries. For example, using X-bar notation (Chomsky, 1986), Lapointe and Dell distinguish phrase fragments (a) from function word fragments (b) (see figure 17.4). The phrase fragments are assumed to contain markers where function word fragments are attached (circled DP in figure 17.4).

Figure 17.4. Phrase and function word fragments (Lapointe & Dell, 1989). NP = noun phrase, DP = determiner phrase, N = noun, Det = determiner.

Once these fragments are selected, unification ensues in order to form the surface sentence structure. This involves attaching the head of each NP fragment to the proper NP slot in the VP fragment. The NP assigned the thematic role of agent typically occupies the NP slot to the left of the verb, and the NP assigned the thematic role of patient/goal occupies the NP slot to the right. As noted above, animate lemmas are more likely to be agents of sentences.

Ordering of Lexical Items into Planning Frames

The temporal relationship between phrase building and sentence planning is crucial. There is general agreement that the availability of lexical items during functional processing affects the selection of a structural frame; that is, that constituent assembly is a flexible process that adapts to the level of activation of individual lexical elements. As lexical items become available, they are *incrementally* inserted into the sentence frame (Bock & Levelt, 1994; Levelt, 1989). For example, lexical items activated first will be placed in the subject position of sentences. Data supporting this idea come from a series of experiments conducted by Bock (1986, 1987). In these experiments, subjects were asked to describe pictures following a prime word that was either phonologically or semantically related to one of the nouns in the picture. Results showed a tendency for speakers to alternate between active and passive sentence forms in order to use semantically primed targets as the subjects of sentences. Words with accessible phonological forms also were found to precede those with less accessible forms even if this required syntactic and morphological changes, as in conversion from an active to a passive sentence (Bock, 1987). This means that, for example, to describe an event in which a reporter destroys a diary, semantic or phonological priming of *diary* would cause *diary* to occur as the subject of the ensuing sentence, resulting in production of a passive sentence such as "The diary was destroyed by the reporter." Selection of *diary* for the subject position would then trigger the passive verb lemma for *destroy*, which, in turn, would lead to selection of an sentence frame with an NP and a PP slot (Bresnan, 1982; Levelt, 1989).

Lexical flexibility is also apparent in insertion of items later in the sentence. A relevant example pertains to production of dative verbs that can occur either in a double object dative (for example, "The reporter sent his editor the story") or prepositional dative (for example, "The reporter sent a story to his editor"). The incremental theory of sentence production postulates that the item that is most active at the time the postverbal position is to be filled will be selected, thereby influencing which syntactic structure is eventually constructed (Bock, 1982; Kempen & Hoenkamp, 1987). In the examples here, if *letter* is more highly activated when the postverbal slot needs to be filled, a prepositional dative construction will ensue; if *editor* is more highly activated, a double object dative will be produced.

Incrementality suggests that selection of a planning frame—for example, the prepositional dative sentence frame—cannot occur before the lexical items supporting the planning frame (*letter* in the example above) are selected. However, in some cases lemmas may need to be retrieved after the planning frame is selected. For example, if *story* were retrieved before *reporter* due to discourse factors, the passive-verb lemma of *send*, which maps the theme argument onto subject position, would be the only appropriate choice for further processing (Levelt, 1989). Such adjustments would require feedback communication from positional to functional processing, which is not yet an integral part of sentence production models.

Another theory of constituent assembly is the competitive model. It postulates that alternative syntactic plans actively compete to determine the syntactic structure that is finally produced (McClelland & Rumelhart, 1981; Dell & O'Seaghdha, 1994). For example, double object and prepositional dative structures will actively compete, and the structure that is computed with the greatest speed is ultimately produced. Thus, according to the competitive model, lexical items such as *send*, which allow syntactic flexibility, are more difficult than items that do not occur in different syntactic structures. This postulate, however, has not been completely supported by research. Ferreira (1996), for example, compared sentence production using verbs that could occur in prepositional and double object dative constructions (such as *send*) with verbs that could occur only in prepositional dative constructions (such as *donate*) to test the predictions of incremental and competitive models. Subjects were presented with nouns and a verb in random order and were required to produce a sentence using the words provided. Fewer errors and shorter reaction times were found with verbs that allowed syntactic flexibility. These results failed to support competition between alternate syntactic structures, since competition would predict more errors and longer reaction times for verbs that allow syntactic flexibility.

Further insight into the processes involved in sentence planning comes from the aphasia literature. It is well known that some aphasic patients show a pattern of preserved or partially preserved production of simple sentence structures such as actives, but they have difficulty producing noncanonical sentences such as passive structures (Bates, Freiderici, Wulfeck, & Juarez, 1988; Menn, Reilly, Hayashi, et al., 1998). In an extensive cross-linguistic study, Bates and colleagues (1988) found that the ability to produce canonical word order is spared in most aphasic subjects. Difficulty producing passive sentences has been attributed to failure to retrieve the passive lemma of a verb (Heeschen, 1993), difficulties with surface morphosyntax (Menn et al., 1998), and/or deficits in microplanning (Berndt, 1991). For example, CH, a patient from our laboratory, produced the following when asked to describe a picture of a cow kicking a horse and to start his sentence with *horse*:

The horse . . . The horse kicks the cow. The horse kicks the cow. The horse is kicking. The horse is going to kick. Jeese! The horse kicks. The horse is kicking. How is the horse. The horse.

Interestingly, however, using the sentence priming task of Bock and colleagues, aphasic patients show ability to produce noncanonical sentences such as passives (Hartsuiker & Kolk, 1998; but see Marin & Schwartz, 1998). Agrammatic aphasic patients also can be trained to produce noncanonical structures such as passive sentences with concomitant generalization to structures that are structurally similar (Ballard & Thompson, 1999; Jacobs & Thompson, 2000; Thompson & Shapiro, 1995; Thompson, Shapiro, Tait, Jacobs, & Schneider, 1996; Thompson, Shapiro, Ballard, Jacobs, & Tait, 1997). Crucially, generalization is constrained to sentences that are, according to linguistic theory, formed by similar movement operations from d- to s-structure. For example, training patients to produce passive sentences (for example, "The thief was chased by the artist") results in generalization to subject-raising structures (for example, "The thief seems to have chased the artist"), both of which are derived from a type of movement known as NP movement (Chomsky, 1986). However, training passive sentences does not affect the ability to produce object cleft sentences such as "It was the artist who the thief chased" or *who* questions such as "Who did the thief chase?"), both of which rely on a different type of movement (Wh-movement).

These findings suggest that the problem underlying noncanonical sentence production involves the assembly of sentence constituents into a noncanonical order; that is, with movement. When provided with syntactic primes, the syntactic frame is in essence provided for the patient; therefore, the normal operations required to derive complex sentences are not required. And when they regain ability to formulate noncanonical sentences relying on one type of assembly, or movement, patients generalize this skill to untrained sentences that require the same assembly routine, but they do not generalize to sentences with different assembly requirements. This suggests, then, that part of positional-level processing is to perform the movement operations required to derive noncanonical sentences. This possibility, however, is not compatible with current models of sentence production, in that movement is not considered a viable component of the process of constituent assembly. Further research aimed at examining the relation between certain sentence types using Bock's syntactic priming paradigm (Bock, 1990) may shed light on this issue. More frequent elicitation of object clefts following *who*-question primes and, similarly, a higher proportion of passive sentences following subject-raising primes would provide data further indicating that separate operations are involved in computing Wh- and NP movement–derived sentences.

Summary of Constituent Assembly. To summarize, psycholinguistic and neuropsychological data suggest modular and computational separation between lexical and phrasal/sentential processes, although the two are highly interdependent. That is, activated lemmas determine the choice of sentence frames to a large extent. Further, factors such as animacy, agenthood, and prominence in discourse influence the ordering of elements in a sentence and, thereby, control the ultimate syntactic structure of the utterance. Available data also support an incremental rather than a competitive model of constituent assembly. However, patterns of production of noncanonical sentences in aphasia showing links between linguistically similar sentences structures suggest the potential for the involvement of additional operations in constituent assembly.

Inflection

Inflectional processes (also termed morpheme retrieval by Bock [1999]) involve generation of details, such as (in English) information about number, tense, and aspect of words. In addition, generation of function words such as auxiliary verbs, determiners, and prepositions, which provide the grammatical structure of sentences, is considered to be part of inflectional processes. Function words and affixes comprise elements of the closed class versus the open class that includes major lexical items (nouns, verbs, adjectives, and adverbs). A key point is that retrieval of closed-class elements is assumed to involve mechanisms that are different from retrieval of open-class words discussed earlier. The observation that individuals with agrammatic aphasia show selective impairment of open-class versus closed-class (function) words in both spontaneous production and in reading supports this distinction (Biassou, Obler, Nespoulous, Dordain, & Harris, 1997; Friederici & Schonle, 1980; Gardner & Zurif, 1975; Nespoulous, Dordain, Perron, et al., 1988). However, processes that derive inflectional affixes may differ from those that derive function words.

Inflectional Generation. Within the framework of early sentence production models posed by Garrett (1980, 1982), closed-class elements comprise the rudimentary material that creates the sentence frame, serving to mark the sentence frame for functions and grammatical features (for example, plural, past tense). This postulate is supported by speech errors known as *stranding* errors; for example, "They were turking talkish" (talking Turkish) (Garrett, 1988). Here, the root *turk* and the stem *talk* are exchanged, while the affixes are left in place—in other words, stranded. The observation that closed-class elements are rarely misplaced in stranding errors suggests that these elements are features of the planning frame and are, therefore, not subject to exchange processes. This implies that stranding is not a frame generation problem; rather, these errors result from normal frame generation coupled with some failure of lexical access.

However, speech errors known as shift errors (Garrett, 1975), which involve misplacement of closed-class material, suggest that inflectional material does not provide a static frame for lexical insertion. Consider, for example, the following error: "Mermaid moves their legs together" (for "Mermaids move their legs together") (Garrett, 1993). In this utterance it is the misattachment of plural *-s* to the verb *move* that renders the utterance erroneous. Shift errors not only differentiate inflection and constituent ordering, but also inflection and phonological encoding because shifted elements often bear the stress features of their new error-induced positions. Garrett (1993) reasoned that stranding occurs at the multiphrasal planning stage (constituent assembly in Bock and Levelt's [1994] model) and that shifts arise as a consequence of later operations.

In this account, for example, lemmas are considered to be the source of number agreement features in English. In functional processing terms, subject-verb agreement dependencies require that selected nouns and finite (tense and number carrying) verbs that are linked to the nominative function have the same number. To this end, the verb inherits the subject's number feature. In this manner, relevant relationships among words are created during lemma selection, and, subsequently, during positional processing, phrase fragments appropriate for generation of the intended dependencies are created. Speech errors that support this notion are termed errors of attraction, in which the number of the matrix verb agrees with the wrong sentence constituent; that is, some noun other than the head noun. Consider, for example, the following error: "Most cities are true of that" (for "That is true of most cities") (Stemberger, 1985b). Here number agreement of the verb conforms to the number of the noun occupying the subject position.

The origin of frame features that control the appearance of inflections, however, is unclear. For example, there is a debate in the literature about how regular and irregular word forms are computed. It is believed by some that all regularly and irregularly inflected forms are retrieved as whole units from the lexicon (Seidenberg, 1997), implying that regular forms do not represent the composition of a stem and an affix. In this view, sentence frame generation would not be controlled by inflectional affixation. The position, however, is challenged by the observation that some patients with aphasia show selective impairment in production of irregular versus regular forms, and vice versa, indicating that separate processes underlie their production (Penke, Janssen, & Krause, 1999; Ullman, Izvorski, Love, Yee, Swinney, & Hickock, in press). Moreover, Penke and colleagues (1999) showed that in their German-speaking agrammatic aphasic subjects, production of irregular words was found to be frequency sensitive, as are open-class words. This suggests that, open-class words, like irregular forms are accessed directly from the mental lexicon. These findings lend support to the notion that regularly inflected forms consist of a stem and an affix, believed to be computed in a rule-based manner—that is, through indirect election—and that irregularly inflected forms are generated from the lexicon and no affix is called for (Clahsen, 1999; Kim, Pinker, Prince, & Prasada, 1991; Pinker, 1991; Stemberger, 1985b).

Function Word Processing versus Inflectional Affixation. An important part of inflectional processing, relevant to sentence frame generation, involves the selection of function words, such as auxiliary verbs, determiners, prepositions, and so on, which help to provide the grammatical structure of sentences. Function words do not correspond to lexical concepts and, therefore, are considered to be accessed indirectly, as are inflectional morphemes. There are reasons to believe, however, that function words and inflectional affixes are under the control of unique operations in generation of the sentence frame. As noted above, Lapointe and Dell (1989) observed that function words are more likely to be omitted, and inflections are more likely to be substituted in agrammatic aphasia. Based on their observations they proposed that affixes are generated as part of the phrase fragment but that function words are not, in contrast to Garrett's (1975) original proposal. Instead, they suggested that function words are generated as separate fragments, which are inserted into the sentence frame by an additional operation. In this view, function words are distinguished from both inflectional affixes and open-class words.

Dissociations noted in aphasic individuals' ability to produce bound morphemes and function words supports this distinction (Miceli, Silveri, Romani, & Caramazza, 1989; Rochon, Saffran, Berndt, & Schwartz, 2000; Saffran, Berndt, & Schwartz, 1989). For example, in their analysis of narrative discourse in individuals with aphasia, Rochon and colleagues (2000) found structural measures of narrative speech such as the proportion of well-formed sentences and structural elaboration of sentences to correlate highly with bound morpheme production measures, but not with production of free morphemes. This finding suggests that generation of sentence structure is more closely linked to generation of bound inflections than is the retrieval of function words.

Summary of Inflection. To summarize, inflectional insertion is considered to occur at the positional level of sentence production and to involve processes that are distinguishable from those involved in constituent assembly. The cur   at thinking is that inflectional features, which generate the final surface structure of sentences are specified during lexical access through a process of indirect election. However, processes that compute inflectional affixes are likely separate from those that generate function words.

CONCLUSION

Cognitive models of sentence production have been revised and refined since Garrett proposed the original framework in 1975. Despite numerous modifications, the basic tenets of ensuing speech production models remain largely unchanged, and include a modular organization with distinct levels of processing between an abstract idea to be expressed and the final phonological makeup of the utterance. We have reviewed several types of evidence supporting this framework. In particular, the speech error data indicate that an impressively regular set of linguistic restrictions apply during sentence production. Further, experimental data in several domains support distinctions among processing levels and serve to elucidate the nature of component processes. Finally, patterns of breakdown and recovery of sentence production seen in individuals with aphasia, to the extent that they represent focal/discrete disruption of the normal language production system, further support the framework discussed here. However, as should be evident from our discussion, the component processes involved at each level require further specification and elaboration. Further, a crucial issue that remains unresolved concerns the temporal relationship between processing levels and the nature of interaction (if any) between them. Research examining the sentence production process, however, presents a challenge. As pointed out by Bock and Levelt (1994), manipulation of components of the language production system is difficult (if not impossible) to do without disrupting the fundamental features of underlying communicative intent. Nevertheless, further research of the type discussed here, as well as computational modeling and other innovative methods of experimentation, will lead us to a greater understanding of the sentence production process.

REFERENCES

Badecker, W., Miozzo, M., & Zanuttinni, R. (1995). The two-stage model of lexical retrieval: Evidence from a case of anomia with selective preservation of grammatical gender. *Cognition, 57,* 193–216.

Ballard, K. J., & Thompson, C. K. (1999). Treatment and generalization of complex sentence production in agrammatism. *Journal of Speech, Language, and Hearing Research, 42*(3), 690–707.

Bates, E., & Devescovi, A. (1989). Crosslinguistic studies of sentence production. In B. MacWhinney & E. Bates (Eds.), *The crosslinguistic study of sentence processing.* Cambridge: Cambridge University Press.

Bates, E., Friederici, A. D., Wulfeck, B. B., & Juarez, L. A. (1988). On the preservation of word order in aphasia: Cross-linguistic evidence. *Brain and Language, 33,* 323–364.

Baynes, K., Share, L. J., & Redfern, B. B. (1995). *Dual access to the lexicon in production: A targeted rehabilitation study.* Paper presented at the Academy of Aphasia, San Diego, CA.

Belletti, A., & Rizzi, L. (1988) Psych-Verbs and θ-theory. *Natural Language and Linguistic Theory, 6,* 291–352.

Berndt, R. S. (1991). Sentence processing in aphasia. In M. T. Sarno (Ed.), *Acquired aphasia* (2nd ed.). San Diego, CA: Academic Press.

Biassou, N., Obler, L. K., Nespoulous, J. L., Dordain, M., & Harris, K. S. (1997). Dual processing of open- and closed-class words. *Brain and Language, 57*(3), 360–73.

Bock, K. (1977). The effect of a pragmatic presupposition on syntactic structure in question answering. *Journal of Verbal Learning and Verbal Behavior, 16,* 723–734.

Bock, K. J. (1982). Toward a cognitive psychology of syntax: Information processing contributions to sentence formulation. *Psychological Review, 89,* 1–47.

Bock, K. (1986). Syntactic persistence in language production. *Cognitive Psychology, 18,* 355–387.

Bock, K. (1987). An effect of accessibility of word forms on sentence structures. *Journal and Memory and Language, 26,* 119-137.

Bock, K. (1990). Structure in language. *American Psychologist, 45*(11), 1221-1236.

Bock, K. (1995). Sentence production: From mind to mouth. In J. L. Miller & P. D. Eimas (Eds.), *Speech, language, and communication*. San Diego, CA: Academic Press.

Bock, K. (1999). Language production. In R. A. Wilson & F. Keil (Eds.), *The MIT encyclopedia of cognitive sciences*. Cambridge, MA: MIT Press.

Bock, K., & Levelt, W. (1994). Language production: Grammatical encoding. In M. A. Gernsbacher (Ed.), *Handbook of psycholinguistics*. San Diego, CA: Academic Press.

Bock, K., & Loebell, H. (1990). Framing sentences. *Cognition, 35*, 1–39.

Bock, K., & Warren, R. K. (1985). Conceptual accessibility and syntactic structure in sentence formulation. *Cognition, 21*, 47-67.

Bresnan, J. (Ed.). (1982). *The mental representation of grammatical relations*. Cambridge, MA: MIT Press.

Caramazza, A., & Hillis, A. E. (1989). The disruption of sentence production: A case of selected deficit to positional level processing. *Brain and Language, 35*, 625–650.

Caramazza, A., & Hillis, A. E. (1990a). Where do semantic errors come from? *Cortex, 26*, 95–122.

Caramazza, A., & Hillis, A.E. (1990b). Spatial representation of words in the brain implied by studies of a unilateral neglect patient. *Nature, 346*, 267–269.

Caramazza, A., & Miceli, G. (1991). Selective impairment of thematic role assignment in sentence processing. *Brain and Language, 41*, 402–436.

Caramazza, A., & Miozzo, M. (1997). The relation between syntactic and phonological knowledge in lexical access: Evidence from the tip-of-the-tongue phenomenon. *Cognition, 64*, 309–343.

Chomsky, N. (1986). *Barriers*. Cambridge, MA: MIT Press.

Clahsen, H. (1999). Lexical entries and rules of language: A multidisciplinary study of German inflection. *Behavioral and Brain Sciences, 22*, 991–1060.

Cutler, A. (1982). The reliability of speech error data. In A. Cutler (Ed.), *Slips of the tongue and language production*. Amsterdam: Mouton.

Damasio, A. R. (1990). Category related recognition deficits as a clue to the neural substrates of knowledge. *Trends in Neuroscience, 13*, 95-98.

De Blesser, R., & Kauschke, C. (2000). Acquisition and loss of nouns and verbs: Parallel or divergent patterns? Paper presented at the British Psychological Society Cognitive Psychology Section XVII Annual Conference. University of Essex.

Dell, G. (1986). A spreading activation theory of retrieval in sentence production. *Psychological Review, 93*, 283–321.

Dell, G. S., & O'Seaghdha, P. G. (1994). Inhibition in interactive activation models of linguistic selection and sequencing. In D. Dagenbach & C. H. Carr (Eds.), *Inhibitory processes in attention, memory, and language*. San Diego, CA: Academic Press.

Dell, G. S., & Reich, P. A. (1981). Stages in sentence production: An analysis of speech error data. *Journal of Verbal Learning and Behavior, 20*, 611–629.

Drew, R. L., & Thompson, C. K. (1999). Model-based semantic treatment for naming deficits in aphasia. *Journal of Speech, Language, and Hearing Research, 42*(4), 972-89.

Fay, D., & Cutler, A. (1977). Malapropisms and the structure of the mental lexicon. *Linguistic Inquiry, 8*, 505–520.

Ferreira, F. (1994). Choice of passive verb is affected by verb type and animacy. *Journal of Memory and Language, 33*, 715–736.

Ferreira, V. S. (1996). Is it better to give than to donate? Syntactic flexibility in language production. *Journal of Memory and Language, 35*, 724–755.

Fodor, J. A. (1983). *Modularity of mind*. Cambridge, MA: MIT Press.

Friederici, A. D., & Schnole, P. W. (1980). Computational dissociation of two vocabulary types. *Neuropsychologia, 13*, 181–190.

Fromkin, V. A. (1971). The non-anomalous nature of anomalous utterances. *Language, 47*, 27-52.

Gainotti, G., Miceli, G., Caltagirone, C., Silveri, C., & Masullo, C. (1981). Contiguity versus similarity of paraphasic substitutions in Broca's and in Wernicke's aphasia. *Journal of Communication Disorders, 14*, 1–9.

Gardner, H., & Zurif, E. (1975). *Bee* but not *be*: Oral reading of single words in aphasia and alexia. *Neuropsychologia, 13*, 181–190.

Garrett, M. F. (1975). The analysis of sentence production. In G. Bower (Ed.), *Psychology of Learning and Motivation, Vol. 9*. New York: Academic Press.

Garrett, M. F. (1980). Levels of processing in sentence production. In B. Butterworth (Ed.), *Language production*. London: Academic Press.

Garrett, M. F. (1982). Production of speech: Observations from normal and pathological language use. In E. A. W (Ed.), *Normality and pathology of language functions*. London: Academis Press.

Garrett, M. F. (1988). Processes in language production. In N. Frederick (Ed.), *Linguistics: The Cambridge survey, Vol. 3*. Cambridge: Cambridge University Press.

Garrett, N. F (1993). Errors and their relevance for models of language production. In G. Blanken, J. Dittman, H. Grimm, J. C. Marshall, & C.-W. Wallesh (Eds.), *Linguistic disorders and pathologies*. Berlin: Walter de Gruyter.

Glaser, W. R. (1992). Picture naming. *Cognition, 42*(1-3), 61–105.

Glaser, W. R., & Dungelhoff, F. J. (1984). The time course of picture-word interference. *Journal of Experimental Psychology: Human Perception and Performance, 10*, 640–654.

Grimshaw, J. (1990). *Argument structure*. Cambridge, MA: MIT Press.

Hartsuiker, R. J., & Kolk, H. H. J. (1998). Syntactic facilitation in agrammatic sentence production. *Brain and Language, 62*, 221–254.

Heeschen, C. (1993). Morphosyntactic characteristics of spoken language. In G. Blanken, J. Dittman, H. Grimm, J. C. Marshall, & C.-W. Wallesh (Eds.), *Linguistic disorders and pathologies*. Berlin: Walter de Gruyter.

Hillis, A., & Caramazza, A. (1991) Category-specific naming and comprehension impairment: A double dissociation. *Brain, 114*, 2081–2094.

Hillis, A. E., Rapp, B. C., Romani, C., & Caramazza, A. (1990). Selective impairment of semantics in lexical processing. *Cognitive Neuropsychology, 7*, 191–244.

Jacobs, B. J., & Thompson, C. K. (2000). Cross-modal generalization effects of training noncanonical sentence comprehension and production in agrammatic aphasia. *Journal of Speech, Language, and Hearing Research, 43*(1), 5–20.

Jescheniak, J. D., & Schriefers, H. (1998). Discrete serial versus cascaded processing in lexical access in speech production: Further evidence from coactivation of near-synonyms. *Journal of Experimental Psychology, 24*, 1256–1274.

Kay, J., & Ellis, A. (1987). A cognitive neuropsychological case study of anomia: implications for psychological models of word retrieval. *Brain, 110*, 613-629.

Kegl, J. (1995). Levels of representation and units of access relevant to agrammatism. *Brain and Language, 50*, 151-200.

Kempen, G., & Hoenkamp, E. (1987). An incremental procedural grammar for sentence formulation. *Cognitive Science, 11*, 201-258.

Kim, J. J., Pinker, S., Prince, A., & Prasada, S. (1991). Why no mere mortal has ever flown out to center field. *Cognitive Science, 15*, 173-218.

Kim, M., & Thompson, C. K. (2000). Verb retrieval in agrammatism. *Brain and Language, 74*, 1-25.

Kiss, K. (2000). Effects of verb complexity on agrammatic aphasic's sentence production. In R. Bastiaanse & Y Gordzinsky (Eds.), *Grammatical disorders in aphasia*. London: Whurr Publishers.

Laine, M., Kujala, P., Niemi, J., & Uusipaikka, E. (1992). On the nature of naming difficulties in aphasia. *Cortex, 28*(4), 537-54.

LaPointe, S. G., & Dell, G. S. (1989). A synthesis of some recent work in sentence production. In N. Carlson & M. K. Tanenhaus (Ed.), *Linguistic structure in language processing*. Dordrecht: Kluwer Academic Publishers.

Levelt, W. (1989). *Speaking: From intention to articulation*. Cambridge, MA: MIT Press.

Levelt, W. (1993). Language use in normal speakers and its disorders. In G. Blanken, J. Dittman, H. Grimm, J. C. Marshall, & C.-W. Wallesh (Eds.), *Linguistic disorders and pathologies*. Berlin: Walter de Gruyter.

Levelt, W. (1999). Producing spoken language: A blueprint of the speaker. In C. M. Brown & P. Hagoort (Eds.), *The neurocognition of language*. New York: Oxford University Press.

Levelt, W. J. M., Roelofs, A., & Meyer, A. S. (1999). A theory of lexical access in speech production. *Behavioral and Brain Sciences, 22*, 1-75.

Levin, B., & Rappaport-Hovav, M. (1995). *Unaccusativity*. Chicago: University of Chicago Press.

MacDonald, J. L., Bock, K., & Kelly, M. H. (1993). Word and world order: Semantic, phonological and metrical determinants of serial position. *Cognitive Psychology, 25*, 188-230.

Marin, J. W., & Schwartz, M. S. (1998). Facilitating sentence planning in nonfluent aphasia. *Brain and Language, 65*, 175-177.

Marshall, J., Pring, T., & Chiat, S. (1998). Verb retrieval and sentence production in aphasia. *Brain and Language, 63*(2), 159-83.

Martin, N., Dell, G. S., Saffran, E. M., & Schwartz, M. F. (1994). Origins of paraphasia in deep dysphasia: Testing the consequences of a decay impairment to an interactive spreading activation model of lexical retrieval. *Brain and Language, 47*, 609-660.

Martin, R. C., & Blossom-Stach, C. (1986). Evidence of syntactic deficits in a fluent aphasic. *Brain and Language, 28*(2), 196-234.

McClelland, J. L., & Rumelhart, D. E. (1981). An interactive activation model of context effects in letter perception. Part I: An account of basic findings. *Psychological Review, 88*, 375-407.

Menn, L., Reilly, K. F., Hayashi, M., Kamio, A., Fujita, I., & Sasanuma, S. (1998). The interaction of preserved pragmatics and impaired syntax in Japanese and English aphasic speech. *Brain & Language, 61*(2), 183-225.

Miceli, G., Silveri, M. C., Nocentini, U., & Caramazza, A. (1988). Patterns of dissociation in comprehension and production of nouns and verbs. *Aphasiology, 2*(3/4), 351-358.

Miceli, G., Silveri, C., Romani, C., & Caramazza, A. (1989). Variation in the pattern of omissions and substitutions of grammatical morphemes in the spontaneous speech of so-called agrammatic patients. *Brain and Language, 36*, 447-492.

Miceli, G., Silveri, M. C., Villa, G., & Caramazza, A. (1984). On the basis for the agrammatic's difficulty in producing main verbs. *Cortex, 20*(2), 207-20.

Nespoulous, J.-L., Dordain, M., Perron, C., Ska, B., Bub, D., Caplan, D., Mehler, J., & Lecours, A. R. (1988). Agrammatism in sentence production without comprehension deficits: Reduced availability of syntactic structures and/or of grammatical morphemes? A case study. *Brain and Language, 33*, 273-295.

Pease, D., & Goodglass, H. (1978). The effects of cueing on picture naming in aphasia. *Cortex, 14*, 178-189.

Penke, M., Janssen, U., & Krause, M. (1999). The representation of inflectional morphology: Evidence from Broca's aphasia. *Brain and Language, 68*, 225-232.

Pinker, S. (1991). Rules of language. *Science, 253*, 530-535.

Rochon, E., Saffran, E. M., Berndt, R. S., & Schwartz, M. F. (2000). Quantitative analysis of aphasic sentence production: Further developments and new data. *Brain and Language, 72*, 193-218.

Roelofs, A. (1992). A spreading-activation theory of lemma retrieval in speaking. *Cognition, 42*(1-3), 107-142.

Saffran, E. M., Berndt, R. S., & Schwartz, M. F. (1989). The quantitative analysis of agrammatic production: Procedure and data. *Brain and Language, 37*, 440-479.

Saffran, E. M., Schwartz, M. F., & Marin, O. S. M. (1980). The word order problem in agrammatism II: Production. *Brain and Language, 10*, 263-280.

Schneider, S. L., & Thompson, C. K. (In press). Verb production in agrammatic aphasia: The influence of semantic and syntactic properties on generalization. *Journal of Speech, Langauge, and Hearing Research*.

Schriefers, H., Meyer, A. S., & Levelt, W. J. M. (1990). Exploring the time course of lexical access in speech production: Results from picture-word interference experiments. *Journal of Memory and Language, 29*, 86-102.

Schwartz, M. F. (1987). Patterns of speech production deficit within and across aphasia syndromes: Application of a psycholinguistic model. In M. Coltheart, G. Sartori, & R. Job (Eds.), *The cognitive neuropsychology of language*. Hillsdale, NJ: Lawrence Erlbaum.

Seidenberg, M. S. (1997). Language acquisition and use: Learning and applying probabilistic constraints. *Science, 275*, 1599-1603.

Stemberger, J. P. (1982). Syntactic errors in speech. *Journal of Psycholinguistic Research, 11*, 313-345.

Stemberger, J. P. (1985a). *The lexicon in a model of language production*. New York: Garland Publishing.

Stemberger, J. P. (1985b). An interactive activation model of language production. In A. Ellis (Ed.), *Progress in the psychology of language*. London: Lawrence Erlbaum.

Stemberger, J. P. (1995). Phonological and lexical constraints on morphological processing. In L. B. Feldman (Ed.), *Morphological aspects of language processing*. Hillsdale, NJ: Lawrence Erlbaum.

Thompson, C. K. (2000). A syntactic account of verb production deficits in agrammatic aphasia. Paper presented at the British Psychological Society Cognitive Psychology Section XVII Annual Conference, University of Essex.

Thompson, C. K., Lange, K. L., Schneider, S. L., & Shapiro, L. P. (1997). Agrammatic and nonbrain damaged subject's verb and verb argument structure production. *Aphasiology, 11,* 473–490.

Thompson, C. K., & Shapiro, L. P. (1995). Training sentence production in agrammatism: Implications for normal and disordered language. *Brain and Language, 50,* 201-224.

Thompson, C. K., Shapiro, L. P., Ballard, K. J., Jacobs, B. J., & Tait, M. E. (1997). Training and generalized production of wh- and NP movement structures in agrammatic aphasia. *Journal of Speech, Language, and Hearing Research, 40,* 228–244.

Thompson, C. K., Shapiro, L. P., Tait, M. E., Jacobs, B. J., & Schneider, S. L. (1996). Training Wh-question production in agrammatic aphasia: Analysis of argu-

ment and adjunct movement. *Brain and Language,* 52(1), 175–228.

Ullman, M. T., Izvorski, R., Love, T., Yee, E., Swinney, D., & Hickok, G. (In press). Neural correlates of the lexicon and grammar: Evidence from the production, reading and judgement of inflection in aphasia. *Brain and Language.*

Vigliocco, G., Antonini, T., & Garrett, M. F. (1997). Grammatical gender is on the tip of Italian tongues. *Psychological Science, 8,* 314–317.

Warrington, E. & McCarthy, R. (1983). Category specific access dysphasia. *Brain, 106,* 859–878.

Warrington, E., & Shallice, T. (1984). Category specific semantic impairments. *Brain, 107,* 829–854.

Young, A., Newcombe, F., Hellawell, D., & DeHaan, E. (1989). Implicit access to semantic information. *Brain and Language, 11,* 186–209.

Zingeser, L. B., & Berndt, R. S. (1990). Retrieval of nouns and verbs in agrammatism and anomia. *Brain and Language, 39,* 14–32.

18

The Neural Basis of Syntactic
Processing: A Critical Look

David Caplan

Sentences convey relationships between the meanings of words, such as who is accomplishing an action or receiving it. The syntactic structure of a sentence is the principal determinant of this "propositional" information (Chomsky, 1965, 1981, 1986, 1995). There is near universal agreement that syntactic structures are constructed from semantic and pragmatic representations as part of the production of spoken, written, and signed language, and from lexical, prosodic, and other perceptual cues in comprehension (see Frazier & Clifton, 1996; Just & Carpenter, 1992; MacDonald, Pearlmutter, & Seidenberg, 1994, for different models of the parsing process, and Levelt, 1989; Bock & Levelt, 1994, for discussion of the process of constructing syntactic structures in speech production). The neural basis for syntactic processing may differ in these different tasks. In this review, I shall deal with studies of comprehension, because it is the domain in which the most studies have been done.

THE GROSS FUNCTIONAL NEUROANATOMY
OF SYNTACTIC PROCESSING IN LANGUAGE COMPREHENSION

There is good evidence that syntactic processing in sentence comprehension involves the perisylvian association cortex—the pars triangularis and opercularis of the inferior frontal gyrus (Brodmann's areas (BA) 45 and 44: Broca's area), the angular gyrus (BA 39), the supramarginal gyrus (BA 40), and the superior temporal gyrus (BA 22: Wernicke's area)—in the dominant hemisphere. Data regarding the functional neuroanatomy of syntactic comprehension were originally derived from deficit-lesion correlations and, more recently, come from functional neuroimaging and electrophysiological studies in normal subjects. All these sources of data indicate that the perisylvian association cortex is involved in this function.

Patients with lesions in parts of this cortex have been described who have had long-lasting impairments of this function (Caramazza & Zurif, 1976). We have estimated that over 90 percent of patients with aphasic disorders who have lesions in this region have disturbances of syntactic comprehension (Caplan, 1987a). Disorders affecting syntactic comprehension after perisylvian lesions have been described in all languages that have been studied, in patients of all ages, with written and spoken input, and after a variety of lesion types, indicating that this cortical region is involved in syntactic processing, independent of these factors (see Caplan, 1987b, for review). Functional neuroimaging studies by Stromswold and colleagues (1996),

Caplan and colleagues (1998, 1999, 2000), Just and colleagues (1996), Dapretto and Bookheimer (1999), Stowe and colleagues (1998), and others have documented increases in regional cerebral blood flow (rCBF) using positron emission tomography (PET) or blood oxygenation level dependent (BOLD) signal using functional magnetic resonance imaging (fMRI) in tasks in which subjects' processing of more versus less syntactically complex sentences was compared. Event-related potentials (ERPs) whose sources are likely to be in this region (the left anterior negativity (LAN)—see below) have been described in relationship to a variety of syntactic processes, including responses to category and agreement violations, comprehension of complex relative clauses, and others (Kluender & Kutas, 1993a, 1993b; Neville, Nical, Barss, Forster, & Garret, 1991). These data all converge on the conclusion that syntactic processing in comprehension is carried out in the dominant perisylvian cortex.

Regions outside the perisylvian association cortex might also support support syntactic processing. If so, one might find evidence for this localization in the form of lesions in these areas leading to disorders of this function. To date, there are no studies that document syntactic comprehension disorders following lesions to nonperisylvian-association cortex, to my knowledge. This does not disprove the hypothesis that nonperisylvian regions support syntactic processing, since future studies may document such associations and because the role of these regions may be ancillary to that of perisylvian cortex for this function.

Evidence for the involvement of nonperisylvian regions in syntactic processing does come from functional neuroimaging and ERP studies.

Mazoyer and colleagues (1993) found increased rCBF in the anterior left temporal lobe when subjects heard stories in French, in French with all the content words replaced with nonwords, or a French story in which every content word was replaced with a semantically unrelated word from the same grammatical category, compared to when they listened to stories in a language they did not know (Tamil) or to lists of words. Bavelier and colleagues (1997) also found increased BOLD signal in anterior temporal, as well as perisylvian, cortex when subjects read sentences compared to reading word lists. Both these studies have been taken as evidence that the anterior temporal cortex is involved in syntactic processing. However, these studies are hard to interpret for several reasons: there were many differences between the activation and baseline conditions in these studies other than the fact that the activation conditions have recognizable syntactic structure (for example, differences in lexical items, in the presence of function words, in intonational contours, and so on), and there were no behavioral tests of what subjects did when they processed these stimuli.

Nonetheless, more controlled activation studies of syntactic processing have also activated nonperisylvian regions. The cingulate gyrus and nearby regions of medial frontal lobe have shown increased blood flow when subjects process syntactically more complex sentences (Caplan et al., 1998, 1999, 2000a). In several studies (Caplan et al., 1998; Carpenter, Just, Keller, Eddy, & Thulborn, 1999), there has been activation in superior parietal lobe in syntactic tasks. These activations have been attributed to non-domain-specific attentional processes (cingulate and midline frontal activation) and to visual-spatial processing (parietal activation), and they may reflect the involvement of short-term memory in comprehending the more complex sentences. It is also possible that these activations are due to syntactic processing per se. The involvement of the superior parietal lobe in syntactic processing is supported by electrophysiological data (event-related potentials), to be discussed later.

The nondominant hemisphere may also be involved in syntactic comprehension. We found that fourteen patients with nondominant hemisphere lesions showed effects of syntactic complexity on performance in an enactment task, which were independent of sentence length (Caplan, Hildebrandt, & Makris, 1996). Normal control subjects did not show these effects. We concluded that right hemisphere lesions affected syntactic comprehension. However, the control subjects performed at ceiling on the syntactically simple sentences, so the effect of the syntactic manipulation in that group may not have been apparent, and this conclusion needs to be reinvestigated. Just and colleagues (1996) reported activation results supporting a role for nondominant hemisphere homologues of Broca's and Wernicke's areas in syntactic comprehension; these areas increased their BOLD signal in response to processing syntactically complex sentences, though to a lesser extent than Broca's and Wernicke's areas themselves. A role for the nondominant hemisphere in this function is possible.

Finally, it has been suggested that subcortical structures involved in laying down procedural memories for motor functions—in particular, the basal ganglia—are involved in "rule-based" processing in language (Ullman, Corkin, et al., 1997, Ullman, Bergida, et al., 1997). To date, data on the role of these structures in rule-based processes have come from studies of morphological processes, and the extent to which they may be involved in rule-based syntactic processing is unclear. However, these subcortical structures are worth mentioning in this survey as possible neural loci of syntactic processing.

THE FUNCTIONAL ORGANIZATION OF THE PERISYLVIAN ASSOCIATION CORTEX FOR SYNTACTIC PROCESSING

A major focus of investigation has been how the perisylvian association cortex is organized to support syntactic comprehension. Different researchers endorse strongly localizationist models (Grodzinsky, 1990, 1995, 2000; Swinney & Zurif, 1995; Zurif, Swinney, Prather, Solomon, & Bushell, 1993), distributed net models (Damasio, 1992; Mesulam, 1990), and models that postulate individual variability in the neural substrate for this function (Caplan, 1987a, 1994; Caplan, Baker, & Dehaur, 1985, 1996). Localizationist models have focused on Broca's area as the locus of all or part of syntactic processing. Distributed models have argued that the entire perisylvian association cortex constitutes a neural net in which this function takes place, although theorists who have developed these models have also maintained that, within this net, Broca's area plays a more important role than other regions. Researchers who postulate individual variability maintain that different individuals use different parts of this cortex to process syntax, or different parts of syntax.

Deficit-Lesion Correlational Studies

Data from deficit-lesion correlational studies bear on these models. There are many such studies (for reviews, see Berndt et al., 1996; Grodzinsky, 2000).[1] These studies show that deficits in syntactic comprehension occur in all aphasic syndromes (Berndt et al., 1996; Caplan et al., 1985, 1997) and following lesions throughout the perisylvian cortex (Caplan et al., 1996). Conversely, patients of all types and with all lesion locations have been described with normal syntactic comprehension (Caplan et al., 1985; Caplan, 1987a). We shall briefly review our own studies, which are typical in this regard.

---

[1]Typically, syntactic comprehension deficits are established by showing that patients can understand semantically irreversible sentences with complex syntactic structures (for example, "The apple the boy ate was red") and semantically reversible sentences with simple syntactic structures (for example, "The boy chased the girl") but not semantically reversible sentences with complex structures (for example, "The boy the girl pushed was tall"). In the last sentence type the relationships between the nouns and verbs cannot be inferred from real-world knowledge or derived by simple heuristics (for example, take the noun immediately before the verb as the agent of the following verb) but depend upon a complex syntactic structure. In most cases, patients are required to indicate that they understand the thematic roles in these sentences using picture matching or enactment tasks. Relatively few syntactic structures are typically examined; often only passives and relative clauses are examined. Some aphasic patients have been shown to be able to make judgments about the grammaticality of sentences they do not understand (Linebarger, Schwartz, & Saffran, 1983; Linebarger, 1995; Wulfeck, 1988), suggesting that they have trouble mapping semantic values such as thematic roles onto syntactic structures that they have created. Several studies have shown normal, or near normal, on-line processing by patients who do poorly on off-line tasks (for example, Tyler, 1985). For these reasons, caution must be observed in taking the pattern of performance described above in sentence-picture matching or enactment (off-line tasks) as definitive evidence for a deficit in the unconscious, obligatory construction of syntactic structures.

In our earliest studies (Caplan, Baker, & Dehaut, 1985; Caplan, 1987a), we used the object manipulation (OM) task with nine syntactic structures in three studies of aphasic patients. In each study, we divided the patients into groups using hierarchical cluster analysis. We found that mean group performance deteriorated on sentences that had more noun phrases, more verbs and prepositions, and in which noun phrases could not be linearly mapped onto the canonical order of thematic roles. We also found that more impaired groups of patients performed more poorly on sentences that were harder for the whole subject population. We suggested that this pattern could result from variable reductions in the availability of a processing resource that is used in syntactic comprehension. In addition, there were indications that patients in some groups were less able to perform certain syntactic operations than others, though the evidence for this was weak. Examination of the relationship of these clusters to lesion location and to aphasic syndromes revealed that patients with lesions in all parts of the perisylvian association cortex and classified by speech pathologists as belonging to every aphasic syndrome fell into all clusters, from worst-performing to best-performing levels. Caplan (1987a) found that a small number of patients performed at normal levels. Most of these patients were ones with relatively pure speech output disturbances—dysarthria and apraxia of speech—though some had other aphasic diagnoses.

We replicated this study using a sentence-picture matching (SPM) task (Caplan, Waters, & Hildebrant, 1997), in which we tested two groups of aphasic patients with left hemisphere strokes (N = 52 and 17) on ten examples of each of ten sentence types. Performance was very similar to that on the OM task. We also tested the group of seventeen patients on both the OM and SPM tasks, and found that performance was significantly correlated. Performance on the SPM task was also not related to lesion location or to aphasic syndrome, with the same exception that patients who performed best tended to be those with relatively pure speech output disturbances.

The data regarding lesion location in these studies were limited to review of reports of radiological procedures, other laboratory reports, and neurological examinations. While lesions were attributed to patients conservatively, these attributions were admittedly inexact. In other work, we examined lesions directly. Caplan and colleagues (1996) reported the effect of lesion site on performance of eighteen patients with (L) CVAs. Volumetric analysis of lesions was undertaken based on CT scans of the brain. These analyses identified the percent of five specific perisylvian regions of interest (ROIs) that was lesioned. Patients were studied using OM on twelve examples of each of twenty-five sentence types. Performance was compared across patients with different lesion sites and correlated with lesion volume in these ROIs. Neither overall accuracy on the twenty-five sentence types, nor an overall score reflecting the effect of syntactic complexity independent of sentence length, nor nineteen separate measures that corresponded to particular syntactic operations, differed in groups defined by lesion location. No correlations between overall accuracy on the entire set of twenty-five sentence types, overall syntactic complexity score, or the nineteen separate measures of particular syntactic operations and normalized lesion volume in the language zone, normalized lesion volume in each of the five perisylvian ROIs, and normalized lesion volume in the anterior and posterior perisylvian ROIs were significant. These correlations remained insignificant when the effect of overall lesion size was partialled out. The results all remained unchanged in ten patients who were studied and scanned at about the same time relative to their lesions (six to twenty-four months post stroke). Detailed analysis of single cases with small lesions of roughly comparable size, who were tested at about the same time after their strokes, indicated that the degree of variability found in quantitative and qualitative aspects of patients' performances was not related to lesion location or the size of lesions in the anterior or posterior portion of the perisylvian association cortex.

Data such as these (see also the review by Berndt, Mitchum, & Haendiges, 1996) argue strongly against localizationist models. The fact that lesions throughout the perisylvian cortex are associated with syntactic processing deficits and that there is no clear relationship between these lesions or aphasic syndromes and these deficits is incompatible with localizationist models. The finding of spared comprehension after strokes in all parts of the perisylvian association cortex is also hard to reconcile with distributed models, since these models predict that there should be evidence of *some* syntactic impairment after *any* perisylvian lesion (but see footnote 1, p. 333). The data are most compatible with an individual variability model, and constitute the main reason that we postulated such a model (Caplan, 1987a, 1994; Caplan et al., 1985, 1996).

There are alternatives to this conclusion. While the presence of deficits after lesions throughout the perisylvian cortex provides strong evidence against localizationist models, the implications of spared performance following lesions throughout this region are less clear. A deficit is a deficit; unless it can be shown that deficits in syntactic processing are secondary to impairments in other functions (such as short-term memory), the implication of a persistent deficit in syntactic processing after a lesion in an area of the brain is that this brain region is necessary for this function in the individual in question. In contrast, the absence of a deficit is always subject to question. It is possible that seemingly unaffected patients have abnormalities of syntactic processing that have yet to be described. This consideration is rendered more likely when we realize that few patients have been tested for on-line syntactic processing or for the ability to construct and interpret a large range of syntactic structures. The deficit-lesion data would therefore be compatible with distributed models, if all patients were shown to have syntactic processing deficits on more rigorous testing. It is also possible that patients who do not have syntactic comprehension disorders when tested months or years after a cerebral insult had such disorders initially. If all perisylvian lesions are initially associated with syntactic comprehension deficits and some of these deficits recover fully, the implication is that syntactic processing requires the entire perisylvian cortex in normal subjects and that it can be sustained by part of that cortex, or by other brain regions, in some individuals.

Advocates of localization have not accepted the conclusion that the data from deficit-lesion correlational analyses rule out localizationist models of syntactic processing. They have argued that a more detailed characterization of syntactic deficits leads to the conclusion one syntactic process is localized in one cortical region. Specifically, Grodzinsky and his colleagues have argued that Broca's aphasics, and not other aphasics, have impairments in a syntactic process known as the coindexation of traces. Grodzinsky (2000) has also argued that this problem in coindexing traces is the *only* syntactic processing problem that Broca's aphasics have. This hypothesis is known as the trace deletion hypothesis (TDH). The hypothesis has a positive-valence counterpart: it implies that traces are coindexed in the region of the brain in which lesions produce Broca's aphasia—Broca's area.

The TDH is relevant to the nature of normal syntactic representations and their normal processing. Chomsky's model of syntax postulates the existence of traces, but others' models do not (Bresnan, 1972; Gazdar, Klein, Pullum, & Sag, 1985), and advocates of the position that the coindexation of traces is localized have also argued that their data support Chomsky's model. In Chomsky's syntactic theory (Chomsky, 1986, 1995), traces are noun phrases (NPs) that are not pronounced that are found in sentences in which an NP has to be related to a distant syntactic position to receive a thematic role because the NP has moved from an initial position. In Chomsky's theory, this occurs in passive sentences, sentences with relative clauses, and several other sentence types. A deficit in coindexation of traces would lead to poor comprehension of sentences with traces and good comprehension of sentences without them, with the qualification that patients would be expected to be able to understand some sentences that have traces by using compensatory heuristics. A frequently used heuristic assigns the thematic role of "agent" to a noun that does not have a thematic role, or to a noun before a verb (but see Beretta & Munn, 1998, for discussion). The pattern of performance that provides support for the TDH is good comprehension of sentences with traces in subject position, such as sentence

(1 below), and poor performance on sentences with traces in object position, such as passive sentences (2), and object-relativized sentences (3).

1. It was the boy who [t] hugged the girl.
2. The girl was hugged [t] by the boy.
3. It was the girl who the boy hugged [t].

This pattern of performance certainly occurs in Broca's aphasics and in patients with lesions in and around Broca's area, as predicted by the TDH. There are, however, two problems for the TDH. There are Broca's aphasics who do not show the TDH performance pattern but rather perform well on sentences such as 2 and 3. Second, among the patients with lesions that do not affect Broca's area, there are many who *do* show the TDH performance pattern. Both these points have been subject to considerable discussion.

The first of these points was emphasized in the paper we have referred to previously by Berndt and colleagues (1996), which documented good performances in about one-third of Broca's aphasics on passive sentences. This paper triggered a response from Grodzinsky and colleagues (1999), who reanalyzed the data on passive sentences presented in Berndt et al. (1996) and argued that these good performances were part of a Gaussian distribution of performance of these patients on these sentences. Berndt and Caramazza (1999) challenged Grodzinsky and colleagues' (1999) reply on the grounds of patient selection, pointing out that Grodzinsky and colleagues (1999) eliminated twenty-one cases from those collected by Berndt and colleagues (1996) and added twenty-one other cases from studies of their own, and that this biased the selection against patients who performed well on passive sentences. Zurif and Pinango (1999) and Drai and Grodzinsky (1999) responded to these arguments, arguing that the twenty-one excluded cases were not "Broca's aphasics," that only ten of the twenty-one included cases might have been selected because they had the pattern of comprehension predicted by the TDH, and that essentially the same basic pattern of performance on passive sentences was seen in the original cases in Berndt et al. (1996) as in the group reported in Grodzinsky et al. (1999). Caramazza and colleagues (2001) then criticized the Grodzinsky and colleagues (1999) paper on statistical grounds. Caramazza and colleagues (2001) argued that formal evaluation showed that the performances of the patients selected by Grodzinsky and colleagues (1999) did not form a Gaussian distribution. At this point, the data favor the view that some Broca's aphasics perform above chance on reversible passive sentences, contrary to the TDH (see also comments by Drai, Grodzinsky, & Zurif, 2001; Caplan, 2001).

The second claim of the TDH that has been discussed is that aphasic patients other than Broca's aphasics do not have disturbances affecting the coindexation of traces. This is not the case with respect to off-line tests of syntactic comprehension: the pattern of performance that we have taken as evidence of a problem coindexing traces occurs in all aphasic syndromes (Berndt et al., 1996; Caplan et al., 1985, 1997; even Grodzinsky reports such results: see Balogh & Grodzinsky, 1999). Since aphasic syndromes are not necessarily 100 percent related to lesion locations, it is important to note that this pattern is also found following lesions throughout the perisylvian cortex (Caplan et al., 1996). Again, these findings would seem to speak decisively against the TDH. However, again, Grodzinsky has replied to this argument against his hypothesis. His response is that the mechanism that produces disturbances affecting coindexation of traces is different in patients with anterior and posterior lesions, as shown by on-line studies (Zurif et al., 1993; Swinney, Zurif, Prather, & Love, 1996). We therefore now turn to these studies.

Swinney and his colleagues (Zurif et al., 1993; Swinney & Zurif, 1995; Swinney et al., 1996) have studied on-line "gap filling" in Broca's aphasics. These authors tested altogether eight Broca's aphasics, all of whom performed below normal in sentence-picture matching for reversible passive sentences. The on-line task they used was cross-modal lexical priming (CMLP). In this task, subjects listen to a sentence and make a lexical decision about a word presented visually at a point in the ongoing sentence. The visual targets of interest occurred at the point of a trace in the sentence and were or were not semantically related to the antecedent of the trace. Normal subjects show priming for related words at this point (and not just before this point); that is, they show priming for a word such as *doctor* at point 2 (but not at the control point 1) in sentences such as (4) and (5) below.

4. The nurse serving on the renal transplant unit [1] who [2] administered the injection replaced the vial.
5. The nurse serving on the renal transplant unit [1] who the injection dismayed [2] replaced the vial.

The Broca's aphasics failed to show this effect. Grodzinsky attributes the Broca's aphasics' lack of priming to a failure to coindex the trace. Swinney and his colleagues attribute it to a delay in this process due to slowed lexical activation.

The reason that Grodzinsky (and Swinney, Zurif, and their colleagues) have argued that the mechanism involved in non-Broca's aphasics' off-line problems with sentences containing traces is different from that found in Broca's aphasics is that Swinney and his colleagues found that eight fluent aphasics showed CMLP in this paradigm; that is, they behaved like normal subjects and showed facilitation for a word such as *doctor* at point 2 (but not at the control point 1) in sentences such as (4) and (5). Therefore, though the mechanism underlying the fluent patients' off-line disorder is not known, Grodzinsky has claimed that it differs from that of the Broca's aphasics when on-line processing is considered.

However, the distinction between Broca's and fluent aphasics' CMLP performances is not as clear as Swinney, Zurif, Grodzinsky, and their colleagues say. In the first study (Zurif et al., 1993), four Wernicke's patients who showed CMLP effects for traces also performed better than the four Broca's aphasics who did not show the CMLP effect on off-line tests of the ability to understand sentences that required the coindexation of traces (that is, passive sentences). The differences in on-line performance might have been due to the relative impairment of the patients rather than their aphasia type or lesion site (Caplan, 1995). In addition, a study by Blumstein and colleagues (1998) contradicts the Swinney/Zurif results. Blumstein and her colleagues repeated the Swinney study using purely auditory materials (the target word was presented in the voice of a speaker of the opposite sex from the speaker of the sentence). They found priming for words semantically related to the antecedent of a trace in eight Broca's aphasics, but no priming for words separated from a prime by an equal number of syllables in control sentences without traces. Balogh and colleagues (1998) argued that the Blumstein et al. results reflect end-of-sentence "wrap up" reactivation of previously presented lexical items, not syntactically based coindexation of traces. However, this cannot be true of two sentence types in Blumstein and colleagues' experiment 1 (their "wh-questions" and "relative clause as subject" materials), in which the trace was not at the end of the sentence and in which the Broca's aphasics showed priming effects. Five fluent (Wernicke's) aphasics did *not* show priming in the Blumstein et al. study, also the opposite result from that reported by Swinney and his colleagues. Blumstein and her colleagues raise the possibility that the absence of statistically significant priming may be due to the small number of patients in this group.

All of these studies must be tempered by the consideration that the experiments were not designed to test the performance of individual patients. In the Zurif and Swinney studies, a deliberate decision was made to use a between-subjects design that made it impossible to ascertain whether priming effects were present in individual subjects. In the Blumstein et al. experiment, too few examples of each type were given to look for significant effects in single subjects (no item statistics are reported in the Blumstein et al. paper). Therefore, these results may hide individual performances that go against the central tendencies of either group of patients. Also, the materials used by Swinney and his colleagues are subject to another concern raised by McKoon and her colleagues. McKoon and colleagues (1994) and McKoon and Ratcliff (1994) argued that the priming effects found with these materials may be due to a better pragmatic fit of the related than the unrelated words to the pragmatic context at the point of the trace, not to the coindexation of the trace per se. Nicol and colleagues (1994) have responded to McKoon and colleagues' concerns by arguing that CMLP exists for the antecedents of traces even when pragmatic factors do not produce such priming (see also Love & Swinney, 1996), but it is not clear whether the stimuli used in the protocol with the Broca's aphasics they tested were confounded with these pragmatic effects.

Overall, at this point in time, the evidence is consistent with the view that, among both Broca's and fluent aphasics, there are some patients that do and and some that do not coindex traces normally on-line.

Finally, the TDH claims that Broca's aphasics do not have disturbances affecting syntactic processing other than a disturbance of coindexation of traces. But this is not clear. Grodzinsky (1995, 2000) cites literature that shows normal processing of phrase structure, coindexation of pronouns, and other grammatical structures in Broca's aphasics. However, the literature cited by Grodzinsky is lacking in individual cases who have been studied on the full range of structures relevant to the TDH. Grodzinsky assumes that because a small number of Broca's aphasics have been shown to be able to understand some types of syntactic structures (for example, Grodzinsky et al., 1993), all Broca's aphasics can be assumed to understand these structures. But this assumption is unwarranted. Only detailed case studies in which individual aphasic patients have been tested on the range of structures needed to establish a deficit restricted to the coindexation of traces can show that an aphasic patient has such a restricted deficit. Case studies in which aphasic patients have been tested on this range of structures have shown a variety of deficits (Caplan & Hildebrandt, 1988a, 1988b; Caplan et al., 1996; Hildebrandt, Caplan & Evans, 1988). All of the patients who have had disturbances affecting traces have also had disturbances affecting other structures, in particular the ability to coindex other items such as pronouns, reflexives, and other empty categories postulated in Chomsky's model of syntax. No clear picture has emerged for Broca's aphasics (Caplan, 2000a).

We have gone through a long discussion to arrive at the conclusion that, on the basis of available evidence, the claim that Broca's area is the sole locus of coindexation of traces is to be rejected. The conclusion that we draw on the basis of present evidence is that the coindexation of traces can go on in all regions of the perisylvian cortex. For syntactic operations, existing deficit-lesion correlational data do not support a localizationist model. They are compatible with a model that recognizes individual differences in localization of syntactic operations.

The phenomenon of coindexation of traces is the best studied syntactic operation in the literature on deficit-lesion correlations; we know less about the localization of other syntactic operations than we do about this process. It is fair to say that the literature on other syntactic operations—subject-verb agreement, noun-adjective agreement, coindexation of reflexives and other phonologically empty referentially dependent NPs, and other syntactic phenomena—is too sparse with respect to number of cases studied, the type of neuroimaging data obtained and/or reported, and aspects of the psycholinguistic evaluation of the studied cases (the availability of on-line studies, for instance) to allow any conclusions about the functional neuroanatomy of these operations to be advanced with any degree of confidence.

Functional Neuroimaging Studies

Positron emission tomography (PET) and, more recently, functional magnetic resonance imaging (fMRI) have become a major source of data regarding the location of the neural tissue involved in language processing. PET and fMRI detect vascular responses to neural events associated with motor, sensory, and cognitive processes. These vascular responses are often called "activation"; it must be recognized that they may in part reflect increases in firing rates of neurons whose physiological effects are inhibitory as well as those with excitatory consequences.

PET and fMRI afford superior localization to deficit-lesion because of the large size of most lesions, and because the variability in many factors in most series of patients (age, education, neural structures affected, time since acute event, intervening therapy, and so on) makes it hard to attribute a particular deficit to a lesion in particular structure independent of other factors. PET and fMRI allow one to study a homogeneous group of subjects and to detect changes in vascular response associated with particular experimental manipulations. Methods for data collection, normalization of brain contours, and statistical analysis have advanced extremely rapidly for these imaging technologies. This has greatly added to the accuracy and sensitivity of these techniques; it has the unavoidable downside of resulting in a rapidly changing domain of study in which different experimental paradigms and different data acquisition and analysis methods are confounded. Coupled with the fact that there are only a limited number of studies of syntactic processing that are based on these imaging techniques, only very preliminary suggestions about the functional neuroanatomy of this ability can be made at present on the basis of activation studies.

The most widely utilized experimental approach in studies that use these techniques is to contrast two conditions—an "experimental" condition and a "baseline" condition that are thought to differ in a limited number of functional operations (ideally, to differ in only one operation). This "subtraction" approach can be used to progressively hone in on more specific operations, and to compare putatively identical operations across different tasks. Studies of syntactic processing that have utilized this technique have provided evidence relevant to the functional organization of the perisylvian cortex for syntactic processing.[2] I shall first review a series of PET studies from our lab, and then turn to other reports in the literature.

Our utilization of the subtraction approach consisted of presenting sentences that were controlled for lexical content and propositional meaning and that varied in syntactic form. We contrasted more complex subject-object (SO) sentences (for example, "The juice that the child spilled stained the rug") with less complex object-subject (OS) sentences (for example, "The child spilled the juice that stained the rug"). Subjects either read or listened to a sentence and made a speeded decision as to whether it was plausible or not. In all experiments, longer RTs and sometimes more errors occurred in the more complex sentences.

The first four experiments we conducted were with college-educated young right-handed subjects. Eight male subjects, aged nineteen to twenty-eight, participated in experiment 1, which used whole sentence visual presentation (Stromswold et al., 1996). There was an in-

---

[2]The first studies in this area compared sentence processing against a range of baseline tasks. Mazoyer and colleagues (1993) used PET to compare rCBF when native speakers of French were at rest with rCBF when they listened to lists of French words, stories in a foreign language, a French story with pseudowords instead of content words, a French story with semantically anomalous content words, and a story in normal French. They found left-sided perisylvian activation in the conditions with comprehensible sentences, and anterior temporal foci in conditions that involved syntactically well formed stimuli. Also using PET, Stowe and colleagues (1994) compared reading sentences word by word to rest and found several activated left perisylvian sites. Bavelier and colleagues (1997) used high magnetic field (4 Tesla) fMRI to compare rCBF when subjects read sentences and processed consonant strings presented item by item. They found patchy activation throughout the left perisylvian cortex whose location varied significantly in different individuals. We also have found activation throughout the left perisylvian cortex, as well as in frontal and occipital regions and, to a lesser extent, in the right hemisphere, in an fMRI study in fluent English/Mandarin bilinguals that compared sentence comprehension in both languages against fixation and nonsense character baselines, with some individual differences in the exact areas of activation across subjects but a high degree of overlap of activations in the two languages within each subject (Chee et al., 1999). Using fMRI, Carpenter and colleagues (1999) found increased BOLD signal in temporal and parietal lobe during the sentence reading portion of a sentence-picture matching task that required verification of spatial relations. Overall, these studies indicate that sentence comprehension involves the dominant hemisphere, and suggest that areas outside the perisylvian cortex may be involved in this function. However, the experiments were not designed to isolate syntactic processing and their implications for the functional neuroanatomy of syntactic processing are therefore limited.

crease in rCBF in the pars opercularis of Broca's area when PET activity associated with OS sentences was subtracted from that associated with SO sentences. Experiment 2 (Caplan et al., 1998) was a replication of this study with eight female subjects, aged twenty-one to thirty-one. There again was an increase in rCBF in the pars opercularis of Broca's area when PET activity associated with OS sentences was subtracted from that associated with SO sentences. There was also activation in the medial frontal and cingulate gyri. Experiment 3 (Caplan et al., 1999) utilized auditory presentation. Sentences in the activation condition consisted of cleft object sentences (for example, "It was the juice that the child spilled") and sentences in the baseline condition consisted of cleft subject sentences (for example, "It was the child that spilled the juice"). Sixteen subjects, eight male and eight female, aged twenty-two to thirty-four, were tested. There was an increase in rCBF in the pars triangularis of Broca's area when PET activity associated with cleft subject sentences was subtracted from that associated with cleft object sentences. There was also activation in the medial frontal gyrus and in the left superior parietal area. Experiment 4 (Caplan et al., 2000) repeated experiments 1 and 2 under conditions of concurrent articulation, which engages the articulatory loop and prevents its use for rehearsal (Baddeley, Thomson, & Buchanan, 1975). Eleven subjects, five male and six female, aged nineteen to thirty-five, were tested. After having practiced in the psychology lab, they undertook the judgment task while simultaneously saying the word *double* at a rate of one utterance per minute, paced metronomically. There was an increase in rCBF in the pars opercularis of Broca's area when PET activity associated with OS sentences was subtracted from that associated with SO sentences. There were also increases in rCBF in the centromedial nucleus of the left thalamus, the posterior cingulate, and the medial frontal gyrus.

Overall, this series of experiments presents a coherent picture, according to which Broca's area is involved in processing more complex relative clauses. The fact that the activation in Broca's area associated with more complex relative clauses persisted under concurrent articulation conditions strongly suggests that Broca's area is involved in some aspect of syntactic processing that differs in the two sentence types, not simply in rehearsing the more complex sentences more than the simple ones. No other regions of the perisylvian association cortex were activated in these experiments, suggesting that Broca's area plays a special role in this process in this population. rCBF also increased in the cingulate and in medial frontal lobe structures in several experiments. These regions—particularly the cingulate—have been activated in many experiments, and we have followed Posner and colleagues (1987, 1988) in attributing this activation to non-domain-specific arousal and directed attention associated with increases in mental effort. The centromedian nucleus of the left thalamus was also activated in the articulatory suppression experiment. This nucleus is part of a circuit that subserves attentional processes. The remaining region of activation in these experiments occurred with auditory presentation in the superior parietal lobe, slightly to the left of the midline.

Dapretto and Bookheimer (1999) also have found activation in Broca's area associated with syntactic processing. In this study, subjects made judgments about the synonymity of two sentences. Two conditions were presented. In the first condition, the sentences had the same form but had one change in vocabulary. Subjects were to say that the sentences were the "same" if the different words were synonyms (for example, "The lawyer questioned the witness," "The attorney questioned the witness"), and that they were "different" if they were not synonyms (for example, "The man was attacked by the doberman," "The man was attacked by the pitbull"). In the second condition, the words in the sentences remained the same but the syntactic structure of the sentence changed. Subjects were to say that the sentences were the "same" if the thematic roles (agent of the verb, theme of the verb, theme of a preposition) did not differ (for example, "The policeman arrested the thief," "The thief was arrested by the policeman"). They were to say that the sentences were "different" if there was a change in thematic roles (for example, "The teacher outsmarted the student," "The teacher was outsmarted by the student"). Subjects saw the same number of active and passive sentences in each condition. The first condition activated Brodmann's area (BA) 47, both against a baseline resting condition and against the second condition. The second condition activated Broca's area (BA 44), both against a baseline resting condition and against the first condition. Dapretto and Bookheimer say that the first condition requires lexical semantic processing and the second condition requires syntactic processing. They therefore conclude that BA 47 is specialized for representing and/or processing lexical semantic information and BA 44 for syntactic structure.

However, not all experiments have produced activation in Broca's area, or exclusively in Broca's area, in association with syntactic processing. We have failed to find any reliable activation in the comparison of passive against active sentences (Caplan, 2000b). Stowe and colleagues (1998) measured PET activity when subjects read lists of words, simple sentences, syntactically complex sentences, and syntactically ambiguous sentences, and performed linear regression analyses on the PET data based on weights for the conditions that simulated different psychological processes. The combination of weights related to "sentence processing load" (list < simple sentences < complex sentences < ambiguous sentences) predicted rCBF in the posterior left temporal lobe. Just and colleagues (1996) reported an fMRI study in which subjects read and answered questions about conjoined, subject-subject, and subject-object sentences. These authors reported an increase in rCBF in both Broca's area and in Wernicke's area of the left hemisphere, as well as smaller but reliable increases in rCBF in the homologous regions of the right hemisphere, when subjects were presented with the more complex subject-subject and subject-object sentences.

Caplan and Waters (1999c) studied thirteen elderly subjects, aged sixty-one to seventy. The elderly subjects showed the expected behavioral effects of longer RTs for SO than OS sentences. However, unlike the young subjects previously studied, there was no increase in rCBF in Broca's area, but rather in the inferior parietal lobe. There was also an increase in rCBF near the midline of the superior frontal gyrus. Reaction times were longer and error rates were higher in this subject group than in the young subjects in experiments 1 through 4 described above, and the subjects in this group averaged fourteen years of education as opposed to sixteen years in previous studies. Educational level and performance level were therefore confounded with age as possible factors relevant to the rCBF differences between this and previous studies. A follow-up experiment controlled for these variables. Eight young subjects (aged nineteen to twenty-eight) with a mean of fourteen years of education were tested on the protocol (unpublished data). Errors and RTs in these young subjects were lower than those of the older subjects, and did not differ from those of young subjects in our previous studies. There was an increase in rCBF in the superior parietal lobe near the midline (BA 7) and in the superior frontal lobe.

Experimental designs are limited in potentially important ways in standard fMRI and PET. Sentences must be blocked by type, raising the possibility that subjects may use task-specific strategies to understand sentences in these experiments (Carpenter et al., 1999). The activation results reflect both plausible and implausible sentences in plausibility judgment tasks, and include processing the assertions to be verified and recalling the stimulus sentences in question-answering tasks. In addition, neither PET nor conventional fMRI can measure activation associated with specific parts of specific sentence types. The recently developed method of event-related fMRI offers significant advantages in experimental design, such as allowing intermixing of stimulus types, and allows for the measurement of the time course of activity associated with specified types of sentences and with specific parts of sentences (Rosen, Buckner, & Dale, 1998).

We used this technique to examine the difference in activation between sentences with more and less complex relative clauses—subject-object (SO) relatives: "The reporter *covering the big story carefully* who the photographer admired appreciated the award," and subject-subject (SS) relatives: "The reporter *covering the big story carefully* who admired the photographer appreci-ated the award"). We developed a stimulus set consisting of matched pairs of sentences with these structures, in which the head noun was separated from the relative clause by a five-word participial phrase to allow for a period of time during which activation associated with the two sentences would be expected not to differ. We piloted these materials using the self-paced reading technique, and established that an increased processing load (indexed by longer read-ing times) occurred at the expected point in the relative clause. We then presented these materials using word-by-word rapid serial visual presentation (RSVP) to ten young proficient subjects in a plausibility judgment task. Comparison of the time course of activation (measure-ment of blood oxygenation level dependent [BOLD] signal) for the more complex SO and less complex SS plausible sentences revealed significantly greater BOLD signal for the SO sen-tences in the late time periods in the left angular gyrus and a trend toward such an increase in the adjacent portion of Wernicke's area. This demonstrates a localized hemodynamic re-sponse to the more complex portion of a syntactically more complex sentence type.[3]

The results of these last experiments continue to demonstrate focal increases in rCBF and in BOLD signal in contrasts of sentences with complex and simpler syntactic structures. How-ever, increases in rCBF and BOLD signal occurred in a variety of locations in the perisylvian association cortex, not just Broca's area. Differences in imaging technique, data analysis, and experimental paradigms make it impossible to draw firm conclusions about the role of these different areas in this process. For instance, it is possible that the posterior perisylvian activa-tion seen in these studies is associated with increased memory loads in particular tasks: the Just et al. (1996) study required subjects to remember a sentence while verifying an assertion about it, and our fMRI study presented long sentences word-by-word.[4] However, if the differ-ences in localization are not due to the methodological differences across studies, the entire set of studies provides evidence for many perisylvian sites being activated by processing more complex syntactic structures, even within a neurobiologically homogeneous group of subjects. These studies have also demonstrated that regions of the brain involved in arousal and atten-tion sometimes become active during processing of more complex syntactic structures; whether this is because of their role in these nonlinguistic processes or because they also are directly involved in assigning and interpreting syntactic structure is unclear.

ELECTROPHYSIOLOGICAL STUDIES OF SYNTACTIC PROCESSING

Event-related potentials (ERPs) are electrophysiological responses to specific sensory, motor, and cognitive events. They are discernable in the electroencephalographic (EEG) record by averaging over multiple trials, thereby increasing the signal-to-noise ratio for the part of the waveform related to a specific event. They are mostly used in normal subjects, though some studies have investigated brain-damaged patients. ERPs are of positive or negative polarity, have millisecond-level temporal resolution, and can be recorded from electrodes over all the scalp. These features allow for the differentiation of different waves on the basis of their polarity, time course, and spatial localization, which has allowed researchers to develop models of the relationship between different aspects of ERPs and particular aspects of sentence pro-cessing. The temporal resolution of ERPs allows them to be used to study on-line processes. ERPs can occur without subjects' overtly responding to a linguistic stimulus, and thus, like eye

---

[3]Mason and colleagues (1999) studied BOLD signal changes associated with reading sentences with reduced relative clauses. They found that BOLD signal increased in ambiguous compared to unambiguous sentences, and in sentences in which the ambiguity was resolved in favor of the less preferred (reduced relative clause) structure. These increases in BOLD signal began to occur 4500 msec after the onset of the sentence. However, their abstract does not report the location of these BOLD signal increases.

[4]The Stowe et al. (1998) study cited above that also found temporal lobe activation used a more complicated design and analysis that is hard to interpret.

movements, are capable of providing information relevant to the unconscious processes involved in language processing without the superimposition of a laboratory task upon such processing. Though spatial distribution of ERPs is relevant to their differentiation, the location of the source of an ERP is difficult to determine in most studies on syntactic processing to date. Therefore, ERPs are of limited utility in approaching questions about the location of the neural structures involved in syntactic processing. However, a considerable amount of work has been directed at identifying aspects of the ERP waveform that may be associated with different aspects of sentence processing.

To my knowledge, the first study that suggested such correspondences was the paper by Kutas and Hillyard (1983) that is best known for its identification of the N400 wave that is associated with the occurrence of a semantically anomalous word in a sentence (for example, "I take my coffee with cream and cement"). This negative wave with a maximum in the mid-to-posterior scalp regions, often lateralized to the right scalp, has been extensively investigated and appears to be sensitive to the ease of integration of new lexical material into a developing semantic or conceptual context.[5] Kutas and Hillyard (1983) also described a second negative wave, distinguishable from the N400 by its slightly earlier occurrence but mostly because of its distribution over the left anterior scalp electrodes, that arose when subjects were presented with sentences that contained errors in noun number, verb number and verb tense. This wave—subsequently called the left anterior negativity (LAN)—and a related earlier negative wave known as the early left anterior negativity (ELAN), have been described by a host of researchers in response to various syntactic violations (Neville et al., 1991; Friederici, Steinhauer, Mecklinger, & Meyer, 1998; Kluender & Kutas, 1993a, 1993b; Munte, Heinze, & Mangun, 1993; Rosler, Putz, Friederici, & Hahne, 1993) and are candidates for electrophysiological correlates of syntactic processing.

Osterhout and Holcomb (1992) described a second wave that has been associated with syntactic processing—the P600, or syntactic positive shift (SPS) (Hagoort, Brown, & Groothusen, 1993). The P600/SPS is a later, positive wave, arising about 500 msec or more after certain syntactic violations, with a centro-posterior scalp distribution, that is often maximal over the right hemisphere electrodes. Osterhout and Holcomb found that this wave occurred after violations of subcategory restrictions on verbal complements, as in "The man persuaded to eat" contrasted with "The man hoped to eat." Hagoort and colleagues (1993) found that it occurred after violations of subject-verb number agreement and violations of category sequences (which they called "phrase structure" violations). The P600/SPS has also been described and explored in numerous studies (Gunter, Stowe, & Mulder, 1997; McKinnon & Osterhout, 1996; Osterhout & Holcomb, 1992, 1993, 1995; Rosler et al., 1993).

One issue that is relevant to the theme of this chapter is the location of these waves. The P600/SPS is found in central and high parietal electrodes and is often maximal over right scalp leads. If these scalp locations reflect directly underlying generators, these waves identify neural tissue that has not been associated with syntactic processing on the basis of deficit-lesion correlational analyses, though some PET studies have found activation in these region in syntactic contrasts, as noted above. The LAN, often assumed to have a left frontal generator, possibly in Broca's area, may be largely generated by an electrophysiological source in the left temporal lobe, according to one recent magnetoencephalographic study (Friederici et al., in press).

A second issue that arises in connection with the location of these waves is that their scalp distributions vary to some degree in different studies. The LAN has been noted over left anterior electrodes in many studies but has been found to be maximal over left hemisphere

---

[5]Though the N400 is therefore considered a "semantic" or "lexical" wave, it has been used to document the aspects of syntactic processing. For instance, Garnsey and colleagues (1989) demonstrated its occurrence after the verb of the relative clause (*ate*) in sentences such as "The rock that the man ate . . . ," and argued on this basis for the immediacy of the assignment of the head noun of the relative clause to the position of object.

sites in others. For instance, Neville and colleagues (1991) found that phrase structure violations (for example, "The scientist criticized of proof the theorem") produced a negative left hemisphere wave beginning around 300 msec that was maximal over left temporal and parietal sites; in the same study, these authors reported that the left early negative wave associated with specificity constraint violations (for example, "What did the scientist criticize Max's proof of?") was maximal over left frontal sites. Munte, Matzke, and Johannes (1997) had subjects either read or make grammaticality judgments about sentences with pseudowords in which there were or were not subject-verb number agreement violations. In the reading task, there was a left negativity from about 280 to 800 msec with a very broad distribution ranging from left anterior through midline parietal electrodes. For the grammaticality judgment task, the negativity was seen only in central and parietal electrodes, and only from 280 to 500 msec. Discrepancies in the exact location of the P600/SPS have also been described. Coulson, King, and Kutas (1998a) review the location (and temporal course) of the P600/SPS waves that have been described in relationship to five different types of syntactic violations, pointing out that, in response to phrase structure violations, this wave's location ranges from the right anterior electrodes (Osterhout & Holcomb, 1992) through the occipital leads (Neville et al., 1991), to a broad distribution (Hagoort et al., 1993). The distribution of these waves can lead to interpretive problems. For instance, which two of the three waves associated with semantic violations, phrase structure violations, and specificity violations in Neville and colleagues' (1991) figure 2, are most similar is not obvious to (my) visual inspection, yet the second and third of these waves are taken as examples of the LAN and the first as an instance of the semantically driven N400. Researchers have deemphasized the importance of either the (E)LAN (Brown & Hagoort, 2000) or the P600/SPS (Coulson et al., 1998a, 1998b) as reflections of syntactic processing on the grounds of the inconsistency in scalp topography and temporal course of these waves in different studies.

A third, related issue is that not all studies have found waves that are expected, and the explanation for the absence of waves in some studies has been that they are obscured by superimposed waves of opposite polarity. For instance, we noted above that Osterhout and Holcomb (1992) described a P600 after violations of subcategory restrictions such as "The man persuaded to eat." Hagoort and colleagues (1993), however, did not find this wave after a different type of subcategory violation—the presence of a direct object after an intransitive verb (for example, "The son of the rich industrialist boasts the car"; note that, in Dutch, the sentential complement continuation [" . . . was a limited edition"] is impossible). Hagoort and colleagues explain the absence of this expected P600/SPS by saying that it was obscured by a concurrent N400. In a similar vein, Munte and colleagues (1997) found an LAN in a grammaticality judgment task with subject-verb agreement violations in pseudoword prose but not in a similar task with real words. They attributed the lack of an LAN to the overlap of the LAN with an earlier-than-usual positive wave associated with these violations. The principles that underlie deciding when waves superimpose and cancel one another out are not clear; we must ask if these failures to find expected waves are indications of different effects of particular stimuli, tasks, or subjects on ERPs associated with these types of ungrammatical sentences, and what this implies about the nature of these waves.

These issues notwithstanding, there have been several attempts to develop general models of the role of the (E)LAN and P600/SPS in syntactic processing. Probably the most encompassing theory has been developed by Friederici and her colleagues. The ELAN has been found following lexical category violations (Neville et al., 1991; Friederici, Pfeifer, & Hahne, 1993; Friederici, Hahne, & Mecklinger, 1996). The LAN has occurred after inflectional agreement and verb argument structure violations (Munte et al., 1993, 1997; Munte & Heinze, 1994; Osterhout & Mobley, 1995; Gunter et al., 1997; Coulson et al., 1998a, 1998b). This has suggested to Friederici (1999) that the ELAN reflects the recognition of syntactic category membership and the ELAN the recognition of agreement and lexically specified subcategorization information. The LAN persists in sentences with pseudowords (Munte et al., 1997). It is not affected by the probability of occurrence of a syntactic violation in a stimulus set (Hahne & Friederici, 1999; Gunter et al., 1999). Because of the sensitivity of these waves to violations of category, lexical and morphological structure, and their insensitivity to meaningfulness and the probability of a violation in the stimulus set, Friederici (1995, 1999) has suggested that the LAN and the ELAN reflect the early, automatic, "first-pass," building of syntactic structure.

The P600/SPS has also been detected at the point at which violations of syntactic structure can be identified (Gunter et al., 1997; McKinnon & Osterhout, 1996; Osterhout & Holcomb, 1992, 1993, 1995; Rosler et al., 1993). Unlike the (E)LAN, it has also occurred when a less likely syntactic structure occurs (Gunter at al., 1997). The P600/SPS is sensitive to the probability of occurrence of a syntactic violation in the stimulus set (Coulson et al., 1998a; Hahne & Friederici, 1999). Because of this, Hahne and Friederici (1999) argued that the P600/SPS is associated with controlled syntactic processing. The P600/SPS does not occur in sentences with pseudowords (Munte et al., 1997) and does occur in syntactically ambiguous sentences at the point at which they are disambiguated toward their less preferred reading (Mecklinger, Schriefers, Steinhauer, & Friederici, 1995). Because of these features, Friederici (1999) has suggested that the P600/SPS reflects making revisions to structures that have been created ("second-pass" parsing). Finally, Friederici and her colleagues have identified two late positive waves associated with disambiguation toward a less preferred syntactic structure: an earlier wave beginning around 350 msec after the disambiguating segment and a late wave at 500 to 900 msec latency (Mecklinger et al., 1995). They have suggested that the first of these waves reflects detection of the syntactic ambiguity (or a syntactic ungrammaticality) and the second its repair.

Friederici's model can be questioned on several grounds. One problem for Friederici's view of the (E)LAN is that Kluender and Kutas (1993a, 1993b) and King and Kutas (1995) have described a LAN when subjects processed embedded questions and relative clauses, which the authors have related to the working memory load in these sentences. Because it occurs in conjunction both with a variety of syntactic violations and at points in sentences at which syntactic working memory load is high, there is, at present, no model that identifies a single syntactic operation with the (E)LAN. There are also problems with Friederici's theories about the P600/SPS. Although this wave does not occur in sentences with pseudowords containing agreement violations (Munte et al., 1997), it does occur in syntactic prose (sentences in which all content words are randomly selected, so that the resulting material is syntactically well formed but semantically incoherent; Brown & Hagoort, 2000), making the hypothesis that it is triggered by reanalysis in the service of semantic integration unlikely. A second problem is that the early positive wave is sometimes seen without the late one (Mecklinger et al., 1995), while other experiments have yielded the late positive wave without the early one (Friederici et al., 1998). It is hard to see how either of these patterns could arise in subjects who understand syntactically ambiguous sentences with unpreferred meanings correctly, if these late positive waves are associated with detection and revision processes, respectively.

A third issue that arises about the P600/SPS that is relevant both to Friederici's model and to more general issues pertaining to the nature of this wave stems from the observation that the task conditions under which the P600/SPS has appeared are the opposite of those that are associated with controlled processing. Hahne and Friederici (1999) found that the P600/SPS occurred when ungrammatical sentences made up 20 percent of the stimuli in a set, but not when they made up 80 percent of the stimuli. Coulson and colleagues (1998b) found that it occurred in grammatical sentences at a point at which they differed from ungrammatical sentences (for example, "Ray fell down and skinned his/he knee") when the grammatical sentences made up a small proportion (20 percent) of the stimuli. Thus the P600/SPS reflects improbability. Controlled processes, in contrast, are subject to expectations set by task parameters, and therefore are more likely to be engaged by a high proportion of relevant stimuli

(Posner & Snyder, 1975). This speaks against Friederici's suggestion that the P600/SPS results from controlled processing. An alternative hypothesis is that the P600/SPS is related to a complex wave known as the P300 (Coulson et al., 1998a, 1998b). One part of the P300 complex, the P3b wave, is associated with unexpected events and therefore is similar to the P600/SPS in this regard, as well as in polarity, scalp distribution, and, in some studies, time course. Bolstering the idea that the P600/SPS is part of the more general P300 complex is the fact that the P600/SPS does not appear to be specific for syntactic processing. Munte, Heinze, Matzke, Wieringa, and Johannes (1998) had subjects read short passages in which target nouns were replaced by semantically incorrect nouns, morphologically incorrect nouns, or orthographically incorrect nouns and found that all these stimuli elicited similar P600s. If the P600/SPS is best considered a part of the P300 complex (for an opposing view, see Osterhout, McKinnon, Bersick, & Corey, 1996; Osterhout & Hagoort, 1999), this wave would not be a correlate of reanalysis processes specifically related to syntactic structures per se.

I will conclude this part of this brief review by noting that, while currently accepted views of ERP correlates of syntactic processing recognize two (potentially divisible) possible syntactic waves—an early left negativity and a late centro-parietal positivity—all possible variants of positivity and negativity crossed by early and late temporal occurrence characterize the ERPs that have been associated with this function. The early left negativity and the late centro-parietal positivity are documented above. An early positivity, at about 350 msec, roughly the time period at which the LAN arises, was described by Mecklinger and colleagues (1995) at a point that signals the presence of an unpreferred syntactic structure—the auxiliary in previously ambiguous object relative sentences. A (somewhat) late negativity, at around 400 to 600 milliseconds, arose in association with an earlier disambiguation toward the same less preferred structure—the first NP in the relative clause—in a study by Friederici and colleagues (1998). Until the specific aspects of syntactic processing that drive these different waves are better understood, these different types of ERPs, with their presumably different cerebral generators, are all candidates for correlates of what may be, at least in part, the same aspects of syntactic processing.

Overall, the ERP literature has developed theories of the relationship of different waves to different syntactic processes, but the relationship of these components to psycholinguistic processes remain to be firmly established. The implications of these studies for the neuroanatomical structures that support parsing are limited because the exact neural structures that generate different ERP components are hard to identify. However, new technologies, such as magnetoencephalography, that can be coupled with electrophysiological techniques, are very likely to yield much more information on this subject.

OVERVIEW

I have argued that many brain regions have been implicated in syntactic processing in comprehension, and that available evidence points to significant individual variability in the localization of aspects of this process. Accepting this as a point of departure, the next question to ask is whether there is any systematicity to the pattern of individual differences in the localization of syntactic operations. Factors that could affect localization can be grouped into different classes: endogenous, biologically determined factors, such as sex, handedness, and age; exogenous, socially determined factors, such as language spoken; and factors that cannot be clearly assigned to either of these categories uniquely but may reflect both, such as verbal working memory capacity and language processing proficiency. It is possible that any of these factors, or others, determine localization; that is, that women differ systematically from men, or left-handers from right-handers, or highly proficient language users from less proficient language users, with respect to what neural areas within the perisylvian association cortex support aspects of syntactic processing. The effects of these factors could be absolute or relative; that is, these factors might *determine* localization or *constrain variability* in localization. The latter mechanism is clearly at work in patterns of lateralization, with handedness constraining variability in the pattern of which hemisphere is dominant for representing and processing language.

The hypothesis that there is significant individual variability in the localization of syntactic processing in sentence comprehension would superficially suggest that the organization of the perisylvian cortex for syntactic processing differs from the functional neuroanatomy of other brain regions for other functions, in which such individual variability is minimal, if it exists at all. However, on closer inspection, these better-understood function-structure relationships are limited to early aspects of perception and late aspects of motor planning and execution. Very little is known about the details of localization of higher functions within a general region. Exactly what region of the dorsolateral prefrontal cortex is involved in functions such as shifting attention, for instance, and is this region the same in all individuals? The notion of individual variability for syntactic processing within perisylvian cortex may not be an entirely iconoclastic suggestion within cognitive neuropsychology. Nonetheless, it is underdetermined by available data, as are all other models of the functional neuroanatomy of syntactic processing. The encouraging feature of current research is that the investigative techniques now available offer unparalleled opportunities to make progress in this domain.

REFERENCES

Baddeley, A. D., Thomson, N., & Buchanan, M. (1975). Word Length and the Structure of Short-term Memory. *Journal of Verbal Learning and Verbal Behavior, 14,* 575-589.

Balogh, J. E., & Grodzinsky, Y. (1999). Levels of linguistic representation in Broca's aphasia: Implicitness and referentiality of arguments. In Y. G. R. Bastiaanse (Ed.), *Grammatical disorders in aphasia: a neurolinguistic perspective.* London: Whurr Publishers.

Balogh, J., Zurif, E. B., Prather, P., Swinney, D., & Finkel, L. (1998): Gap filling and end of sentence effects in real-time language processing: Implications for modeling sentence comprehension in aphasia. *Brain and Language, 61,* 169-182

Bavelier, D., Corina, D., Jezzard, P., Padmanabhan, S., Clark, V. P., Karni, A., Prinster, A., Braun, A., Lalwani, A., Rauschecker, J. P., Turner, R., & Neville, H. (1997). Sentence reading: A Functional MRI Study at 4 Tesla. *Journal of Cognitivie Neuroscience, 9,* 664-686.

Beretta, A., & Munn, A. (1998). Double-agents and trace deletion in agrammatism. *Brain and Language, 65,* 404-421.

Berndt, R., & Caramazza, A. (1999): How "regular" is sentence comprehension in Broca's aphasia? It depends on how you select the patients, *Brain and Language, 67,* 242-247

Berndt, R., Mitchum, C., & Haendiges, A. (1996). Comprehension of reversible sentences in "agrammatism": a meta-analysis. *Cognition, 58,* 289-308.

Blumstein, S., Byma, G., Hurowski, K. Huunhen, J., Brown, T., & Hutchison, S. (1998). On-line processing of filler-gap constructions in aphasia. *Brain and Language, 61*(2), 149-169.

Bock, K., & Levelt, P. (1994). Language production: Grammatical Encoding. In M. Gernsbacher (Ed.), *Handbook of psycholinguistics.* New York: Academic Press.

Bresnan. J. (1972). The passive in lexical theory. In J. Bresnan (Ed.), *The mental representation of grammatical relations.* Cambridge: MIT Press.

Brown, C., & Hagoort, P. (2000). On the electrophysiology of language comprehension: Implications for the human language system. In M. P. Matthew, W. Crocker, & C. Clifton, Jr. (Eds.), *Architectures and mechanisms for language processing.* Cambridge: Cambridge University Press.

Caplan, D. (1987a). Discrimination of normal and aphasic subjects on a test of syntactic comprehension. *Neuropsychologia, 25,* 173-184.

Caplan, D. (1987b). *Neurolinguistics and linguistic aphasiology.* Cambridge: Cambridge University Press.

Caplan, D. (1994). Language and the brain. In M. Gernsbacher (Ed,), *Handbook of psycholinguistics.* New York: Academic Press.

Caplan, D. (1995). Issues arising in contemporary studies of disorders of syntactic processing in sentence comprehension in agrammatic patients. *Brain and Language, 50,* 325-338.

Caplan, D (2000a). Lesion location and aphasic syndrome do not tell us whether a patient will have an isolated deficit affecting the co-indexation of traces. *Behavioral and Brain Sciences, 23,* 25-27.

Caplan, D (2000b). Positron emission tomographic studies of syntactic processing. In L. Shapiro, Y. Grodzinsky, & D. Shapiro (Eds.), *The neurology of language.* San Diego: Academic Press.

Caplan, D. (2001). The measurement of chance performance in aphasia, with specific reference to the comprehension of semantically reversible passive sentences: A note on issues raised by Caramazza, Capitani, Rey, and Berndt (2000) and Drai, Grodzinsky, and Zurif (2000). *Brain and Language, 76,* 193-201.

Caplan, D., Alpert, N., & Waters, G. S. (1998). Effects of syntactic structure and propositional number on patterns of regional cerebral blood flow. *Journal of Cognitive Neuroscience, 10,* 541-552.

Caplan, D, Albert, N., & Waters, G. S. (1999) PET Studies of sentence processing with auditory sentence presentation. *Neuroimage, 9,* 343-351

Caplan, D., Alpert, N., Waters, G., & Olivieri, A. (2000). Activation of Broca's area by syntactic processing under conditions of concurrent articulation. *Human Brain Mapping*, 9, 65-71.

Caplan, D., Baker, C., & Dehaut, F. (1985). Syntactic determinants of sentence comprehension in aphasia. *Cognition*, 21, 117-175.

Caplan, D., Hildebrandt, N., & Makris, N. (1996). Location of lesions in stroke patients with deficits in syntactic processing in sentence comprehension. *Brain*, 119, 933-949.

Caplan, D., & Waters, G. (1999). Age effects on the functional neuroanatomy of syntactic processing in sentence comprehension. In S. Kemper & R Kliegel (Eds.), *Constraints on language: Aging, grammar and memory*. Boston: Kluver.

Caplan, D., Waters, G., & Hildebrandt, N. (1997). Determinants of sentence comprehension in aphasic patients in sentence-picture matching tasks. *Journal of Speech and Hearing Research*, 40, 542-555.

Caramazza, A., Capitani, E., Rey, A., & Berndt, R. S. (2001). Agrammatic Broca's aphasia is not associated with a single pattern of comprehension performance. *Brain and Language*, 76, 158-184.

Caramazza, A., & Zurif, E. B. (1976). Dissociation of algorithmic and heuristic processes in language comprehension: Evidence from aphasia. *Brain and Language*, 3, 572-582.

Carpenter, P. A., Just, M. A., Keller, T. A., Eddy, W. F., & Thulborn, K. R. (1999) Time course of fMRI-activation in language and spatial networks during sentence comprehension. *Neuroimage*, 10, 216-224

Chee, M. W. L,. Caplan, D., Soon, C. S., Sriram, N., Tan, E. W. L, Thiel, T., & Weekes. B. (1999). Processing of visually presented sentences in Mandarin and English studied with fMRI. *Neuron*, 23, 127-137.

Chomsky, N. (1965). *Aspects of the theory of syntax*. Cambridge, MA: MIT Press.

Chomsky, N. (1981). *Lectures on covernment and binding*. Dordrecht: Foris.

Chomsky, N. (1986). *Knowledge of language*. New York: Praeger.

Chomsky, N. (1995). *Barriers*. Cambridge, MA: MIT Press.

Coulson, S., King, J. W., & Kutas, M. (1998a). Expect the unexpected: Event-related brain potentials to morphosyntactic violations. *Language and Cognitive Processes*, 13, 21-58.

Coulson, S., King, J. W., & Kutas, M. (1998b). ERPs and domain specificity: Beating a straw horse. *Language and Cognitive Processes*, 13, 653-672.

Damasio, A. R. (1992). Aphasia. *New England Journal of Medicine*, 326, 531-539.

Dapretto, M., & Bookheimer, S. Y. (1999). Form and content: Dissociating syntax and semantics in sentence comprehension. *Neuron*, 24, 427-432.

Drai, D., & Grodzinksy, Y. (1999). Comprehension regularity in Broca's aphasia? There's more of it than you ever imagined. *Brain and Language*, 70, 139-

Drai, D., Grodzinsky, Y., & Zurif, E. (2001). Broca's aphasia is associated with a single pattern of comprehension performance: A reply. *Brain and Language*, 76, 186-192.

Frazier, L., & Clifton, C. (1996). *Construal*. Cambridge, MA: MIT Press.

Friederici, A. D. (1995). The time course of syntactic activation during language processing: A model based on neuropsychological and neurophysiological data. *Brain and Language*, 49, 259-281

Friederici, A. D. (1999). Diagnosis and reanalysis: Two processing aspects the brain may differentiate. In J.

D. Fodor & F. Ferreira (Eds.), *Reanalysis in sentence processing*. New York: Kluver.

Friederici, A. D., Pfeifer, E., & Hahne, A. (1993). Even-related brain potentials during natural speech processing: Effects of semantic, morphological, and syntactic violations. *Cognitive Brain Research*, 1, 183-192.

Friederici, A. D., Hahne, A., & Mecklinger, A. (1996). Temporal structure of syntactic parsing: Early and late event-related brain potentials effects. *Journal of Experimental Psychology: Learning, Memory, and Cognition*, 22, 1219-1248.

Friederici, A. D., Steinhauer, K., Mecklinger, A., & Meyer, M. (1998). Working memory constraints on syntactic ambiguity resolution as revealed by electrical brain responses. *Biological Psychology*, 47, 193-221.

Friederici, A. D., Wang, Y., Herrmann, C. S., Maess, B., & Oertel, U. (In press). Localization of early syntactic processes in frontal and temporal cortical areas: A magnetoencephalographic study. *Human Brain Mapping*.

Garnsey, S. M., Tanenhaus, M. K., & Chapman, R. M. (1989). Evoked potentials and the study of sentence comprehension. *Jounral of Psycholinguistic Research*, 18, 51-60.

Gazdar, G., Klein, E., Pullum, J., & Sag, I. (1985). *Generalized phrase structure grammar*. Cambridge, MA: Harvard University Press.

Grodzinsky, Y. (1990). *Theoretical perspectives on language deficits*. Cambridge, MA: MIT Press.

Grodzinsky, Y. (1995). A restrictive theory of agrammatic comprehension. *Brain and Language*, 50, 27-51.

Grodzinsky, Y (2000): The neurology of syntax: Language use without Broca'a area. *Behavioral and Brain Sciences*, 23, 47-117.

Grozinsky, Y., Pinango, M. M., Zurif, E. A., & Drai, D. (1999). The critical role of group studies in neuropsychology: Comprehension regularities in Broca's aphasia. *Brain and Language*, 67, 134-147.

Grodzinsky, Y., Wexler, K., Chien, Y. C., Marakovits, S., & Solomon, J. (1993). The breakdown of binding relations. *Brain and Language*, 45, 396-422.

Gunter, T. C., Stowe, L. A., & Mulder, G. (1997). When syntax meets semantics. *Psychophysiology*, 34, 660-676.

Gunter T., Vos, S. et al. (1999). Memory or aging? That's the question: An electrophysiological perspective on language. In S. Kemper & R. Kliegel (Eds), *Constraints on language: Aging, grammar and memory*. Boston: Kluver.

Hagoort, P., Brown, C., & Groothusen, J. (1993). The syntactic positive shift (SPS) as an ERP measure of syntactic processing. *Language and Cognitive Processes*, 8, 485-532.

Hahne, A., & Friederici, A. D. (1999). Electrophysiological evidence for two steps in syntactic analysis: Early automatic and late controlled processes. *Journal of Cognitive Neuroscience*, 11, 194-205.

Hildebrandt, N., Caplan, D., & Evans, K. (1988). The man left without a trace: A case study of aphasic processing of empty categories. *Cognitive Neuropsychology*, 4, 257-302.

Just, M. A., & Carpenter, P. A. (1992). A capacity theory of comprehension: Individual differences in working memory. *Psychological Review*, 99(1), 122-149.

Just, M. A., Carpenter, P. A., Keller, T. A., Eddy, W. F. & Thulborn, K. R. (1996). Brain activation modulated by sentence comprehension. *Science*, 274, 114-116.

King, J. W., & Kutas, M. (1995). Who did what and when?

Using word- and clause-level ERPs to monitor working memory usage in reading. *Journal of Cognitive Neuroscience, 7*, 376-395.

Kluender, R., & Kutas, M. (1993a). Bridging the gap: Evidence from ERPs on the processing of unbounded dependencies. *Journal of Cognitive Neuroscience, 5*, 196-214.

Kluender, R., & Kutas, M. (1993b). Subjacency as a processing phenomenon. *Language and Cognitive Processes, 8*, 573-633.

Kutas, M., & Hillyard, S. A. (1983). Event-related potentials to grammatical errors and semantic anomalies. *Memory and Cognition, 11*, 539-50.

Levelt, W. J. M. (1989). *Speaking: From intention to articulation.* Cambridge, MA: MIT Press.

Linebarger, M. C. (1995). Agrammatism as evidence about grammar. *Brain and Language, 50*, 52-91.

Linebarger, M. C., Schwartz, M. F., & Saffran, E. M. (1983). Sensitivity to grammatical structure in so-called agrammatic aphasics. *Cognition, 13*, 361-392.

Love, T., & Swinney, D. (1996). Coreference processing and level of analysis on object-relative constructions: Demonstration of antecedent reactivation with the cross-modal priming technique. *Journal of Psycholinguistic Research, 25*, 5-24.

MacDonald, M. C., Pearlmutter, N. J., & Seidenberg, M. S. (1994). Lexical nature of syntactic ambiguity resolution. *Psychological Review, 101*, 676-703.

Mason, R. A., Just, M. A., Keller, T., A., & Carpenter, P. A. (1999): Ambiguity in the brain: How syntactically ambiguous sentences are processed. *Psychonomics Society, L.A.*

Mazoyer, B., Tzourio, N., Frak, V., Syrota, A., Murayama, N., Levrier, O., & Salamon, G. (1993). The cortical representation of speech. *Journal of Cognitive Neuroscience, 5*, 467-479.

McKinnon, R., & Osterhout, L. (1996). Constraints on movement phenomena in sentence processing: evidence from event-related brain potentials. *Language and Cognitive Processes, 11*(5), 495-523.

McKoon, G., & Ratcliff, R. (1994). Sentential context and on-line lexical decision. *Journal of Experimental Psychology: Learning, Memory, and Cognition, 20*, 1239-1243.

McKoon, G., Ratcliff, R., & Ward, R. (1994). Testing theories of language processing: An empirical investigation of the on-line lexical decision task. *Journal of Experimental Psychology: Learning, Memory, and Cognition, 20*, 1219-1228

Mecklinger, A., Schriefers, H., Steinhauer, K., & Friederici, A. D. (1995). Processing relative clauses varying on syntactic and semantic dimensions: An analysis with event-related potentials. *Memory and Cognition, 23*, 477-494.

Mesulam, M.-M. (1990). Large-scale neurocognitive networks and distributed processing for attention, language, and memory. *Annals of Neurology, 28*(5), 597-613.

Munte, T. F., & Heinze, H. (1994). ERP negativities during syntactic processing of written words. In H. J. Heinze, T. F. Munte, & G. R. Mangun (Eds.), *Cognitive Electrophysiology.* La Jolla, CA: Birkhauser Boston.

Munte, T. F., Heinze, H., & Mangun, G. R. (1993). Dissociation of brain activity related to syntactic and semantic aspects of language. *Journal of Cognitive Neuroscience, 5*, 335-344.

Munte, T. F., Heinze, H., Matzke, M., Wieringa, B. M., & Johannes, S. (1998). Brain potentials and syntactic violations revisited: No evidence for specificity of the syntactic positive shift. *Neuropsychologia, 36*, 217-226.

Munte, T. F., Matzke, M., & Johannes, S. (1997). Brain activity associated with syntactic incongruities in words and pseudo-words. *Journal of Cognitive Neuroscience, 9*, 318-329.

Neville, H., Nicol, J. L., Barss, A., Forster, K. I., & Garret, M. F. (1991). Syntactically based sentence processing classes: Evidence from event-related brain potentials. *Journal of Cognitive Neuroscience, 2*, 151-165.

Nicol, J., Fodor, J., & Swinney, D. (1994). Using cross-modal lexical decision tasks to investigate sentence processing. *Journal of Experimental Psychology: Learning, Memory, and Cognition, 20*, 1229-1238.

Osterhout, L., & Hagoort, P. (1999). A superficial resemblance doesn't necessarily mean that you're part of a family: Counter arguments to Coulson, King, and Kutas (1998) in the P600/SPS-P300 debate. *Language and Cognitive Processes, 14*(1), 1-14.

Osterhout, L., & Holcomb, P. (1992). Event-related brain potentials elicited by syntactic anomaly. *Journal of Memory and Language, 31*, 785-806.

Osterhout, L., & Holcomb, P. (1993). Event-related potentials and syntactic anomaly: Evidence of anomaly detection during the perception of continuous speech. *Language and Cognitive Processes, 8*, 413-437.

Osterhout, L., & Holcomb, P. J. (1995). Event-related brain potentials and language comprehension. In M. Rugg & M. Coles (Eds.), *Electrophysiological studies of human cognitive function.* Oxford: Oxford University Press.

Osterhout, L., McKinnon, R., Bersick, M., & Corey, V. (1996). On the language specificity of the brain response to syntactic anomalies: Is the syntactic positive shift a member of the P300 family? *Journal of Cognitive Neuroscience, 8*, 507-526.

Osterhout, L., & Mobley, L. A. (1995). Event-related brain potentials elicited by failure to agree. *Journal of Memory and Language, 34*, 739-773.

Posner, M. I., Inhoff, A. W., Friedrich, F. J., & Cohen, A. (1987). Isolating attentional systems: A cognitive-anatomical analysis. *Psychobiology, 15*, 107-121.

Posner, M. I., Peterson, S. E., Fox, P. T., & Raichle, M. E. (1988). Localization of cognitive operations in the human brain. *Science, 240*, 1627-1631.

Posner, M. I., & Snyder, C. R. (1975). Attention and cognitive control. In R. L. Solso (Ed.), *Information processing and cognition.* New York: Lawrence Erlbaum.

Rosler, F., Putz, P., Friederici, A., & Hahne, A. (1993). Event-related potentials while encountering semantic and syntactic constraint violations. *Journal of Cognitive Neuroscience, 5*, 345-362.

Stowe, L. A., Broere, C. A. J., Paans, A. M., Wijers, A. A., Mulder, G., Vaalbur, W., & Zwarts, F. (1998). Localizing components of a complex task: sentence processing and working memory. *Neuroreport, 9*, 2995-2999.

Stowe, L. A., Wijers, A. A., et al. (1994). PET-studies of language: An assessment of the reliability of the technique. *Journal of Psycholinguistic Research, 23*, 499-527.

Stromswold, K., Caplan, D., Alpert, N., & Rosch, S. (1996). Localization of syntactic comprehension by positron emission tomography. *Brain and Language, 52*, 452-473.

Swinney, D., & E. Zurif (1995). Syntactic processing in aphasia. *Brain and Language, 50*, 225-239.

Swinney, D., Zurif, E., Prather, P., & Love, T. (1996). Neurological distribution of processing resources underlying language domprehension. *Journal of Cognitive Neuroscience, 8,* 174–184.

Tyler, L. (1985). Real-time comprehension processes in agrammatism: A case study. *Brain & Language, 26,* 259–275.

Ullman, M. T., Bergida, R., & O'Craven, K. M. (1997). Distinct fMRI activation patterns for regular and irregular past tense, *NeuroImage, 5,* S549.

Ullman, M. T., Corkin, S., Coppola, M., Hickok, G., Growdon, J., Koroshetz, W., & Pinker, S. (1997). A neural dissociation within language: Evidence that the mental dictionary is part of declarative memory and grammatical rules are processed by the procedural system. *Journal of Cognitive Neuroscience, 9,* 289–299.

Wulfeck, B. B. (1988). Grammaticality judgments and sentence comprehension in agrammatic aphasia. *Journal of Speech and Hearing Research, 31,* 72–81.

Zurif, E., & Pinango, M. M. (1999). The existence of comprehension patterns in Broca's aphasia. *Brain and Language, 70,* 133–138.

Zurif, E., Swinney, D., Prather, P., Solomon, J., & Bushell, C. (1993). An on-line analysis of syntactic processing in Broca's and Wernicke's aphasia. *Brain and Language, 45,* 448–464.

19

Assessment and Treatment of Sentence Processing Disorders: A Review of the Literature

Jane Marshall

INTRODUCTION

Many people with aphasia can produce and understand single words, but not sentences. Clinically this problem demands attention, mainly because it severely limits the range of meanings that the person can convey and comprehend.

Typical production problems are illustrated by the samples of aphasic speech (in table 19.1).The first four speakers all have difficulties conveying events, although the reasons for their difficulties vary. SW has limited verb access, a problem shared by many aphasic people (for example, McCarthy & Warrington, 1985; Miceli, Silveri, Villa, & Caramazz, 1984; Kohn, Lorch, & Pearson, 1989; Caramazza & Hillis, 1991; Zingeser & Berndt, 1990; Mitchum & Berndt, 1994; Bates, Chen, Tzeng, Li, & Opie, 1991; Daniele, Giustolisi, Silveri, Colosimo, & Gainotti, 1994; Berndt, Haendiges, Mitchum, & Sandson, 1997a; Breedin, Saffran, & Schwartz, 1998; Bastiaanse & Jonkers, 1998). BG accesses a useful verb, but fails to combine it with sentence structure. PB also has structural difficulties, although of a different kind. His speech is not agrammatic and contains syntactic structures that are generally compatible with the subcategorization of the verb. Yet he cannot map the nouns appropriately onto those structures. Again, such word order problems have been observed elsewhere (Martin & Blossom-Stach, 1986). The last speaker, VB, has more success communicating events and states, mainly because she can compose verb argument structure. Her problem seems specific to function words and inflections. Yet, this is not without semantic consequences. For example, it is difficult for her to convey subtleties of time, aspect, and focus.

Some (but not all) of these speakers had parallel difficulties in comprehension. They understood nouns well, but failed when verbs or sentences were tested. Structures expressing reversible relations, such as "the man is chasing the woman," were particularly problematic. Functionally, this led to problems whenever meaning could not be inferred from context or pragmatic cues.

In the last twenty years clinicians have developed numerous assessment and therapy techniques in response to sentence-level problems. This chapter will provide an overview of these techniques. The first section will cover assessment, initially of production and then of compre-

Table 19.1
Samples of Aphasic Speech

SW (talking about her daughter)
I would get Saffron and I would have to . . . because warm hair, got to . . .
(Leoni, 1998, unpublished data)

BG (written description of a picture in which a man buys flowers for his girlfriend)
Interflora   Love Aah !!!   Telephone   paid   wallet
(Tragopoulou, 1998, unpublished data)

PB (describing a picture in which a man buys a cat from a woman)
one woman and a cat is buying the man and paying the money the till
(Marshall, Chait, & Pring, 1997)

VB (description of a friend)
Valerie is big . . . fat round hip . . . she quite tall . . . she work British Telecom . . . she always borrow pattern and not bring back
(Marshall et al., 1999)

hension, and will conclude with a discussion about the diagnostic process. The second section will summarize a range of therapy approaches for different levels of sentence impairments. The final discussion will briefly appraise a number of clinical issues, such as generalization of effects, the mechanism by which therapy achieves change, and possible goals for sentence-level therapies.

ASSESSMENT OF SENTENCE PRODUCTION

Sampling and Analyzing Spontaneous Speech

Generating a hypothesis about an individual's sentence processing impairment usually requires a sample of connected speech. There are various methods of sampling, each with its own advantages and disadvantages. Samples of conversation arguably offer the most "naturalistic" illustration of a person's output. However, there are difficulties with this method. Evaluating errors may be problematic if the topic is unknown, although Thompson and colleagues (1996) introduced some control over this by asking subjects to base their conversation on a provided TV news clip. Also the conversational partner may strongly influence the output produced by the aphasic person, and obtaining appropriate control data is difficult.

These problems have encouraged some researchers to turn to narrative techniques, such as recounting familiar stories (for example, Saffran, Berndt, & Schwartz, 1989; Byng & Black, 1989). Here the topic is known, and the aphasic person's production can be compared to narratives from nonimpaired control subjects. Saffran and colleagues provide useful criteria for the inclusion and exclusion of data and guidance for the administration of the task. The anxiety that recounting fairy stories is stigmatizing can be avoided by eliciting narratives from more age-appropriate sources, such as silent videos.

Another advantage of narratives is the availability of reasonably efficient analytical procedures (for example, Saffran et al., 1989; Byng & Black, 1989; Thompson, Shapiro, Tait, Jacobs, & Schneider, 1996). These explore different properties of the data, such as morphological, lexical, and structural aspects and verb argument structure. Such analyses can be used to generate hypotheses about where processing is breaking down. For example, an abnormal verb-to-noun ratio suggests that a lexical impairment with verbs is contributing to the problem, whereas depressed morphological measures may indicate that processing function words and inflections is a site of particular difficulty.

Narrative samples cannot meet all needs. Some aphasic people find such an unconstrained task difficult and require more cues to generate output. Storytelling is culturally laden, and may have been rarely undertaken by the aphasic person even before their stroke. Narratives also cannot be used to elicit particular sentence forms.

Elicitation of Particular Structures

Clinicians may be interested in whether the aphasic person can produce particular structures, or in whether structural variables influence success. These questions require alternative elicitation procedures, which can target specific forms. A number of studies have employed picture description; for example, to elicit two or three argument structures (Marshall, Chiat, & Pring, 1997) or to elicit actives and passives (Mitchum, Haendiges, & Berndt, 1995). The latter is achieved by showing the person a picture of an event, and asking them to begin either with the agent noun (for actives) or the theme (for passives). Question and other moved argument forms have also been elicited; for example, through lead-in dialogues (Springer, Willmes, & Haag, 1993) or by combining modelling and pictures (Thompson et al., 1996; Ballard & Thompson, 1999).

None of these techniques is trouble free. It is very difficult to develop event pictures that reliably target particular structures. For example, a picture in which a man feeds hay to a horse may elicit the target (three argument) structure, or any number of alternatives, such as "the horse is eating" or "the man wants the horse to eat." Imposing constraints, in the hope of eliciting particular structures, can render the task highly abnormal. As a result, even if the person succeeds, it may be difficult to conclude that he or she could access the same structures in more natural conditions.

Investigating Lexical Aspects of Production

Many aphasic people access verbs less successfully than nouns (for example, see Berndt et al., 1997a), and this difficulty is strongly associated with sentence production problems (for example, Berndt et al., 1997b). Furthermore, people showing the inverse pattern (where nouns are more impaired than verbs), typically preserve sentence production skills (for example, Zingeser & Berndt, 1988; Marshall, Pring, Chiat, & Robson, 1996).

Such findings suggest that sentence impairments may originate with a lexical difficulty with verbs. This is supported by evidence that naming verb pictures is more difficult than naming matched noun pictures for some aphasic people (for example, Byng, 1988; Mitchum & Berndt, 1994; although see Bastiaanse & Jonkers, 1998, for evidence that naming scores may not correlate with verb production in spontaneous speech). Some studies have explored whether sentence production is facilitated when lexical production is cued; for example, by providing the verb (see Marshall, Pring, & Chait, 1998). Such cueing effects support the view that the sentence impairment is at least partly attributable to lexical difficulties.

Lexical aspects of sentence production are explored rather differently by the TRIP test (Thematic Roles in Production; Whitworth, 1996). Whitworth argues that lexical retrieval in sentences and in isolation are fundamentally different. The TRIP test enables the clinician to compare naming of the same nouns in response to single item and event pictures. Evidence of successful naming in isolation, but poor naming in sentences suggest that the person is unable to access nouns as part of a thematic structure.

Removing Speech from Investigations of Production

Failure to generate output may have numerous explanations, one of which could be peripheral problems with speech. It can be useful, therefore, to explore production without asking the person to speak. One method is to use writing, although this may be impossible for the aphasic person. Another approach uses sentence anagrams, where the aphasic person is asked to assemble sentences from provided written fragments (for example, Saffran, Schwartz, & Marin, 1980; Jones, 1986). If the person succeeds on the task, they may retain sentence ordering skills, even though those skills are not realized in production.

Marshall and colleagues (1993, 1997) developed a modified version of the anagram task. They presented their subjects with four written fragments; for example:

the water (direct object)
the glass (distracter)
pours (verb)
the man (subject)

The person had to construct an SVO sentence from these fragments, in so doing rejecting the distracter fragment. Success here not only indicates sentence ordering skills, but also requires subtle knowledge of the verb's assignment rules. For example, the person has to know that *pour* maps the theme of the event, rather than the goal, onto the direct object.

Interpreting performance on sentence anagram tasks can be difficult, mainly because the task imposes both input and output demands. For example, although the person has to produce a sentence, this may be achieved largely through input; that is, by assembling the fragments randomly and then judging the outcome. Other subjects may fail the task because they cannot read the fragments (although this can be assisted during administration).

No single output task can "diagnose" the production impairment. Rather, clinicians have to seek patterns across a range of tasks. Thus impaired performance with sentence anagrams, together with reduced or disordered verb argument structure in speech may indicate difficulties at the functional level of production. In this case, further corroboration would be sought from input testing.

ASSESSMENT OF SENTENCE COMPREHENSION

Identification of a sentence comprehension impairment is typically achieved via sentence-to-picture matching tasks. Here the person hears or reads a sentence and has to match it to one of a number of pictures, with distracters bearing various relationships to the target. Tasks can explore a range of structures (for example, Bishop, 1982; Kay, Lesser, & Coltheart, 1992), and different types of predicate (for example, Byng & Black, 1999).

Since the 1970s, we have known that many aphasic people fail sentence-to-picture matching tasks whenever sentences express plausibly reversible meaning relations, and when one of the distracters represents the reversal of the target (for example, Caramazza & Zurif, 1976; Saffran, Schwartz, & Marin, 1980; Jones, 1984; Black, Nickels, & Byng, 1992; Druks & Marshall, 1995; Berndt, Mitchum, & Wayland, 1997). In general, reversal errors occur more frequently with complex, moved argument forms such as passives, although some individuals make errors even with simple actives.

Sentence-to-picture matching is not the only technique for exploring comprehension. For example, subjects can be asked to demonstrate comprehension by manipulating objects to act out sentences (for example, Caplan, Baker, & De Haut, 1985) or by judging the semantic plausibility of sentences (for example, Schwartz, Linebarger, Saffran, & Pate, 1987).

Marshall and colleagues (1996) developed a sentence comprehension task that does not require intact noun comprehension. In this task the person is shown a reversible event picture (see figure 19.1). A written, or spoken, sentence is provided to describe the event, in which the people are referred to with place names. So for figure 19.1, the sentence is: "Ealing chases Aberdeen." The person is then asked to identify the person referred to in the first noun phrase; for example, "who is Ealing?" Half the stimuli involve simple, SVO sentences, and half involve

Figure 19.1. A sample stimulus from the sentence comprehension test developed by Marshall and colleagues (1996). "Ealing chases Aberdeen." "Who is Ealing?"

moved argument structures. Success on this task, and with all sentence types, demonstrates that the person can comprehend verb argument relations. Failure is more difficult to interpret. For example, the person may be thrown by the sheer oddity of the task!

Although the occurrence of reversible errors in sentence comprehension is widely acknowledged, the source of such errors is a topic of considerable controversy (for example, see Grodzinsky, 1986, Caplan & Hildebrandt, 1988; Black et al., 1992; Miyake, Carpenter, & Just, 1994, Berndt, Mitchum, & Wayland, 1997). In terms of clinical diagnosis, it is likely that different people fail the sentence comprehension task for different reasons (for example, see Byng, Nickels, & Black, 1994). Therefore further tasks are needed to help the clinician pin down the level of deficit.

Grammaticality Judgment Tasks

One explanation for poor sentence comprehension may be an inability to parse the syntactic structure of sentences. This hypothesis would be supported by evidence that comprehension declines as a factor of syntactic complexity. Further corroboration might be sought from tests of grammaticality judgment, in which the person is asked to judge whether heard sentences are syntactically correct or not. Stimuli can violate a range of syntactic rules, such as constituent order ("pours the water the man") and the use of auxiliaries ("is the boy is having a good time").

There is compelling evidence that many people who fail tests of reversible sentence comprehension can nevertheless carry out grammaticality judgments (for example, Linebarger, Schwartz, & Saffran, 1983; Berndt, Salasoo, Mitchum, & Sandson, 1988; Schwartz, Saffran, Fink, Myers, & Martin, 1994; Marshall et al., 1997). This led to the proposal that sentence comprehension impairments may have a semantic, rather than syntactic origin. It was argued that aphasic people could not interpret the product of the parse, or determine which phrase was performing which role with respect to the verb. One explanation for such "mapping impairments" could be inadequate verb information, and particularly an inability to retrieve the thematic properties of verbs.

Tests of Verb Knowledge

A number of input tests have been developed to explore verb knowledge. Some simply explore core meaning, or the nature of the state/event referred to by the verb. Possible tests here include verb-to-picture matching with semantic distracters (for example, Marshall et al., 1993, 1997) or matching verbs to video scenes of events.

Some tests specifically explore access to verbs' thematic properties. Byng (1988) developed a Verb Video Test, which compared comprehension of related verbs with comprehension of reverse role verbs. In this task, the person hears (or reads) a verb, which has to be matched to one of two scenes presented on video. Related items oppose verbs with semantically related core meanings (such as *fall* and *rise*). Reverse-role items oppose verbs that describe the same event, but with different thematic perspectives (for example, *give* and *take*). Byng's subjects readily distinguished the related verbs, but not the reverse role verbs.

There are other thematic verb tasks. Breedin and colleagues (1994) used a verb odd-one-out paradigm, in which some stimuli required core meaning judgments (for example, *harvest, reap, plant*) and others required thematic judgments (for example, *buy, sell, purchase*). Marshall and colleagues (1997) used a picture pointing task. Here the person was shown a picture of an interactive event, such as a woman giving a boat to a boy, and asked to point to one of the participants in response to a verb. So, for the given example, on one occasion the experimenter asked, "Who is giving?" and on another, "Who is taking?" PB, the person in the study, was at chance on this, despite being able to distinguish related verbs (such as *eat* and *drink*) in another verb-to-picture matching task.

As suggested above, tests such as these have shown that many people cannot access the thematic properties of verbs, even though core meaning may be retained (for example, Byng, 1988; Marshall et al., 1997). This is one indicant of a lexically based mapping impairment. Importantly, not all aphasic people show this pattern, and there are at least two documented cases where subjects performed better on thematic tasks than on core meaning tasks (Breedin et al., 1994; Marshall, Chiat, Pring, & Robson, 1996). Such double dissociations suggest that different aspects of verbs may be vulnerable to different types of brain damage. Clinically, these findings argue for assessments that can uncover different skills and weaknesses with verbs and provide a basis for individually tailored therapy.

Assessment of Working Memory

Some commentators suggest that sentence comprehension may be compromised by an inability to retain a phonological record of sentences; that is, because of a working memory deficit (Just & Carpenter 1992; Miyake et al., 1994; Harrmann, Just, & Carpenter, 1997).

Memory limitations are consistent with length effects in comprehension. For example, in a sentence-to-picture matching task, the person may fail with full passive forms but cope better with their truncated counterparts (such as "the woman was pushed"). Similarly, Mitchum and colleagues (1995) found that their subject, ML, performed worse when sentences were padded with (irrelevant) adjectives and adverbs; for example, "The *friendly* man is *gently* pushing the *stubborn* woman."

Repetition, either of word lists or sentences, can offer further insights into working memory. So ML, above, not only failed to comprehend padded sentences but was also poor at repeating them (Mitchum et al., 1995). Interestingly, material within the verb phrase was often omitted in the padded condition.

Byng and colleagues (1994) developed a number of tasks to explore sentence retention. In one, subjects were shown three character pictures—for example, of a nun, a cowboy, and an astronaut. They then heard an SVO sentence involving two of the characters, and had to point to the relevant pictures, in their order of mention. In another task, the person heard two sentences and had to judge whether or not they were identical. Different sentences had reversed word order; for example, "the nun splashes the queen" versus "the queen splashes the nun."

There is considerable debate about the role of working memory in sentence comprehension (for example, Caplan & Waters, 1990). One possibility is that memory impairments interact with other deficits, compounding the individual's problems. This seemed to be the case for ML above (Mitchum et al., 1995). He displayed evidence of poor verb processing. So, when memory capacity was exceeded, as in the padded sentence repetition task, verb information was particularly vulnerable to omission. It seems that clinicians need to be alert to the memory limitations of their subjects, not necessarily as an explanation for the comprehension deficit, but as a possible contributor.

On-Line Procedures

All the above assessment techniques are off-line. They require the person to carry out a conscious task, such as pointing to a picture, in response to a given stimulus. It is assumed that processing of the stimulus is complete before the task is executed.

Recently, a number of researchers have supplemented off-line tasks with on-line techniques (for example, Tyler, 1992; Shapiro & Levine, 1990; Zurif, Swinney, Prather, Solomon, & Bushell, 1993, Tyler, Ostriu, Cooke, & Moss, 1995). Here, the skills or knowledge being tested are exposed to less conscious manipulation on the part of the test subject. The procedures also tap processing as it takes place, and so provide insights into its time course.

One typical on-line procedure uses lexical decision, where the probe word is presented within different linguistic contexts. Of interest is how these contexts affect judgment times. Such tasks can expose interesting skills in aphasic people, which might be missed by more conventional testing. For example, Shapiro and colleagues (1990, 1993) presented lexical decision probes within a variety of sentences. The verbs used in the sentences had various argument structures. Some allowed for just one structure, such as *put*, which takes an obligatory three-place structure, while others allowed for multiple structures, such as *send*, which can be used either with two arguments or with three. Previous testing with nonaphasic people had shown that the complexity of a verb's argument structures affected latencies on the lexical decision task, in that verbs with multiple argument structures delayed decision times (Shapiro, Zurif, & Grimshaw, 1987). These findings were replicated with a group of people with Broca's aphasia. It seemed that the Broca's subjects, like "normals," were retrieving all the argument options of a verb during sentence processing, even in sentences that they could not comprehend.

On-line findings have interesting clinical potential. For example, Shapiro and colleagues' research suggests that some aphasic people have latent verb knowledge, which they fail to exploit in sentence comprehension. Therapy could aim to bring such knowledge more to a level of consciousness. It is currently not realistic to argue for on-line assessment to be part of routine clinical practice. Nevertheless, researchers might aim to provide this resource, on a consultancy basis, to clinicians who wish to explore the sentence processing skills of their clients in more depth.

TESTS OF EVENT KNOWLEDGE

Events and states do not automatically map onto language. Rather, speakers express a particular idealization or construal of events:

> The meaning of a sentence ... is a highly schematic construal of an event or state, an austere idealization into a structure built of foundational notions such as causation, motion and change. The same situation, even the same state of knowledge about a situation, must first be mapped onto

one of the many possible idealizations of it before it can be described in words. (Pinker, 1989, p. 360)

Pinker argues for a level of cognitive processing that acts as a mediator between our general ideas and the production of language. Furthermore, this thinking is linguistically driven. In other words, we have to adopt idealizations over events that can be mapped onto the words and structures available in our language. Slobin (1996), in a similar discussion, refers to this as "thinking for speaking."

"Thinking for speaking" might be illustrated via the event in figure 19.2. Even a simple event like this presents the speaker with a number of options. English allows us to focus on the manner in which the sand is moved (in which case we might select a verb like *shovel*) or on the effect on the wheelbarrow (in which case we might select *fill*). Such idealizations do not merely affect verb selection, but also the mapping of arguments around the verb. So, if we construe the event as having an effect on the barrow, we might opt for sentence (1) below, whereas if our focus is more on the sand we might opt for (2):

1. The man is loading the wheelbarrow with sand.
2. The man is loading sand into the wheelbarrow.

Recently, it has been suggested that some aphasic people may be unable to formulate language-appropriate idealizations of events (for example, Marshall, Pring, & Chiat, 1993; Byng et al., 1994; Dipper, 1999, Black & Chiat, in press). To test this, assessments of event processing skills have been developed.

Dipper (1999) used a video task to investigate whether subjects were aware that an event was taking place. Twenty scenes were presented, half of which depicted events (for example, someone washing up) and half states (for example, washing up on a draining board). Subjects had to indicate whether or not something was happening. To exclude the possibility that subjects were basing their decision purely on the detection of motion, Dipper introduced the illusion of movement when filming the states; for example, by using camera panning (for a similar task using pictures see Byng et al., 1994).

Figure 19.2. An event that illustrates "thinking for speaking." Different perspectives are possible; for example: "The man is loading the wheelbarrow with sand"; "The man is loading sand into the wheelbarrow."

Other tasks explore whether or not subjects can categorize events. In the Event Perception Test the person has to match two representations of the same verb, in the presence of a distracter (Marshall et al., 1999); and in Dipper's Event Photograph Task subjects are asked to identify the odd one out from three photos; for example, where two represent "have" states and one an "act" event (Dipper, 1999).

The Role Video (Marshall et al., 1993) investigates whether the person can identify the role structure of events. In this task, the person is shown a video clip of an event, such as a man ironing a shirt. The person is then provided with three photographs and asked to pick the one that shows the outcome of the event. One distracter retains the theme, but shows an outcome from a different type of event; for example, a picture of a torn shirt. The other shows an outcome from the same type of event, but with a different theme; for example, a picture of ironed trousers. Half the stimuli involve interactive events, such as a woman punching a man. Here, one of the distracters shows the outcome of the role reversal; for example, a picture of a woman with a bandaged eye. Thus, in this task the person has to judge both what type of event has taken place, and who was performing which role.

The above tasks are preliminary attempts to explore whether or not the person can make language-relevant judgments about events. It is possible to raise objections to all the tasks. For example, it is difficult to ensure that subjects are basing their judgments on the relevant parameters and not some trivial feature of the stimuli. Nevertheless, such tasks have been helpful in suggesting that "early" difficulties in event processing may contribute to a problem with sentences (for example, Marshall et al., 1993).

DIAGNOSIS

In a typical speech and language therapy clinic only a selection of the above measures will be administered, and anyway many are not widely available. This raises the question of what constitutes a clinically viable assessment regime.

Without being overprescriptive, I would suggest that the following tests offer a core assessment of sentence skills:

- a test of reversible sentence comprehension, ideally involving different predicates and structures;
- a test of verb comprehension, ideally exploring both core and thematic meaning;
- an analysis of connected speech; for example, from a narrative sample or picture description; and
- a test of noun and verb naming.

The reversible sentence comprehension test should identify a comprehension impairment and start to generate hypotheses about the sources of that impairment. For example, performance may be affected by sentence length or complexity. This may signal a difficulty in parsing or in short-term memory. Evidence of improved performance in the written modality might signal the latter. Alternatively, it may emerge that errors are most related to predicate type. For example, sentences with agentive predicates (like *splash*) may be understood, whereas sentences with nonagentive predicates (like *admire*) are not. This might suggest that sentence difficulties originate with a semantic problem with verbs, in which case the verb comprehension test may provide corroborating evidence. This should also indicate which verb properties are most accessible. For example, the person may cope well with core meaning distinctions but not thematic distinctions. On the production side, the regime should highlight diagnostic patterns, such as verb omission, reduced production of closed-class words, and structural poverty. Of course, in individual cases this basic regime could be supplemented by further assessments, such as tests of working memory, grammaticality judgments, or explorations of event knowledge.

The nature of sentence processing impairments is still poorly understood, even by researchers who can devote considerable mental energy to the question. It is not, therefore, realistic to expect clinicians to arrive at cast-iron diagnoses of their patients' difficulties. Rather, they need assessments that will enable them to select a therapy approach with reasonable confidence. A number of studies demonstrate that it is possible to develop a therapy hypothesis from a highly economical assessment regime (for example, see Nickels, Byng, & Block, 1991) and within routine clinical settings (for example, see Swinburn, 1999; Greenwood, 1999). These studies may not have fully diagnosed the individual's sentence processing impairments. However, in all cases it seemed that the impairment was sufficiently understood for successful therapy to commence.

THERAPY

Therapies Based on the Mapping Hypothesis

In the 1980s, Schwartz and colleagues published a series of influential papers arguing that people with Broca's aphasia can process syntactic information—for example, in carrying out grammaticality judgments—but cannot relate that information to meaning. It is claimed that their difficulties reflect an inability to map thematic roles onto sentence positions, either because they cannot access thematic information from verbs, or because they lack assignment procedures (for example, Saffran et al., 1980; Schwartz, Saffran, & Marin, 1980; Linebarger et al., 1983; Schwartz, Linebarger, & Saffran, 1985; Schwartz et al., 1987).

The mapping hypothesis had clear implications for therapy. Rather than training surface sentence forms, therapy should aim to clarify connections between meaning and structure. Numerous therapy studies have since been influenced by the hypothesis (for example, Jones, 1986; Byng, 1988; Nickels et al., 1991; Le Dorze, Jacob, & Conderre, 1991; Byng et al., 1994; Schwartz et al., 1994; Mitchum et al., 1995; Haendiges, Berndt, & Mitchum, 1996; Crerar, Ellis, & Dean, 1996; Marshall et al., 1997; Mitchum, Greenwald, & Berndt, 1997; Berndt & Mitchum, 1998; and see Marshall, 1995, for review).

Various techniques are employed in mapping therapy. One approach, developed by Jones (1986), involves the metalinguistic analysis of verb argument structure (see also Le Dorze et al., 1991; Schwartz et al., 1994). Therapy stimuli take the form of written sentences. The person is first asked to segment each sentence into syntactic phrases and find and mark the verb. Then the patient or theme is identified (for example, "What is s/he V-ing?"); followed by the agent (for example, "Who is V-ing?"). These roles are marked with relevant Wh-words or underlined in different colors. Therapy progresses from simple to more complex, moved argument sentences. Schwartz and colleagues (1994) also manipulated predicate type, in that one group of sentences involved verbs that assign the role of stimulus/experiencer (such as *love*).

Jones's therapy requires certain skills on the part of the aphasic person. They need to comprehend Wh-questions, since these feature prominently in the task, and be able to read (although Le Dorze and colleagues bypassed this problem by using "pictorial sentences"). The treatment also assumes that the person can identify phrase boundaries, although this is consistent with the mapping hypothesis.

Other treatments impose less stringent demands. Mitchum and colleagues (1995) used variants on a sentence-to-picture matching task. These included verification, in which the person had to confirm whether or not a spoken sentence matched a picture, and forced choice, in which the person had to match a spoken sentence to one of two pictures. Feedback either confirmed a correct judgment, or identified errors while repeating the target (see also Haendiges, Berndt, & Mitchum, 1996; Berndt & Mitchum, 1998).

Word order tasks also feature in mapping therapy. Byng (1988) and Nickels and colleagues

(1991) asked participants to describe pictures by ordering sentence fragments. Pictures were presented in related pairs; for example, one might show a monk writing a letter and the other a robber writing a letter. The person had to select one picture and compose a description using given sentence fragments. When this was accomplished, they were asked to change the sentence so that it would describe the other picture; for example, by swapping the first noun phrase.

From these brief descriptions, it is clear that mapping therapies encompass a wide range of treatment techniques and strategies. Indeed, there are further variants that have not been presented (for example, see Byng, 1988; Marshall et al., 1997). Despite this, they are united by a common aim—that is, to clarify how sentence structure expresses meaning—and they all emphasize where event participants are mapped in relation to the verb. Many of the therapies also engage a level of conscious reflection on the part of the aphasic person. For example, Nickels and colleagues (1991) did not automatically correct the production errors made by their subject, AER, preferring to promote self-judgment and correction. In this way therapy aims to develop an underlying linguistic skill, rather than simply drilling sentences (see Byng & Black, 1995, for similar arguments).

Although positive, outcomes from mapping therapy have been variable. The two seminal studies (Jones, 1986; Byng, 1988) suggested that treatment could significantly (and in the case of Byng, rapidly) improve sentence skills. There were also intriguing signs of generalization. Both studies indicated that input therapy could benefit production; and Byng (1988) showed that therapy focusing on just one predicate type (prepositions) could bring about improved production and comprehension of others. Such findings led to the proposal that one mapping mechanism might be common to production and comprehension, and with procedures shared by different predicates.

Subsequent studies, however, have qualified these early claims. Many have failed to achieve generalization from comprehension to production (for example, see Mitchum et al., 1995) and improvements are often confined to the treated predicate type. For example, PB received therapy focusing on three argument structures. After treatment, descriptions of three argument events improved, but not descriptions of two argument events (Marshall et al., 1997). Similarly, AER (Nickels et al., 1991) only improved with two argument, agentive sentences, which were the treated type. Studies have also reported subjects who either failed to benefit at all or only very minimally (for example, see Schwartz et al., 1994; Byng et al., 1994).

These different outcomes almost certainly reflect a number of factors. In some cases progress may be hindered by additional deficits, such as limitations in working memory (for example, see Mitchum et al., 1995), or problems with event conceptualization (eg Byng et al., 1994). Mitchum and colleagues (1995) also suggest that early claims for input to output generalization may have been overstated, in that post-therapy production may have simply contained more verb arguments, rather than improved mapping per se. They also argue that therapy may have included a production element, even if this was not specifically focused in the task. Nevertheless, the various approaches to mapping therapy have improved either sentence comprehension or production, with most of the people involved. Furthermore, most studies achieve a degree of generalization, if only with untreated examples of the target sentence type. Such generalization suggests that therapy has not simply drilled sentences, but has restored competence in mapping arguments of at least the target predicate types.

Selection of a mapping approach is encouraged by evidence of a mapping impairment. Typical signs are: poor comprehension of reversible sentences, verb omissions, and reduced verb argument structure in output. People with pure mapping impairments should be able to carry out grammaticality judgments, or detect syntactic errors in sentences. A further indicant may be poor verb comprehension, particularly with tasks that require access to thematic information. Interestingly, mapping impairments are not confined to agrammatic speakers. At least two of the subjects who have participated in mapping treatment studies had fluent forms of aphasia (Mitchum et al., 1995; Marshall et al., 1997).

Therapy Working at the Level of the Event

A recent variant of mapping therapy aimed to improve knowledge of event roles, rather than the positioning of those roles in the sentence (Marshall et al., 1993). The subject, MM, showed typical signs of a mapping impairment. Production was nonfluent, with few verbs and no verb argument structure. Reversal errors occurred in comprehension, even with simple SVO structures. Verb comprehension was poor, particularly in tasks requiring thematic knowledge. In addition to these difficulties, MM made errors on event processing tasks. For example, with the Role Video she could select outcomes for nonreversible events, but not reversible ones. With the latter, she tended to select the role distracter. So, when shown an event in which a woman shoots a man she chose the photo of the woman dead on the floor as the outcome.

From these findings, the authors hypothesized that MM's difficulties with verbs and verb argument structures were underpinned by a failure to conceptualize the role structure of events. Therapy targeted this level. The task required her to make a number of decisions about events, presented on video. These decisions were supported by photographs illustrating the various event participants. So, for example, MM was required to identify the agent and theme of the event by picking the relevant photos. She also had to specify the nature of the action, by selecting an appropriate outcome photograph (so for an event in which a man ironed a shirt she selected a picture of an ironed shirt as opposed to a torn shirt). Therapy was made more complex by increasing the number of photographs from which MM had to select and by progressing from nonreversible to reversible events.

Therapy was entirely confined to such event tasks: it involved no production or comprehension of sentences. Despite this, after therapy MM produced more verbs and verb argument structure on a picture description task. The authors account for this by arguing that therapy helped MM to develop language-appropriate event construals, which map more readily onto verbs and verb structures.

Previous mapping therapy studies have included an element of event analysis (for example, Nickels et al., 1991). However, this study is unusual in that therapy was limited to such analysis. It would be interesting to know whether other subjects might benefit from this approach, particularly those with very severe impairments who cannot cope with the linguistic demands of other therapies.

Therapy Aiming to Improve Verb Retrieval

Many aphasic people name verbs less successfully than nouns. It is therefore unsurprising that treatments have been developed aiming to improve verb production (for example, Fink, Martin, Schwartz, Saffran, & Myers, 1992; Mitchum, Haendiges, & Brendt, 1993; Mitchum & Berndt, 1994; Fink, Schwartz, Sobel, & Myers, 1998; Marshall et al., 1998; Marshall, 1999).

Of particular interest is whether verb retrieval therapy merely improves verb naming, or whether there are associated gains in sentence production. So far, results are contradictory. Mitchum and colleagues (1993, 1994) aimed to improve verb production in two individuals, one in speech and the other in writing. Both subjects named nouns more successfully than verbs, omitted verbs in spontaneous production, and depended on light or semantically nonspecific verbs. The task involved repeated naming of target verbs, from a number of different depictions. Errors were corrected by providing the target word. Following this therapy, both subjects named treated verbs more successfully. However, sentence generation with those verbs was still impaired.

This outcome contrasts with that achieved with EM (Marshall et al., 1998). EM's speech was typically agrammatic, with virtually no sentence structure and few verbs. Verb naming was poor, regardless of the task and despite considerable success with nouns.

EM's deficit seemed particularly focal, in that many skills with verbs were retained. She comprehended verbs well, even on tasks that required access to thematic knowledge. EM could also read verbs aloud (regardless of regularity) and write them; for example, in naming tasks (she could also write sentences). These findings suggested that semantic representations of verbs were preserved, together with their phonological and orthographic forms. Her problems were confined to spoken naming, and were therefore attributed to a deficit in accessing phonology from semantics.

One final assessment suggested that EM's difficulties with sentence production were related to her verb retrieval problem. EM was asked to generate spoken sentences from sixty-four provided nouns and verbs, which were matched for frequency. The cue words were presented in random order, verbs being uninflected. EM responded very positively to the verb cues; for example, she generated twenty-seven correct sentences from them, compared to just eleven with the nouns. Furthermore, her sentences revealed a degree of syntactic variation. For example:

"the girl was drowned in the pool" (cued with "drown")
"the girl ripped the trousers in the tree" (cued with "rip")

It seemed that merely providing the phonology of the verb all but eliminated EM's agrammatism. This was a positive prognosticator for therapy. If therapy could recover spontaneous access to verbs, improved sentence production should follow.

Therapy was influenced by treatment studies for anomia, which indicate that word production can be facilitated by tasks that combine semantic and phonological processing (for example, Howard, Paterson, Franklin, Orchard-Lisle, & Morton, 1985; Marshall, Pound, White-Thomson, & Pring, 1990; Le Dorze, Boulay, Gaudreau, & Brassard, 1994; Nickels & Best, 1996). Tasks included word-to-picture matching, odd one out judgements, and producing verbs from given scenarios. Many tasks provided written options for selection. Given EM's good reading aloud, this ensured that she was able to access phonology while also processing the meaning of the target verbs. EM was also encouraged to cue herself by writing verbs and then reading them aloud.

After therapy, EM's ability to access the treated verbs in a picture description task improved significantly (but not controls) and there was a corresponding improvement in her sentence production with these verbs. Thus, with EM, verb retrieval therapy not only improved verb production, but also stimulated more sentences.

There was an important limitation in the results achieved with EM (see Marshall, 1999). A second evaluation task asked her to retell two brief narratives. One employed fourteen of the treated verbs and the other fourteen of the controls. This task assessed whether EM could use the treated verbs not just in picture description, but in more open conditions. Results were poor, in that there were only minimal changes post therapy in verb and sentence production even with the treated verbs.

These results invited a reappraisal of EM's deficit. It seemed that production was dependent on the conceptual demands of the task. When her thinking was directed by a picture, EM could access the treated verbs. In more open tasks she could not. This chapter has already argued that verb production imposes particular conceptual demands. Speakers have to construe events in ways that are consistent with their language. It is possible, indeed likely, that this thinking is aided by constrained tasks, like picture description, which help the speaker focus on the properties of the main event. Less constrained tasks, like narrative, offer no such aids.

A second program of therapy aimed to help EM to formulate constrained messages that could be mapped onto simple verb argument structures. The main task involved recounting clips of commercial videos (*Ruthless People* and *Roxanne*). EM was provided with a number of strategies to assist narrative production; for example, think of one event at a time, act out each event, and then try to describe your gesture. She was also familiarized with ten general verbs (such as *put* and *go*) that might be used to describe a wide range of events. There was evidence during therapy that these strategies effectively cued EM's production:

EM   oh dear . . . no
JM   OK. He's got to the door. Think about what he does next. Just the first thing.
      Try acting it out.
EM   (mimes putting something on the floor) put the bag on the ground . . . (mimes
      opening it) open the bag . . . (mimes reaching in) pick up the credit card . . . oh no
JM   (mimes inserting the card in the door)
EM   put the card in the . . . crack

Such gains were also observed in post-therapy measures of narrative production, in that there was an increase in verb and verb argument production and less dependence on single noun phrases. We hypothesized that therapy changed EM's conceptual preparations for language. It helped EM to formulate highly focused idealizations that could be more readily mapped onto the verbs and verb argument structures available to her.

Accounts of verb therapy suggest that we can help people regain access to treated verbs, but with limited generalizations to controls. Some individuals also show improved sentence production with the treated verbs, although this seems to depend upon the relationship between the verb and the sentence impairment. Finally, the study conducted with EM suggests that we should be alert to the conditions in which verb access can be achieved. Some individuals may need particular help to access verbs in open conditions, such as narrative.

Selecting verb retrieval therapy is encouraged by evidence of reduced verb access, particularly in relation to nouns. However, this is a common aphasic symptom, which often accompanies other deficits, such as mapping impairments. Furthermore, other therapies, such as mapping treatments, can have a positive impact on verb production (for example, see Byng, 1988; Schwartz et al., 1994; Marshall et al., 1993).

The clinician might focus therapy purely on verb access if there is evidence that the verb deficit is the main contributor to the output problem, as seemed to be the case for EM. Verb therapy might also be attempted if other treatments have been unhelpful, or if there is a residual verb problem, even after the successful application of another approach.

Morphosyntactic Treatments

Most of the treatments described so far focus on semantic or lexical aspects of sentence processing. This section will describe treatments targeting morphosyntactic aspects. Several such treatments have been developed, all aiming to elicit and shape the production of target sentence structures (for example, Naeser, 1975; Kearns & Salmon, 1984; Thompson & McReynolds, 1986; Springer et al., 1993).

One approach, which has been quite extensively evaluated, is the Helm Elicited Language Programme for Syntax Stimulation (HELPSS). This program is influenced by studies conducted by Goodglass and colleagues (1972) and Gleason and colleagues (1975), which suggested that agrammatic production was due to impaired access to syntax rather than its loss. The studies also identified a hierarchy of structures, progressing from those that are easy to achieve in agrammatism to those that are most difficult. The HELPSS program offers graded practice of this hierarchy of structures. Taking each structure in turn, first the individual has to repeat a model provided by the therapist, then produce the target in response to a completion cue. Production is assisted in both cases by pictures. HELPSS has improved scores on the Northwest Syntax Screening Test, and induced better descriptions of the Cookie Theft Picture, both with individuals and small groups of agrammatic subjects (Helm-Estabrooks, Fitzpatrick,

& Barrisi, 1981; Helm-Estabrooks & Ramsberger, 1986). Generalization to untreated exemplars of the target structures has also been demonstrated, although not to untreated sentence types (Doyle et al., 1987).

HELPSS is a general approach designed for all agrammatic speakers. It is not underpinned by psycholinguistic theory. In contrast, Mitchum and her colleagues applied morphosyntactic therapies following a model-based analysis of the sentence impairment (Mitchum et al., 1993; Mitchum & Berndt, 1994). The individuals involved in these studies were first given verb retrieval therapy (see above). This resulted in improved verb access, but with limited generalization to sentence production. The authors therefore hypothesized that there was an additional impairment in recovering the morphosyntactic elements of the verb phrase (at Garrett's positional level of production; see Cynthia K. Thompson and Yasmeen Faroqi-Shah, chapter 17 in this volume).

This impairment was targeted in a second therapy program, aiming to facilitate the production of three basic grammatical frames (expressing future, present, and past tenses). Therapy was based on fourteen sets of sequential pictures, showing an action about to happen, the action being carried out, and the action just completed. The task involved ordering and describing these pictures. Tense markers were cued by specific verbal instructions; for example, the present was triggered by the instruction that the action was happening "right now." Further cues provided the uninflected verb, and increasing portions of the sentence.

This therapy improved the sentence production of both participants, with several important generalizations. First, verb morphology improved even with untreated verbs. Second, the effects generalized to tasks that differed from those used in therapy (although not to open narrative). Finally, there were cross-modality effects, in that EA, whose treatment was confined to written tasks, nevertheless achieved better spoken production after therapy. These generalizations suggested that the participants had acquired a general competence in building the target grammatical frames. Furthermore, this competence seemed modality free, which suggested that the positional-level representation is abstract in nature, rather than phonological or orthographic.

Morphosyntactic therapy might be applied if the deficit is felt to be at the positional level of production, where the syntactic frame is constructed. This would be signalled by impaired production of grammatical morphology and absent or disordered constituent structure. This approach might also be chosen if semantic skills are intact; for example, as shown by good sentence comprehension.

Treatment for Complex Structures

Thompson and her colleagues have developed a treatment approach based on Chomsky's government binding theory (for example, Thompson, Shapiro, & Roberts, 1993; Thompson & Shapiro, 1995; Thompson et al., 1996; Thompson et al., 1997; Thompson, 1998; Ballard & Thompson, 1999). It is argued that people with agrammatism cannot process sentences in which elements have been moved from their deep structure positions—that is, because of a difficulty with traces and coindexing. So, for example, sentence (1) below is more likely to be understood or produced than sentences (2) and (3).

1. The soldier is pushing the woman in the street.
2. It is the woman i who the soldier is pushing trace i in the street.
3. Who i is the soldier pushing trace i in the street?

Linguistic-specific treatment (LST) aims to restore skills in processing phrase movement. In a typical treatment task, subjects first hear models of the target sentence structure, such as Wh-questions like (3 above). They are then provided with a written canonical sentence, which they have to transform into the target structure. The sentence elements are written on separate cards, to permit movement, and the person is given relevant Wh-word and question mark cards. In the first therapy step, the verb and its thematic roles are identified. So, for example, the therapist might point to the verb and say: "This is *pushing*; it is the action of the sentence" and then point to the object noun phrase, saying: "This is the *woman*; she is the person being pushed." When all roles have been identified, the object NP is replaced by the relevant Wh-card (who) and the question mark added to the end of the sentence. The aphasic person is now asked to produce the modified sentence: "The soldier is pushing *who* in the street?" After this, the therapist demonstrates subject/auxiliary verb inversion. Finally, the Wh-word is moved to the beginning of the sentence, and the aphasic person is asked to produce the resultant question form. All steps are then repeated, with less input from the therapist. These therapy stages aim to clarify the verb argument relations of the sentence and demonstrate how they are expressed in the noncanonical structure.

A number of evaluations have shown that LST brings about improved production of the target sentence forms, with generalizations to untreated exemplars. Generalizations to untreated sentence types have also been demonstrated, which are broadly in line with the linguistic theory behind the therapy. So, for example, Thompson and colleagues (1997) found that training Wh-movement with object clefts improved other Wh-movement structures, such as Wh-questions, but not syntactically unrelated forms, such as passives (and see Ballard & Thompson, 1999). Some studies have suggested that improvements are not confined to the treatment task, but extend to open narrative (for example, Thompson et al., 1996; Thompson, 1998) although findings here have been variable (see Ballard & Thompson, 1999).

Selecting LST as a treatment approach might be determined by a number of factors. The therapy is based on a theory of agrammatism, which presumably excludes people with other forms of sentence impairment. Candidates should also show particular difficulties with moved argument forms; for example, in sentence comprehension. There is some evidence that this approach may have rather limited success with people who have severe impairments (see Ballard & Thompson, 1999). Given that the treatment focuses on the production of complex forms this is perhaps not surprising.

A final question concerns functional relevance. Although many aphasic people struggle with the structures targeted by LST, they may nevertheless express the meanings carried by such structures. For example, many people can communicate questions despite severe problems with Wh-forms. The appropriacy of training grammatically correct question production might therefore be challenged. We might also ask whether being able to produce clefts substantially furthers the communicative competence of aphasic people. Here the evidence of generalization seems critical. Such generalization suggests that LST can establish linguistic principles that are applicable to a number of related structures. In other words, the benefits of therapy are not simply in training target structures, but in restoring aphasic peoples' command over a grammatical feature of their language. There is evidence that such enhanced grammatical competence *does* have functional benefits. For example, JD (Thompson, 1998) showed post-therapy gains in narrative production and in his scores on the ASHA FACS (American Speech-Language-Hearing Association Functional Assessment of Communication Skills for Adults; Frattali, Thompson, Holland, Wohl, & Ferketic, 1995).

Therapy Using Nonverbal Media

Sentence skills may be targeted through mediums other than formal language. One approach, developed by Weinrich and colleagues, uses an iconic computerized visual communication system (C-VIC; Weinrich, 1991; Weinrich, McCall, Weber, Thomas, & Thronburg, 1995; Weinrich, Shelton, McCall, & Cox, 1997).

C-VIC offers a number of advantages over natural language. "Words" take the form of iconic symbols, which are accessed hierarchically, thus easing lexical retrieval. It employs a simplified syntax of canonical "word" order, with no function words or inflections. The system can provide the aphasic person with production cues, such as sentence templates and models.

These simplifications can help even severely aphasic people achieve "sentence" production following C-VIC training. Crucially, there is evidence that benefits generalize to natural language. For example, Weinrich and colleagues (1995) found that training prepositional C-VIC structures improved the production and comprehension of English prepositional sentences. A subsequent experiment again showed C-VIC to English generalizations, this time for simple active sentences. Such generalizations suggest that C-VIC calls upon "normal" language processing skills, such as lexical retrieval and the construction of verb argument relations.

Interestingly, the limitations in the effects of C-VIC are also rather similar to the limitations of therapies based on natural language. For example, benefits seem confined to treated structures. So, training with actives brought about no improvements in passive production (Weinrich et al., 1995). Generalization to narrative, or even multisentence production, has also been difficult to achieve (Weinrich et al., 1997).

DISCUSSION

Generalization of Therapy Effects

The reviewed treatment approaches demonstrate that aphasic sentence processing skills can respond positively to therapy. In virtually all cases, experimental design enables us to locate the source of change to the content of treatment, rather than nonspecific effects. Furthermore, studies have included people with severe and chronic aphasia.

Although the picture emerging from this review is generally positive, the degree of change varies from study to study, particularly in terms of generalization. This is a crucial issue. Clinically, evidence of generalization enhances the claim that therapy is of functional benefit. Theoretically, generalization can help to identify processing changes that may have occurred as a result of our intervention.

In many of the reviewed studies, generalizations are limited to the target treatment structure. So, for example, therapy involving SVO sentences may improve the production or comprehension of this form, with generalization to untreated exemplars, but with no generalization to untreated forms (for example, see Nickels et al., 1991; Weinrich et al., 1995). Within-type generalizations suggest that the person has learned one grammatical frame or procedure, with no applications to untreated sentence types. Nevertheless, the ability to use the structure with novel lexical content is functionally important, since it shows that the person has achieved some creativity with that structure.

Some studies achieve more widespread generalizations to untreated sentence types (for example, Byng, 1988; Thompson et al., 1997). Such cross-type generalization argues for the acquisition of a general grammatical procedure that can be applied to different structures. This in turn has implications for models of language processing. So, for example, the results achieved by Thompson and colleagues (1997) may indicate that the language system includes procedures for processing phrase movement, which are shared by linguistically related structures. Of interest is whether treatment targeting complex forms is more likely to achieve cross-type generalization than therapy targeting simple forms. The studies conducted by Thompson and colleagues suggest that this may be the case. However, there is also counterevidence. For example, Marshall and colleagues (1997) found that treatment for SVOO structures achieved no generalization to SVO forms. The issue may not be one of complexity per se, but rather of shared processing. In other words, the effects of therapy can only generalize to structures that call upon the enhanced skills. This may explain the results achieved by Marshall and colleagues (1997), in that mapping three argument forms, involving goals and sources, may be qualitatively different from mapping two argument forms, involving agents and patients.

Another generalization issue concerns cross-modality effects, or generalization from input to output and vice versa. Such generalization is potentially important, since it indicates that production and comprehension may share processing components. In particular, we might envisage that production and comprehension share a central semantic processor; for example, dealing with the verb and its arguments. In which case, therapies targeting such semantic features should have the best prognosis for cross-modality generalization. Yet, results here are contradictory, with some studies achieving generalization (for example, Jones, 1986; Schwartz et al., 1994) and others not (for example, Mitchum et al., 1995). Furthermore, many studies cannot contribute to this debate, since therapy involved both production and comprehension elements (for example, Nickels et al., 1991; Marshall et al., 1997). Even when therapy is confined to one modality, it is difficult to ensure that elements of the other do not sneak in. For example, the person may read aloud or repeat sentences provided for comprehension, thus introducing output to an input task. Overall, it is very difficult to draw any firm conclusions about this aspect of generalization.

There is more evidence that treatment can generalize across different output modalities. For example, Mitchum and colleagues (1993) improved speech production as a result of writing therapy, and Weinrich and colleagues (1995) improved English sentences through C-VIC training. Such generalizations suggest that therapy has enabled the person to compute abstract grammatical representations that can be mapped onto different forms of output. In modelling terms, this indicates that at least some levels of sentence production are modality free. The finding is also important clinically, since it suggests that clinicians can base therapy on the person's preferred output modality with the expectation that effects may generalize to others.

The final generalization issue concerns cross-task generalization, or extensions to tasks beyond those used in treatment. In particular, therapy should aim to generalize production from elicited to spontaneous conditions. Although some studies have achieved such generalization (for example, Byng, 1988; Schwartz et al., 1994; Thompson, 1998) many have not (for example, Marshall et al., 1993; Mitchum et al., 1993; Weinrich et al., 1997).

Different factors may obstruct generalization to spontaneous speech. Narrative tasks, which are typically used to assess spontaneous production, impose numerous nonlinguistic demands; for example, involving memory and organization. It may be that such demands limit the resources available to the language processor. In other cases, limitations in spontaneous production may reflect subtle difficulties in event processing, or "thinking for speaking." So, constrained tasks, which assist such processing, are achieved, while open tasks are not. If this is the case, we need to pay more attention to this aspect of processing in our therapy.

Mechanisms of Change

It has been repeatedly stated that we do not understand how therapy affects the working of the language processing system (for example, Caramazza, 1989; Hillis, 1993), although, as suggested above, we can gather some clues from the effects of therapy and patterns of generalization.

It would be particularly interesting to know whether therapy recovers on-line access to linguistic representations and processes, or whether it develops alternative strategies and devices. The limited effects of therapy may suggest the latter. For example, the person may be able to apply painstaking strategies within constrained tasks, but not in open and spontaneous narrative. Another method of probing this would be to compare on- and off-line evaluations. Evidence of improvement only on off-line tasks would argue for strategic gains, whereas gains on both would argue for more automatic, on-line gains.

The nature of change is functionally important. If therapy builds conscious strategies we can only reasonably expect the intermittent use of such strategies. So, the person may choose to apply his or her enhanced sentence skills in some contexts, but not in others. Indeed, part of our therapy might help the person make such decisions to best effect. For example, we might encourage them to apply the skills whenever meaning cannot be inferred from context alone. If, on the other hand, therapy restores automatic access to linguistic skills, much more widespread and generalized use of the skills can be expected.

Clinical Applications

Most of the reviewed studies were conducted in the research context. This begs the question of whether similar approaches can be used in the routine clinical environment.

Schwartz and colleagues (1995) specifically address this question. They argue for a modular approach to therapy. Here assessment aims to identify three broad types of sentence impairment: mapping deficits, morphosyntactic deficits, and verb deficits. Treatment packages can then be made available to treat these three levels of impairment. The authors acknowledge that these bandings are not sensitive to the multiple variations found in aphasic people. However, as yet it is unclear how to respond therapeutically to such variations. Therefore, this modular approach seems both an efficient and realistic proposal for current clinical practice. Furthermore, clinicians can modify the basic packages during therapy administration, in response to individual differences. For example, mapping therapy with some individuals may place a greater than usual emphasis on event analysis, and morphosyntactic therapy can be applied to different structures and with different modalities. As our ideas develop, we might add to the basic packages. For example, as suggested below, nonverbal therapy might make an interesting addition.

Goals of Sentence Therapy

This chapter began by stating that aphasic sentence disorders matter because they limit the meanings that can be conveyed or comprehended. Therapy, therefore, should aim to expand these meanings. This may not equate to grammatically perfect language. So, for example, we may decide that therapy goals have been met even if the person is producing truncated or telegrammatic forms, providing they are expressing more meaning than they were before. This encourages us to take a broad view of what constitutes a sentence. It remains true that sentences must contain a predicate, and optionally arguments of that predicate. The sentence must also communicate the relationship between these elements. Yet how that is done is up for grabs. Often, at least for English speakers, the relationship will be conveyed through word order. Yet this does not have to be the case. The person may sequence gestures, or computer icons, or even structured drawings (for example, Sacchett, Byng, Marshall, & Pound, 1999). Such creative possibilities offer great potential for future sentence-level therapy.

REFERENCES

Ballard, K., & Thompson, C. (1999). Treatment and generalisation of complex sentence production in agrammatism. *Journal of Speech, Language and Hearing Research, 42,* 690–707.

Bastiaanse, R., & Jonkers, R. (1998). Verb retrieval in action naming and spontaneous speech in agrammatic and anomic aphasia. *Aphasiology, 12,* 951–969.

Bates, E., Chen, S., Tzeng, O., Li, P., & Opie, M. (1991). The noun-verb problem in Chinese aphasia. *Brain and Language, 41,* 203–233.

Berndt, R. S., Haendiges, A., Mitchum, C., & Sandson, J. (1997a). Verb retrieval in aphasia 1: Characterising single word impairments. *Brain and Language, 56,* 107–137.

Berndt, R. S., Haendiges, A., Mitchum, C., & Sandson, J. (1997b). Verb retrieval in aphasia 2: Relationship to sentence processing. *Brain and Language, 56,* 68–106.

Berndt, R. S., & Mitchum, C. (1998). An experimental treatment of sentence comprehension. In N. Helm-Estabrooks & A. Holland (Eds.), *Approaches to the treatment of aphasia.* San Diego, CA: Singular Publishing.

Berndt, R. S., Mitchum, C., & Wayland, S. (1997). Patterns of sentence comprehension in aphasia: A consideration of three hypotheses. *Brain and Language 60,* 197–221.

Berndt, R. S., Salasoo, A., Mitchum, C., & Blumstein, S.

(1988). The role of intonation cues in aphasic patients' performance on the grammaticality task. *Brain and Language, 34,* 65–97.

Bishop, D. (1982). *Test for reception of grammar.* Oxford: MRC, Oxford and Thos. Leach.

Black, M., & Chiat, C. (In press). Putting thoughts into verbs: Developmental and acquired impairments. In W. Best, K. Bryan, & J. Maxim (Eds.), *Semantic processing theory and practice.* London: Whurr Publishers.

Black, M., Nickels, L., & Byng, S. (1992). Patterns of sentence processing deficit: Processing simple sentences can be a complex matter. *Journal of Neurolinguistics, 6,* 79–101.

Breedin, S., Saffran, E., & Coslett, H. (1994). Reversal of the concreteness effect in a patient with semantic dementia. *Cognitive Neuropsychology, 11,* 617–660.

Breedin, S., Saffran, E., & Schwartz, M. (1998). Semantic factors in verb retrieval: An effect of complexity. *Brain and Language 63,* 1–31.

Byng, S. (1988). Sentence processing deficits: Theory and therapy. *Cognitive Neuropsychology, 5,* 629–676.

Byng, S., & Black, M. (1989). Some aspects of sentence production in aphasia. *Aphasiology, 3,* 241–263.

Byng, S., & Black, M. (1995). What makes a therapy? Some parameters of therapeutic intervention in aphasia. *European Journal of Disorders of Communication, 30,* 303–316.

Byng, S., & Black, M. (1999). *The reversible sentence comprehension test.* Telford, England: Winslow Press.

Byng, S., Nickels, L., & Black, M. (1994). Replicating therapy for mapping deficits in agrammatism: remapping the deficit? *Aphasiology, 8,* 315–341.

Caplan, D., Baker, C., & De Haut (1985). Syntactic determinants of sentence comprehension in aphasia. *Cognition, 21,* 117–175.

Caplan, D., & Hildebrandt, N. (1988). *Disorders of syntactic comprehension.* Cambridge, MA: MIT Press.

Caplan, D., & Waters, G. (1990). Short term memory and language comprehension: A critical review of neuropsychological literature. In G. Vallar & T. Shallice (Eds.), *Neuropsychological impairments of short term memory.* Cambridge: Cambridge University Press.

Caramazza, A. (1989). Cognitive neuropsychology and rehabilitation: an unfulfilled promise. In X. Seron & G. Deloche (Eds.), *Cognitive approaches in neuropsychological rehabilitation.* Hillsdale, NJ: Lawrence Erlbaum.

Caramazza, A., & Hillis, A. (1991). Lexical organisation of nouns and verbs in the brain. *Nature 349,* 788–790.

Caramazza, A., & Zurif, E. (1976). Dissociation of algorithmic and heuristic processes in language comprehension: Evidence from aphasia. *Brain and Language, 3,* 572–582.

Crerar, A., Ellis, A., & Dean, L. (1996). Remediation of sentence processing deficits in aphasia using a computer based microworld. *Brain and Language, 52,* 229–275.

Daniele, A., Giustolisi, L., Silveri, M., Colosimo, C., & Gainotti, G. (1994). Evidence for a possible neuroanatomical basis for lexical processing of nouns and verbs. *Neuropsychologia 32,* 1325–1341.

Dipper, L. (1999). Event processing for language: An investigation of the relationship between events, sentences, and verbs, using data from 6 people with non-fluent aphasia. Unpublished Ph.D. thesis, University College London.

Druks, J., & Marshall, J. C. (1991). Agrammatism: An analysis and critique, with new evidence from four Hebrew speaking aphasic patients. *Cognitive Neuropsychology, 8,* 415–433.

Druks, J., & Mashall, J. C. (1995). When passives are easier than actives: Two case studies of aphasic comprehension. *Cognition, 55,* 311–331.

Fink, R., Martin, N., Schwartz, M., Saffran, E., & Myers, J. (1992). Facilitation of verb retrieval skills in aphasia: A comparison of two approaches. *Clinical Aphasiology, 21,* 263–275.

Fink, R., Schwartz, M., Sobel, P., & Myers, J. (1998). Effects of multilevel training on verb retrieval: Is more always better? *Brain and Language, 60,* 41–44.

Frattali, C., Thompson, C., Holland, A., Wohl, C., & Ferketic, M. (1995). *American Speech-Language-Hearing Association functional assessment of communication skills for adults.* Rockville, MD: ASHA.

Gleason, J., Goodglass, H., Green, E., Ackerman, N., & Hyde, M. (1975). The retrieval of syntax in Broca's aphasia. *Brain and Language, 24,* 451–471.

Goodglass, H., Gleason, J., Bernholtz, N., & Hyde, M. (1972). Some linguistic structures in the speech of a Broca's aphasic. *Cortex, 8,* 191–212.

Greenwood, A. (1999). Early stages in treating a person with non-fluent aphasia. In S. Byng, K. Swinburn, & C. Pound (Eds.), *The aphasia therapy file.* Hove, England: Psychology Press.

Grodzinsky, Y. (1986). Language deficits and the theory of syntax. *Brain and Language, 27,* 135–159.

Haarman, H., Just, M., & Carpenter, P. (1997). Aphasic sentence comprehension as a resource deficit: A computational approach. *Brain and Language 59,* 76–120.

Haendiges, A., Berndt, R. S., & Mitchum. (1996). Assessing the elements contributing to a mapping deficit: A targeted treatment study. *Brain and Language, 52,* 276–302.

Helm-Estabrooks, N., Fitzpatrick, P., & Barrisi, B. (1981). Response of an agrammatic patient to a syntax stimulation program for aphasia. *Journal of Speech and Hearning Disorders, 47,* 385–389.

Helm-Estabrooks, N., & Ramsberger, G. (1986). Treatment of agrammatism in long-term Broca's aphasia. *British Journal of Disorders of Communication, 21,* 39–45.

Hillis, A. (1993). The role of models of language processing in rehabilitation of language impairments. *Aphasiology, 7,* 5–26.

Howard, D., Patterson, K., Franklin, S., Orchard-Lisle, V., & Morton, J. (1985). The treatment of word retrieval deficits in aphasia: A comparison of two therapy methods. *Brain, 108,* 817–829.

Jones, E. (1984). Word order processing in aphasia: Effects of verb semantics. *Advances in Neurology, 42.* New York: Raven.

Jones, E. (1986). Building the foundations for sentence production in a non-fluent aphasic. *British Journal of Disorders of Communication, 21,* 63–82.

Just, M., & Carpenter, P. (1992). A capacity theory of comprehension: Individual differences in working memory. *Psychological Review, 99,* 122–149.

Kay, J., Lesser, R., & Coltheart, M. (1992). *Psycholinguistic assessment of language processing in aphasia.* Hove, England: Lawrence Erlbaum.

Kearns, K., & Salmon, S. (1984). An experimental analysis of auxiliary and copula verb generalisation in aphasia. *Journal of Speech and Hearing Disorders, 49,* 152–163

Kohn, E., Lorch, M., & Pearson, D. (1989). Verb finding in aphasia. *Cortex, 25,* 57–69.

Le Dorze, G., Boulay, N., Gaudreau, J., & Brassard, C. (1994). The contrasting effects of a semantic versus a formal-semantic technique for the facilitation of naming in a case of anomia. *Aphasiology, 8,* 127–141.

Le Dorze, G., Jacob, A., & Coderre, L. (1991). Aphasia rehabilitation with a case of agrammatism: A partial replication. *Aphasiology, 5,* 63–85.

Linebarger, M., Schwartz, M., & Saffran, E. (1983). Sensitivity to grammatical structure in so-called agrammatic aphasics. *Cognition, 13,* 361–392.

Marshall, J. (1995). The mapping hypothesis and aphasia therapy. *Aphasiology, 9,* 517–539.

Marshall, J. (1999). Doing something about a verb impairment: Two therapy approaches. In S. Byng, K. Swinburn, & C. Pound (Eds.), *The aphasia therapy file.* Hove, England: Psychology Press.

Marshall, J., Chiat, S., Pring, T., & Robson, J. (1996). An investigation of semantic jargon. Part 2: Verbs. *Journal of Neurolinguistics, 9,* 251–260.

Marshall, J., Chiat, S., & Pring, T. (1997). An impairment in processing verbs' thematic roles: A therapy study. *Aphasiology, 11,* 855–876.

Marshall, J., Chiat, S., & Pring, T. (1999). *The event perception test.* Telford, England: Winslow Press.

Marshall, J., Pound, C., White-Thomson, M., & Pring, T. (1990). The use of picture/word matching tasks to assist word retrieval in aphasic patients. *Aphasiology, 4,* 167–184.

Marshall, J., Pring, T., & Chiat, S. (1993). Sentence processing therapy: Working at the level of the event. *Aphasiology, 7,* 177–199.

Marshall, J., Pring, T., & Chiat, S. (1993). Sentence processing therapy: working at the level of the event. *Aphasiology, 7,* 177–199.

Marshall, J., Pring, T., & Chiat, S. (1998). Verb retrieval and sentence production in aphasia. *Brain and Language, 63,* 159–188.

Marshall, J., Pring, T., Chiat, S., & Robson, J. (1996). Calling a salad a federation: An investigation of semantic jargon. Part 1: Nouns. *Journal of Neurolinguistics, 9,* 237–250.

Martin, R., & Blossom-Stach, C. (1986). Evidence of a syntactic deficit in a fluent aphasic. *Brain and Language, 28,* 196–234.

McCarthy, R., & Warrington, E. (1985). Category specificity in an agrammatic patient: The relative impairment of verb retrieval and comprehension. *Neuropsychologia, 23,* 709–727.

Miceli, G., Silveri, M., Villa, G., & Caramazza, A. (1984). On the basis for the agrammatic's difficulty in producing main verbs. *Cortex 20,* 207–220.

Mitchum, C., & Berndt, R. S. (1994). Verb retrieval and sentence construction: Effects of targeted intervention. In M. Riddoch & G. Humphreys (Eds.), *Cognitive neuropsychology and cognitive rehabilitation.* Hove, England: Lawrence Erlbaum.

Mitchum, C., Greenwald, M., & Berndt, R. S. (1997). Production specific thematic mapping impairment: A treatment study. *Brain and Language, 60,* 121–123.

Mitchum, C., Haendiges, A., & Berndt, R. S. (1993). Model-guided treatment to improve written sentence production: A case study. *Aphasiology, 7,* 71–109.

Mitchum, C., Haendiges, A., & Berndt, R. S. (1995). Treatment of thematic mapping in sentence comprehension: Implications for normal processing. *Cognitive Neuropsychology, 12,* 503–547.

Miyake, A., Carpenter, P., & Just, M. (1994). A capacity approach to syntactic comprehension disorders: Making normal adults perform like aphasic patients. *Cognitive Neuropsychology, 11,* 671–717.

Naeser, M. (1975). A structured approach to teaching aphasics basic sentence types. *British Journal of Disorders of Communication, 10,* 70–76.

Nickels, L., & Best, W. (1996). Therapy for naming disorders. Part 1: Principles, puzzles, and progress. *Aphasiology, 10,* 109–136.

Nickels, L., Byng, S., & Black, M. (1991). Sentence processing deficits: A replication of therapy. *British Journal of Disorders of Communication, 26,* 175–201.

Pinker, S. (1989). *Learnability and cognition: The acquisition of argument structure.* Cambridge MA: MIT Press.

Sacchett, C., Byng, S., Marshall, J., & Pound, C. (1999). Drawing together: Evaluation of a therapy programme for severe aphasia. *International Journal of Language and Communication Disorders, 34,* 265–289.

Saffran, E., Berndt, R. S., & Schwartz, M. (1989). The quantitative analysis of agrammatic production: Procedure and data. *Brain and Language, 37,* 440–479.

Saffran, E., Schwartz, M., & Marin, O. (1980). The word order problem in agrammatism 2: Production. *Brain and Language, 10,* 263–280

Schwartz, M., Fink, R., & Saffran, E. (1995). The modular treatment of agrammatism. *Neuropsychological Rehabilitation, 5,* 93–127.

Schwartz, M., Linebarger, M., & Saffran, E. (1985). The status of the syntactic deficit theory of agrammatism. In M.-L. Kean (Ed.), *Agrammatism.* Orlando: Academic Press.

Schwartz, M., Linebarger, M., Saffran, E., & Pate, D. (1987). Syntactic transparency and sentence interpretation in aphasia. *Language and Cognitive Processes, 2,* 85–113.

Schwartz, M., Saffran, E., Fink, R., Myers, J., & Martin, N. (1994). Mapping therapy: A treatment programme for agrammatism. *Aphasiology, 8,* 19–54.

Schwartz, M., Saffran, E., & Marin, O. (1980). The word order problem in agrammatism 1: Comprehension. *Brain and Language, 10,* 249–262.

Shapiro, L., Gordon, B., Hack, N., & Killackey, J. (1993). Verb argument structure processing in complex sentences in Broca's and Wernicke's aphasia. *Brain and Language, 45,* 423–447.

Shapiro, L., & Levine, B. (1990). Verb processing during sentence comprehension in aphasia. *Brain and Language, 38,* 21–47.

Shapiro, L., Zurif, E., & Grimshaw, J. (1987). Sentence processing and the mental representation of verbs. *Cognition, 27,* 219–246

Slobin, D. (1996). From "thought and language" to "thinking for speaking." In J. Gumperz & S. Levinson (Eds.), *Rethinking linguistic relativity.* Cambridge: Cambridge University Press.

Springer, L., Willmes, K., & Haag, E. (1993). Training in the use of wh-questions and prepositions in dialogues: A comparison of two different approaches in aphasia therapy. *Aphasiology, 7,* 251–270.

Swinburn, K. (1999). An information example of a successful therapy for a sentence processing deficit. In S, Byng, K. Swinburn. & C. Pound (Eds.), *The aphasia therapy file.* Hove, England: Psychology Press.

Thompson, C. (1998). Treating sentence production in agrammatic aphasia. In N. Helm-Estabrooks & A, Holland (Eds.), *Approaches to the treatment of aphasia.* San Diego, CA: Singular.

Thompson, C., & McReynolds, L. (1986). Wh-interrogative production in agrammatic aphasia: An experimental analysis of auditory-visual stimulation and direct-production treatment. *Journal of Speech and Hearing Research, 29,* 193–206.

Thompson, C., & Shapiro, L. (1995). Training sentence production in agrammatism: Implications for normal and disordered language. *Brain and Language, 50,* 201–224.

Thompson, C., Shapiro, L., Ballard, K., Jacobs, B., Schneider S., & Tait, M. (1997). Training and generalized production of wh- and NP- movement structures in agrammatic aphasia. *Journal of Speech, Language, and Hearing Research, 40,* 228–244.

Thompson, C., Shapiro, L., & Roberts, M. (1993). Treatment of sentence production deficits in aphasia, a linguistic specific appraoch to wh-interrogative training and generalization. *Aphasiology, 7,* 111–133

Thompson, C., Shapiro, L., Tait, M., Jacobs, B., & Schneider, S. (1996). Training wh question production in agrammatic aphasia: Analysis of argument and adjunct movement. *Brain and Language, 52,* 175–228.

Tyler, L. (1992). *Spoken language comprehension: An experimental approach to disordered and normal processing.* Cambridge MA: MIT Press.

Tyler, L., Ostrin, R., Cooke, M., & Moss, H. (1995). Automatic access to lexical information in Broca's aphasics:

Against the automaticity hypothesis. *Brain and Language, 48,* 131–162.

Weinrich, M. (1991). Computerized visual communication as an alternative communication system and therapeutic tool. *Journal of Neurolinguistics, 6,* 159–176.

Weinrich, M., McCall, D., Weber, C., Thomas, K., & Thornburg, L. (1995). Training on an iconic communication system for severe aphasia can improve natural language production. *Aphasiology, 9,* 343–364.

Weinrich, M., Shelton, J., McCall, D., & Cox, D. (1997). Generalization from single sentence to multi sentence production in severely aphasic patients. *Brain and Language, 58,* 327–352.

Whitworth, A. (1996). *Thematic roles in production.* London: Whurr Publishers.

Zingeser, L., & Berndt, R. S. (1988). Grammatical class and context effects in a case of pure anomia: Implications for models of language production. *Cognitive Neuropsychology, 5,* 473–516.

Zingeser, L., & Berndt, R. S. (1990). Retrieval of nouns and verbs in agrammatism and anomia. *Brain and Language, 39,* 14–32.

Zurif, E., Swinney, D., Prather, P., Solomon, J., & Bushell, C. (1993). An on-line analysis of syntactic processing in Broca's and Wernicke's aphasia. *Brain and Language, 45,* 448–464.

Part 7

Other Types of Models
and Treatment Approaches

How Can Connectionist
Cognitive Models
of Language Inform Models
# of Language Rehabilitation?

Nadine Martin
Matti Laine
Trevor A. Harley

INTRODUCTION

Cognitive models of language theories have served well as frameworks within which to evaluate acquired language impairments. This is because brain damage does not result in a random malfunctioning of language abilities, but leads to systematic patterns of behavioral breakdown that respect the underlying regularities and rules of language. In recent years, the practice of interpreting aphasic deficits within a cognitive (or psycholinguistic) model has been extended to include recommendations for therapy approaches based on a subject's psycholinguistic profile. This endeavor began with great enthusiasm but was met almost immediately with many difficult challenges. It has become increasingly clear that the issues to be addressed in rehabilitation theory and practice are complex and require an understanding of mental processing that is not yet fully realized in cognitive models. In this chapter, we aim to acquaint the reader with some of the issues that need to be addressed in order to understand the cognitive underpinnings of rehabilitation and how scientists have used psycholinguistic models to approach these issues. With this background, we will discuss the recent emergence of connectionist psycholinguistic models that characterize dynamic aspects of language processing and their potential role in the development of theories of rehabilitation.

There are two broad classes of psycholinguistic models, and each type is well suited to characterize particular aspects of the language system. Functional models have been around in one form or another since the 1950s. These models (also known as "box and arrow" models; for example, Morton, 1982; Howard & Franklin, 1988; Caplan, 1992) are intended to identify the mental components of the language system (the information processing units that map input to stored linguistic representations) and their functional roles in encoding and decoding language. Connectionist models are a more recent development, but their use has increased dramatically in the last two decades. These models provide an additional means to investigate the properties of processing mechanisms of the language system (for example, Dell, 1986; Harley, 1993; Hinton & Shallice, 1991; Plaut & Shallice, 1993). By the middle of the 1980s, there was little disagreement about the general structure of the language system (for example, Ellis, 1985; Morton, 1982; Caplan, 1992). Moreover, it was a well-established practice in aphasia research to use psycholinguistic models to interpret effects of brain damage on language (for example, Caplan, 1992) and, in turn, to use aphasic language performance as tests of those models (for example, Caramazza, 1984). This interplay between functional psycholinguistic models and language deficits greatly increased our understanding of the cognitive components of the language system. Diagnostically, the taxonomy of impairments to various cognitive structures and functions has proven invaluable. Unfortunately, this knowledge has not readily advanced our understanding of mechanisms underlying recovery from language impairment or the influences of treatment on impaired language. This is because recovery from and treatment of language impairments are phenomena that depend on the integrity of processes that encode and decode language as well as those processes that mediate learning and relearning of language. Functional models are not intended to provide descriptions of these processes and, consequently, cannot adequately address questions concerning cognitive and behavioral changes that accompany recovery and treatment. Connectionist models, on the other hand, are meant to account for dynamic processes of language and memory, and it is this potential that makes them particularly relevant to rehabilitation science.

The advent of "connectionism" has led to much anticipation that connectionist models will greatly advance our understanding of dynamic aspects of language processing. Although this may well be the case someday, the use of this approach is still in its early stages, and despite major strides, we are a long way off from addressing some important rehabilitation issues. There are at least two reasons for this. First, the cognitive mechanisms underlying recovery and treatment are likely to be very complex. There may be multiple alternative cognitive adaptations and strategies that underlie mechanisms of recovery and treatment. Moreover, it is likely that these cognitive mechanisms are influenced by a variety of "human" factors that cannot be addressed in connectionist models (for example, age, education, intelligence, motivation). Second, rehabilitation science presents many difficult questions. It is important at the outset to identify and prioritize general and specific issues to be addressed. On the broadest level, for example, we want to know how the cognitive system recovers. Does it reorganize? Does it adapt to use unimpaired systems when possible? Are parallel structures and processes in the contralesional hemisphere engaged as part of recovery or treatment? There are a host of specific questions as well. How do our therapy techniques affect language processing—normal and impaired? How do such techniques make representations accessible? Can we learn to predict what techniques will improve effects of therapy? How do we facilitate processing of words and under what conditions? How can we promote generalization of training to untrained items? How can we increase the speed of learning? How can we ensure that what is learned (or relearned) remains accessible after training is completed?

To answer these and other related questions, we need to understand the processing dynamics of the language system. That is, we need to identify the principles that govern access, retrieval, and storage of information as well as learning new information. Given the enormity of this task and the relative newness of the science, it is no surprise that we still have much to learn. And yet, because connectionist modeling has great potential to further our understanding of cognitive processes relevant to rehabilitation, it is important to periodically take stock of this approach as it is applied to rehabilitation issues. It is our goal in this chapter to provide such a report and evaluate the progress of connectionist cognitive models toward fulfilling that goal. The rest of the chapter is organized as follows. The following section clarifies some basic definitions and issues that pertain to connectionist cognitive models. Next, we discuss questions and issues that need to be addressed in a theory of rehabilitation; then we review past and current efforts of connectionist psycholinguistic models to address these questions. Last, we conclude with a brief discussion of the future of connectionist models and rehabilitation.

CONNECTIONIST COGNITIVE MODELS OF LANGUAGE: SOME CLARIFICATIONS AND DEFINITIONS

The use of connectionist models to study language has increased dramatically in a very short period. Moreover, these models are fairly complex compared to the functional descriptive models that dominated cognitive neuropsychology for a number of years. It is useful, therefore, to review some fundamental questions about connectionist models and cognitive models in general.

How Does a Cognitive Model of Language Represent Language Theory?

When evaluating the validity and usefulness of a connectionist model (or any cognitive model), it is important to keep in mind that models are not theories themselves, but rather are representations of a theory. As such, they sometimes make simplifying assumptions because the questions being investigated do not require certain theoretical detail. In this way, simplifying assumptions make it easier to investigate a particular behavior. Ideally, simplifying assumptions should not gloss over operations or variables that will clearly affect the behavior being examined. This may be unavoidable, however, because it is no easy task to characterize in a model every variable that will affect a particular language behavior. For example, the seemingly simple process of word production is carried out over several stages of representation, including a conceptual stage that initiates the process. Many models of word production do not detail the complex stage of conceptual activation (a modeling task in and of itself!), but do assume that it has some general influences (for example, imageability effects) on word retrieval that are evident in empirical studies. These influences may be built in to the model with the understanding that a model more capable of providing these details will be developed in the future.

A final point to be made about the use of models to represent theories is that no model or simulation can ensure that it has reached the ultimate truth about phenomena with 100 percent certainty. Models can only be falsified. A successful simulation shows but one way in which a phenomenon could happen, and there are always other possible ways. Thus, models and model simulations should be evaluated in conjunction with empirical data. If there are no other discriminating data available between two or more models of a phenomenon, the principle of Occam's razor is typically used; that is, the simplest solution is deemed to be the best.

What is a Computational Model?

Computational modeling is a relatively new method for studying cognitive processes underlying language and other behaviors. This tool is particularly important to connectionist models because they formulate hypotheses about the parameters of dynamic processes. It has been argued by some (for example, McCloskey, 1991; Forster, 1994) that computational simulations of phenomena do not constitute explanations of those phenomena. This depends on what is meant by explanation. The computational implementation of a model is a tool that is used to test a theory's hypotheses about processing dynamics and their role in language generation. As such, it can demonstrate the theory's account (or explanation) of a particular phenomena.

As our theories advance to include postulations of complex and dynamic cognitive phenomena, it will become increasingly difficult to predict from a theory how certain processes will fare in a given context (for example, a specific kind of functional deficit). Although guesses can be made, it is useful to have a computational model of the theory that can be used to simulate a process under specific conditions. When a theoretical model is implemented on the computer, it can be used to generate predictions about dynamic processes that are not intuitively obvious. However, as noted above, some additional assumptions are always necessary when using models to evaluate a particular aspect of a theory. This is especially true when models are computationally implemented. There are many linguistic processes and operations that have not yet been simulated in any detailed fashion on a computer, even if they are articulated in a theoretical model. Consequently, some simplifying assumptions are made to accommodate the limitations of the implemented version of the model. For example, the word production model of Dell (1986; Dell & O'Seaghdha, 1991) uses a small lexicon (five words), and the words have only three phonemes. Obviously, this does not represent the actual size and content of the mental lexicon. However, this "mini-lexicon" enables the theorist to examine issues about processing (for example, effects of semantic and phonological similarity among words in the lexicon on word retrieval) without the complications of implementing a larger lexicon with words of varying lengths and syllable structure. As computational studies address the problems of representing phonemic and syllable structure of words, simulated lexicons can be elaborated accordingly, and issues about word retrieval can be examined in a more realistic simulation of the lexical network.

How Do Connectionist Models Differ from Other Models of Cognition?

Grainger and Jacobs (1999) provide a comprehensive analysis of cognitive model types and their relations to each other. Within their scheme, connectionist models are first identified as quantitative models. This differentiates them from "box and arrow"–type functional models (for example, Caplan, 1992). Additionally, functional models postulate the existence of functional operations (for example, retrieval) in the language system, but unlike connectionist models, they do not detail the processes that mediate those operations (for example, spreading activation, competitive learning), although the theories they represent might do so. Another feature of connectionist models is that they use algorithmic computations, which differentiates them from mathematical models (for example, Massaro & Friedman, 1990). However, they must be further differentiated from symbolic models (for example, the ACT model of Anderson, 1983), which also use algorithmic computations. Connectionist models differ from symbolic models in two ways: first, linguistic concepts are represented as simple processing units (network nodes) that are massively interconnected, and second, processing of information in connectionist models is accomplished without explicitly coded rules. Symbolic models, on the other hand, have their roots in formal logic and view cognition as the manipulation of symbols that are stored and retrieved from memory and transformed according to rules.

Although our definition of connectionist models seems clear enough thus far, there remain a few misconceptions. First, it is not unusual for connectionist models to be falsely equated with distributed network models (Bechtel & Abrahamsen, 1991). Although distributed (PDP) models certainly are prime examples of connectionist models, not all connectionist models have distributed representations. Connectionist models are further divided into two types depending on whether they have localist or distributed representations. Whereas localist models are used to simulate performance of an already developed system, distributed models are capable of learning and therefore can be applied to problems that involve acquisition of new information. More will be said about these two types of connectionist models in the next section.

Norris (1993) makes the point that connectionist models are sometimes falsely equated with interactive theories of processing. This misconception has been fueled by the prevalence of connectionist theories that assume interaction. Norris views connectionism as a tool to simulate processing characteristics of language regardless of what that theory of processing is. Network models were used, for example, in Norris's (1993) demonstration of a bottom-up feedforward theory of word recognition and in Laine, Tikkala, and Juhola's (1998) simulation of modular stages of word production. These models use network architectures to simulate language generation as a dynamic process, but they are actually hybrid models that combine "box and arrow" models with connectionist tools to simulate the functioning of the model. The existence of hybrid models suggests that any given functional model can be easily translated directly into a connectionist model, but this is not entirely true. Such a transformation requires the modeler to make more assumptions than the original "box and arrow" model did. Even so, once those assumptions are made, the new model can retain some basic features of the original architecture (for example, the simulation of Laine and colleagues [1998] included the seriality and discreteness assumptions of Levelt's [1989] model of word production).

In sum, the core description of a connectionist model is that it is a computationally implemented network architecture with localist or distributed representations that are massively interconnected and processed via activation and/or learning algorithms. The networks of a connectionist model are comprised of elementary units that can be activated to some degree and are connected to each other such that active units excite or inhibit other units. The system is dynamic in that it spreads excitatory and inhibitory activation among its units. Although this unique set of features defines connectionist models, there are an increasing number of variant models that incorporate only some aspects of that ideal.

What are Localist and Distributed Connectionist Models?

A localist connectionist model of language combines representations of single linguistic units (for example, phonemes or words) with dynamic processes that serve to retrieve those representations over the course of language generation and comprehension. Localist representations are used in models that have built-in parameters and are capable of performing a task at the outset. These models are used to examine performance by the language system in its fully developed state either intact or lesioned in some way to simulate impairment. Figure 20.1 shows one example of a localist connectionist model of word production (adapted from Dell & O'Seaghdha, 1991). Numerous similar models of word production have been developed by a number of researchers (for example, MacKay, 1987; Stemberger, 1985; Harley, 1984; 1993; Schade & Berg, 1992). Grainger and Jacobs (1999) note that localist connectionist models differ from the early spreading activation networks such as those used by Collins and Loftus (1975). Whereas the connections in a localist model represent simple causal relations between

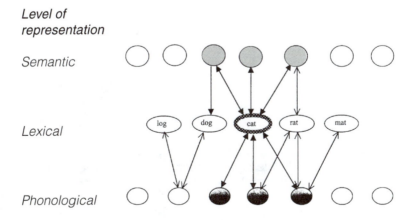

Figure 20.1. An interactive activation model of word production (adapted from Dell & O'Seaghdha, 1991). Activation spreads forward and feeds back across three layers of representational nodes: semantic, lexical, and phonological.

two representations (for example, the word *dog* and its semantic features), the connections in the Collins and Loftus network represent information about the relationship of the connected representations (for example, a dog has fur).

In distributed connectionist models, representations are not single units, but rather are patterns of activity over many units. It is the strength of these activated units that determines the extent to which the patterns act as conceptual unit. An example of a distributed model is shown in figure 20.2. This figure shows a representation of the PDP architecture used by Dell, Juliano, and Govindjee (1993) in their study of phonological speech errors in word production. This is one of many distributed models that have been developed to investigate written or spoken word processing (for example, Hinton & Shallice, 1991; Seidenberg & McClelland, 1989; Plaut, 1996). Distributed models are learning models and therefore can be used to examine issues that revolve around learning and relearning. While there are some issues in cognition that can be addressed by either type of model, there are other issues that are best handled by one type or the other. These are discussed below.

What Are Some Uses of a Localist Connectionist Model?

Localist connectionist models are relatively easy to understand and have been viewed by some as a useful bridge between functional models and more complex connectionist models (Grainger & Jacobs, 1999). They have several useful applications. Localist models can be used to explore effects of "fixed" variables on processing of language. By "fixed," we mean those variables that are relatively constant once a language is learned; for example, a word's frequency, its imageability, or its relation to other words in the network. Of course, even a seemingly fixed variable (for example, word frequency) is subject to changes in the relative strength of its effect on word processing. Such alterations would be temporary and due to competing effects of other variables. It is also likely that the relative strength of a fixed variable varies depending on the task. For example, in picture naming, the words being retrieved are all imageable, but vary in frequency. Thus, in this task, word frequency would have a prominent influence on word retrieval. In a word repetition task, both imageability and frequency, of the words can be

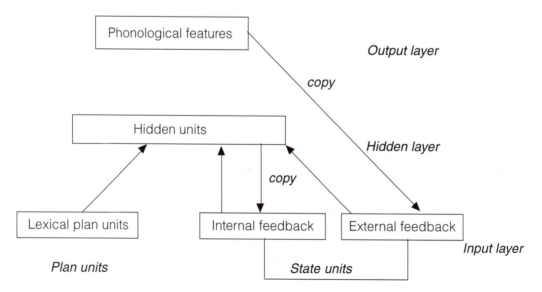

Figure 20.2. An adaptation of the PDP architecture used by Dell, Juliano, and Govindjee (1993). There are three layers (input, output, hidden). Each rectangle within a layer represents a set of units (phonological, hidden, lexical, internal context, and external context).

manipulated, allowing both variables to influence performance. Understanding the effects of fixed variables on word processing has relevance to both diagnostic and therapeutic aspects of rehabilitation. Diagnostically, effects of variables such as imageability, frequency and familiarity have been associated with the integrity of specific stages of word representation. With respect to rehabilitation issues, these variables are reflected in the choice of materials used in therapy (for example, the concreteness or abstractness of words). Awareness of the influences of these variables on language function enables a therapist to maximize or minimize their effects by choosing therapy materials and activities appropriate to the severity and type of impairment.

Another area in which localist models have proved particularly useful is the investigation of speech error phenomena in both normal and aphasic speakers. Much of our understanding of how the language processing system is organized comes from the study of speech errors. This research has yielded a set of constraints on error occurrence that is presumed to derive from the underlying organization of language production. A fundamental mechanism of word retrieval in localist models is a process of competitive activation and (in some models) inhibition among activated nodes in the lexical network. When a word is activated, that activation spreads to other related word nodes in what is termed its "lexical neighborhood." These nodes all compete for activation and either the target word is selected or, in error, a close "neighbor." This mechanism plays an important role in word recognition (see Frauenfelder & Peters, 1999), word production (for example, Dell, 1986; Schade & Berg, 1992), and error production (Dell & Reich, 1981; Harley, 1984). The competition among lexical nodes is affected by their linguistic relationships (for example, semantic, phonological) to each other, effects of variables such as frequency and imageability, and the parameters of processing mechanisms (for example, activation strength) in the model. Although it is possible that the representations of linguistic concepts are distributed, a localist version of that distribution is useful when examining the behavior of representations within a neighborhood of other activated representations. This is because it is easier to see how the characteristics of those representations affect characteristics of the output. Distributed models also can be used to simulate language performance, but the layers of hidden units in a distributed network, where much of the "learning" takes place, make it difficult to understand how various representations and processing assumptions influenced the output of the network (for example, McCloskey, 1991; Forster, 1994).

What Are Some Uses of a Distributed Connectionist Model?

Like localist models, distributed models are able to simulate effects of relatively stable variables on word processing. Although, as noted above, it is more difficult to understand how those effects take place in a distributed model, recently developed techniques to analyze the activity of the hidden units have helped to address this concern. Distributed connectionist models add something more to the arsenal of tools available to study language processing. Because they are learning models, distributed models can be used to examine questions about cognitive processes involved in learning and relearning. Moreover, they can be used to examine interactions between learning and fixed variables such as frequency of words to be learned. A distributed model also would be used if we want to identify underlying regularities of a phenomenon that could be captured by interactions between the elements of a distributed representation. In semantics, for example, the features that presumably comprise semantic representations of an object are the subunits that make one semantic representation similar to another. When features of two objects are shared, they are connected. This connection contributes to processes of learning and generalization of learning. These are certainly concepts that are important to rehabilitation.

Computer simulations using distributed networks can reveal interesting emergent properties that are not readily apparent in the model. In very complex systems, which the language system surely is, we might not be able to deduce or intuit all of the implications for recovery that will emerge from a model before that modeling is carried out. This ability of connectionist models to reveal emergent properties not immediately apparent in a theory will be very important to the future of research in cognitive rehabilitation. Throughout the literature on model-based therapy programs there are instances in which a therapy program designed on the apparent logic of a model did not work as planned (for example, Nettleton & Lesser, 1991). Moreover, there are likely many instances of failed model-based therapies that are never reported. There are many possible reasons for an unpredicted outcome, but one of them is that the logic of the model was misunderstood. Complex dynamic systems do not always behave in intuitively predictable ways. A computational instantiation of such a system enables the generation of predictions about its behavior. This feature will be discussed further in our review of connectionist investigations of recovery and treatment.

Is It Better to Use a Localist or Distributed Model?

Localist and distributed models each have features that are well suited to the investigation of different phenomena. Dell and Juliano (1996) compared the abilities of two models of phonological encoding (a localist and a distributed model) to account for some constraints associated with phonological speech errors. The first constraint, phonotactic regularity, holds that speech errors rarely result in sound sequences that are not already present in a language. The second constraint, the consonant-vowel category effect, states that in single sound substitutions, consonants replace consonants and vowels replace vowels. The third constraint, known as the syllable constituent effect, refers to instances when adjacent vowel and consonants are replaced. This occurs more often with rhyme (final vowel-consonant, VC) constituents than with initial consonant-vowels (CV). Finally, there is the initialness effect; initial consonants are more likely to engage in slip errors than noninitial consonants.

Dell and Juliano (1996) found that although both models could account for most of these phenomena fairly well, the PDP model was unable to produce movement errors (for example, the phoneme exchange error: *left hemisphere → heft lemisphere*), thus preventing it from accounting for some very important phenomena in speech production. Despite this, Dell and Juliano conclude that each model has some unique advantages that are suitable to the study of speech error phenomena. They note that the localist interactive activation model is better able to account for more phenomena in speech production than the distributed model and that it is better integrated with linguistic theory. On the other hand, a virtue of the PDP model is that its account of error effects is simple and straightforward: they emerge as products of a massed influence of the vocabulary. Also, because the PDP model can learn, it can be used to study phenomena of change as a function of experience (short-term training effects and long-term developmental changes).

This is but one example of a comparison between applications of PDP and localist connectionist models to a particular theoretical question. There should be more instances of this kind of comparison in future studies. As a general rule, it should be kept in mind that cognitive models of all types are *tools*. As such, their value is best weighed according to their suitability for investigating a particular processing issue.

ISSUES RELEVANT TO THE DEVELOPMENT OF A COGNITIVE THEORY OF REHABILITATION

A complete theory of rehabilitation requires both neurophysiological and cognitive accounts of the fundamental mechanisms underlying cognitive changes associated with recovery and rehabilitation. Nonetheless, there are some specific issues of recovery and treatment that can be addressed within the framework of cognitive-behavioral dynamics independently of the underlying neural mechanisms. Information from this line of investigation should have immediate application to methodologies used in cognitive rehabilitation. In this section, we will identify questions that need to be answered to develop ideal programs of treatment for word retrieval and other language disorders. In the sections that follow, we will describe the contributions of connectionist models to those efforts.

What Skills Should be Targeted in Therapy?

There are two parts to this question. First, we need to identify the language deficit. Diagnosis of a deficit needs to be accurate and described at a level of detail that will be useful to the clinician. Once a diagnosis is made, there is a second, related question of whether to treat the deficit directly or to focus therapy on the remaining strengths of communication ability. In one sense, this question goes back to the early days of rehabilitation medicine when it was uncertain whether treatment would improve damaged abilities. If there was hope that brain functions could be restored or reconstituted, then direct treatment seemed warranted. If no such hope existed, it seemed more appropriate to focus therapy on promoting functional communication. Although this controversy remains unresolved, the question of treating a deficit directly is raised in a slightly different way with respect to therapy approaches that aim to restore the damaged function. As our models of cognition have become more sophisticated, it is increasingly apparent that even when the goal is to restore a functional system, there are circumstances in which one would not approach the impaired subsystem head on. Rather, depending on the deficit, it might be advisable to teach to the strength of the damaged system in hopes of stimulating activity in the impaired subsystem. These options will be discussed further later in this chapter.

How Do Our Therapy Techniques Affect Language Processing— Normal and Impaired?

This is one of the most important and challenging questions of rehabilitation theory. To answer this question, we need a greater understanding of how brain damage affects both the representations and processes of language. Most cognitive models distinguish between linguistic representations and the processes that access and retrieve those representations. Presumably, brain damage can affect either or both of these components. For example, difficulty in understanding semantic aspects of language could be due to impaired semantic representations or to impairment of processes that access and retrieve those representations. Although these two aspects of language function have long been recognized, treatment research has focused primarily on the remedial effects of linguistic content and less on the dynamic components of the task itself. Therapy tasks are often chosen on the basis of a match between their linguistic content and the representations that are impaired or inaccessible (for example, semantic tasks for semantic impairment).

As our cognitive models become more explicit about processes involved in accessing and retrieving linguistic representations, there can be more speculation about how impairments to those processes might affect language. For example, one model (Dell, Schwartz, Martin, Saffran, & Gagnon, 1997) attributes word production disorders to either or both of two possible deficits to the processing components of language function: a slowing of the rate of activation or an increase in the rate of decay of activated representations. To the extent that such processing deficits are shown to be real, it will be important to consider how these deficits are treated in therapy. It may not be sufficient to say that an individual's word processing impairment is due to a deficit in accessing semantics. Rather, the access deficit could be defined further with respect to the underlying processing impairment that is impeding access (for example, weak activation or too-fast decay). Moreover, these two kinds of impairments (or others postulated by other models) might respond differently to different kinds of tasks depending on the extent to which those tasks promote activation of the target and competing representations.

Another issue to consider in choosing therapy tasks is how stimulation of one level of representation (for example, semantic) affects processing at another level of representation (for example, phonological). In cascading and interactive activation models it is postulated that impairment at later stages of encoding can be influenced by tasks that strengthen activation at earlier stages. Presumably, an effect of therapy would be to strengthen activation transmission to subsequent stages. If this is the case, it might be advisable, for example, to treat a phonologically based word retrieval deficit with semantically stimulating materials and activities.

These are but a few examples of the kinds of "treatment" questions that would be posed given a theory of processing. There has been investigation into some of these issues (for example, Nettleton & Lesser, 1991; Laine & Martin, 1996), but much more needs to be done. If brain damage affects processing (and consequently activation of representations), a therapy plan should consider the characteristics of the content (words, pictures, and other stimuli) as well as those of the tasks used in therapy. Moreover, the choice of task should be made with an understanding of the process that has gone wrong, how it has gone wrong, and how the dynamics of the therapy task will affect the impaired process. These issues will be discussed further later in this chapter.

What Techniques Facilitate Processing and Under What Conditions?

This question is directly related to the previous question. Rehabilitation science currently lacks an understanding of the dynamics of the therapy tasks. This knowledge would help us to determine what tasks facilitate or impede improvement. Most speech therapy tasks that are used to improve comprehension or production involve one or both of two fundamental phenomena: *priming* and *contextual* effects. Priming is the concept of one event (for example, hearing a word) affecting another (saying the same or another word). When a word is activated and/or retrieved, its residual activation can influence processing of subsequent words for a period of time. Also, the activation of one word representation spreads to other related word representations, increasing their level of activation. Spreading activation is one mechanism that is presumed to mediate priming. Additionally, processes that are under the subject's strategic control can be invoked; these include postlexical semantic matching and expectancy-based processing (for example, Neely, 1991).

Priming takes a number of forms. The target word can be primed directly by presenting the word itself or a task that elicits that word. Semantic priming occurs when facilitation cues that are semantically related to the target word are presented. Examples of semantic cues include the definition of a word, words that are in the same category (banana → apple), or a phrase cue that includes semantic information about the target ("You pound nails with a _____"). Any activity that probes semantic information about the target word or related concepts will prime the target and related word representations. Phonological priming involves providing part of the word's phonological form (for example, initial phoneme, the rime). For instance, /ba/ will prime phonological representations of numerous words, including *Bob, bottle, bog, bomb*. Once a word representation has been primed, it is presumed that its activation is raised for a period of time, making it temporarily more accessible.

A second factor that affects word retrieval is the linguistic context in which a word is retrieved. In the process of word retrieval, linguistic context is formed as part of the natural course of spreading activation; when representations of a word to be spoken are activated, related representations are also "primed" to some degree, creating a context in which the target word will be activated. We will call this *internal priming*. Context is also created by *external priming*. External priming can create different contexts for word retrieval. A prime word that is semantically or phonologically related to the target word creates a related context. Unrelated primes do not create related contexts, although semantic and phonological neighboring word representations would be activated somewhat by internal priming from spreading activation. Priming and context are two interdependent phenomena: priming creates the context, and, in turn, context adds to the priming.

There are number of important issues about priming and contextual effects. How do they affect normal and impaired processing? Research to date indicates that priming and context can be facilitative or disruptive to naming performance in normal (for example, Martin, Weisberg & Saffran, 1989) and impaired speakers depending, in part, on the nature of their naming impairment (Laine & Martin, 1996; Martin & Laine, 2000). When does priming facilitate processing and when does it interfere? Therapy tasks typically employ external priming and context quite liberally. In some cases, priming and context are used to directly facilitate retrieval of the target word (for example, phonemic and semantic cues). In other tasks, priming directly activates both the target and competitors and thus presents a more challenging situation for the subject. This sort of priming may or may not be facilitative. For example, in the synonymy judgment and yes/no questions (for example, Is an apple yellow? Do birds have feathers?), the task is to judge what could be conflicting or overlapping information and to choose between words that are related. These and other tasks (for example, word-to-picture matching) activate words that overlap in features and thus can make the task of retrieving the target word more difficult. It would be a worthwhile enterprise to describe therapy tasks in terms of whether the priming and context effects they promote are facilitative (prompt target retrieval directly), challenging (priming competitor representations as well as the target word), or both. Once treatment tasks were analyzed in this way, we could determine circumstances in which one approach would be better than another for promoting immediate and long-lasting improvements in retrieval.

Priming and context effects are products of language processing. This means that impaired language processes will alter these effects in different ways. It is for this reason that we need to have a clear understanding of processes that access and transmit linguistic representations and what goes wrong with them when they are impaired. Connectionist models should be able to determine parameters of priming and contextual effects via simulation, and this basic research should serve as a foundation to investigate the effects of therapy techniques on impaired and healthy language processes.

What Factors Promote Generalization of Learning from Trained to Untrained Items?

The question of how generalization works has long been an issue in rehabilitation research. Understanding the mechanisms underlying generalization of learning from trained to untrained items is important to the overall efficacy of a treatment program. Otherwise, training would have to be item-specific. A related issue is whether training generalizes across modalities; for example, from input tasks to output abilities. In naming treatments, this generalization is only observed some of the time, and we are not yet certain of the factors that promote this generalization. Some factors thought to affect generalization of training include linguistic relatedness among items being trained (priming and context effects), prototypicality of items in a category being trained, and set size of items being trained. Connectionist models are equipped to explore mechanisms of spreading activation and learning that presumably mediate generalization. However, it is important to emphasize that these issues require empirical investigation as well. Connectionist models can be used as frameworks for such studies because they can generate and test hypotheses about how these factors influence generalization under normal conditions and under conditions of impairment (for example, Plaut, 1996).

What Factors Contribute to Learning and the Endurance of Treatment Effects?

There are a number of issues about the nature of learning that need to be addressed in order to tackle more specific questions about the endurance of treatment effects. We need to understand the differences and similarities between learning new information and the "relearning" of information after a stroke (Laine, 2000). These may or may not involve the same processes. There is evidence that aphasia can impede learning of new information (Martin & Saffran, 1999) and that the effectiveness of learning is linked to the integrity of short-term memory and lexical system (both often impaired in aphasia). It is likely that effective treatments will require both relearning and new learning. Thus, to address specific questions about the effectiveness of treatment, we will need to gain further understanding of the fundamentals of learning. How is information encoded into short- and long-term memory? What factors affect speed of learning? What is the nature of forgetting?

There are several developments in connectionist modeling that ultimately should contribute to our understanding of the factors that affect learning. For example, efforts to model short-term memory and long-term learning and their links to language (for example, Gupta & MacWhinney, 1997) will no doubt provide information about factors that influence the speed of learning and the endurance of learned information. Also, explorations into the sensitivity of PDP models to memory interference might be another way to approach this question. This line of investigation would explore the degree to which a model could retain learned information when new, further learning occurs. As we learn more about these and other fundamental issues of learning, we can apply this information to empirical and computational investigations of learning in the aphasic population.

CONTRIBUTIONS OF CONNECTIONIST MODELS TO REHABILITATION: PROGRESS AND POTENTIAL

In theory, connectionist models can describe the dynamics of cognitive systems, and herein lies their potential contribution to rehabilitation. The investigation of some issues requires distributed models that learn, while other questions could be addressed using either localist or distributed connectionist models. Of the questions relevant to rehabilitation science that were listed earlier, functional models were able to adequately address the question of what deficit should be treated. They also provided some insight into the kinds of therapy materials and activities to use for a specific deficit. Connectionist models now or in the future should be able to address many of the other questions. Below, we discuss preliminary efforts of connectionist models to address some of these questions.

How Does the Damaged Language System Repair Itself?

A complete answer to this question will require investigations of both behavioral and neurophysiological changes that occur with recovery. For example, it is important to know whether physical systems are restored or whether other physical structures (for example, tissue surrounding a lesion site or structures in the intact hemisphere) assume function. Cognitive models can explore behavioral changes that would be expected to accompany recovery or relearning. Such changes may or may not parallel measurable physiological changes.

One important question about the nature of recovery is whether the impaired language system recovers in a way that returns the system to its premorbid state or whether new patterns of functioning (physical and cognitive) emerge. Cognitive theories can address the behavioral side of this question. Martin, Dell, Saffran, and Schwartz (1994) and Martin, Saffran, and Dell (1996) studied the patterns of language recovery of an aphasic individual, NC, whose naming and repetition were seriously compromised. They documented the kinds of speech errors that NC produced early in the course of his recovery and again after a year or so of recovery. NC's error patterns were noteworthy because they included semantic errors in repetition and form-related word errors (formal paraphasias) in naming. This error pattern was difficult to account for in a functional model without multiple lesion sites (for example, Howard & Franklin, 1988). Another challenge to an account of this error pattern is that it is unlike typical error patterns of normal speakers. Although normal speakers produce formal paraphasias in production (termed "malapropisms"), the predominant error type is semantic (Dell et al., 1997; Harley & MacAndrew, in press). In repetition, normals make few errors, and so a true record of what kind of error would predominate is unavailable. However, the simulation of an interactive activation model used by Martin and colleagues (1994), based on Dell and O'Seaghdha's (1991) model (see figure 20.1) indicates that semantic errors would be extremely unlikely. Indeed, they are very rare in cases of repetition impairment. The comparison of normal speech error patterns with this subject's error pattern is an important one to the issue of recovery. Martin and colleagues wanted to know whether NC's "abnormal" speech error pattern would resolve back to a more normal error pattern, or whether some new pattern of error would emerge with recovery. If the former recovery pattern were observed, it would provide evidence that recovery involves, at least in part, some return to premorbid behavioral patterns.

The first step in studying this problem was to account for NC's "abnormal" error pattern in acute stages. This was examined within the framework of Dell and O'Seaghdha's (1991) interactive spreading activation model. This model assumes that activation processes that mediate lexical retrieval are regulated by two parameters, connection strength (the rate of activation spread) and decay rate (the rate of activation decline toward resting level). Noise and the number of time steps to production are additional parameters. Martin and Saffran (1992) and Martin, Shelton, and Yaffee (1994) hypothesized that NC's error pattern resulted from a pathologically rapid decay of primed nodes in the semantic-lexical-phonological network. This prediction was partly intuitive, based on NC's severely impaired short-term memory and his complaint that words spoken to him would "disappear" before he could grasp what they were. Martin and colleagues (1994) confirmed in a computer simulation that the model also made this prediction. In a series of simulations, the model reproduced NC's error pattern in both naming and repetition, with the same functional lesion to the model. In a second part of this same study, Martin and colleagues (1994) examined NC's error pattern after some recovery. At that time, NC no longer made semantic errors in repetition of single words or formal paraphasias in naming. They compared this pattern to the model's simulation of naming and repetition performance after the decay rate was reduced from .8 (abnormally high) to a lower rate that was closer to normal. The simulation again produced an error pattern comparable to NC's (no semantic errors in repetition, no formal paraphasias in naming).

Dell and colleagues (1997) used a version of the model described above to account for the error patterns of eighteen aphasic subjects by increasing the normal decay rate (increasing it) and/or reducing the normal connection weight. In this same study, they investigated the recovery patterns of a subset of those eighteen subjects (those who were available) and showed that the changes in their error patterns could be simulated by altering the impaired parameters back toward their normal levels (that is, lowered decay rate, increased connection weight). These two studies of recovery (Martin et al., 1994; Dell et al., 1997) provide evidence that the path of recovery for impaired cognitive mechanisms underlying speech production follows a trajectory toward their normal premorbid state.

In another study of patient NC, Martin and colleagues (1996) examined his recovery of word processing abilities in conjunction with recovery of a severe auditory-verbal STM impairment that was also present in his profile. They found that as NC recovered, his performance on auditory-verbal STM tasks improved (span increased to two items), and his pattern of error in word repetition changed as well (fewer semantic errors, more formal paraphasias and neologisms). Other features of his span performance resembled patterns associated with STM-based repetition impairments (reduced recency effects and reduced word length effects). In a series of computer simulation and empirical studies, Martin and colleagues (1996) showed that NC's repetition performance could be accounted for by varying two parameters of the interactive activation model of repetition adapted from Dell and O'Seaghdha's (1991) model of production: decay rate and temporal interval. In their previous study of NC's recovery, the model demonstrated that such a reduction would result in greater accuracy and fewer semantic errors in immediate repetition of single words (Martin et al., 1994), a pattern that simulated NC's performance as he recovered. Martin and colleagues (1996) confirmed a further prediction of the model regarding NC's repetition error pattern: semantic errors would emerge in the repetition error pattern even after the decay rate had recovered somewhat, *if* the amount of time between input and output in a repetition task was increased. This was demonstrated in two tasks: repetition of two words and repetition of a single word after a delay. In each of these tasks, semantic errors reemerged as predicted. These results provide support for the view that auditory-verbal STM and lexical processing are related. NC's changes in recovery also support the view that deep dysphasia and STM-based repetition disorders are quantitative variants of the same underlying disturbance.

The studies of Martin and colleagues demonstrate how a connectionist model (in this case a localist connectionist model) can account for the complexities of behavioral changes that accompany recovery. Also, they show that apparently distinct disturbances (short-term memory and word processing) are at least functionally related. The studies discussed so far are examples of how computational simulations can provide accounts of phenomena that are not easily explained. Martin and colleagues postulated a relationship between lexical retrieval and temporal components of word processing. While this hypothesis was supported by the data, the computational simulation revealed the interactive activation model's account of this relationship. This series of studies is an excellent example of how connectionist modeling and experimental investigations of patients can interact to produce a more comprehensive study of cognitive neuropsychological issues. There are undoubtedly many other such puzzles in cognitive neuropsychology that involve complex behaviors and that would benefit from a study that combines empirical computational methods of analysis.

How Do Therapy Techniques Affect Normal and Impaired Processes?

At present, there have been few studies that explore directly the effects of therapy techniques on normal and impaired processes. We shall describe one of these below and also some empirical studies that explore this question. A major goal of cognitive neuropsychological research has been to determine how representations and processes are affected by brain damage. We certainly need theories of normal and impaired processing before we can explore the dynamics of therapy techniques and their interactions with those processes. There are a number of studies using localist and distributed connectionist models that have explored effects of damage to linguistic representations and processes on language output (for example, Hinton & Shallice, 1991; Plaut & Shallice, 1993; Plaut, 1996; Dell et al., 1997; Foygel & Dell, 2000; Rapp & Goldrick, 2000). Models such as these can serve as frameworks in future studies to examine more complex questions concerning the interaction of external stimuli and inner processes of the language system.

Damage and Retraining in a Distributed Connectionist Model:
The Effects of Site of Functional Lesion

One question that is important to understanding effects of treatment is whether those effects vary depending on where the site of functional lesion is located within a psycholinguistic model. Are deficits affecting semantic processes and representations more or less amenable to treatment than those affecting phonological or orthographic processing? The answer to this question could depend on what kind of treatment is being administered. However, there also could be an effect of site of functional lesion on relearning that is independent of the treatment being administered. In the first study we discuss below, Plaut (1996) explored the issue of whether relearning is differentially affected by the site of functional lesion using a distributed network model of reading.

In Plaut's (1996) model of reading, there are three levels of representation: orthographic, intermediate, and semantic. There are also clean-up units connected to the semantic representations that serve to refine the semantic representation as learning proceeds. Functional lesions are simulated by removing connections between the following representations: (1) orthographic and intermediate, (2) intermediate and semantic, and (3) semantic and clean-up units. Plaut explored the effectiveness of retraining in relation to the site of functional lesion. Retraining in this model involved presenting a set of words that had been learned by the model before it was lesioned. Of this set of words, the now-lesioned model recognized only half. Because retraining was the same for each site of functional lesion, this study provides no insight into differential effects on relearning related to task differences or how such task differences might interact with functional lesion site. Thus, Plaut's study is more a simulation of recovery in response to general language stimulation rather than an examination of specific treatment effects. Nevertheless, it provides important information about recovery of semantic versus orthographic lesions (and in the auditory modality, phonological lesions).

Plaut demonstrated that relearning and generalization varied depending on the site of functional lesion and that more relearning occurred in the case of semantic-to-clean-up lesions than in lesions affecting earlier stages of processing (orthographic-to-intermediate units and intermediate units-to-semantic units). The network model demonstrates this as a function of the degree of structure in the subtasks performed by each part of the network. Mapping of orthographic representations onto partially organized semantic representations (the intermediate representations) is not very structured. More structure is observed in the mapping of the intermediate representations onto the semantic representations, and finally, the interactions of the semantic representations and the clean-up units have the greatest amount of structure.

Although Plaut's analysis of the network's behavior is logical, the conclusion, that greater improvement and generalization would be observed following lesions to the semantic level than to the orthographic (or phonological) lesions, is counterintuitive. First, it is inconsistent with much of what we know about top-down contextual effects on word processing. Semantic representations that are processed later in the course of word processing influence processing of earlier-stage phonological representations (for example, McClelland & Rumelhart, 1981; Tanenhaus, Dell, & Carlson, 1987; Marslen-Wilson & Welsh, 1988). Extending this idea to impairments of word processing, when phonological input processing is impaired, top-down influences are available to facilitate comprehension. When the incoming spoken word is degraded by phonological impairment, presumably several semantic representations would be activated. This semantic information would be used to disambiguate the input and help the listener determine what words were actually spoken. When semantic processes are impaired, phonological input would provide no information about semantic structure and therefore would do little to facilitate semantic processing. At the same time, knowing the phonological form of the word is insufficient to achieve comprehension of that word. It is difficult to resolve this pattern of interactive influences during input processing with the notion that semantic lesions recover more quickly than phonological lesions.

A second, more practical reason to question the prediction of Plaut's model is that there are no empirical data to support this pattern of recovery. In fact, it was challenged in a study by Weekes and Coltheart (1996) that investigated the effects of a treatment program for surface dyslexia. That patient showed significant generalization of training effects despite the fact that his impairment was orthographic and not semantic. Although Plaut argues that this patient's functional lesion may have involved semantic deficits as well as orthographic deficits, the fact remains that this counterintuitive prediction about prognosis needs to be verified with empirical data.

What do we know about prognosis for recovery in relation to psycholinguistic impairment? Many studies have examined factors such as severity of impairment, age, and neurological site of lesion. These studies provide some relevant evidence. Kertesz and McCabe (1977) examined recovery patterns associated with various clinical syndromes (Wernicke's, Broca's, conduction, and so forth). They found that the least amount of recovery was observed in global aphasia and Wernicke's aphasia, and the greatest amount in Broca's aphasia. This latter group demonstrates impaired phonological processing, particularly in output, but semantic processing and comprehension are relatively spared. Conduction aphasics, who also have good semantic processing and impaired phonological processing, showed a relatively high rate of recovery. Wernicke's aphasia is associated with poor input processing abilities, including both phonological and semantic deficits. Unfortunately, these aphasia categories do not effectively associate input and output semantic and phonological (or orthographic) abilities with recovery potential. Nonetheless, the robust recovery in Broca's and conduction aphasics, who demonstrate good semantic processing and relatively impaired phonological processing, suggests a pattern that is inconsistent with the predictions of Plaut's (1996) model.

A proper test of Plaut's predictions requires a recovery study that effectively isolates the prognostic relevance of functional lesion sites comparable to those postulated in Plaut's model. A recent study by Schwartz and Brecher (2000) provides some relevant data. They used Dell and colleagues' (1997) model as theoretical framework and examined recovery of naming abilities from the perspective of changes in error pattern in relation to severity. They observed that the rate of phonological errors increased with severity and that the rate of semantic errors did not. This finding was consistent with the model's predictions that phonological errors are severity-sensitive and that semantic errors are severity-insensitive. On the basis of these findings, Schwartz and Brecher predicted that with partial recovery, error patterns would show a greater decrease in the rate of phonological errors than in the rate of semantic errors. Their study of the partial recovery of seven subjects confirmed this prediction. This finding, that phonological errors, characteristic of phonological lesions, were more likely to resolve with recovery than semantic errors (characteristic of some types of semantic lesions and some types of phonological output deficits (for example, Caramazza & Hillis, 1990), fails to provide support for the predictions of Plaut's model. Although Schwartz and Brecher's study does not account for the recovery track of semantic errors that arise from phonological output deficits, it does at least show that phonological errors drop out of the error pattern with recovery sooner than semantic errors. It would be an interesting extension of this study (and a more complete test of Plaut's model) to determine if semantic errors resulting from phonological output deficits also recovered sooner than semantic errors resulting from semantic deficits.

Although data to support the predictions generated by Plaut's (1996) model are lacking, they remain plausible and should be investigated further. Plaut's study is another example of the way in which connectionist models (with or without a distributed network) can lead to interesting emergent properties of complex systems that might not be apparent before modeling. These predictions cannot be taken as fact, however, until verified by empirical data. Combined computational and empirical studies should prove to be a very effective approach to solving many of the intricate puzzles in language theory and rehabilitation.

Interactions of Treatment and Site of Functional Lesion:
Exploring Differential Effects of Semantic and Phonological Context on Word Retrieval

As described earlier, Martin and colleagues (1994) and Dell and colleagues (1997) used a localist connectionist model to characterize the picture naming abilities of aphasic patients and also to examine dynamics of their recovery (Martin et al., 1996; Schwartz & Brecher, 2000). They characterized a patient's deficits in terms of processing impairments and postulated two such impairments: a weakened connection weight that affects the strength of information transmission and an increased decay rate that affects the integrity of activated representations. These studies attempt to define what can go wrong with processing and what the consequences of those impairments are for speech output. The next step is to explore the interaction of the fundamental components of therapy techniques, priming and context, with the kinds of representational and processing damage that can occur. The approach to this line of research would be similar to that of the many studies that examined the effects of therapy tasks on semantic versus phonological impairments, except that the focus would be on decay rate versus connection weight impairments. Ultimately, it should be possible to vary both the processing parameters and the locus of functional lesion to define aphasic impairment (see Foygel & Dell, 2000, for relevant steps toward this goal).

Empirically, Laine and Martin (1996) and Martin and Laine (2000) have begun to explore the interaction of treatment (priming) with site of functional lesion, using the Dell model as a theoretical framework. They employed a paradigm that exploits both priming and context through massed repetition priming of picture names that are linguistically (semantically or phonologically) related. One goal of this and related studies using this paradigm is to determine whether a subject's naming ability is facilitated or impeded by any of these contexts. Laine and Martin (1996; Martin & Laine, 2000) specifically investigated whether priming type (semantic or phonological) interacts with the linguistic impairment (semantic and/or phonological) that underlies the naming deficit. They demonstrated in several studies that some patients improve when the words being trained are semantically (categorically) related (Laine & Martin, 1996; Kiviniemi et al., 2000), while others improve when the words being trained are phonologically related (Martin & Laine, 2000).

Future investigations using this paradigm could investigate the possible interaction of processing impairment with tasks that promote priming of a neighborhood of related representations. Within the framework of Dell and colleagues' (1997) model, this would involve identifying differential effects of priming on naming impairments attributed to connection weight impairments (slowed activation) and decay rate impairments (premature decay of activated representations). Connection weight lesions lead to reduced activation of the target and competing representations. Therefore, priming should boost the activation of these representations toward a normal state and facilitate activation of the target word. In contrast, deficits caused by too-rapid decay of activated representations do not reduce activation, but rather upset the balance between activation of the target word and competing neighborhood representations. In this case, it is conceivable that priming would be disruptive to naming because too many related and competing representations would be activated. Although the hypothesis has not yet been tested computationally, it is consistent with general performance features of Dell and colleagues' (1997) model. But how does one determine what kind of processing problem is present? Computer simulations are useful for addressing this kind of question. Again, using Dell and colleagues' (1997) modeling study as an example, simulations of connection weight and decay rate impairments yielded distinctive error patterns associated with each type and severity of lesion. Each subject's error profile was then matched to the model's predicted error patterns, enabling classification of the subject's processing impairment within the framework of the model. This method could be used in future studies requiring such a classification.

The Dell model is but one framework within which we can try to understand the effects of therapy tasks on normal and impaired processing. It is noteworthy because it has sparked an interest in processing impairments in aphasia. Recent studies have investigated the ability of other models to account for the error patterns that were modeled in the Dell et al. (1997) study as well as data that could not be fit to that model (for example, Rapp & Goldrick, 2000; Ruml & Caramazza, 2000; Foygel & Dell, 2000). These models are taking the initial assumptions of the Dell et al. model and modifying them in several important ways. For example, an important aspect of the aphasic simulations using the Dell et al. model was that the parameter impairments were set globally throughout the lexical network. That is, it was assumed that the processing deficit (increased decay rate or reduced connection weight) affected semantic, lexical, and phonological processing equally. This characterization of aphasic impairment seemed at odds with neuropsychological data indicating the existence of cases with clear dissociations of semantic and phonological stages of naming. It is true that the interaction of the global deficit and the temporal course of processing from semantic to lexical and then to phonological representations can result in error patterns that appear to selectively involve one or another level of representation to some extent. Nonetheless, there remain cases with patterns of error on naming and other tasks that indicate a clear dissociation between semantic and phonological abilities. For this reason, other models that capture the possibility of such dissociations are being tested against the naming data from Dell and colleagues (1997) and other patients reported in the literature (for example, Rapp & Goldrick, 2000; Ruml & Caramazza, 2000; Foygel & Dell, 2000).

The studies discussed above are meant to illustrate the very first steps that connectionism is taking toward an eventual contribution to rehabilitation of naming deficits. These and other models that attempt to characterize naming and object specification (for example, Schade & Eikmeyer, 1999) indicate that the time is ripe to begin thinking about how training techniques might affect those same processing parameters, whether they are impaired or not. Future efforts by connectionist models should be able to determine parameters of these contextual effects via simulation by exploring, for example, effects of linguistic relatedness or neighborhood size on word access.

How Do We Promote Generalization of Training to Untrained Items?

Generalization of treatment effects from a set of trained items to other untrained items is one of the more important issues in rehabilitation. Connectionist models, both localist and distributed, have mechanisms that would mediate such generalization.

Generalization in a Localist Model

In localist connectionist models, spreading activation is the means by which generalization effects would occur. Training on one item would presumably cause spreading activation to other related words. In this model, both semantic and phonological spreading activation should contribute to the effect. Some evidence for this notion comes from the contextual priming studies of Laine and Martin (1996; Martin & Laine, 2000), in which sets of related and unrelated items were trained with a repetition priming procedure. In those studies, they examined the effects of context on rates of correct responses as well as on rates of contextual and noncontextual errors. Contextual errors are those errors that came from within the set of items being trained and would be an example of external priming. Noncontextual errors are those errors that are not items in the set. They are presumed to result from internal priming and as evidence of spreading activation to related items. These same processes, according to Martin and Laine, play a role in generalization of learning.

A Study of Generalization in a Distributed Model

In distributed models, generalization is mediated by overlapping semantic features among items being trained. Plaut (1996) demonstrated in a computational study of reading that relearning is strongly influenced by the regularity of structure in mapping one representation onto another. In the network he used, the mapping between orthography and semantics was determined by the semantic organization of the words. This suggested that if a set of words to be trained was representative of the semantic structure of the entire set of words, generalization to untrained words in the set could be expected. Plaut proposed that the typicality of a concept (that is, the proximity to the central tendency of a category) is a variable that would affect the estimate of the semantic structure. His experiments showed that generalization was greater when the network was retrained on both typical and atypical members of the category. Plaut attributes this effect to the probability that atypical members of a category include more information about the structure and central tendency of that category than do more typical members. At first glance, this prediction of Plaut's model could appear to be counterintuitive. In therapy, the general inclination is to train the most typical and familiar objects of a category. This practice might result in item-specific improvement, but not much generalization to untrained items. Plaut's model provides an insight that suggests more generalization will occur if a wider representation of the category is trained. This intriguing hypothesis remains to be investigated empirically. The outcome of such an investigation would have direct implications for methods used to treat anomia.

Other Learning Issues Relevant to Rehabilitation: Models That Link Language, Short-Term Memory and Learning

The connectionist models we have discussed thus far address automatic aspects of language processing. Controlled strategic processes that are important to the formation of compensatory strategies are currently outside the scope of these models and may be for some time to come. However, there is another realm of investigation and a host of connectionist models that ultimately should provide some information relevant to our understanding of controlled processing and its role in rehabilitation. Studies of short- and long-term memory, verbal learning, and the connections of these systems with language processing aim to understand the processes involved in learning and factors that affect those processes. Empirical data from a variety of populations (for example, developmental, normal and impaired adults, bilinguals) bear on these issues, and there are an increasing number of models designed to account for some of these findings (for example, Baddeley, 1986; Burgess & Hitch, 1992; Hartley & Houghton, 1996; Gupta & MacWhinney, 1997; Page & Norris, 1999). Ultimately, this line of research should reveal factors that affect speed and longevity of learning (and relearning) and other issues of learning that are relevant to rehabilitation.

A full account of this line of research is beyond the scope of this chapter. However, the work of Gupta and MacWhinney (1997) provides a good example of a model that attempts to link verbal STM and vocabulary acquisition. The model employs connectionist processing elements and learning algorithms, and provides an explicit account of lexical access and retrieval. The model also offers an account of word learning, nonword repetition, and immediate serial recall, and relates these three phenomena to each other and to the lexical processing system. Importantly, Gupta (1996) demonstrated that all three abilities depend crucially on the strength of long-term phonological knowledge in the system. Word learning and immediate serial recall also depend on the strength of long-term phonological and long-term semantic knowledge. This model is very promising as an account of links between verbal STM, verbal learning, and language processing. Moreover, its potential extends to accounts of the language, memory, and learning problems observed in aphasia. This and other similar models should serve well as frameworks within which to explore the breakdown of the interactions of STM, language, and learning in brain damage. Clearly, such studies should have implications for treatment of language impairment.

CONCLUSIONS: WHAT ARE SOME FUTURE DIRECTIONS OF CONNECTIONIST MODELING OF REHABILITATION?

In recent years, there has been an increase in the use of psycholinguistic theories to guide treatment of language disorders. This practice presupposes that both clinical and theoretical enterprises will benefit from this alliance. This mutual benefit is possible as long as theories can address the issues that are pertinent to treatment. In order to do this, theories must afford detailed descriptions of dynamic aspects of processing, the effects of brain damage on those processes, and the effects of specific treatment procedures on healthy and impaired processes (Hillis & Caramazza, 1994; Plaut, 1996; Harley, 1996). In this chapter, we have reviewed the history of the practice of using cognitive models to guide therapy. This line of research has been challenging and filled with controversy. Progress has been made, and yet much more needs to be done.

Functional models of language advanced the practice of model-based treatment and essentially rekindled a conviction of the value of therapy for neurogenic language impairments. The most important contribution of these models has been the framework they provide for diagnosing linguistic impairments associated with aphasia. Eventually, their shortcomings as complete frameworks for treatment became apparent, and yet, this so-called failing was actually an important contribution. The realization that treatment research required a theory of process came about, in part, because functional models of language proved insufficient to address issues pertaining to the dynamics of recovery and treatment.

The emergence of connectionist models provides new tools that can help theories of rehabilitation begin to address the dynamics of treatment methods (Harley, 1996). Although it is clear from this review that there are only a few studies that directly apply connectionist models to treatment issues, we should not be discouraged about their potential contribution to rehabilitation science. There is an active use of connectionist models to address more fundamental issues of processing characteristics, short- and long-term memory, and learning. The understanding of these fundamental processes ultimately will be applicable to treatment. We would hope that in ten years' time, a chapter such as this one would be quite different. Such a chapter might include, as background, a greater understanding of the fundamental issues of processing and learning that are currently being explored in connectionist models. In addition, we anticipate that there will be more studies combining empirical and computational data about the effects of specific treatments on different types of linguistic and processing impairments.

ACKNOWLEDGMENTS

This chapter was written with the support of a grant from the National Institutes of Health (NIDCD 01924-07) awarded to Temple University (PI: Nadine Martin), a grant from the James S. McDonnell Foundation (98-25 CRH-QUA.109) awarded to Matti Laine and Nadine Martin, and a grant from the Academy of Finland (43301) awarded to Matti Laine. We gratefully acknowledge this support.

REFERENCES

Anderson, J. R. (1983). *The architecture of cognition*. Cambridge, MA: Harvard University Press.

Baddeley, A. D. (1986). *Working memory*. Oxford, England: Clarendon Press.

Baum, S. (1992). Phonological, semantic and mediated priming. *Brain and Language, 60,* 347–359.

Burgess, N., & Hitch, G. J. (1992). Toward a network model of the articulatory loop. *Journal of Memory and Language, 31,* 429–460.

Caplan, D. (1992). *Language: Structure, processing, and disorders.* Cambridge, MA: MIT Press.

Caramazza, A. (1984). The logic of neuropsychological research and the problem of patient classification in aphasia. *Brain and Language, 21,* 9–20.

Caramazza, A., & Hillis, A. E. (1990). Where do semantic errors come from? *Cortex, 26,* 95–122.

Collins, A. M., & Loftus, E. F. A. (1975). A spreading activation theory of semantic processing. *Psychological Review, 82,* 407–428.

Dell, G. S. (1986). A spreading activation theory of retrieval in language production. *Psychological Review,* *93,* 283–321.

Dell, G. S., & Juliano, C. (1996). Computational models of phonological encoding. In T. Dijkstra & K. DeSmedt (Eds.), *Computational psycholinguistics* London: Taylor and Francis.

Dell, G. S., Juliano, C., & Govindjee, A. (1993). Structure and content in language production: A theory of frame constraints in phonological speech errors. *Cognitive Science, 17,* 149–195.

Dell, G. S., & O'Seaghdha, P. G. (1991). Stages in lexical access in language production. *Cognition, 42,* 287–314.

Dell, G. S., & Reich, P. (1981). Stages in sentence production: An analysis of speech error data. *Journal of Verbal Learning and Verbal Behavior, 29,* 611–629.

Dell, G. S., Schwartz, M. F., Martin, N., Saffran, E. M., & Gagnon, D. A. (1997). Lexical access in aphasic and non-aphasic speakers. *Psychological Review, 104*(4), 801–838.

Dell, G. S., Schwartz, M. F., Martin, N., Saffran, E. M., & Gagnon, D. A. (2000). The role of computational models in neuropsychological investigations of language: Reply to Ruml and Caramazza. *Psychological Review, 107,* 635–645.

Ellis, A. (1985). The production of spoken words: A cognitive neuropsychological perspective. In A. W. Ellis (Ed.), *Progress in the psychology of language, Vol. 2.* London: Lawrence Erlbaum.

Foygel, D., & Dell, G. S. (2000). Models of impaired lexical access in speech production. *Journal of Memory and Language, 43,* 182–216.

Forster, K. (1994). Computational modeling and elementary process analysis in visual word recognition. *Journal of Experimental Psychology: Human Perception and Performance, 20,* 1292–1310.

Frauenfelder, & Peters (1999). Simulating the time course of spoken word recognition: An analysis of lexical competition in TRACE. In J. Grainger & A. M. Jacobs (Eds.), *Localist connectionist approaches to human cognition.* Mahwah, NJ, and London: Lawrence Erlbaum.

Geschwind, N. (1965). Disconnection syndromes in animals and man, Part I. *Brain, 88,* 237–294.

Goodglass, H., & Kaplan, E. (1983). *The assessment of aphasia and related disorders.* Philadelphia: Lea & Febiger.

Grainger, J., & Jacobs, A. M. (1999). On localist connectionism and psychological science. In J. Grainger & A. M. Jacobs (Eds.), *Localist connectionist approaches to human cognition.* Mahwah, NJ, and London: Lawrence Erlbaum.

Gupta, P. (1996). Word learning and verbal short-term memory: A computational account. In *Proceedings of the eighteenth annual conference of the Cognitive Science Society.* Hillsdale, NJ: Lawrence Erlbaum.

Gupta, P., & MacWhinney, B. (1997). Vocabulary acquisition and verbal short-term memory: Computational and neural bases. *Brain and Language, 59,* 267–333.

Harley, T. A. (1984). A critique of top-down independent levels models of speech production: Evidence from non-plan internal speech errors. *Cognitive Science, 8,* 191–219.

Harley, T. A. (1993). Phonological activation of semantic competitors during lexical access in speech production. *Language and Cognitive Processes, 8,* 291–309.

Harley, T.A. (1996). Connectionist modeling of the recovery of language functions following brain damage. *Brain and Language, 52,* 7–24.

Harley, T. A., & MacAndrew, S. B.,G. (In press). Constraints upon word substitution speech errors. *Journal of Psycholinguistic Research.*

Hartley, T., & Houghton, G. (1996). A linguistically constrained model of short-term memory for nonwords. *Journal of Memory and Language, 35,* 1–31.

Hillis, A. E. (1990). Effects of separate treatments for distinct impairments within the naming process. In T. Prescott (Ed.), *Clinical aphasiology,* vol. 19. Austin, TX: Pro-Ed.

Hillis, A. E., & Caramazza, A. (1994) Theories of lexical processing and rehabilitation of lexical deficits. In M. J. Riddoch & G. W. Humphreys (Eds.), *Cognitive neuropsychology and cognitive rehabilitation.* Hove, England: Lawrence Erlbaum.

Hinton, G. E., & Shallice, T. (1991). Lesioning an attractor network: Investigations of acquired dyslexia. *Psychological Review, 99,* 74–95.

Howard, D., & Franklin, S. (1988). *Missing the meaning? A cognitive neuropsychological study of processing words by an aphasic patient.* Cambridge MA: MIT Press.

Kertesz, A., & McCabe, P. (1977). Recovery patterns and prognosis in aphasia. *Brain, 100,* 1–18.

Kiviniemi, K., Laine, M., Tarkiainen, A., Jarvensivu, T., Martin, N., & Salmelin, R. (2000). Anomia treatment modifies naming-related cortical activation: Evidence from an MEG study. *Brain and Language, 74,* 433–435.

Laine, M. (2000). The learning brain. *Brain and Language, 71,* 132–134.

Laine, M., & Martin, N. (1996). Lexical retrieval deficit in picture naming: Implications for word production models. *Brain and Language, 53,* 283–314.

Laine, M., Tikkala, A., & Juhola, M. (1998). Modelling anomia by the discrete two-stage word production architecture. *Journal of Neurolinguistics, 10*(2), 139–158.

Levelt, W. J. M. (1989). *Speaking: From intention to articulation.* Cambridge, MA: MIT Press.

MacKay, D. G. (1987). *The organization of perception and action: A theory for language and other cognitive skills.* New York: Springer-Verlag.

Marslen-Wilson, W. D., & Welsh, A. (1988). Processing interactions and lexical access during word recognition in continuous speech. *Cognitive Psychology, 10,* 29–63.

Martin, N., Dell, G. S., Saffran, E. M., & Schwartz, M. F. (1994). Origins of paraphasias in deep dysphasia: Testing the consequences of a decay impairment to an interactive spreading activation model of language. *Brain and Language, 47,* 609–660.

Martin, N., & Laine, M. (2000). Effects of contextual priming on word retrieval in anomia. *Aphasiology, 14*(1) 53–70.

Martin, N., & Saffran, E. M. (1992) A computational account of deep dysphasia: Evidence from a single case study. *Brain and Language, 43,* 240–274.

Martin, N., & Saffran, E. M. (1999). Effects of word processing and short-term memory deficits on verbal learning: Evidence from aphasia. *International Journal of Psychology, 34*(5/6), 339–346

Martin, N., Saffran, E. M., & Dell G. S. (1996). Recovery in deep dysphasia: Evidence for a relation between auditory-verbal STM and lexical errors in repetition. *Brain and Language, 52,* 83–113.

Martin, N., Weisberg, R. W., & Saffran, E. M. (1989). Variables influencing the occurrence of naming errors: Implications for models of lexical retrieval. *Journal of Memory and Language, 28,* 462–485.

Martin, R. C., Shelton, J., & Yaffee, L. (1994). Language processing and working memory: Neuropsychological evidence for separate phonological and semantic capacities. *Journal of Memory and Language, 33*, 83–111.

Massaro, D. W., & Friedman, D. (1990). Models of integration given multiple sources of information. *Psychological Review, 97*, 225–252.

McClelland, J. L., & Rumelhart, D. E. (1981). An interactive activation model of context effects in letter perception, part I: An account of the basic findings. *Psychological Review, 88*, 375–407.

McCloskey, M. (1991). Networks and theories: The place of connectionism in cognitive science. *Psychological Science, 6*, 387–395.

Morton J. (1982). Disintegrating the lexicon: An information processing approach. In J. Mehler, E. C. T. Walker, & M. F. Garrett (Eds.), *Perspectives on mental representation: Experimental and theoretical studies of cognitive processes and capacities*. Hillsdale, NJ: Lawrence Erlbaum.

Neely, J. H. (1991). Semantic priming effects in visual word recognition: A selective review of current findings and theory. In D. Besner & G. W. Humphreys (Eds.), *Basic processes in reading: Visual word recognition*. Hillsdale, NJ: Lawrence Erlbaum.

Nettleton, J., & Lesser, R. (1991). Therapy for naming difficulties in aphasia: Application of a cognitive neuropsychological model. *Journal of Neurolinguistics, 6*, 139–157.

Norris, D. (1993). Bottom-up connectionist models of interaction. In G. T. M. Altmann & R. Shillock (Eds.), *Cognitive models of speech processing: The second sperlonga meeting*. Hillsdale, NJ: Lawrence Erlbaum.

Page, M., & Norris, D. (1998). Modeling immediate serial recall with a localist implementation of the primacy model. In J. Grainger & A. M. Jacobs (Eds.), *Localist connectionist approaches to human cognition*. Mahwah, NJ, and London: Lawrence Erlbaum.

Plaut, D. (1996). Relearning after damage in connectionist networks: Toward a theory of rehabilitation. *Brain and Language, 52*, 25–82.

Plaut, D., & Shallice, T. (1993). Deep dyslexia: A case study of connectionist neuropsychology. *Cognitive Neuropsychology, 10*(5), 377–500.

Poeppel, D. (1996). A critical review of PET studies of phonological processing. *Brain and Language, 55*, 317–351.

Rapp, B., & Goldrick, M. (2000). Discreteness and interactivity in spoken word production, *Psychological Review, 107*, 460–499.

Robertson, I. H., & Murre, J. M. J. (1999). Rehabilitation of brain damage: Brain plasticity and principles of guided recovery. *Psychological Bulletin, 125*, 544–575.

Ruml, W., & Caramazza, A. (2000). An evaluation of a computational model of lexical access. *Psychological Review, 107*, 609–634.

Schade, U., & Berg, T. (1992). The role of inhibition in a spreading activation model of language production, part 2: The simulational perspective. *Journal of Psycholinguistic Research, 22*, 435–462.

Schade, U., & Eikmeyer, H.-J. (1999). Modeling the production of object specifications. In J. Grainger & A. M. Jacobs (Eds.), *Localist connectionist approaches to human cognition*. Mahwah, NJ, and London: Lawrence Erlbaum Associates.

Schwartz, M. F., & Brecher, A. (2000). A model-driven analysis of severity, response characteristics, and partial recovery in aphasics' picture naming. *Brain and Language, 73*, 62–91.

Seidenberg, M. S., & McClelland, J. L. (1989). A distributed, developmental model of word recognition and naming. *Psychological Review, 96*, 523–568.

Stemberger, J. P. (1985). An interactive model of language production. In A. W. Ellis (Ed.), *Progress in the psychology of langauge, vol. 1*. Hillsdale, NJ: Lawrence Erlbaum.

Tanenhaus, M. K., Dell, G. S., & Carlson, G. (1987). Context effects in lexical processing: A connectionist approach to modularity. In J. L. Garfield, *Modularity in knowledge representation and natural-language understanding*, Cambridge, MA: MIT Press.

Weekes, B., & Coltheart, M. (1996). Surface Dyslexia and surface dysgraphia: Treatment studies and their theoretical implications. *Cognitive Neuropsychology, 13*(2), 277–315.

21

Biological Approaches
to the Treatment of Aphasia

Steven L. Small

INTRODUCTION

Presently, behavioral treatment constitutes the mainstay of treatment of aphasia. By trying to *remediate* (that is, eliminate deficits) or to *compensate* (that is, bypass deficits), speech-language pathologists seek to ameliorate the communication skills of patients with brain lesions and language disorders. For over a century, clinicians have sought to use pharmacological agents to remediate aphasia or to aid compensation, and this work has generally been unsuccessful (Small, 1994). However, in several limited areas, the use of drug treatment as an adjunct to traditional (behavioral) speech therapy has shown some promise. Furthermore, the future for pharmacological and other biological treatments is bright, with new research in neurotrophins and cell transplants holding tremendous promise (Small, 2000). This chapter will review the current state of aphasia pharmacotherapy as well as the most promising ideas for biological approaches in the future.

There is increasing evidence that behavioral interventions of various kinds can influence the anatomical structure of the brain. This has been best seen in studies of the motor system, where a relative increase in the use of one muscle group compared to another can lead to motor cortical changes reflecting this change (Merzenich et al., 1984). Further, in animals given experimental cortical lesions and then trained on motor tasks, cortical reorganization occurs adjacent to the damaged region (Jenkins & Merzenich, 1987). This provides tantalizing data for neurobiological approaches to rehabilitation.

While these results were obtained in sensorimotor systems, they give hope that cognitive reorganization could occur and lead to neuroanatomical changes for both remediation and compensation of aphasia.

With functional neuroimaging, it is possible to visualize and quantify such neurobiological changes. One study illustrated this phenomenon in a patient with phonological dyslexia (an acquired reading disorder most notable for the inability to read or pronounce nonwords; see Friedman, 1988, for a review). This patient sought help with her reading, fifteen years after a large left fronto-temporal stroke and severe aphasia and hemiparesis. She was taught to read by "sounding words out" using word and nonword exemplars and a progressive cueing approach (Kendall, McNeil, & Small, 1998). She underwent functional MR imaging before, during, and after therapy, and her primary focus of brain activation during reading changed from left inferior parietal to left occipito-temporal (Small, Flores, & Noll, 1998).

Data such as this suggest an approach to aphasia treatment that focuses on biology rather than education, whether the intervention used is specifically biological (for example, neuropharmacological) or behavioral (for example, neurolinguistic). If certain types of aphasia therapies, whether linguistic, neuropsychological, stimulation-based, pharmacological, or surgical, can alter brain anatomy and physiology, and if particular patterns of such altered states can be shown to be associated with better outcome, there is a precise and scientific method of designing, monitoring, and evaluating treatment. This would alter significantly both the goals of aphasia therapy and the responsibility of therapists (Small, 2000).

In this chapter, I discuss the current state of biological interventions for chronic stroke in animal model systems, and, more specifically, for the language manifestations of chronic stroke in humans. Although this discussion will mainly concern pharmacotherapy, other contemporary modalities of possible biological intervention in the future, such as tissue transplantation, are also addressed.

PHYSIOLOGY AND PHARMACOLOGY OF LANGUAGE: ANIMAL MODELS

This section reviews the existing data on brain chemistry and pharmacotherapy following both experimental stroke in animal models and stroke in humans. Of course, the animal data characterize systems other than language, but are relevant to language because of similarities in basic neuronal system architecture of the cerebral cortex. The pharmacological studies in humans originate from studies of both motor and language rehabilitation. The combined results of this research constitute a degree of future promise for drug therapy of aphasia.

Acute Stroke

In this chapter, I restrict attention to the subacute and chronic phases of stroke. The treatment of acute stroke, or "brain attack," has recently become of tremendous interest to the clinical scientific community and to the public at large, particularly in light of the apparent hemodynamic similarities between stroke and myocardial infarction ("heart attack"), the discrepancy between available treatments for acute stroke and what is available for its myocardial counterpart, and the results of a successful trial of thrombolytic therapy (The NINDS rt-PA Stroke Study Group, 1995).

In addition to thrombolytics, recent research has delved into various approaches to limit the size of infarctions, particularly by preventing the secondary effects of the brain injury. These approaches include neuroprotectants, calcium channel blockers, and glutamate receptor antagonists, among others (Fisher & Bogousslavsky, 1998).

Another recent innovation involves exploitation of brain areas of diffusion-perfusion mismatch, where perfusion MR imaging shows regional hypoperfusion, yet diffusion-weighted imaging (which is highly sensitive to irreversible infarct) does not indicate that this region is irrecoverably damaged. In a remarkable recent report of five aphasic patients with significant such mismatches, an intravenous dose of phenylephrine, administered to increase the mean arterial blood pressure and overcome the disproportionate area of hypoperfusion, led to reversals of language deficits without progression of infarction (Hillis et al., 2001).

It is important for aphasiologists to know of these approaches to the treatment of acute stroke for two main reasons. First is the obvious fact that preventing aphasia is preferable to treating it. Second is the fact that many acute therapeutic interventions for stroke may also play a role in the subacute and chronic time periods (for example, neuroprotectants) to augment other treatments for aphasia. Despite this overlap, the forthcoming sections deal with animal experimentation and human trials of biological therapies aimed at the longer-term sequelae of stroke and aphasia.

Chronic Stroke

Catecholamines: Dopamines and Norepinephrine

The main catecholamines in the brain are dopamine and norepinephrine, two neurotransmitters that are prevalent throughout the brain and serve in many neural systems. Neurons that use norepinephrine (previously called noradrenaline) are called adrenergic neurons. The connections that these cells make with other neural cells are of many different types, but are broadly classified as either alpha (α) or beta (β). These synaptic connections can be stimulated with agonists or blocked with antagonists, and the roles of these α-adrenergic agonists and antagonists are quite different in many respects from those of β-adrenergic compounds.

The role of these agents in animal models of stroke recovery has generally involved either measuring the concentrations of these agents or administering the agents directly or giving substances that act to increase their concentrations in the brain. Measuring these agents can involve either direct assessment of their presence in the brain or spinal fluid or studying the main sources of their production in the brain, such as the substantia nigra for dopamine or the locus coeruleus for norepinephrine. Since the catecholamines do not cross the blood-brain barrier, either they must be administered directly into the brain or spinal fluid, or other agents must be administered that act as catecholamine agonists or increase catecholamine concentrations. Dextro-amphetamine is the most popular experimental drug of this latter sort, acting nonspecifically to increase the concentrations of all the catecholamines at synaptic junctions.

The concentrations of catecholamines in the rat and cat brainstem (Brown, Carlson, Ljungren, Seisjö, & Snider, 1974; Cohen, Woltz, & Jacobson, 1975) and the subcortex of the rat (Robinson, Shoemaker, & Schlumpf, 1980) are decreased following cerebral cortical infarction. After the acute phase following rat unilateral cortical infarction (forty days), there remain decreases in ipsilateral norepinephrine concentrations in the cortex and brainstem, and decreases in ipsilateral brainstem (but not cortical) dopamine concentrations (Robinson, Shoemaker, Schlumpf, Valk, & Bloom, 1975). This catecholamine deficit may result from right cortical but not left cortical infarction (Robinson, 1979). Such experimental stroke also causes widespread depression of glucose utilization in the cortex on both sides, the ipsilateral red nucleus, and the locus coeruleus bilaterally (Feeney, Sutton, Boyeson, Hovda, & Dail, 1985).

Recent interest in these catecholamine systems has focused on the role of cerebral cortical norepinephrine, particularly the dorsal noradrenergic bundle (Goldstein & Bullman, 1997). This bundle contains ascending fibers from the locus coeruleus, the brainstem nucleus that is the primary site of origin of norepinephrine in the brain. In this work, lesions to this bundle had an effect on recovery of animals with contralateral sensorimotor cortical injuries, but had no effect on animals with sham cortical injuries. The general conclusion of this research on central norepinephrine (NE) suggests that efforts to deplete NE, to block α-adrenergic (NE) receptors, or to decrease NE release impede recovery, whereas drugs that increase NE release or block reuptake facilitate recovery (Goldstein, 1999).

These basic neuropharmacological data regarding the role of catecholamines in stroke recovery have led to a number of therapeutic studies in animal models (Goldstein, 2000a). In the early studies of this type, a single dose of dextro-amphetamine (d-amphetamine), which augments postsynaptic catecholamines, including both norepinephrine and dopamine, led to accelerated recovery in a beam-walking task in rats with unilateral motor cortex ablation (Feeney, Gonzalez, & Law, 1982; Goldstein, Miller, Cress, Tyson, & Davis, 1988). By contrast, a single dose of haloperidol, a dopamine antagonist, blocked the amphetamine effect. When given alone, haloperidol delayed spontaneous recovery, whereas phenoxybenzamine, an α-adrenergic antagonist, reproduced the deficits in recovered animals. Treatment with intraventricular norepinephrine, but not dopamine, reproduced the beneficial effect of d-amphetamine (Boyeson &

Feeney, 1984). The absence of an effect of dopamine was paradoxical, since the dopamine-antagonist haloperidol had such a profound effect in delaying recovery. Analogous results have been obtained with *d*-amphetamine therapy of motor system injury in the cat (Feeney & Hovda, 1983; Hovda & Feeney, 1984).

These motor system results generalize to the visual system (Feeney & Hovda, 1985). Bilateral ablation of the primary visual cortex of the cat causes impairment of visual depth perception. When given both visual experience and dextro-amphetamine, such cats demonstrate marked improvement in function. The effect is not seen when the dextro-amphetamine is unaccompanied by visual experience or when the visual experience is accompanied by saline instead of active drug.

As the locus coeruleus (LC) is the origin of diffuse arborizations of noradrenergic neurons throughout the cortex, the role of the LC in stroke recovery has been evaluated (Feeney et al., 1985). Although experimental stroke itself causes widespread cerebral cortical depression of glucose utilization, this can be accelerated by prior ablation of the LC. Dextro-amphetamine reverses this metabolic depression, and haloperidol exacerbates it.

Animal models thus suggest that endogenous and exogenous catecholamines, particularly norepinephrine, acting through α receptors, play an important role in recovery from stroke. These data also suggest that the effect of catecholamine augmentation therapy depends on concomitant experience. Thus, motor recovery following stroke, while facilitated by pharmacotherapy, depends on the presence of motor practice, just as visual recovery depends on visual experience. These data also provide potentially valuable information about drugs commonly used in the rehabilitation setting (for example, haloperidol), but which might have adverse effects upon recovery (discussed further later in this chapter).

Serotonin (5-Hydroxytriptophan; 5-HT)

Although antidepressant medications are commonly thought to affect the brain predominantly by increasing serotonin, they generally affect a wider variety of monoamines, including the catecholamines (Frazer, 1997). Several studies have investigated both tricyclic antidepressants and the newer "selective" serotonin reuptake inhibitors (SSRI) in their effects on stroke recovery in animal models (Boyeson, 1996; Boyeson & Harmon, 1993; Boyeson, Harmon, & Jones, 1994). One study, aiming to assess the issue of transmitter selectivity, also evaluated the role of serotonin itself in mediating this process. Of particular interest were the results that neither the SSRI fluoxetine nor direct administration of serotonin were effective in improving motor function in a rat model (Boyeson et al., 1994). The results with the tricyclics, with much less specific effects on monoamine uptake, were not as clear, particularly since desipramine (Boyeson & Harmon, 1993) and amitryptylline (Boyeson et al., 1994) seemed to have opposite effects.

Gamma Amino Butyric Acid (GABA)

Intracortical infusion of GABA exacerbates the hemiparesis produced by a small motor cortex lesion in rats (Schallert et al., 1992). The short-term administration of diazepam (a benzodiazepine and indirect GABA agonist) permanently impedes sensory cortical recovery from the anteromedial neocortical injury. Furthermore, administration of phenobarbital, which may have some agonist effects on GABA receptors, also impedes recovery from brain injury (Hernandez & Holling, 1994; Montanez, Kline, Gasser, & Hernandez, 2000). As in the case of the catecholamines, these animal data may provide useful clinical information by suggesting that certain drugs, namely those that might have agonist effects on GABA receptors, be avoided in the rehabilitation setting.

PHARMACOTHERAPY OF APHASIA

History

In an early case report, Linn (1947) describes two aphasic patients with language disorders from traumatic brain injury. The patients had language testing before and after the injection of intravenous amobarbital sodium. While language performance of the first patient improved, he attributed the result to improved attention and "energy." The second patient went from a state of near mutism to a markedly improved state, which endured only when the drug was administered. Unfortunately, the patient eventually developed tolerance to the treatment. The article concludes that sodium amytal may help with the "psychological component" present in organic disease.

The most realistic explanation for improvement in these patients with traumatic brain lesions relates to the short-acting anticonvulsant properties of amobarbital. One could speculate that the beneficial effect of this drug in the alleviation of aphasia following brain trauma was the direct result of stopping ongoing partial seizures in the left temporal lobe. Aphasic seizures constitute a well-documented form of partial epilepsy (Lesser, 1991; Rosenbaum, Siegel, Barr, & Rowan, 1986; Wells, Labar, & Solomon, 1992), and it would be interesting to reexamine Dr. Linn's patients with this in mind.

Furthermore, a carefully controlled clinical study involving twenty-seven hospitalized patients with aphasia failed to replicate Dr. Linn's finding (Bergman & Green, 1951). Comprehensive language and cognitive testing of these patients before and after administration of intravenous amobarbital found that while many patients felt that they were more fluent during the amobarbital infusion, no patient showed objective improvement in function.

West and Stockel (1965) selected twenty-nine patients with right hemiparesis and aphasia from stroke for a double-blind placebo-controlled crossover study of meprobamate therapy combined with behavioral speech therapy. In each six-month cycle, a patient had one three-month period of meprobamate plus speech therapy and another of placebo plus speech therapy. General physical and neurological examinations, laboratory evaluations, and comprehensive language and cognitive measures were performed before and after four such cycles. After careful statistical analysis, the authors determined that the medication did not produce better results than speech therapy alone. While this double-blind crossover study produced valid results for a subpopulation of patients with aphasia, eligibility required a right hemiparesis, excluding many patients with aphasia.

Sarno and colleagues (1972) studied the effects of hyperbaric oxygen on sixteen chronic aphasic patients with right hemiplegia and aphasia from left hemisphere stroke. Comprehensive neurological and cognitive evaluation before and after treatment with hyperbaric air or hyperbaric oxygen failed to show improvement in auditory comprehension or functional communication during or following therapy.

Modern Studies

Modern studies of pharmacological treatment of aphasia have focused on neurotransmitter systems, particularly catecholaminergic systems. A number of studies have been conducted, not all well designed (see Small, 1994, for some critical analysis), aiming to assess several different agents. This section reviews the existing literature on drug therapy of aphasia. Table 21.1 summarizes those drugs that have been suggested to help in the treatment of aphasia and for which there exist at least one controlled study supporting such a beneficial effect. It is important to note that not a single one of these drugs has been adequately shown to help aphasia recovery to the degree that would be necessary to recommend its general use. Several

Table 21.1
Drugs With Potentially Helpful Effects on Aphasia Recovery

Agent	Typical drug use	Mechanism
Bromocriptine	Parkinsonism	Dopamine receptor agonist
Dextro-amphetamine (sympathomimetic)	Narcolepsy/depression	Increases release of dopamine, norepinephrine
Piracetam ("nootropic")	"Memory enhancement"	Cholinergic and excitatory amine facilitation (plus vascular, hematological effects)

biological approaches that have been tested for aphasia recovery have been shown to be ineffective (for example, meprobamate, hyperbaric oxygen; see discussion above) or very poorly supported by published literature (for example, amobarbital, selegiline). At present, it can be concluded that the drugs in table 21.1 remain promising candidates for helping aphasia recovery, but have not yet been proven to do so.

Studies of brain catecholamines in animals following stroke led to an analogous study in humans. In this study, it was found that the concentration of catecholamines in the human cerebrospinal fluid is decreased following cerebral cortical infarction (Meyer, Stoica, Pascu, Shimazu, & Hartman, 1973). This theoretical motivation and a number of empirical speculations have led to studies aimed at augmenting these transmitters in the brains of patients following stroke.

Dopamine Agonists

Several studies have examined the role of dopamine. Albert and his colleagues (Albert, 1988; Albert, Bachman, Morgan, & Helm-Estabrooks, 1988) described a case suggesting that the dopamine agonist bromocriptine helped restore speech fluency in a patient with transcortical motor aphasia resulting from stroke. The patient was tested before treatment with bromocriptine, during treatment, and then following cessation of treatment. Fluency improved when the patient was taking bromocriptine and evaporated following cessation of the drug. This case is particularly difficult to interpret, given the lack of many specific neurological details and of careful controls on the evaluation process. The absence of an underlying basal ganglia disorder was never documented, so the effect could have been due to treatment of underlying Parkinson's disease, for example. Furthermore, the possibilities of a placebo effect or performance variability was not discussed.

Another case report failed to find a similar benefit from bromocriptine in a man with transcortical motor aphasia from ischemic stroke (MacLennan, Nicholas, Morley, & Brookshire, 1991). Multiple baselines for testing and withdrawal periods were used to study this patient, who showed no improvement in language performance, despite his perception to the contrary. The authors concluded that a placebo effect may be responsible for the apparent improvement in language function seen in some patients.

Recently, two patients with "left frontoparietal infarcts" and "nonfluent aphasia" were treated with bromocriptine for three months in an escalating dose, and underwent comprehensive language testing prior to therapy and monthly during therapy (Gupta & Mlcoch, 1992). Both patients improved markedly in speech fluency and not in other aspects of language function. The presence of multiple baselines, with lack of improvement in language measures other than fluency, gives this study some weight. However, its value is limited by certain design flaws, including inability to rule out placebo effects and lack of any withdrawal phase.

A prospective open-label trial of bromocriptine in treatment of nonfluent aphasia (Sabe, Leiguarda, & Starkstein, 1992) studied seven patients with left frontal ischemic infarctions and a nonfluent aphasia. Every two weeks, the dose of bromocriptine was escalated and then deescalated, with language and neuropsychological testing before and during treatment. Statistical analysis of behavioral measures correlated improvement with escalating doses and deterioration with declining doses of the drug in patients with moderate aphasia. Severely impaired patients did not improve. The open-label nature of this study, with few controls, no withdrawal periods, and improvement in all baselines diminishes the generalizability of these results.

Nonspecific Catecholaminergic Treatment: Sympathomimetics

Dextro-amphetamine is perhaps the most widely studied biological treatment for the chronic effects of stroke, including aphasia (Walker-Batson, 2000), yet both its clinical efficacy and mode of action remain unclear (Goldstein, 2000a). Since dextro-amphetamine has nonspecific effects on catecholamine transmission, it affects both dopamine and norepinephrine. Despite the ambiguity about its mechanism of action and its nonspecificity, the combination of strong evidence from animal model systems and some suggestive evidence from human studies still make this a promising drug for treatment of aphasia. Since the biological basis of recovery from aphasia has much in common with that of motor weakness, this section summarizes relevant studies of dextro-amphetamine use in human patients to improve language and/or motor recovery from stroke.

In a study of motor rehabilitation from stroke, eighty-eight elderly patients who had been classified as "rehabilitation failures" because of poor progress in physical therapy were given dextro-amphetamine as an adjunct to physical therapy (Clark & Mankikar, 1979). Patients with dementia or depression were excluded from the study. The dose schedule was increased from 2.5 mg twice daily to a maximum of 10 mg twice daily as tolerated. With some dramatic cases among them, a full 55 percent of all subjects improved, and 58 percent of these were able to leave the hospital. Of those who experienced limiting side effects (26 percent of all patients) or did not improve (19 percent of all patients), only 23 percent were able to leave the hospital. The improvement was particularly evident in the younger groups (sixty-eight to eighty-four years old) compared to the older group (eighty-five to ninety-four years old).

These data are enticing, given the dramatic nature of the functional outcome measure; that is, some patients left the hospital and others could not. However, many problems limit the degree to which this optimistic interpretation is justified, including the role of placebo effects, possibility of better care given to patients receiving medicine, and the consistency of motor testing, particularly without blinding of the tester.

A double-blind placebo-controlled study attempted to replicate this beneficial effect of dextro-amphetamine in motor stroke rehabilitation (Crisostomo, Duncan, Propst, Dawson, & Davis, 1988). One group of four patients received dextro-amphetamine and physical therapy, and another group of four patients received placebo and physical therapy. Neurological evaluations conducted on the days immediately before and after therapy demonstrated a positive effect of the drug on motor functioning after ischemic stroke. The results of this study coupled with its careful design provide some degree of optimism for amphetamine pharmacotherapy in stroke rehabilitation.

An early study of aphasia pharmacotherapy focused on the amphetamine-related drug methylphenidate and the benzodiazepine chlordiazepoxide. In this double-blind placebo-controlled crossover study, a language battery was performed one hour after drug (or placebo) administration (Darley, Keith, & Sasanuma, 1977). Statistical analysis of the data revealed no difference in language performance between any of the conditions for the patients as a group. A recent study evaluated motor recovery in stroke patients, some of whom were given methylphenidate in a prospective, randomized, double-blind manner, and found a significant difference in motor and depression scores on some measures but not others (Grade, Redford, Chrostowski, Toussaint, & Blackwell, 1998). A separate study suggested that methylphenidate may play a valuable role in the treatment of poststroke depression (Lazarus et al., 1992), an important result that must be taken into account in interpretation of a wide variety of other studies of poststroke recovery.

Walker-Batson and colleagues (1991) have reported a study of six patients with ischemic cerebral infarction, all in the distribution of the left middle cerebral artery. All patients were aphasic, and were evaluated by the Porch Index of Communicative Ability (Porch, 1967). Each patient took dextro-amphetamine every four days, (about) an hour prior to a session of speech and language therapy, for a total of ten sessions. When evaluated after this period, the patients performed at significantly above 100 percent of their expected levels, according to the PICA norms. Similar positive results were recently reported in a randomized, placebo-controlled trial of d-amphetamine or placebo, plus therapy (Walker-Batson et al., 2001).

In a motor study conducted by the same research group, ten hemiplegic patients were randomized to receive either dextro-amphetamine or placebo in conjunction with physical therapy. The results suggested a significant difference between the two groups in motor function, both at the end of the ten-session experimental period and after one year. Of potential significance, the studies showing beneficial effects of dextro-amphetamine—that is, this study (Walker-Batson, Smith, Curtis, Unwin, & Greenlee, 1995), the aphasia study by the same group (Walker-Batson et al., 1991), and the other study of motor rehabilitation (Crisostomo et al., 1988)—share the common feature of evaluating the drug as an enhancement to behavioral or physical therapy, rather than as a monotherapeutic panacea.

Piracetam

Piracetam is a derivative of GABA, but instead of GABA agonist or antagonist activity, acts as a "nootropic agent" on the central nervous system, facilitating neural communication in systems that use acetylcholine or excitatory amines as neurotransmitters (Giurgea, Greindl, & Preat, 1983; Vernon & Sorkin, 1991). It is said that this agent improves learning and memory, but it is not clear which of its multitudinous biological effects (for example, neuroprotective, circulatory) are responsible for the purported cognitive benefit.

A large multicenter trial (De Deyn, Reuck, Deberdt, Vlietinck, & Orgogozo, 1997) compared outcomes of patients receiving this drug within twelve hours of acute stroke. The results showed no effect on the primary outcome measure of neurological status at four weeks. There was some question whether or not there was an effect in an early-treatment subgroup (that is, within seven hours), particularly on several of the secondary outcome measures, including recovery from aphasia (De Deyn, et al., 1997; Orgogozo, 1999). One of the secondary measures in this study was recovery from aphasia at twelve weeks, and there appeared to be significantly better recovery from aphasia in the piracetam-treated group than the control group, particularly for the early-treatment subgroup (Huber, 1999).

Additional studies of piracetam using the Aachen Aphasia Test (AAT) scores as outcome measures have suggested effects even in postacute and chronic aphasia. In one study involving 158 patients with recent stroke (six to nine weeks earlier), 67 of whom had aphasia on entry (30 randomized to piracetam, 37 to placebo), multivariate analysis of AAT scores at twelve weeks showed significant improvement in the piracetam group compared to the placebo group, which was no longer evident at twenty-four weeks (Enderby, Broeckx, Hospers, Schildermans, & Deberdt, 1994). In a later study (Huber, Willmes, Poeck, Van Vleymen, & Deberdt, 1997), sixty-six patients with chronic aphasia (four weeks to thrity-six months) were treated behaviorally (five individual and five group sessions per week, each one hour long) for six weeks, and in a double-blind random fashion, half were given piracetam and half placebo. The author of the study (Huber, 1999) showed that the improvement scores differed between the two groups in a single subtest of the AAT (written language). Unfortunately, the results overall were disappointing.

Depression

A crucial issue that must be addressed as part of aphasia rehabilitation is depression, since it can adversely affect language recovery. Following stroke, it has been demonstrated that patients with depression have more cognitive impairment than patients with comparable lesions but no depression (Downhill & Robinson, 1994). Furthermore, in stroke patients matched for severity and lesion localization, patients with depression had worse recovery than their nondepressed counterparts in functional status and cognitive performance (Morris, Raphael, & Robinson, 1992).

Of particular interest is the relationship between depression and site of lesion, since the majority of patients with aphasia have lesions in the left perisylvian region. In fact, the data suggest not only that depression is more common in patients with left hemisphere stroke than right, but that this difference in the incidence of depression seems to hold only in patients with radiographic evidence of typical hemispheric asymmetries (Starkstein et al., 1991). The implications of this for aphasia rehabilitation are clear, particularly in light of the pharmacotherapy data presented above, which do not indict any antidepressant medications as having adverse effects for aphasia recovery. Treatment of depression should be considered a fundamental part of any aphasia rehabilitation program.

The role of antidepressant drugs in aphasia rehabilitation, apart from their demonstrated role in the treatment of depression per se, is not yet clear. Certainly, the data cited above on the effects of depression on recovery, and the role of these drugs in alleviating depression, suggest that they would play a large role in any rehabilitation program. However, as pharmacological agents to be used to enhance recovery, the data are complicated, with the rehabilitative effects often different in animal models and human studies (see table 21.2). This is an area ripe for further work.

FUTURE BIOLOGICAL APPROACHES TO APHASIA TREATMENT

In addition to pharmacology of aphasia, it might be possible in the future to directly alter the aphasic brain to increase synaptic connectivity among existing brain regions or between exist-

Table 21.2

Antidepressant Drugs with Discordant Effects in Animal Models of Stroke
and Human Stroke Recovery

Agent	Class	Animal	Human
Fluoxetine	Selective serotonin reuptake inhibitor (SSRI)	0	+
Trazodone	"Atypical" antidepressant	–	+
Amitriptylline/nortriptylline/desimipramine	Tricyclic antidepressant	+ and 0	0
Methylphenidate	Sympathomimetic	+	+ and 0

+ = benefit; – = harm; 0 = no effect; combinations reflect multiple studies. Some reasons for this are discussed by Goldstein (2000a).

ing brain regions and new tissue that has been artificially implanted. There is increasing therapeutic interest in the direct repair of damaged brain tissue, through a combination of tissue or cell transplantation and administration of growth factors. Genetic manipulations have been proposed as a possible way to achieve both of these interventions. In this section, we will review some of the ongoing research in these areas, and speculate about their possible role in aphasia therapy.

Neurotrophins (Nerve Growth Factors)

Growth factors have been advocated for a variety of purposes in the treatment of stroke, particularly in the acute phase of ischemic brain injury (Zhang et al., 1999), but also as neuroprotective agents useful in the chronic phase of recovery from brain injury (Olson et al., 1994). Evidence on the normal brain suggests that brain-derived neurotrophic factor (BDNF) plays a role in neural plasticity, with local BDNF levels increasing in the context of visual (Castren, Zafra, Thoenen, & Lindholm, 1992) or sensory experience (Rocamora, Welker, Pascual, & Soriano, 1996). It is also likely that this trophin plays a fundamental role in the perinatal development of visual cortical structure (Harris, Ermentrout, & Small, 1997).

Gene Therapy

Gene transfer into the central nervous system might ultimately play a role in delivering such trophins or other agents into damaged brain areas, and thus to help stimulate recovery or increased synaptic connectivity. Vector systems under development for such gene transfer include viruses as well as precursor (stem) cells that give rise to neural or to glial (supportive) cells (Zlokovic & Apuzzo, 1997). At the present time, however, it is not functionally feasible to adequately deliver genetic material to the brain to treat stroke (Zlokovic & Apuzzo, 1997).

Transplantation

Neural stem cells are multipotential precursors to neurons and glia, and are typically found in the subventricular zone and in the dentate gyrus (Palmer, Markakis, Willhoite, Safar, & Gage, 1999). These cells will proliferate and differentiate into neurons and glial cells in vitro (Vescovi, Gritti, Galli, & Parati, 1999). When implanted into the adult animal brain, these cells migrate along the same routes taken by the original (endogenous) precursor cells, and seem to respond normally to the endogenous signals that direct their differentiation in a variety of ways (Fricker et al., 1999).

Attempts have been made to induce differentiation into neurons and glial cells, and further into specific types of such cells. By implanting precursor cells into the dentate gyrus, they can be induced to differentiate into neurons (Eriksson et al., 1998). This process can be influenced by both extrinsic factors, such as environmental manipulations, and by intrinsic factors, such as neurotrophins (Kempermann, Kuhn, & Gage, 1998). In vitro, such cells have been induced to differentiate even further; for example, into catecholaminergic neurons (Vescovi et al., 1999). Neurally differentiated stem cells have been shown to form electrically active and functionally connected neurons (Auerbach, Eiden, & McKay, 2000).

Specifically with regard to stroke and treatment of cortical lesions, fetal neocortical cells have been successfully transplanted into the site of cortical lesions (Johansson, 2000), and have even been shown to migrate selectively into areas of experimental cell death (Macklis, 1993; Snyder, Yoon, Flax, & Macklis, 1997). It is hoped the use of neural progenitor (stem) cells can reduce reliance on fetal cells (Vescovi et al., 1999). In vitro, the progenitor cells can be greatly expanded in the presence of certain neurotrophins (Fricker et al., 1999), and can thus become a source for implantation.

DRUGS TO AVOID IN APHASIA RECOVERY

One important consequence of this research into the pharmacology of aphasia is the realization that drugs are not only potential therapeutic adjuncts, but that they can also serve as inhibitors of successful recovery. If some pharmacological manipulation appears to play a role in accelerating or improving recovery, the opposite manipulation could delay or prevent recovery. With this in mind, several investigators have performed retrospective studies of medication use during aphasia rehabilitation and made some important findings.

The first study of the inadvertent pharmacological interference with aphasia recovery (Porch, Wyckes, & Feeney, 1985) was a retrospective review that was motivated by two significant observations. The first observation was that hypertension is an important risk factor for cerebrovascular disease, and that patients with stroke frequently require medications to reduce blood pressure. The second observation was that some of these agents, particularly catecholamine antagonists, might be expected to disturb stroke recovery. A retrospective review of the medications of thirty-two patients presenting for language evaluation following stroke (Porch et al., 1985) showed that the nineteen patients taking medicines performed more poorly on the Porch Index of Communicative Ability (PICA) (Porch, 1967) than the thirteen who were not taking medicines. Although this study was poorly controlled and the results cannot be easily accepted, it was important for recognizing the effect of drugs on rehabilitative outcome.

More recently, a single investigator has taken up this important area of research, and has performed a number of studies in both animals and man addressing the effects of common medications taken by people who have strokes (Goldstein, 1993, 1995, 1998, 2000a, 2000b). His work is generally well controlled and the results are important. This research program was initiated with the observation that over 80 percent of all patients were taking some medicine at the time of their stroke, and that 65 percent were taking multiple medications. Included in this list were such drugs as α-adrenergic blockers and benzodiazepines, which are known to impede stroke recovery in animal studies (as discussed earlier).

This research program has included both investigations in animal models and clinical studies of patients. By building on the observational and interventional studies in animals that were discussed previously, Goldstein and his colleagues have furthered basic knowledge about the role of catecholamine systems in experimental stroke, and have examined the incidental effects of catecholamine-affecting agents on human stroke recovery. An initial report noted that a number of drugs that impair recovery in experimental stroke (for example, drugs that affect catecholamine or GABA systems) are commonly given to stroke patients for coincident medical problems (Goldstein, 1993).

This led to a formal retrospective (chart review) study of patients taking these specific drugs at the time of their strokes (Goldstein, 1995). A total of ninety-six patient records were reviewed, and patients were grouped on whether or not they were taking one or more of the following drugs: clonidine, prazosin, any dopamine receptor antagonist (for example, neuroleptics), benzodiazepines, phenytoin, or phenobarbital. Statistical analysis revealed that whereas patient demographics and stroke severity were similar between groups, motor recovery time was significantly shorter in the group that was not taking one of these drugs.

This work has profound relevance to aphasia rehabilitation as it is currently practiced, independent of the explicit biological interventions discussed here. In order to maximize functional recovery, it is important not only to insure adequate behavioral treatment, but also to insure the appropriate neurobiological substrate for this treatment (or, more concretely, to insure that this substrate is not pharmacologically inhibited from responding to the therapy).

Table 21.3
Drugs with Potentially Deleterious Effects on Stroke Recovery

Drug (class of agent)	Common symptom or sign occurring during stroke rehabilitation	Relationship to neurotransmitter systems
Diazepam (benzodiazepine)	Anxiety	γ aminobutyric acid (GABA) agonist
Chlordiazepoxide (benzodiazepine)	Anxiety	γ aminobutyric acid (GABA) agonist
Clonidine	Hypertension	α_2 adrenergic agonist
Phenoxybenzamine	Hypertension (pheochromocytoma)	α_1 adrenergic antagonist
Prazosin	Hypertension	α_1 adrenergic antagonist
Haloperidol (butyrphenone)	Psychosis	D2 dopaminergic antagonist
Phenobarbital (barbiturate)	Seizures	γ aminobutyric acid (GABA) agonist
Phenytoin (hydantoin)	Seizures	Not transmitter-specific

It is thus advisable for patients in aphasia therapy to avoid drugs that might interfere with catecholamine (NE or dopamine) or GABA function, or are thought to delay recovery by empirical study. A summary of these potentially deleterious agents is shown in table 21.3.

CONCLUSIONS

Existing studies on biological approaches to the treatment of aphasia do not yet paint an unambiguous picture. Nonetheless, there are increasingly reliable data suggesting a potential beneficial effect of increased central nervous system catecholamines on human motor recovery and aphasia rehabilitation. In the realm of motor system recovery, both human and animal studies suggest that dextro-amphetamine can facilitate recovery when combined with practice. Weaker evidence also suggests that when coupled with practice in oral communication, increasing brain norepinephrine and/or dopamine might facilitate improvement in speech and language impairments after stroke. Larger multicenter studies of this question are currently in progress.

Although pharmacotherapy and other biological treatments cannot be used as a replacement for speech therapy, pharmacotherapy might play a role as adjunct, and other biological therapies, such as cell transplantation, might play a role in concert with carefully designed adaptive learning approaches. In the published cases where pharmacotherapy improved language functioning in people with aphasia, it was used adjunctively. It is very likely that pharmacotherapy can play a valuable role as an adjunct to behavioral rehabilitation to decrease performance variability, and to improve mean performance in patients with mild to moderate language dysfunction from cerebral infarctions. Furthermore, the future of combined biological and behavioral interventions appears bright, although there remain significant basic research problems to be solved before this will emerge from the laboratory.

ACKNOWLEDGMENTS

This research was supported by the National Institute of Deafness and other Communication Disorders, National Institutes of Health, under grant NIH DC R01-3378. Their support is gratefully acknowledged.

REFERENCES

Albert, M. L. (1988). Aphasia is now treatable. *Hospital Practice, 23,* 31–38.

Albert, M. L., Bachman, D. L., Morgan, A., & Helm-Estabrooks, N. (1988). Pharmacotherapy for Aphasia. *Neurology, 38,* 877–879.

Auerbach, J. M., Eiden, M. V., & McKay, R. D. (2000). Transplanted CNS stem cells form functional synapses in vivo. *European Journal of Neuroscience, 12*(5), 1696–1704.

Bergman, P. S., & Green, M. (1951). Aphasia: Effect of intravenous sodium amytal. *Neurology, 1,* 471–475.

Boyeson, M. G. (1996). Effects of fluoxetine and maprotiline on functional recovery in poststroke hemiplegic patients undergoing rehabilitation therapy [letter; comment]. *Stroke, 27*(11), 2145–2146.

Boyeson, M. G., & Feeney, D. M. (1984). The role of norepinephrine in recovery from brain unjury (abstract). *Annual Meeting of the Society for Neuroscience, 10,* 68.

Boyeson, M. G., & Harmon, R. L. (1993). Effects of trazodone and desipramine on motor recovery in brain-injured rats. *American Journal of Physical Medicine and Rehabilitation, 72*(5), 286–293.

Boyeson, M. G., Harmon, R. L., & Jones, J. L. (1994). Comparative effects of fluoxetine, amitriptyline and serotonin on functional motor recovery after sensorimotor cortex injury. *American Journal of Physical Medicine and Rehabilitation, 73*(2), 76–83.

Brown, R. M., Carlson, A., Ljungren, B. L., Seisjö, B. K., & Snider, S. R. (1974). Effect of ischemia on monoamine metabolism in the brain. *Acta Scandinavica Physiologica, 90,* 789–791.

Castren, E., Zafra, F., Thoenen, H., & Lindholm, D. (1992). Light regulates expression of brain-derived neurotrophic factor mRNA in rat visual cortex. *Proceedings of the National Academy of Sciences, USA, 89*(20), 9444–9448.

Clark, A. N. G., & Mankikar, G. D. (1979). D-amphetamine in elderly patients refractory to rehabilitation procedures. *Journal of the American Geriatrics Society, 27*(4), 174–177.

Cohen, H. P., Woltz, A. G., & Jacobson, R. L. (1975). Catecholamine content of cerebral tissue after occlusion or manipulation of middle cerebral artery in cats. *Journal of Neurosurgery, 43,* 32–36.

Crisostomo, E. A., Duncan, P. W., Propst, M., Dawson, D. V., & Davis, J. N. (1988). Evidence that amphetamine with physical therapy promotes recovery of motor function in stroke patients. *Annals of Neurology, 23,* 94–97.

Darley, F. L., Keith, R. L., & Sasanuma, S. (1977). The effect of alerting and tranquilizing drugs upon the performance of aphasic patients. *Clinical Aphasiology, 7,* 91–96.

De Deyn, P. P., Reuck, J. D., Deberdt, W., Vlietinck, R., & Orgogozo, J. M. (1997). Treatment of acute ischemic stroke with piracetam: Members of the Piracetam in Acute Stroke Study (PASS) Group. *Stroke, 28*(12), 2347–2352.

Downhill, J. R., Jr., & Robinson, R. G. (1994). Longitudinal assessment of depression and cognitive impairment following stroke. *Journal of Nervous and Mental Disease, 182*(8), 425–431.

Enderby, P., Broeckx, J., Hospers, W., Schildermans, F., & Deberdt, W. (1994). Effect of piracetam on recovery and rehabilitation after stroke: A double-blind, placebo-controlled study. *Clininical Neuropharmacology, 17*(4), 320–331.

Eriksson, P. S., Perfilieva, E., Bjork-Eriksson, T., Alborn, A. M., Nordborg, C., Peterson, D. A., & Gage, F. H. (1998). Neurogenesis in the adult human hippocampus [see comments]. *Nature Medicine, 4*(11), 1313–1317.

Feeney, D. M., Gonzalez, A., & Law, W. A. (1982). Amphetamine, haloperidol, and experience interact to affect rate of recovery after motor cortex injury. *Science, 217,* 855–857.

Feeney, D. M., & Hovda, D. A. (1983). Amphetamine and apomorphine restore tactile placing after motor cortex injury in the cat. *Psychopharmacology, 79,* 67–71.

Feeney, D. M., & Hovda, D. A. (1985). Reinstatement of binocular depth perception by amphetamine and visual experience after visual cortex ablation. *Brain Research, 342,* 352–356.

Feeney, D. M., Sutton, R. L., Boyeson, M. G., Hovda, D. A., & Dail, W. G. (1985). The locus coeruleus and cerebral metabolism: Recovery of function after cortical injury. *Physiological Psychology, 13*(3), 197–203.

Fisher, M., & Bogousslavsky, J. (1998). Further evolution toward effective therapy for acute ischemic stroke [see comments]. *JAMA, 279*(16), 1298–1303.

Frazer, A. (1997). Pharmacology of antidepressants. *Journal of Clinical Psychopharmacology, 17*(2), 2S–18S.

Fricker, R. A., Carpenter, M. K., Winkler, C., Greco, C., Gates, M. A., & Bjorklund, A. (1999). Site-specific migration and neuronal differentiation of human neural progenitor cells after transplantation in the adult rat brain. *Journal of Neuroscience, 19*(14), 5990–6005.

Friedman, R. (1988). Acquired alexia. In F. Boller & J. Grafman (Eds.), *Handbook of neuropsychology: Vol. 1.* Amsterdam: Elsevier Science Publishers.

Giurgea, C. E., Greindl, M. G., & Preat, S. (1983). Nootropic drugs and aging. *Acta Psychiatrica Belgium, 83*(4), 349–358.

Goldstein, L. B. (1993). Basic and clinical studies of pharmacologic effects on recovery from brain injury. *Journal of Neural Transplantation and Plasticity, 4*(3), 175–192.

Goldstein, L. B. (1995). Common drugs may influence motor recovery after stroke: The sygen in acute stroke study investigators. *Neurology, 45*(5), 865–871.

Goldstein, L. B. (1998). Potential effects of common drugs on stroke recovery. *Archives of Neurology, 55*(4), 454–456.

Goldstein, L. B. (1999). Pharmacological approach to functional reorganization: The role of norepinephrine. *Rev Neurol (Paris), 155*(9), 731–736.

Goldstein, L. B. (2000a). Effects of amphetamines and small related molecules on recovery after stroke in animals and man. *Neuropharmacology, 39*(5), 852–859.

Goldstein, L. B. (2000b). Should antihypertensive therapies be given to patients with acute ischemic stroke? *Drug Safety, 22*(1), 13–18.

Goldstein, L. B., & Bullman, S. (1997). Effects of dorsal noradrenergic bundle lesions on recovery after sensorimotor cortex injury. *Pharmacology, Biochemistry, & Behavior, 58*(4), 1151–1157.

Goldstein, L. B., Miller, G. D., Cress, N. M., Tyson, A. G., & Davis, J. N. (1988). Studies of an animal model for the recovery of function after stroke (abstract). *Annals of Neurology, 22,* 159-160.

Grade, C., Redford, B., Chrostowski, J., Toussaint, L., & Blackwell, B. (1998). Methylphenidate in early poststroke recovery: A double-blind, placebo- controlled study. *Archives of Physical Medicine & Rehabilitation, 79*(9), 1047-1050.

Gupta, S. R., & Mlcoch, A. G. (1992). Bromocriptine treatment of nonfluent aphasia. *Archives of Physical Medicine and Rehabilitation, 73,* 373-376.

Harris, A. E., Ermentrout, G. B., & Small, S. L. (1997). A Model of Ocular Dominance Column Development by Competition for Trophic Factor. *Proceedings of the National Academy of Science, USA, 94*(18), 9944-9949.

Hernandez, T. D., & Holling, L. C. (1994). Disruption of behavioral recovery by the anti-convulsant phenobarbital. *Brain Research, 635*(1/2), 300-306.

Hillis, A., Kane, A., Tuffiash, E., Ulatowski, J. A., Barker, P. B., Beauchamp, N., et al. (2001). Reperfusion of specific brain regions restores selective lexical functions. *Brain and Language, 79,* 495-510.

Hovda, D. A., & Feeney, D. M. (1984). Amphetamine with experience promotes recovery of locomotor function after unilateral frontal cortex injury in the cat. *Brain Research, 298,* 358-361.

Huber, W. (1999). The role of piracetam in the treatment of acute and chronic aphasia. *Pharmacopsychiatry, 32, suppl. 1.,* 38-43.

Huber, W., Willmes, K., Poeck, K., Van Vleymen, B., & Deberdt, W. (1997). Piracetam as an adjuvant to language therapy for aphasia: A randomized double-blind placebo-controlled pilot study. *Archives of Physical Medicine and Rehabilitation, 78*(3), 245-250.

Jenkins, W. M., & Merzenich, M. M. (1987). Reorganization of neocortical representations after brain injury: A neurophysiological model of the bases of recovery from stroke. *Progress in Brain Research, 71,* 241-266.

Johansson, B. B. (2000). Brain plasticity and stroke rehabilitation: The Willis lecture. *Stroke, 31*(1), 223-230.

Kempermann, G., Kuhn, H. G., & Gage, F. H. (1998). Experience-induced neurogenesis in the senescent dentate gyrus. *Joural of Neuroscience, 18*(9), 3206-3212.

Kendall, D. L., McNeil, M. R., & Small, S. L. (1998). Rule-based treatment for acquired phonological dyslexia. *Aphasiology, 12*(7/8), 587-600.

Lazarus, L. W., Winemiller, D. R., Lingam, V. R., Neyman, I., Hartman, C., Abassian, M., Kartan, U., Groves, L., & Fawcett, J. (1992). Efficacy and side effects of methylphenidate for poststroke depression. *Journal of Clinical Psychiatry, 53*(12), 447-449.

Lesser, R. P. (1991). Aphasia as the initial manifestation of epilepsy. *Mayo Clinic Proceedings, 66*(3), 325-326.

Linn, L. (1947). Sodium amytal in treatment of aphasia. *Archives of Neurology and Psychiatry, 58,* 357-358.

Macklis, J. D. (1993). Transplanted neocortical neurons migrate selectively into regions of neuronal degeneration produced by chromophore-targeted laser photolysis. *Journal of Neuroscience, 13*(9), 3848-3863.

MacLennan, D. L., Nicholas, L. E., Morley, G. K., & Brookshire, R. H. (1991). The effects of bromocriptine on speech and language runction in a man with transcortical motor aphasia. *Clinical Aphasiology, 21,* 145-155.

Merzenich, M. M., Nelson, R. J., Stryker, M. P., Cynader, M. S., Schoppmann, A., & Zook, J. M. (1984). Somatosensory cortical map changes following digit amputation in adult monkeys. *Journal of Comparative Anatomy, 224,* 591-605.

Meyer, J. S., Stoica, E., Pascu, I., Shimazu, K., & Hartman, A. (1973). Catecholamine concentrations in CSF and plasma of patients with cerebral infarction and haemorrhage. *Brain, 96,* 277-288.

Montanez, S., Kline, A. E., Gasser, T. A., & Hernandez, T. D. (2000). Phenobarbital administration directed against kindled seizures delays functional recovery following brain insult [in-process citation]. *Brain Research, 860*(1/2), 29-40.

Morris, P. L., Raphael, B., & Robinson, R. G. (1992). Clinical depression is associated with impaired recovery from stroke. *Medical Journal of Australia, 157*(4), 239-242.

Olson, L., Backman, L., Ebendal, T., Eriksdotter-Jonhagen, M., Hoffer, B., Humpel, C., Freedman, R., Giacobini, M., Meyerson, B., Nordberg, A., et al. (1994). Role of growth factors in degeneration and regeneration in the central nervous system: Clinical experiences with NGF in Parkinson's and Alzheimer's diseases. *Journal of Neurology, 242, Suppl. 1*(1), S12-15.

Orgogozo, J. M. (1999). Piracetam in the treatment of acute stroke. *Pharmacopsychiatry, 32, suppl. 1.,* 25-32.

Palmer, T. D., Markakis, E. A., Willhoite, A. R., Safar, F., & Gage, F. H. (1999). Fibroblast growth factor-2 activates a latent neurogenic program in neural stem cells from diverse regions of the adult CNS. *Journal of Neuroscience, 19*(19), 8487-8497.

Porch, B. E. (1967). *Porch index of communicative ability, vol. 1: Theory and development.* Palo Alto, CA: Consulting Psychologists Press.

Porch, B., Wyckes, J., & Feeney, D. M. (1985). Haloperidol, thiazides, and some antihypertensives slow recovery from aphasia (abstract). *Annual Meeting of the Society for Neuroscience, 11,* 52.

Robinson, R. G. (1979). Differential behavioral and biochemical effects of right and left hemisphere cerebral infarction in the rat. *Science, 205,* 707-710.

Robinson, R. G., Shoemaker, W. J., & Schlumpf, M. (1980). Time course of changes in catecholamines following right hemisphere cerebral infarction in the rat. *Brain Research, 181,* 202-208.

Robinson, R. G., Shoemaker, W. J., Schlumpf, M., Valk, T., & Bloom, F. E. (1975). Effect of experimental cerebral infarction in rat brain on catecholamines and behavior. *Nature, 255,* 332-334.

Rocamora, N., Welker, E., Pascual, M., & Soriano, E. (1996). Upregulation of BDNF mRNA expression in the barrel cortex of adult mice after sensory stimulation. *Journal of Neuroscience, 16*(14), 4411-4419.

Rosenbaum, D. H., Siegel, M., Barr, W. B., & Rowan, A. J. (1986). Epileptic aphasia. *Neurology, 36*(6), 822-825.

Sabe, L., Leiguarda, R., & Starkstein, S. E. (1992). An open-label trial of bromocriptine in nonfluent aphasia. *Neurology, 42,* 1637-1638.

Sarno, M. T., Sarno, J. E., & Diller, L. (1972). The effect of hyperbaric oxygen on communication function in adults with aphasia secondary to stroke. *Journal of Speech and Hearing Research, 15,* 42-48.

Schallert, T., Jones, T., Weaver, M., Shapiro, L., Crippens, D., & Fulton, R. (1992). Pharmacologic and anatomic considerations in recovery of function. *Physical Medicine and Rehabilitation, 6,* 375-393.

Small, S. L. (1994). Pharmacotherapy of aphasia: A critical review. *Stroke, 25*(6), 1282-1289.

Small, S. L. (2000). The future of aphasia treatment. *Brain and Language, 71*(1), 227–232.

Small, S. L., Flores, D., & Noll, D. C. (1998). Different neural circuits subserve reading before and after therapy for acquired dyslexia. *Brain and Language, 62*, 298–308.

Snyder, E. Y., Yoon, C., Flax, J. D., & Macklis, J. D. (1997). Multipotent neural precursors can differentiate toward replacement of neurons undergoing targeted apoptotic degeneration in adult mouse neocortex. *Proceedings of the National Academy of Sciences, USA, 94*(21), 11663–11668.

Starkstein, S. E., Bryer, J. B., Berthier, M. L., Cohen, B., Price, T. R., & Robinson, R. G. (1991). Depression after stroke: The importance of cerebral hemisphere asymmetries. *Journal of Neuropsychiatry and Clinical Neuroscience, 3*(3), 276–285.

The NINDS rt-PA Stroke Study Group (1995). Tissue plasminogen activator for acute ischemic stroke. *New England Journal of Medicine, 333*(24), 1581–1587.

Vernon, M. W., & Sorkin, E. M. (1991). Piracetam: An overview of its pharmacological properties and a review of its therapeutic use in senile cognitive disorders. *Drugs Aging, 1*(1), 17–35.

Vescovi, A. L., Gritti, A., Galli, R., & Parati, E. A. (1999). Isolation and intracerebral grafting of nontransformed multipotential embryonic human CNS stem cells. *J Neurotrauma, 16*(8), 689–693.

Walker-Batson, D. (2000). Use of pharmacotherapy in the treatment of aphasia. *Brain Lang, 71*(1), 252–254.

Walker-Batson, D., Curtis, S., Natarajan, R., Ford, J.,

Dronkers, N., Salmeron, E., Lai, J., & Unwin, H. (2001). A double-blind placebo-controlled study of the use of amphetamine in the treatment of aphasia. *Stroke, 32*, 2093–2098.

Walker-Batson, D., Devous, M. D., Curtis, S., Unwin, D. H., & Greenlee, R. G. (1991). Response to amphetamine to facilitate recovery from aphasia subsequent to stroke. *Clinical Aphasiology, 21*, 137–143.

Walker-Batson, D., Smith, P., Curtis, S., Unwin, H., & Greenlee, R. (1995). Amphetamine paired with physical therapy accelerates motor recovery after stroke: Further evidence. *Stroke, 26*(12), 2254–2259.

Wells, C. R., Labar, D. R., & Solomon, G. E. (1992). Aphasia as the sole manifestation of simple partial status epilepticus. *Epilepsia, 33*, 84–87.

West, R., & Stockel, S. (1965). The effect of meprobamate on recovery from aphasia. *Journal of Speech and Hearing Research, 8*, 57–62.

Zhang, W. R., Kitagawa, H., Hayashi, T., Sasaki, C., Sakai, K., Warita, H., Shiro, Y., Suenaga, H., Ohmae, H., Tsuji, S., Itoh, T., Nishimura, O., Nagasaki, H., & Abe, K. (1999). Topical application of neurotrophin-3 attenuates ischemic brain injury after transient middle cerebral artery occlusion in rats. *Brain Research, 842*(1), 211–214.

Zlokovic, B. V., & Apuzzo, M. L. (1997). Cellular and molecular neurosurgery: Pathways from concept to reality, part II: Vector systems and delivery methodologies for gene therapy of the central nervous system. *Neurosurgery, 40*(4), 805–812; discussion 812–813.

22

Assessment and Treatment of Pragmatic Aspects of Communication in Aphasia

Audrey L. Holland
Jacqueline J. Hinckley

INTRODUCTION

This chapter on pragmatic aspects of the assessment and treatment of aphasic adults will cover a number of topics that are important for understanding the goals and methods of aphasia management geared to everyday language use. The chapter will begin with a brief history of pragmatic concerns in relation to aphasia treatment. Next, it will provide a rationale for clinicians who focus treatment on pragmatic issues. The chapter will include both theoretical and practical perspectives, as well as a brief examination of what a pragmatic perspective might mean for current constraints on health care. Next, we will furnish examples of the broad range of activities related to both assessment and treatment that can find shelter under the pragmatic umbrella. Finally, we will look into our crystal ball, discussing what pragmatic approaches to treatment of aphasia might have to offer in the future, as various sources of information from other disciplines, and different paradigms, begin to influence treatment.

The vast area of pragmatics in relation to aphasia will not be covered here; rather, we will concentrate on some issues that appear to have the greatest relevance for aphasia treatment. For this chapter, we define *pragmatic intervention* in a narrow way as well; that is, we will be discussing intervention that emphasizes the language and communication used in everyday social situations. Thus, our review incorporates what is often referred to as "functional communication."

HISTORY OF PRAGMATIC CONCERNS IN THE TREATMENT OF APHASIA

Four themes intersect to create the background out of which pragmatic approaches to the treatment of aphasia arose. All of these themes began to influence aphasia treatment in the 1960s and early 1970s, and have their origins in reactions to behaviorist explanations of language. Social communication theory, ethnomethodology, and conversational analysis, and a developing emphasis on functional communication, converged with a philosophical focus on language, and these theoretical frameworks were applied to the practice of aphasia therapy. A parallel confluence of approaches in cognitive psychology, linguistics, and computer science resulted in cognitive neuropsychological approaches to aphasia therapy. Whereas cognitive neuropsychological models have a primary goal to explain the cognitive processes and operations within the organism that are responsible for language, pragmatic models explain the use of language by the individual within the social context to achieve actions and goals.

The pragmatic focus evolved in philosophical circles, and evaluated metaphysical disputes based on their consequences in real life (McDermott, 1977). In pragmatic philosophy, an important characteristic of human beings is their role as actors (Austin, 1962; Searle, 1969; Grice, 1975). American pragmatist philosophers concentrated on descriptions of the world and truth as it was immediately perceived, rather than discussing what it ought to be (Murphy, 1990). Interestingly, pragmatists were considered by philosophers from other traditions to be provincial or trite in their approach, primarily because they accepted real actions and their consequences as "truth." (A similar fate sometimes still befalls aphasia clinicians with a pragmatic outlook.)

Pragmatists who were interested in language emphasized that actions are accomplished with words that go beyond the grammar of the sentence (Austin, 1962). Austin noted that listeners usually immediately perceive the function of a communicative statement, even though that function may not be apparent through analysis of its words and grammar. These communicative statements were called "speech acts" by Searle (1969), who categorized and described them as: (1) what is actually said (the "locutionary" act; for example, "Put your mother on the phone"); (2) the function of the statement (the "illocutionary" act; for example, a request to get Mom to come to the telephone); and (3) the effect that is produced (the "perlocutionary " act; for example, the son gets Mom). Searle's linguistic characterizations and analysis were motivated by his interest in the philosophical problems of meaning and truth. True to these philosophical roots, pragmatic approaches to language assessment and treatment retain the themes of action and the importance of immediate circumstances.

Simultaneous with this impetus, social communication theory, exemplified by the work of Goffman (1959, 1974) and Hymes (1972, 1974), was also beginning to stress the importance of understanding language beyond the confines of its formal structure. That is, language, in addition to nonverbal behaviors such as gesture, proxemics, prosody, and so forth, was being studied by social scientists as communication, the most pervasive form of human interaction.

The next theme in these early pragmatic influences included contributions from ethnomethodology to the study of conversation itself, probably the most basic use of language. Specifically, conversational analysis, conducted by researchers such as Sachs, Schegloff, and their colleagues (1973, 1974) initiated study of the organization and patterns of conversation. The three strong complementary influences of philosophy, social communication theory, and ethnomethodology form the theoretical basis of a pragmatic perspective in clinical aphasiology.

Reestablishing an aphasic person's ability to communicate has probably been the implicit goal of language clinicians since they first began working with aphasic individuals around World War II. However, it was not until 1968, when Sarno first specifically articulated the need for clinicians to become concerned directly with "functional communication," that the history of the role of pragmatics in language rehabilitation began. With the development of a rating scale, the Functional Communication Profile (FCP; Sarno, 1969), the fourth theme arose, from the practices of functional restoration that defined physiatry, as well as occupational and physical therapy. With these influences, aphasia treatment began its move from didactic and often abstract language training based on then-current models of learning, to fledgling issues in everyday language use.

Theoretical origins and clinical implications were finally merged after the publication of Bates's influential *Language in Context* (1976). As a result of this work, students of language acquisition and child development were reintroduced to some long-dormant linguistic concepts relating to central questions of how language is used by its speakers, and to what purposes.

Clinical work with language-disordered children was almost immediately affected, and across the clinical discipline of speech language pathology, pragmatic issues such as the importance of context began to be addressed.

A RATIONALE FOR PRAGMATIC APPROACHES TO TREATMENT

Theoretical Orientation

Pragmatic approaches to aphasia treatment differ in many ways from the other clinical approaches described in this book. First, the focus of treatment is on the personal accomplishment of actions for which we typically use language, rather than on the internal workings of the system. Patient, caregiver, and clinician perspectives on pragmatic treatments are also subtly altered toward social experiences.

The difference in focus between pragmatic treatment and more language-driven treatments for aphasia can be illustrated by a model of the effects of a child's first language on developing literacy in a second language. Cummins (1983) distinguished what he called "basic interactive communication skills (BICS)" from "cognitive, academic, language proficiency (CALP)." He noted that BICS were heavily contextual and were crucial for appropriate socialization, and that CALP was not nearly as context-defined, but crucial for success in intellectual pursuits, such as succeeding in school. Both traditional and cognitive neuropsychological approaches focus on CALP, while pragmatic approaches focus on BICS. According to Cummins (1983), BICS are the bedrock upon which CALP is built.

Indeed, aphasic individuals frequently have relatively preserved pragmatic abilities, in particular those that can be nonverbally managed, such as turn-taking and sensitivity to use and comprehension of nonverbal cues (Prutting & Kirchner, 1983; Schienberg & Holland, 1980; Katz, LaPointe, & Markel, 1978). Verbal pragmatic forms suggesting pragmatic strengths include comprehension of indirect requests (Wilcox, Davis, & Leonard, 1978) and high sensitivity to linguistic context (Kimbarow & Brookshire, 1983; Clark & Haviland, 1977). It is commonplace to observe that aphasic individuals perform maximally in situations in which they know the rules, and when they are free to communicate with flexibility. In fact, recent work by Kagan (1998) has shown that aphasic patients actually communicate more effectively when others are trained to provide specific supports for aphasic adults' communication. This is consistent with the idea that social interactive abilities are fundamental to communication, and when social support is provided, communication improves.

A cornerstone of the rationale for pragmatic aphasia treatment is that when clinicians focus heavily on pragmatics, they are simultaneously likely to focus on the relative strengths of their aphasic patients, rather than their deficits. The notion of putting good pragmatic skills at the service of impaired lexicon, grammar, and phonology paves the way for a broad array of clinical approaches. These include developing acceptable strategies for circumventing language difficulties, enlisting nonverbal communication as a support for failing language, and guiding others to provide scaffolding and support for maximizing aphasic success.

Patient and Family Perspectives

Pragmatic work with aphasic adults typically features everyday language use, making it appealing to patients, caregivers, and third-party payors as well. The perspective of patients and their caregivers has become more important as health care systems compete for enrollees, and patients are recognized as consumers of a health care product. People with aphasia, as well as their caregivers, need and value the reestablishment of basic communication skills to accomplish daily activities, to develop and maintain social relationships, to work, and to play.

Pragmatic approaches serve the consumer's perspective well, in that the focus is on communication activities such as conversation and typical personal activities that should match the patient's ultimate hopes and expectancies. Pragmatic approaches foreground the interpersonal strategies that patients and their friends and family members need to communicate effectively. While emphasizing what patients can do with language, clinicians must also inquire about the activities that their clients most hope to be able to do—and then use these as goals.

Reimbursement Perspectives

Another rationale for pragmatic approaches is the pattern of reimbursement by third-party payors, who often use arbitrarily determined guidelines to judge appropriate treatment methods. Third-party payors should be most interested in effecting long-term changes in productivity and independence, so that patients require fewer general health care and disability resources over the long term. Lack of productive and enjoyable activities can lead to depression and the occurrence of other related health changes (Kim, Warren, Madill, & Hadley, 1999; Koenig & Kuchibhatla, 1999). Therefore it is in payors' best interests to facilitate important, functional outcomes to decrease the total costs of health care and disability for persons with aphasia after stroke and brain injury. Pragmatic approaches are certainly not the only means to achieve ultimate functional outcomes; however, by targeting the personally relevant use of language throughout the assessment and intervention process, the chances of a good functional outcome may be increased (Wertz, 1999). The most efficient techniques for leading us to desired outcomes is an issue that continues to require investigation.

Rehabilitation Perspective

Recently (1999), the World Health Organization released its Beta-2 version of the International Classification of Impairments, Disabilities, and Handicaps, the ICIDH-2. Table 22.1 summa-

Table 22.1
International Classification of Impairments, Disabilities, and Handicaps
with Special Reference to Aphasia

Comparison of 1980 and 1999 versions.

1980	1999
Impairment	Impairment
Any loss or abnormality of psychological, physiological, or anatomical structure or function.	Definition unchanged.
For example, the aphasia itself, as measured by score on an aphasia test such as the BDAE or WAB.	
Disability	Activity limitations
A restriction or lack of ability to perform an activity within the range of normal ability. Results from the impairment (in this case aphasia). Its functional consequences.	Extent to which one's activities have been curtailed by the impairment.
For example, as a result of aphasia, the person cannot make himself understood, or has stopped using the telephone.	Example as with disability.
Handicap	Participation restrictions
A disadvantage that results from the disability and impairment that prevents an individual from fulfilling an age-appropriate societal role.	Extent to which one's ability to participate in society has been curtailed.
For example, because the person cannot now talk as before, he or she has had to stop practicing law.	Example as with handicap.

rizes both the original and revised versions of this classification scheme. The greatly revised and more clearly stated new model has changed its anchor terms, and developed explicit rating procedures that promise to have worldwide impact on rehabilitation. Meant not only to encompass illness and disablement, the ICIDH-2 now also incorporates health and wellness issues. The new terminology describes positive attributes, body structure and function, personal activities, and participation in society and then contrasts them with their negative terms. The now-familiar term *impairment* has been retained from the earlier ICIDH model, but *disability* has been replaced by "activity limitations" and *handicap* by "participation restrictions." New and clearer methods for assessing these limitations and restrictions are now included, with the intent of looking beyond impairments to their effects on the activities of everyday life and the toll of such limitations on the ability to participate in society. Largely in line with this conceptualization, Worrall (1999a) has begun to use the ICIDH-2 model as a meta-theory for pragmatic assessment and treatment for aphasia.

PRAGMATIC APPROACHES TO ASSESSMENT

The unique perspective of pragmatic approaches to aphasia treatment necessitates the use of some unique assessment procedures. We recognize that there is no substitute for tests that inventory the nature and extent of aphasic impairment. However, a pragmatic perspective suggests that instruments such as the *Boston Diagnostic Assessment Examination* (BDAE; revised edition, 2000) need to be supplemented with other assessment procedures. We acknowledge that in this period of shrinking health care dollars, extensive assessment of any type is likely to be precluded, except for research purposes. Nonetheless, we would be remiss if we failed to mention the powerful tools of observation, discourse analysis, and conversational analysis, before we describe more streamlined functional assessment measures.

Direct Observation

Authentic human communication requires that individuals interact within social contexts, making careful observation a critical part of the assessment process. There are three categories of contextual influences on communication that must be kept in mind. These are the linguistic context, the paralinguistic context, and the extralinguistic context. The linguistic context includes features of discourse, such as cohesion, topic, gist, and theme. Prosody, intonation, and emotional processing contribute to the paralinguistic context. The setting in which the communication takes place and the characteristics of the communication partner are components of the extralinguistic context that will also shape communication. Ideally, these contextual effects should be described and systematically varied if one wishes to obtain representative communication samples.

Possibly the most important clinical observations concern the natural transactions and interactions that occur with aphasic patients and others in typical daily environments. A one-hour-observation is often sufficient for a representative sample (Holland, 1982). Provided that observers tightly define the variables of interest, Boles and Bombard (1998) demonstrated that a ten-minute observational sample might be sufficient.

Another form of structured observation employs ethnographic methods, derived from sociological and anthropological models. Parr (1992, 1995) has documented the usefulness of such an approach for assessing the reading and writing abilities of aphasic adults. Davidson (1998) has used extensive participant observation to document the recurrent topics of talk in normally aging and aphasic adults. Observations such as these should help to identify communication strengths as well as problems, and also may help to set appropriate therapy goals in context-sensitive and patient-oriented ways that other types of assessment cannot.

Discourse Analysis

Discourse analysis is an objective alternative for measuring communicative performance in relation to various aspects of context. Multiple samples should be obtained that will vary elements of the linguistic, paralinguistic, and extralinguistic context. Analysis procedures can measure microstructural elements of the discourse such as intersentential cohesion, macrostructural elements such as topic or theme, and superstructural elements such as story grammar occurring within the verbal output (Cherney, Shadden, & Coelho, 1998).

Picture description activities, such as use of the well-known Cookie Theft drawing from the BDAE, provide examples of expository discourse. In the case of picture description, the activity is a monologue, atypical of daily communication activities. However, this type of sample is quick and easy to collect and analyze, according to a number of possible schemes, such as those proposed by Brookshire and Nicholas (1994) and Nicholas and Brookshire (1995). Both microstructural and macrostructural analyses can be carried out on expository discourse samples, but such a sample does not provide an opportunity for examining other pragmatic behaviors.

Narrative discourse presents a more functional context, in which aphasic individuals can be asked to recount important life events, tell bedtime stories to their grandchildren, or to describe movie plots to friends. Procedural discourse is also a valuable assessment context from a functional perspective. Clinicians can gather procedural discourse samples such as "tell me how to make toast and jam," or more complicated topics such as how to play a familiar sport or game.

There are a few structured discourse analysis procedures and profiles that have been used with aphasic adults. The Profile of Communicative Appropriateness (Penn, 1988) results in a rating of appropriate use of various pragmatic abilities within conversational, narrative, and procedural discourse samples. Prutting and Kirchner's (1983) Pragmatic Protocol was developed to score fifteen minutes of conversational discourse between the patient and a caregiver on the appropriateness or presence of verbal and nonverbal pragmatic abilities. Similarly, the Discourse Abilities Profile (Terrell & Ripich, 1989) is based on narrative, procedural, and conversational samples. The Assessment Profile of Pragmatic Linguistic Skills (Gerber & Gurland, 1989) provides a format for analyzing successful interactions, breakdowns, and repairs. Strategies for improving the ability to recognize and repair communication breakdowns are often fruitful avenues for intervention for both aphasic adults and their partners.

Conversational Analysis

Conversation differs from these preceding genres in that it is dyadic in nature, with two or more partners interacting to develop or to coconstruct meaning (Jacoby & Ochs, 1995; Goodwin, 1995). In conversation with an aphasic partner, the nonaphasic partner often disproportionately carries the burden of communication. Nevertheless, neither aphasic nor nonaphasic speakers are singly responsible for the development of a conversation's meaning. Conversation is a joint process, of intricate sequencing, turn-taking, repairing miscommunications, and so on, most often with the two processes of transaction and interaction occurring simultaneously. Information is exchanged as the transactional feature of conversation, but the social connection—that is, the interaction—between conversational partners is also a crucial feature (Brown & Yule, 1983).

Possibly the most revealing tool for the assessment of pragmatic skills is conversational analysis. *Conversation* as used here is not necessarily limited to individuals with mild to moderate aphasia. For example, in a compelling analysis of videotaped interactions between a severely aphasic man and his partners, Goodwin (1996) illustrated the cooperative process whereby this man demonstrates his ability to participate actively in making decisions. Goodwin pointed out that this man's participation occurs because his conversational partners treat him as a coparticipant. They search for, recognize, and trust that his limited words and gestures are all attempts to convey meaning. Finally, they verify with him the adequacy of their interpretations.

Conversational analysis is a tool that permits fine-grain analysis of naturally occurring stratagems and behaviors that contribute to aphasic patients' communicative strengths. Work in this area is exemplified by the contributions of Damico and his coworkers, Simmons-Mackie (1996a, 1996b) and Oelschlaeger (1998, 1999). Although conversational analysis is probably too labor-intensive to be a viable clinical assessment, it serves as a research base on which clinicians can rely in their attempts to understand the range and complexity of pragmatic skills shown by their aphasic patients.

Formal Measures and Scales to Rate Pragmatic Abilities

CADL-2

There are few formal measures of pragmatic skills designed for individuals with aphasia. To date, only one has undergone extensive field-testing and standardization in English. That is the test of Communicative Activities of Daily Living, recently revised (CADL-2; Holland, Frattali, & Fromm, 1999). CADL-2 is derived from Searle's concepts of speech acts, noted earlier. It samples a number of communication activities that occur in daily living, using pictures and prompts to create appropriate contexts for the activities tested. CADL-2, which is considerably shorter than its predecessor, uses a three-point scoring system for scoring observed communicative behaviors that include social communication, requesting information, or correcting misinformation. It also samples everyday reading and writing activities, using numbers, sequential relationships, humor, and comprehension of metaphor. For most CADL-2 items, all modes of communication (that is, gestures, speech, reading, and so on) are considered equivalent for conveying messages, and scoring is independent of the modality in which the response occurred. However, the information that is provided by noting the modality of responding can be important for planning subsequent clinical activities. CADL-2 provides a valid estimate of performance on a number of everyday communication activities. Although it is no substitute for observation, CADL-2 permits clinicians to sample a broad range of functional communication skills in approximately thirty-five minutes. The manual also provides guidelines (developed by Bartlett, 1999) using individual CADL-2 data in planning treatment.

Rating Scales and Interview Formats

There are a number of different scales and protocols that can provide useful information about activities and their limitations brought on by aphasia. Only a few examples will be discussed here. The first assessment measure relating to pragmatic issues was the Functional Communication Profile (FCP; Sarno, 1969), mentioned earlier. The FCP is a short rating scale of rehabilitation center related functional behaviors, and it is still in use. The Functional Assessment of Communication Skills for Adults (ASHA FACS; Frattali, Thompson, Holland, Ferketic, & Wohl, 1995) was designed explicitly for clinicians to rate functional communication behaviors of individuals with aphasia or traumatic brain injury. It uses a seven-point scale, anchored at "does" and "does not do," and samples the domains of social communication; basic needs; reading, writing, and number activities; and daily planning. Clinicians base their ratings on their own observations of their aphasic clients, but they can consult other health care workers and families to facilitate completing the rating scale. The ASHA FACS is easy to score, and, given a modicum of contact with patient and family, can be administered in fifteen minutes. The ASHA FACS was extensively pilot- and field-tested and has demonstrated good inter- and intrarater reliability. Many ASHA FACS items can serve as appropriate targets for clinical intervention. For example, getting help in an emergency, making needs or wants known, or requesting information of others (all ASHA FACS items) can serve as targets for treatment.

The Communicative Effectiveness Inventory (CETI; Lomas et al., 1989) is a sixteen-item inventory designed to measure partner perception of aphasic individuals' communication effectiveness. The scale items were selected by family members from a much larger set of items as being most important for communication. Family members rate each behavior as to whether it can be done as well as before the aphasia-producing event. Much like ASHA FACS, many of the behaviors that comprise the CETI can be considered excellent targets of direct intervention.

A recently published semistructured interview format is the Functional Communication Therapy Planner (FCTP; Worrall, 1999b). First, an extensive questionnaire is completed. Then the FTCP interview takes place as a collaboration between patient, family, and clinician. The FCTP assesses real-world communication needs and provides a method for setting realistic, but pertinent, goals for treatment.

All of these measures are geared to the assessment of activities and activity limitations, in ICIDH-2 terms. The natural alignment of functional and pragmatic approaches also extends to ICIDH-2's next level, that of restrictions in societal participation. Assessment at the level of participation should also be made. The ultimate goal of good therapy (pragmatically oriented or not) is related to improving the quality of an aphasic person's life in this broadest sense as well. Although there are literally dozens of measures that assess aspects of quality of life (QoL), remarkably few of them adequately tap the importance of communication in living as fully as possible. (See discussions of these issues by Hirsch & Holland, 1999; Cruice, Worrall, & Hickson, in press.) In addition, most experts agree that QoL is difficult to measure by proxy, and having a communication disorder complicates many aphasic peoples' ability to make subjective ratings. Among QoL measures that have potential for use in measuring quality of life following aphasia, Stern's (1999) visual analogue scale for measuring mood states in aphasia can be considered useful, and recent work by Hirsch (1999) suggests that simple one-question surveys can be quite effective. The American Speech-Language-Hearing Association is currently developing a measure using a series of visual analogue scales with which aphasic patients describe the quality of their communicative lives (Paul-Brown, Frattali, Holland, & Thompson, unpublished). Finally, it should be noted that measures of pragmatic communication probably require even more sensitivity to cultural differences than do measures that assess the extent of language impairment. The measures described here all have been scrutinized for their sensitivity. As new measures are developed, they must also be evaluated as to cultural appropriateness.

TREATMENT

We now turn our attention to pragmatically oriented treatment for aphasia. The processes underlying the clinical techniques discussed here do not differ in kind from those used in more traditional treatments. That is, principles of learning, coupled with counseling and topped off with carefully designed and specified practice, are at the heart of pragmatic treatment. What *is* different is the nature of the tasks that comprise the treatment. Clinical stimuli and tasks are geared to everyday events, or to interactions, or to communication strategies that can be used when language skills inevitably break down. Further, because of the emphasis on an individual's own pattern, style, and opportunity for communication, the process is far less clinician-driven, far more the result of collaboration between aphasic individuals, their families, and their clinicians than are most other approaches. In the ideal case, patients and families choose goals that are cast in everyday terms, with clinician guidance and counseling as to how realistic they are, what modifications of those goals might be acceptable, and so forth. Finally, not only aphasic individuals themselves, but partners and others who have significant opportunities to communicate with a given aphasic person are often the targets of pragmatic therapy themselves. In what follows, we provide a number of examples of pragmatic approaches to treatment. As with assessment, we have been selective, aiming simply to illustrate the breadth of approaches that constitute the pragmatic treatment spectrum. Throughout, by generous use of examples, we have tried to provide a sense of the kinds of activities that can be incorporated into pragmatic approaches.

Practicing Scenarios in Context

As suggested earlier, one way to achieve long-term functional outcomes is to target the precise context in which a patient wants to communicate effectively, and then work to improve the communication skills typically used in that context. These contexts or settings can be identified by discourse type and partner; for example, conversation with others. Milman and Holland (unpublished) worked with an aphasic woman who chose to address her frustration in being unable to maintain control of casual conversations with strangers. With the patient's extensive input, they developed an opening scenario that succinctly told the story of her aphasia, and immediately moved on to her asking questions of conversational partners. These questions were aimed at finding out what the partner's interests were. This strategy was successful in permitting the aphasic woman to maintain "the upper hand" in such conversations.

Another way to identify contexts for intervention is to choose highly specific situations based on personal relevance. For example, two adults with aphasia were successfully trained to identify and communicate different types of emergencies effectively via telephone to a virtual emergency operator accomplice, who did not know the exact emergency that was to be communicated (Hopper & Holland, 1998). A third patient was taught to use an augmentative communication device, programmed to state specific emergencies. Similarly, Davidson (1998) describes teaching an aphasic person with dysarthria to deal with that aspect of his communication problem that was the most bothersome to him—namely, being able to place bets via the phone to his bookie. Consulting with a travel agent about an upcoming trip, placing a phone call to set up a hair appointment, buying a gift for a spouse, or conducting bank business are all potential contexts for which specific communication skills and strategies can be developed and trained.

Key elements in the success of scenarios such as these are that (1) they have been developed in consultation with aphasic individuals concerning their perceived needs, and (2) the tasks are heavily practiced. Presumably because the tasks represent self-selected behaviors that have obvious personal payoff for them, aphasic patients involved in this form of intervention routinely do their homework and keep logs of their daily practice.

Training Strategies

Another pragmatic approach is to help patients and their partners to use strategies that facilitate communication between them. Conversational coaching (Holland, 1991, Hopper, Holland, & Rewega, in press) is a formalized approach to strategy teaching. Briefly, baseline observation begins the process. This observation explores what strategies both partners already use, which of them seem effective and which are not, as well as what currently unused strategies might also be fruitfully incorporated into their exchanges. Examples are boundless, but include such things as asking for clarification, requesting circumlocution, and verifying what is understood, on the part of the conversational partner, and devices like accompanying speech or substituting for it, with gestures, drawing, or partial word writing, requesting the partner to slow down, using circumlocution without being requested to do so. These strategies are written on cards, explained, and described to both partners. Training itself involves individually prepared verbal monologues (for example, "Audrey's encounter with the coyote in her yard") or short videotaped stories (for example, "Real People" TV newsreels). These monologues or videotapes are then shown only to the aphasic partner, whose job next is to retell the content to the naive partner. The clinician participates by coaching both aphasic and nonaphasic partners to use their strategies effectively for communicating the content of the monologue or TV event. In a recent study involving one dyad (Hopper, Holland, & Rewega, in press), significant training effects were found after only ten sessions. More important, treatment effects were maintained over a six-month interval, probably because these partners learned simple strategies that could be easily applied to everyday talk.

Another formal approach to training conversational skills targets both aphasic persons and caregivers (FICA; Alarcon & Rogers, 1999). Conversational discourse between them is analyzed, and then they both are interviewed about communication situations that are more or less comfortable and effective for them. The clinician then targets conversational strategies for both aphasic and nonaphasic partners. For example, the aphasic person might be trained to use other communication channels to communicate the message effectively, while the caregiver might be trained to provide more response time, or to use a specific hierarchy of cues, or to talk more slowly. Family conversation is used as a specific context for intervention.

Less formal approaches to strategy training rely on the creativity of the clinician. Marshall (1993) described a problem-solving approach used in a group setting with adults with mild aphasia. In this approach, patients brought up typical daily challenges, and worked together with other group members and the clinician to identify solutions. Communicating in an emergency and preparing for a doctor's appointment are two examples of situations that arose from the patients' discussion and were handled by the development of helpful strategies. This problem-solving approach can also be used in individual sessions.

Specific conversational skills and strategies can also be identified and trained. Making requests, revising, and clarifying have all been trained successfully among adults with aphasia (Newhoff & Apel, 1989; Doyle, Goldstein, Bourgeois, & Nakles, 1989). For example, if aphasic persons rarely use requests for revisions, they can be spurred to do so by occasional foreign, nonsense, or slurred words that a clinician might embed in her conversations with her aphasic client. She might need to use cues such as "Did you understand what I said?" or "Did that all make sense to you?" Of critical importance, clinicians must explain the goal of these activities so that they are well understood, and import techniques that specify the strategy being trained, such as writing the strategy out on a card.

Modeling is a powerful tool for training strategies, and probably contributes to the success of the PACE (Davis & Wilcox, 1985) technique. In this approach, the patient and therapist take turns giving and receiving clues and descriptions of pictures. This method of treatment invokes three communication principles: (1) new information is exchanged; (2) both participants act as senders and receivers of information; (3) any mode of communication, including gesturing, drawing, pointing to words in a communication notebook, and so on is acceptable. When the clinician uses the very strategies that her clients could benefit from using, the effectiveness of the training typically becomes apparent to clients, who in turn are more likely to adopt the strategies. The ecological value of PACE lies in the exchange of unknown, new information, a feature PACE shares with conversational coaching, described earlier.

Training Others

Pragmatic approaches prioritize the context in which communication occurs, making it necessary to acknowledge the importance of training others in the environment to communicate more effectively with aphasic patients. Because communication in context is a fundamental characteristic of pragmatically based intervention, some of the procedures already described have included the training of others. The following examples specifically emphasize training others in the environment, allowing the aphasic person's communication changes to be natural and incidental because they are not a direct target of the intervention.

One of these training approaches is supported conversation (Kagan, 1998). Volunteers and clinicians are trained to think of aphasia as masking the inherent competence of aphasic speakers. Specific conversational techniques are demonstrated to partners as revealing the competence that lies beneath the language difficulties imposed by aphasia. Next, formal training is provided to demonstrate how to use these techniques, along with practice in talking both to normal speakers who simulate aphasia, and to aphasic speakers themselves. Some of the techniques include ways to listen more effectively, how to encourage multimodal communicative attempts, and how to ask questions of aphasic people more appropriately. Many useful and "aphasia friendly" materials for supporting conversation are available as accompaniments to the techniques as well (Kagan, Winckel, & Shumway, 1996).

Lyon (1988, 1997) has developed a therapeutic approach in which a person with aphasia is matched, based on common interests and activities, with a volunteer. This volunteer, now a communication partner, is trained to facilitate the communication of the aphasic person. A key feature of Lyon's approach is that pleasurable activities serve as the milieu for training, and communication flows when it is the natural by-product of the activity. Examples might include going bowling, attending movies or concerts, or cooking together. Communication occurs as part of the context of something personally relevant, important, and enjoyable, and the training of the communication partner ensures success.

The family system can be viewed as a central context for aphasic people, and intervention can be derived from models of family systems (Lubinski, 1994; Newhoff & Apel, 1989). The unwelcome entrance of aphasia into a family alters its entire ecology; social roles and family responsibilities are very likely to be affected. Using interviewing techniques, and considering the family as a whole, can often lead the clinician to recommend environmental strategies that will aid patients and families to recover together.

Burns, Dong, and Oehring (1995) describe a general approach to family management following aphasia in which any of the techniques described here can comfortably fit. The essence of Burns and colleagues' approach is a subtle shift from perceiving patients and their families as the recipients of clinician-planned and -determined activities, to developing with them a partnership in clinical decision-making. Empowering the family is a key theme.

Group Approaches

The importance of involving other people in the treatment approaches described above foreshadows the following brief discussion of aphasia group treatment approaches within a pragmatic framework. Treatment occurring in group settings is proliferating (see, for example, books concerning group treatment by Elman [1999], Avent, [1997], and Marshall, [1999]). Because many activities of aphasia groups emphasize functional aspects of everyday communication, and because one of the most powerful of the therapeutic tools employed in group treatment is conversational interaction, there is an almost inevitable emphasis on pragmatic issues. The powerful effects of modeling and social support are nowhere else so accessible as in a group format. Although equal turn-taking and the clinician's use of targeted strategies as mentioned in the description of PACE might provide some minimal modeling, it can never be as meaningful as that of the experience of a group of true peers.

Evidence concerning the value of group intervention is still incomplete, but data are available, including the Wertz et al. (1981) VA cooperative study comparing individual, impairment-oriented treatment and pragmatically oriented group treatment, work by Aten, Caliguiri, and Holland (1982), and, most recently, the study by Elman and Bernstein-Ellis (1999). These studies indicate that group treatment is beneficial in improving communication abilities as measured by both functional and impairment-based assessments. Brumfitt and Sheeran (1997) have documented improvements in psychosocial areas such as feelings of self-worth, and attitude toward communication, as well as communication improvement in response to short-term group therapy (ten sessions). It is apparent that group therapy can readily facilitate improvements on many levels—impairment, disability, and participation in life.

THE FUTURE OF PRAGMATIC APPROACHES

Where are we going?

By selecting examples of the pragmatic approach in assessment and treatment, we have tried to showcase some of its strengths, including: (1) client-driven identification of problems and goals with a resulting focus on personally relevant contexts; (2) active exploitation of preserved communication skills as bridges to communication success; and (3) incorporation of the personal support system of the client as a realistic and necessary target of intervention. We have seen how these strengths play out in various assessment and treatment procedures.

An underlying theme of this discussion has been the growing relationship between pragmatic treatment for aphasia and a social model of rehabilitation. We have used words and phrases that imply this relationship, such as the ICIDH-2 terminology, but also *empowerment, collaboration in clinical decision-making, participant, transaction, interaction,* and many more. Jordan and Kaiser (1996) provide an excellent review of the relationship between aphasia and the disability movement. The current health care emphasis on the social consequences of illness and disability create a ripe atmosphere for the application of pragmatic approaches. As noted earlier, this is leading to a popularization of many pragmatic or functional approaches, including group therapy, and the measurement of additional outcomes of treatment, such as activity and participation limitations and wellness.

Due to its external focus, however, the pragmatic approach could potentially be criticized for a lack of description about the internal processes that contribute to the use of the client's communication system. This is not the primary goal of the pragmatic approach, in contrast to approaches based on cognitive neuropsychological theory. Inasmuch as both approaches are applied to intervention, a reasonable explanation of the nature of the change mechanisms should be part of a complete discussion of the approach.

Embedded in a pragmatic intervention approach are elements of the social cognitive theories of learning, which began to appear at about the same time as the developing interest in pragmatics. For example, Bandura's (1977, 1978) theory describes an interactive, multidimensional relationship between cognitive factors, the environment, and behavior. According to Bandura, behavior change occurs as a result of environmental cues, mediated by an individual's beliefs and level of emotional arousal. The environment, including the social context, figures centrally in this theory of learning. The power of modeling by peers, verbal persuasion, mastery experiences, and stress reduction results in increases in task approach and persistence, which ultimately yields the desired performance (Berry & West, 1993). Self-esteem, self-efficacy, and personality are important variables in the therapeutic process that have only infrequently been formally addressed (Brumfitt, 1993), but are accounted for in this theoretical model.

The conceptual relationships of social cognitive theory map onto typical processes and procedures in pragmatically oriented intervention. Clinicians and caregivers participate equally in targeted social interaction, and thereby serve as models. Modeling is an obvious fundamental process in group treatment, a nurturing environment in which other group members demonstrate effective communication strategies as well as social support and encouragement. Specific situation training provides potential mastery experiences that will lead to permanent behavior change in the selected contexts. Clinicians often serve a coaching, counseling, or facilitator role, which relates to the important influence of verbal persuasion on persistence, self-efficacy, and task performance in the social cognitive model. Future treatment research from a pragmatic perspective might benefit from testing the relationships modeled in social cognitive theory.

We can look to other influences as well. These include what can be learned from second language acquisition, which increasingly stressed language practice in highly contextualized scenarios that represent probable real-world encounters. Further, understanding of what maximizes adults' ability to learn in general should also play a role in aphasia rehabilitation, an enterprise that, obviously, largely concerns adults. Both of these models of learning can be applied to elaborate the description of the change processes during pragmatic intervention. With such a foundation, clinical researchers will be in a position to compare the various types of outcomes obtained from different treatment procedures.

The current emphasis in pragmatics is to utilize our knowledge of pragmatic abilities and impairments to achieve the best functional outcomes possible. A pragmatic approach to aphasia relies on a real-world perspective. Clinicians must always ask, "How will this affect this person's daily life, and that of his or her family?" Pragmatic functions of language, such as being able to invite, deny, or request, are essential to daily social interactions. In the last thirty years, we have refined our ability to assess pragmatic abilities and measure the functional outcomes of our treatment efforts. We know that we can effect important, pragmatic changes among adults with aphasia through intervention. The future will bring more elaborated versions of the mechanisms of this change as well as more data on the efficiency of particular types of procedures for individuals with very different aphasic characteristics.

ACKNOWLEDGMENTS

This work was funded in part by National Multipurpose Research and Training Center Grant DC 01409 from the National Institute on Deafness and Other Communication Disorders (first author) and by a grant from the James F. McDonnell Foundation (second author). The work was completed while the first author was the Flora Stone Mather Visiting Professor, Case Western Reserve University, Cleveland, Ohio.

REFERENCES

Alarcon, N., & Rogers, M. (1999). Quality of communication between individuals with aphasia and conversational Partners. Paper presented at the Convention of the American Speech-Language-Hearing Association. San Francisco, CA.

Aten, J., Caliguiri, M., & Holland, A. (1982). The efficacy of functional communication therapy for chronic aphasic patients. *Journal of Speech and Hearing Disorders, 47,* 93–96.

Austin, J. L. (1962). *How to do things with words.* Cambridge, MA: Harvard University Press.

Avent, J. (1997). *Manual for cooperative group treatment of aphasia.* Boston: Butterworth-Heineman.

Bandura, A. (1977). Self-efficacy: Toward a unifying theory of behavioral change. *Psychological Review, 84,* 191–215.

Bandura, A. (1978). The self system in reciprocal determinism. *American Psychologist, 77,* 344–358.

Bartlett, C. (1999). How to use CADL-2 in treatment. Monograph accompanying CADL-2. Austin TX: Pro-Ed.

Bates, E. (1976). *Language in context.* New York: Academic Press.

Berry, J. M., & West, R. L. (1993). Cognitive self efficacy in relation to personal mastery and goal setting across the lifespan. *International Journal of Behavioral Development, 16,* 351–379.

Boles, L., & Bombard, T. (1998). Conversational discourse analysis: Appropriate and useful sample sizes. *Aphasiology, 12,* 547–560.

Brookshire, R., & Nicholas, L. (1994). Speech-sample size and test-retest stability of connected speech measures for adults with aphasia. *Journal of Speech and Hearing Research, 37,* 399–407.

Brown, G., & Yule, G. (1983). *Discourse analysis.* Cambridge: Cambridge University Press.

Brumfitt, S. (1993). Losing your sense of self: What aphasia can do. *Aphasiology, 7,* 569–574.

Brumfitt, S. M., & Sheeran, P. (1997). An evaluation of short-term group therapy for people with aphasia. *Disability and Rehabilitation, 19,* 221–230.

Burns, M., Dong, K., & Oehring, A.(1995). Family involvement in the treatment of aphasia. *Topics in Stroke Rehabilitation, 2,* 68–77.

Cherney, L. R., Shadden, B. B., & Coelho, C. A. (1998). *Analyzing discourse in communicatively impaired adults.* Gaithersburg, MD: Aspen.

Clark, H. H., & Haviland, S. E. (1977). Comprehension and the given-new contract. In R. O. Freedle (Ed.), *Discourse production and comprehension.* Norwood, NJ: Ablex.

Cruice, M., Worrall, L., & Hickson, L. (In press). Quality of life measurement in speech pathology and audiology. *Asian Journal of Communication Disorders.*

Cummins, J. (1983). Language proficiency and academic achievement. In J. W. Oller (Ed.), *Issues in language testing research.* Rowley, MA: Newbury House.

Davidson, B. (1998). *What do older Australians talk about?* Paper presented at the VIII International Conference on Aphasia Rehabilitation. Kwa Maritane, South Africa.

Davis, G. A., & Wilcox, M. J. (1985). *Adult aphasia rehabilitation: Applied pragmatics.* San Diego, CA: College-Hill Press.

Doyle, P. J., Goldstein, H., Bourgeois, M. S., & Nakles, K. O. (1989). Facilitating generalized requesting behavior in Broca's aphasia: An experimental analysis of a generalization training procedure. *Journal of Applied Behavior Analysis, 22,* 157–170.

Elman, R. J. (1999). *Group treatment for neurogenic communication disorders: The expert clinician's approach.* Woburn, MA: Butterworth-Heinemann.

Elman, R., & Bernstein-Ellis, E. (1999). The efficacy of group communication treatment in adults with chronic aphasia. *Journal of Speech, Language, and Hearing Research, 42,* 411–419.

Frattali, C., Thompson, C., Holland, A., Ferketic, M., & Wohl, C. (1995). *Functional assessment of communication skills for adults (ASHA FACS).* Rockville, MD: American Speech-Language-Hearing Association.

Gerber, S., & Gurland, G. (1989). Applied pragmatics in the assessment of aphasia. *Seminars in Speech and Language: Aphasia and Pragmatics, 10,* 263–281.

Goffman, E. (1959). *The presentation of self in everyday life.* New York: Anchor.

Goffman, E. (1974). *Frame analysis.* New York: Harpers.

Goodwin, C. (1995). Co-constructing meaning in conversations with an aphasic man. *Research and Social Interaction (Special issue on co-construction), 28,* 233–260.

Goodwin, C. (1996). *Co-construction of meaning in global aphasia.* Telerounds 17, University of Arizona.

Grice, H. P. (1975). Logic and conversation. In P. Cole & J. Morgan (Eds.), *Speech Acts: Syntax and Semantics, Vol. 3.* New York: Academic Press.

Hirsch, F., & Holland, A. (1999). Assessing quality of life after aphasia. In L. Worrall & C. Frattali (Eds.), *Functional communication in aphasia.* New York: Thieme.

Holland, A. (1982). Observing functional communication of aphasic adults. *Journal of Speech and Hearing Disorders, 47,* 50–56.

Holland, A. L. (1991). Pragmatic aspects of intervention in aphasia. *Journal of Neurolinguistics, 6,* 197–211.

Holland, A., Frattali, C., & Fromm, D. (1999) *Communicative activities of daily living (CADL-2).* Austin, TX: Pro-Ed.

Hopper, T., & Holland, A. (1998). Situation-specific treatment for aphasia. *Aphasiology, 12,* 933–944.

Hopper, T., Holland, A., & Rewego, M. (In press). Conversational coaching: Treatment outcomes and future directions. *Aphasiology.*

Hymes, D. (1972). On communicative competence. In J. Pride & J. Holmes (Eds.), *Sociolinguistics: Selected readings.* Baltimore: Penguin.

Hymes, D. (1974). *Foundations in sociolinguistics: An ethnographic approach.* Philadelphia: University of Pennsylvania Press.

Jacoby, S., & Ochs, E. (1995). Co-construction: An introduction. *Research on Language and Social Interaction, 28,* 171–183.

Jordan, L., & Kaiser, W. (1996). *Aphasia: A social approach.* London: Chapman and Hall.

Kagan, A. (1998). Supported conversation for adults with aphasia: Methods and resources for training conversation partners. *Aphasiology, 12,* 816–831.

Kagan, A., Winckel, J., & Shumway, E. (1996). *Pictographic communication resources manual.* Toronto: Aphasia Centre, North York.

Katz, R. C., LaPointe, L. L., & Markel, N. N. (1978). Coverbal behavior and aphasic speakers. In R. Brookshire (Ed.), *Clinical Aphasiology Conference proceedings.* Minneapolis, MN: BRK.

Kim, P., Warren, S., Madill, H., & Hadley, M. (1999). Quality of life of stroke survivors. *Quality of Life Research, 8,* 293–301.

Kimbarow, M., & Brookshire, R. (1983). The influence of communicative context on aphasic speakers' use of pronouns. In R. Brookshire (Ed.), *Clinical Aphasiology Conference proceedings.* Minneapolis, MN: BRK.

Koenig, H. G., & Kuchibhatla, M. (1999). Use of health services by medically ill depressed elderly patients after hospital discharge. *American Journal of Geriatric Psychiatry, 7,* 48–56.

Lomas, J., Pickard, L., Bester, S., Elbard, H., Finlayson, A., & Zoghabib, C. (1989). The communicative effectiveness index: Development and psychometric evaluation of a functional communication measure for adult aphasia. *Journal of Speech and Hearing Disorders, 54,* 113–124.

Lubinski, R. (1994). Environmental systems approach to adult aphasia. In R. Chapey (Ed.), *Language intervention strategies in adult aphasia.* Baltimore: Williams and Wilkins.

Lyon, J. G. (1988). Communicative partners: Their value in reestablishing communciation with aphasic adults. In T. Prescott (Ed.), *Clinical aphasiology, Vol. 18.* Austin, TX: Pro-Ed.

Lyon, J. G., Cariski, D., Keisler, L., Rosenbek, J., Levine, R., Kumpula, J., Ryff, C., Coyne, S., & Blanc, M. (1997). Communication partners: Enhancing participation in life and communication for adults with aphasia in natural settings. *Aphasiology, 11,* 693–708.

Marshall, R. C. (1993). Problem-focused group treatment for clients with mild aphasia. *American Journal of Speech-Language Pathology, 2,* 31–37.

Marshall, R. C. (1999). *An introduction to group aphasia treatment.* Boston: Butterworth-Heineman.

McDermott, J. J. (1977). *The writings of William James.* Chicago: University of Chicago Press.

Murphy, J. P. (1990). *Pragmatism: From Peirce to Davidson.* San Francisco: Westview Press.

Newhoff, M., & Apel, K. (1989). Environmental communication programming with aphasic persons. *Seminars in Speech and Language: Aphasia and Pragmatics, 10,* 315–328.

Nicholas, L., & Brookshire, R. (1995). The presence, completeness, and accuracy of main concepts in the connected speech of non-brain-damaged adults and adults with aphasia. *Journal of Speech and Hearing Research, 38,* 145–156.

Oelschlaeger, M., & Damico, J. (1998). Spontaneous verbal repetition: A social strategy in aphasic conversation. *Aphasiology, 12,* 971–978.

Oelschlaeger, M., & Damico, J. (1999). Participation of a conversation partner in the word searches of a person with aphasia. *American Journal of Speech-Language Pathology, 8,* 62–71.

Parr, S. (1992). Everyday reading and writing practices of normal adults: Implications for aphasia assessment. *Aphasiology, 6,* 273–283.

Parr, S. (1995). Everyday reading and writing in aphasia: Role change and the influence of pre-morbid literacy practice. *Aphasiology, 9,* 223–238.

Penn, C. (1988). The profiling of syntax and pragmatics in aphasia. *Clinical Linguistics and Phonetics, 2,* 179–208.

Prutting, C. A., & Kirchner, D. (1983). Applied pragmatics. In T. Gallagher & C. A. Prutting (Eds.), *Pragmatic assessment and intervention issues in language.* San Diego, CA: College-Hill Press.

Sachs, H., Schegloff, E., & Jefferson, G. (1974). A simpler systematics for the organization of turn taking in conversation. *Language, 50,* 696–735.

Sarno, M. T. (1969). *Functional communication profile: A manual of directions,* (Rehabilitation Monograph 42). New York: NYU Medical Center.

Schegloff, E., & Sacks, H. (1973). Opening up closings. *Semiotica, 7,* 289–327.

Schienberg, S., & Holland, A. L. (1980). Conversational turn-taking in Wernicke's aphasia. In R. H. Brookshire (Ed.), *Clinical aphasiology conference proceedings.* Minneapolis, MN: BRK.

Searle, J. R. (1969). *Speech acts.* Cambridge: Cambridge University Press.

Simmons-Mackie, N., & Damico, J. (1996a). The contribution of discourse markers to communicative competence in aphasia. *American Journal of Speech-Language Pathology, 5,* 37–43.

Simmons-Mackie, N., & Damico J., (1996b). Accounting for handicaps in aphasia: Assessment from an authentic social perspective. *Disability and Rehabilitation, 18,* 540–549.

Stern, R. (1999). Analyzing mood states in aphasia. *Seminars in Speech and Language, 20*(1), 33–50.

Terrell, B., & Ripich, D. (1989). Discourse competence as a variable in intervention. *Seminars in Speech and Language: Aphasia and Pragmatics, 10,* 282–297.

Wertz, R. T, Collins, M., Weiss, D., Kurtzke., Friden, T., Brookshire, R., Pierce, J., Holtzapple, P., Hubbard, D., Porch, B., West, J., Davis, L., Matovich, V., Morley, G., & Resurreccion., E. (1981). Veterans Administration cooperative study on aphasia: A comparison of individual and group treatment. *Journal of Speech and Hearing Research, 24,* 580–594.

Wertz, R. T. (1999). One hundred years of aphasia treatment. Symposium presented at the Annual Convention of the American Speech-Language-Hearing Association. San Francisco, CA.

Wilcox, M., Davis, G., & Leonard, L. (1978). Aphasics' comprehension of contextually conveyed meaning. *Brain and Language, 6,* 362–377.

World Health Organization. (1999). *ICIDH-2: International classification of functioning and disability.* Beta-2 draft, full version. Geneva: World Health Organization.

Worrall, L. (1999a). Functional communication: Theory and practice. Seminar presented at the Department of Communication Sciences, University of British Columbia, Vancouver, Canada.

Worrall, L. (1999b). *Functional communication planner.* Oxon, England: Winslow.

The Nature and Implications of Right Hemisphere Language Disorders: Issues in Search of Answers

Connie A. Tompkins
Wiltrud Fassbinder
Margaret T. Lehman-Blake
Annette Baumgaertner

Historically the study of neurologically based adult language disorders has focused on aphasia, which in most individuals is a consequence of damage to the language-dominant left cerebral hemisphere. However, language impairments associated with right hemisphere damage (RHD) have received increasing attention of late. On the rehabilitation front, it has become clear that adults with left hemisphere damage and aphasia are not the only ones whose communication disorders can affect their daily function, social interaction, and quality of life. As a result, one important goal of the quest to understand RHD language disorders is to derive implications for diagnosis, prognosis, and clinical intervention. From a more theoretical perspective, language impairments in adults with RHD have been studied as a window on the nature of language representation and processing in the so-called minor hemisphere. The research on RHD converges with other investigations, including those of individuals with intact (Beeman & Chiarello, 1998) and surgically disconnected right hemispheres (Baynes & Eliassen, 1998; Zaidel, 1998) and of people who are recovering from aphasia (Cappa, 1998; Kinsbourne, 1998) to indicate that the right hemisphere potential for language processing is far from minor.

In line with this volume's emphasis on language disorders, this chapter focuses on the most definitive evidence about language functioning after RHD, which comes from investigations of right-handed adults whose neurologic pathology is confined to the right cerebral hemisphere. Such damage typically is a result of cerebrovascular accidents rather than etiologies with more diffuse cerebral consequences such as traumatic brain injury or Alzheimer's disease.

The material in this chapter is organized into four major parts. In the first section of this chapter, we outline some conceptual and methodological issues that influence the conduct and interpretation of RHD language research. Next, we provide an overview of accumulated evidence about RHD language disorders in lexical-semantic and discourse function, and discuss current attributions about the nature of these difficulties. We focus on these domains because of the wealth of evidence for their potential disruption after RHD, in contrast to phonological and syntactic functions that RHD leaves essentially unimpaired. Language processing in the intact right hemisphere also is addressed briefly in this section, as one framework from which to interpret RHD disorders. While prosodic (for example, Baum & Pell, 1999) and emotional (for example, Van Lancker & Pachana, 1998) processing deficits also are hallmarks of RHD, and contribute crucially to social communicative exchange, space limitations preclude discussing them here. We then consider how evidence and perspectives on RHD language disorders and normal right hemisphere language function inform one another. Finally, we address briefly some issues related to clinical management of RHD language disorders. Throughout the chapter we identify unresolved questions and directions for further investigation.

DESIGNING AND READING THE RESEARCH: CONCEPTUAL AND METHODOLOGICAL CONSIDERATIONS

Those who plan and interpret studies of RHD language and communication must grapple with a number of challenges. Chief among these are a dearth of explicit, testable models of the cognitive and linguistic domains or systems that support social exchange, and philosophical issues concerning the validity of predicting from normal to disordered functions (or vice versa). These issues will be discussed in the third section of this chapter.

Theory building is further complicated by the fact that we do not know whether there is more than one variant of RHD language disorders, as there is for the aphasias (Joanette & Goulet, 1994), or even whether there are predictable sets of symptoms that routinely cooccur in those who have the disorders. While some work hints that different patterns of strength and weakness correspond to pre- or post-Rolandic lesion location (for example, Joanette, Lecours, Lepage, & Lamoureux, 1983), the logical prerequisite to this observation, that discrete performances covary with lesion site, does not always hold (for example, Lojek-Osiejuk, 1996; Tompkins, Baumgaertner, Lehman, & Fassbinder, 2000; Tompkins, Lehman, & Baumgaertner, 1999). Another major problem is that there is little consensus on how to define or even what to call RHD language deficits, either in totality or as individual components of an aggregate "syndrome." Conceptual and terminological imprecision, and apparent overlap, are common in referring to targets of inquiry like nonliteral language processing, inferencing, integration, and reasoning from a theory of mind (see discussions in Stemmer & Joanette, 1998; Tompkins, 1995). This definitional difficulty both derives from and contributes to most of the other challenges detailed in this chapter (for further discussion see, for example, Joanette & Ansaldo, 1999; Myers, 1999; Stemmer & Joanette, 1998).

Other notable considerations in the investigation of RHD language and communication include those related to the following.

Accounting for Inter- and Intrasubject Variability

Adults with RHD form a heterogeneous group, varying widely in lesion characteristics, presence and severity of impairments, and reactions to and eventual outcomes of their condition (Tompkins, Lehman, Wyatt, & Schulz, 1998). Adding to these sources of between-subject performance differences are individual attributes that are unrelated to the neurological event, such as age-related sensory changes, educational attainment, and premorbid knowledge, skills, and cognitive capacities. Characteristics like handedness (Pujol, Deus, Losilla, & Capdevila, 1999; Shapleske, Rossell, Woodruff, & David, 1999), sex (Gur et al., 1999; Shapleske et al., 1999), or age (Cherry & Hellige, 1999) also may interact with hemispheric contributions to language functioning. Intrasubject performance variability is evident in adults with RHD as well. Some of this undoubtedly reflects physiologic and psychologic adaptation and compensation to the consequences of the neurologic insult, though little is known yet about this kind of change over time. Some also can be task-induced, for example, by purposeful manipulation of attentional processing requirements (see, for example, Tompkins & Lehman, 1998). Such pervasive variability poses a variety of hurdles for RHD language research. Among them, it is a formidable challenge for any study to account for a full range of potential components of and contributors to communication performance. It is also essentially impossible to match subsets of RHD participants for between-subjects designs. And, particularly in combination with frequently poor subject descriptions, it can be extremely difficult to generalize results.

Selecting Participant Samples

In the RHD language disorders literature, sample sizes generally are quite small and sampling biases are common, such as selecting research participants solely from those who receive rehabilitation for their deficits. A somewhat less obvious sampling issue concerns the question of which RHD subjects to study. Some suggest that to understand RHD language disorders, one should investigate only individuals who have them (Myers, 1999). While this position currently is not possible to implement, as there is no independent, theoretically and psychometrically sound measure for documenting the presence, nature, or severity of RHD language disorders, one might approximate this goal by sampling from patients with lesions that are more likely to be associated with language impairments (middle cerebral artery infarcts). However, a subject sample that is not selected for language disorders confers advantages as well, for discovering subgroups of the RHD population, developing prognostic profiles, and/or inferring potential mechanisms of deficit by assessing factors associated with spared and impaired performances. Of course, an unselected sample will include an unknown mix of individuals with and without language disorders, so results that reflect only the group mean performance may be entirely uninformative.

Designating Disordered Performances

Beyond the general difficulty of determining who has a RHD language disorder, clinicians and researchers face a more specific challenge. For many variables of interest, especially in the realm of pragmatics and interpersonal communication, normative information is not available, and individual differences and sociocultural variations are not well understood. Relatedly, there has been little in the way of cross-linguistic or cross-cultural work on RHD language disorders. Control groups are a start, but given their typically small sizes in the RHD literature, the variety of attributes that may influence performance, and the potentially vast range of "normal," it often remains quite difficult to decide what constitutes a "deficit."

Establishing Control Groups to Rule Out Nonspecific Effects on Performance

When the research goal is to determine whether RHD specifically is responsible for performances of interest, it becomes especially problematic to select an appropriate control group. Adults with left hemisphere damage (LHD) and aphasia often cannot be used, because their basic linguistic processing difficulties may invalidate their performance with complex stimuli and task instructions typical of RHD language studies. When participants with LHD are included, issues arise of equating the two groups for severity (Duffy & Myers, 1991). Adults with left brain lesions who are sufficiently accurate on the experimental tasks may be less neurologically involved than the RHD group, particularly if the RHD sample is relatively severe (for example, includes only people who receive cognitive-language rehabilitation). It is important in such circumstances that conditions be included to probe for compelling double dissociations in performance, or for paradoxical functional facilitation effects (Kapur, 1996). It also helps to evaluate potentially different reasons for quantitatively similar performances of participants with right and left hemisphere lesions (Kasher, Batori, Soroker, Graves, & Zaidel, 1999; Tompkins, 1990). However, as noted by Joanette and Goulet (1994), such a rarefied sample of adults with LHD raises questions about its representativeness. It is less difficult to constitute a control group when the research question asks only whether certain kinds of deficits can occur in adults with RHD. In such cases, nonspecific performance differences can be reduced by using control groups of patients with peripheral nervous system involvement (Lojek-Osiejuk, 1996), or of neurologically normal adults who have experienced the "patient" role (for example, people with orthopedic injuries; Blonder, Burns, Bowers, Moore, & Heilman, 1993).

Inferring Lesion-Behavior Correspondences

Few studies of adults with RHD have attempted to discover relationships between cognitive and communicative performances and right hemisphere lesion sites, despite the potential diagnostic, prognostic, and explanatory value of doing so. This may be partly due to the fact that most participants in RHD language studies have middle cerebral artery occlusions with lesions that do not respect anatomic boundaries, even for comparisons as gross as "anterior" versus "posterior." But as noted above, reports of performance differences are inconsistent even when such anatomic distinctions are made. The typically small sample sizes and inherent heterogeneity in RHD language studies clearly complicate efforts to align lesion and language characteristics. An equally large obstacle at present may be the various "unknowns" about the specific physiologic consequences of neurologic injury (discussed later in this chapter).

Other Methodological Issues Related to Operationalizing and Measuring the Constructs Involved in RHD Language Research

It is quite difficult to apply many of the psycholinguistic or neuropsychological research paradigms that allow fine-grained analysis of component strengths and weaknesses in adults with RHD. Performance on tasks that involve precisely timed stimulus presentation methods may be confounded by concomitant deficits, such hemispatial neglect or visuoperceptual difficulties, or by general and/or specific slowing (Howes & Boller, 1975; Tompkins, 1990). Considerations like these almost certainly have contributed to the fact that the overwhelming majority of research has used off-line methods and metalinguistic tasks to evaluate language processing in adults with RHD. This fact also has skewed the accumulated observations, because such methods introduce multiple demands that may confound or obscure the processes of interest. In comparison, less cognitively demanding implicit or on-line measures have revealed strengths that were not evident from off-line, metalinguistic tasks; thus such methods may help to sort out potential reasons for impaired end-product performance (see Tompkins & Baumgaertner, 1998; Tompkins & Lehman, 1998, for summary). Of course, on-line measurement has its own set of problems, such as determining how and where to probe to evaluate a process as it is happening. Well-elaborated theoretical models of the mechanisms in question will be needed to help address such issues. On a different methodological point, is it also challenging to validate stimulus materials. Norms do not exist for many stimulus parameters of interest, such as extent of semantic feature overlap or degree of relatedness. And those that are available, such as category norms, usually are based on young adults' metalinguistic judgments, which raises questions about the validity of applying them with older adults or in more implicit tasks.

EVIDENCE AND ATTRIBUTIONS ABOUT RHD LANGUAGE DISORDERS

Lexical-Semantic Processing

Individuals with RHD may exhibit deficits on measures that require lexical comprehension and retrieval, like word-picture matching, picture naming, semantic judgment, and verbal fluency tasks. Results across different studies using the same tasks often are contradictory, but that is not particularly surprising because the lack of independent selection criteria for language disorders makes it possible that random samples of adults with RHD do not contain enough individuals with language deficits to find effects (Joanette, Goulet, & Hannequin, 1990).

A major problem in evaluating studies of RHD lexical-semantic disorders is that these investigations usually do not specify a model of lexical semantics, or an account of how lexical-semantic representations or computations are hypothesized to be impaired. Broadly speaking, such impairments could reflect degradation of stored representations, or disorders of processes that map phonologic or orthographic lexical information onto meaning (or vice versa). For activation of related meanings as evaluated in priming studies, effects could derive from associations between phonological or orthographic information, associations of word meanings based on semantic similarity or cooccurrence probability, or an interaction of these factors. The studies reviewed here do not allow a clear differentiation of such factors. Thus, the term *lexical-semantic* as used herein must subsume all such aspects of the lexical-semantic system.

One line of research has investigated whether RHD can result in subtle, but general deficits in the lexical-semantic system (Gainotti, Caltagirone, Miceli, & Masullo, 1983; Lesser, 1974). To date there is no definitive evidence of such impairments in individuals with RHD. Results from investigations of word-picture matching and picture naming are inconclusive. Although many studies have shown that individuals with RHD can be impaired on such tasks (Adamovich & Brooks, 1981; Gainotti et al., 1983; Lesser, 1974), none has provided statistically significant evidence that errors made by participants with RHD could not be the result of visual perceptual impairment (Chieffi, Carlomagno, Silveri, & Gainotti, 1989; Gainotti et al., 1983). The common finding that individuals with RHD make more visual-semantic errors than pure visual errors could reflect an interaction of visual-perceptual and semantic deficits, or the products of impaired visual-perceptual recognition as filtered through an intact lexical-semantic system.

Results of priming studies provide even less evidence of lexical-semantic disorders, in that individuals with RHD have no deficit in associative lexical priming at short and long stimulus onset asynchronies (Gagnon, Goulet, & Joanette, 1989; Henik, Dronkers, Knight, & Osimani, 1993; Tompkins, 1990). However, while such findings suggest that lexical-semantic activation processes are preserved to some degree, they do not rule out the possibility that these processes are in some way less efficient after RHD (Tompkins, 1990). For example, in a study of lexical metaphor, reaction times of participants with RHD were slower even after being adjusted for basic response speed (Tompkins, 1990), a finding that could reflect slowed activation.

Other data are consistent with the possibility of a subtle lexical-semantic deficit, but perhaps only when processing is relatively demanding of cognitive effort. In several studies using metalinguistic tasks, individuals with RHD had difficulty specifically in conditions that required retrieval of semantic information, as compared to phonological or orthographic aspects of words. For example, disordered performance on word-picture matching tasks occurred with semantic but not phonological distractors (Lesser, 1974); word similarity judgments were deficient for stimuli with semantic but not phonological or orthographic relationships (Chiarello & Church, 1986); and impairments were evident only in the semantic condition of a verbal fluency study that directly compared word generation for specified semantic categories with that for specified initial letters (Joanette & Goulet, 1989). From these results, the authors inferred an impairment in lexical-semantic processing after RHD. However, such an inference is valid only if stimuli in the contrasting conditions have the same resource demands. That this is a questionable assumption has been shown for verbal fluency tasks. When semantic and orthographic conditions are equated for the number of words control subjects produce on average to each criterion, individuals with RHD are impaired in both conditions (Goulet, Joanette, Sabourin, & Giroux, 1997). This suggests a general inefficiency in the search to retrieve items for this task, more than a problem of lexical-semantics. Overall, then, the evidence to date does not definitively indicate whether a lexical-semantic deficit is a direct consequence of RHD, or whether the accumulated results reflect more generalized difficulties with attentional or working memory processes.

Another line of research has investigated whether RHD impairs the processing of specific meaning domains, as carried by nonliteral, emotional, and/or concrete words. Because the priming of metaphoric word meanings is spared in adults with RHD (Tompkins, 1990), a specific deficit for nonliteral meanings, if it exists, again may be linked to demands for effortful processing. In this regard, individuals with RHD do more poorly on semantic judgment tasks involving metaphoric or emotional meanings than do control subjects with LHD and without brain damage, but RHD participants perform equally to LHD subjects in judging literal or affectively neutral meanings (Borod, Andelman, Olber, Tweedy, & Welkowitz, 1992; Brownell, Simpson, Bihrle, Potter, & Gardner, 1990). Individuals with RHD also are less likely to group word triplets based on metaphoric relations (Brownell, Potter, Michelow, & Gardner, 1984). However, as argued above, to infer a specific impairment in the effortful processing of "meta-phoric" or "emotional" semantic meanings, it would be necessary to demonstrate that such differences do not derive from an interaction of general processing limitations and differences in processing difficulty between domains. On the whole, these findings do not rule out domain-specific lexical-semantic deficits, but neither do they provide compelling evidence.

Individuals with RHD also have been predicted to have difficulty processing concrete word meanings (Gainotti et al. 1983; Rainville, Goulet, & Joanette, 1995). Although perhaps intu-itively at odds with evidence implicating the intact right hemisphere in computing nonliteral interpretations, this proposal was first based on the finding that in some studies using divided visual field presentation there was a reaction time advantage for concrete words over abstract words only in the left visual field/right hemisphere (Ellis & Shepherd, 1974). The right hemi-sphere thus was proposed to facilitate concrete word recognition, possibly through activation of imageable aspects of word meanings. In adults with RHD, the logic goes, this facilitation would be disrupted, creating particular difficulties for concrete word processing. Evidence to date is not consistent with this hypothesis. Goulet and Joanette (1994) assessed differences in spoken production of concrete and abstract words, using semantically constrained sentences in which subjects had to fill in a missing word (for example, "the butcher cuts the meat with a . . . "). They found that individuals with RHD were better at supplying abstract words than concrete words. However, this result is hard to interpret because the degree of semantic constraint was not controlled between conditions, and only five stimuli were used in each condition. Two other studies that addressed the concreteness effect failed to find it (Rainville et al., 1995; Warrington, McKenna, & Orpwood, 1998). Of course it remains possible that subtle differences in the processing of abstract and concrete words after RHD are not captured by the off-line tasks used in these investigations.

Results of a PET study of individuals with healthy brains (Beauregard, Chertkow, Bub, & Murtha, 1997), however, suggest that right hemisphere structures have no specific role in processing concrete lexical items. Beauregard and colleagues obtained images during the pre-sentation of concrete, abstract, and emotional words, as well as during a prestimulus phase that was assumed to reflect preparatory and attentional processes in anticipation of the experi-mental task. When this control condition was subtracted from the experimental conditions, right hemisphere activation was evident only for the emotional word stimuli. Interpretation must remain tentative, though, because aspects of stimulus selection likely affected the results in ways that cannot be determined. For example, concreteness values were based on the intuition of the investigators. Also, concrete words were selected from one semantic category but words in the other conditions came from many categories.

Other imaging evidence related to the abstract/concrete dichotomy is conflicting. Consistent with the prediction of a concreteness effect, an event-related potential study (Kounios & Holcomb, 1994) found a stronger effect for concrete words over the right hemisphere than the left. But three other imaging studies (PET and fMRI) found activation in the right hemisphere for the processing of abstract, not concrete, words (D'Esposito et al., 1997; Kiehl et al., 1999; Perani et al., 1999). These contradictory findings most likely reflect differences in stimulus control.

Recently, models of right hemisphere lexical-semantic processing derived from divided visual field studies in people with healthy brains have been applied to account for lexical-semantic deficits in RHD. As suggested in the example above, the underlying assumption in relating these models to RHD disorders is one of direct mapping. That is, RHD results in a loss or diminution of function that has been attributed to the intact right hemisphere. At the same time, adults with RHD become overly reliant on intact left hemisphere processes. The direct mapping assumption is problematic, as discussed in detail later in this chapter. However, two prominent applications of normal processing models are considered next.

One hypothesis is that RHD will disrupt the activation of, for example, metaphoric meanings or subordinate interpretations of lexical ambiguities (the "intelligence-related" interpretation of the adjective *sharp*; or the "sides-of-a-river"' interpretation of the noun *bank*). This prediction is based on evidence suggesting that only the right hemisphere serves the purpose of activating weak associates of lexical items, or distant semantic relations (for reviews, see Beeman, 1998; Chiarello, 1998). To date, however, no study with RHD participants has directly investigated this hypothesis by manipulating semantic associativeness or degree of semantic feature overlap. While it is safe to assume that the metaphoric prime-target pairs used by Tompkins (1990) were less associated than their literal controls, the degree of associativeness might be too high to serve even as an indirect test of this hypothesis.

A second hypothesis, which is linked to the previous one, is that the left hemisphere quickly selects dominant or contextually appropriate meanings while the right hemisphere maintains activation of subordinate meanings and remote associates (see Beeman, 1998; Chiarello, 1998). Assuming a direct mapping between normal and disordered right hemisphere functions, this hypothesis predicts that individuals with RHD should not have access to nondominant or alternative interpretations. Also, assuming that left hemisphere processes predominate, adults with RHD should show inhibition effects for subordinate meanings of ambiguous words or remotely associated words. Such inhibition effects have been reported for right visual field/left hemisphere presentations in priming studies with non-brain-damaged individuals (Burgess & Simpson, 1988; Nakagawa, 1991), though not always (Anaki, Faust, & Kravetz, 1998). While applications to RHD have received little empirical investigation, priming of (subordinate) metaphoric interpretations of lexical ambiguities at a long interstimulus interval (Tompkins, 1990) is at odds with notion that such meanings are unavailable over extended periods of time to adults with RHD.

In summary, definite evidence is still lacking as to whether RHD affects the lexical-semantic system. To address this issue, studies are needed that are based on models of lexical-semantic processing, and from which directly testable predictions can be derived. To differentiate lexical-semantic deficits from generalized processing difficulties, various attentional, retrieval, and/or timing demands of the experimental tasks need to be directly manipulated.

Discourse Processing

RHD language disorders are particularly evident in the domain of pragmatics, which involves the context-appropriate social use of language. Much of the relevant research has focused on discourse processing as a manifestation of pragmatic functioning (for current reviews and perspectives see Beeman, 1998; Brownell & Martino, 1998; Myers, 1999; Stemmer & Joanette, 1998; Tompkins & Lehman, 1998). A growing literature suggests possible impairments in building, extracting, or applying the mental structures that guide discourse processing. These problems seem especially marked when the communicative task requires adults with RHD to revise mental models in order to update or repair initial interpretations, or to construct a coherent model by linking multiple or disparate representations of text elements, internal knowledge, and external contexts.

Among potential difficulties with creating, manipulating, or using discourse structure after RHD are those of: (1) supplying sufficiently informative content in discourse and conversation (Lojek-Osiejuk, 1996; Roman, Brownell, Potter, Seibold, & Gardner, 1987; Trupe & Hillis, 1985; see summary in Myers, 1999); (2) conveying, and perhaps appreciating, central themes of single discourse units (Benowitz, Moya, & Levine, 1990; Hough, 1990; Myers & Brookshire, 1996; Schneiderman, Murasugi, & Saddy, 1992) or of several related ones (Lojek-Osiejuk, 1996); (3) organizing and ordering elements of discourse structure (Lojek-Osiejuk, 1996; Schneiderman et al., 1992); and (4) assimilating these elements into a conceptual whole (Brownell, Carroll, Rehak, & Wingfield, 1992; Myers & Brookshire, 1995; Schneiderman et al., 1992; Wapner, Hamby, & Gardner, 1981). The extent and nature of this last problem, often described as a difficulty with integrating various sources of information in discourse processing, has been examined more fully in investigations of specific types of discourse units or processing operations. This literature describes potential impairments of the following.

Relating Mental Representations of Stimuli and Their Associated Contexts to Determine or Convey Nonliteral Intended Meanings

Problems of this sort have been reported for various tasks involving nonliteral forms and intents, such as selecting punchlines for jokes (Bihrle, Brownell, & Powelson, 1986; Brownell, Michel, Powelson, & Gardner, 1983); recognizing conversational irony and its implications (Kaplan, Brownell, Jacobs, & Gardner, 1990); determining connotative meanings of words (Schmitzer, Strauss, & DeMarco, 1997); interpreting idioms (Myers & Linebaugh, 1981); and processing indirect requests (Stemmer, Giroux, & Joanette, 1994; Weylman, Brownell, Roman, & Gardner, 1989). RHD does not seem to affect the activation or representation of nonliteral intended meanings (Stemmer et al., 1994; Tompkins, 1990, 1991; Tompkins, Boada, & McGarry, 1992) or their canonical structures (Bihrle et al., 1986; Rehak et al., 1992), and adults with RHD can represent relevant elements of the (verbal) stimulus contexts in nonliteral processing tasks (Brownell, Pincus, Blum, Rehak, & Winner, 1997; Myers & Brookshire, 1994, 1996; Stemmer et al., 1994). Thus, the problem primarily seems to be one of synthesizing knowledge representations, and perhaps of selecting from competing possibilities activated by the ambiguity inherent in nonliteral forms (Tompkins et al., 1999; 2000).

Reconciling Multiple, Seemingly Incongruent Inferences to Arrive at a Full Understanding of a Discourse Unit

Adults with RHD have particular difficulty in contexts that support or induce conflicting interpretations (Brownell, Potter, Bihrle, & Gardner, 1986; Frederiksen & Stemmer, 1993; Tompkins, 1991; Tompkins et al., 1999, 2000), including those that violate canonical expectations (for example, Rehak et al., 1992; Stemmer et al., 1994). Together with other work (Lehman-Blake & Tompkins, 2001), this observation suggests that inference generation per se is not a primary interpretive roadblock for adults with RHD (but see Beeman, 1993). Rather, the problem in such instances seems to be one of effortful integration, as would be needed to revise or repair interpretations based on ostensibly competing inferences (Stemmer & Joanette, 1998; see also Tompkins & Lehman, 1998).

Reasoning from a Theory of Mind

This involves an understanding of the ways in which knowledge, beliefs and motivations guide one's own behavior and that of others (Kaplan et al., 1990; Siegal, Carrington, & Radel, 1996; Winner, Brownell, Happe, Blum, & Pincus, 1998). Adults with RHD are less likely, for example, to use knowledge about communication partners' shared familiarity with a third party to determine how formally to address that person in a conversation (Brownell et al., 1997); to provide explanatory remarks that mitigate the imposition of indirect requests (Brownell & Stringfellow, 1999); or to appreciate the implications of and motivations for conversational tangents and redundancies (Rehak, Kaplan, & Gardner, 1992). Again, these difficulties cannot be attributed to a failure to understand or represent individual elements of the scenarios in question, as detail questions are accurately answered (Brownell et al., 1997; Rehak et al., 1992; Winner et al., 1998).

Many findings like those above are difficult to interpret, due to confounds introduced by the typically metalinguistic assessment tasks. However, such results seem to implicate primarily a set of attention-demanding, effortful integrative and organizational mental operations that are involved in discourse processing. As noted earlier, deficits of discourse representation and integration are not absolute. Adults with RHD perceive and represent many elements of both given and inferred information. They use explicit connectors to integrate components of a text (Brownell et al., 1992) and do well when interpretation is straightforward, as is the case for consistent passages (Brownell, Potter, Bihrle, & Gardner, 1986; Lehman-Blake & Tompkins, in press; Tompkins, Bloise, Timko, & Baumgaertner, 1994) and canonical forms (Brownell & Stringfellow, 1999; Hough, 1990; Rehak et al., 1992; Stemmer et al., 1994). They can make lower-order theory of mind inferences (Siegal et al., 1996; Winner et al., 1998) and empathy judgments (Rehak et al., 1992), and determine appropriate personal reference from status information (Brownell et al., 1997). These kinds of findings are consistent with other evidence that nonlanguage variables related to cognitive effort and/or task processing demands contribute importantly to observed performances of adults with RHD (see discussion in Tompkins & Lehman, 1998).

Most of the emerging theoretical accounts of RHD discourse processing deficits, described just below, center on concepts like effortful integration and inferencing, social cognition, and/or suppression of contextually inappropriate alternatives. There is some overlap among these accounts, in that many, if not all, specify to some extent the nature of RHD difficulties in constructing coherent, integrated mental structures to enable discourse production and comprehension. For example, Brownell and Martino (1998) refer to problems with "self-directed inference" (p. 325). This concept refers to comprehenders' efforts to discover and elaborate an interpretive framework when overlearned interpretive routines are inadequate and the text itself provides insufficient guidance as to how its elements fit together. Reasoning from a theory of mind also is gaining popularity as an explanatory construct, as implied above (see, for example, Brownell & Martino, 1998; Sabbagh, 1999). Tompkins and colleagues (1999, 2000) appeal to a general psycholinguistic mechanism that is central to building an integrated discourse representation (Gernsbacher, 1990). Their studies demonstrate that suppression function, or the ability to dampen mental activations that are contextually incompatible, predicts some aspects of discourse comprehension performance by adults with RHD. The suppression deficit hypothesis accommodates a variety of existing data, and intersects in interesting ways with each of the other accounts of RHD discourse processing deficits (Tompkins et al., 2000;

Tompkins & Lehman, 1998). Suppression deficits also could contribute to a difficulty with constructing and integrating new conceptual models, the unifying explanation proposed by Stemmer and Joanette (1998).

However, Brownell and colleagues (Brownell & Martino, 1998; Brownell et al., 1997) contend that difficulties in creating or using coherent discourse representations are not sufficient to explain discourse processing deficits in RHD adults. They suggest an additional essential ingredient, that adults with RHD experience a kind of social disconnection, or diminished interest in people. As partial evidence of a separate affective dimension to the RHD communicative profile, Brownell and colleagues note that adults with RHD infrequently invoke internal attributions for a character's actions, even though they can integrate textual information and stored knowledge to generate plausible external attributions (Brownell, Blum, & Winner, 1994). This kind of evidence might be at least partly subsumable under the suppression account. If, for example, external attributions are in some way more straightforward, more automatically invoked, or more strongly activated than internal attributions, particularly in a metalinguistic task, a dearth of the latter might be related to a difficulty inhibiting the former.

Finally, because the expression of deficits in each of these domains seems to be moderated by processing abilities and demands, as described above (see also Cherney, Drimmer, & Halper, 1997; Coslett, Bowers, & Heilman, 1987; Myers & Brookshire, 1994, 1996), general factors related to processing capacity and processing load need to be considered in a full account of RHD impairments and skills.

Potential explanatory constructs also derive from a growing normal cognitive neuroscience literature. The bulk of evidence has accrued from studies using split visual field stimulus presentation or contemporary neuroimaging techniques. Much of this work attributes to the right hemisphere some specialized computations or unique modes of operation that, when disrupted, might produce the kinds of discourse processing problems assumed to be typical of adults with RHD. These mechanisms, usually characterized in terms that place them in opposition with presumed left hemisphere mechanisms revolve around concepts like coarse (versus fine) coding (for example, Beeman, 1998) or differential specificity of lexical and pictorial semantic processors (Chiarello, 1998). Another perspective is that the right hemisphere activates knowledge structures without selection (Richards & Chiarello, 1997) or with little constraint by sentence context (Faust, 1998), while the left hemisphere uses contextual constraints to select quickly from among the activated possibilities. In an alternative formulation, the right and left hemispheres rely on different kinds of constraints to achieve meaning integration (Federmeier & Kutas, 1999; Titone, 1998).

Beeman (1998) illustrates one way in which constructs like these are suggested to account for discourse-level deficits of adults with RHD, by arguing that such deficits arise from impairments of the lexical-semantic processing propensities of the two cerebral hemispheres. In people with healthy brains, initial meaning activation proceeds in parallel in each hemisphere, but the left hemisphere quickly selects a narrow range of contextually relevant information, while the right hemisphere continues to activate and maintain a more diffuse network of distant associates and subordinate meanings (see summaries in Beeman, 1998; Chiarello, 1998). By this account, RHD renders the language user overly dependent on rapid selection processes of the left hemisphere, hampering the ability to transcend or override dominant or straightforward interpretations, or to derive inferences from the overlap of distantly related concepts. Potential difficulties with this kind of reasoning are considered in the next section of this chapter.

Other evidence from individuals with healthy brains adds to the explanatory landscape. While no direct tests have been made, hemispheric differences in anatomy and neurochemistry (see brief summaries in Beeman, 1998; Federmeier & Kutas, 1999) have been linked by several investigators to theoretical positions about right hemisphere language and its disorders. For example, Beeman (1998) marshals evidence about right brain connectivity at the cellular level to support the coarse coding hypothesis. And with reference to the suppression deficit hypothesis, Tompkins and colleagues (1997, 2000) find intriguing the report that neurotransmitter systems involved in filtering irrelevant stimuli are more concentrated in the right hemisphere, and more disrupted by RHD (Tucker & Williamson, 1984).

Recent neuroimaging studies of people with intact brains also are beginning to offer clues about the neural substrates of discourse processing. Right hemisphere regions are sometimes, and in some conditions, activated in processing "theory of mind" tasks (for example, Baron-Cohen et al., 1994; Gallagher et al., 2000; but see Fletcher et al., 1995, for emphasis on a left hemisphere region). Portions of the right hemisphere also may be activated for tasks presumed to require holistic or global processing (for example, Bottini et al., 1994; Evans, Shedden, Hevenor, & Hahn, 2000; but see Fink, Marshall, Halligan, & Dolan, 1999, for a qualification to the hypothesis of hemispheric asymmetries for local versus global processing). Crozier and colleagues (1999) report right hemisphere participation for about half of their subjects for detecting errors in the sequence of actions in familiar scripts; St. George, Kutas, Martinez, and Sereno (1999) document right brain activation in reading untitled as opposed to titled stories; and Bottini and colleagues (1994) implicate right cortical regions in metaphor appreciation. However, cautious interpretation is warranted because in many such studies, stimulus controls are not sufficient to rule out credible alternative explanations for right hemisphere participation, such as differential plausibility (Bottini et al., 1994; Gallagher et al., 2000) or imageability (for example, Baron-Cohen et al., 1994). Other investigators attribute elevated right hemisphere activation to more general processing factors, such as attentional demands associated with relative novelty (Martin, 1999) or increased syntactic complexity (Just, Carpenter, Keller, Eddy, & Thulborn, 1996; Keller, Carpenter, & Just, 2001). It will be particularly interesting in the future to draw upon such work to infer how anatomic and physiologic factors interact with cognitive capabilities and task demands in determining which RHD adults will evidence language disorders, and how those disorders are manifest. Some additional cautions for interpreting neuroimaging studies of right hemisphere language are provided later in this chapter.

It would be surprising if any single explanatory concept could account for RHD discourse deficits, and combined attributions are appearing in a general form in the literature (see, for example, Brownell et al., 1997; Myers, 1999; Tompkins & Lehman, 1998). Two long-range challenges are to sort out how various potential explanatory constructs interact with one another to produce the picture(s) of strength, weakness, and performance variation that typify the RHD population, and to construct an integrated framework that captures the range of phenomena that support social communication (further discussion provided later in this chapter). To approach these goals will require a great deal of work to develop existing accounts so that specific, a priori predictions can be derived and tested. These efforts in turn will benefit from more research that examines component processes and their interactions as explicitly set out in relevant models, including those of discourse processing (Frederiksen, Bracewell, Breuleux, & Renaud, 1990) and other aspects of pragmatic function (see Stemmer, 1999a, for examples). Also, it will be important to continue to track multiple sources of performance variability. Such pursuits will help us determine both the extent to which nonlanguage cognitive functions (for example, individual differences in attentional or working memory processes) are responsible for observed impairments, and the ways in which such functions intersect with hemispheric specializations to generate normal and disordered language performances. Furthermore, on-line investigations are needed, with systematic manipulation of stimulus features and demands, to evaluate RHD adults' real-time representation and use of crucial elements of internal knowledge and external context. Related to this issue, an intriguing but as yet unexplored possibility is that slowing of perceptual processes and other discrete mental operations (for example, suppression of contextually inappropriate alternatives) could propagate through the system to create a variety of consequences for ongoing discourse integrative processes (Just & Carpenter, 1992; for other slowing hypotheses, see Salthouse [1996] with respect to cognition in normal aging, and Kolk [1995] and Swinney, Zurif, and Nicol [1989] for language production and comprehension, respectively, in aphasia).

CORRESPONDENCE IN LITERATURES ON NORMAL AND DISORDERED RIGHT HEMISPHERE LANGUAGE FUNCTION

This volume contains many examples of the ways in which various sources of data on language and the brain inform one another, and contribute to clinical decisions. Evidence of impaired and preserved performance in neurologic language disorders allows inferences about the nature of intact language representation and processing systems; evidence and perspectives on normal language are used to predict and explain language difficulties that result from brain damage; and theories of both deficient and normal function have implications for assessment and treatment.

For right hemisphere language processes and disorders, efforts to hypothesize and evaluate mutual constraints, and to apply the results in rehabilitation, have barely begun. This is hardly surprising. One of the most obvious reasons is that right hemisphere language capacities and deficits have been a focus of systematic study for only about the last ten to fifteen years. In addition, investigations of normal and disordered right hemisphere language functioning have not yet evaluated the same phenomena and mental computations, so generalizations between the two literatures have not been directly tested. While this sounds fairly easy to remedy, philosophical, conceptual, and methodological considerations present substantial challenges for predicting and interpreting the outcomes of such tests. A number of these considerations were discussed earlier. Elaborated more fully below are issues concerning the theoretical foundations of RHD language research, and the processes of predicting and generalizing between the literatures on normal and disordered right hemisphere language function.

Theory-driven research in RHD language is crucial both for identifying performance dissociations that fuel hypotheses about the intact right hemisphere's contribution to language, and for understanding the nature of RHD language deficits themselves. The primarily atheoretic, exploratory character of early investigations of RHD language and communication was to be expected. However, theories are now essential to help unify the accumulating observations, circumscribe and operationalize key phenomena to investigate, and identify central premises to test. While there are few explicit and testable theories of the cognitive and linguistic underpinnings of social communication, RHD language research in recent years has increasingly consulted available models to guide the investigation of some of the cognitive and communicative processes of interest. Examples are found in work on indirect requests (Brownell & Stringfellow, 1999; Stemmer et al., 1994), inferences (Dipper, Bryan, & Tyson, 1997; Lehman, 1999), and other more general aspects of discourse processing (Lojek-Osiejuk, 1996; Tompkins et al., 2000).

Beyond the need to use theoretical models at all lies the question of what kind of models ultimately will best inform our efforts. RHD language disorders presumably reside at some complex intersection of the multiple linguistic, affective, and cognitive operations, levels, and domains that enable the social interactive use of language. Efforts to investigate RHD language disorders systematically have been hampered by a dearth of theoretical frameworks that address the range of, and interactions among, potentially relevant computations, dimensions, and systems. Ongoing research has led to useful hypotheses about the nature of RHD language disorders, but these proposals are largely unconnected to any broader theoretical perspective(s). Thus, an integrated conceptual framework is needed to provide a structure for understanding the interactions among processing components and levels, and for clarifying the relationships among seemingly diverse results and hypotheses. Building such a model is a long-range enterprise, but some outlines are emerging to move us along this path. For example, Stemmer and

Joanette (1998) describe the utility of a multilayer model of discourse that incorporates conceptual, propositional, and linguistic levels of representation and processing (Frederiksen et al., 1990; but see Joanette & Goulet, 1994, for some of its limitations). And Stemmer (1999b) advocates situating research on RHD communicative exchange within a broad framework that addresses the way in which any action is shaped by the synergistic interplay between characteristics of an individual and his or her environment.

Another thorny source of difficulty for linking the RHD and intact right hemisphere language literatures, though neither new nor specific to right hemisphere research, relates to the unknown nature of the inferential bridge between normal and disordered hemisphere function. As noted earlier, investigators who generalize between these literatures typically assume, and sometimes propose explicitly, that performance after RHD reflects a diminution or loss of right hemisphere contributions to the processes in question, and a consequent overreliance on left hemisphere modes or operations (Beeman, 1993, 1998; Burgess & Simpson, 1988; Chiarello, 1998; Molloy, Brownell, & Gardner, 1990; Richards & Chiarello, 1997). But such an assumption may be rather tenuous, for the reasons discussed below.

First, the interconnectedness of the cerebral hemispheres, whether only one or both are functioning normally, creates a major question mark in mapping results from damaged to normal brains, or vice versa. For example, visual word recognition research summarized by Banich and Nicholas (1998) indicates that the two intact hemispheres interact in ways that are not predictable from the processing of either one alone. Also, as Tucker (1981) notes, it is unclear how the hemispheres coordinate, cooperate, facilitate, and/or inhibit one another when one is damaged. If the neurological impairment releases some right hemisphere process from inhibition, the output of that process may be exaggerated rather than diminished.

Another complication for the prevailing assumption about the relationship between normal and disordered right hemisphere language functions is that performance after RHD almost certainly reflects dynamics other than those owing to the directly disrupted neural tissue. These include electrical and chemical changes in regions remote from the structural lesion (Andrews, 1991; Reinecke et al., 1999; Witte & Stoll, 1997; see also Cappa, 1998), recruitment of undamaged portions of the damaged hemisphere (for example, Warburton, Price, Swinburn, & Wise, 1999; see also Cappa, 1998), and intentional and incidental compensations that the language user develops as she or he tries to navigate the world with an altered system. These dynamics likely change over time, as well, further obscuring the picture to be obtained from adults with RHD.

Finally, this uncertain state of affairs is evident in data that do not align easily with predictions that assume a direct mapping between normal and disordered performance. As mentioned earlier, in people with intact brains, activation of the subordinate meanings of lexical ambiguities is rapidly suppressed by the left hemisphere, but maintained by the right hemisphere for a longer period of time (Burgess & Simpson, 1988). As a result, many researchers (for example, Beeman, 1993, 1998; Burgess & Lund, 1998; Chiarello, 1988, 1998; Molloy et al., 1990) suggest that adults with RHD should not be able to activate and/or maintain alternative interpretations over prolonged periods. This kind of reasoning does not accord easily with evidence from RHD adults summarized above, demonstrating preserved activation and representation of nonliteral meanings (Rehak et al., 1992; Stemmer et al., 1994; see also Tompkins & Lehman, 1998), and sustained interference from activated alternative inferences (Tompkins et al., 1999, 2000). And as noted previously, even a more direct generalization, to lexical-level processing by adults with RHD, does not accord with data that documents priming of the metaphoric interpretations of lexical ambiguities at an interval that should have enabled the intact left hemisphere to inhibit them (Tompkins, 1990). This rather inexact correspondence of RHD and normal literatures (see Tompkins et al., 2000, for additional examples) has received little attention, and a better fit may remain elusive until more progress is made in understanding the nature of interactions between intact and damaged hemispheres, as well as physiologic and psychological mechanisms of brain damage and recovery.

Neuroimaging studies of people with intact brains present some similar challenges for inferring the links between normal and disordered function. As above, proceeding from the dominant assumption that RHD engenders an overreliance on left hemisphere operations, it is not always easy to tie RHD language evidence to inferences drawn from intact brain imaging. For example, in a PET study, Fletcher and colleagues (1995) report left medial frontal activation when story comprehension requires the attribution of mental states. Noting the importance of this same left brain region to conditional associative learning tasks, Fletcher and colleagues tentatively propose that the key to its participation is a need for "integration of information in the light of other stimuli" (p. 121), as when an interpretation differs from a canonical expectation. But rather than being a strength for adults with RHD, this sounds quite a bit like the kind of processing that causes them particular difficulty. In addition, while normal variability is rarely addressed in neuroimaging studies of language, it can be vast (Crozier et al., 1999). This variation, along with infrequent attention to individual attributes that may modulate hemispheric contributions to language functioning, renders even more problematic the process of generalizing between "normal" and "disordered" literatures.

A number of more general issues further complicate the conduct and interpretation of neuroimaging studies of right hemisphere language mechanisms. For example, in order to draw inferences about neural activity from fMRI, valid models are needed of how activation/signal differences change in relation to underlying neural events. However, such models do not yet exist (D'Esposito & Aguirre, 1999). Similarly, the variability of the hemodynamic response within and across subjects is just beginning to be explored (D'Esposito, Zarahn, Aguirre, & Rypma, 1999; Lohmann et al., 1999). To make matters all the more difficult, the effects of interactions between type and nature of a stimulus event and mode of response on changes in regional cerebral blood flow are little understood, even at a perceptual level (Binder, 1997; Jennings, McIntosh, Kapur, Tulving, & Houle, 1997). All such issues contribute to the fact that researchers are continually exploring appropriate ways to exploit the rapidly evolving sophistication in fMRI technology (Birn, Bandettini, Cox, & Shaker, 1999; D'Esposito et al., 1999). But in the final analysis, results and interpretations derived from studies using any technology are only as valid as the theoretical context in which they are examined.

A subsidiary issue, raised earlier, involves the validity of generalizing between younger and older brains. The research on right hemisphere language processing in intact brains almost exclusively investigates the former, but because cerebrovascular accident is rare in young people, RHD studies overwhelmingly evaluate the latter. This dictates caution in applying to one population the theories, methods, or evidence that were developed with the other.

Despite such hurdles, the existing RHD and normal right hemisphere language literatures are mutually informative. One major contribution of RHD language studies has been to highlight within- and between-subject variability that, we would argue, should be accommodated by theories of normal right hemisphere language processing (see also Stemmer, 1999b) and evaluated for its neural bases (Just et al., 1996; Keller et al., 2001). For instance, evidence of RHD language performance that covaries with processing demands points to the need for more research at the intersection of attention (or working memory) and language. More generally, existing RHD language data present a source of clues for reasoning backwards, to infer what normal (right hemisphere) language systems might be like. Currently, this evidence mostly licenses the weak inference that the intact right hemisphere participates in some way (and through an unknown interaction with the left hemisphere) to carry out functions that are disrupted by RHD. This underscores the value of converging evidence from a variety of sources to advance the enterprise of cognitive neuropsychology. At the same time, normal models and data regarding, for example, right hemisphere lexical-semantic processing have generated an emerging picture of component operations, time course considerations, and conditions most likely to reveal right hemisphere contributions to language (Beeman & Chiarello, 1998; Federmeier & Kutas, 1999). Either for theoretical or clinical purposes, contributions like these can help determine the kinds of phenomena to evaluate in adults with RHD. However, until we have a better understanding of the nature of the problem in mapping between intact and damaged brain systems, it will not be particularly surprising when predictions from one of these sources of right hemisphere language data are not borne out in the other.

CONSIDERATIONS FOR CLINICAL MANAGEMENT OF RHD LANGUAGE DISORDERS

Current clinical practice in evaluation and treatment of RHD language disorders is primarily symptom-driven and atheoretical (Myers, 1999; Tompkins, 1995). This too is not entirely surprising, because clinical applications of necessity lag behind theory development. But a theoretically oriented approach offers the opportunity to identify and capitalize on processes that may underlie various communicative strengths and weaknesses, potentially enhancing generalization of treatment gains to a range of skills and contexts that rely on those processes. Thus, well-substantiated hypotheses about facilitators of and barriers to communication become a key ingredient in assessment and treatment planning.

To illustrate, we consider several clinical implications from the evidence and hypotheses described above. Of immediate clinical relevance, the manipulation of task processing demands can induce substantial performance variations in adults with RHD, particularly in relation to each individual's attentional or working memory capacity. Thus, regardless of whether facilitation or compensation is the primary rehabilitation goal, a variety of processing factors potentially can be modified to make things more or less difficult for any given patient (see Tompkins, 1995, for suggestions). More generally, research that clarifies the extent to which language performance after RHD reflects attentional, working memory, or other nonlanguage cognitive impairments, rather than language deficits per se, will have direct implications for the assumptions underlying the development of treatment approaches.

The suppression deficit hypothesis has ramifications for clinical management as well. This hypothesis derives from evidence that discourse comprehension difficulties in adults with RHD are associated with a tendency to activate and hold on too long to interpretations that become contextually irrelevant (Tompkins et al., 2000). The suppression account thus provides a principled foundation for some common treatment practices, such as working with RHD adults to distinguish central or relevant information from that which is peripheral or irrelevant.

At the same time, the suppression deficit hypothesis and the findings upon which it is based suggest some common clinical techniques that may be less appropriate. For example, comprehension skills of adults with RHD often are assessed and treated with tasks that require them to supply more than one interpretation for words or phrases that have multiple meanings, such as indirect requests, idioms, or lexical ambiguities. But if adults with RHD automatically activate multiple meanings, and their primary difficulty involves discarding those that are contextually inappropriate, the exercise of generating alternative meanings may be pointless or even detrimental. In this case, treatment might focus more fruitfully on tasks that involve determining the contextual relevance or appropriateness of alternative meanings that the clinician explicitly furnishes or implicitly primes. Tompkins and Baumgaertner (1998) provide some concrete treatment suggestions related to this goal and to others that are designed to help RHD clients "stay on track." Myers (1999) also offers a variety of ideas about how treatment might differ if one hypothesizes suppression deficits as a basis for RHD language difficulties, as opposed to a lack of activation of inferences or alternative interpretations (for example, Beeman, 1993, and extrapolations from research on normal right hemisphere language processing, as above).

Despite the potential clinical utility of a theory of deficient (or preserved) language performance, such a theory is far from sufficient as a basis for treatment planning. Even for an exquisitely defined deficit, no such theory can prescribe what should happen in treatment, in either general or specific terms (Caramazza, 1989; Hillis, 1994). Rather, a theory of a deficit provides only a pointer to potential assessment or remediation goals and strategies. There is also little evidence that theory-driven treatment results in better outcomes than time-tested atheoretical approaches (Hillis, 1998). Furthermore, deficit-oriented therapy may miss the bigger picture, which largely equates the therapeutic benefit for any particular client with its effects on consequences that go beyond the "impairment" itself (see, for example, Frattali, 1998). These include the client's ability to perform specific daily life activities, and to handle potential psychological, social, economic, and environmental repercussions of the condition under treatment. While there is no direct evidence to suggest that deficit-oriented treatment cannot contribute to improvements at these other levels of outcome, neither is there any strong evidence of whether deficit-oriented treatment is necessary or sufficient to this end.

For adults with RHD language disorders, a multifaceted and long-range program of research will be required to establish what kinds of treatments work best (see discussion in Tompkins et al., 1998). Research that investigates a full range of outcomes of RHD language disorders, and that ascertains the nature of interactions among these different levels of outcome, will be central to understanding how we might achieve meaningful treatment results. Unfortunately, nearly no work of this sort exists. Rigorous treatment efficacy studies also are desperately needed, but currently none is to be found for RHD language disorders. Beyond incorporating design parameters that maximize internal validity (Kearns, 1992), such investigations should use an assortment of measures at a variety of levels of outcome, evaluate evidence of maintenance and generalization to meaningful tasks and contexts, and include social validation or other consumer satisfaction assessments for patients and family members (see Tompkins et al., 1998). Treatment studies also are needed to investigate the value of targeting variables that mediate, moderate, or modify the relationships among deficits and higher-level outcomes (Schulz & Williamson, 1993), in addition to or rather than targeting the deficits themselves. More generally, intervention planning for anyone with a neurologically based language disorder ultimately will benefit from efforts to understand the "how" of treatment, with reference to the variety of cognitive, neurophysiological, and psychosocial processes that produce a favorable climate for adaptive learning and generalization in the presence of brain damage (see, for example, Blomert, 1998; Caramazza & Hillis, 1992; Gordon, 1999; Holland, 1992; Linebaugh, 1999).

ACKNOWLEDGMENT

This work was supported in part by grant DC01820 from the National Institute on Deafness and Other Communication Disorders. Dr. Baumgaertner is currently affiliated with the Department of Neurology, University of Hamburg Medical Center.

REFERENCES

Adamovich, B. L., & Brooks, R. L. (1981). A diagnostic protocol to assess the communication deficits of patients with right hemisphere damage. In R. H. Brookshire (Ed.), *Clinical aphasiology: Vol. 11.* Minneapolis, MN: BRK.

Anaki, D., Faust, M., & Kravetz, S. (1998). Cerebral hemisphere asymmetries in processing lexical metaphors. *Neuropsychologia, 36,* 691–700.

Andrews, R. J. (1991). Transhemispheric diaschisis: A review and comment. *Stroke, 22,* 943–949.

Banich, M. T., & Nicholas, C. D. (1998). Integration of processing between the hemispheres in word recognition. In M. Beeman & C. Chiarello (Eds.), *Right hemisphere language comprehension: Perspectives from cognitive neuroscience.* Mahwah, NJ: Lawrence Erlbaum.

Baron-Cohen, S., Ring, H., Moriarty, J., Schmitz, B., Costa, D., & Ell, P. (1994). Recognition of mental state terms: Clinical findings in children with autism and a functional neuroimaging study of normal adults. *British Journal of Psychiatry, 165,* 640-649.

Baum, S. R., & Pell, M. D. (1999). The neural bases of prosody: Insights from lesion studies and neuroimaging. *Aphasiology, 13,* 581-608.

Baynes, K., & Eliassen, J. C. (1998). The visual lexicon:

Its access and organization in commissurotomy patients. In M. Beeman & C. Chiarello (Eds.), *Right hemisphere language comprehension: Perspectives from cognitive neuroscience*. Mahwah, NJ: Lawrence Erlbaum.

Beauregard, M., Chertkow, H., Bub, D., & Murtha, S. (1997). The neural substrate for concrete, abstract, and emotional word lexica: A positron emission tomography study. *Journal of Cognitive Neuroscience, 9*, 441–461.

Beeman, M. (1993). Semantic processing in the right hemisphere may contribute to drawing inferences from discourse. *Brain and Language, 44*, 80–120.

Beeman, M. (1998). Coarse semantic coding and discourse comprehension. In M. Beeman & C. Chiarello (Eds.), *Right-hemisphere language comprehension: Perspectives from cognitive neuroscience*. Mahwah, NJ: Lawrence Erlbaum.

Beeman, M., & Chiarello, C. (Eds.). (1998). *Right-hemisphere language comprehension: Perspectives from cognitive neuroscience*. Mahwah, NJ: Lawrence Erlbaum.

Benowitz, L. I., Moya, K. L., & Levine, D. N. (1990). Impaired verbal reasoning and constructional apraxia in subjects with right hemisphere damage. *Neuropsychologia, 28*, 231–241.

Bihrle, A. M., Brownell, H. H., & Powelson, J. A. (1986). Comprehension of humorous and nonhumorous materials by left and right brain-damaged patients. *Brain and Cognition, 5*, 399–411.

Binder, J. (1997). Functional magnetic resonance imaging: Language mapping. *Neurosurgery Clinics of North America, 8*, 383–392.

Birn, R. M., Bandettini, P. A., Cox, R. W., & Shaker, R. (1999). Event-related fMRI of tasks involving brief motion. *Human Brain Mapping, 7*, 106–114.

Blomert, L. (1998). Recovery from language disorders: Interactions between brain and rehabilitation. In B. Stemmer & H. A. Whitaker (Eds.), *Handbook of neurolinguistics*. San Diego, CA: Academic Press.

Blonder, L. X., Burns, A. F., Bowers, D., Moore, R. W., & Heilman, K. M. (1993). Right hemisphere facial expressivity during natural conversation. *Brain and Cognition, 21*, 44–56.

Borod, J. C., Andelman, R., Olber, L. K., Tweedy, J. R., & Welkowitz, J. (1992). Right hemisphere specialization for the identification of emotional words and sentences: Evidence from stroke patients. *Neuropsychologia, 30*, 827–844.

Bottini, G., Corcoran, R., Sterzi, R., Paulesu, E., Schenone, P., Scarpa, P., Frackowiak, R. S. J., & Frith, C. D. (1994). The role of the right hemisphere in the interpretation of figurative aspects of language: A positron emission tomography activation study. *Brain, 117*, 1241–1253.

Brownell, H. H., Blum, A., & Winner, E. (1994). Attributional bias in RHD patients with impaired discourse comprehension. *Brain and Language, 43*, 121–147.

Brownell, H. H., Carroll, J. J., Rehak, A., & Wingfield, A. (1992). The use of pronoun anaphora and speaker mood in the interpretation of conversational utterances by right hemisphere brain-damaged patients. *Brain and Language, 43*, 121-147.

Brownell, H. H., & Martino, G. (1998). Deficits in inference and social cognition: The effects of right hemisphere brain damage on discourse. In M. Beeman & C. Chiarello (Eds.), *Right hemisphere language com-

prehension: Perspectives from cognitive neuroscience*. Mahwah, NJ: Lawrence Erlbaum.

Brownell, H. H., Michel, D., Powelson, J., & Gardner, H. (1983). Surprise but not coherence: sensitivity to verbal humor in right-hemisphere patients. *Brain and Language, 18*, 20–27.

Brownell, H. H., Pincus, D., Blum, A., Rehak, A., & Winner, E. (1997). The effects of right-hemisphere brain damage on patients' use of terms of personal reference. *Brain and Language, 57*, 60–79.

Brownell, H. H., Potter, H. H., Bihrle, A. M., & Gardner, H. (1986). Inference deficits in right brain-damaged patients. *Brain and Language, 27*, 310–321.

Brownell, H. H., Potter, H. H., Michelow, D., & Gardner, H. (1984). Sensitivity to lexical denotation and connotation in brain-damaged patients: A double dissociation. *Brain and Language, 22*, 253–265.

Brownell, H. H., Simpson, T. L., Bihrle, A. M., Potter, H., & Gardner, H. (1990). Appreciation of metaphoric alternative word meanings by left and right brain-damaged patients. *Neuropsychologia, 28*, 375–383.

Brownell, H. H., & Stringfellow, A. (1999). Making requests: Illustrations of how right-hemisphere brain damage can affect discourse production. *Brain and Language, 68*, 442–465.

Burgess, C., & Lund. K. (1998). Modeling cerebral asymmetries in high-dimensional space. In M. Beeman & C. Chiarello (Eds.), *Right hemisphere language comprehension: Perspectives from cognitive neuroscience*. Mahwah, NJ: Lawrence Erlbaum.

Burgess, C., & Simpson, G. (1988). Cerebral hemispheric mechanisms in the retrieval of ambiguous word meanings. *Brain and Language, 33*, 86–103.

Cappa, S. F. (1998). Spontaneous recovery from aphasia. In B. Stemmer & H. A. Whitaker (Eds.), *Handbook of neurolinguistics*. San Diego, CA: Academic Press.

Caramazza, A. (1989). Cognitive neuropsychology and rehabilitation: An unfulfilled promise? In X. Seron & G. DeLoche (Eds.), *Cognitive approaches to rehabilitation*. Hillsdale, NJ: Lawrence Erlbaum.

Caramazza, A., & Hillis, A. E. (1992). For a theory of remediation of cognitive deficits. In J. A. Cooper (Ed.), *Aphasia treatment: Vol 2. Current approaches and research opportunities*. Bethesda, MD: National Institutes of Health.

Cherney, L., Drimmer, D., & Halper, A. (1997). Informational content and unilateral neglect: A longitudinal investigation of five subjects with right hemisphere damage. *Aphasiology, 11*, 351–364.

Cherry, B. J., & Hellige, J. B. (1999). Hemispheric asymmetries in vigilance and cerebral arousal mechanisms in younger and older adults. *Neuropsychology, 13*, 111–120.

Chiarello, C. (1988). Semantic priming in the intact brain: Separate roles for the right and left hemispheres? In C. Chiarello (Ed.), *Right hemisphere contributions to lexical semantics*. New York: Springer Verlag.

Chiarello, C. (1998). On codes of meaning and the meaning of codes: Semantic access and retrieval within and between hemispheres. In M. Beeman & C. Chiarello (Eds.), *Right hemisphere language comprehension: Perspectives from cognitive neuroscience*. Mahwah, NJ: Lawrence Erlbaum.

Chiarello, C., & Church, K. L. (1986). Lexical judgments after right- or left-hemisphere injury. *Neuropsychologia, 24*, 623–630.

Chieffi, S., Carlomagno, S., Silveri, M. C., & Gainotti, G. (1989). The influence of semantic and perceptual factors on lexical comprehension in aphasic and right brain-damaged patients. *Cortex, 25,* 591-598.

Coslett, H. B., Bowers, D., & Heilman, K. M. (1987). Reduction in cerebral activation after right hemisphere stroke. *Neurology, 37,* 957-962.

Crozier, S., Sirigu, A., Lehericy, S., van de Moortele, P., Pillon, B., Grafman, J., Agid, Y., Dubois, B., & LeBihan, D. (1999). Distinct prefrontal activations in processing sequence at the sentence and script level: An fMRI study. *Neuropsychologia, 37,* 1469-1476.

D'Esposito, M., & Aguirre, G. K. (1999). Event-related MRI: Implications for cognitive psychology. *Psychological Bulletin, 125,* 155-164.

D'Esposito, M., Detre, M. A., Aguirre, G. K., Stallcup, M., Alsop, D. C., Tippet, L. J., & Farah, M. J. (1997). A functional MRI study of mental image generation. *Neuropsychologia, 35,* 725-730.

D'Esposito, M., Zarahn, E., Aguirre, G. K., & Rypma, B. (1999). The effect of normal aging on the coupling of neural activity to the bold hemodynamic reponse. *Neuroimage, 10,* 6-14.

Dipper, L. T., Bryan, K. L., & Tyson, J. (1997). Bridging inference and relevance theory: An account of right hemisphere inference. *Clinical Linguistics and Phonetics, 11,* 213-228.

Duffy, J. R., & Myers, P. S. (1991). Group comparisons across neurologic communication disorders: Some methodological issues. *Clinical Aphasiology, 19,* 1-14.

Ellis, H. D., & Shepherd, J. W. (1974). Recognition of abstract and concrete words presented in left and right visual fields. *Journal of Experimental Psychology, 103,* 1035-1036.

Evans, M. A., Shedden, J. M., Hevenor, S. J., & Hahn, M. C. (2000). The effect of variability of unattended information on global and local processing: Evidence for lateralization at early stages of processing. *Neuropsychologia, 38,* 225-239.

Faust, M. (1998). Obtaining evidence of language comprehension from sentence priming. In M. Beeman & C. Chiarello (Eds.), *Right hemisphere language comprehension: Perspectives from cognitive neuroscience.* Mahwah, NJ: Lawrence Erlbaum.

Federmeier, K. D., & Kutas, M. (1999). Right words and left words: Electrophysiological evidence for hemispheric differences in meaning processing. *Cognitive Brain Research, 8,* 373-392.

Fink, G. R., Marshall, J. C., Halligan, P. W., & Dolan, R. J. (1999). Hemispheric asymmetries in global/local processing are modulated by perceptual salience. *Neuropsychologia, 37,* 31-40.

Fletcher, P. C., Happe, F., Frith, U., Baker, S. C., Dolan, R. J., Frackowiak, R. S. J., & Frith, C. D. (1995). Other minds in the brain: A functional imaging study of "theory of mind" in story comprehension. *Cognition, 57,* 109-128.

Frattali, C. (1998). *Measuring outcomes in speech-language pathology.* New York: Thieme.

Frederiksen, C. H., Bracewell, R. J., Breuleux, A., & Renaud, A. (1990). The cognitive representation and processing of discourse: Function and dysfunction. In Y. Joanette & H. H. Brownell (Eds.), *Discourse ability and brain damage: Theoretical and empirical perspectives.* New York: Springer Verlag.

Frederiksen, C. H., & Stemmer, B. (1993). Conceptual processing of discourse by a right hemisphere brain-damaged patient. In H. H. Brownell & Y. Joanette (Eds.), *Narrative discourse in neurologically impaired*

and normal aging adults. San Diego, CA: Singular Publishing Group.

Gagnon, J., Goulet, P., & Joanette, Y. (1989). Activation automatique et contrôlée du savoir lexico-sémantique chez les cérébrolésés droits. *Langages, 96,* 95-111.

Gainotti, G., Caltagirone, C., Miceli, G., & Masullo, C. (1983). Selective impairment of semantic-lexical discrimination in right-brain-damaged patients. In E. Perecman (Ed.), *Cognitive processing in the right hemisphere.* New York: Academic Press.

Gallagher, H. L., Happe, F., Brunswick, N., Fletcher, P. C., Frith, U., & Frith, C. D. (2000). Reading the mind in cartoons and stories: An fMRI study of "theory of mind" in verbal and nonverbal tasks. *Neuropsychologia, 38,* 11-21.

Gernsbacher, M. A. (1990). *Language comprehension as structure building.* Hillsdale, NJ: Lawrence Erlbaum.

Gordon, J. K. (1999). Can learning theory teach us about aphasia therapy? *Aphasiology, 13,* 134-140.

Goulet, P., & Joanette, Y. (1994). Sentence completion task in right-brain-damaged right-handers: Eisenson's study revisited. *Brain and Language, 46,* 257-277.

Goulet, P., Joanette, Y., Sabourin, L., & Giroux, F. (1997). Word fluency after a right-hemisphere lesion. *Neuropsychologia, 35,* 1565-1570.

Gur, R. C., Turetsky, B. I., Matsui, M., Yan, M., Bilker, W., Hughett, P., & Gur, R. E. (1999). Sex differences in brain gray and white matter in healthy young adults: Correlations with cognitive performance. *Journal of Neuroscience, 19,* 4065-4072.

Henik, A., Dronkers, N. F., Knight, R. T., & Osimani, A. (1993). Differential effects of semantic and identity priming in patients with left and right hemisphere lesions. *Journal of Cognitive Neuroscience, 5,* 45-55.

Hillis, A. E. (1994). Contributions from cognitive analyses. In R. Chapey (Ed.), *Language intervention strategies in adult aphasia* (3rd ed.). Baltimore: Williams & Wilkins.

Hillis, A. E. (1998). Treatment of naming disorders: New issues regarding old therapies. *Journal of the International Neuropsychological Society, 4,* 648-660.

Holland, A. (1992). Some thoughts on future needs and directions for research and treatment of aphasia. In J. A. Cooper (Ed.), *Aphasia treatment: Vol. 2. Current approaches and research opportunities.* Bethesda, MD: National Institutes of Health.

Hough, M. S. (1990). Narrative comprehension in adults with right and left hemisphere brain-damage: Theme organization. *Brain and Language, 38,* 253-277.

Howes, D., & Boller, F. (1975). Evidence for focal impairment from lesions of the right hemisphere. *Brain, 98,* 317-332.

Jennings, J. M., McIntosh, A. R., Kapur, S., Tulving, E., & Houle, S. (1997). Cognitive subtractions may not add up: The interaction between semantic processing and response mode. *Neuroimage, 5,* 229-239.

Joanette, Y., & Ansaldo, A. I. (1999). Clinical note: Acquired pragmatic impairments and aphasia. *Brain and Language, 68,* 529-534.

Joanette, Y., & Goulet, P. (1989). Hémisphère droit et langage: Au-delà d'une certaine compétence lexico-sémantique. *Langages, 96,* 83-94.

Joanette, Y., & Goulet, P. (1994). Right hemisphere and verbal communication: Conceptual, methodological, and clinical issues. *Clinical Aphasiology, 22,* 1-24.

Joanette, Y., Goulet, P., & Hannequin, D. (1990). *Right hemisphere and verbal communication.* New York: Springer Verlag.

Joanette, Y., Lecours, A. R., Lepage, Y., & Lamoureux, M. (1983). Language in right-handers with right-hemisphere lesions: A preliminary study including anatomical, genetic, and social factors. *Brain and Language, 20,* 217–248.

Just, M. A., & Carpenter, P. A. (1992). A capacity theory of comprehension: Individual differences in working memory. *Psychological Review, 99,* 122–149.

Just, M. A., Carpenter, P. A., Keller, T. A., Eddy, W. F., & Thulborn, K. R. (1996). Brain activation modulated by sentence comprehension. *Science, 274,* 114–116.

Kaplan, J. A., Brownell, H. H., Jacobs, J. R., & Gardner, H. (1990). The effects of right hemisphere damage on the pragmatic interpretation of conversational remarks. *Brain and Language, 38,* 315–333.

Kapur, N. (1996). Paradoxical functional facilitation in brain-behaviour research. *Brain, 119,* 1775–1790.

Kasher, A., Batori, G., Soroker, N., Graves, D., & Zaidel, E. (1999). Effects of right- and left-hemisphere damage on understanding conversational implicatures. *Brain and Language, 68,* 566–590.

Kearns, K. P. (1992). Methodological issues in aphasia treatment research: A single-subject perspective. In J. A. Cooper (Ed.), *Aphasia treatment: Vol. 2. Current approaches and research opportunities.* Bethesda, MD: National Institutes of Health.

Keller, T. A., Carpenter, P., & Just, M. A. (2001). The neural bases of sentence comprehension: An fMRI examination of syntactic and lexical processing. *Cerebral Cortex, 11,* 223–237.

Kiehl, K. A., Liddle, P. F., Smith, A. M., Mendrek, A., Forster, B. B., & Hare, R. D. (1999). Neural pathways involved in the processing of concrete and abstract words. *Human Performance, 7,* 225–233.

Kinsbourne, M. (1998). The right hemisphere and recovery from aphasia. In B. Stemmer & H. A. Whitaker (Eds.), *Handbook of neurolinguistics.* San Diego:, CA Academic Press.

Kolk, H. (1995). A time-based approach to agrammatic production. *Brain and Language, 50,* 282–303.

Kounios, J., & Holcomb, P. J. (1994). Concreteness effects in semantic processing: ERP evidence supporting dual-coding theory. *Journal of Experimental Psychology: Learning, Memory, and Cognition, 20,* 804–823.

Lehman, M. T. (1999). Factors influencing predictive inference generation. Unpublished doctoral dissertation.

Lehman-Blake, M. T., & Tompkins, C.A. (2001). Predictive inferencing in adults with right hemisphere brain damage. *Journal of Speech, Language, and Hearing Research, 44,* 639–654.

Lesser, R. (1974). Verbal comprehension in aphasia: An English version of three Italian tests. *Cortex, 10,* 247–263.

Linebaugh, C. W. (1999). Merging the models: What, why, how and when in aphasia therapy. *Aphasiology, 13,* 143–147.

Lohmann, H., Knecht, S., Deppe, M., Junker, J., Ringelstein, E. B., & Henningsen, H. (1999). Variability of the maximal hemodynamic response in a language task. *Neuroimage, 9,* S989.

Lojek-Osiejuk, E. (1996). Knowledge of scripts reflected in discourse of aphasics and right-brain-damaged patients. *Brain and Language, 29,* 68–80.

Martin, A. (1999). Automatic activation of the medial temporal lobe during encoding: Lateralized influences of meaning and novelty. *Hippocampus, 9,* 62–70.

Molloy, R., Brownell, H. H., & Gardner, H. (1990). Dis-

course comprehension by right-hemisphere stroke patients: Deficits of prediction and revision. In Y. Joanette & H. H. Brownell (Eds.), *Discourse ability and brain damage.* New York: Springer Verlag.

Myers, P. S. (1999). *Right hemisphere damage: Disorders of communication and cognition.* San Diego, CA: Singular Publishing Group.

Myers, P. S., & Brookshire, R. H. (1994). The effects of visual and inferential complexity on the picture descriptions of non-brain-damaged and right-hemisphere-damaged adults. *Clinical Aphasiology, 22,* 25–34.

Myers, P. S., & Brookshire, R. H. (1995). Effects of noun type on naming performance of right-hemisphere-damaged and non-brain-damaged adults. *Clinical Aphasiology, 23,* 195–206.

Myers, P. S., & Brookshire, R. H. (1996). Effect of visual and inferential variables on scene descriptions by right-hemisphere-damaged and non-brain-damaged adults. *Journal of Speech and Hearing Research, 39,* 870–880.

Myers, P. S., & Linebaugh, C. W. (1981). Comprehension of idiomatic expressions by right-hemisphere-damaged adults. In R. H. Brookshire (Ed.), *Clinical aphasiology: Vol. 11.* Minneapolis, MN: BRK.

Nakagawa, A. (1991). Role of anterior and posterior attention networks in hemispheric asymmetries during lexical decisions. *Journal of Cognitive Neuroscience, 3,* 313–321.

Perani, D., Cappa, S. F., Schnur, T., Tettamanti, M., Collina, S., Rosa, M. M., & Fazio, F. (1999). The neural correlates of verb and noun processing: A PET study. *Brain, 122,* 2337–2344.

Pujol, J., Deus, J., Losilla, J. M., & Capdevila, A. (1999). Cerebral lateralization of language in normal left-handed people studied by functional MRI. *Neurology, 52,* 1038–1043.

Rainville, P., Goulet, P., & Joanette, Y. (1995). Contribution of the right hemisphere to the processing of concrete words. *Clinical Aphasiology, 23,* 207–216.

Rehak, A., Kaplan, J. A., & Gardner, H. (1992). Sensitivity to conversational deviance in right-hemisphere-damaged patients. *Brain and Language, 42,* 203–217.

Rehak, A., Kaplan, J. A., Weylman, S. T., Kelly, B., Brownell, H. H., & Gardner, H. (1992). Story processing in right-hemisphere brain-damaged patients. *Brain and Language, 42,* 320–336.

Reinecke, S., Lutzenburg, M., Hagemenn, G., Bruehl, C., Neumann, H. T., & Witte, O. W. (1999). Electrophysiological transcortical diaschisis after middle cerebral artery occlusion (MCAO) in rats. *Neuroscience Letters, 261,* 85–88.

Richards, L., & Chiarello, C. (1997). Activation without selection: Parallel right hemisphere roles in language and intentional movement? *Brain and Language, 57,* 151–178.

Roman, M., Brownell, H. H., Potter, H. H., Seibold, M. S., & Gardner, H. (1987). Script knowledge in right hemisphere-damaged and in normal elderly adults. *Brain and Language, 31,* 151–170.

Sabbagh, M. A. (1999). Communicative intentions and language: Evidence from right-hemisphere damage and autism. *Brain and Language, 70,* 29–69.

Salthouse, T. A. (1996). The processing-speed theory of adult age differences in cognition. *Psychological Review, 103,* 403–428.

Schmitzer, A. B., Strauss, M., & DeMarco, S. (1997). Contextual influences on comprehension of multiple-meaning words by right hemisphere brain-damaged and non-brain-damaged adults. *Aphasiology, 11,* 447–460.

Schneiderman, E. I., Murasugi, K. G., & Saddy, J. D. (1992). Story arrangement ability in right brain-damaged patients. *Brain and Language, 43,* 107–120.

Schulz, R., & Williamson, G. M. (1993). Psychosocial and behavioral dimensions of physical frailty. *The Journals of Gerontology, 8,* 1–5.

Shapleske, J., Rossell, S. L., Woodruff, P., & David, A. (1999). The planum temporale: A systematic, quantitative review of its structural, functional, and clinical significance. *Brain Research Reviews, 29,* 26–49.

Siegal, M., Carrington, J., & Radel, M. (1996). Theory of mind and pragmatic understanding following right hemisphere damage. *Brain and Language, 53,* 40–50.

St. George, M., Kutas, M., Martinez, A., & Sereno, M. I. (1999). Semantic integration in reading: Engagement of the right hemisphere during discourse processing. *Brain, 122,* 1317–1325.

Stemmer, B. (Ed.). (1999a). Pragmatics: Theoretical and clinical issues. [Special Issue]. *Brain and Language, 68*(3).

Stemmer, B. (1999b). Discourse studies in neurologically impaired populations: A quest for action. *Brain and Language, 68,* 402–418.

Stemmer, B., Giroux, F., & Joanette, Y. (1994). Production and evaluation of requests by right-hemisphere brain-damaged individuals. *Brain and Language, 47,* 1–31.

Stemmer, B., & Joanette, Y. (1998). The interpretation of narrative discourse of brain-damaged individuals within the framework of a multilevel discourse model. In M. Beeman & C. Chiarello (Eds.), *Right hemisphere language comprehension: Perspectives from cognitive neuroscience.* Mahwah, NJ: Lawrence Erlbaum.

Swinney, D., Zurif, E., & Nicol, J. (1989). The effects of focal brain damage on sentence processing: An examination of the neurological organization of a mental module. *Journal of Cognitive Neuroscience, 1,* 25–37.

Titone, D. (1998). Hemispheric differences in context sensitivity during lexical ambiguity resolution. *Brain and Language, 65,* 361–394.

Tompkins, C. A. (1990). Knowledge and strategies for processing lexical metaphor after right or left hemisphere brain damage. *Journal of Speech and Hearing Research, 33,* 307–316.

Tompkins, C. A. (1991). Automatic and effortful processing of emotional intonation after right or left hemisphere brain damage. *Journal of Speech and Hearing Research, 34,* 820–830.

Tompkins, C. A. (1995). *Right hemisphere communication disorders: Theory and management.* San Diego, CA: Singular Publishing Group.

Tompkins, C. A., & Baumgaertner, A. (1998). Clinical value of online measures for adults with right hemisphere brain damage. *American Journal of Speech-Language Pathology, 7,* 68–74.

Tompkins, C. A., Baumgaertner, A., Lehman, M. T., & Fassbinder, W. (2000). Mechanisms of discourse comprehension impairment after right hemisphere brain damage: Suppresion in lexical ambiguity resolution. *Journal of Speech, Language, and Hearing Research, 43,* 62–78.

Tompkins, C. A., Baumgaertner, A., Lehman, M. T., & Fossett, T. R. D. (1997). Suppression and discourse comprehension in right brain-damaged adults: A preliminary report. *Aphasiology, 11,* 505–519.

Tompkins, C. A., Bloise, C. G. R., Timko, M. L., & Baumgaertner, A. (1994). Working memory and inference revision in brain-damaged and normally aging adults. *Journal of Speech and Hearing Research, 37,* 896–912.

Tompkins, C. A., Boada, R., & McGarry, K. (1992). The access and processing of familiar idioms by brain-damaged and normally aging adults. *Journal of Speech and Hearing Research, 35,* 626–637.

Tompkins, C. A., & Lehman, M. T. (1998). Interpreting intended meanings after right hemisphere brain damage: An analysis of evidence, potential accounts, and clinical implications. *Topics in Stroke Rehabilitation, 5,* 29–47.

Tompkins, C. A., Lehman, M. T., & Baumgaertner, A. (1999). Suppression and inference revision in right brain-damaged and non-brain-damaged adults. *Aphasiology, 13,* 725–742.

Tompkins, C. A., Lehman, M. T., Wyatt, A., & Schulz, R. (1998). Functional outcome assessment of adults with right hemisphere brain damage. *Seminars in Speech and Language, 19,* 303–321.

Trupe, E. H., & Hillis, A. (1985). Paucity vs. verbosity: Another analysis of right hemisphere communication deficits. In R. H. Brookshire (Ed.), *Clinical aphasiology: Vol. 15.* Minneapolis, MN: BRK.

Tucker, D. M. (1981). Lateral brain function, emotion, and conceptualization. *Psychological Bulletin, 89,* 19–46.

Tucker, D. M., & Williamson, P. A. (1984). Asymmetric neural control systems in human self-regulation. *Psychological Review, 91,* 185–215.

Van Lancker, D., & Pachana, N. A. (1998). The influence of emotion on language and communication disorders. In B. Stemmer & H. A. Whitaker (Eds.), *Handbook of neurolinguistics.* San Diego, CA: Academic Press.

Wapner, W., Hamby, S., & Gardner, H. (1981). The role of the right hemisphere in the apprehension of complex linguistic materials. *Brain and Language, 14,* 15–32.

Warburton, E., Price, C. J., Swinburn, K., & Wise, R. J. S. (1999). Mechanisms of recovery from aphasia: Evidence from positron emission tomography studies. *Journal of Neurology, Neurosurgery, and Psychiatry, 66,* 155–161.

Warrington, E. K., McKenna, P., & Orpwood, L. (1998). Single word comprehension: A concrete and abstract word synonym test. *Neuropsychological Rehabilitation, 8,* 143–154.

Weylman, S., Brownell, H. H., Roman, M., & Gardner, H. (1989). Appreciation of indirect requests by left- and right-brain-damaged patients: The effects of verbal context and conventionality of wording. *Brain and Language, 36,* 580–591.

Winner, E., Brownell, H., Happe, F., Blum, A., & Pincus, D. (1998). Distinguishing lies from jokes: Theory of mind deficits and discourse interpretation in right hemisphere brain-damaged patients. *Brain and Language, 62,* 89–106.

Witte, O. W., & Stoll, G. (1997). Delayed and remote effects of focal cortical infarctions: Secondary damage and reactive plasticity. *Advances in Neurology, 73,* 207–227.

Zaidel, E. (1998). Language in the right hemisphere following callosal disconnection. In B. Stemmer & H. A. Whitaker (Eds.), *Handbook of neurolinguistics.* San Diego, CA: Academic Press.

Author Index

Adkins, E., 207–227
Aguirre, G., 215, 221, 223
Albert, M., 210, 402
Aliminosa, D., 111, 115
Allison, T., 220
Allport, D., 193, 198, 200, 201, 202
Amitrano, A., 172
Arbib, M., 213, 221
Arguin, M., 192
Aten, J., 423
Austin, J., 414
Avent, J., 423

Balogh, J., 337
Bandura, A., 424
Banich, M., 441
Barry, C., 198
Basso, A., 210, 237–238
Bastiaanse, R., 174
Bates, E., 324, 414
Baumgaertner, A., 443
Bavelier, D., 332
Bayles, K., 222
Baynes, K., 317
Beauregard, M., 434
Beauvois, M., 54, 189, 190
Becker, J., 156
Beeman, M., 438
Beeson, P., 41, 67, 71–99, 101–120, 111, 114, 118
Behrmann, M., 112, 238
Belin, P., 260
Bell, B., 156
Benson, D., 144, 153
Berndt, R., 39, 132, 171, 172, 302, 336
Bernstein-Ellis, E., 423
Best, W., 230, 231, 236
Biassou, N., 289
Black, M., 201
Black, S., 116
Blair, J., 34
Blossom-Stach, C., 318

Blumstein, S., 257, 276, 285, 337
Boatman, D., 269–280, 281–291
Bock, K., 311, 312, 313, 318, 320, 321, 323, 324–325, 327
Boland, J., 297, 298, 300
Boles, L., 417
Bombard, T., 417
Bookheimer, S., 154, 222, 332, 340
Bosje, M., 174
Bottini, G., 439
Boyle, M., 170, 178
Brecher, A., 390
Breedin, S., 198, 199, 200, 201, 257, 299, 302, 356
Broca, P., 72
Brookshire, R., 418
Brown, J., 117
Brownell, H., 437, 438
Bruce, C., 174
Brumfitt, S., 423
Bub, D., 192
Budin, C., 211
Burns, M., 423
Burton, M., 251–267, 262
Byng, S., 38, 112, 169, 201, 245, 356, 360, 361

Caliguiri, M., 423
Caltagirone, C., 315
Campbell, R., 192, 200
Campion, J., 144
Cannestra, A., 154–155
Capasso, R., 172
Capitani, E., 210
Caplan, D., 302, 303, 304, 308, 331–350, 332, 334, 341
Cappa, S., 214
Caramazza, A., 6, 12, 53, 58, 59, 60–61, 65, 110, 113, 118, 123–142, 130, 133, 134, 138, 144, 149, 163, 172, 187, 188, 189, 192, 195, 211, 315, 316, 336
Cardell, E., 115
Carlomagno, S., 112, 114
Celsis, P., 259
Chao, L., 151

449

Cheney, H., 115
Chertkow, H., 143–161, 150, 151, 163
Chialant, D., 12, 123–142, 144, 163, 201
Chiat, S., 173, 199, 200, 201, 320
Chomsky, N., 302, 335
Cipolotti, L., 215
Coelho, C., 170, 178
Collins, A., 379–380
Coltheart, M., 6, 34, 38, 193–194, 389
Comer, J., 212
Coslett, H., 190, 191, 198, 199
Costa, A., 12, 123–142, 144
Coughlan, A., 220
Coulson, S., 344, 345
Crozier, S., 439
Cruz, R., 222
Cubelli, R., 6
Cummins, J., 415
Cupples, L., 193

Damasio, A., 150, 157, 158, 211, 212, 216
Damasio, H., 150, 157, 158, 213
Damian, M., 257
Damico, J., 419
Dapretto, M., 222, 332, 340
Davidson, B., 417, 421
Davies, K., 156
Dehaene, S., 212
Dejerine, J., 72, 78
Dell, G., 136, 137, 138, 139, 312, 316, 322, 326, 378,
    380, 382, 386, 387, 388, 390, 391–392
Deloche, G., 230
Demb, J., 220
Demonet, J., 220
De Mornay Davies, P., 198
Dennis, M., 210
dePartz, M.-P., 39, 40, 112
De Renzi, E., 146, 192
Derouesne, J., 54
D'Esposito, M., 215, 221, 223
Devinsky, O., 149, 157–158
Dipper, L., 358, 359
Dong, K., 423
Doyle, P., 176
Doyle, W., 149
Drai, D., 336
Drew, R., 317
Dudek, G., 192

Ellis, A., 315
Ellsworth, T., 175, 179
Elman, J., 254, 255
Elman, R., 423
Ennis, M., 176
Evans, K., 302
Exner, S., 72

Fadiga, L., 213
Farah, M., 145, 192, 211, 212, 213, 221, 223
Farmer, A., 236
Faroqi-Shah, Y., 12, 127, 311–328

Ferreira, C., 213
Ferreira, F., 319
Ferreira, V., 324
Fiez, J., 263
Fletcher, P., 442
Foygel, D., 139
Franssen, M., 174
Freud, S., 15
Friederici, A., 223, 345, 346
Friedman, R., 27–43, 37, 39, 40
Funnell, E., 31, 127, 144, 185–205, 233

Gade, A., 148
Gaffan, D., 195
Gagnon, D., 136
Gainotti, G., 211, 315
Gandour, J., 263
Garrett, M., 312, 313, 321, 322, 325, 327
Garrett, N., 326
Gates, A., 34
Gelman, R., 130
Gerlach, C., 148
Gibson, E., 306, 307, 308, 309
Giusiano, B., 213
Gleason, J., 364
Glosser, G., 213
Goffman, E., 414
Gold, B., 223
Goldstein, L., 407
Gonzalez Rothi, L., 37, 144, 163–182
Goodglass, H., 36, 150, 210, 211, 364
Goodwin, C., 418
Gordon, B., 149, 212, 220
Gorno-Tempini, M., 215
Goulet, P., 432, 434
Govindjee, A., 380
Grabowski, T., 157, 158
Grafton, S., 213, 217, 221
Graham, N., 77, 78
Grainger, J., 378, 379
Greenwald, M., 164, 173
Griffiths, H., 201
Grimshaw, J., 320
Grodzinsky, Y., 335, 336, 337, 338
Gupta, P., 393

Haendiges, A., 302
Hagoort, P., 343, 344
Hahne, A., 345
Harley, T., 375–396
Hart, J., 127, 149, 207–227
Hatfield, F., 113, 235
Haxby, J., 152
Haywood, M., 6
Heinze, H., 346
Helenius, P., 144
Helm Estabrooks, N., 236
Herbster, A., 156
Hermann, B., 156
Heywood, C., 195
Hichwa, R., 157, 158

Hickok, G., 261
Hildebrandt, N., 302, 303, 304, 308
Hillis, A., 3-14, 15-25, 38, 53, 65-66, 110, 111, 113, 115, 118, 133, 169, 174, 187, 192, 195, 198, 211, 236-237, 315, 316
Hillyard, S., 343
Hinckley, J., 413-427
Hirsch, F., 420
Hodges, J., 154, 214, 222, 299
Holcomb, P., 343, 344
Holland, A., 174, 236, 413-427
Horner, J., 35, 229
Horton, S., 245
Howard, D., 17, 174, 175, 233, 235, 236
Humphreys, G., 192, 196, 212
Hymes, D., 414

Inglis, L., 193
Insalaco, D., 41
Ishai, A., 214

Jackendoff, R., 200
Jacobs, A., 378, 379
Jescheniak, J., 317
Joanette, Y., 432, 434, 441
Job, R., 211
Johannes, S., 344, 346
Jokeit, H., 214
Jones, E., 360
Jones, G., 197-198
Jordan, L., 424
Juhola, M., 378
Juliano, C., 380, 382
Just, M., 332, 333, 342

Kagan, A., 415
Kaiser, W., 424
Kalinyak-Fliszar, M., 176
Kanwisher, N., 146
Kaplan, E., 36
Kashiwagi, A., 37
Kashiwagi, T., 37
Kaszniak, A., 211
Katz, R., 231
Kay, J., 34, 233, 315
Kegl, J., 320
Kelly, M., 318
Kertesz, A., 223, 390
Kim, M., 320
King, J., 344, 345
Kintsch, W., 185, 201, 203
Kiran, S., 235
Kirchner, D., 418
Kluender, R., 345
Kolk, H., 440
Kraut, M., 207-227
Kuhl, P., 255
Kutas, M., 343, 344, 345, 439

Laiacona, L., 210
Laiacona, M., 128

Laine, M., 39, 41, 317, 378, 391, 392
Lambon-Ralph, M., 129
LaPointe, L., 35
LaPointe, S., 312, 322, 326
Law, I., 148
Leischner, A., 117
Lesser, R., 34, 116, 212
Levelt, W., 144, 154, 311, 312, 313, 315, 321, 322, 325, 327, 379
Lieberthal, T., 238
Linebarger, M., 296, 300
Linebaugh, C., 176
Linn, L., 401
Loftus, E., 379-380
Lorch, M., 117
Lott, S., 37, 39
Lowell, S., 170
Luders, H., 157
Luria, A., 174
Lyon, J., 423

MacGinitie, W., 34
MacWhinney, B., 393
Maher, L., 37, 169
Manning, L., 192, 200
Marshall, J., 173, 199, 200, 233, 234, 235, 320, 354, 356, 367
Marshall, R., 236, 422, 423
Martin, A., 151, 213, 216
Martin, N., 136, 316, 375-396
Martin, R., 257, 302, 305, 306, 308, 318
Martinez, A., 439
Martino, G., 437
Masullo, C., 315
Matzke, M., 344, 346
Mauri, A., 212
Mazoyer, B., 332
McCabe, P., 390
McCarthy, G., 220
McCarthy, R., 132, 210, 211
McClelland, J., 254, 255
McCloskey, M., 62-63
McDonald, J., 318
McKenna, P., 210
McKoon, G., 338
McMullen, P., 211
Mecklinger, A., 346
Meyer, A., 144
Meyer, M., 211
Miceli, G., 60-61, 172, 315
Mintun, M., 156
Mitchum, C., 39, 172, 302, 356, 360, 361, 362, 365, 368
Mohr, J., 155
Moo, L., 207-227
Moody, S., 41
Moore, C., 146, 147, 152, 156, 158, 214
Morris, J., 235
Moss, H., 215
Moss, S., 37
Moyer, S., 40, 41
Mummery, C., 154, 214, 217, 222, 223

Munte, T., 344, 346
Myers, P., 443

Neary, D., 201
Nebes, R., 156
Neville, H., 344
Newton, P., 198
Nichelli, P., 6
Nicholas, C., 441
Nicholas, L., 418
Nickels, L., 39, 174, 229, 230, 231, 235, 236, 360–361
Nicol, J., 338, 440
Nielsen, J., 209
Niemi, J., 39
Nobre, A., 220
Norris, D., 378

Ochipa, C., 169
Oehring, A., 423
Ogle, J., 72
Ojemann, G., 16, 149, 155, 156
Oliveira, R., 117
Ollinger, J., 156
Opitz, B., 223
O'Seaghdha, P., 387, 388
Osterhout, L., 343, 344
Ostrin, R., 300

Paivio, A., 196–197, 199
Parlato, V., 114
Parr, S., 417
Pashek, G., 175
Patterson, K., 154, 214, 222, 230, 233, 236
Paulson, O., 148
Penke, M., 326
Pentore, R., 6
Perani, D., 150, 215, 217, 222
Perrine, K., 149
Petersen, S., 151, 156, 220
Peterson, S., 17
Pietrini, V., 211
Pinango, M., 336
Pinker, S., 358
Pisoni, D., 255
Plaut, D., 198, 389–390, 392–393
Poeppel, D., 261
Poncet, M., 213
Posner, M., 151, 218, 340
Pound, C., 116
Praamstra, P., 144
Premack, D., 130
Price, C., 17, 146, 147, 152, 156, 158, 214, 215, 222, 223
Pring, T., 173, 199, 230, 320
Prutting, C., 418

Quinlan, P., 196

Raichle, M., 151
Ramage, A., 116

Rapcsak, S., 67, 71–99, 101–120, 211, 212
Rapp, B., 58, 64, 187, 315
Ratcliff, R., 338
Rauschecker, J., 277
Raymer, A., 144, 163–182
Redfern, B., 317
Ricci, P., 223
Riddoch, M., 192, 196
Rizzolatti, G., 213, 221
Robson, J., 173, 199
Rochon, E., 326
Roeltgen, D., 80
Romani, C., 187, 305, 306, 308, 315
Rosen, H., 156
Rothi, J., 167
Rothi, L., 164
Rubens, A., 211, 212
Ruml, W., 138, 139

Sacchett, C., 212
Sachs, H., 414
Saetti, M., 192
Saffran, E., 136, 190, 191, 192, 198, 199, 201, 296, 299, 300, 316, 353, 386, 387
Saillant, B., 189
Salmelin, R., 144
Sandson, J., 302
Sarno, M., 401, 414
Sartori, G., 211, 212
Schegloff, E., 414
Schneider, S., 320
Schriefers, H., 316, 317
Schwartz, M., 136, 192, 201, 296, 299, 300, 315, 316, 360, 369, 386, 390
Schwartz, T., 149
Searle, J., 414
Sedivy, J., 296
Segal, J., 207–227
Semenza, C., 211
Seron, S., 230
Seron, X., 111, 112
Shallice, T., 56, 127, 128, 186, 187, 188, 195, 198, 199, 210
Shapiro, K., 134
Shapiro, L., 357
Share, L., 317
Shaywitz, B., 220
Sheeran, P., 423
Shelton, J., 130, 134, 387
Shewell, C., 230
Silveri, C., 315
Silveri, M., 211, 212
Simmons-Mackie, N., 419
Slobin, D., 358
Small, S., xvi, 251–267, 397–411
Snowden, J., 201
Spencer, K., 173, 176
Spitzer, M., 213, 216
Spivey, M., 297, 298
Spivey-Knowlton, M., 296

Spreen, O., 34
St. George, M., 439
Stemberger, J., 315, 316
Stemmer, B., 441
Stern, R., 420
Stewart, L., 150
Stockel, S., 401
Stowe, L., 332
Stromswold, K., 331
Subbiah, I., 6
Swinney, D., 336, 337, 338, 440

Tanenhaus, M., 297, 298
Temple, C., 210
Thompkins, C., 429–448
Thompson, C., 12, 127, 235, 311–328, 353, 365, 366,
    367
Thompson-Schill, S., 215, 218, 221, 222, 223
Tikkala, A., 378
Tippett, L., 213
Tomoeda, C., 222
Tompkins, C., 435, 437, 439, 443
Tranel, D., 150, 157, 158, 212
Trueswell, J., 296
Tucker, D., 441
Tulving, E., 185
Tuomainen, J., 41
Tyler, L., 215, 299, 300, 301
Tyrrell, P., 211

Ungerleider, L., 152

Vandenberghe, R., 221
Van der Linden, M., 112

Venneri, A., 6
von Cramon, D., 223

Walker-Bateson, D., 404
Wallace, M., 212
Walters, G., 156
Wambaugh, J., 176
Warren, R., 318
Warrington, E., 127, 128, 132, 186, 187, 194, 195, 199,
    210, 211, 220
Waters, G., 304, 341
Weekes, B., 38, 389
Weinrich, M., 366, 367, 368
Wernicke, C., 72
Wertz, R., 231, 423
West, R., 401
Whatmough, C., 143–161, 163
Whitaker, H., 149
Whitworth, A., 353
Whurr, M., 117
Wieringa, B., 346
Wiggs, C., 152
Wilson, B., 230
Wise, R., 154
Worrall, L., 417

Yaffee, L., 387
Yamadori, A., 210

Zatorre, R., 154, 262, 263
Zelkowicz, B., 156
Zettin, M., 211
Zingeser, L., 171
Zurif, E., 336, 337, 440

Subject Index

Aachen Aphasia Test (AAT), 404
Action Naming Test, 171
Afferent dysgraphia, 92–93
Agnosia, auditory, 287–289
Agraphia, 15
Alexia. *See also* Reading disorders
  neuroanatomical aspects of reading, 15
  semantic treatment approach, 37–38
  tactile-kinesthetic treatment approach (T–K), 36–37
  Alzheimer's disease (AD)
  and auditory processing disorders, 289
  preserved syntax and disrupted semantics, 299
  semantic agraphia and homophone confusions, 74, 77
  semantic processing in naming, 149, 151
American Speech-Language-Hearing Association (ASHA), 420
American Speech-Language-Hearing Association Functional Assessment of Communication Skills for Adults (ASHA FACS), 366
Anomia, 163. *See also* Naming disorders
Aphasia, biological approaches to treatment of
  acute stroke, 398
  animal models, 398
  catecholamines in chronic stroke, 399
  chronic stroke, 399
  depression, 405
  dopamine agonists, 402–403
  drugs to avoid in aphasia recovery, 407–408
  future biological approaches, 405–407
  gamma amino butyric acid (GABA), 400
  gene therapy, 406
  neurotrophins (nerve growth factors), 406
  pharmacotherapy of aphasia, 401–405
  piracetam, 404–405
  Porch Index of Communicative Ability (PICA), 404, 407
  serotonin (5-Hydroxytriptophan; 5-HT), 400
  sympathomimetics, 403–404
  transplantation, 406–407
Apraxia, defined, 11
Apraxic agraphia, 90

Assessment Profile of Pragmatic Linguistic Skills, 418
Auditory disorders, diagnosis and treatment of. *See also* Speech processing, models of
  auditory agnosia, 287–289
  auditory sound agnosia (nonverbal auditory agnosia), 288
  auditory verbal agnosia, 287–288
  conductive hearing loss, 282
  cortical deafness, 288–289
  diagnosis and treatment of acquired auditory processing disorders, 285–289
  dysarticulation of the ossicles, 282
  electrocochleography (ECoG), 283
  global aphasia, 286–287
  glomus tumors, 282
  hearing loss, diagnosis and treatment of, 281–285
  Landau-Kleffner syndrome, 289
  Meniere's disease, 283, 284
  mixed hearing loss, 284–285
  neural plasticity in adult auditory system, 289–290
  otitis media, 282
  otoacoustic emissions (OAE), 283
  otosclerosis, 282
  receptive aphasias, diagnosis and treatment of, 285–287
  sensorineural hearing loss, 283–284
  transcortical sensory aphasia, 286
  tuning forks, types and tests, 284–285
  Wernicke's aphasia, 285–286
Auditory speech processing, neurobiological bases of. *See also* Speech processing, models of
  auditory belt, 276
  auditory cortex, 274–277
  auditory nerve or eighth cranial nerve, 271
  auditory parabelt, 276–277
  central auditory system, 271–277
  cochlear nucleus (CN), 272–273
  connectivity of auditory cortex, 277–278
  contralateral connections of auditory cortex, 278
  dichotic listening, 274
  efferent auditory pathways, 278
  inferior colliculus (IC), 273–274
  inner ear, 271

Auditory speech processing, neurobiological bases of
    (cont'd)
    ipsilateral connections of auditory cortex, 277
    lateral lemniscus (LL), 273
    medial geniculate body (MGB), 274
    Michael's syndrome, 271
    middle ear, 270–271
    Mondini's syndrome, 271
    outer ear, 269–270
    peripheral auditory system, 269–271
    primary auditory cortex, 275–276
    superior olivary complex (SOC), 273

Bigraphs, in treatment of alexias, 40
Boston Diagnostic Aphasia Examination (BDAE), 36,
    104, 232, 285, 417, 418
Boston Naming Test (BNT), 171, 176, 231
British Aphasiology Society, 239

Cognitive architecture, defined, 47
Cognitive theory of rehabilitation, 382–386
Communication Effectiveness Inventory (CETI), 420
Communicative Activities of Daily Living (CADL-2), 419
Connectionist models
    computational modeling, 12, 377–378
    connectionist cognitive models, 377–378
    connectionist models differing from other models
        of cognition, 378–379
    contributions of connectionist models to
        rehabilitation, 386–393
    damage and retraining in a distributed connectionist
        model: effects of site of functional lesion, 388–
        390
    damaged language system repairing itself, 386–388
    effects of therapy techniques on normal and impaired
        processes, 388–392
    factors promoting generalization of learning from
        trained to untrained items, 385
    factors that affect learning and endurance of
        treatment effects, 386
    future directions of connectionist modeling of
        rehabilitation, 394
    generalization of training to untrained items, 392–
        393
    interactions of treatment and site of functional
        lesion, 390–392
    localist and distributed connectionist models, 379–382
    models as representations of a theory, 377
    models that link language, short-term memory and
        learning, 393
    priming and contextual effects, 384–385

Deep agraphia, 82, 83
Deep dyslexia, 8, 32, 197, 199
    treatment, 38–39
Diffusion-weighted imaging (DWI), 16, 20, 21, 22, 23
Dipper's Event Photograph Task, 359
Discourse Abilities Profile, 418
Dorsal stream in neuroanatomical aspects of reading,
    19
Dysarthria, defined, 11

Dysarticulation of the ossicles, 282

Electrocorticography (ECoG), 219, 283
Epilepsy and auditory processing disorders, 289
European Aachen Aphasia Test, 285
Event Perception Test, 359
Event-related potential (ERP), 332, 342
    in naming, 144
    in speech processing studies, 259, 260, 264

Florida Semantics Battery, 165, 168, 176
Functional Assessment of Communication Skills for
    Adults (ASHA FACS), 419–420
Functional Communication Profile (FCP), 414, 419
Functional Communication Therapy Planner (FCTP),
    420

Hearing loss. See Auditory disorders, diagnosis and
    treatment of
Helm Elicited Language Programme for Syntax
    Stimulation (HELPSS), 364–365
Herpes simplex encephalitis (HSE), 209
Homophones, 8–9, 29, 74, 77

Input surface dyslexia, 8

Johns Hopkins University Dysgraphia Battery, 106
Johns Hopkins University Dyslexia Battery, 34

Landau-Kleffner syndrome, 289
Lemma
    in models of naming, 123, 124–126
    in models of reading process, 12
    in models of sentence production, 313–315
Letter-by-letter reading, clinical diagnosis and treatment,
    29

Magnetic resonance
    diffusion-weighted imaging (DWI), 16, 20, 21, 22,
        23
    perfusion-weighted imaging (PWI), 16, 20, 21, 22,
        23
Magnetoencephalography (MEG), 259, 260, 264
Meniere's disease, 283, 284
Michael's syndrome, 271
Mondini's syndrome, 271
Multiple oral rereading (MOR) technique, 40–41

Naming, models of
    category-deficits as artifacts of poor experimental
        control, 127–128
    constraints imposed by modality-specific-deficits on
        number of processing layers, 126–127
    decay rate, 137
    discrete versus cascade processing, 135–136
    domain-specific theories of category-specific deficits,
        130–131
    feed-forward cascade activation model, 135
    globality assumption, 137
    grammatical category-specific deficits, 131–134
    interactive model of cascade activation, 135–136

lemma level, 123, 124–126
levels of processing, 124–127
lexeme level, 124–126
lexical representation, 124
mechanisms of lexical activation and selection, 134–139
modality-neutral-level hypothesis, 124–126
model fitting the data for fluent aphasics, 138–139
open-class words/closed-class words, 131
organized unitary content hypothesis (OUCH), 130, 131
semantic category-specific deficits, 127–131
semantic representation, 124
sensory functional hypothesis (SFH), 128–130, 131
testing interactivity assumption, 137
Naming, neuroanatomical aspects of
activation of phonology and word retrieval, 153–154
Broca's and/or Wernicke's areas, 149, 153–154, 155, 156
event-related potential (ERP), 144
imaging studies, 143, 145
lesion studies, 143, 144–145
naming deficits associated with basal temporal language area and temporal pole lesions, 156–158
perceptual processes, 144–145
semantic processing in naming, 148–153
speech initiation and articulation, 155–156
visual object recognition, 145–148
Naming disorders, clinical diagnosis and treatment of
assessment, 164–167
case example, 176–178
contrasting naming treatments, 175–176
cross-modality comparisons, 165
gesture, 174–175
graphemic mechanisms, 174
phonological judgment treatment, 173
phonological tasks, 171–172
phonologic cueing hierarchy, 172–173
phonologic impairments, 170–173
phonologic treatments, 172–173
semantic category rhyme therapy, 173
semantic comprehension treatments, 169
semantic distinctions treatment, 169–170
semantic feature matrix training, 170
semantic tasks and assessment, 167–168
semantic treatments for naming impairments, 168–170
substantive naming treatments, 174–175
treatment, 167–173
Neglect dyslexia, 18–19, 27
New Adult Reading Test Revised (NART), 34
Northwest Syntax Screening Test, 364

Organized unitary content hypothesis (OUCH), 130, 131, 188, 196
Orthography-to-phonology (OPC) mechanisms
in models of reading process, 6–8, 9, 10, 12, 150
neuroanatomical aspects, 22–23
Otosclerosis, 282

Parkinson's disease, micrographia in, 91–92, 117
Perfusion-weighted imaging (PWI), 16, 20, 21, 22, 23
Phoneme-grapheme conversion system (PG system), 50–51. See also Phonological-to-orthographic conversion
Phonemes, in models of reading process, 11
Phonologically plausible errors (PPEs), 58, 60, 65
Phonological-to-orthographic conversion (POC), 102, 104. See also Phoneme-grapheme conversion system
Pick's disease, 75
Porch Index of Communicative Ability (PICA), 404, 407
Pragmatic concerns in treatment of aphasia
Assessment Profile of Pragmatic Linguistic Skills, 418
basic interactive communication skills (BICS), 415
cognitive, academic, language proficiency (CALP), 415
Communication Effectiveness Inventory (CETI), 420
Communicative Activities of Daily Living (CADL-2), 419
conversational analysis, 418–419
direct observation, 417
Discourse Abilities Profile, 418
discourse analysis, 418
formal measures and scales to rate pragmatic abilities, 419–420
Functional Assessment of Communication Skills for Adults (ASHA FACS), 419
Functional Communication Profile (FCP), 414, 419
Functional Communication Therapy Planner (FCTP), 420
future of pragmatic approaches, 424
group approaches, 423–424
history of pragmatic concerns in treatment of aphasia, 413–415
International Classification of Impairments, Disabilities, and Handicaps (ICIDH-2), 416–417
PACE technique, 422, 423
patient and family perspective, 415–416
practicing scenarios in context, 421
pragmatic approaches to assessment, 417–420
Pragmatic Protocol, 418
Profile of Communicative Appropriateness, 418
quality of life (QoL), 420
rating scales and interview formats, 419–420
rationale for pragmatic approaches, 415–417
rehabilitation perspective, 416–417
reimbursement perspectives, 416
supported conversation, 423
training others, 422–423
training strategies, 421–422
treatment, 420–424
Profile of Communicative Appropriateness, 418
Pseudowords (PWs), 8, 30–31, 35
Psycholinguistic Assessment of Language Processing in Aphasia (PALPA), 34, 106, 231–233
Pure word deafness, 287–288
Pyramids and Palm Trees, 168, 231–233

Reading, neuroanatomical aspects of
access to orthographic representations in the lexicon, 19–20

Reading, neuroanatomical aspects of (*cont'd*)
diffusion-weighted imaging (DWI), 16, 20, 21, 22, 23
dorsal stream, 19
fMRI studies, 17, 18, 23
functional imaging, 17–18
lesion-deficit correlation approach, 15–16, 23
lexical-semantic representations, 21
neglect dyslexia, 18–19
orthography-to-phonology (OPC) mechanisms, 22–23
perfusion-weighted imaging (PWI), 16, 20, 21, 22, 23
PET studies, 17, 18
phonological representations, 21–22
subtraction method of study, 17
viewer-centered, stimulus-centered, and object-centered spatial representations of words, 18–19
Wernicke's area, 21, 23
Reading disorders, clinical diagnosis and treatment of.
See also Alexia
access to lexicon through visual modality, 29–30
assessing underlying cognitive deficit, 27–28
Boston Diagnostic Aphasia Exam (BDAE), 36
clinical assessment tools, 34–36
concreteness effects in oral reading, 31
deficit in accessing phonology from orthography by training bigraphs, 39–40
deficit in accessing phonology from orthography by training grapheme-phoneme correspondence rules, 38–39
digit span, 31
Gates-MacGinitie Reading Tests, 34–35
Gray Oral Reading Test, Third Edition, (GORT-3), 35–36
homophones, 29
identity of letters, 28
impairment in reading certain classes of words using paired associate learning, 40
integrity of orthographic representations, 28–29
length effect, 29–30
letter knowledge, 28
lexical decision, 28–29
morphologic paralexias, 33
multiple oral rereading (MOR) approach, 40–41
naming and pointing to letters named, 28
neglect, 27
New Adult Reading Test Revised (NART), 34
part of speech effects, 33
phonologic processing, 30–31
Psycholinguistic Assessment of Language Processing in Aphasia (PALPA), 34
Reading Comprehension Battery for Aphasia, Second Edition (RCBA-2), 35
reading pseudowords, 30
recognition of letters, 28
recognition of orally spelled words, 30
selective attention deficit, 28
semantic paralexias, 32
semantic representation, 31–33

sentence and text reading, 33–34
spelling, 30
tactile-kinesthetic (T-K) letter identification, 36–37
visual processing, 27
Wechsler Memory Scale, 31
word-picture matching, 31
Reading process, models of
cognitive processes underlying reading, 4
computational models, 12
computational requirements for reading, 3–4
input surface dyslexia, 8
lemma, 12
lexical-semantic representations, 4, 8–9
motor programming and articulation, 4, 11
orthographic representations (units of the orthographic lexicon), 4, 6–8
orthography-phonology correspondence (OPC), 6–8, 9, 10, 12
phonetic selection, 11
phonological representations, 4, 9–11
pseudowords (PWs), 8
reading unfamiliar words, 4
regularization errors, 8
stimulus-centered representations, 4, 5–6
"summation," 9
surface dyslexia, 8
threshold of activation, 10
viewer-centered representations, 4, 5
word-centered (object-centered) representations, 4, 6
Regional cerebral blood flow (rCBF), 332, 340
Regularization errors, 8
Right hemisphere language disorders
clinical management of RHD language disorders, 443–444
conceptual and methodological considerations, 430–432
control groups to rule out nonspecific effects on performance, 431–432
designating disordered performances, 431
discourse processing, 435–440
inferring lesion-behavior correspondences, 432
inter-and intrasubject variability, 430–431
issues related to operationalizing and measuring the constructs in RHD language research, 432
lexical-semantic processing, 433–435
reasoning from a theory of mind, 437–440
reconciling multiple, seemingly incongruent inferences to arrive at a full understanding of a discourse unit, 436–437
relating mental representations of stimuli and their associated contexts to determine or convey nonliteral intended meanings, 436
Rinne tuning fork, 284

Schwabach tuning fork, 284
Selective attention deficit in reading disorders, 28
Semantic dementia. *See also* Alzheimer's disease (AD)
semantic agraphia and homophone confusions, 74, 77
semantic memory and event scripts, 203

semantic processing in naming, 149, 151
Semantic memory
  action naming better than object naming, 200–201
  category-specific disorders for objects, 194–196
  content organization within a single semantics system, 194
  disconnection between verbal semantics and visual semantics, 189–190
  dual route theory, 191
  and event scripts, 201–203
  hypothesis of content organization within a single semantic system, 188–189
  identifying semantic memory deficits, 186–187
  imageable, concrete, and abstract words, 196–200
  input hypothesis, 188
  material-specific semantic systems, 187–189
  modality-specific content hypothesis, 188, 192–194
  modality-specific format hypothesis, 187
  modality-specific input hypothesis, 189–192
  optic aphasia and a unitary semantic system, 190
  optic aphasia and right hemisphere semantics, 190
  semantic access theory, 191–192
  separable semantic systems, 186–201
  superadditive theory, 192
Semantic paralexias, 32
Semantics, neural substrates of
  electrocorticography (ECoG), 219
  herpes simplex encephalitis (HSE), 209
  neural "hybrid" model of semantics, 219, 224
  neural substrates of semantic categories, 209–217
  organization of semantic representations, 208–217
  select studies of category organization, 210–215
  timeslicing, 219
"Semantic therapy"
  Aphasia Therapy Interaction Coding System, 244
  assessment, 231–234
  BOX, lexical therapy, 230
  characterizing "doing therapy" data, 244
  "chronic aphasic" patients, 231
  developing a framework for describing interactions in therapy, 239–245
  developing a working hypothesis, 234
  "diagnostic therapy," 234
  formal and informal assessments, 231–234
  macro and micro-learning goals, 244–245, 246
  planning treatment: using models, 235–245, 246
  response management process, 241–243
  semantic therapy treatment in the literature, 236–239
  stimulus selection for therapy, 234–235
Sensory functional hypothesis (SFH), 128–130, 131
Sentence comprehension deficits
  "constraint-based" approaches, 298
  disruptions of specific aspects of syntactic parsing, 302–304
  future research direction, 307–309
  independence of syntax and semantics, 299–301
  interactions between syntax and semantics, 300–301
  mapping between grammatical and thematic roles, 301–302

  preserved syntax and disrupted semantics, 299–300
  PRO (missing elements), 303
  role of the verb, 302
  working memory and sentence comprehension, 304–307
Sentence processing disorders, assessment and treatment of. See also Syntactic processing, neural basis of
  American Speech-Language-Hearing Association Functional Assessment of Communication Skills for Adults (ASHA FACS), 366
  Chomsky's government binding theory, 365
  computerized visual communications system (C-VIC), 366–367
  diagnosis, 359–360
  Dipper's Event Photograph Task, 359
  elicitation of particular structures, 353
  event knowledge, tests of, 357–359
  Event Perception Test, 359
  generalization of therapy effects, 367–368
  goals of sentence therapy, 369
  grammaticality judgment tasks, 355
  Helm Elicited Language Programme for Syntax Stimulation (HELPSS), 364–365
  linguistic-specific treatment (LST), 365
  "mapping impairments," 355
  mechanisms of change, 368–369
  morphosyntactic treatments, 364–365
  Northwest Syntax Screening Test, 364
  on-line procedures, 357
  Role Video, 359, 362
  sampling and analyzing spontaneous speech, 352–353
  sentence comprehension, assessment of, 354–357
  sentence production, assessment of, 352–354
  therapies based on the mapping hypothesis, 360–361
  therapy aiming to improve verb retrieval, 362–364
  therapy using nonverbal media, 366–367
  therapy working at level of the event, 362
  treatment for complex structures, 365–366
  verb knowledge, tests of, 356
  Verb Video Test, 356
  working memory, assessment of, 356–357
Sentence production, models of
  animacy in function assignment, 318
  building phrase structure, 321–323
  component processes of sentence production, 312–327
  conceptual intrusion, 316
  constituent assembly, 321, 325
  experimental studies of lexical selection, 316–317
  factors involved in function assignment, 318
  function word processing versus inflectional affixation, 326–327
  generating the message, 313
  inflection, 325–327
  interactive activation (IA) model, 316–317
  lemma access, 313–315
  lexical selection in functional processing, 313–317
  ordering of lexical items into planning frames, 323–325

Sentence production, models of (*cont'd*)
  positional processing, 321–327
  reaction times (RTs), 316
  role of the verb in function assignment, 319–320
  role-reversal errors, 318
  tip-of-the-tongue (TOT) phenomenon, 311, 313, 315, 317
  word form access/lexeme selection, 315–316
Spatial dysgraphia, 92–93
Speech processing, models of. *See also* Auditory disorders, diagnosis and treatment of
  Broca's and Wernicke's aphasia, 257, 258
  Cohort model of word recognition, 254
  functional neuroanatomy of speech perception, 258–263
  inferior frontal cortex, 261–263
  inferior parietal cortex, 261
  Merge model of word recognition, 256
  models of word recognition, 254–256
  Neighborhood Activation Model of word recognition, 256
  neuroimaging studies, 258–263
  posterior temporal cortex, 259–261
  TRACE model of word recognition, 254, 255–256
Spelling, cognitive architecture of
  cognitive architecture, defined, 47
  direct route/nonsemantic route in lexical processes, 49
  distinction between lexical and sublexical processing, 54–56
  dysgraphic performance revealing architecture of spelling process, 51–67
  feedback from graphemes to lexical representations, 62–63
  graphemic buffering component or process, 59–62
  integration of lexical and sublexical processes, 64–67
  lexical processes, 48–49
  lexical semantic system, 49
  lexical substitutions, 63
  orthographic autonomy, 51–54
  orthographic output lexicon, 49
  phoneme-grapheme conversion system (PG system), 50–51
  phonologically plausible errors (PPEs), 58, 60, 65
  postlexical processes, 49–50
  relationship between oral and written spelling, 57–59
  sublexical processes, 50–51
Spelling and writing, neuroanatomical correlates of
  afferent control systems, 92–93
  allographic conversion, 87–89
  Alzheimer's disease (AD), 74, 75, 77
  Brodmann areas, 75, 76–77, 78, 79, 80
  central components, 73–87
  Exner's writing center, 90, 91
  graphemic buffer dysfunction, 81, 84–87
  lexical-semantic spelling route, 73–79
  micrographia in Parkinson's disease, 91–92, 117
  motor programming and neuromuscular execution, 89–92, 93

peripheral components, 87–93
phonological spelling route(s), 79–84
Pick's disease, 75
semantic dementia, 74, 75, 77
structural and functional imaging techniques, 72
subword-level phonological spelling, 79–80, 82, 93
supplementary motor area (SMA), 90, 91, 93
Wernicke's and Broca's areas, 71, 74, 80, 82, 86
word-level phonological spelling, 79, 82, 93
Spelling disorders, clinical diagnosis and treatment of
  anagram and copy treatment (ACT), 111
  clinical evaluation of spelling, 102–107
  copy and recall treatment: CART, 111
  graphemic buffer, assessment of, 108
  interactive use of lexical and phonological spelling routes, 114
  lexical relay strategy, 113
  lexical-semantic route, 102–105
  output modalities other than handwriting, 116–117
  peripheral writing processes, assessment of, 108–109
  phonological spelling route, assessment of, 107–108
  treatment approaches to spelling impairments, 109–117
  writing to dictation, 106–107
  written naming task, 106
Supplementary motor area (SMA), 90, 91, 93
Surface dyslexia, 8, 79
Syntactic processing, neural basis of
  Chomsky's syntactic theory, 335, 338
  cross-modal lexical priming (CMLP), 336–338
  deficit-lesion correlational studies of perisylvian association cortex, 333–338
  electrophysiological studies of syntactic processing, 342–346
  event-related potentials (ERP), 342
  functional neuroimaging studies, 338–342
  functional organization of the perisylvian association cortex, 333–342
  object manipulation (OM), 334
  perisylvian regions of interest (ROIs), 334
  rapid serial visual presentation (RSVP), 342
  regional cerebral blood flow (rCBF), 332, 340
  sentencepicture matching (SPM), 334
  syntactic positive shift (SPS), 343
  trace deletion hypothesis (TDH), 335–336, 338

Thematic Roles in Production (TRIP) test, 353
Tip-of-the-tongue (TOT) phenomenon, 311, 313, 315, 317
TRACE model of word recognition, 254, 255–256

Verb Video Test, 356

Weber tuning fork, 284, 285
Wechsler Memory Scale, 31
Western Aphasia Battery, 104, 176, 232, 285
World Health Organization, International Classification of Impairments, Disabilities, and Handicaps (ICIDH-2), 416–417